booksonline

Read this book online today:

With SAP PRESS BooksOnline we offer you online access to knowledge from the leading SAP experts. Whether you use it as a beneficial supplement or as an alternative to the printed book, with SAP PRESS BooksOnline you can:

• Access your book anywhere, at any time. All you need is an Internet connection.
• Perform full text searches on your book and on the entire SAP PRESS library.
• Build your own personalized SAP library.

The SAP PRESS customer advantage:

Register this book today at *www.sap-press.com* and obtain exclusive free trial access to its online version. If you like it (and we think you will), you can choose to purchase permanent, unrestricted access to the online edition at a very special price!

Here's how to get started:

1. Visit *www.sap-press.com.*
2. Click on the link for SAP PRESS BooksOnline and login (or create an account).
3. Enter your free trial license key, shown below in the corner of the page.
4. Try out your online book with full, unrestricted access for a limited time!

Your personal free trial **license key**
for this online book is:

2zaw-49m3-e5ns-hyir

Configuring Controlling in SAP® ERP

SAP PRESS is a joint initiative of SAP and Galileo Press. The know-how offered by SAP specialists combined with the expertise of the Galileo Press publishing house offers the reader expert books in the field. SAP PRESS features first-hand information and expert advice, and provides useful skills for professional decision-making.

SAP PRESS offers a variety of books on technical and business related topics for the SAP user. For further information, please visit our website: *www.sap-press.com*.

Janet Salmon
Controlling with SAP—Practical Guide
2012, 582 pp., hardcover
ISBN 978-1-59229-392-6

John Jordan
100 Things You Should Know About Controlling with SAP
2011, 289 pp., hardcover
ISBN 978-1-59229-341-4

John Jordan
Product Cost Controlling with SAP (Second Edition)
2012, 652 pp., hardcover
ISBN 978-1-59229-399-5

Rogerio Faleiros and Alison Kreis Ryan

Configuring Controlling in SAP® ERP

Galileo Press

Bonn • Boston

Galileo Press is named after the Italian physicist, mathematician and philosopher Galileo Galilei (1564—1642). He is known as one of the founders of modern science and an advocate of our contemporary, heliocentric worldview. His words *Eppur si muove* (And yet it moves) have become legendary. The Galileo Press logo depicts Jupiter orbited by the four Galilean moons, which were discovered by Galileo in 1610.

Acquisitions Editor Meg Dunkerley
Developmental Editor Emily Nicholls
Technical Reviewer Rodrigo Glauser
Copyeditor Julie McNamee
Cover Design Graham Geary
Photo Credit iStockphoto.com/Veni
Layout Design Vera Brauner
Production Graham Geary
Typesetting SatzPro, Krefeld (Germany)
Printed and bound in the United States of America

ISBN   978-1-59229-401-5

© 2012 by Galileo Press Inc., Boston (MA)
1st edition 2012

Library of Congress Cataloging-in-Publication Data
Faleiros, Rogirio Naques, 1978-
Configuring controlling in SAP ERP / Rogerio Faleiros,
Alison Kreis Ryan. -- 1st ed.
p. cm.
Includes bibliographical references and index.
ISBN 978-1-59229-401-5 (alk. paper) -- ISBN 1-59229-401-4
(alk. paper) 1. Cost control--Data processing. 2. SAP ERP.
I. Ryan, Alison Kreis. II. Title.
HD47.3.F45 2012
658.15'52028553--dc23
2012008960

FSC
www.fsc.org
MIX
Paper from
responsible sources
FSC® C014174

Contents at a Glance

Dear Reader,

It is my pleasure to present SAP PRESS readers with the first comprehensive guide to configuring Controlling. You'll find that this book is relevant to a wide range of readers, just as the CO component stretches to fit infinite unique and pressing business needs. It is the first of its kind to explore each and every CO subcomponent and help you achieve your customizing objectives, complementing the business management process.

In *Configuring Controlling in SAP ERP*, the authors have successfully blended their backgrounds as super users and IT managers. Alison and Rogerio were dedicated to mastering the editorial learning curve associated with a first-time writing effort, and doggedly weathered the challenges that time zone differences, travel schedules, and full-time jobs present. Their meticulous attention to detail—and the dedication of their evenings and weekends—ensured that this book delivers unmatched coverage of the Controlling component. I am confident that your work will benefit from Alison and Rogerio's thorough presentation of this highly nuanced topic.

We appreciate your business, and welcome your feedback. Your comments and suggestions are the most useful tools to help us improve our books for you, the reader. We encourage you to visit our website at *www.sap-press.com* and share your feedback about this work.

Thank you for purchasing a book from SAP PRESS!

Emily Nicholls
Editor, SAP PRESS

Galileo Press
Boston, MA

emily.nicholls@galileo-press.com
www.sap-press.com

Contents

8   Profit Center Accounting 449

Acknowledgments

My decision to write a book was not made alone—it was shared with loved ones, who encouraged me to move forward on the project. When reflecting on the time spent writing, I will always remember those who gave me the strength I needed to continue, even in the most difficult times. These are the people who I would like to thank—my parents, my brother, my sister, and especially my wife, Favi Faleiros, who was by my side throughout the project, giving me the support I needed. I also want to thank my son, Gustavo Faleiros, who was born in the middle of the writing process. Just looking at his smiling face was my source of energy.

Rogerio Faleiros

Writing a book like this is quite a project. It requires many hours, including long nights and weekends that would otherwise have been spent with family. I would not have been able to dedicate the necessary time without the active support and encouragement of family and friends, especially from my husband, Chris Ryan, and my mother, Nell Kreis. Finally, also encouraging me in spirit throughout the project was my father, Fritz Kreis, who taught me that all things are possible, if only you are willing to work for them.

Alison Kreis Ryan

We both would like to thank our technical reviewer, Rodrigo Glauser, for his time and valuable suggestions, and also the editorial staff at Galileo Press for their coaching and patience as we worked through the process of writing, editing, and proofing this book. Many individuals contributed to the project, and we could not have completed it without them.

Preface

Having worked with SAP ERP Controlling (CO) for many years, we've noticed a gap in the available documentation related to customizing SAP ERP CO. We could find references for some subcomponents, but could never put our hands on a book or article that singularly covered all aspects of CO.

After searching for the information in many places and discovering a disconcerting lack of available resources, we decided to write our own book that offered readers a resource to take them step by step through all the subcomponents contained in SAP ERP CO, gleaned from many years working with CO in customizing as a key user and IT manager.

So here it is. In *Configuring Controlling in SAP ERP*, we offer you the best practices for customizing all of the areas of SAP ERP CO together in one practical reference.

Introduction

Throughout history—that is, since the first days of commercial enterprises—civilizations have found it necessary to create methods to monetarily measure the income, expenses, and profits of businesses. Modern financial accounting procedures date from the mercantilist era and were established to address this need in a consistent manner: to standardize the financial statements certified by external auditors and, in turn, provided to financial institutions, investors, and creditors.

As companies started to grow and became increasingly competitive, a gap began to emerge between the different needs of company management and financial institutions. These management information needs were the drivers for the development of the basic principles of cost accounting.

The functions of coordinating, monitoring, and optimizing all business processes in an organization are together called *controlling*. To operate, controlling requires information from all areas of the company. The materials manager provides information about inventories, purchased materials, preferred vendors, and forecasted material needs. The production area provides information about materials consumed, production times, and production lines. The sales and distribution area gives details about what products were sold, customers, prices, quantities, payment terms, and delivery terms. The financial accounting area provides information about depreciation, taxes, cash flow, and so on. The information from the entire company environment together allows the controlling function to provide information in a way that helps manage the business more effectively. The controlling function is therefore a management tool for decision making and includes the steps of planning, controlling, and reporting the results.

In SAP ERP, these business functions are addressed in a component called Controlling (CO).

Who This Book Is For

This book is designed for SAP ERP consultants with some knowledge of SAP ERP Financials who want to learn how to customize CO in SAP ERP. If you self-identify with this group, this book will guide you through all of the concepts and steps to establish the customization needed to activate the CO component in SAP ERP Financials.

For an IT manager or project manager who is interested in SAP ERP CO customizing or is planning to implement new functionalities inside SAP ERP CO, this book provides a complete picture of what functionality is available in the CO component. It highlights the key factors to consider in determining the optimal configuration for the organization.

How This Book Is Structured

This book covers all aspects of customization of the SAP ERP CO component. The book provides a complete understanding of how the CO component works, the configuration alternatives, the important business considerations, and how to do the customizations. We highlight key configuration decisions in each area that should be made with a company's future plans and flexibility in mind. The book also provides tips and tricks for topics that have a significant impact on accounting and reporting.

Beginning with general controlling, and continuing through each of the controlling topics or subcomponents, you'll learn how to determine the key decision points and how to do the necessary customization in SAP ERP, and you'll gain an understanding of the functional and business impacts of customizing inside the component. Here is an overview of the book by chapter:

▶ **Chapter 1: General Controlling**
This chapter provides an introduction to the CO component and the necessary customizing information to activate it. You'll learn the difference between internal and external accounting, and how CO can help an organization meet the requirements of both. It shows the available and important options related to the controlling area customizing to help you determine the best combination of alternatives to manage your business reporting needs. You will learn

how to create the controlling area and number ranges, the importance of versions in CO, how to create substitutions and validations to help classify postings in the CO component, and how to assign company codes to a controlling area.

- **Chapter 2: Cost Element Accounting**
  Chapters 2, 3, and 4 together will help you to answer the following question: *"What costs occur within our organization, and how can SAP ERP provide information so that they can be effectively managed?"* In Chapter2, specifically, you will learn how Cost Element Accounting provides the capability for reconciling costs in CO with the Financial Accounting (FI) component and also classifying costs and revenues that are posted to CO. It shows you step by step how to establish a customized cost element structure for your business.

- **Chapter 3: Cost Center Accounting**
  This chapter explains how Cost Center Accounting works and the benefits of using it. You'll see how to customize Cost Center Accounting in CO—from cost center master data to the cost center information system—and also learn how to establish the customizing for cost center planning and cost center budgeting, as well as which tools are available to be used for actual values.

- **Chapter 4: Internal Orders**
  You'll learn in this chapter about an excellent tool to help you analyze your company costs using CO. You'll learn the basic concepts of internal orders, how and when they can be used, how to customize the planning and budgeting, and how to customize the period-end closing for internal orders.

- **Chapter 5: Activity-Based Costing**
  In this chapter, you'll learn about this powerful subcomponent that, combined with Cost Center Accounting and internal orders, can provide new tools to help you answer the following question: *"How can we reduce our overhead or other service costs?"* You'll learn how to establish the most effective customizing in the subcomponent to meet your organization's needs.

- **Chapter 6: Product Cost Controlling**
  This chapter shows you how to add to your controlling analysis the possibility to simulate and create cost estimates for different purposes. You'll learn how to customize the subcomponent to simulate these costs and also how to do the necessary customizing to analyze actual costing. You'll see how it provides extensive reporting tools to analyze and manage production costs, helping you answer the following question: *"What are the manufacturing costs of a product?"*

▶ **Chapter 7: Profitability Analysis**

In this chapter, you'll learn how to customize the subcomponent to answer the following question: *"How profitable are individual market segments?"* You will learn the difference between costing-based and accounting-based CO-PA and how to customize both the planning and actual CO-PA.

▶ **Chapter 8: Profit Center Accounting**

In this chapter, you will learn how to customize both actual and planning functions of the Profit Center Accounting (EC-PCA) subcomponent to help you answer the following question: *"How profitable are individual enterprise areas?"* You'll also learn how to customize the transfer price functionality within EC-PCA to measure profits between businesses within your organization.

▶ **Chapter 9: Conclusion**

In the final chapter, we'll review the main purpose of each of the SAP ERP CO subcomponents covered in this book. You'll also learn about the dependencies between them so that you can develop your implementation plan with a full understanding of which components you want to activate and which portions are required to support the desired functionality.

SAP ERP CO contains a wide variety of available functionalities in the subcomponents that you will learn about in this book. Although you may not have a need for all of the subcomponents, by reading about all of them, you will have a good understanding of each and how they relate to help you develop a customized implementation plan for your organization.

Looking ahead, in Chapter 1, you'll learn about the basic organizational concepts of SAP ERP CO, which will form the foundation for your understanding and customization of all of the subcomponents contained in SAP ERP CO.

Understanding the basic organizational concepts of Controlling in SAP ERP Financials is the critical first step to customizing the component by establishing the structure to obtain the best results for your business processes.

1   General Controlling

This chapter explains the foundational structure components of the Controlling component in SAP ERP. We'll discuss all of the main components contained in SAP ERP and how they interrelate, explain the differences between internal and external accounting, and describe how the Controlling component (CO) can be customized to help manage the business—all the while highlighting the most important factors to consider in establishing the foundation for CO.

We'll walk through the step-by-step processes to establish this foundation and show you how to create the main CO organizational structural component, the controlling area, including all of the available settings for the customizing, how to create and assign the number ranges, and how to assign company codes.

We will also discuss some best practices for production start-up and how activating CO affects the archiving process.

SAP ERP is an integrated system, meaning an operation in one component can affect other components. Figure 1.1 illustrates how CO can receive values from other components. This doesn't mean that CO is the principal component, but it illustrates how CO can interact with other SAP ERP components.

The following is a brief description of the SAP ERP components shown in Figure 1.1 and their primary functions:

▶ Financial Accounting (FI) records all financial postings and is used mainly for external or statutory accounting.

▶ Project Systems (PS) can be configured to track all of the information related to a project, such as budget, percentage completed, and tasks to do.

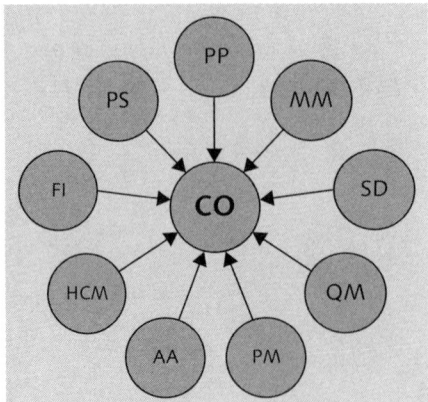

Figure 1.1 SAP ERP CO Integration

- Production Planning (PP) records information related to production such as bills of material (BOM), routing, production confirmation, and Material Requirements Planning (MRP).

- Materials Management (MM) is used to keep all information related to materials, such as vendor, purchasing, storage location, and others.

- Sales and Distribution (SD) contains all transactions related to customers, such as distribution channel, pricing, and sales.

- Quality Management (QM) can be used to track the quality of a material, track whether it is a purchased or produced material, and create a quality history record for the material.

- Plant Maintenance (PM) is used to record the entire maintenance process, including schedules, equipment, maintenance orders, and material requisitions.

- Asset Accounting (AA) provides all of the financial information about assets, including depreciation terms, localization, asset inventory lists, and others.

- Human Capital Management (HCM) manages all information about the employer and employees, such as labor, holidays, health insurance, and other benefits.

All of these components interact with CO, creating both actual values and planning values.

CO also has internal divisions or subcomponents to help manage the data received from other components (see Figure 1.2).

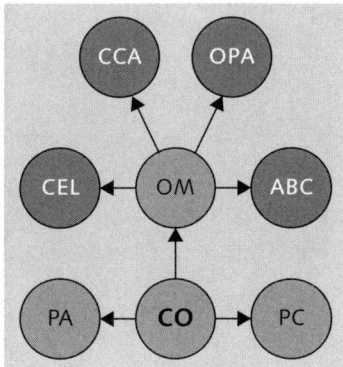

Figure 1.2 CO Subcomponents

Because it's not necessary to use all of the CO subcomponents, we recommend that you determine which will add value to your business and then selectively set up and use those that are appropriate. This section includes brief descriptions of each and how they can be used. (The subcomponents are discussed in more detail in later chapters.)

▶ **Overhead Management (CO-OM)**
Contains four subcomponents: Cost Element Accounting (CO-OM-CEL or just CO-CEL), Cost Center Accounting (CO-OM-CCA or just CO-CCA), Internal Orders (CO-OM-OPA or just CO-OPA), and Activity-Based Costing (CO-OM-ABC or just CO-ABC). The postings are classified by cost elements, cost centers, internal orders, and business processes.

▶ **Product Costing (CO-PC)**
Allocates the costs of the production process to the individual products. These values are then used in financial and other postings related to manufactured materials.

▶ **Profitability Analysis (CO-PA)**
Combines data coming from SD and CO-PC to allow reporting that can provide detailed information for managers, including profit and loss (P&L) by customer, product, product line, plant, sales office, and others.

Now that we've seen the subcomponents included in CO, let's look at the differences between CO and FI and how these subcomponents interact with FI.

CO configuration in SAP ERP allows an organization to define the structures to maintain information to meet both internal and external accounting needs. One question that is often asked when working with SAP ERP for the first time is "What is the difference between FI and CO?" Both contain accounting data but have important differences in structure and use.

FI is responsible for *external* (or statutory) accounting and is focused on meeting the needs of entities outside the company such as banks, government institutions, and insurance companies. This includes accounting tools such as balance sheets and P&L statements. External accounting meets the legal requirements imposed by legislation and taxing authorities.

CO is responsible for *internal* (or management) accounting and is focused on meeting the needs for information from within the organization. Internal accounting is designed to provide information for management at all levels to direct and control its strategic and daily operations. Some common examples of this are cost reports with actual and budget comparisons by functional area or cost center; a P&L by product, customer, or other sales classification to monitor margins and profitability; or detailed production cost reports comparing actuals to targets.

One way to look at the purposes and uses of the two components is basically that FI will capture *how much* was spent, and CO will capture *how* it was spent. Figure 1.3 illustrates the differences between these two components.

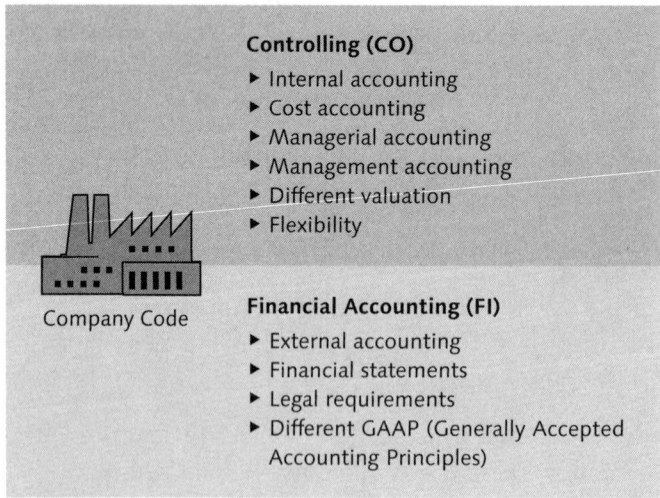

Figure 1.3 Differences Between FI and CO

It's important that the system customizing is established to facilitate the flexible and accurate management of information to meet the requirements of both external and internal accounting. Figure 1.4 illustrates the relationship of these areas and how the CO architecture in SAP ERP can be used to meet the needs of both.

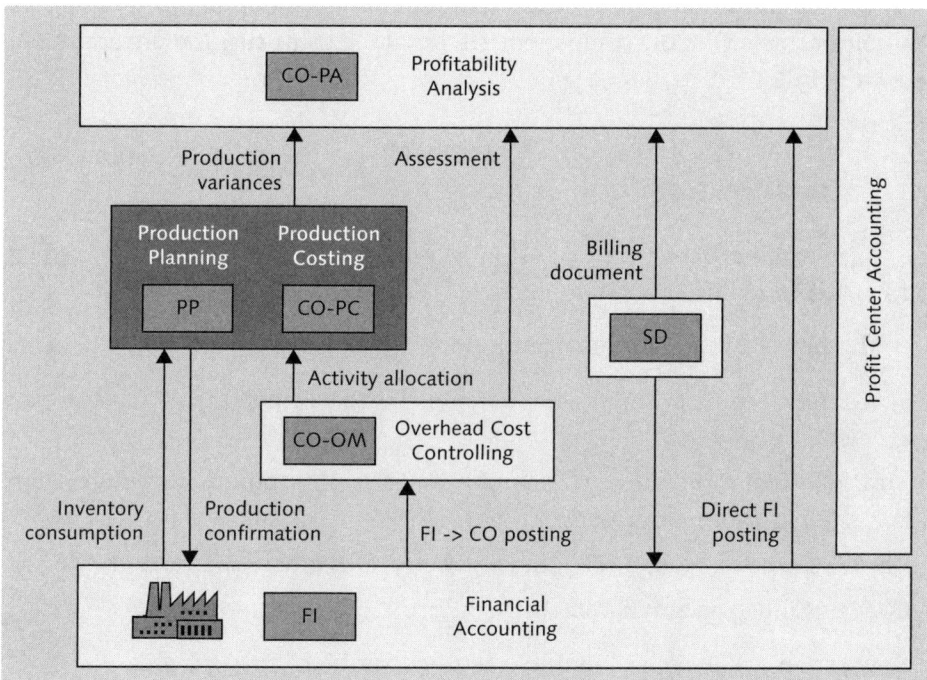

Figure 1.4 Controlling Architecture

Figure 1.4 shows the basic architecture of CO in SAP ERP. The various components of CO are shown, with arrows indicating typical flows of costs and activity type quantities. The arrow from FI to CO-OM represents FI expenses posting in the OM subcomponent, such as depreciation or salaries.

The arrow pointing from CO-OM to CO-PC shows that costs can flow from Overhead Cost Controlling to Product Cost Controlling, using the activity allocation to do the posting.

Similarly, costs can flow from CO-OM to CO-PC and from SD to CO-PA, where they can be used together with revenue data to calculate operating results and determine how well various segments of the business are performing. The arrow from FI to CO-PA shows direct revenue posting to the PA subcomponent. The arrow between FI and the CO-PC subcomponent reflects direct inputs to the production process such as raw materials consumption. There is also a return flow to FI, when production costs are capitalized as semi-finished or finished goods inventory.

Now that we've shown how the main components contained in SAP ERP and the subcomponents of the CO component interrelate, let's discuss the organizational structure of CO.

1.1 Organization

The organizational structure in SAP ERP is how you customize the system to address legal and business requirements.

Here are some examples of the organizational structures used in the components:

- **FI:** Company code, business area, functional area, segment, and financial management area.
- **MM:** Plant, location, purchase organization, storage location, warehouse number, shipping point, and loading point.
- **SD:** Sales organization, distribution channel, sales office, and sales group.
- **CO:** Controlling area and operating concern.

In this section, we'll explain all of the settings for the controlling area.

Decisions made at the organizational structure level impact the way the SAP ERP system works and directly affect the information that can be generated by the system. Throughout this chapter, we'll demonstrate the configuration process for each of the steps using a hypothetical organization situation called XYZ Enterprise.

XYZ Enterprise is a manufacturing and distribution company with operations in the United States, Brazil, and Germany. It's headquartered in the United States, and all consolidated results are reported in US dollars.

The organizational components defined for XYZ will be discussed to demonstrate the alternatives available in customizing and the rationale for selecting each.

Before starting the controlling area customizing, you have an important decision point, which is the definition of the currency types.

The currency type definition for controlling area and company code directly impacts how the organization structures are defined. An incorrect definition in this step can make it impossible to consolidate company codes situated in different countries at the same controlling area level.

Table 1.1 shows the list of currency types available to use in the controlling area.

Currency Type	Description
10	Company code currency
20	Controlling area currency
30	Group currency
40	Hard currency
50	Index-based currency
60	Global company currency

Table 1.1 Currency Types Available for Controlling Areas

Currency type customization is subjective, which means that there is no customizing path where you can define all of the currencies at the same time. The currency types are determined during the customizing of other areas' SAP ERP items. For example, when you are setting up the different SAP ERP clients (such as development, quality or test, and production) you must choose a currency for the client, which indirectly defines the currency type 30. This is one of the most common areas that can cause issues in SAP ERP, and it's difficult or impossible to change or correct later. It's crucial to analyze all of the requirements and consider them in the definition of the structures before beginning the customizing.

> **Note**
>
> All of the currency types should be defined in the project blueprint with consideration of all active components and the company needs. Never change the currency type in an environment with data because it will cause a system inconsistency.

The following list describes all of the available currencies types for controlling area customizing:

▶ **Currency type 10**

Currency type 10 is defined at the company code level. Each company code in SAP ERP has its own currency, and when you set this currency, you are actually creating the currency type 10 for that company code.

To maintain the company code currency, use Transaction OX02, or follow the IMG menu path ENTERPRISE STRUCTURE • DEFINITION • FINANCIAL ACCOUNTING • EDIT, COPY, DELETE, CHECK COMPANY CODE, which brings you to the screen shown in Figure 1.5.

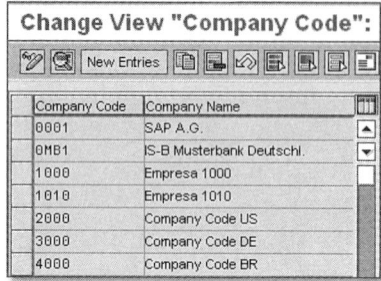

Figure 1.5 Edit Company Code

By double-clicking on an entry in the COMPANY CODE column (e.g., company code 2000), you can view the basic information for each company code, as shown in Figure 1.6.

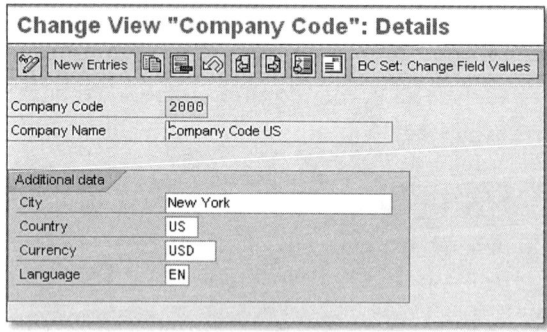

Figure 1.6 Maintain Company Code Settings

The CURRENCY field in Figure 1.6 is defined as "USD"—currency type 10 for company code 2000.

▶ **Currency type 20**

Currency type 20 (controlling area currency) is the currency type defined in the controlling area settings. We don't recommend that you use this type in a multi-currency organization because there is a possibility that the currency assigned to currency type 20 may not be available at the company code level. If this is the case, the system cannot assign the company code to the controlling area.

▶ **Currency type 30**

Each SAP Client has its own currency. Any company code that uses currency type 30 as one of the three available will share the same currency. Currency type 30 is usually used for consolidation. A company doing business in many countries, for example, can assign currency type 30 to all company codes, and it will be available to consolidate the balance sheet, profit and loss, and other financial statements in the same currency.

To maintain the SAP Client currency, use Transaction SCC4, or follow menu path TOOLS • ADMINISTRATION • ADMINISTRATION • CLIENT ADMINISTRATION • CLIENT MAINTENANCE, which brings you to the screen shown in Figure 1.7.

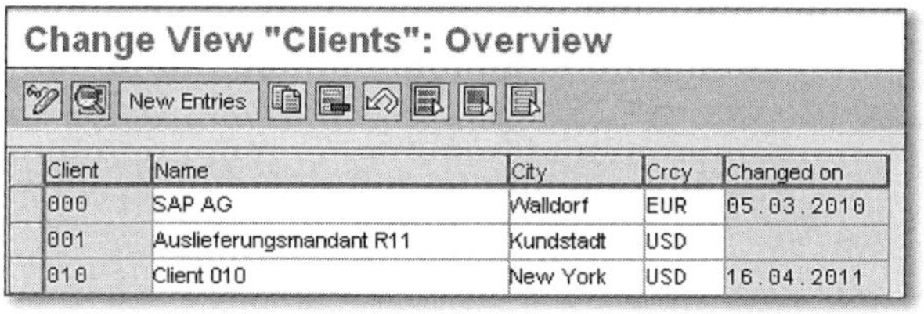

Change View "Clients": Overview

Client	Name	City	Crcy	Changed on
000	SAP AG	Walldorf	EUR	05.03.2010
001	Auslieferungsmandant R11	Kundstadt	USD	
010	Client 010	New York	USD	16.04.2011

Figure 1.7 Client Maintenance

The currency (CRCY column shown in Figure 1.7) assigned to CLIENT 010 is USD. This means the client currency type or currency type 30 is USD.

▶ **Currency types 40 and 50**

Currency types 40 and 50 are defined in the country customizing. These can be used in countries where inflation is relevant, and accountants need a hard or indexed currency to be available for financial statements.

You maintain the currencies using Transaction OY01 or by following the IMG menu path NETWEAVER • GENERAL SETTINGS • SET COUNTRIES • DEFINE COUNTRIES IN MYSAP SYSTEMS, which brings you to Figure 1.8.

Figure 1.8 Country Global Parameters

To see the information for the country, double-click in the COUNTRY column (e.g., US), and the corresponding country settings will open. There are two currency fields available in the settings: INDEX-BASED CURR. and HARD CURRENCY, which are currency types 50 and 40, respectively. You can see in Figure 1.9 that COUNTRY US uses USD as index-based currency or currency type 50, and EUR as hard currency or currency type 40.

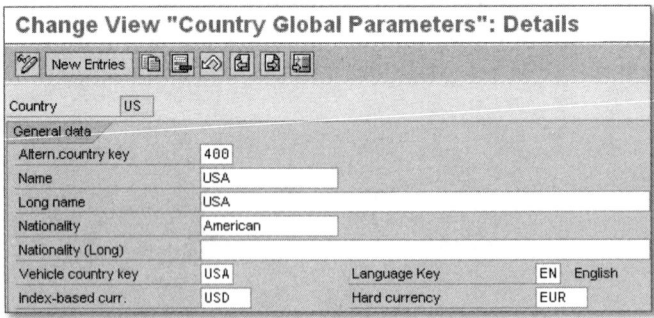

Figure 1.9 US Country Global Parameters

► **Currency type 60**

Currency type 60 is seldom used as a controlling area currency. It is normally defined in the trading partner customization. Company codes assigned to the same trading partner will share the same currency.

To maintain the trading partner currency, either use Transaction OX15, or follow the IMG menu path ENTERPRISE STRUCTURE • DEFINITION FINANCIAL ACCOUNTING • DEFINE COMPANY, which will open the screen shown in Figure 1.10.

Double-clicking on an entry in the COMPANY column, (e.g., 2000) will open the screen shown in Figure 1.11, Internal Trading Partner Details. (Note that the term "company" is synonymous with "trading partner" in SAP ERP.)

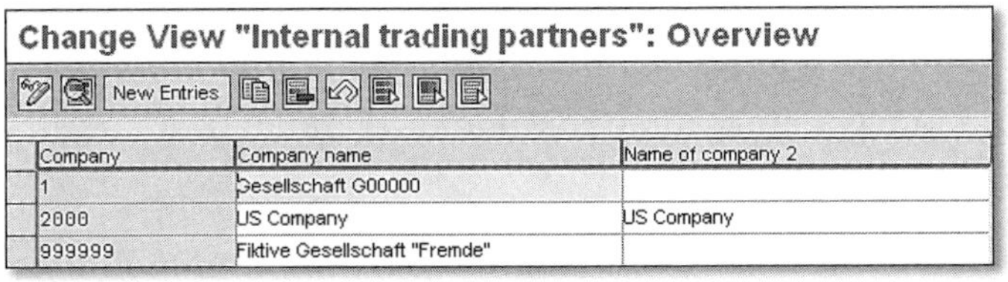

Change View "Internal trading partners": Overview

New Entries

Company	Company name	Name of company 2
1	Gesellschaft G00000	
2000	US Company	US Company
999999	Fiktive Gesellschaft "Fremde"	

Figure 1.10 Trading Partner Customizing

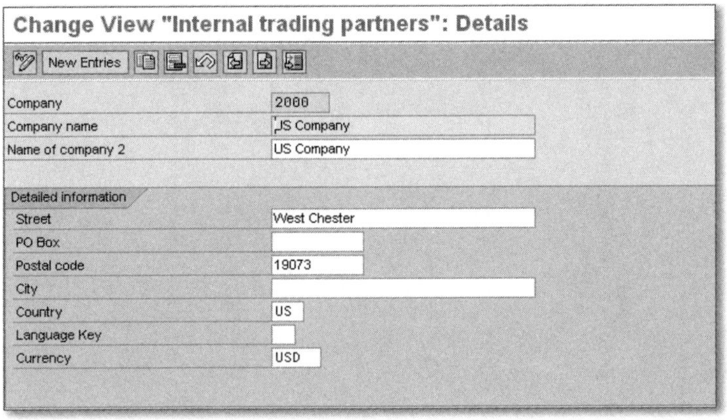

Change View "Internal trading partners": Details

New Entries

Company	2000
Company name	US Company
Name of company 2	US Company

Detailed information

Street	West Chester
PO Box	
Postal code	19073
City	
Country	US
Language Key	
Currency	USD

Figure 1.11 Trading Partner Detail

The CURRENCY field in this screen (e.g., USD) is the global company currency or currency type 60.

It is useless to have the currency type created if you don't assign the currency type to the company code. Each company code can have three currency types assigned. This allows the accounting to be maintained in three different currencies. To customize the currency at the company code level, use Transaction OB22, or follow the IMG menu path FINANCIAL ACCOUNTING (NEW) • FINANCIAL ACCOUNTING GLOBAL SETTINGS (NEW) • LEDGERS • LEDGER • DEFINE CURRENCIES OF LEADING LEDGER (see Figure 1.12 and Figure 1.13).

Change View "Additional Local Currencies For Company Code": Overview

New Entries   BC Set: Change Field Values

CoCd	Company Name	City	Country
2000	Company Code US	New York	US
3000	Company Code DE	Walldorf	DE

Figure 1.12 Additional Local Currencies for Company Code

Double-click in one company code to see the details, as shown in Figure 1.13. In this screen, you customize the second and third currency for a company code, and the exchange rate type that will be used to convert the first currency to the second and third.

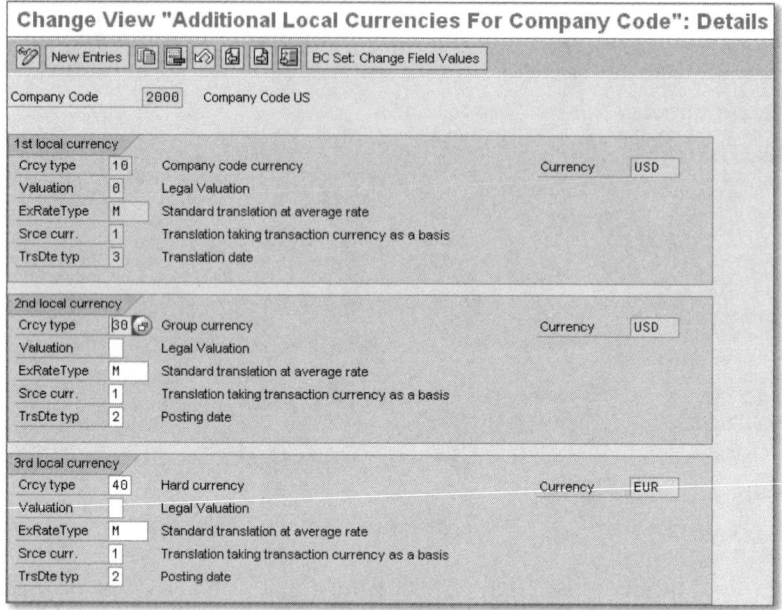

Figure 1.13 Additional Local Currencies for Company Code Details

You can see in this example that for company code 2000, the group currency, (currency type 30) was assigned as the second local currency, and hard currency (currency type 40) was assigned as the third local currency. These settings at the company code level are important because when you customize the controlling area, the combination of available local currencies should determine how you set the controlling area currency.

1.1.1 Creating the Controlling Area

The controlling area is the main and highest organizational unit in CO. All cost objects, such as cost centers, internal order activity types, and statistical key figures, must have a controlling area assigned. Additionally, all cost allocations, distributions, and assessments must be performed within a controlling area and cannot cross between different controlling areas.

A controlling area is also used to consolidate multiple company codes that are contained within the same controlling area. You can assign more than one company code to one controlling area, or you can assign just one company code to each controlling area. The advantage in assigning more than one company code is that you can perform accounting and reporting across company codes.

The assignment of a company code to the controlling area must be made with consideration given to the processes that the company has in logistics and accounting. A good blueprint in this phase will determine the best way to create the controlling area and get the best results in the future regarding reporting and available processes.

When you customize the controlling area, you are selecting which CO subcomponents this controlling area will have and which company codes will be assigned to it. The creation, settings definition, and company code assignment for a controlling area can all be done in the same step. Use Transaction OKKP, or go to CONTROLLING • GENERAL CONTROLLING • ORGANIZATION • MAINTAIN CONTROLLING AREA. Figure 1.14 shows the screen used to make the customizations. You can create a new controlling area by clicking on NEW ENTRIES, or you can copy an existing one.

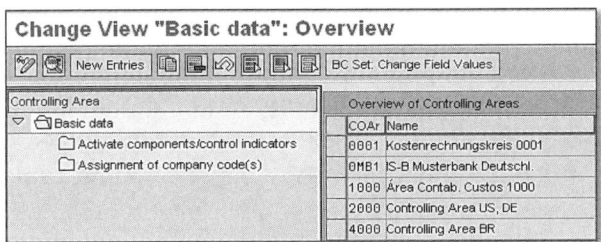

Figure 1.14 Controlling Area Definition

By clicking NEW ENTRIES, you can see the first settings for the controlling area, such as controlling area identification, currency, chart of accounts, and fiscal year variant. Figure 1.15 shows the screen for controlling area 2000 as an example.

Next, we'll explain the characteristics for each option and what impact the selections may cause in CO.

After giving identification for the controlling area (a four-digit alphanumeric field), the first customizing is the ASSIGNMENT CONTROL. This will identify the kind of controlling area, that is, whether it will be a controlling area with multiple company codes or a controlling area with only one company code.

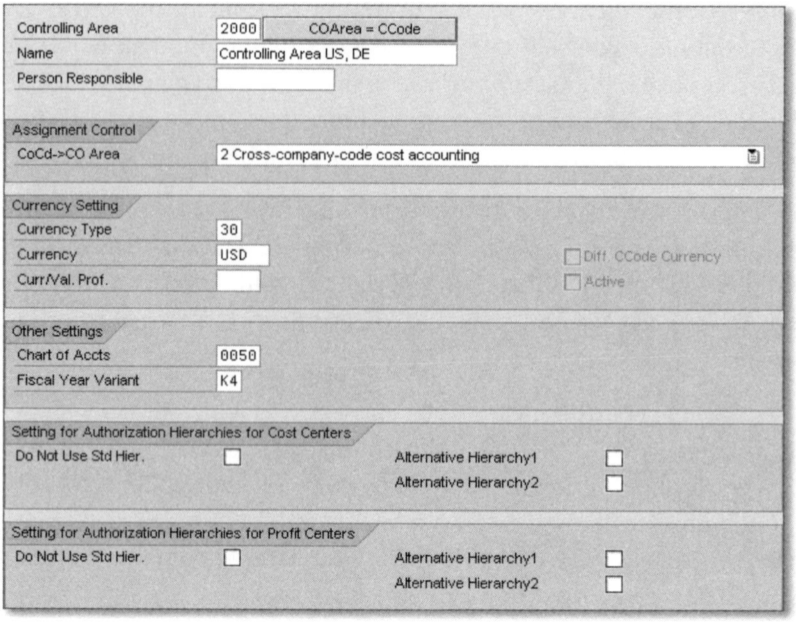

Figure 1.15 Controlling Area Definition

If you set the field so that the controlling area is the same as the company code (COAREA = CCODE), you are saying that a relationship of one controlling area for each company code will be adopted by the system. Because all of the cost reports and cost transactions in SAP have to be executed by controlling area, it's impossible to consolidate costs of two different company codes in the same report using standard functionality with this option. It can only be done using custom-developed reports. No cross-company-code costing can be performed when using this option.

Setting the COCD->CO AREA field to CROSS-COMPANY-CODE COST ACCOUNTING allows the controlling area to have more than one company code assigned. Using this option, you can consolidate different company codes in the same controlling area and use cross-company-code costing. This is the recommended setting for company code assignment.

The next important fields in the controlling area settings are the CURRENCY TYPE and CURRENCY. This is the place to set the currency type that we've already explained. Be careful when choosing the correct currency type for the controlling area. You should consider the organization's needs as they are today and how they may change in the future. If you choose a currency type that restricts the company code assignment, you will lose flexibility. Because values flow from FI to CO and vice versa, the company code and controlling area must share a common currency. One currency type that can be assigned to all company codes and across controlling areas is currency type 30.

Every time a document is created in CO, the system updates the line items in the total tables with three different currencies:

1. The controlling area currency, which is the currency definition we've just described

2. The company code currency or object currency

3. The transaction currency, which is the currency in which the document was posted

For example, in a controlling area with USD currency and a company code in Germany with EUR currency, the system will save the values in USD for controlling area currency, in EUR for company code currency, and in a third currency that is the transaction currency.

The next fields available for the controlling area initial settings are the CHART OF ACCTS and FISCAL YEAR VARIANT. In cross-company-code cost accounting, the chart of accounts must be the same for all company codes, and the fiscal year variants assigned to the controlling area and company codes can differ only in the number of special periods.

Also available in this customizing screen are the SETTING FOR AUTHORIZATION HIERARCHIES FOR COST CENTERS and SETTING FOR AUTHORIZATION HIERARCHIES FOR PROFIT CENTERS sections. Use the settings in these sections if you want to change the way the system checks the user authorizations for cost centers and profit centers. You can change the authorization check from the standard hierarchy to the alternative hierarchy 1 or 2.

After you create the basic settings for the controlling area, the next step is to assign the company codes to the controlling area. To do this, you should go back to the first customizing screen shown previously in Figure 1.15, select the controlling area on the right side of the screen, and click on ASSIGNMENT OF COMPANY CODE(S). Figure 1.16 shows the details.

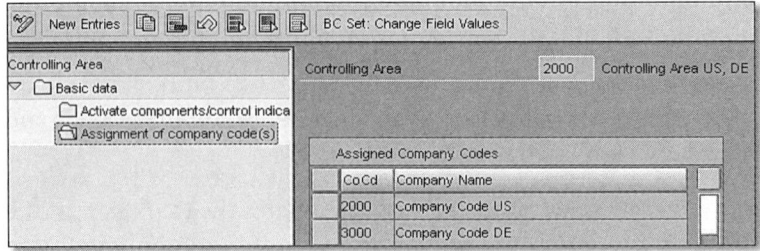

Figure 1.16 Company Code Assignment to a Controlling Area

In the next screen, click on NEW ENTRIES, and add the company code on the right side. A cross-company-code controlling area will accept more than one company code, as long as the consistency prerequisites, such as chart of accounts, currency type, and fiscal year variant, are met.

After assigning the company codes, go back to the initial settings, and you can see two new fields on the controlling area basic data. One is the CCTR STD. HIERARCHY, and the other is the document type for the reconciliation ledger (see Figure 1.17).

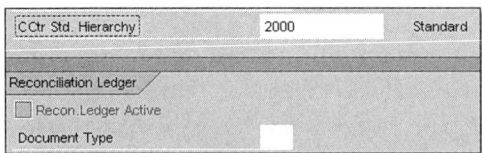

Figure 1.17 New Fields on Controlling Area Basic Settings

The standard hierarchy is the first node of the cost center structure, and all cost centers in the controlling area must be in a node of the standard hierarchy. You must create the first node here, and afterwards you can maintain the standard hierarchy by adding or removing new nodes and creating cost centers. Maintaining the hierarchy is done in a separate transaction, which is covered in detail in Chapter 3, Cost Center Accounting.

When the New General Ledger is active, the real-time integration function can be used to reconcile CO and FI.

> **Note**
>
> SAP recommends using real-time integration in place of the reconciliation ledger. The reconciliation ledger will not be supported by SAP in the long term.

Our example company, XYZ, has three different company codes already configured in FI. Company code is the smallest unit of organization in terms of financial accounting for external reporting (balance sheet, P&L statement). A company must be constituted to meet the requirements of tax, business, and financial accounting. All financial postings must be linked to a company. The company is identified by a four-digit alphanumeric code that must be unique. XYZ's three company codes correspond to the different legal entities in the XYZ consolidated group.

The customizing listed in Table 1.2 and Table 1.3 was made relative to currency and company code for XYZ using the previously described steps.

Company Code	Company Code Description
2000	Company Code US
3000	Company Code DE
4000	Company Code BR

Table 1.2 Company Codes for XYZ Enterprise

Company Code	Crcy Type 1	Crcy Type 2	Crcy Type 3
2000 – Company Code US	10 – USD	30 – USD	40 – EUR
3000 – Company Code DE	10 – EUR	30 – USD	40 – EUR
4000 – Company Code BR	10 – BRL	30 – USD	40 – EUR

Table 1.3 Company Codes and Currency Types for XYZ

By choosing this model for XYZ, since all company codes share two currencies types, the company will be able to produce consolidated financial statements in a common currency, in this case, USD or EUR.

Controlling area is the highest organizational level within CO. Recall that a controlling area may include one or more company codes. The controlling area and all company codes included within that controlling area must use the same operative chart of accounts. For XYZ, one controlling area was defined, and all three company codes are assigned to that controlling area. This configuration was defined for XYZ to provide the most flexible accounting and reporting options for the entire enterprise. Using one controlling area with the currency assignments configured at the company code level will allow daily transactions to be recorded in the local currencies, cross-company-code accounting, and costing and assessments. Reporting will be available for any subgrouping of the three legal entities within the controlling area or for the entire consolidated group.

Now that you've assigned the company code(s) to the controlling area, the next step is to create the controlling area number ranges. Activating the individual subcomponents in CO is discussed in detail in later chapters.

1.1.2 Maintain Number Ranges for Controlling Documents

Because every posting in CO creates a document, the next step in the customizing is to define the CO document number ranges. The postings in CO are classified by business transactions. For example, business transaction COIN is used for CO through-postings from FI, so you should create the number range and then assign the business transaction to the number range. The CO number ranges are independent of the fiscal year. We recommend that you use different number ranges for planning and actual business transactions so you can identify which line item is planning and which is actual just by looking at the document number in line-item reports.

> **Note**
>
> When you create the number range for a controlling area, a transport request is not created. Don't transport the number ranges; always create the groups and the number ranges directly in each environment.

You can create CO number ranges using Transaction KANK or by following the IMG menu path CONTROLLING • GENERAL CONTROLLING • ORGANIZATION • MAINTAIN NUMBER RANGES FOR CONTROLLING DOCUMENTS. Figure 1.18 shows the customizing screen.

You must create a group first to assign the number ranges to it. Click the button to maintain GROUPS (the pencil icon) as shown in Figure 1.18 (the GROUPS eyeglasses icon is to display groups). The screen shown in Figure 1.19 appears.

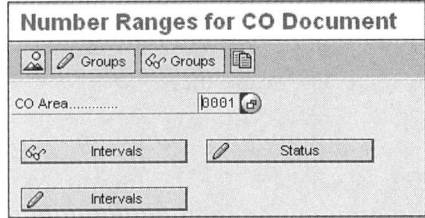

Figure 1.18 Number Ranges for the CO Document

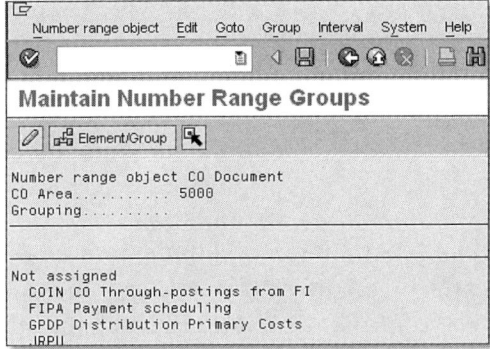

Figure 1.19 Maintain Number Range Groups

Go to the GROUP menu, and select INSERT. A new pop-up window will appear where the group name and the number range can be added, as shown in Figure 1.20.

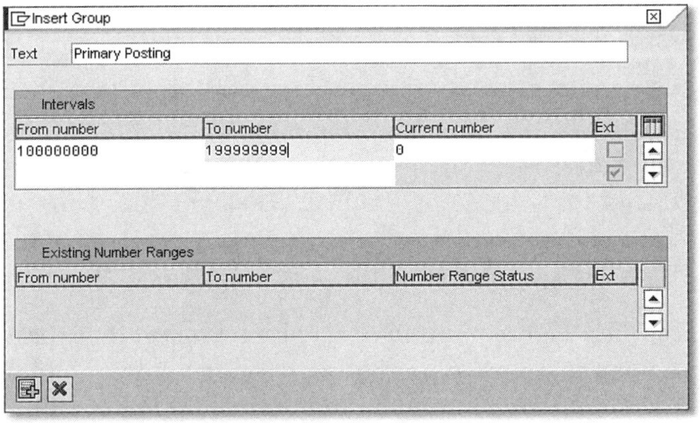

Figure 1.20 Creating the Number Range Group

After creating the number range group, the controlling business transaction should be assigned to the group. Figure 1.21 shows an example of how to assign business transactions to the group just created for primary postings.

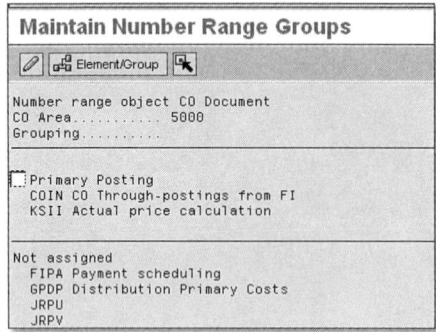

Figure 1.21 Number Range Group Assignment

To assign the transaction, select the CO business transaction with the SELECT ELE-MENT button (icon with arrow pointing to the square in the corner). Leave the cursor in the group that you want to assign the controlling business transaction, and click the ELEMENT/GROUP button. Repeat this process until all business transactions are assigned to a group.

The SAP ERP system includes standard default assignments of business transactions to number ranges for controlling area 0001. You can copy the number ranges from this controlling area and change just the business transactions that you don't want to use that are included in the model. This process makes the number range creation faster and easier.

If you're going to copy the number ranges from another controlling area such as 0001, first compare both controlling areas to see if the activated components for the controlling areas are the same. If they are not, activate the same components for both controlling areas, and copy the number ranges. Then you can return to the controlling area settings and deactivate the components that you aren't going to use.

To copy the number range, click the COPY button (icon with two sheets of paper), and select the controlling area FROM and TO, as shown in Figure 1.22.

Next you need to customize the versions for the controlling area.

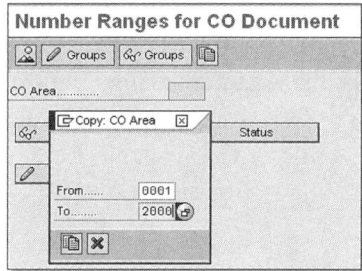

Figure 1.22 Number Range Copying

1.1.3   Maintain Versions

Every posting, planning, and budget for CO occurs in at least one version of CO in SAP ERP. A version consists of a set of indicators that is fiscal year-dependent and is used for planning and actual postings in a controlling area.

SAP ERP automatically generates the 000 version while creating the controlling area. Actual values created by primary costs and internal allocation of costs are recorded in that version. As a result, the 000 version should be used for comparisons of actual costs to planned costs. Versions allow the creation of an independent group of actual and planned data depending on the fiscal year.

The CO version definition is generic and allows data integrity when working with different CO subcomponents: CO-PA, CO-CCA, CO-ABC, EC-PCA. However, each CO subcomponent requires additional specific versions beyond the basic setting. The number of versions is virtually unlimited.

You can create and change the CO versions using Transaction OKEQ or by going to CONTROLLING • GENERAL CONTROLLING • ORGANIZATION • MAINTAIN VERSIONS, which brings you to the screen shown in Figure 1.23.

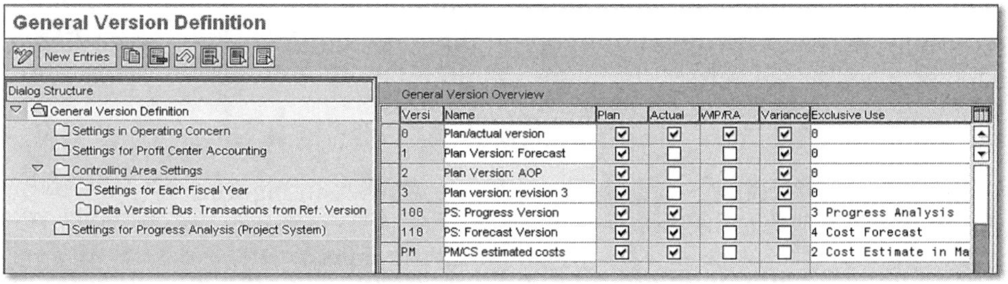

Figure 1.23 Maintain Controlling Versions

To create a version, you can either copy an existing version or create a new one. When copying a version, be sure to copy the dependent data (you'll be prompted to do so by the system). Afterwards, be sure to check the data and change the settings according to your requirements. With the new version created, you should now select the initial options for the version. Five options are available for the GENERAL VERSION DEFINITION (as shown on the right side of Figure 1.23):

- ▶ PLAN
  Allows planning values in the version.

- ▶ ACTUAL
  Indicates that the version will receive the actual transactions from direct or internal postings, primary postings, and secondary postings. Only version 000 can be flagged as actual, unless the version is a delta version or an exclusive use version.

- ▶ WIP/RA
  Permits Work in Process (WIP) and Results Analysis (RA) for the version.

- ▶ VARIANCE
  Permits calculation of variances for the version.

- ▶ EXCLUSIVE USE
  Indicates that the version is exclusive for some CO subcomponents, such as Transfer Price, Cost Estimate in Maintenance Order, Progress Analysis, Cost Forecast, or Material Ledger.

> **Note**
>
> The selection of the options must be consistent with the definitions for the controlling area. For example, it isn't possible to select VARIANCE in the version if it isn't set on the controlling area definition.

The SETTINGS IN OPERATING CONCERN and SETTINGS FOR PROFIT CENTER ACCOUNTING are explained in Chapter 7, Profitability Analysis, and Chapter 8, Profit Center Accounting, respectively.

After creating the basic settings for the version, you now need to create the version settings in the controlling area. In the controlling area settings, you define the options for each year that this version will be valid, such as the exchange rate type, options for the activity type rate calculation, and others. To create the version, select the version on the right side of the screen, and double-click on the CONTROLLING AREA SETTINGS node on the left. The system will ask if you want to create the version in the controlling area. Click YES, and you will see the screen shown in Figure 1.24.

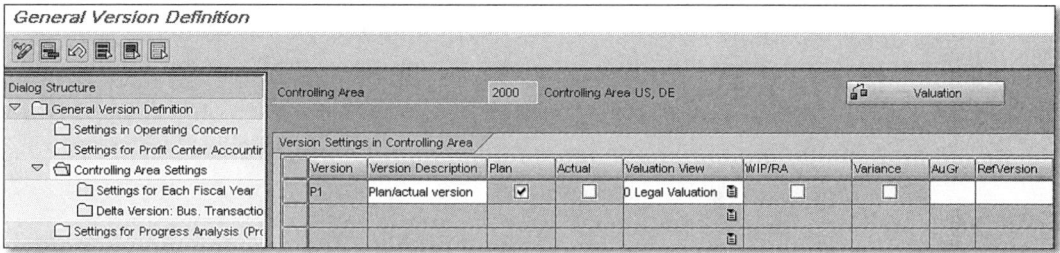

Figure 1.24 Creating Controlling Area Settings for Version

The same options that were available in the GENERAL VERSION DEFINITION node are available in the CONTROLLING AREA SETTINGS node, so that the same version can be assigned to different controlling areas. The fields selected here should be consistent with the options selected for GENERAL VERSION DEFINITION. If you set all options available for the version in the basic settings, you can select the desired options for the specific controlling area settings, but if you haven't selected the field in the basic settings, you can't select it here. Two additional options are also available: VALUATION VIEW and REF VERSION (refer to Figure 1.24). The VALUATION VIEW option is used if the valuation and currency profile is activated in the controlling area. The REF VERSION option is used to create delta versions.

After you've created the controlling area settings, create the year-dependent setting for the version in the controlling area. Mark the version on the right side of the screen, and double-click on the SETTINGS FOR EACH FISCAL YEAR node. You can either copy a current entry or create a new one. Figure 1.25 shows the version settings for the year.

The first tab that you will customize is the PLANNING tab. You will set the planning options for this version in the selected controlling area.

In the GENERAL INDICATORS section, you can see VERSION LOCKED, INTEGRATED PLANNING, and COPYING ALLOWED checkboxes:

▶ Setting the VERSION LOCKED indicator means that this version will be locked for planning purposes for cost centers. If the INTEGRATED PLANNING flag is set, the VERSION LOCKED setting will also affect the planning in internal orders and projects.

▶ Setting the INTEGRATED PLANNING flag creates the integration of planning between cost centers and other CO subcomponents such as Profit Center Accounting or Internal Orders.

▶ Setting the COPYING ALLOWED flag allows planning versions to be copied from this version.

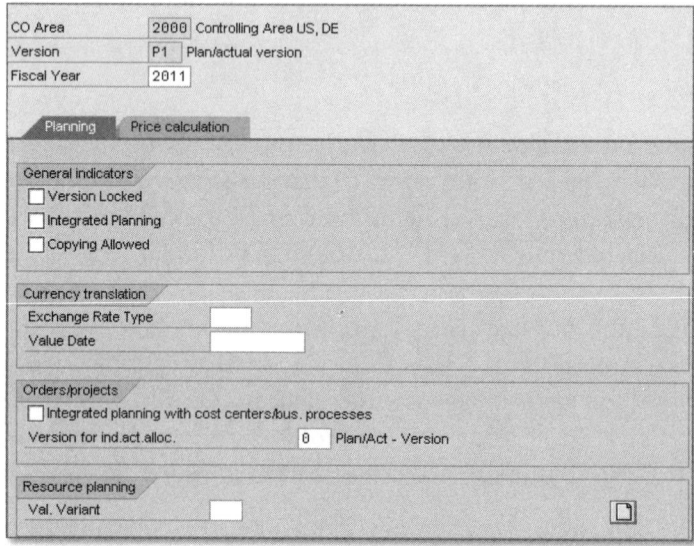

Figure 1.25 Year-Dependent Version Setting (Planning)

In the CURRENCY TRANSLATION section, you can configure the EXCHANGE RATE TYPE and the VALUE DATE fields to define which exchange rate type will be used when planning in a different currency than the controlling area currency. The system will use the exchange rate type assigned in the customizing to create the conversion. If you leave the VALUE DATE field blank, SAP ERP determines an exchange rate based on the starting date of each period. If you set a value date, the system will use the exchange rate from this date for all planning in this year, even when the period is not the same as the value date.

In the ORDERS/PROJECTS section, you can also set the INTEGRATED PLANNING WITH COST CENTERS/BUS. PROCESSES checkbox in the version customizing for the orders and projects. By setting this code, you are saying that settlement, periodic reposting, and indirect activity allocations are allowed. When you don't set this checkbox, you need to specify in the VERSION FOR IND.ACT.ALLOC field from which version the system will get the activity price to use for planning. If the field is blank, SAP ERP will adopt version 0 as reference.

The next tab you need to customize is the PRICE CALCULATION tab. In this customizing, you set the behavior of the system when calculating the activity type price for planning and determine whether it is a real version for the actual price calculation as well.

In Figure 1.26, you can see the available options for the version. The version shown is an actual and plan version, so customizing for both planning and actual price calculations are available.

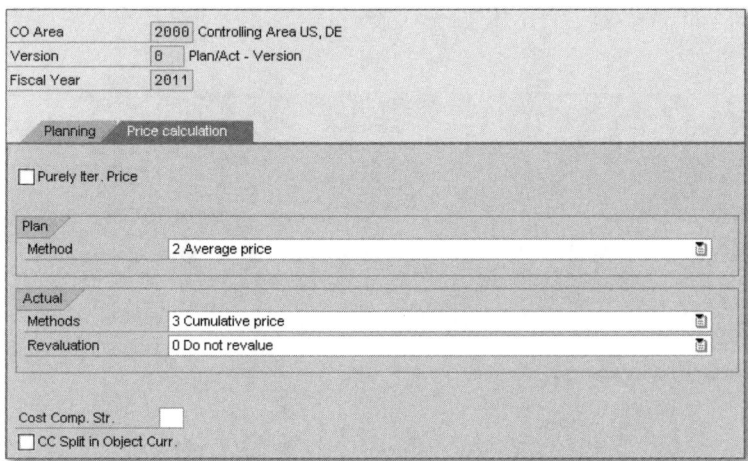

Figure 1.26 Price Calculation Settings

The first field is PURELY ITER. PRICE, which is used only if you set the activity price manually during the planning process.

For the PLAN section, you can set the METHOD field by selecting either PERIODIC PRICE or AVERAGE PRICE. If you are planning the activity price by year and set the transaction to calculate from period 1 to period 12, with PERIODIC PRICE selected, the system will calculate the activity price for each period by dividing the planning cost amount by the activity price quantity in the period. The cost center balance by period will be zero. Table 1.4 shows an example of periodic price calculation.

	Cost	Activity	Price
Period 1	10,000 USD	50 hours	200 USD/hr
Period 2	15,000 USD	100 hours	150 USD/hr
Period 3	5,000 USD	100 hours	50 USD/hr

Table 1.4 Periodic Price Calculation

With AVERAGE PRICE selected, the system will add up all costs from the period on the selection screen and divide the amount per the total quantity of activity type in the period. The balance in the cost center in this case won't be zero by month but only in total for the same range of periods used for the price calculation. Table 1.5 shows the results of the same data as in the periodic price example when AVERAGE PRICE is selected instead. In this case, the system will use the price 120 USD/hr for all periods.

	Cost	Activity	Price
Period 1	10,000 USD	50 hours	200 USD/hr
Period 2	15,000 USD	100 hours	150 USD/hr
Period 3	5,000 USD	100 hours	50 USD/hr
Average	30,000 USD	250 hours	120 USD/hr

Table 1.5 Average Price Calculation

For actual price calculation (shown in the ACTUAL section of the screen), you have three options available: PERIODIC PRICE, AVERAGE PRICE, and a new option called CUMULATIVE PRICE. Cumulative price is similar to average price, but when running the revaluation, the system will create a new posting in the previous periods adjusting the cumulative price. For this method, the period lock can't be used because every time a new price is calculated, the system posts a difference in previous periods. Table 1.6 shows a cumulative price example.

	Cost	Activity	Price
Period 1	10,000 USD	50 hours	200 USD/hr
Period 1	25,000 USD	150 hours	166,67 USD/hr
Period 3	30,000 USD	250 hours	120 USD/hr

Table 1.6 Cumulative Price Calculation

Revaluation can only be used for actual price calculation because during the month, the system uses the activity price planned for posting of transactions. At the month-end closing, you can revalue the prices using the actual costs and the actual activity type quantities. You have three options available in the version customizing: Do Not Revaluate, Revaluate in Own Business Transaction, and Revaluate in Original Transaction. By selecting Do Not Revaluate, the transactions remain as originally calculated using planned activity pricing, and the cost center balance won't be zero in the period. Revaluate in Own Business Transaction means the system will post the difference in a separate transaction, and you can see in the reports the difference between actual and planned prices. Using the last option, Revaluation in Original Transaction, the system will post the actual price in the same transaction as the planned price, and you can't see the difference between actual and planned price.

You can also define delta versions in the versions customizing. When working with statistical Activity-Based Costing, a delta version must be used to save the delta statistical posting. The SAP system provides the delta version solution to work with specific or nonspecific CO subcomponents, and it's possible to select which data will be used to create the delta posting. To create a delta version, you must assign which version will be the reference version in the controlling area settings for the version. To make the assignment, navigate back to controlling area settings by double-clicking on the Controlling area settings node on the left side of the screen, which will bring you to the screen shown in Figure 1.27.

In this case, version P2 will have version 0 as the reference version. To select which business transactions you want to pull from the reference version, mark the version on the right side of the screen, and double-click on Delta Version: Bus. Transactions from Ref. Version on the left side of the screen. Figure 1.28 shows the business transactions options.

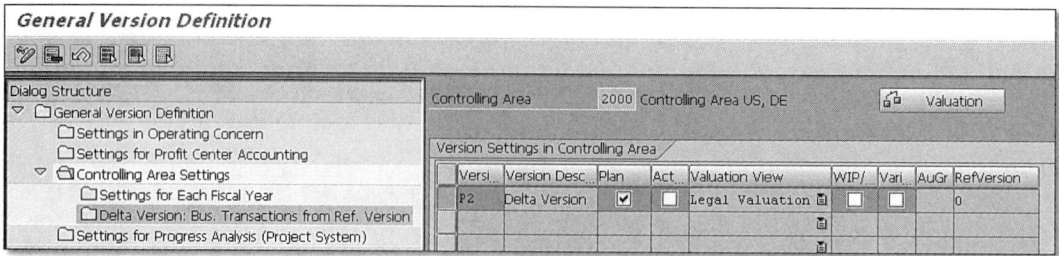

Figure 1.27 Reference Version

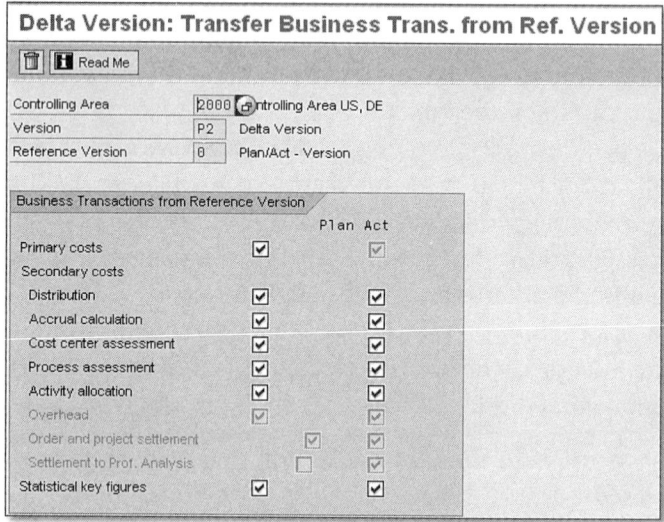

Figure 1.28 Business Transaction from Reference Version

Note

If a business transaction is selected, postings will not be allowed from that business transaction. For example, if the Act (actual) checkbox is selected for the COST CENTER ASSESSMENT entry, it isn't possible to run actual cost center assessments in this version.

Now that you understand the basic organizational settings for CO, the controlling area, number ranges, and versions, the next topic to address is the customizing available for account assignment logic.

1.2 Account Assignment Logic

To ensure that correct information is recorded in CO, rules for validations and substitutions, commonly referred to as account assignment logic, can be created. These validation or substitution rules are assigned to the controlling area.

One example of validation is used in the XYZ Company. For all of the manufacturing operations, XYZ has a validation to restrict which cost elements can be posted in production cost centers. This allows for consistent and standardized production cost reporting and worldwide benchmarking.

XYZ also uses a substitution to determine a fixed cost center for a defined cost element. This is intended to avoid mistakes in cost center selection when posting to the defined cost element.

In the following subsections, we will use these examples to show how each is customized in the SAP system.

1.2.1 Define Validation

The first step in the validation customizing is to choose which event you want to activate the CO validation. Three events are available for this step:

▶ (0001) – LINE ITEM
Subjects each line item in the document to the validation.

▶ (0002) – INTERNAL CO POSTING: SEND/REC VAL
Validates only CO internal postings.

▶ (0100) – DOCUMENT HEADER
Checks only the document header; fields from document line item are not available with this option.

Figure 1.29 shows the first customizing screen for the validation, where you define the controlling area, event, validation name, and whether it is active. To create the validation, use Transaction OKC7, or follow the IMG menu path CONTROLLING • GENERAL CONTROLLING • ACCOUNT ASSIGNMENT LOGIC • DEFINE VALIDATION.

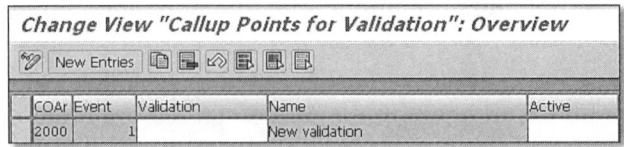

Figure 1.29 Validation Customizing

Double-click in the line, and a new screen will appear. In this screen, once you expand the node COST ACCOUNTING, the three events available for the validation are listed, as shown in Figure 1.30.

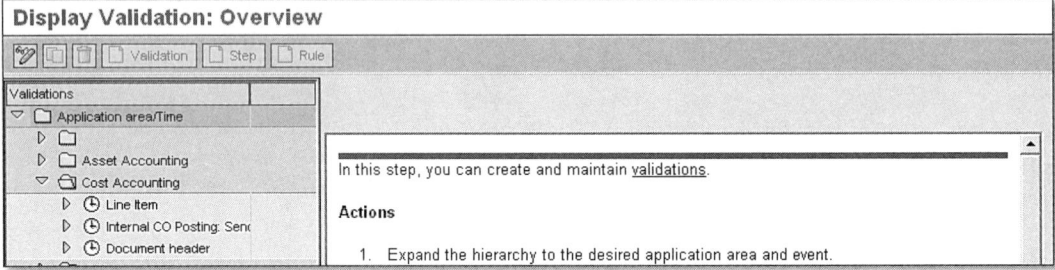

Figure 1.30 Cost Accounting Validation

Open the node where the validation will be created, LINE ITEM, INTERNAL CO POSTING: SEND/REC VAL, OR DOCUMENT HEADER. Click on the change mode button (pencil icon), and create a new validation for the desired event. For this example, we will create one at LINE ITEM.

The validation is divided into three phases, as shown in Figure 1.31:

► PREREQUISITE
Determines if the entered information on the field is to be checked. If the condition is met, the validation goes to the CHECK phase.

► CHECK (after the prerequisite is reached)
Checks if the information entered meets the validation criteria established. If not, the validation goes to MESSAGE.

► MESSAGE
If the prerequisite condition is met, and the check is not true, you can set an error or warning message.

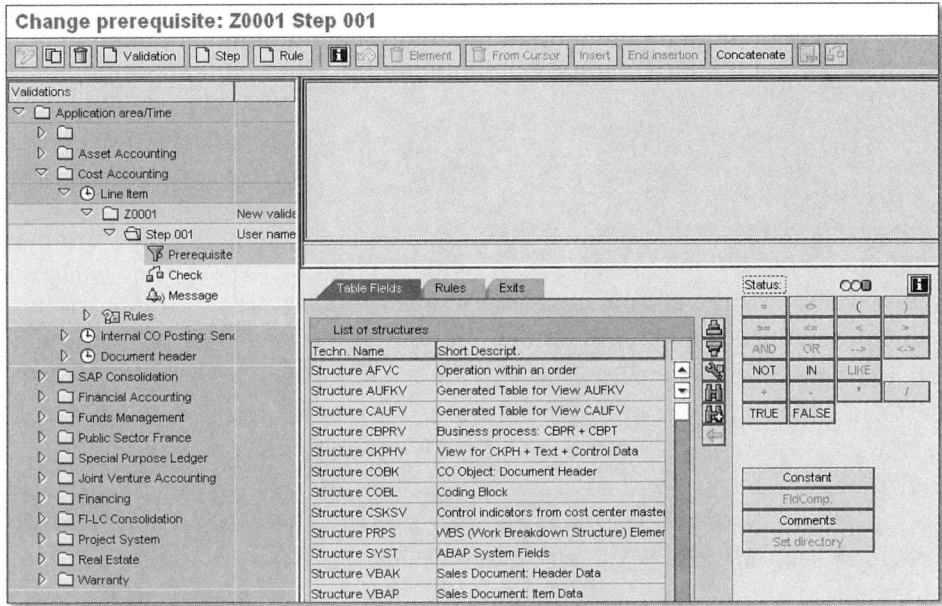

Figure 1.31 Validation Screen

In the validation rules, checks are set up using the structures shown in Table 1.7 (and in the LIST OF STRUCTURES section of Figure 1.31) when available in the document.

Structure	Description
AFVC	OPERATION WITHIN AN ORDER
AUFKV	GENERATED TABLE FOR VIEW AUFKV
CAUFV	GENERATED TABLE FOR VIEW CAUFV
CKPHV	BUSINESS PROCESS: CBPR + CBPT
CBPRV	VIEW FOR CKPH + TEXT + CONTROL DATA
COBK	CO OBJECT: DOCUMENT HEADER
COBL	CODING BLOCK
CSKSV	CONTROL INDICATORS FROM COST CENTER MASTER RECORD
PRPS	WORK BREAKDOWN STRUCTURE (WBS) ELEMENT MASTER DATA

Table 1.7 Available Structures for Validations

Structure	Description
SYST	ABAP System Fields
VBAK	Sales Document: Header Data
VBAP	Sales Document: Item Data

Table 1.7 Available Structures for Validations (Cont.)

When working with validations, we recommend that you create sets of parameters to contain the requirements. For example, if the Prerequisite is the user name, instead of fixing the user name in the prerequisite, it's better to define the user name inside of a set of parameters. This approach is recommended because sets of parameters can be maintained directly in the production environment. If the name is fixed in the Prerequisite or in the Check, a transport request is needed to make changes. The fields available to create the set are the fields on the structures available for the validation (see Table 1.7).

> **Note**
>
> To create a set of parameters, use Transaction GS01, or, to modify a set of parameters, use Transaction GS02. The sets must be defined using the structures available on the validation and will be automatically added as a valid set to the validation.
>
> When transporting the validation, you have the option to transport the set along with the validation. If the set already exist in the quality and production environments, it will be overwritten and will adopt the values from the development environment. If you plan to transport the sets along with the validation, you should maintain the set in the development environment with the same entries as in the production environment to avoid this kind of problem.

For XYZ, we will create a validation step with the following rule: For each document posted in CO, the system will first check the Prerequisite, if the cost center in the line item of the document being posted is in the set ZKOSTL (COBL-KOSTL). The set in this case represents the production cost centers. If this Prerequisite condition is met, the system will then check if the cost element is in the set ZSAKNR (COBL-SAKNR). In this case, the set contains the valid cost elements to post in the production cost centers. If the Check condition is not met, an error message will appear stating that the cost element is not allowed for posting to the cost center.

To create the first check, on the screen shown in Figure 1.31, mark PREREQUISITE on the left side of the screen, and double-click in the structure that has the field to be tested, (in our case, the structure COBL). Find the field COBL-KOSTL, and double-click in the field. Now the field will appear in the right box on the top of the screen. On the right will be a list of the operators available, (we selected IN, SET DIRECTORY, and ZKOSTL).

Repeat the same step for the CHECK. On the left side of the screen, select the structure, the field, and the set. Figure 1.32 shows the completed validation.

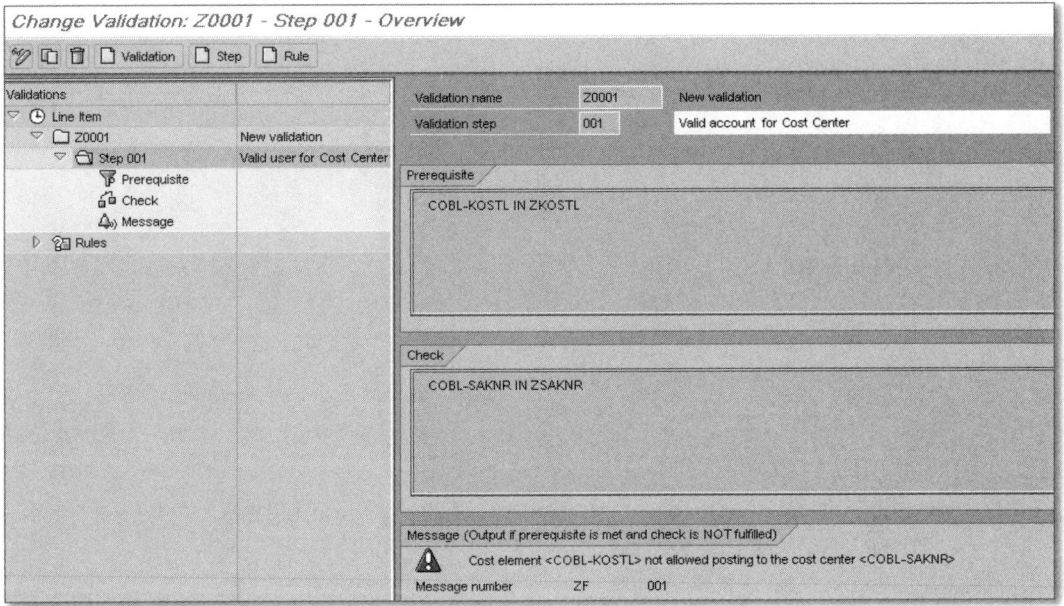

Figure 1.32 Complete Validation Step

A message is also needed for the validation. Select MESSAGE on the left side of the screen, as shown in Figure 1.33.

The field MESSAGE TYPE is used to choose the kind of message provided by the validation (error, warning, or information).

CO provides up to four variables to be used in the message. In this case, we have selected the COBL-SAKNR (GL account) and COBL-KOSTL (cost center). Click on CHANGE to create or modify the message as shown in Figure 1.34.

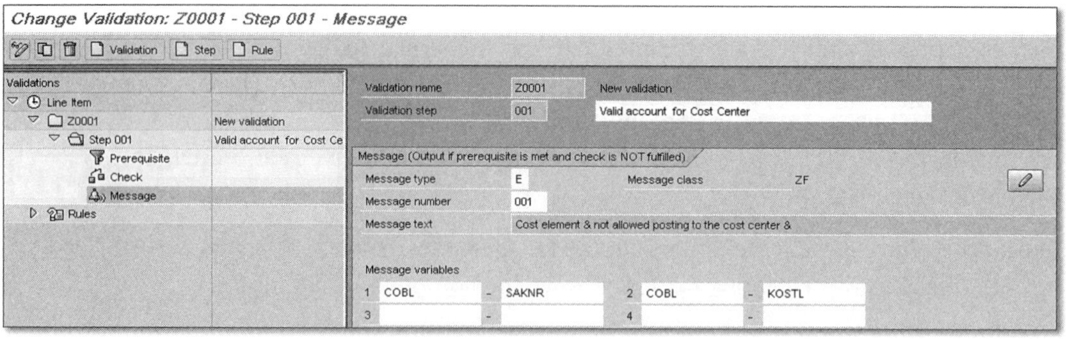

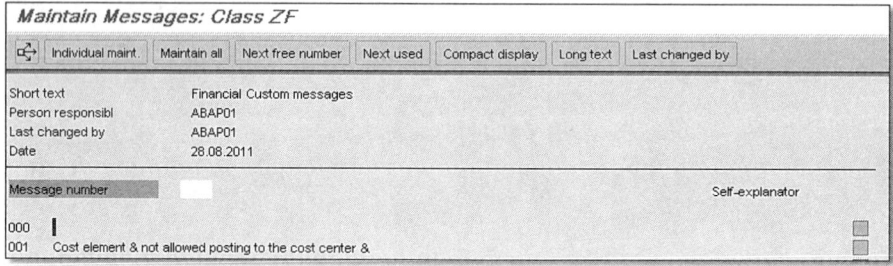

Change Validation: Z0001 - Step 001 - Message
Validation
Step
Rule
Validations
Line Item
Z0001
New validation
Step 001
Valid account for Cost Ce
Prerequisite
Check
Message
Rules
Validation name
Z0001
New validation
Validation step
001
Valid account for Cost Center
Message (Output if prerequisite is met and check is NOT fulfilled)
Message type
E
Message class
ZF
Message number
001
Message text
Cost element & not allowed posting to the cost center &
Message variables
1 COBL - SAKNR
2 COBL - KOSTL
3
4

Figure 1.33 Message for Validation

Maintain Messages: Class ZF
Individual maint.
Maintain all
Next free number
Next used
Compact display
Long text
Last changed by
Short text
Financial Custom messages
Person responsibl
ABAP01
Last changed by
ABAP01
Date
28.08.2011
Message number
Self-explanator
000
001 Cost element & not allowed posting to the cost center &

Figure 1.34 Message Detail

At the bottom of Figure 1.34, note that the first symbol "&" in the message will show the COBL-SAKNR (GL account) and the second symbol "&" will show the COBL-KOSTL (cost center). If more message variables are used, the addition of the symbol "&" in the message will add the variable to the message.

Another good way to create validations in CO is to use a user exit to perform the PREREQUISITE or the CHECK phase.

When using a user exit to create the validation, the first step is to copy the standard program delivered by SAP ERP and assign the new program to the customizing.

The user exit validation program provided by SAP ERP is Program RGGBR000. Copy this program to a custom program (for XYZ, we will be using Program ZRGGBR000). After copying, assign the program to the customizing using GBLR in the APPL. AREA column (shown in Figure 1.35). You can assign the program to validation customizing using Transaction GCX2 or by following the IMG menu path FINANCIAL ACCOUNTING (NEW) • SPECIAL PURPOSE LEDGER • BASIC SETTINGS • USER EXITS • MAINTAIN CLIENT-SPECIFIC USER EXITS.

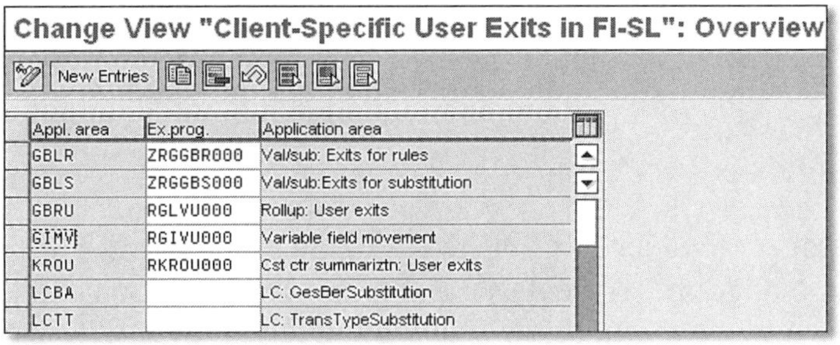

Figure 1.35 Assign Custom Program to Validation

To use the user exit, you must define the kind of parameters the exit will have. Table 1.8 shows the available parameters for the user exit.

User Exit Type	Description	Application
C_EXIT_PARAM_NONE	No parameters are defined for the user exit. Only the return value b_result (T = True or F = False) is passed from the user exit.	Rules, validations, and substitutions (prerequisite)
C_EXIT_PARAM_FIELD	Same as user exit type 1, except one parameter (the field to be substituted) is defined in the user exit. For example, a substitution routine can be created that analyzes the cost center irrespective of the field used.	Substitution
C_EXIT_PARAM_CLASS	All data is passed as one parameter; this exit type can be used in validations and substitutions.	Rules, validations, and substitutions (prerequisite)

Table 1.8 Validation/Substitution User Exit Parameters

Consider the following example of user exit code:

```
exits-name  = 'Z001'.
exits-param = c_exit_param_none.
exits-title = text-100.
APPEND exits.
```

```
FORM z100  USING b_result.
  if cobl-werks = '2001'.
    b_result = b_true.
  else.
    b_result = b_false.
  endif.

endform.
```

In this case, the user exit z001 will be available to use in the validation customizing. Figure 1.36 shows the recently created user exit Z001 – Plant Validation.

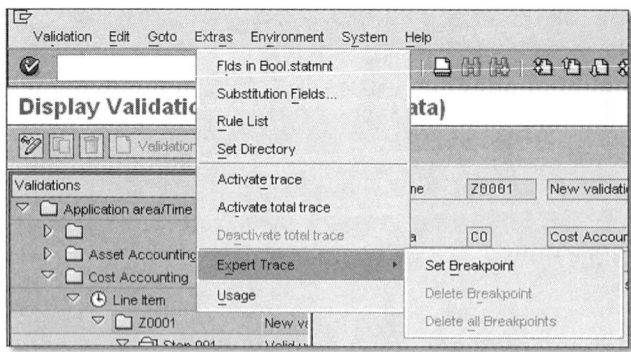

Techn. Name	Short Descript.
U100	Check account combination
US001	Example single record validation in EIS
Z001	Plant Validation
UFP01	UFP01
UFP02	UFP02

Figure 1.36 Exits Tab

There is another good tool available to use in the validation customizing. Go to the Extras menu, and activate ABAP trace for the validation by clicking on Expert Trace (see Figure 1.37). This allows you to debug the validation on the screen. You can also see all of the fields available to use in the validation by clicking on the Flds in Bool.statmnt menu item.

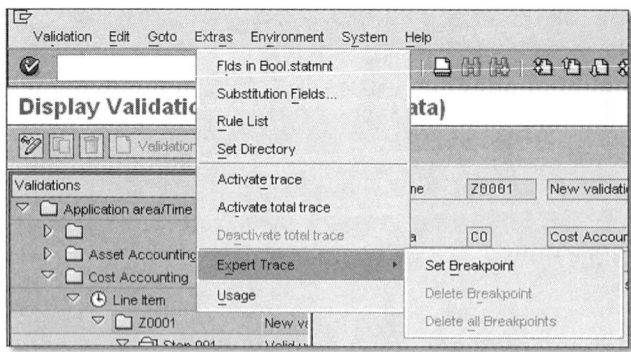

Figure 1.37 Menu Extras

Once you have defined your validations, the last step is to transport them to the production environment. The transport method for validations is different from the regular transport method. Upon saving the customizing, the screen to select or create a transport request will appear.

To create a transport for the validation definition, mark the validation name on the left side of the screen and choose VALIDATION • TRANSPORT from the menu bar as shown in Figure 1.38.

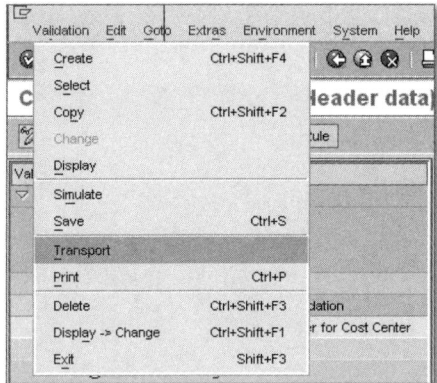

Figure 1.38 Validation Transport Request

The next screen is used to select which options are to be added to the transport request, as shown in Figure 1.39.

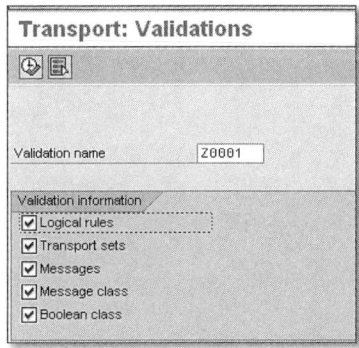

Figure 1.39 Transport Validations

When you run the transaction, the screen to select or create a new transport request will appear.

This transport request will just transport the steps definition for the validation; that is, it will not transport the option as active or not active.

To activate or deactivate the validations, return to the first screen of the validation. Enter the COAr (controlling area), the EVENT, and the VALIDATION, which you can see in Figure 1.40. The last column, ACTIVE, will show whether it is active or not: "1" is active, and "0" is not active. The option can be changed in this screen.

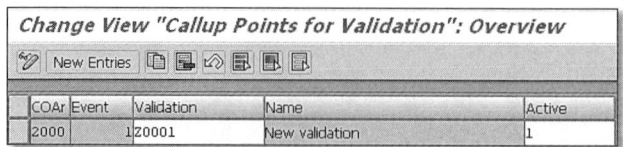

Figure 1.40 Validation Activation

After the validation has been transported to the production environment, and you have verified or maintained the sets used, you must activate the validation for it to take effect.

1.2.2 Define Substitutions

Substitutions use the same structures as those defined for the validation (refer to Table 1.7). The difference between validation and substitution is that the substitution will change the value for one or more fields without the knowledge of the user, respecting the predefined rules.

For substitutions, the following events are available:

► (0001) – LINE ITEM
Changes values from line items posted in CO.

► (0010) – ORDER
Substitutes values when a CO document has orders as cost object only.

► (0100) – DOCUMENT HEADER
Substitutes fields in CO document headers.

To create the substitution, either use Transaction OKC9, or follow the IMG menu path CONTROLLING • GENERAL CONTROLLING • ACCOUNT ASSIGNMENT LOGIC • DEFINE SUBSTITUTION. Figure 1.41 shows the customizing screen.

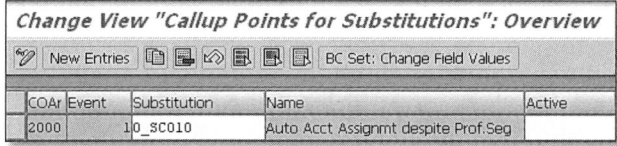

Figure 1.41 Substitution Definition

The first step is to create the substitution to be called in this screen. Double-click in the line, and a new customizing screen will appear as shown in Figure 1.42.

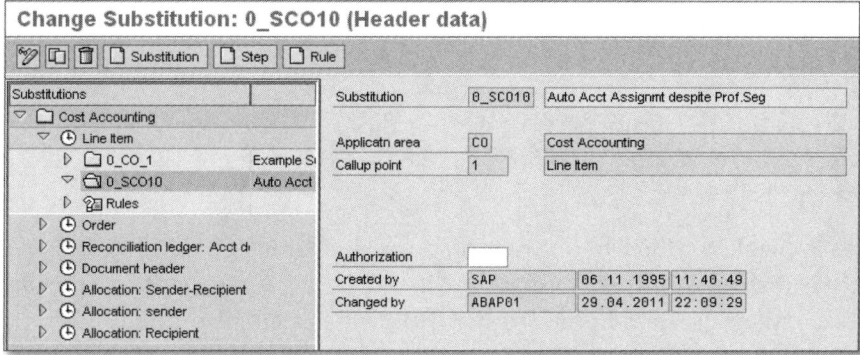

Figure 1.42 Change Substitution

You can use one of the available substitutions or create a new one. For the XYZ example, we will create a new one called Z0001 – substitution.

After creating the substitution, you must create the steps for this substitution by clicking the STEP button as shown in Figure 1.43.

The substitution is divided into two phases:

► PREREQUISITE
Determines whether the entered information on the field is to be checked. If the condition is met, it goes to the SUBSTITUTION phase.

► SUBSTITUTION (after the PREREQUISITE is reached)
Changes the field value to the one fixed in the customizing.

Substitution works very much like validation, so we will only focus on the differences between them.

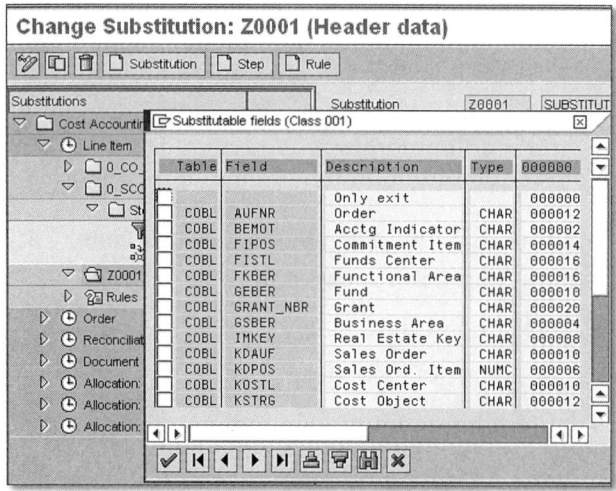

Figure 1.43 Substitution Field Selection

The fields available for the PREREQUISITE phase are the same as in a validation. The difference is that the substitution doesn't use the CHECK. If the PREREQUISITE condition is met, then the field in the SUBSTITUTION will get the new value.

The example of substitution shown in Figure 1.44 is designed to fix a cost center for a cost element so that any postings to this cost element will use the defined cost center, regardless of the user's entry.

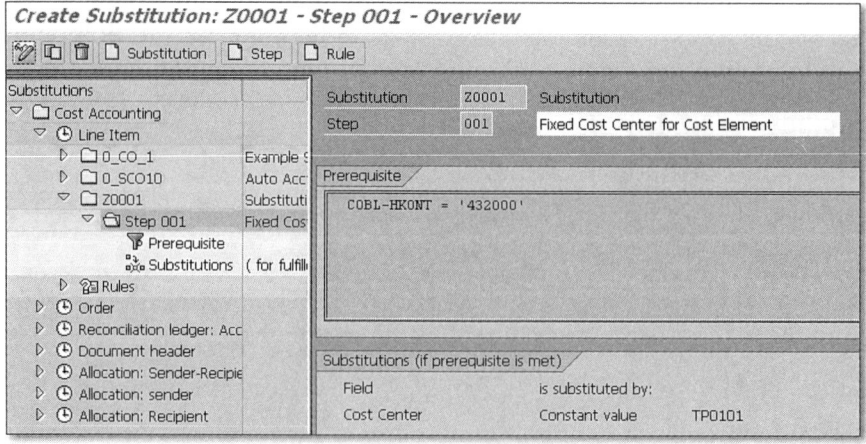

Figure 1.44 Substitution Step

When using a user exit to create a substitution, the first step is to copy the standard program delivered by SAP ERP and assign the new program in the customizing.

The user exit substitution program provided by SAP is Program RGGBS000. Copy this program to a custom program. In this example, we will use Program ZRGGBS000. The process to assign the program is the same as already described and shown earlier in Figure 1.35 for the validation.

The user exit process and transporting the substitution definition use the same procedures as in the validation.

Not all fields for the structure shown earlier in Table 1.7 are available for validation and substitution; you can expand the available fields for the substitution by maintaining the View VWTYGB01 in Transaction SM30 and changing the field EXCLUDE as shown in Figure 1.45.

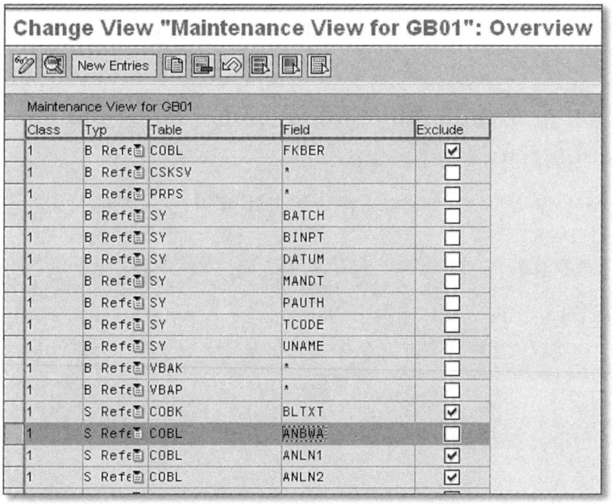

Change View "Maintenance View for GB01": Overview

New Entries

Maintenance View for GB01

Class	Typ		Table	Field	Exclude
1	B	Refe	COBL	FKBER	☑
1	B	Refe	CSKSV	*	☐
1	B	Refe	PRPS	*	☐
1	B	Refe	SY	BATCH	☐
1	B	Refe	SY	BINPT	☐
1	B	Refe	SY	DATUM	☐
1	B	Refe	SY	MANDT	☐
1	B	Refe	SY	PAUTH	☐
1	B	Refe	SY	TCODE	☐
1	B	Refe	SY	UNAME	☐
1	B	Refe	VBAK	*	☐
1	B	Refe	VBAP	*	☐
1	S	Refe	COBK	BLTXT	☑
1	S	Refe	COBL	ANBWA	☐
1	S	Refe	COBL	ANLN1	☑
1	S	Refe	COBL	ANLN2	☑

Figure 1.45 Available Fields for Substitution

Now that you've configured your organizational structures and accounting assignment logic, it's time to plan how to smoothly integrate these elements into your production environment.

1.3   Production Start-Up Preparation

In this section, we'll discuss the options and recommended approach to send the controlling area customizing to your production environment. It's important to understand the implications and define the best strategy for your organization before transporting any new elements to the production environment.

To prepare for production start-up, the data to be transported must be defined, and you need to delete any test data from the environment. If any inconsistencies are found in the transport request, create a new transport request.

1.3.1   Transport System Settings

In the transport request, all of the settings for the organization, master data, planning, actual postings, validations, and substitutions can be added inside the controlling area.

The transport of master data (cost elements, cost centers, activity types, statistical indices, orders) is done in two steps:

1. The system eliminates the master data that already exist on the target system in the same area or cost accounting chart of accounts.

2. The system imports the master data contained in the order of adjustment.

> **Note**
>
> If there is any master data in the target system that is not in the sender system (created manually or through other transport requests), the master data in the target system will be erased. The transactional data in the controlling tables will not be changed, so the transport request may cause an inconsistency in the system and require the creation of the master data manually in the target system again.

If more than one controlling area uses the same chart of accounts, to avoid causing inconsistencies in the master data transport, follow these steps:

1. Create the cost elements in all controlling areas that use the same chart of accounts.

2. Always transport together the controlling area and chart of accounts definitions for cost elements. You can see these two marked to transport in the screen shown in Figure 1.46.

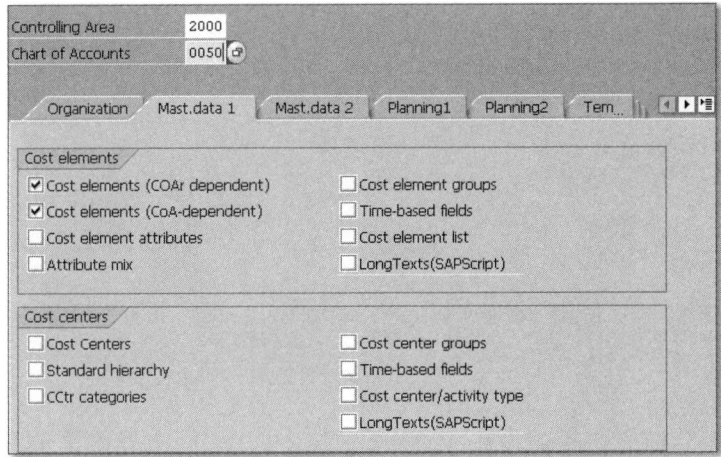

Figure 1.46 Cost Element Transporting Options

To create the transport request for controlling area settings, use Transaction OKE5, or follow the IMG menu path CONTROLLING • GENERAL CONTROLLING • PRODUCTION START-UP PREPARATION • TRANSPORT SYSTEM SETTINGS • TRANSPORT SETTINGS FOR ORGANIZATION. Figure 1.47 shows the customizing screen.

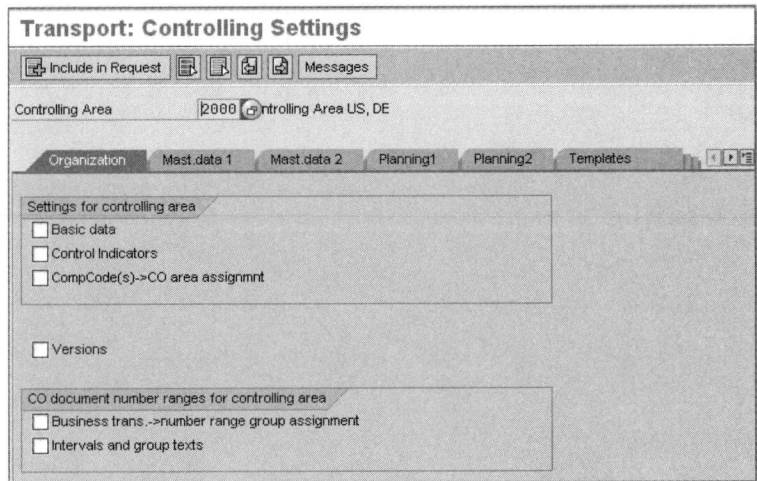

Figure 1.47 Transport Controlling Area Settings

By selecting the available tabs and the options in each tab, the information can be added to the transport request by clicking on INCLUDE IN REQUEST.

After defining the transport request, remember that because the master data will be transported along with the other controlling area settings, you must be sure to delete any test data before the transport is sent.

1.3.2   Delete Test Data

If transaction data or master data was created during testing in the quality or test system, it must be deleted for the production start.

You can delete information for the following data groups:

▶ Transaction data

▶ Cost elements

▶ Cost centers

▶ Activity types

▶ Orders

▶ Cost objects

▶ Base planning objects

> **Note**
>
> Never use this option in a productive system. It will erase all of the controlling area data, including master data and transactional data.

You can delete the controlling area data using these transactions:

▶ OKC3: Delete Transaction Data

▶ OKC5: Delete Cost Elements

▶ OKC4: Delete Cost Centers

▶ OKC6: Delete Activity Types

▶ OKO5: Delete Orders

▶ KKPV: Delete Cost Objects

▶ KKE5: Delete Base Planning Objects

All of the options available for the deletion of data are in the customizing folder: IMG menu path CONTROLLING • GENERAL CONTROLLING • PRODUCTION START-UP PREPARATION • DELETE TEST DATA. Figure 1.48 shows one example.

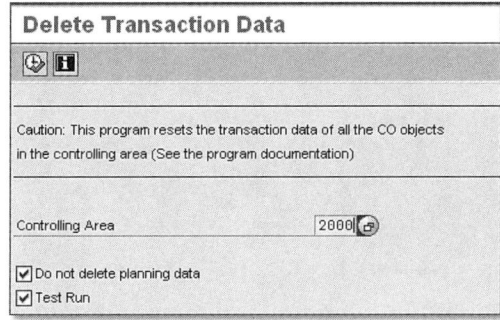

Figure 1.48 Delete Transactional Data

Another option you can consider before your production start-up is deactivating the update for all currencies on each posting to CO objects.

1.3.3 Set "Update All Currencies" Indicator

The "UPDATE ALL CURRENCIES" INDICATOR section allows a reduction of the amount of memory used when posting data to CO objects (e.g., cost centers or orders). However, it only works if the database system compresses empty fields.

In the controlling area definition, the indicator will show whether values are to be updated in the controlling area currency *only* (indicator not active) or also in the transaction currency and in the object currency (indicator active).

The deactivation of this parameter must meet these three conditions:

1. The database system compresses empty fields.

2. The relevant controlling area and the company codes assigned to it use the same currency (currency type 10).

3. There will not be any organizational changes for this controlling area in the future. Such changes would include assigning new company codes with different currencies, or entering currency settings that differ between the company code and controlling area.

When creating a controlling area, the system by default proposes this indicator active, and it can be deactivated by following the IMG menu path CONTROLLING · GENERAL CONTROLLING · PRODUCTION START-UP PREPARATION · SET "UPDATE ALL CURRENCIES" INDICATOR (see Figure 1.49).

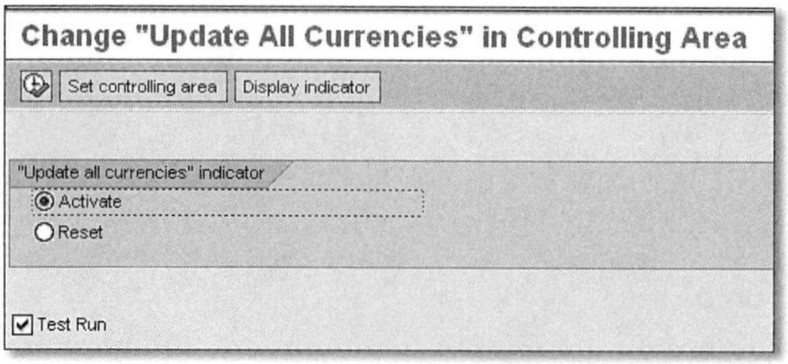

Figure 1.49 Update All Currencies in the Controlling Area

> **Note**
>
> If transaction data already exists for the controlling area in question, the indicator should not be changed. It may cause program errors and data inconsistencies.

When preparing for production start-up of CO in an SAP ERP environment that already contains historical transactions in other components, the final item you need to consider is whether to transfer the postings of already-existing documents to your newly activated CO component.

1.3.4 Follow-Up Posting

If the CO component is activated in an already productive system, the old documents can be transferred to CO. The system uses the original documents to create the CO entries.

You can post documents from the following areas:

▶ FI documents

▶ MM documents

▶ SD documents

▶ Down payments

▶ Reconciliation Ledger

In most cases, you can select the company code, fiscal year and period. To create the follow-up posting, use Transaction OKBA for FI documents, Transaction OKBB for MM documents, Transaction OKBC for SD documents, Transaction OKBG for down payments, and Transaction KAL1 for the Reconciliation Ledger.

Or, you can go to the folder in the IMG menu path CONTROLLING • GENERAL CON-
TROLLING • PRODUCTION START-UP PREPARATION • FOLLOW-UP POSTING. Figure 1.50
shows an example of the screen to transfer FI documents.

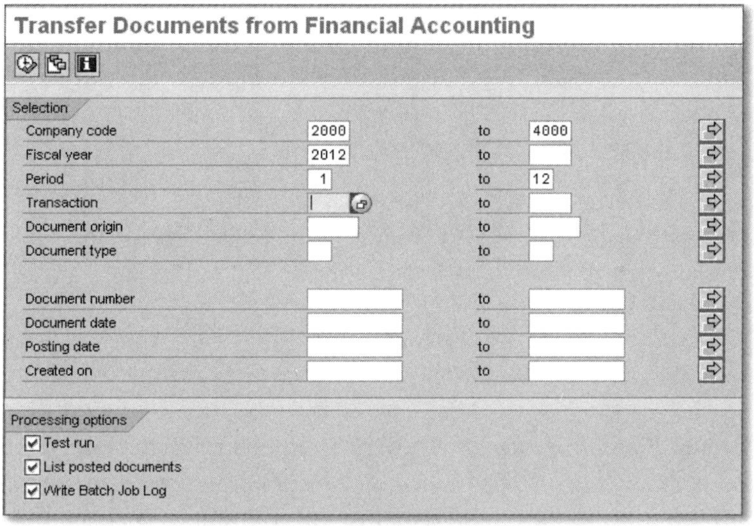

Figure 1.50 Transfer Documents from Financial Accounting

To manage the changes in group master data, you can activate the change documents for the master data groups in CO. This means that the system logs all
changes to the group structure and the group name, together with the date of the
change and the user who made the change.

We recommend that you avoid activating the change log for all of the groups.
Only the most important ones should be selected, such as cost center groups, cost
element groups, and others. It isn't advisable to activate change documents for
order groups because they are subject to many changes in the system. The change
logs will increase the system response time when creating or changing a group, as
well as increase the size of the database. Figure 1.51 shows the available options.
To activate or deactivate the option, either use Transaction GSCD, or follow the
IMG menu path CONTROLLING • GENERAL CONTROLLING • PRODUCTION START-UP
PREPARATION • ACTIVATE CHANGE DOCUMENTS FOR GROUPS.

Now that you've learned how to develop your production startup plan, we need
to discuss how activating CO impacts your archiving strategy.

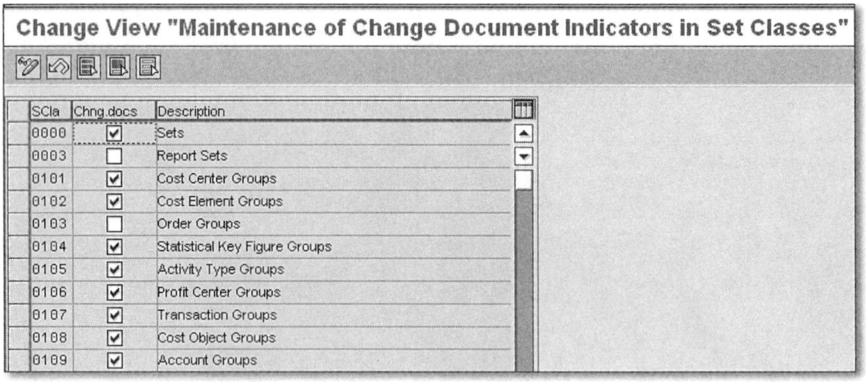

Figure 1.51 Change Documents for Controlling Master Data Groups

1.4 Archiving

Activating CO in SAP ERP will increase the need for storage for new tables, a variety of new documents that will be generated for each transaction posted, and additional master data. These data-storage requirements will continue to increase over time without some strategy to archive the data. The cost of storage and the effects on system performance cannot be ignored by the organization. It's considered best practice to have a clearly defined archiving strategy for the SAP ERP environment that will meet the organization's needs for information and at the same time maintain system performance and system storage costs at optimal levels.

SAP NetWeaver Information Lifecycle Management (SAP NetWeaver ILM) is a tool to manage the retention time, archive data, and destroy data from the system after the retention time has passed.

The archiving part of SAP NetWeaver ILM is divided into four areas:

▶ Maintaining or creating the audit areas
▶ Setting up policies and maintaining rules
▶ Archiving and storing data
▶ Destroying data

Establishing an archiving strategy requires a collaborative effort among many of the organization's areas, including representatives from IT, the audit team, the tax team, the finance team, and business management. We will focus here on explaining the implications of activating CO on an organization's overall archiving strategy.

To archive data in SAP ERP, the system uses an archive object that links all of the necessary database information to archive and delete an item. Each of the SAP ERP components has an archive object assigned. The archive object in the controlling area is called CO_ITEM. To process archiving, the system uses one program to write (CO_ITEM_WRI) and another program to delete (CO_ITEM_DEL) the lines.

The archiving strategy should consider the prerequisites for each archive object, the legal retention time, the media to save the archived data, and how to destroy the data.

The system doesn't archive any CO line items that meet the following criteria:

▶ Line items that are down payments (value type 12, 58, 59, 61, 63)

▶ Line items for parked documents (value type 60)

▶ Investment measures that are stored as CO line items

▶ Actual line items in current or future periods

▶ Plan line items in current or future fiscal years

▶ Line items that were distributed using Application Link Enabling (ALE)

The write program archives the CO line items for all objects for which a residence time has been specified. It does not process CO line items for object types that have been explicitly excluded from archiving. To maintain the residence time for the CO_ITEM (see Figure 1.52), follow the IMG menu path CONTROLLING • GENERAL CONTROLLING • ARCHIVING • PREPARE ARCHIVING OF CONTROLLING LINE ITEMS.

Figure 1.52 Residence Time for Controlling Line Items

Create at least one entry for each object type to be archived. All entries are optional except for the object type (TY. column). The CTR object type covers both cost center and activity type data (object type ATY can't be maintained separately).

For orders (except for sales orders), the order type can be specified as a subobject type (in the SUBOBJTYPE column).

You can distinguish between objects in different controlling areas by entering the desired controlling area in the COAR column, and also to distinguish between plan and actual line items by entering the desired abbreviation in the VAL. TYPE CAT. column.

To exclude individual lines from archiving, select the DO NOT ARCH checkboxes. Enter the number of residence periods for each line in the RES. PERIODS column. Each CO line item is archived after the corresponding number of residence periods has expired after the posting period. The residence time doesn't include special periods. Documents posted in special periods are assigned to the last period of the fiscal year for determination of residence time.

Actual data in CO line items can be archived by period, but plan data can only be archived annually.

To only archive data from fiscal years when all postings within this year meet the residence time, select the FYEAR (fiscal year complete) column.

1.5 Summary

After reading this chapter, you should now understand the different subcomponents of the SAP ERP Controlling component, and how they can be used to help manage your business. You also learned how to create and activate a controlling area, create number ranges and versions, and set up rules for account assignment logic.

We also discussed the activities related to production start-up and the implications of the activation of CO to your archiving strategy.

Now that you have a thorough understanding of the basic organizational settings in CO and how to best customize it for your organization, let's move on to Chapter 2, where you'll learn about Cost Element Accounting.

Cost Element Accounting is a foundational element in SAP Controlling. You'll learn how to establish a structure to best support the information objectives of your organization.

2   Cost Element Accounting

After completing all of the initial steps to activate SAP ERP Controlling (CO), you can now establish a customized structure of cost elements. Cost elements are required structural components for CO to be activated, and the structure you define in these steps will be used by all of the other subcomponents that you'll learn about in later chapters. In this chapter, you'll learn how Cost Element Accounting (CO-CEL) classifies the costs and revenues that are posted to CO and how it provides the capability for reconciliation of costs in CO with the Financial Accounting (FI) component. You'll learn how to establish your own customized master data structure for CO-CEL, how to use accrual calculations, and how to access and use the most important reports available in SAP ERP for CO-CEL.

CO-CEL allows identification of the nature of revenues and costs in the CO component of SAP ERP. CO uses a combination of cost objects and cost elements to classify postings, and therefore establishing a structure of cost elements is a required step in the activation of CO. The structure determined for the cost elements and cost objects together will determine how CO information will be available for use in reporting and analysis, so—as with all of the areas—you should have a clear blueprint of the desired result to follow when customizing this area. Without a well-planned cost element structure, you will not be able to take full advantage of the accounting and reporting power that the CO component provides.

Cost objects are all of the cost collectors reflected in CO such as cost centers, internal orders, WBS elements, business processes, and production orders.

Cost elements classify costs and revenues in CO by type in a similar manner as accounts are used in FI. This chapter will explain the different types and show you step by step how to customize all aspects of cost elements in your SAP ERP system.

2.1   Master Data

In this section, we'll explain how the cost elements are divided in categories and also how to create the cost elements in a collective way, how to group the cost elements, how to create the cost element attributes, and how to determine time-based fields for cost elements.

Cost elements can be either primary or secondary cost elements:

▶ Primary cost elements are the FI P&L accounts that are reflected in CO (e.g., Energy, Material, Services, Labor, and Maintenance). When an FI account has a corresponding cost element, the posting in FI will be reflected in CO and also be associated with a cost object, such as cost center, internal order, or production order. Figure 2.1 shows one example of a primary cost element viewed using Transaction KA03.

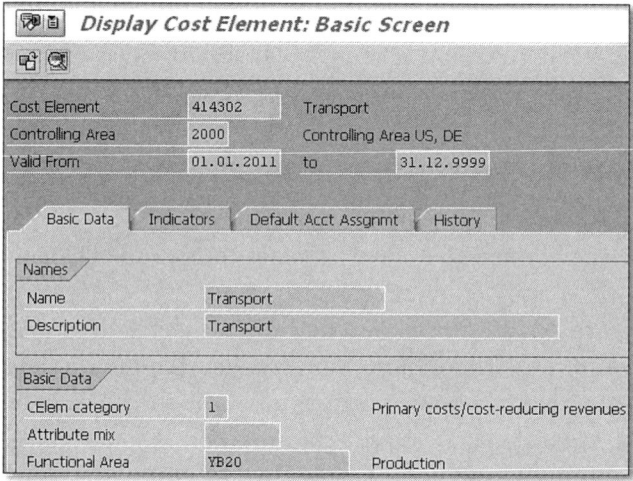

Figure 2.1 Primary Cost Element Example

> **Note**
>
> Cost elements aren't created automatically when a P&L account is created in FI. You must decide when creating new FI accounts whether there should be a corresponding cost element. However, if you want cost elements to be automatically created when P&L accounts are created in FI, you can select the CONTROLLING INTEGRATION option in the chart of accounts definition with Transaction OB13.

► Secondary cost elements are cost elements restricted to CO. They do not exist in FI but are only used to perform internal allocations in CO. For example, an activity performed by a cost center and charged to a production order will use a secondary cost element to credit the cost center and debit the production order. Figure 2.2 shows one example of a secondary cost element viewed using Transaction KA03.

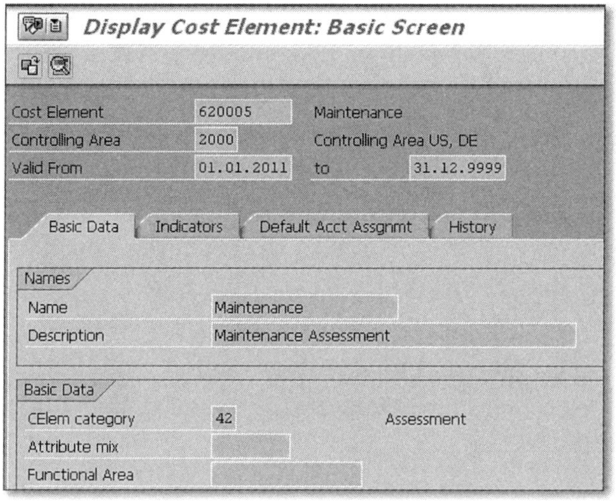

Figure 2.2 Secondary Cost Element Example

Let's consider an example of how the values flow for depreciation expense to demonstrate a process with both primary and secondary cost elements.

Depreciation is posted in a production cost center from the Asset Accounting component (FI-AA), using the cost center in the asset master data. This posting will be made simultaneously in both FI (in the account for depreciation expense) and in CO (using a corresponding primary cost element).

After that, when the production is confirmed, a portion of the depreciation from this production cost center will be sent to the product using an activity type and a secondary cost element in CO. This posting is not reflected in FI.

Cost elements are also divided into categories. The category has a technical control function. It determines the nature of the posting, whether it is a revenue or cost, whether it is a direct or indirect posting (activity type), and finally whether it is an internal or external posting to CO.

There are six categories for primary cost elements and nine categories for secondary cost elements.

The following are descriptions of the primary cost element categories:

▶ **1 – Primary costs/cost-reducing revenues**

These cost elements are used for primary postings; costs from other components, such as depreciation from FI-AA, purchases to a cost center from MM, labor from HCM; and also other direct postings from FI. You can also use this category for cost-reducing revenues, for example, if you have received a payment for rent from a sublease and want to offset this against the main rental cost in CO. Note that this use is different from the cost element categories 11 and 12, designed to be used for true revenues.

▶ **3 – Accrual calculation using the percentage method**

When using the accrual calculations (CO-CCA), a cost element of this type must be defined to post the credit and the debit in the cost objects related to the accrual.

▶ **4 – Accrual calculation using target equal to actual method**

This category is also used for accrual calculation, but in this case, the system uses the target value to post the accrual.

▶ **11 – Revenues**

Use this category for cost elements for revenues. Revenues are displayed in CO with a negative sign (credit). An exception to this is Profitability Analysis (CO-PA). In CO-PA, revenues are displayed with a positive sign (+).

> **Note**
>
> If revenues are posted to cost centers using a cost element with category 11 or 12, the values appear as statistical information only. This means that revenues can be reposted for posting adjustments to other cost centers, but another allocation is not possible. Revenues are ignored in iterative activity price calculation and are therefore not included in the allocation price of an activity type.

▶ **12 – Sales deductions**

This category is used for sales deductions. Sales deductions are adjustment or deduction postings related to revenues, such as discounts and rebates. These are also used in CO-PA. Because revenue postings in CO-PA appear with a positive sign, this cost element category helps to identify which cost elements should have a negative sign in CO-PA.

▶ **22 – External settlements**
Cost elements of this category are used to settle orders, projects, or other cost object postings to objects outside of CO. For example, CO external objects can be assets (Asset Management), materials (Materials Management), or GL accounts (Financial Accounting). The SAP system always creates an FI accounting document when settling to external objects.

The following lists and describes the secondary cost element categories:

▶ **21 – Internal settlements**
This cost element category is used to settle order or project costs to other CO internal objects (e.g., an internal order settling costs to a cost center or to another internal order). Examples of CO internal objects are orders, profitability segments, cost centers, and projects.

▶ **31 – Order/project results analysis**
This category is used to save results analysis data in orders or projects.

▶ **41 – Overhead rates**
When you are using overhead calculation in CO-CCA, this cost element category is used to allocate overhead costs using overhead rates from cost centers to orders. The allocation will credit one cost object and debit another.

▶ **42 – Assessment**
When using assessments in CO-CCA, this category is used to allocate costs from one cost object to another cost object.

▶ **43 – Allocation of activities/processes**
When you allocate costs from a cost center to a production order using an activity type, a cost element with category 43 must be assigned to the activity type.

▶ **50 – Incoming orders: sales revenues**
This cost element category is used for revenues from sales orders with revenues in the current period of the project-related order.

▶ **51 – Incoming orders: other revenues**
Similar to cost element category 50, this one is used for other revenues rather than direct revenues in an incoming order (e.g., imputed interest from sales orders).

▶ **52 – Incoming orders: costs**
This category is similar to categories 50 and 51 but is now used for costs and not revenue.

▶ **61 – Earned values**
This cost element category is used for the earned values from the earned value analysis in the Project Systems (PS) component.

Now that you understand the types of cost elements, and the differences between and uses for the available categories, you can now create cost elements.

2.1.1 Automatic Creation of Primary and Secondary Cost Elements

Individual primary cost elements can be created and modified using Transaction KA01 and Transaction KA02, respectively. Secondary cost elements are created using Transaction KA06 and modified using Transaction KA02. When you have multiple cost elements to create, the process can be long and tedious to do one at a time.

To speed up the creation process, the SAP system provides a tool to automatically create cost elements. You can create multiple primary or secondary cost elements in one step by defining the account range and a cost element category for the range. The automatic cost element creation process is simple and involves three steps:

1. Define default settings.

2. Create a batch input session.

3. Execute a batch input session.

Define Default Settings

In this first step, you can determine the cost element or range of cost elements that will be created as well as the cost element category to be assigned. You can create either primary or secondary cost elements using this process. Primary cost elements will adopt the description from the financial account master data and can be created using account ranges.

Secondary cost elements will adopt the description from the cost element category. Later, you should change the descriptions to the desired user-defined description. It isn't possible to create secondary cost elements using account ranges because they are not directly related to FI accounts.

After creating cost elements, you can change the cost elements using Transaction KA02 (e.g., if you later want to assign an attribute mix to a cost element).

To define the default settings, either use Transaction OKB2, or follow the IMG menu path CONTROLLING • COST ELEMENT ACCOUNTING • MASTER DATA • COST ELEMENTS • AUTOMATIC CREATION OF PRIMARY AND SECONDARY COST ELEMENTS • MAKE DEFAULT SETTINGS. You will need to select which chart of accounts to use as a reference, as shown in Figure 2.3.

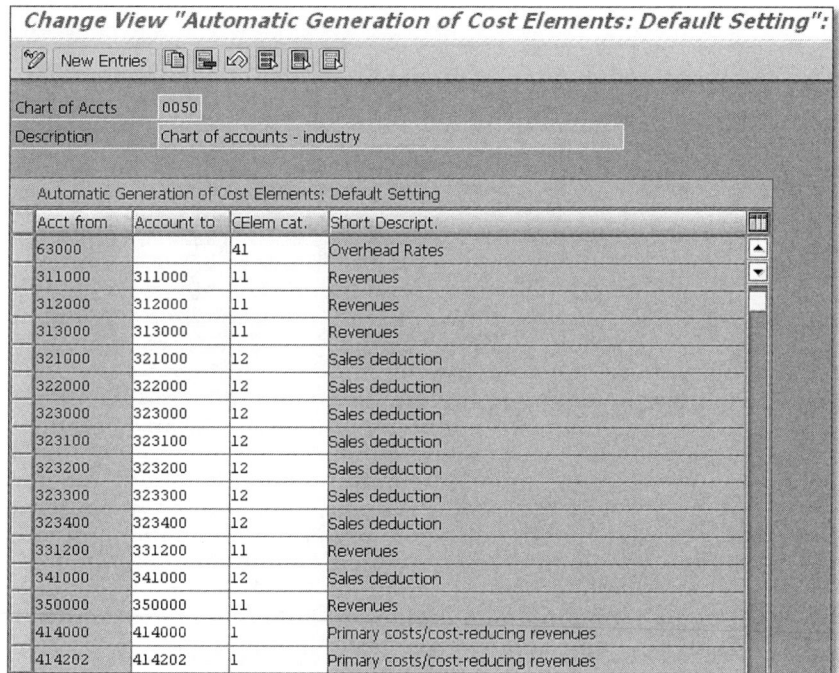

Figure 2.3 Default Settings Customizing Screen

Create a Batch Input Session

From here, the system will use the settings in DEFAULT SETTINGS to create the batch input session. Use Transaction OKB3, or go to IMG menu path CONTROLLING • COST ELEMENT ACCOUNTING • MASTER DATA • COST ELEMENTS • AUTOMATIC CREATION OF PRIMARY AND SECONDARY COST ELEMENTS • CREATE BATCH INPUT SESSION. Enter the appropriate information in the CONTROLLING AREA, VALID FROM, VALID TO, and SESSION NAME fields, and execute as shown in Figure 2.4 and Figure 2.5.

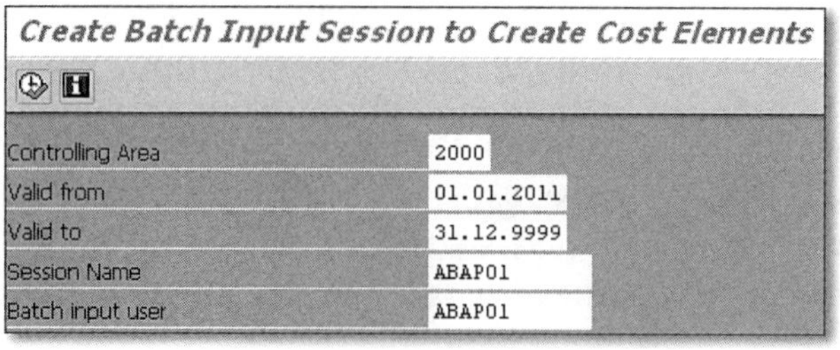

Create Batch Input Session to Create Cost Elements

Controlling Area	2000
Valid from	01.01.2011
Valid to	31.12.9999
Session Name	ABAP01
Batch input user	ABAP01

Figure 2.4 Create Batch Input Session First Screen

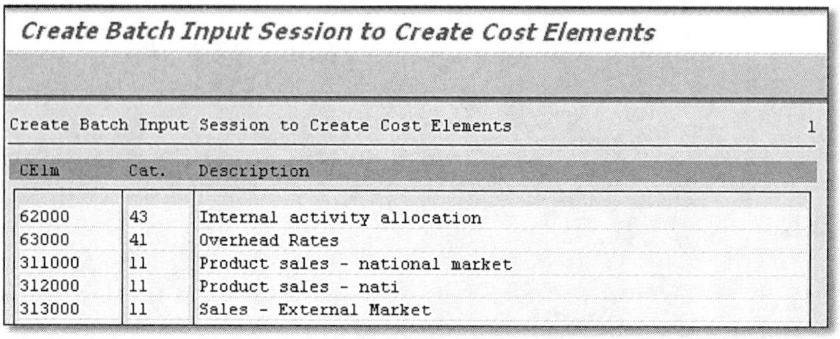

Create Batch Input Session to Create Cost Elements

Create Batch Input Session to Create Cost Elements   1

CElm	Cat.	Description
62000	43	Internal activity allocation
63000	41	Overhead Rates
311000	11	Product sales - national market
312000	11	Product sales - nati
313000	11	Sales - External Market

Figure 2.5 Create Batch Input Session Second Screen

Execute a Batch Input Session

After maintaining the default settings and creating the batch input session, you can execute the batch input session by using Transaction SM35 or by following the IMG menu path CONTROLLING • COST ELEMENT ACCOUNTING • MASTER DATA • COST ELEMENTS • AUTOMATIC CREATION OF PRIMARY AND SECONDARY COST ELEMENTS • EXECUTE BATCH INPUT SESSION, which brings you to the screen shown in Figure 2.6.

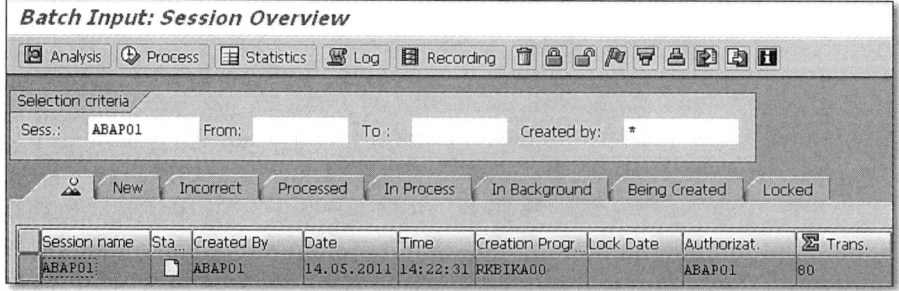

Figure 2.6 Batch Input Session

The system will create all of the cost elements that don't already exist in the system according to the default settings. It won't overwrite the existing ones, which will show as an error after processing the batch input session.

> **Note**
>
> The default settings are configured in the development client and must be transported to the quality and production clients because maintenance of the default settings requires an open configuration. The second and third steps are executed directly in the receiver client. We recommend that you execute these steps in each client (rather than only in the production client) to ensure consistency of data among the different clients.

After creating the cost elements, the next step is to establish a structure for cost element grouping.

2.1.2   Cost Element Groups

The SAP system provides an excellent tool to facilitate grouping of the cost objects' master data in a logical structure. Any of the cost objects (such as cost elements, cost centers, internal orders, or WBS elements) can be grouped. It's really helpful to have a grouping scheme established for use when running reports and also for use in some customizing activities.

Groups can be used on all costing reports, so reporting and analysis requirements should be considered when establishing the logic for grouping. The groups can be created by using objects, by creating hierarchies, or by using parts of other groups. Cost element groups are maintained as master data, so you don't need an open customizing environment to maintain the group. For example, when running a CO report, in the selection screen, you can use a single cost element, a range of cost elements, or a cost element group. You can create a cost element group with the cost elements that are often used for reporting, and every time you need to run the report, you use the cost element group. Figure 2.7 shows an example of the selection screen for the Report S_SL0_21000007 – Cost Elements: Breakdown by Company Code.

Some customizing can be done by cost element range or by using a cost element group. For example, in assessment customizing, if you use a cost element group to define the sender cost elements in assessments, you can maintain the group in the production environment simply by adding or removing cost elements in the group. It's possible to combine both primary and secondary cost elements in groups.

Cost Elements: Objects: Selection

| Variation | Output Parameters... | Data Source... | Extract Parameters... |

Selection values

Controlling Area	2000
Fiscal Year	2011
Period	8

Selection groups

Company Code		to	
Cost Element Group			
Or value(s)		to	

Figure 2.7 Cost Element Report Selection Screen Example

You can create cost element groups using transactions in the user menu or in the customizing menu. Use Transactions KAH1, KAH2, and KAH3 to create, change, or display groups, respectively. You can also use the following IMG menu path CONTROLLING • COST ELEMENT ACCOUNTING • MASTER DATA • COST ELEMENTS • CREATE COST ELEMENT GROUPS. Figure 2.8 shows an example of a cost element group.

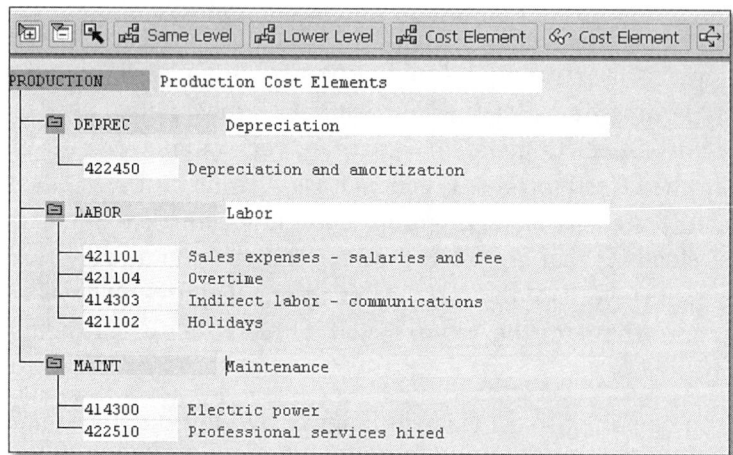

Figure 2.8 Cost Element Group Example

Another characteristic that you can use to segregate cost elements is cost element attributes. These are created and then used to classify the cost elements in a certain way to facilitate reporting.

2.1.3 Cost Element Attributes and Cost Element Attributes Mix

The field ATTRIBUTE MIX, available in the cost element master data in Figure 2.1, can be used as an additional characteristic of the cost element. You can create custom reports to return data using this field.

Two steps are necessary to create the cost element attribute mix. The first is to create the cost element attributes, and the second is to define the cost element attribute mix itself. The cost element attribute is a single attribute that can't be used in the cost element master data. You should group the attributes to create the attribute mix, which is then assigned to cost elements. Each group can contain up to a maximum of eight cost element attributes, divided into columns.

To illustrate this, we'll show the steps to create an attribute mix that can be assigned to all cost elements representing noncash employee-related tax expenses.

To maintain the cost element attributes, use Transaction OKA6, or follow the IMG menu path CONTROLLING • COST ELEMENT ACCOUNTING • MASTER DATA • COST ELEMENTS • DEFINE COST ELEMENT ATTRIBUTES. This brings you to the screen shown in Figure 2.9.

In this example, you can have one or multiple attributes created for a specific item. After you create all of the attributes, you can go to the next customizing step where you can group the cost element attributes to build the cost element attribute mix.

To maintain the cost element attributes mix, use Transaction OKA4, or follow the IMG menu path CONTROLLING • COST ELEMENT ACCOUNTING • MASTER DATA • COST ELEMENTS • DEFINE COST ELEMENT ATTRIBUTE MIX. This brings you to the screen shown in Figure 2.10.

In Figure 2.10, you can see the customizing of the attribute mix by column. In the first column, you can only use attributes that have item = 1 in the cost element attribute; in the second column, you can use only attributes that have item = 2 in the cost element attribute, as shown in Figure 2.9. You can define combinations using these rules up to a limit of eight columns for the attribute mix.

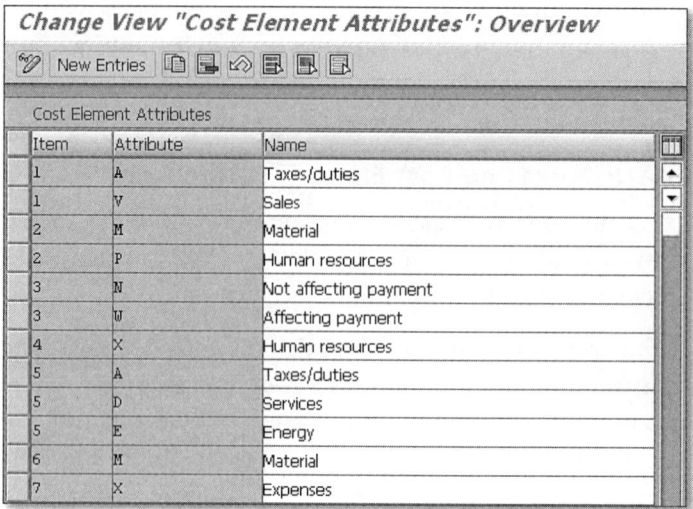

Figure 2.9 Cost Element Attributes

Item	Attribute	Name
1	A	Taxes/duties
1	V	Sales
2	M	Material
2	P	Human resources
3	N	Not affecting payment
3	W	Affecting payment
4	X	Human resources
5	A	Taxes/duties
5	D	Services
5	E	Energy
6	M	Material
7	X	Expenses

New Entries: Overview of Added Entries

Characteristics Mix for Cost Elements

Attrb01	Attrb02	Attrb03	Attrb04	Attrb05	Attrb06	Attrb07	Attrb08
A	P	W	X	D	M	X	
V							
V	M	W	X	D			
A	P	N					

Figure 2.10 Cost Element Attribute Mix

The cost element attribute mix will be named in the system by a combination of all columns. For example, the attribute mix on the last line shown in Figure 2.10 will be named APN – TAXES/DUTIES/HUMAN RESOURCES/NOT AFFECT. This attribute mix would then be assigned to all appropriate cost elements in the master data using Transaction KA02. Figure 2.11 illustrates this step.

The next option in the master data is to define which field in the cost element master data will have the time-based dependencies.

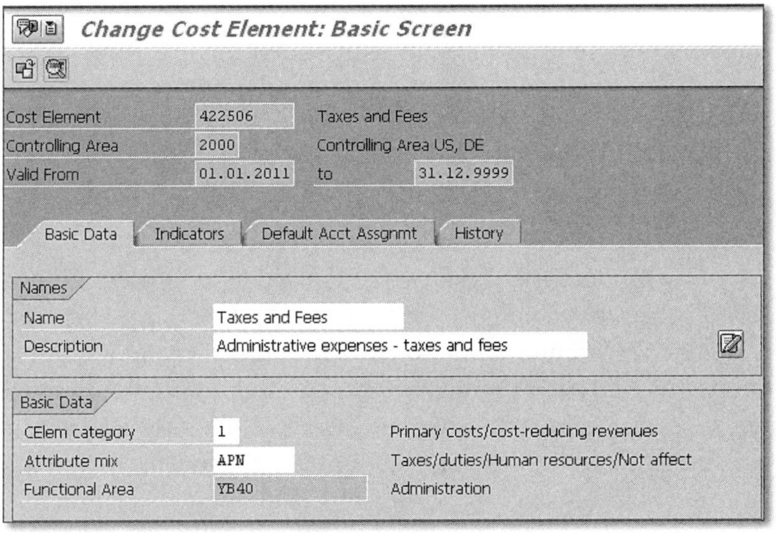

Figure 2.11 Cost Element Attribute Mix Assignment Example

2.1.4 Time-Based Fields for Cost Elements

As part of the customizing for cost elements, you can designate the fields that are time-dependent. A time-dependent definition means that if the master data is changed, the system will consider the posting date to find the correct assignment to the field. For example, if you change the cost center assigned to a cost element in the default account assignment in the cost element master data, the SAP system will respect the day of the change, and for a posting in this cost element, the system will check the posting date against the change date. If the posting date is before the change date, the system uses the old cost center defined in the master data; if the posting date is later then the change date, the system will adopt the new cost center assignment.

SAP ERP determines four different time-based dependencies that are already defined for use in each area:

► Not time-based

► Day-based

► Period-based

► Fiscal-year-based

The types of time-based dependencies used by each area cannot be changed; you only have the option to turn on or turn off the dependency for each area.

> **Note**
>
> Carefully consider which fields should have time-based dependencies because the time-based functionality can consume large amounts of data storage space.

For cost elements, only two fields are available to change the time-based settings, both of which are in the DEFAULT ACCOUNT ASSIGNMENT. To change the time-dependent settings, use Transaction OKEK, or follow the IMG menu path CONTROLLING • COST ELEMENT ACCOUNTING • MASTER DATA • COST ELEMENTS • DETERMINE TIME-BASED FIELDS FOR COST ELEMENTS. This brings you to the screen shown in Figure 2.12. If you mark the cost center or order as time-dependent, the system will consider the changes in the master data for this field by day. For example, you can't change the time dependency from day to year. It's predefined by the system, and you can only select whether the field will have time dependency or not.

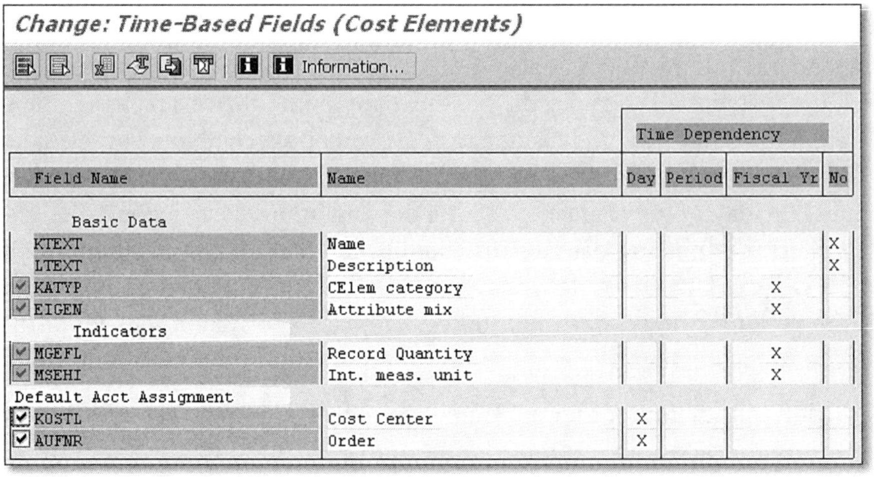

Change: Time-Based Fields (Cost Elements)

🖳 🖳 | 🗐 🔧 🖹 🗟 | 🛄 🛄 Information...

		Time Dependency			
Field Name	Name	Day	Period	Fiscal Yr	No
Basic Data					
KTEXT	Name				X
LTEXT	Description				X
☑ KATYP	CElem category			X	
☑ EIGEN	Attribute mix			X	
Indicators					
☑ MGEFL	Record Quantity			X	
☑ MSEHI	Int. meas. unit			X	
Default Acct Assignment					
☑ KOSTL	Cost Center	X			
☑ AUFNR	Order	X			

Figure 2.12 Cost Element Time-Based Fields

Now that we've discussed the cost element master data, and you know why cost element categories are important, how to create cost elements in a collective way, how to create the cost element attributes and attribute mix, and also how to determine time dependencies in the master data, let's move on to accrual calculations.

2.2   Accrual Calculation

The SAP system has standard functionality to support accruals in both FI and CO. Accruals can be used when you have an expense that is paid in a specific month of the year but that is related to the entire year (e.g., insurance or property tax). To spread this cost across the affected months automatically, you can use accrual calculation.

Accruals made in FI will also be reflected in CO, but accruals made in CO will only be reflected in CO. Before customizing accruals in CO, you should consider which alternative will best serve your needs. In most cases, maintaining accrual data in both areas is desirable, so it should be done in FI. You would only establish accruals in CO for costs that should not be spread in FI, but you want them to be spread across periods for costing purposes.

The following are the three methods for creating accrual calculations in CO (remember that when using CO accruals, no posting will be made in FI):

▶ **Percentage method**
The system will calculate these values by applying a percentage of the posted values in certain cost elements defined in the customizing. A debit will be created in the receiver cost center, and a credit will be made in the cost center or order defined as the accrual object. The system uses a cost element with cost element category 3 (accrual calculation using a percentage method) to perform the postings.

▶ **Target equals actual**
This method is used when a planned cost using activity-dependent planning is used as the reference to calculate the accrual. The system will create the accrual using the planned activity rate and will use the actual activity to create the values. For instance, if you have used activity-dependent planning to set a certain cost at a fixed dollar amount per unit of production, then this type of accrual will post actual costs calculated on the planned per unit cost times the actual units produced. These types of accruals are posted using a cost element with category 4 (accrual calculation using target equal to actual method).

▸ **Plan equals actual**

This method is used when a cost planned using activity-independent planning is used as the referral to calculate the accrual. The system will create the accrual using the planned values in category 4 (accrual calculation using target equal to actual method). For example, if you have a planned value in a specific month that you want to use as reference for the accrual, the system gets the value and creates the accrual postings.

You customize all three of these methods on the same screen. To begin to create an accrual calculation, either use Transaction KSAZ, or follow the IMG menu path CONTROLLING • COST ELEMENT ACCOUNTING • ACCRUAL CALCULATION • PERCENTAGE METHOD • MAINTAIN OVERHEAD STRUCTURE. This brings you to the Maintain CO-OM Accrual Calculation: Overhead Structure screen shown in Figure 2.13.

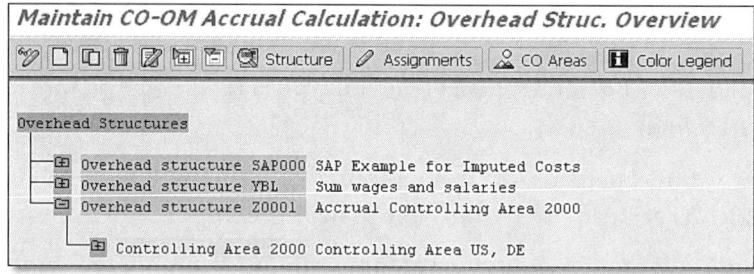

Figure 2.13 Maintain Overhead Structure

Next, we'll explain the steps for each method, beginning with the percentage method.

Percentage Method

For this method, you must create an overhead structure that contains the base, overhead rate (percentage), and credit. From the screen shown previously in Figure 2.13, go to ENVIRONMENT • BASES. This brings you to Figure 2.14. The base determines the cost element range that will be considered when forming the base values for calculating the cost of overhead.

By double-clicking in the BASE desired line, the screen will open and allow entry of the cost elements to be used as the base. We are going to use A-B1 – WAGES as an example. Figure 2.15 shows the cost element range definition.

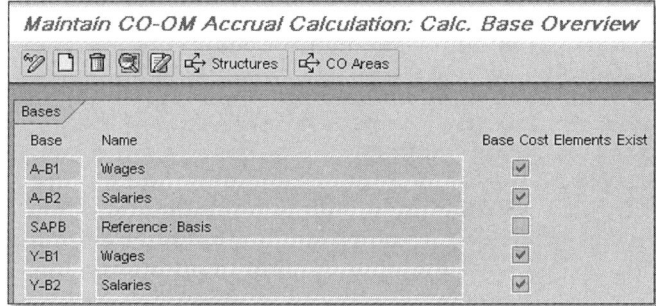

Figure 2.14 Overhead Structure Base Overview

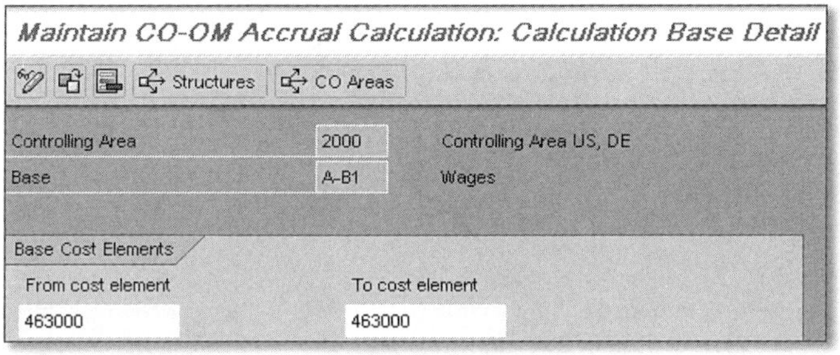

Maintain CO-OM Accrual Calculation: Calculation Base Detail

| Controlling Area | 2000 | Controlling Area US, DE |
| Base | A-B1 | Wages |

Base Cost Elements

From cost element	To cost element
463000	463000

Figure 2.15 Accrual Calculation Base Detail

After you set the cost element range, you must define the overhead rates for the overhead structure. Return to the screen shown in Figure 2.13. Click on the ENVIRONMENT menu, and select OVERHEAD RATES. This will bring you to the screen shown in Figure 2.16.

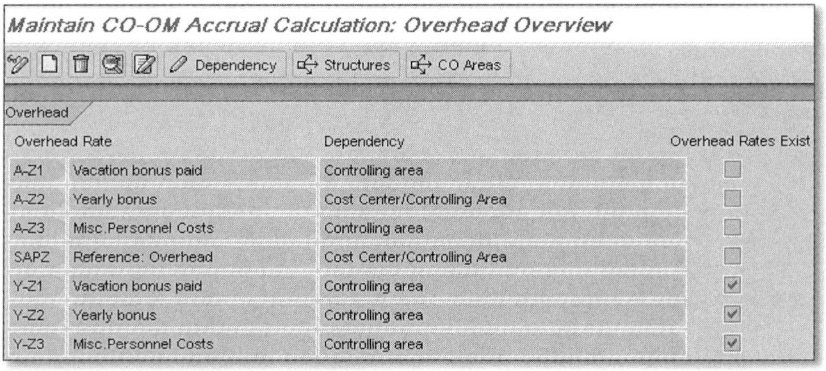

Maintain CO-OM Accrual Calculation: Overhead Overview

Overhead Rate		Dependency	Overhead Rates Exist
A-Z1	Vacation bonus paid	Controlling area	☐
A-Z2	Yearly bonus	Cost Center/Controlling Area	☐
A-Z3	Misc.Personnel Costs	Controlling area	☐
SAPZ	Reference: Overhead	Cost Center/Controlling Area	☐
Y-Z1	Vacation bonus paid	Controlling area	☑
Y-Z2	Yearly bonus	Controlling area	☑
Y-Z3	Misc.Personnel Costs	Controlling area	☑

Figure 2.16 Overhead Rate Overview

In this screen, you can create a new line, or you can maintain the rate by double-clicking in an existing line in the screen shown in Figure 2.17.

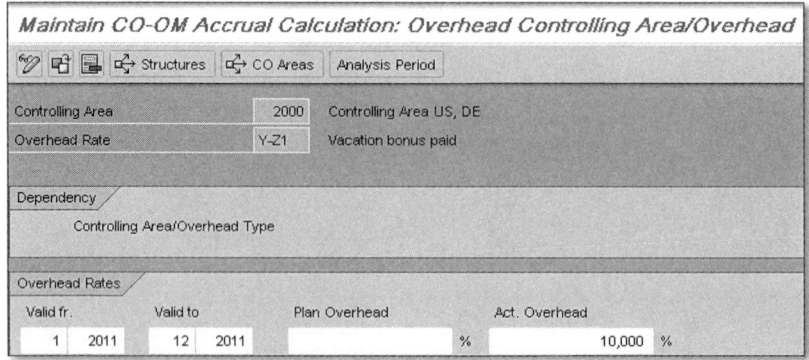

Figure 2.17 Overhead Rate Detail

In this screen, you must establish a valid period for the rate and set the plan or actual rate.

The next step in setting up the CO overhead accrual is to define the credit cost element and cost object. Because CO accruals are not posted in FI, the offset to the accrual cost must be to another CO object. Return to the first screen, shown in Figure 2.13. Go to ENVIRONMENT • CREDITS in the menu bar, which brings you to the screen shown in Figure 2.18.

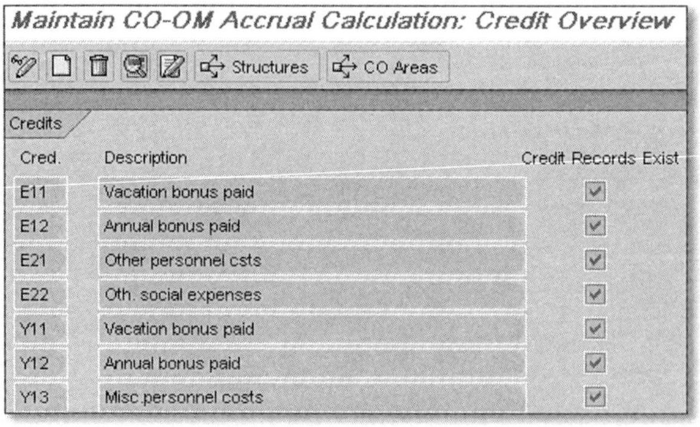

Credits		
Cred.	Description	Credit Records Exist
E11	Vacation bonus paid	☑
E12	Annual bonus paid	☑
E21	Other personnel csts	☑
E22	Oth. social expenses	☑
Y11	Vacation bonus paid	☑
Y12	Annual bonus paid	☑
Y13	Misc personnel costs	☑

Maintain CO-OM Accrual Calculation: Credit Overview

Figure 2.18 Accrual Calculation Credit Overview

By double-clicking in the credit line, you can define the credit cost element and also the credit cost center or order in the screen shown in Figure 2.19.

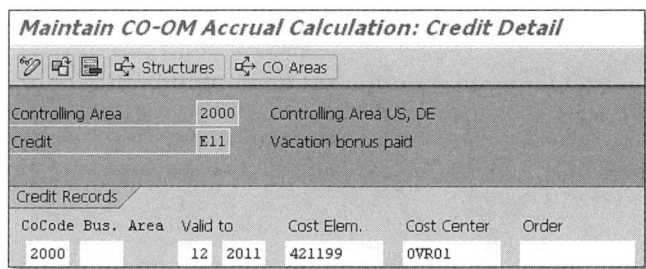

Figure 2.19 Accrual Calculation Credit Detail

The credit will contain the cost elements with category 3. The cost object used for credit can be either a cost center or an internal order and is defined by company code (CoCode), as shown in Figure 2.19. You must define a valid period for the credit.

The overhead structure can be associated with any controlling area. The accrual calculation can use actual or planned costs to calculate the values. Select Assignments (shown previously in Figure 2.13), then select the appropriate option in the Controlling Area field, and click on either the Plan accrual or Actual Accrual buttons, as shown in Figure 2.20.

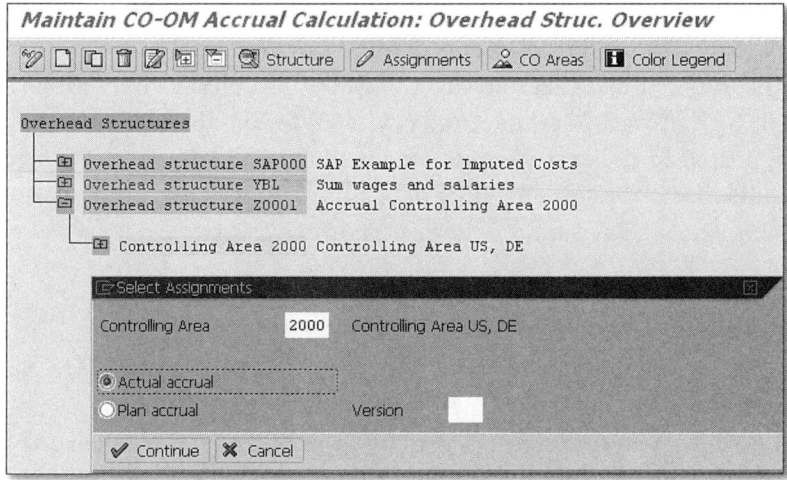

Figure 2.20 Controlling Area Overhead Structure Assignment

Click on the Continue button, and you'll see that the overhead structure is the combination of bases, overhead rates, and credits, as shown in Figure 2.21.

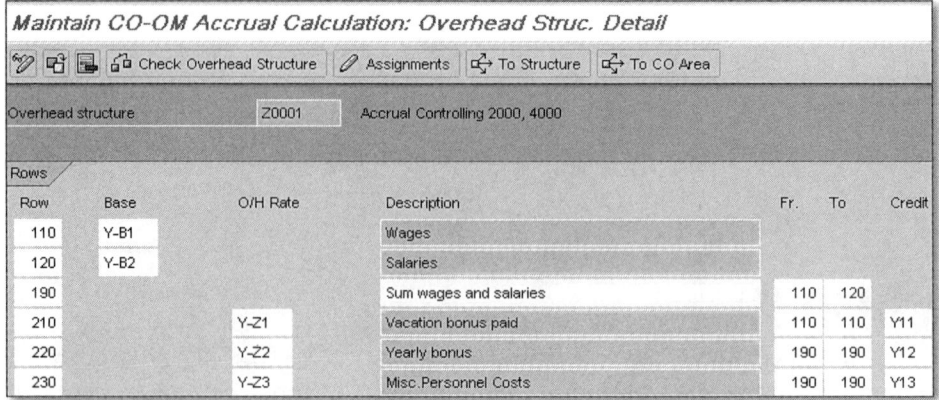

Figure 2.21 Overhead Structure

The rows define the sequence in which the system will read, summarize, and post the values. It should have a base, overhead rate, and credit. You can also summarize lines using the FROM and TO fields, as shown in Figure 2.21, where line 190 is summarizing lines 110 to 120.

The example accrual shown in Figure 2.21 will calculate an amount to accrue using a fixed percentage of the amounts in the cost elements defined as WAGES (BASE Y-B1) for VACATION BONUS PAID (O/H RATE Y-Z1), and also different fixed percentages of the total of the cost elements defined as WAGES and SALARIES (BASE Y-B1 and Y-B2) combined as YEARLY BONUS and MISC. PERSONNEL COSTS, respectively (O/H RATE Y-Z2 ad Y-Z3). Credits (Y11, Y12, Y13) for the three amounts calculated will be posted in the cost element and cost centers defined in the step shown earlier in Figure 2.19 with offsetting debits in the same cost elements and in the cost centers specified at the time the accrual is executed.

Target Equals Actual and Plan Equals Actual Methods

Establishing the setup for these methods is simple. The system will look to the planning values in a cost element with category 4 (accrual calculation using target equal to actual method) whether they are activity or nonactivity-dependent. The customizing is established in the same screen shown earlier in Figure 2.13 by going to the menu ENVIRONMENT and choosing TARGET=ACTUAL CREDITS.

The next step in the customizing is to select the category 4 cost element in the parameters and to choose the credit cost object. Figure 2.22 and Figure 2.23 show the customizing screens. With the settings shown in this example, the system will use the values planned in this cost element to post the accrual and post an offsetting credit to the object defined in Figure 2.22.

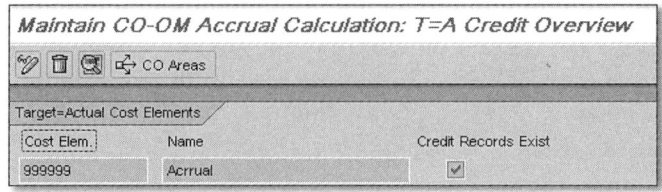

Figure 2.22 Maintain Accrual Cost Element

By double-clicking in the cost element, you can now enter the company code, valid period, and credit cost center or order.

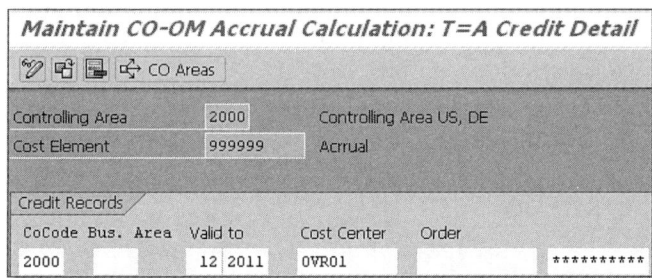

Figure 2.23 Maintain Credit Cost Object and Credit Account

Now that you've learned how to customize CO accrual calculations, let's discuss the information system and why a good structure for CO-CEL is important to meet the needs of the organization.

2.3   Information System

The SAP ERP information system for CO-CEL has many standard reports. The way you customize CO-CEL will directly impact the available data for reporting.

In the decision to create corresponding primary cost elements for FI P&L accounts, you are defining whether it will be possible to see the values in CO reporting. By choosing the correct cost element category for the cost elements, you can correctly classify the values as revenues or expenses.

Using cost element groups, you can create a logical structure for cost elements that can be used in reporting. The logic for the groups can be by area, type of cost, function, or other parameter that will be useful in your reporting. Because they are user-defined, you can create cost element groups in whatever manner you want. If all standard cost element reports provided in SAP ERP aren't sufficient to meet a specific need for cost visibility, you can also use Report Painter and Report Writer to create custom reports, and use additional characteristics in the reports such as the cost element attribute mix.

The details of how to create custom reports using Report Painter or Report Writer are not covered in this book, but many other references cover these areas in detail. (We recommend *Financial Reporting with SAP* by Aylin Korkmaz [SAP PRESS, 2012]). Our focus here is on how to import and generate the standard reports and some tips on how to get the most from the standard reports provided.

Sometimes, reports in SAP ERP stop functioning for a variety of reasons (such as a system shutdown, database corruption, etc.). In this situation, you can import the standard reports again from the SAP ERP client 000. To import the reports, either use Transaction KALI, or follow the IMG menu path CONTROLLING • COST ELEMENT ACCOUNTING • INFORMATION SYSTEM • STANDARD REPORTS • IMPORT STANDARD REPORTS. This brings you to the screen shown in Figure 2.24, where the import can be done online or in the background. In a production environment, especially if many reports will be imported at once, it's recommended to do this in the background to avoid performance impacts.

SAP ERP standard reports that have been just imported must also be generated. Only then is an executable program created that can be run in the information system. To generate the reports, either use Transaction KAL8, or go to CONTROLLING • COST ELEMENT ACCOUNTING • INFORMATION SYSTEM • STANDARD REPORTS • GENERATE STANDARD REPORTS. This brings you to the screen shown in Figure 2.25. The reports can be generated online or in the background. Just as with the import step, we recommend generating the reports in the background rather than online in a production environment, or if you have selected many reports to import at the same time.

Report Writer: Copy Report Groups From Source Client

RGrp	Lib	Description	Created By	Created on	Last gen.	JS
☑ 5AG1	5A1	CElem.: Business Area Allocations	SAP	25.01.1995		50
☑ 5AB1	5A1	CElem.: Company Code Allocations	SAP	25.01.1995		50
☑ 5AB2	5A1	CElem.: Costs by Company Code	SAP	14.06.1996		50
☑ 5AB3	5A1	CElem.: Functional Area Allocations	SAP	10.06.1996		50
☑ 5AF3	5A1	CO/FI Reconcil. CCode Crcy (BArea)	SAP	09.09.1997		50
☑ 5AF4	5A1	CO/FI Reconcil. Group Crcy (BArea)	SAP	09.09.1997		50
☑ 5AF1	5A1	CO/FI Reconciliation in CCde Crcy	SAP	22.06.1994		50
☑ 5AF2	5A1	CO/FI Reconciliation in Group Crcy	SAP	23.06.1994		50
☑ 5AR2	5A1	Cost Elem.: Breakdown by Obj. Type	SAP	08.12.1994		50
☑ 5AK1	5A1	Cost Elem.: Drilldown by Func. Area	SAP	30.08.1995		50
☑ 5AO1	5A1	Cost Elem.: Drilldown by Obj. Type	SAP	23.06.1994		50
☑ 5AC2	5A1	Cost Elem.: Obj. Class in Columns	SAP	29.06.1994		50
☑ 5AA1	5A1	Cost Elements: Accrued Costs	SAP	30.01.1995		50
☑ 5AG3	5A1	Cost Elements: Breakdown by B.Area	SAP	07.06.1996		50
☑ 5AO2	5A1	Cost Elements: Obj. Type in Columns	SAP	27.06.1994		50
☑ 5AR1	5A1	Cost Elements: Object Classes	SAP	11.06.1996		50
☑ 5A21	5A2	Cost Elements: Objects	SAP	13.01.2004		50
☑ 5AW1	5A1	Cost Elements: Work in Process	SAP	09.01.1995		50
☑ 5AG2	5A1	Cost Flow Between Bus. Areas (Rows)	SAP	25.01.1995		50
☑ 5AI1	5A1	Cost Flow Between CoCdes – BusAreas	SAP	30.06.1994		50
☑ 5AC1	5A1	Cost per Object Class, Curr. Cum.	SAP	29.06.1994		50

Figure 2.24 Copy Standard Reports from the Source Client

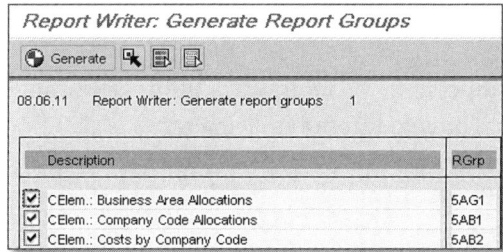

Figure 2.25 Generate Report Groups

Some parameters in the selection screen can be set as default when running cost reports. This helps to expedite the running time because users don't need to resupply all of the information every time they run a report. Some user settings can be specified to populate automatically in the selection screens of the reports, such as controlling area, cost center/cost center group, cost element/cost element group, report period, and currency.

Users can maintain their own user-specific settings using Transaction RPC0, as shown in Figure 2.26.

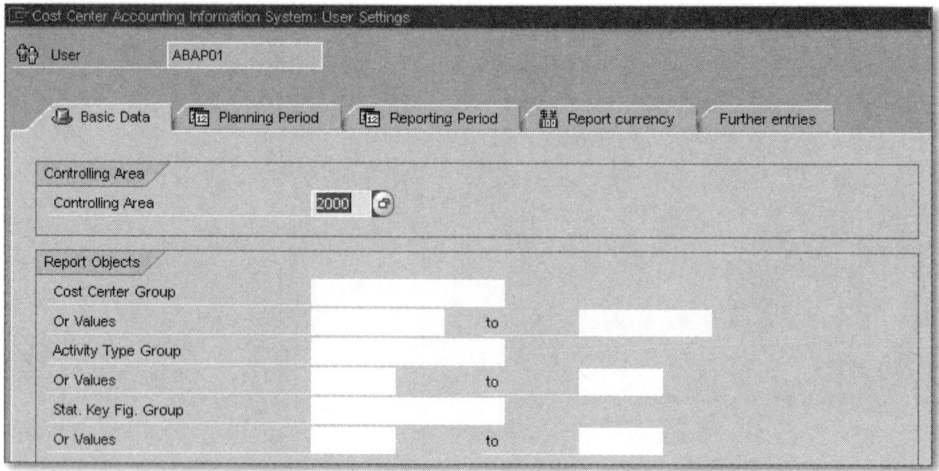

Figure 2.26 User Default Settings

On this screen, each user can define the default selection screen variables for their own user ID. These variables will then be defaulted in the selection screen of all cost element reports but can still be overridden by the user when executing the reports.

In this section, we've discussed some important considerations of the definitions of CO-CEL and how they affect reporting, how to import and generate the standard cost element reports, and how to set some default parameters to make running the reports faster and easier for users.

2.4   Summary

After finishing this chapter, you should now understand the importance of CO-CEL and how it serves as the foundation for CO.

In master data, you've learned about all of the cost element categories and the uses for each one, including the implications to the data in CO when you select a specific category for a cost element. You now know the difference between primary and secondary cost elements, and when to use each. You've learned how to create cost elements in a collective way to decrease the time spent in master data creation. We've also discussed the benefits of groupings and how, by using cost element attributes and attribute mixes, you can add one more level of breakdown to the cost elements. You've also seen how to define a time dependency for cost element master data.

For accrual calculations, you now can distinguish between the available methods of calculation, and the reasons to use accrual calculations in CO rather than accruals in FI.

In the information system, you've learned how the CO-CEL structure can facilitate a powerful and flexible reporting system using both SAP ERP standard reports and custom reports, as well as the need sometimes to import and activate the standard reports again.

Now that the customizing of CO-CEL has been completed, it's time to address the structure and definitions for Cost Center Accounting (CO-CCA) in Chapter 3.

Cost Center Accounting is used in SAP ERP to manage and control overhead and other costs.

3   Cost Center Accounting

This chapter explains how Cost Center Accounting (CO-CCA) works and the benefits of its use. You'll learn step by step how to make CO-CCA operational, including the customizing of the cost center master data, cost center planning, cost center budgeting, and the most important considerations to customizing the actual posting processes, such as assessments, distributions, and cost center variances. You'll also see some of the most important reports available in SAP ERP for CO-CCA.

CO-CCA is used to allow classification and segregation of costs in accounting and reporting by departments or functional areas and by types. Functional areas can be defined, for instance, by production processes or major equipment to capture process cost information in manufacturing, or by departments to segregate costs by the person responsible in other areas. Examples of the types of costs often desired are production, distribution, sales, and administrative.

To use CO-CCA in SAP ERP, you must activate it in the controlling area settings. In Chapter 1, General Controlling, you learned how to create the controlling area and how to assign a controlling area to a company code. Now you'll learn how to activate the CO-CCA and make it operational in SAP ERP, using the same transaction as you used to create the controlling area. Either use Transaction OKKP, or go to CONTROLLING • ORGANIZATION • MAINTAIN CONTROLLING AREA, which will bring you to the customizing screen shown in Figure 3.1.

You'll notice in this screen that there are some default controlling areas provided with SAP ERP, along with the ones you have created using the steps described in Chapter 1. Mark the controlling area in which you are ready to activate CO-CCA on the right side of the screen, and click on ACTIVATE COMPONENTS/CONTROL INDICATORS. Click the NEW ENTRIES button. Figure 3.2 shows the details of the New Entries screen.

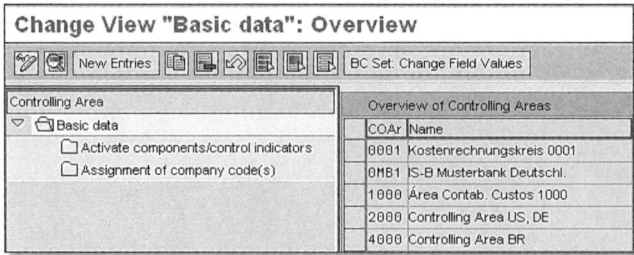

Figure 3.1 Controlling Area Definition

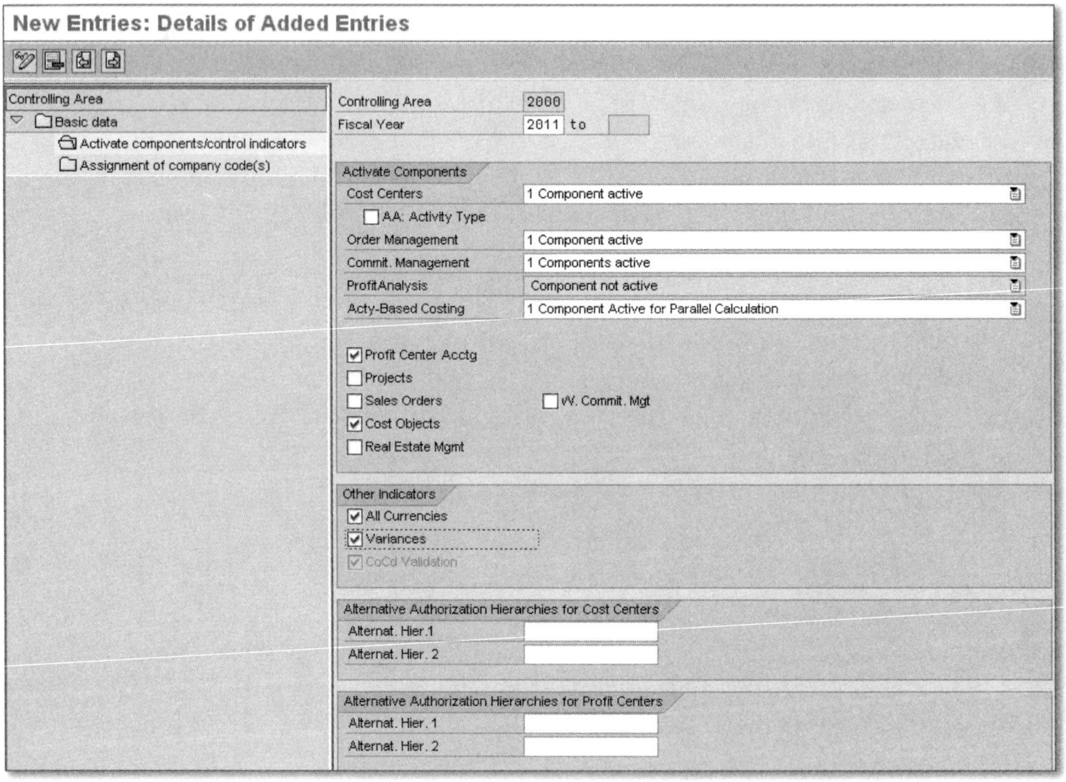

Figure 3.2 Activate Components for the Controlling Area

The first step is to specify the starting year of the settings in the FISCAL YEAR field and then activate the controlling area settings. By selecting COST CENTERS, you can activate the CO-CCA subcomponent by choosing from a list of four available options:

▶ COMPONENT NOT ACTIVE

This is the default setting in the controlling area, indicating that the CO-CCA subcomponent is not active.

▶ COMPONENT ACTIVE

The subcomponent is activated without restriction, the cost centers will work as cost objects, and all CO functionality for CO-CCA will be available.

▶ COMPONENT ACTIVE FOR VALIDATIONS

The subcomponent is not active, you can use the cost center cost objects, but the CO component will not be updated. This is useful only to check and validate postings.

▶ COMPONENT ACTIVE FOR EXISTENCE CHECKS

The subcomponent is not active and used only to validate; in this case, the system will check only if the cost center master data exists or not.

The first or the second options (not active or active, respectively) are most commonly used. You can create validations using the second option as well, and the subcomponent will be fully operational.

Now that you've learned how to activate CO-CCA in SAP ERP, you'll next see how to customize the CO-CCA master data in a manner that will best support the management information needs of your organization.

3.1 Master Data

The decisions you make in establishing your master data will define how you can use your CO-CCA subcomponent. The master data and how you choose to organize the structures will also affect the way that management information will be available in reporting on these areas. The CO-CCA master data structures are divided into four important areas:

▶ Cost centers

▶ Activity types

▶ Statistical key figures

▶ Resources

3.1.1 Cost Center Master Data

The first area to customize in your CO-CCA master data is cost centers. Before you can begin to create cost centers, however, you'll need to determine your definitions for cost center categories.

Cost center categories define the type of activity performed by the cost center such as production, administration, and so on. SAP ERP provides some standard categories, but you can also define your own as needed.

You can use cost center categories to restrict the cost centers that may perform a particular activity or be associated with an activity type in the planning functions. In the activity type master data, you can define which type of cost center can perform that kind of activity. The cost center category is also used to define default values for the cost centers as described in this subsection.

You can define a default functional area for the cost center category and also activate or deactivate the following indicators as default values:

▶ Lock primary postings
▶ Lock secondary postings
▶ Lock revenue postings and revenue planning
▶ Lock commitment update
▶ Lock primary cost planning
▶ Lock secondary cost planning
▶ Lock consumption quantities

The default values will be proposed at the time of cost center creation, and you can change these values when creating or changing cost centers.

To maintain the cost center categories, you can use Transaction OKA2 or follow the IMG menu path Controlling • Cost Center Accounting • Master Data • Cost Centers • Define Cost Center Categories. The screen is shown in Figure 3.3 appears.

By marking the default options in this step of the customizing, every time you create a new cost center and select the cost center category, the system will propose the default information for the cost center.

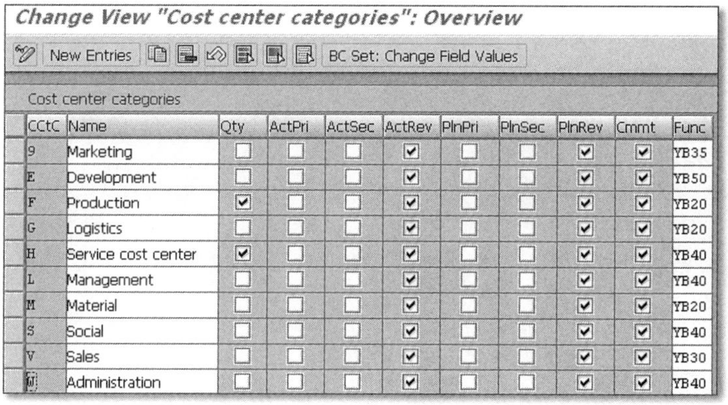

CCtC	Name	Qty	ActPri	ActSec	ActRev	PlnPri	PlnSec	PlnRev	Cmmt	Func
9	Marketing	☐	☐	☐	☑	☐	☐	☑	☑	YB35
E	Development	☐	☐	☐	☑	☐	☐	☑	☑	YB50
F	Production	☑	☐	☐	☑	☐	☐	☑	☑	YB20
G	Logistics	☐	☐	☐	☑	☐	☐	☑	☑	YB20
H	Service cost center	☑	☐	☐	☑	☐	☐	☑	☑	YB40
L	Management	☐	☐	☐	☑	☐	☐	☑	☑	YB40
M	Material	☐	☐	☐	☑	☐	☐	☑	☑	YB20
S	Social	☐	☐	☐	☑	☐	☐	☑	☑	YB40
V	Sales	☐	☐	☐	☑	☐	☐	☑	☑	YB30
W	Administration	☐	☐	☐	☑	☐	☐	☑	☑	YB40

Figure 3.3 Cost Center Categories

You must define a standard hierarchy for the controlling area. The standard hierarchy is basically a cost center group with all cost centers in a controlling area assigned on it. You've defined the first node for the standard hierarchy when creating the controlling area, in Chapter 1, Section 1.1.1. The standard hierarchy consists of two structural elements:

- End nodes, where you assign the cost centers
- Summarization nodes, which are not cost centers but summarize the cost centers in the "nodes" attached to them

You can't associate the same cost center to two different nodes. The same principle is applicable to the nodes; each cost center can be assigned to only one node at a time.

The standard hierarchy can have multiple cost center groups with multiple cost centers, or one group with one cost center. Each cost center that you create must be associated with a group in the standard hierarchy. This ensures that the standard hierarchy contains all of the cost centers of the controlling area.

One example of how a standard hierarchy can be defined is shown in Figure 3.4.

Master data for cost centers is generated within a period of validity. If, for example, a cost center was created as valid for one year, and you want to extend its validity, you need to maintain the cost center again for it to be valid for the additional period desired. The system will consider it as the same cost center because it has the same identification key. Cost center maintenance can be performed by using the specific transactions or through the standard hierarchy.

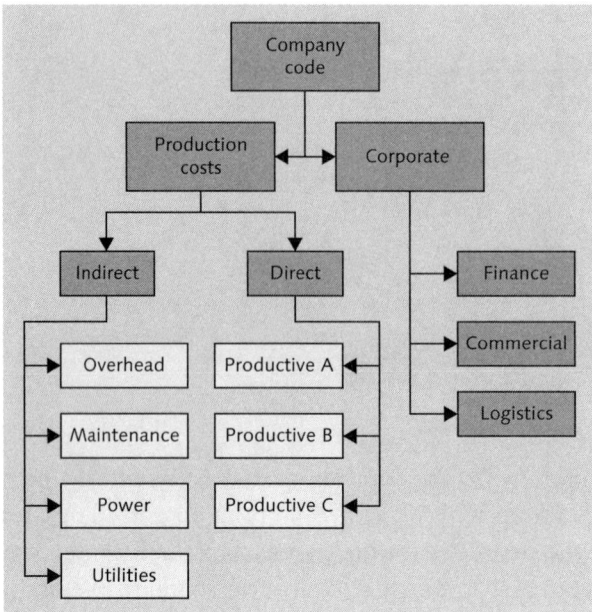

Figure 3.4 Cost Center Hierarchy Example

You can create or modify cost centers using the menu Transactions KS01 and KS02, respectively, but it's easier to maintain them using the standard hierarchy.

To maintain the standard hierarchy (see Figure 3.5), either use Transaction OKEON, or follow the IMG menu path CONTROLLING • COST CENTER ACCOUNTING • MASTER DATA • COST CENTERS • DEFINE STANDARD HIERARCHY.

To manage overhead costs, cost centers are grouped with similar types based on the nature of their functions: decision making, monitoring, or administration. The cost center standard hierarchy is designed to represent these different cost center groupings in a structured manner.

Each node of the standard hierarchy represents a cost center group. You can create or change cost centers using the corresponding function in the menu.

To assign a cost center to another part of the hierarchy, simply reassign the cost center area during the maintenance of the standard hierarchy.

All changes in the cost center master data can be made through the standard hierarchy maintenance. This makes the process of creating or changing a cost center easier.

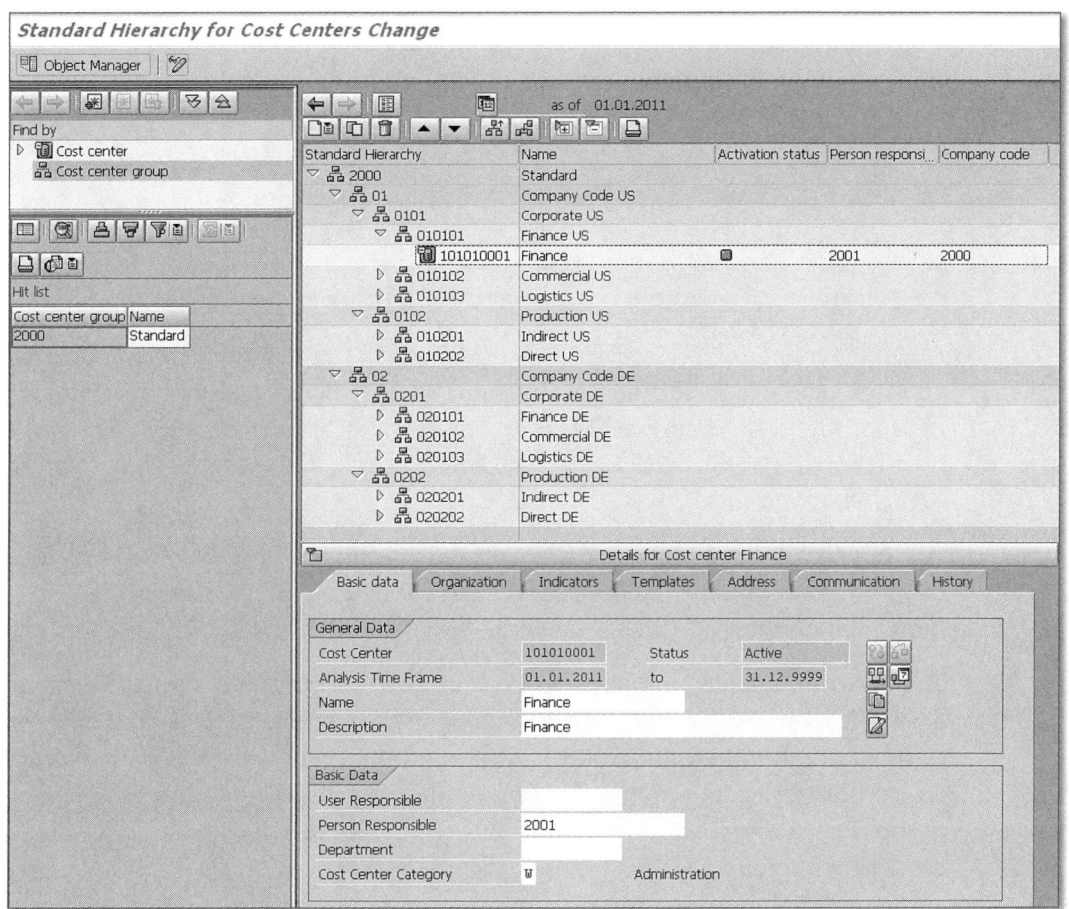

Figure 3.5 Cost Center Standard Hierarchy

As you've seen in Chapter 2 for cost elements, you can also group cost centers. The groups can be created using parts of the standard hierarchy or parts of other groups. Groups can be used for reporting purposes and in the customizing.

To create cost center groups, you can use the user menu or also the customizing menu. In the user menu, Transactions KSH1, KSH2, KSH3 are used to create, change, or display groups, respectively. In the customizing menu, use the following IMG menu path CONTROLLING • COST CENTER ACCOUNTING • MASTER DATA • COST CENTERS • DEFINE COST CENTER GROUPS. Figure 3.6 shows one example of a cost center group, which groups the cost centers related to indirect production costs.

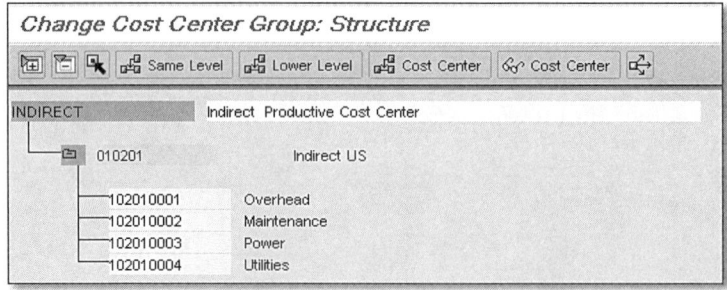

Figure 3.6 Cost Center Group

You can see how a cost center group and a cost element group can be combined in reporting in the example shown in Figure 3.7. This example uses one of the most common reports in CO-CCA, Report S_ALR_87013611 – Cost Centers: Actual/Plan/Variance.

You can see that a group for cost center and a group for cost element were used in the selection screen, which impacts the way the report is displayed and also limits the selection of data displayed.

The report will have a breakdown both by cost center group and cost element group. You can see the cost center grouping in the left side of the Figure 3.7. You can navigate between the groups and expand the group to select an individual cost center inside the group. The results detail is also shown by cost element group, as you can see on the yellow lines of the report, which show subtotals by cost element group.

Cost center customizing also permits definition of some fields as time-based fields, as you saw previously for cost elements. All changes in the fields that are selected to be time-based fields will be tracked, and the system will consider the valid date that matches with the posting date to define the appropriate characteristic to update the CO tables. For example, if the field LOCK ACTUAL PRIMARY COST is marked on the cost center master data and also in the customizing as time-based relevant, and you unmark it, it will be unmarked from the date that you made the change. If you try to post any value with a posting date preceding the change, the system won't allow the posting. Figure 3.8 shows an example of the available fields. You can use Transaction OKEG, or in the customizing menu, use the IMG menu path CONTROLLING • COST CENTER ACCOUNTING • MASTER DATA • COST CENTERS • DEFINE TIME-BASED FIELDS FOR COST CENTERS.

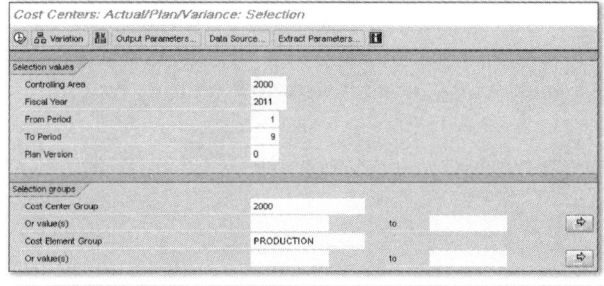

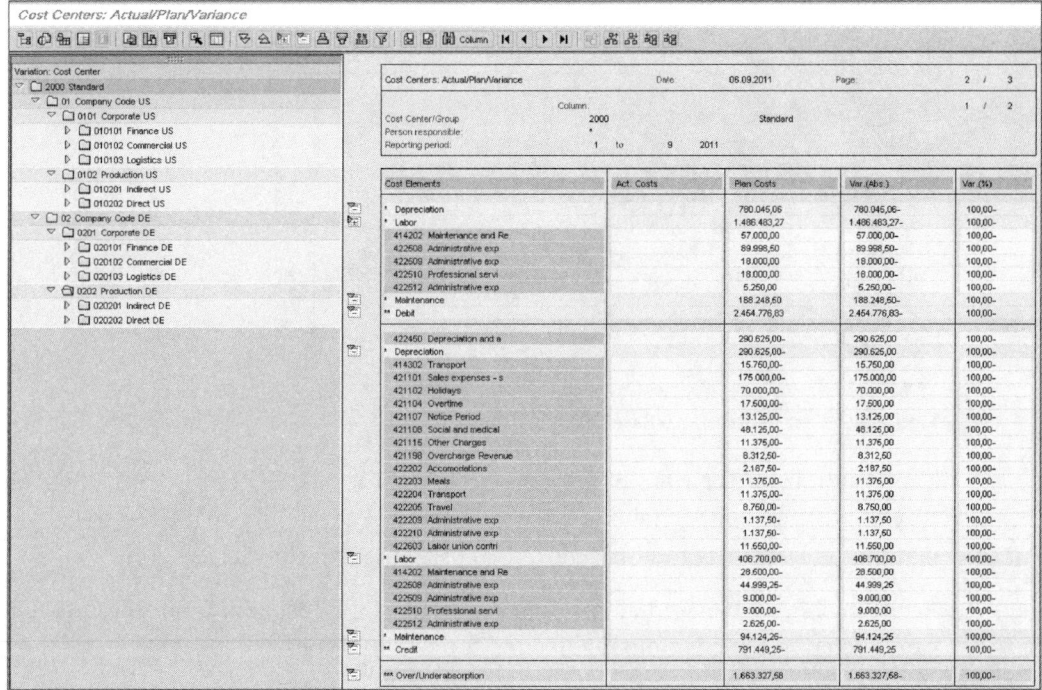

Figure 3.7 Cost Center Reporting Example

You can choose from four time-based dependency options that are available in SAP ERP. These options cannot be changed. The following dependencies are possible:

- ▶ Not time-based
- ▶ Day-based
- ▶ Period-based
- ▶ Fiscal-year-based

> **Note**
>
> Remember that the time-based functionality consumes large amounts of data storage space, so carefully consider which fields should have time-based dependencies.

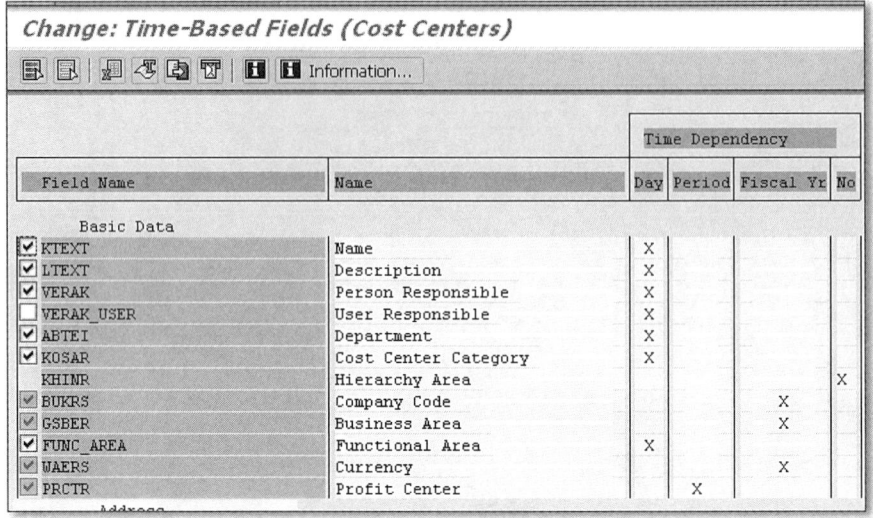

Figure 3.8 Cost Center Time-Based Fields

The customizing for time-based dependencies for cost centers works the same way as for time-based fields for cost elements. You should mark the fields you want to be treated as time-based in the cost center master data.

After finishing the essential customizing settings for cost center master data, you can now go to the customizing needed for activity types.

3.1.2 Activity Types

Activity types classify a specific activity performed by one or more cost centers. In carrying out an activity, a cost center consumes resources, and, of course, the cost of these resources must be allocated to cost objects (cost centers, orders, processes) that are benefiting from the activity performed. The cost center that performs the activity is called the "sender," and the cost center or other cost object that receives activities is known as the "receiver."

In internal activity allocation, the system calculates the total cost to be allocated from the sender to the receiver based on the amount of activity performed by the sender considering the activity quantity and the activity price set for the activity. The SAP system creates a debit for the receiver and a credit for the sender in terms of quantity and value using the secondary cost element defined in the register of the type of activity.

Activity types provide a tracing factor (cost driver) for cost allocations, for example, labor time, machine hours, and so on.

Through integrated planning, you can extract the activity quantity information from the Production Planning (PP) component. PP plans the values in the work centers, and, in CO, these activities are transferred to the cost center associated to the work center and valuated according to the activity price planned. This will be explained further in Section 3.2.4.

In activity type master data, you can set the following options:

▶ Plan activity type category

▶ Actual activity type category

▶ Price indicator

▶ Actual price indicator

▶ Cost element for the activity allocation

▶ Average price

▶ Predistribution of fixed costs

▶ Planned quantity set

▶ Actual quantity set

You can create, change, or display activity types using Transactions KL01, KL02, and KL03, respectively, in the SAP ERP user menu or by following the IMG menu path CONTROLLING • COST CENTER ACCOUNTING • MASTER DATA • ACTIVITY TYPES • CREATE ACTIVITY TYPES. Figure 3.9 shows the options on the activity definition screen, using an example of an activity type for depreciation.

When creating a new activity type, after giving a name and description to the activity type in the NAMES section, you must choose an activity unit to measure the activity performed by the cost object.

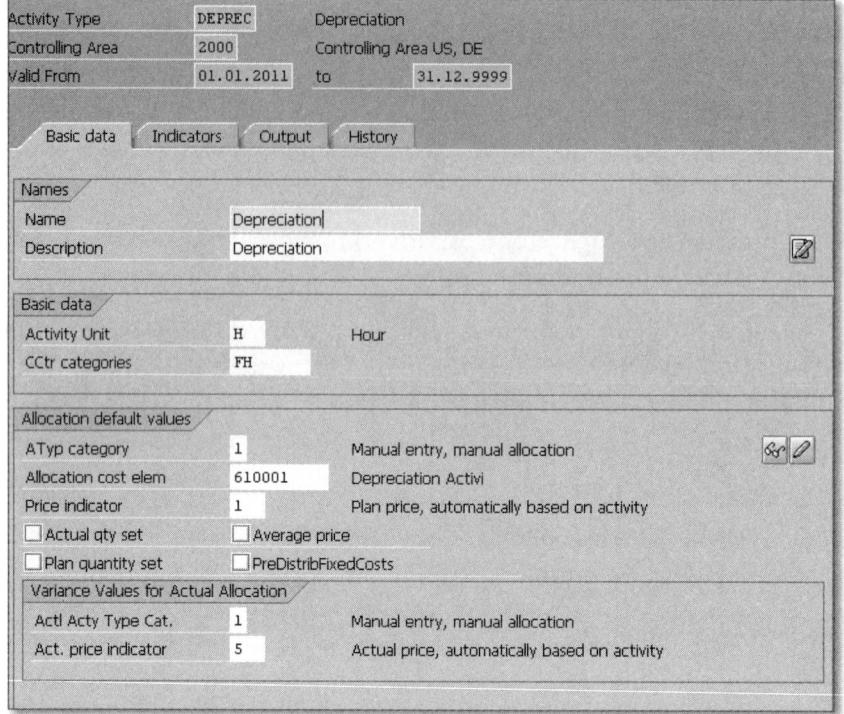

Figure 3.9 Activity Type Definition

In the field CCTR CATEGORIES, you define which cost center categories can be used with this activity type. Remember that you've already customized the cost center categories. This is one place that you can now use those cost center categories. You can associate up to eight categories or enter "*" to accept all cost center categories. In the example shown in Figure 3.9, only cost center categories "F" (production) and "H" (service) are allowed to use this activity type.

The ATYP CATEGORY field is used in both planning and actual transactions. Activity types are divided into four different categories for planning, and these same four plus one additional category for actual. Activity categories determine both the allocation method and the planning quantity.

The following are the allocation methods for activity types:

▶ 1: MANUAL ENTRY, MANUAL ALLOCATION
Activities in this category are used for manual planning and allocation. The planning amount of the activity to be performed by the sender cost center is

made using the planning function of the activity type. This planning will consist of an activity quantity and price (allocation of measurable activities; actual quantity times planned price).

▶ 2: INDIRECT DETERMINATION, INDIRECT ALLOCATION
This category is used when the calculation of the quantities is impossible or extremely tedious. The calculation of planned and actual amounts is made through the indirect activity allocation using a relationship defined between the sender and receiver.

▶ 3: MANUAL ENTRY, INDIRECT ALLOCATION
You can use this category when you manually plan the sender cost center through a special function without informing any receiver cost object. The system, based on the relationship established between sender and receiver, will calculate the amount of activities to be allocated to each receiver. After allocation of indirect activities, the activities will be fully reconciled.

▶ 4: MANUAL ENTRY, NO ALLOCATION
Select this category if you are doing manual planning to the sender cost center and you want the cost to remain there. You can use this category for internal cost center activities.

▶ 5: TARGET = ACTUAL ALLOCATION (ACTUAL ONLY)
This is a special kind of indirect allocation that determines the actual values from the needs of planned activities through an operating index. This category can only be used for actual allocation. The categories for planning should be 1, 2, 3, or 4 (most commonly, category 1).

You can generally combine all categories for actual and planning, but we advise you to choose the same category for planning and actual, so you can compare them both in future analysis. You cannot combine activity type category 4 (manual entry, no allocation) with any categories that allow allocation.

In the definition of the activity type, you must also make an entry in the ALLOCATION COST ELEM field. The activity type uses a cost element category 43 (Internal activity allocation). (You learned about cost element categories in Chapter 2.) If the activity type has never been used, or there is no data in the FISCAL YEAR field, then you can change this cost element. This information is "year time-based," which means for each fiscal year, a different cost element can be defined.

In the PRICE INDICATOR field, you select how the system will calculate the planned and actual activity price. You can separately enter a price indicator that is different from that in the plan in the ACT. PRICE INDICATOR field. You can enter the following values for the plan price indicator:

▶ 1: PLAN PRICE, AUTOMATICALLY BASED ON ACTIVITY
The system calculates the activity price automatically, based on the planned activity and the planned costs.

Fixed price: Fixed planned costs ÷ planned activity

Variable price: Variable planned costs ÷ planned activity

Total price: Fixed price + variable price

▶ 2: PLAN PRICE, AUTOMATICALLY BASED ON CAPACITY
The fixed portion of the activity price will be calculated based on the cost center capacity. This method will often result in over- or under-absorption in the cost center because the cost center can receive more or less activity than its capacity.

Fixed price: Fixed plan costs ÷ capacity

Variable price: Variable plan costs ÷ plan activity

Total price: Fixed price + variable price

▶ 3: DETERMINED MANUALLY
You set the price of the activity type manually.

You can enter the following values for the actual price indicator (ACT. PRICE INDICATOR field):

▶ 5: ACTUAL PRICE, AUTOMATICALLY BASED ON ACTIVITY
Select this option if you want to the system to calculate the actual price based on the actual activity and actual costs.

▶ 6: ACTUAL PRICE, AUTOMATICALLY BASED ON CAPACITY
This works similarly to option 5, but in this case, the system will use the capacity to calculate the activity rate.

▶ 7: MANUALLY DETERMINED FOR ACTUAL ALLOCATIONS
You set the activity type price manually.

If you have set values 1 or 2 for planning and 5 or 6 for actual, SAP ERP calculates new prices when you execute the plan price calculation and actual price calculation, respectively.

The definition made in the version maintenance, Transaction OKKP, for the price calculation method (periodic, average price or cumulative) will impact how SAP ERP calculates the price. In Figure 3.10, you can see the version customizing. In the actual activity price, the revaluation of the activity type will occur only if you've selected a revaluation method from the preceding list.

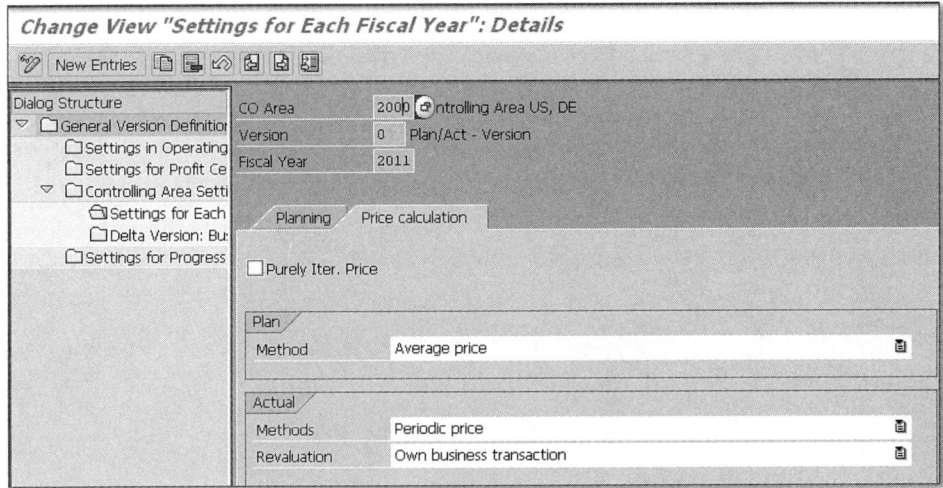

Figure 3.10 Maintain Controlling Area, Price Calculation

Also in the activity type definition screen shown earlier in Figure 3.9, the last options you have in the ALLOCATION DEFAULT VALUES section are four flag indicators:

▶ ACTUAL QTY SET
If this flag is set, the actual activity quantity must be posted manually.

▶ AVERAGE PRICE
Indicates whether the activity prices for the cost center and activity type combination remain constant for the entire fiscal year (average of periods). This field is also year time dependent and can be changed each year if desired.

▶ PLAN QUANTITY SET
Indicates that the planned activity cannot be changed by the planning reconciliation.

▶ PREDISTRIBFIXEDCOSTS
Allows this activity type to be used in fixed cost predistribution.

Because the activity price is a cost object, and all cost objects can be grouped, you can define activity type groups for activity type master data as well. These groups can be useful both in reporting and customizing. Grouping works the same way as you've already seen for cost element and cost center grouping. You can create activity type groups using the user menu or the customizing menu. In the user menu, Transactions KLH1, KLH2, and KLH3 are used to create, change, or display groups, respectively. In the customizing menu, use the following IMG menu path CONTROLLING • COST CENTER ACCOUNTING • MASTER DATA • ACTIVITY TYPES • DEFINE ACTIVITY TYPE GROUPS.

You can also define time-based fields for activity types in the same way as for cost elements and cost centers. You can maintain activity type time-based fields using Transaction OKEI or following IMG menu path CONTROLLING • COST CENTER ACCOUNTING • MASTER DATA • ACTIVITY TYPES • DEFINE TIME-BASED FIELDS FOR ACTIVITY TYPES.

After creating the necessary customizing for activity types, the next step is to define the statistical key figures master data.

3.1.3 Statistical Key Figures

Statistical key figures are numerical measures that assist in the allocation of costs between cost centers, internal orders, and profit centers. As with activity types, statistical key figures can be also be used as criteria for periodic cost allocation (distributions and assessments). They can also be defined for a particular type of activity performed by a cost center (e.g., the number of employees in a cost center, or the amount of power in kilowatt hours [KWH] used in a cost center). They can also be used for reporting both planned and actual costs.

There are two categories for statistical key figures:

▶ **01: Fixed values**
   Fixed values means that its values remain constant over the periods. The quantity is measured once and applies to all periods. For example, the number of employees from a cost center can be considered as a fixed value. However, it can be changed manually by the user if necessary, for example, if an employee is transferred to a different functional area (cost center) and for new hires and terminations.

▶ **02: Total values**

Total values correspond to values accumulated over the period, for example, the number of telephone calls made in the month. These indices need to be updated periodically.

You can also import statistical key figures from the Logistic Information System (LIS) without the need to update them manually. For this, LIS must be active in logistics and in the statistical key figure master data. The relationship with the corresponding key figure in LIS must also be specified.

You can create, change, or display statistical key figure master data using Transactions KK01, KK02, and KK03, respectively, in the SAP ERP user menu or via the IMG menu path CONTROLLING • COST CENTER ACCOUNTING • MASTER DATA • STATISTICAL KEY FIGURES • MAINTAIN STATISTICAL KEY FIGURES (see Figure 3.11).

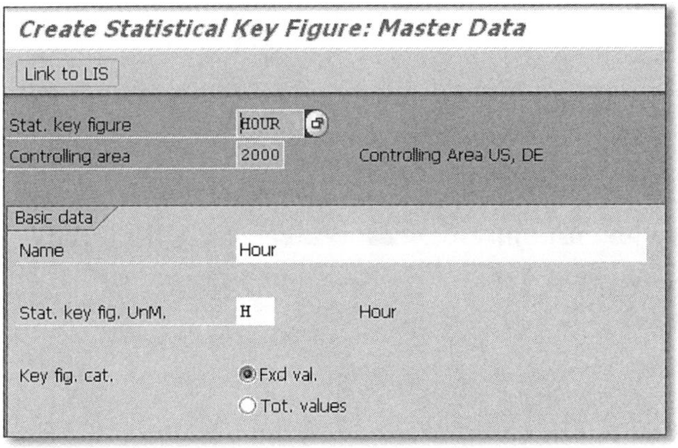

Figure 3.11 Statistical Key Figure

You can group statistical key figures in the same way as for all cost objects. You can create the group using the user menu or using the customizing menu. In the user menu, use Transactions KKH1, KKH2, and KKH3 to create, change, or display groups, respectively. In the customizing menu, use the IMG menu path CONTROLLING • COST CENTER ACCOUNTING • MASTER DATA • STATISTICAL KEY FIGURES • MAINTAIN STATISTICAL KEY FIGURE GROUPS.

Now that you've defined the statistical key figures and understand how they are used, you're ready to learn about resources master data.

3.1.4 Resources

Resources are goods and services purchased for the execution of a particular business activity. In CO-OM, you can use resources for planning purposes only. You can plan resources during the cost centers/activity type planning. By associating more than one resource to a cost element, you can reduce the chart of accounts without losing details relevant to cost analysis.

Three types of records are available:

- **Type R**
  Exists only in CO-OM, and their prices are stored directly in the price tables.
- **Type M**
  Refers to a material and their prices are defined in the material master. In MM, the resources together with the item category describe what the item represents as an estimate of costs (material, activity type, purchasing info records, or overhead).
- **Type B**
  Refers to a base planning object and considers the price of the base planning object to value the resource consumption.

Now that you've learned how to customize the cost center master data, activity types, statistical key figures, and resources for CO-CCA, it's time to learn about the options available in CO-CCA planning.

3.2 Planning

Cost center planning is typically part of the company budget and should be integrated into the overall planning process. Planning can be done for primary costs, secondary costs, activity type quantities consumed, and statistical key figures. The planning is done for a set period of time, usually a fiscal year.

Cost center planning can be handled in various ways, depending on the needs of the organization. Cost center planning can be done online in SAP ERP, providing an immediate result that can be analyzed in the information system.

The cost object groups, such as cost center groups and cost element groups, are an excellent tool that can streamline the planning procedure. For example, you can create a plan for a group of cost elements and a group of cost centers, instead of planning for them individually.

The first step in the planning customizing is to define the basic settings for planning.

3.2.1 Basic Settings for Planning

In basic settings we'll discuss the prerequisites to start the planning customizing, why and how to define exchange rate types and the related exchange rates, and which required options must be set in version maintenance to create the planning.

You can define an optional exchange rate type for cost center planning. This exchange rate should be updated in the version using version maintenance. The exchange rate type stores exchange rates for different purposes, for example, planning, buying rate, selling rate, and average rate. SAP ERP provides standard exchange rate type "P", which is assumed in the automatic generation version of the 000. You can also create your own exchange rate type. You maintain the exchange rate types using Transaction OB07 or by following the IMG menu path CONTROLLING • COST CENTER ACCOUNTING • PLANNING • BASIC SETTINGS FOR PLANNING • DEFINE EXCHANGE RATE TYPES. Figure 3.12 shows the customizing screen.

You can create a new exchange rate type by clicking on the NEW ENTRIES button, or you can mark one and click the COPY button. We created exchange rate type "P1" as a copy of "P", as you can see in Figure 3.12.

After defining the exchange rate type, you can now define the exchange rates to be stored in this type.

Currency types that will be used in SAP ERP must be registered in this transaction with an exchange rate type, expiration date, rate from and to, and currency from and to. Most world currencies are already enrolled in SAP ERP. To maintain the exchange rate, you can use Transaction OB08 or follow the IMG menu path CONTROLLING • COST CENTER ACCOUNTING • PLANNING • BASIC SETTINGS FOR PLANNING • DEFINE EXCHANGE RATE. Figure 3.13 shows the exchange rate maintenance screen with entries for our example exchange rate type P1. Exchange rates were entered based on direct quotation at the first of each month.

Change View "Currency Translation Exchange Rate Types": Overview

New Entries

ExRt	Usage	Ref.crcy	Buy.rt.at	Sell.rt.at	Inv	E...	Fixed
100*	Reference value = group value				☐	☐	☐
1001	Current exchange rate				☐	☐	☐
1002	Average exchange rate				☐	☐	☐
1003	Historical exchange rate				☐	☐	☐
1004	Current exch. rate prior year				☐	☐	☐
200*	Reference value = group value				☐	☐	☐
2001	Current exchange rate				☐	☐	☐
2002	Average exchange rate				☐	☐	☐
2003	Historical exchange rate				☐	☐	☐
2004	Current exch. rate prior year				☐	☐	☐
B	Standard translation at bk.sellin...				☐	☐	☐
EURO	EMU regulation, fixed exchang...	EUR			☐	☑	☑
EURX	EMU regulation, variable excha...	EUR			☐	☑	☐
G	Standard translation at bank bu...				☐	☐	☐
I	Intrastat exchange rate type				☐	☐	☐
M	Standard translation at average...				☐	☐	☐
P	Standard translation for cost pl...				☐	☐	☐
P1	Exchange rate type P1				☐	☐	☐

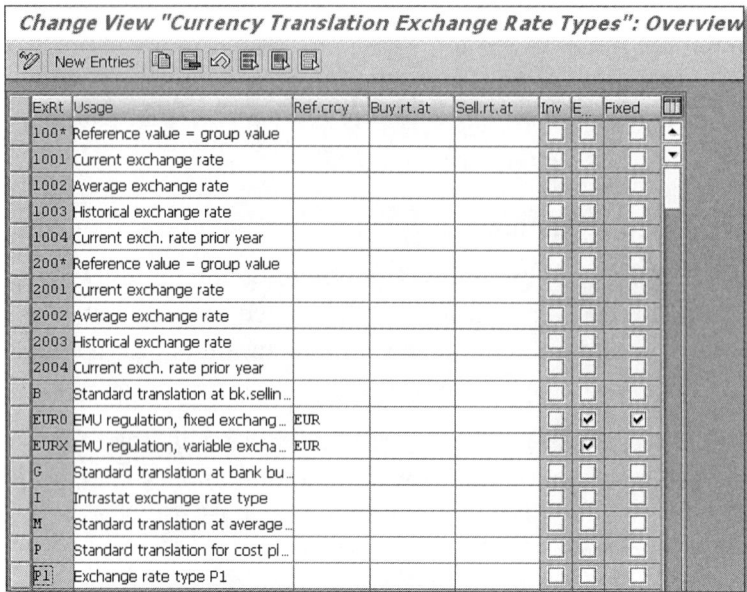

Figure 3.12 Exchange Rate Type

Change View "Currency Exchange Rates": Overview of Selected Set

New Entries

ExRt	ValidFrom	Indir.quot		Ratio (from)	From		Dir.quot.		Ratio (to)	To
P1	12/01/2011		X	1	EUR	=	1.43000	X	1	USD
P1	11/01/2011		X	1	EUR	=	1.40000	X	1	USD
P1	10/01/2011		X	1	EUR	=	1.45000	X	1	USD
P1	09/01/2011		X	1	EUR	=	1.45000	X	1	USD
P1	08/01/2011		X	1	EUR	=	1.40000	X	1	USD
P1	07/01/2011		X	1	EUR	=	1.38000	X	1	USD
P1	06/01/2011		X	1	EUR	=	1.35000	X	1	USD
P1	05/15/2011		X	1	EUR	=	1.37000	X	1	USD
P1	05/01/2011		X	1	EUR	=	1.30000	X	1	USD
P1	04/01/2011		X	1	EUR	=	1.25000	X	1	USD
P1	03/01/2011		X	1	EUR	=	1.22000	X	1	USD
P1	02/01/2011		X	1	EUR	=	1.18000	X	1	USD
P1	01/01/2011		X	1	EUR	=	1.15000	X	1	USD

Figure 3.13 Maintain Exchange Rate

You have the option to select direct quotation (Dir. quot.) or indirect quotation (Indir. quot). Direct quotation is how much a foreign currency costs versus the local currency. Indirect quotation is the opposite.

The last step in basic settings is to maintain the planning version. You've already learned how to create versions in SAP ERP in Chapter 1. It's important to remember that you can assign the recently created exchange rate type to the version using Transaction OKEQ. Figure 3.14 shows how to assign the exchange rate type to a version.

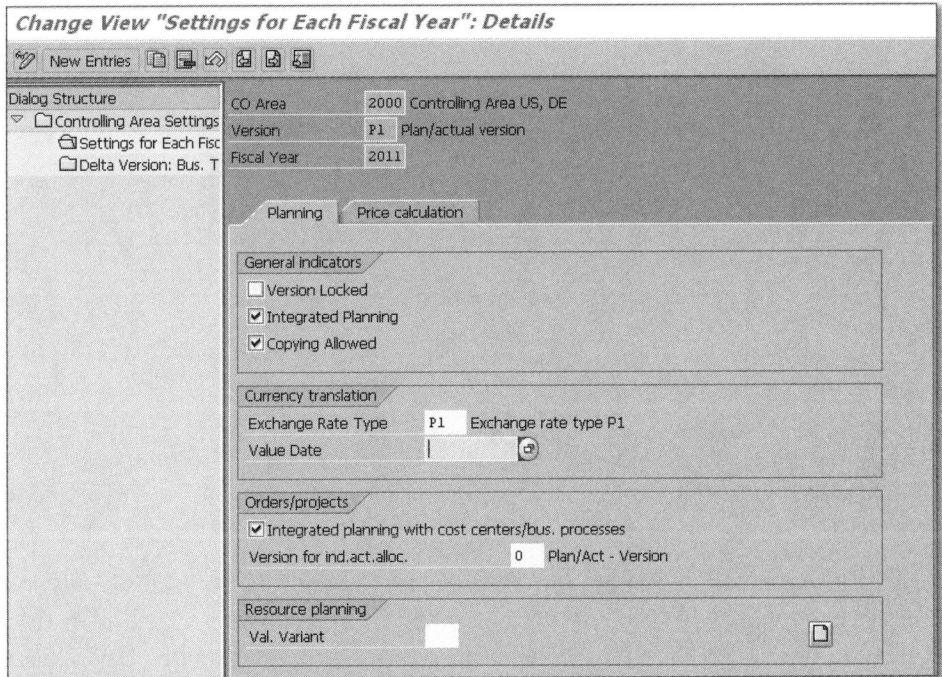

Figure 3.14 Version Settings

In this case, the system will adopt the exchange rate type "P1" for the version, and because the VALUE DATE is empty, the system will use the exchange rate for the first day of the period for each planning period. You can see in Figure 3.13 shown previously that for 05/2011, there are two exchange rates: one for 05/01/2011 of

1.30000 USD/EUR and another for 05/15/2011 of 1.37000 USD/EUR. The system will use the currency rate from 05/01/2011.

Now let's consider a planning example. Using Transaction KP06, we've planned in the cost center 201010001 – FINANCE $10,000 per month for a total of $120,000 for the year. Figure 3.15 shows the planning screen.

Change Cost Element/Activity Input Planning: Period Screen

Version	P1	Plan/actual version
Fiscal Year	2011	
Cost Center	201010001	Finance
Cost Element	422602	Municipal taxes

Pe	Text	Plan Fixed Costs	Plan Variable Costs	Plan fixed consum.	Plan vbl consumpt.	Unit	Q	L
1	January	10.000,00	0,00	0,000	0,000			
2	February	10.000,00	0,00	0,000	0,000			
3	March	10.000,00	0,00	0,000	0,000			
4	April	10.000,00	0,00	0,000	0,000			
5	May	10.000,00	0,00	0,000	0,000			
6	June	10.000,00	0,00	0,000	0,000			
7	July	10.000,00	0,00	0,000	0,000			
8	August	10.000,00	0,00	0,000	0,000			
9	September	10.000,00	0,00	0,000	0,000			
10	October	10.000,00	0,00	0,000	0,000			
11	November	10.000,00	0,00	0,000	0,000			
12	December	10.000,00	0,00	0,000	0,000			
*Pe		120.000,00	0,00	0,000	0,000			

Figure 3.15 Planning Example for Controlling Area Currency

The company code belonging to this cost center has "EUR" as the company code currency.

When running a cost center report in the object currency (EUR, in this case), you can see in Figure 3.16 that the system made the conversion of the plan data entered in the screen shown in Figure 3.15 using the rate for the first day of each month using the exchange rates entered for the rate type "P1" during exchange rate maintenance shown in Figure 3.13.

This example shows the results using the standard cost center Report S_ALR_87013611 – Cost Centers: Actual/Plan/Variance. You should keep in mind that the report currency (controlling area currency, object currency, or transaction currency) can be defined in Transaction RPC0, as already explained in Chapter 2.

```
Periods: Act./Plan                    Date: 04.07.2011           Page:      2 /   2
                                                                 Column:    1 /   1
Cost Center/Group        201010001         Finance
Person responsible       3001
Cost Element/Group       422602            Municipal taxes
Fiscal Year              2011
```

Periods	Act. Costs	Plan Costs	Var.(Abs.)	Var.(%)
1 January		8.695,65	8.695,65-	100,00-
2 February		8.474,58	8.474,58-	100,00-
3 March		8.196,72	8.196,72-	100,00-
4 April		8.000,00	8.000,00-	100,00-
5 May		7.692,31	7.692,31-	100,00-
6 June		7.407,41	7.407,41-	100,00-
7 July		7.246,38	7.246,38-	100,00-
8 August		7.142,86	7.142,86-	100,00-
9 September		6.896,55	6.896,55-	100,00-
10 October		6.896,55	6.896,55-	100,00-
11 November		7.142,86	7.142,86-	100,00-
12 December		6.993,01	6.993,01-	100,00-
* Total		90.784,88	90.784,88-	100,00-

Figure 3.16 Cost Center Report in Object Currency

After creating the basic settings, the next step in the process of customizing your planning settings is customizing for manual planning.

3.2.2 Manual Planning

Manual planning covers the following planning areas:

► Statistical key figures planning

► Activity type planning

► Primary cost planning

► Secondary cost planning

► Budget planning

► Detailed planning

To create cost center planning, you can either use standard planning profiles or create your own. Cost center planning is done through predefined SAP ERP screens containing only the fields that should be updated by the planner and associated to planner profiles. These screens are known as the planning layouts. These layouts should be defined for the areas of planning, for example, cost element and activity type. SAP ERP has some predefined layouts.

There are three kinds of planning layouts:

▶ Planning layouts for cost element planning

▶ Planning layouts for activity type planning

▶ Planning layouts for statistical key figure planning

The main advantage of manipulating the planning layout is that you can change the planning currency. The standard layout uses the controlling area currency as a planning currency. For instance, you may want to make planning entries using the cost object currency instead of the controlling area currency, and this can be made much easier by using a customized planning layout.

You create the planning layouts using Transactions KP65 (for cost element), KP75 (for activity type), and KP85 (for statistical key figure) or by following the IMG menu path CONTROLLING • COST CENTER ACCOUNTING • PLANNING • MANUAL PLANNING • USER-DEFINED PLANNING LAYOUTS • CREATE PLANNING LAYOUTS FOR COST ELEMENT PLANNING. Figure 3.17 shows the customizing screen for Transaction KP65.

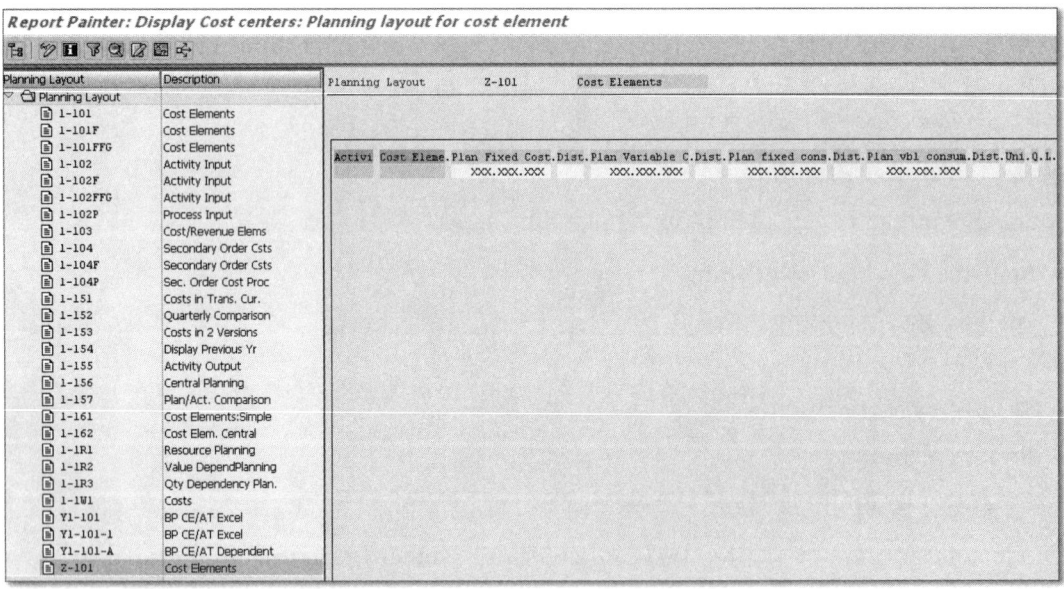

Figure 3.17 Planning Layout

You'll now see how to create a planning layout for cost element planning. The same process applies for the other two.

Controlling area 2000 used in our XYZ organization example from Chapter 1 has USD as the controlling area currency, and because company codes 2000 and 3000 are assigned to this controlling area, both company codes use USD as the controlling area currency. Company code 3000 has EUR as the company code currency. If we use the standard layout, all of the planning values will be entered in USD. We can create a layout that uses the object currency as the planning currency for cost centers in company code 2000. The system will adopt USD as the planning currency, and, for cost centers in company code 3000, the system will adopt EUR, doing the conversion following the exchange rate type linked in the planning version. Figure 3.18 shows how to select the object currency. Double-click in the PLAN FIXED COST column, and, on the resulting screen, you can change the KEY FIGURE field to PLAN FIXED COST IN OBJECT CURRENCY.

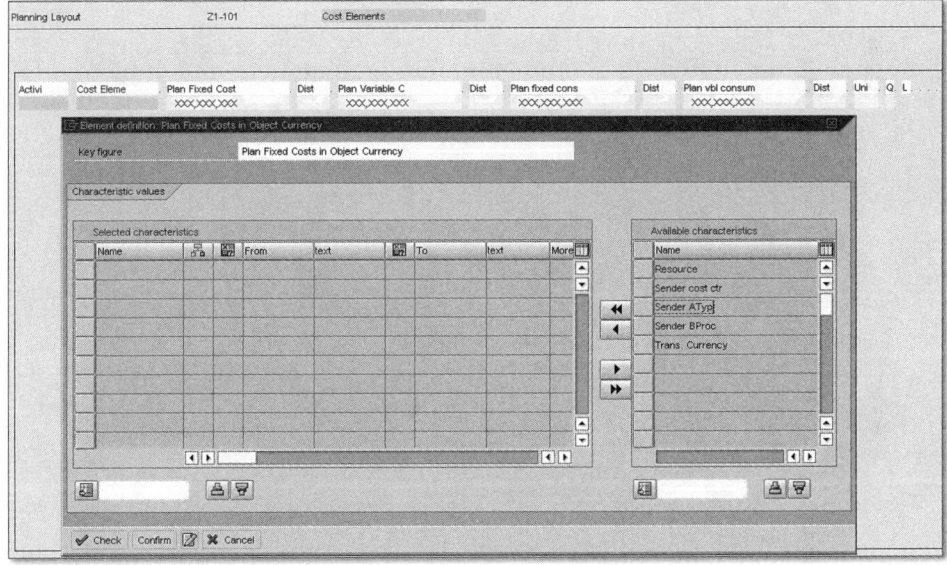

Figure 3.18 Planning Layout Detail

Now that you've created a planning layout that can use the object currency as the planning currency, you must assign this layout to a planner profile. SAP ERP also has several standard profiles available that cover many of the most common planning situations. The SAPALL profile can be used for planning for the three areas with different layouts available in each area. The SAPEASY profile is prepared for a simplified planning. Typically, you copy these profiles and modify them to suit your needs.

Another use for the planning profiles is security. You can restrict the planner profile in the user's security profile and limit the planning access for users.

You create the planner profile using Transaction KP34 or by following the IMG menu path CONTROLLING • COST CENTER ACCOUNTING • PLANNING • MANUAL PLANNING • DEFINE USER-DEFINED PLANNER PROFILES. You can see the first screen showing the overview of the available profiles in Figure 3.19.

Profile	Description	Auth.group
SAP101	Release 3.0/3.1 CO-OM: Prim. Cost/ATyp/StKF	
SAP102	Release 3.0/3.1 CO-OM: Acty Input/ATyp/StKF	
SAP103	Rel: 3.0/3.1 PP Plan: Costs, Rev/ATyp, Price/StKF	
SAP104	Rel. 3.0/3.1 CO-OM: Sec.Ord.Costs/ATyp/A-Dep. StKF	
SAP800	EC-PCA: Planning Profit Center Group (Centralized)	
SAP801	EC-PCA: Profit Center Planning (Decentralized)	
SAPALL	CO Planning: All Planning Areas	
SAPEASY	CO-OM: Prim. Cost/ATyp/StKF -- Basic Layouts	
SAPFAGL	Planner Profile for Planning in Gen. Ledger (New)	
SAPFIGL	Planner Profile for FI-GL Planning	
SAPFMPL	Planner Profile for FM Budget Control System	
SAPFUND	CO Planning Fund Accounting: All Planning Areas	
SAPFUNDA	FM Activity Input	
SAPFUND0	FM Primary Costs/Statistical Key Figures	
SAPFUNDR	FM Revenues	
SAPGRANT	CO Planning with Grants: All Planning Areas	
SAPIM1	Primary Costs/Statistical Key Figures Multi-Crcy	
SAPIM2	Activity Input Multi-Currency	
SAPIM3	Revenues Multi-Currency	
SAPR&R	CO-OM: Resource and Dependency Planning	
SAPREFX	RE-FX: Cost and Revenue Planning	
YBALL_01	BP planning with Excel (reduced)	
YBALL_02	BP Planning: All Planning Areas	
ZSAPALL	CO Planning: All Planning Areas	

Figure 3.19 Planner Profile

You can create a new planner profile or copy an existing one to customize. For this example, we've copied the SAPALL profile to ZSAPALL. Mark the profile on the right side of the screen, and double-click on GENERAL CONTROLLING on the left side of the screen. Figure 3.20 shows the next step, in which you'll determine the settings for the planning areas included in the profile.

The last two columns show how the system will propose the distribution key (CUDK column) for amounts and distribution key for quantities (QTDK column) when planning.

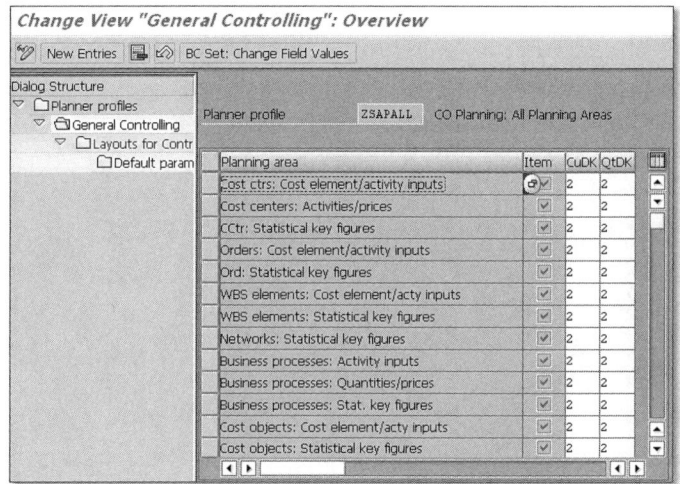

Figure 3.20 Planning Area

Click to select one line in the far left column on the right side of the screen, and then double-click on the LAYOUTS FOR CONTROLLING folder on the left side of the screen as shown in Figure 3.21.

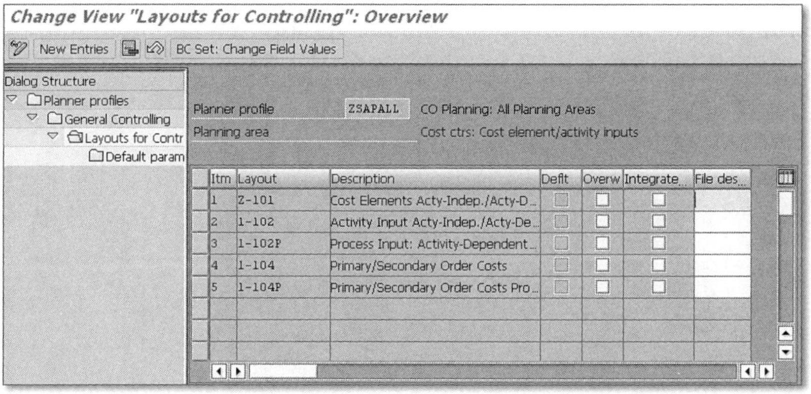

Figure 3.21 Layouts for Controlling

Click on NEW ENTRIES, and select the layout created in the user-defined planning layouts (in our case, Z-101).

The OVERWRITE flag controls whether users can change the proposed values for the distribution key when planning, and the INTEGRATED EXCEL flag means that SAP ERP will open Microsoft Excel to perform the planning.

After saving the planner profile, you should select it using Transaction KP04. Every time you want to change the planner profile, you should perform this action. Figure 3.22 shows the assignment. You can now use this layout to plan and also continue using the standard layouts if you want because they are assigned to the planner profile as well.

Figure 3.22 Set Planner Profile

You can also save the profile in your user master record, so that every time you are going to plan, the system will adopt the planner profile saved in your user master record.

Next, we'll show an example of planning using a different planner layout. We used Transaction KP06 to show how the planning currency was affected by changing the planning layout, as shown in Figure 3.23.

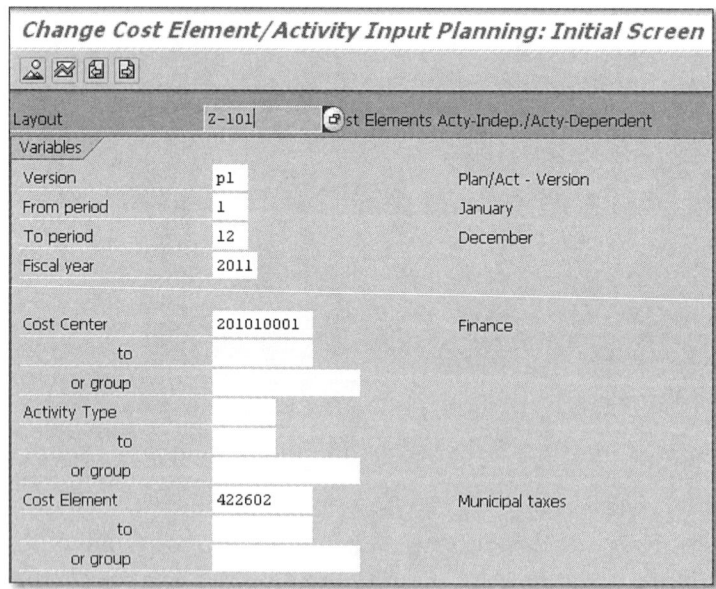

Figure 3.23 Cost Center Planning Example

You can see that the system brought the layout Z-101, and you can navigate between the planning layouts using the arrow icons at the top of the screen (left and right). Figure 3.24 shows the same planning values from Figure 3.15, but now in the object currency, as defined for the layout.

Change Cost Element/Activity Input Planning: Period Screen

Version	P1	Plan/actual version
Fiscal Year	2011	
Cost Center	201010001	Finance
Cost Element	422602	Municipal taxes

Pe	Text	Plan Fix Costs in OC	Plan Var. Costs O	Plan fixed consum	Plan vbl consumpt
1	January	8.695,65	0,00	0,000	0,000
2	February	8.474,58	0,00	0,000	0,000
3	March	8.196,72	0,00	0,000	0,000
4	April	8.000,00	0,00	0,000	0,000
5	May	7.692,31	0,00	0,000	0,000
6	June	7.407,41	0,00	0,000	0,000
7	July	7.246,38	0,00	0,000	0,000
8	August	7.142,86	0,00	0,000	0,000
9	September	6.896,55	0,00	0,000	0,000
10	October	6.896,55	0,00	0,000	0,000
11	November	7.142,86	0,00	0,000	0,000
12	December	6.993,01	0,00	0,000	0,000
*Pe		90.784,88	0,00	0,000	0,000

Figure 3.24 Cost Element Planning, Object Currency

Now that you've learned the settings for manual planning, we'll move on to the planning aids, which are tools provided by SAP ERP to help in the planning process.

3.2.3 Planning Aids

SAP ERP provides some tools to help in the planning process, such as copying planning, deleting planning, revaluating, and transferring planning from other components.

The copy function allows you to copy planning data from another version, referencing either planning or actual postings. Data can be copied either within or between fiscal years, periods, versions, and cost centers. A copy can also be limited to a data type of planning and a currency type. For the copy process, there is no customizing to be done, so just use the transactions available in the SAP ERP user menu:

▶ **KP97 – Copy Planning for Cost Centers**
Copy planning values to different periods or cost centers.

▶ **KP98 – Copy Actual to Plan for Cost Centers**
Copy actual cost center data to planning versions.

▶ **KP90 – Delete Planned Costs**
Delete selected cost element planning data for all cost centers.

▶ **KP91 – Delete Planned Costs**
Delete all cost center planned costs in the version for a fiscal year.

Figure 3.25 shows an example of using Transaction KP97, where we've copied the planning data for all cost centers from one year to another.

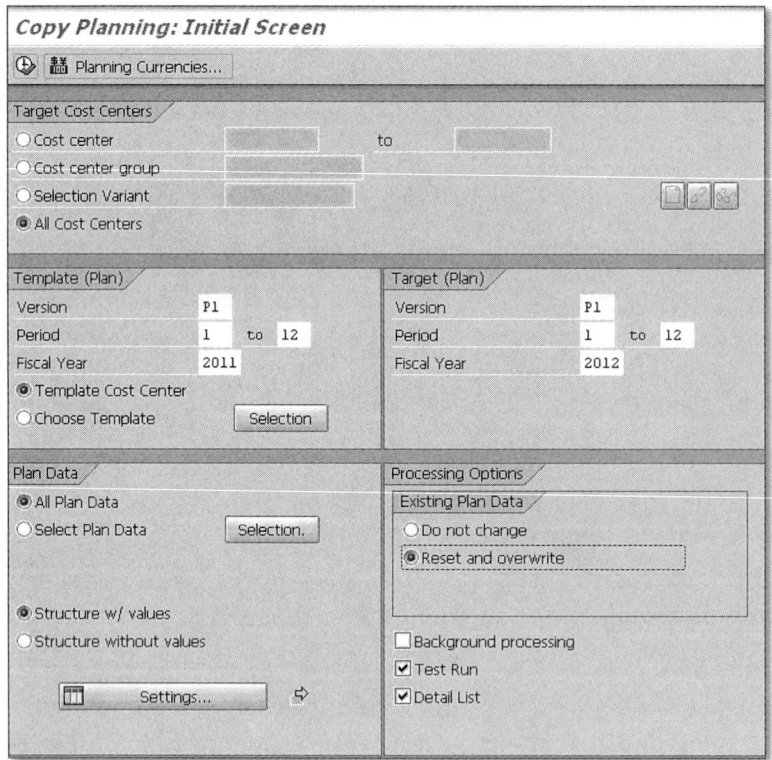

Figure 3.25 Copy Planning Example

> **Note**
>
> The copying process only copies costs from primary cost elements. Costs from secondary cost elements, such as assessments and internal order settlements, are not copied, either actual to plan, or plan to plan.

Another important tool is revaluation, by which you revalue the planning values using a defined percentage. It is possible to create the revaluation by period and with the cost element restricted. This is valid only for cost center planning.

You maintain the customizing for revaluation planning by using Transaction KPU1 or by following the IMG menu path CONTROLLING • COST CENTER ACCOUNT-ING • PLANNING • PLANNING AIDS • DEFINE REVALUATION, as you can see in Figure 3.26.

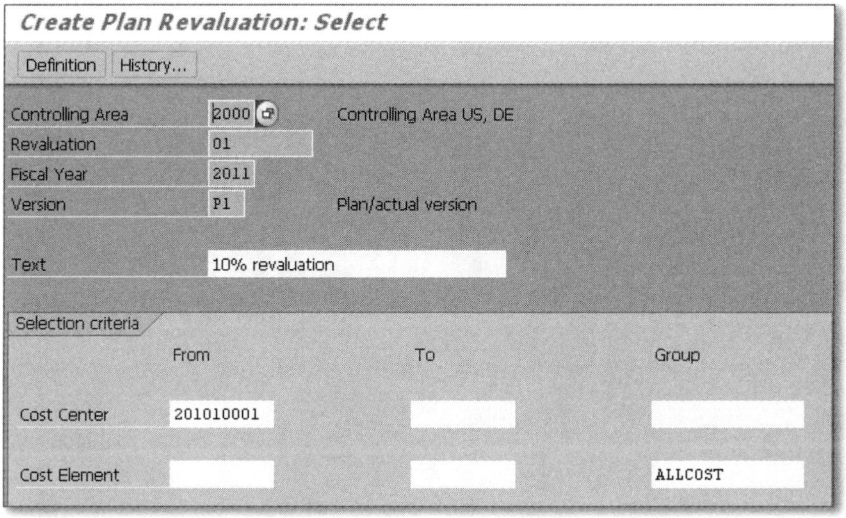

Figure 3.26 Revaluation Example

In this example, we want to increase the planned values by adding 10% for all cost elements in one cost center. Note here that we used the cost element group to define the cost elements that we want to revalue. Click on DEFINITION, and enter the periods and the percentage for costs and consumption in the PERCENT-AGE PER PERIOD section. Figure 3.27 shows the definition screen.

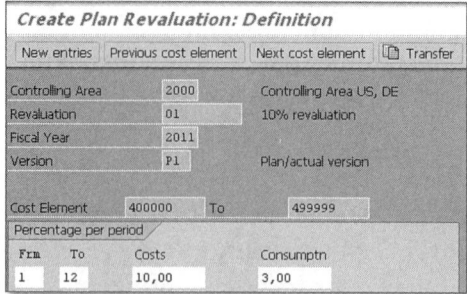

Figure 3.27 Revaluation Percentage Definition

After creating the customized settings, you can run the revaluation using Transaction KSPU from the SAP ERP user menu. Figure 3.28 shows the execution and the cost center report after the revaluation run. Comparing the results to those in Figure 3.15, we can see that 10% was added to the planning values, as we defined in the definition settings.

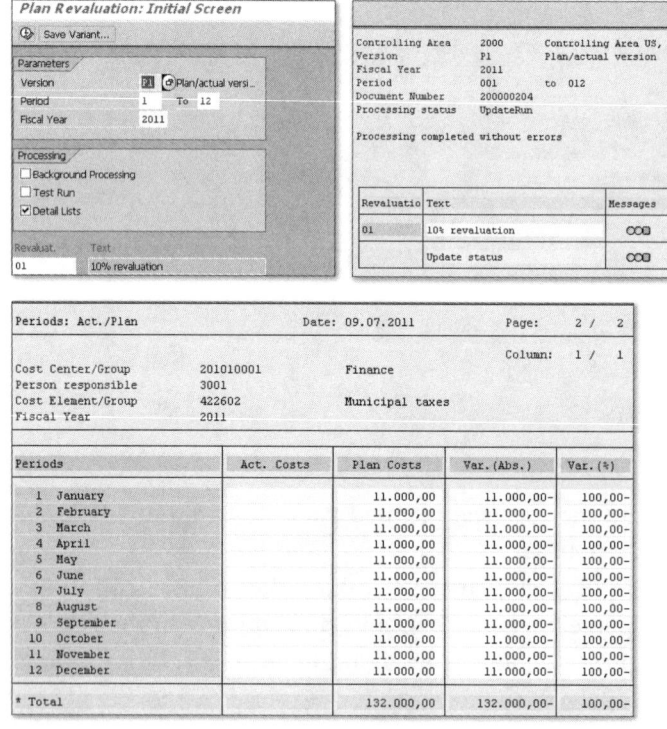

Figure 3.28 Plan Revaluation Execution with Reporting

Another useful tool provided by SAP ERP is the plan data transfer, where you can transfer planning values from other components.

3.2.4 Plan Data Transfer

SAP ERP allows you to import planning data from other components, such as depreciation data from Asset Accounting (AA), human resources costs from HCM, statistical key figures from LIS, and production activity from PP. To enable the import from PP, some customizing is needed.

From PP, you can transfer scheduled activities. You use this functionality to import the planned activity consumption based on the planning done in production using the PP component functions for Sales and Operation Planning (SOP), Materials Requirements Planning (MRP), or Long-Term Planning (LTP). The effective transfer of values takes place, in fact, through the plan reconciliation. The transfer procedure occurs in three steps:

1. Create the cost center planning cost center/activity type for which PP can create the necessary activity. This can be done manually using Transaction KP26 or by copying from another planning or from actual values.

2. Create the production planning using SOP, MRP, or LTP.

3. Run the plan reconciliation using Transaction KPSI.

The first and second steps are day-to-day activities and require no special setup steps, but the plan reconciliation requires that you first establish the customizing. You create the plan reconciliation customizing using Transaction OMIK or by following the IMG menu path CONTROLLING • COST CENTER ACCOUNTING • PLANNING • PLAN DATA TRANSFER • TRANSFER SCHEDULED ACTIVITIES FROM PP. You can see the customizing screen in Figure 3.29.

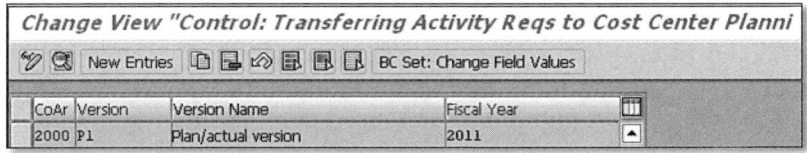

Figure 3.29 Control Transferring Activity Requirements

The customizing is year- and version-dependent, which means for each planning version and year combination, you'll need to create a new entry. The advantage of this functionality is that you can create planning scenarios to allocate to different planning versions in Controlling (CO), simplifying the planning process. Click on NEW ENTRIES to customize the transfer requirement. Figure 3.30 shows the screen where you define the transfer requirements for the combination you want to create.

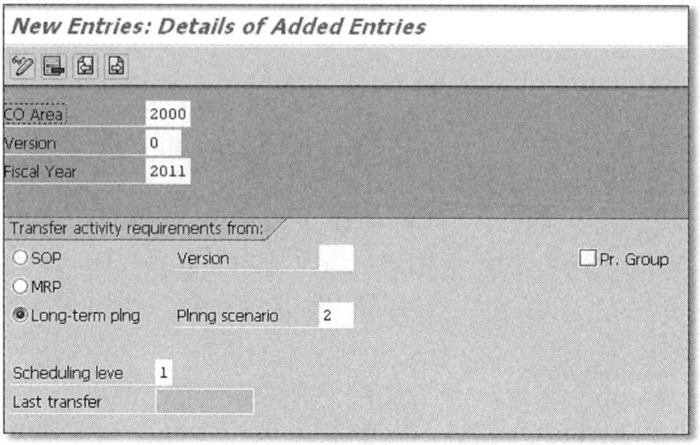

Figure 3.30 Transfer Requirement Detail

This customizing should be done in consultation with the production team because they will determine if the planning should be based on SOP, MRP, or LTP and will also define the correct version or planning scenario to use.

The next step in cost center planning is allocations, where you'll learn how to customize assessments, distributions, and periodic reposting.

3.2.5 Allocations

Allocations are used to send a cost or group of costs from one cost object to another. For example, an allocation can be used to split the energy costs from the overhead cost center to the production cost centers. Four different types of allocations could be used for this example. In this section, we'll explain each, outline the differences between them, and demonstrate how to customize each one.

To perform periodic allocations, you first need to define the cycles. The cycle contains the allocation definition, such as senders and receivers, as well as other rules for the allocation. Moreover, you need to define which cost elements are to be allocated, the activity type quantities, and the criteria that will be used to establish the allocation either directly or indirectly. Cycles are created separately for each of the four types of allocations.

The following are the four types of periodic allocations available in SAP ERP:

► Periodic reposting

► Distribution

► Assessment

► Indirect activity allocation

You must create at least one cycle for each kind of allocation. Note that you can't use a cycle defined for assessment in a distribution. Also, separate cycles must be defined for planned and actual values. In planning, a cycle must be created for each version.

For distributions, assessments, and periodic reposting, the following values are assessed:

► Total planned or actual

► Fixed planned or actual

► Fixed rate of activity type

For indirect activity allocation, the following values are assessed:

► Total planned or actual

► Fixed planned or actual

► Inversely determined quantity

Cycle processing can be hierarchical or iterative, as represented in Figure 3.31 and described here:

► **Hierarchical method**
You should use this method when there is no recursive link between the cost centers, or the cost center will receive no cost from one of its receptors directly or indirectly. In this case, SAP ERP processes the segments in a cycle in succession without repetition. This method can also be used when the sender cost object is part of the receiver and must have a part of the cost allocated.

► **Iterative method**
Use this method in repetitive processing. SAP ERP considers the cyclic structure of the network for cost center allocation (the receiver cost object can also

be a sender cost object). If, for example, a cost center "A" must have its costs allocated to cost centers "A," "B," and "C," and part of the cost from cost center "C" must return to cost center "A" to be allocated again, then iterative processing should be used. Interactive processes are available only for segments in the same cycle.

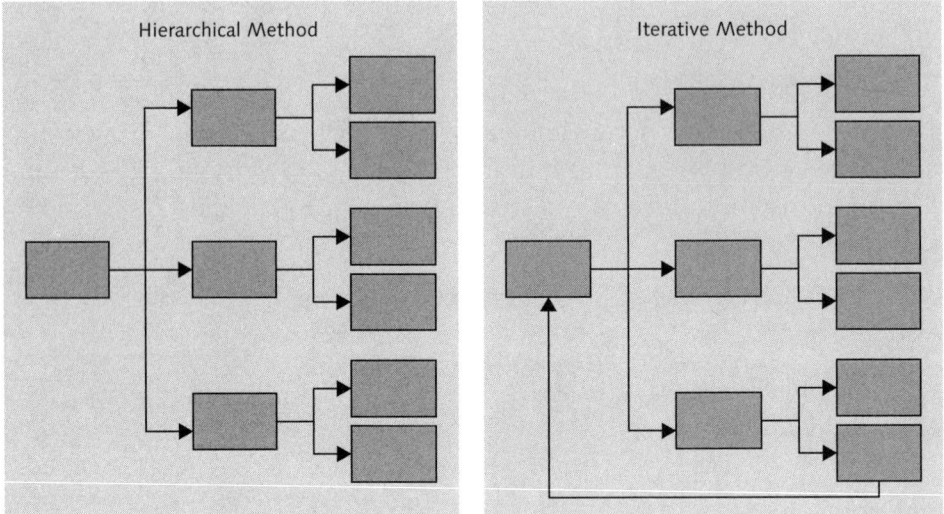

Figure 3.31 Hierarchical Method versus Iterative Method

We'll explain in detail the cycle for periodic reposting, and the same idea is valid for the other kinds of allocations. You'll also learn the differences between the available kinds of allocations.

Periodic Reposting

Periodic reposting reduces the number of postings to be made in FI (for actual posting) and the planning time as well. For example, you can post all planned electricity costs to one cost center or internal order, and then run the periodic reposting to settle these costs to other cost objects following a predefined rule customized in the periodic reposting.

Although very similar to the distribution process, in the periodic reposting, you can't see the credit posting in the total reports. Another difference is that in a distribution, you can't use an internal order as a sender cost object, whereas in the periodic reposting, you can.

In Figure 3.32, you can see the first customizing screen for the planning periodic reposting. Use Transaction KSW7, or follow the IMG menu path CONTROLLING • COST CENTER ACCOUNTING • PLANNING • PLANNING AIDS • PERIODIC REPOSTINGS • DEFINE PERIODIC REPOSTINGS.

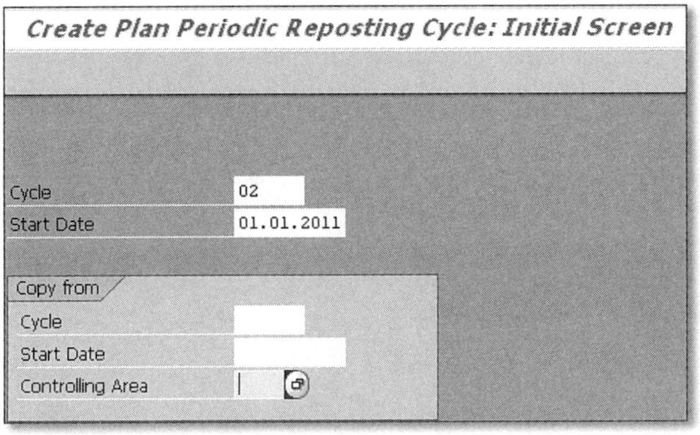

Figure 3.32 Periodic Reposting Initial Screen

On the initial screen, you'll define the cycle name and start date. You also have the option to copy from an existing cycle.

After you've defined the cycle name and start date, the next step is to customize the cycle header, as shown in Figure 3.33.

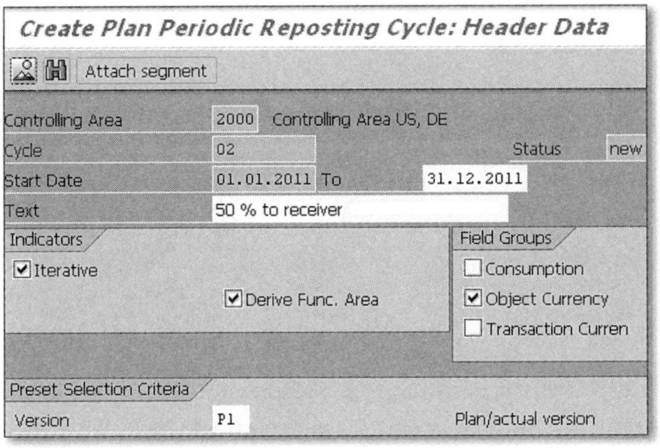

Figure 3.33 Periodic Reposting Cycle Header Data

In Table 3.1, you can see the available options for the cycle header.

Field	Description	Action	Comments
START DATE	Cycle validity date	Define the end date of the valid period for the cycle.	You can only change the To date in this screen because the start date was defined in the first step.
TEXT	Free text	Cycle description.	
INDICATORS	ITERATIVE field	Define if the cycle will be iterative.	
	DERIVE FUNC. AREA field	Define if the cycle will derive the functional area from the cost objects.	
FIELD GROUPS	CONSUMPTION field	Define if the planned consumption will be allocated.	The allocation will always be made in the controlling area currency, plus the currency selected in this section.
	OBJECT CURRENCY field	Define if the allocation will also consider the object currency.	
	TRANSACTION CURRENCY field	Define if the allocation will also consider the transaction currency.	
PRESET SELECTION CRITERIA	VERSION	Define the cycle version that you are going to use to perform the cycle.	This option is only present in planned allocations and not available for actual allocations.

Table 3.1 Periodic Reposting Cycle Header Data

After you create the cycle header, you can attach the segments. By clicking on ATTACH SEGMENT as shown in Figure 3.33, you can create one or more segments to the cycle. Figure 3.34 shows the first screen of segment customizing.

Table 3.2 explains all of the available options for the segment header customizing.

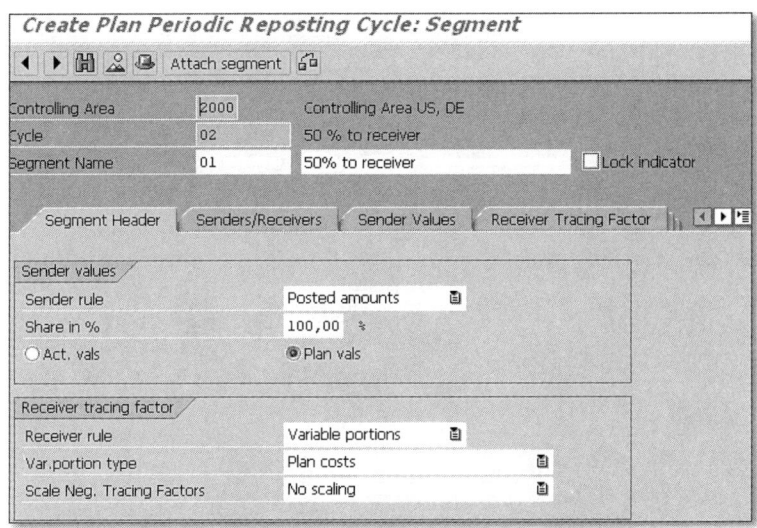

Figure 3.34 Segment Header Tab

Field	Description	Action	Comments
SEGMENT NAME	Alphanumeric identifier.	Define the segment name.	
LOCK INDICATOR	Checkbox.	Lock the segment in the cycle.	When processing cycles, locked segments will be ignored.
SENDER RULE	POSTED AMOUNTS: Consider the values posted in the planning. FIXED AMOUNTS: Consider fixed values on the SENDER VALUES tab. FIXED RATES: On the SENDER VALUES tab, the fixed prices defined for the sender are multiplied by the receiver tracing factors and the result allocated to the receivers.	Choose from the available options.	Specify how the system will distribute the values between the sender and receiver.

Table 3.2 Segment Header Tab

Field	Description	Action	Comments
SHARE IN %	Percentage of the sender costs that will be allocated.	Enter a percentage.	Actual values or planned values.
ACT. VALS OR PLANVALS	Define the reference type value used for the sender. Actual or planned values.	Choose one.	Actual or planned cycle's definitions are maintained in different transactions. This code only refers to which values will be used as sender.
RECEIVER RULE	Define how the values are going to be allocated in the receiver.	Choose one of the options.	
VAR.PORTION TYPE	Determine which object cost will be used as reference for the allocation.	Choose one of the options.	Available only in variable portions.
SCALE NEG. TRACING FACTORS	Define how the system will manage negative values in the allocation.	Choose one of the options.	Available only in variable portions.

Table 3.2 Segment Header Tab (Cont.)

For the RECEIVER RULE field, you can choose from four options (VARIABLE PORTIONS, FIXED AMOUNTS, FIXED PERCENTAGE, and FIXED PORTIONS), as described here:

▶ VARIABLE PORTIONS

The system will use values already recorded in the database to determine the amount for each receiver. When you select variable portions, you'll have two additional options to define: VAR. PORTION TYPE and SCALE NEG. TRACING FACTORS.

The following options for variable portion type are available:

▷ PLAN COSTS: Considers the planning values for the version and cost elements selected on the RECEIVER TRACING FACTOR tab. The system will add up the total planned costs for all costs in the receivers and divide the total of each receiver by the grand total to determine the percentage that each receiver will receive. The sender values will be defined by the combination entered in the SENDERS/RECEIVERS tab.

▶ ACTUAL COSTS: Works the same way as PLAN COSTS, but the system will consider the actual cost as reference for the allocation.

▶ PLAN/ACTUAL CONSUMPTION: These two alternatives also follow the same logic of the preceding, except they consider the consumption quantity and not the cost values.

▶ ACTUAL/PLAN STATISTICAL KEY FIGURES: Works in the same way as PLAN COSTS, but in this case, the system will use the planning or actual statistical key figures defined on the RECEIVER TRACING FACTOR tab to create the receiver percentage. The sender values will be defined by the combination entered in the SENDERS/RECEIVERS tab.

▶ PLAN/ACTUAL ACTIVITY: Uses the same logic as statistical key figures but uses the planning or actual activity type to create the receiver percentage.

▶ STATISTICAL PLAN COST: Follows the same logic but only considers statistical planning values for internal orders or cost centers. A cost center receives statistical values when real planning is posted to an internal order assigned to this cost center, and the order receives the real planning. An internal order gets a statistical planning value when the internal order master data is defined as a statistic. The cost center assigned to this internal order will receive the real planning.

If one of the receivers has the receiver tracing factor positive and partly negative, we can distinguish two cases. If the sum of all receiver tracing factors is greater than zero, both the senders and receivers with negative tracing factors are credited. The receivers with positive tracing factors are debited by a larger amount to compensate for this. If the sum of all receiver tracing factors is less than zero, both the senders and the receivers with positive tracing factors are credited. Receivers with negative tracing factors are debited for a greater amount in return.

For negative tracing factors, the system allows the following alternatives:

▶ NO SCALING: The system uses the negative tracing factor in the calculations.

▶ STANDARD SCALING: Scaling depends on the sum of the receiver tracing factors.
   In standard scaling, if the total is positive or zero, the largest negative tracing factor is set to zero for the amount. The other tracing factors are

increased accordingly. In this case, the sum of all of the receivers' tracing factors will be greater than zero. If the total is negative, the largest positive tracing factor is set at zero. Other tracing factors will be respectively decreased, which means that all receiver tracing factors will be negative.

▶ Absolute value (negative to positive): The tracing factor negative sign is reversed. All tracing factors will be positive.

▶ Negative tracing factor to zero: The negative tracing factors will be set to zero. Nothing will be allocated to this receiver.

▶ Smallest negative tracing factor to zero: The largest negative tracing factor is set to zero. The other tracing factors are increased accordingly. The previous receiver with zero tracing factors will now receive a positive tracing factor.

▶ Smallest negative tracing factor to zero, but zero = zero: The largest negative tracing factor in terms of amount is set to zero. The other tracing factors are increased accordingly. The previous receiver with zero tracing factor will remain with zero as a tracing factor.

▶ Fixed amounts
Considers fixed values defined in the Sender Values tab to determine the values that each receiver will receive. The sender will be credited by the sum of these values.

▶ Fixed percentages
Considers the fixed percentages defined in the Sender Values tab by applying the percentage in the sender values. In this case, if the sum of the percentages set is less than 100%, a residual balance will remain on the sender.

▶ Fixed portions
This option is very similar to the previous option but, in this case, rather than any percentage, values are defined. The system will add up all of the portions and divide by the portion of each receiver to find the percentage assigned to the receiver. The entire balance of the cost center is allocated, unless you set a percentage less than 100% for the sender.

After customizing the segment header, you can go to the Senders/Receivers tab. Figure 3.35 shows the available options.

You can define the senders and receivers by using combinations of orders, cost centers, activity types, functional areas, cost objects, business processes, and cost elements. You can define these by using single values, ranges, or groups.

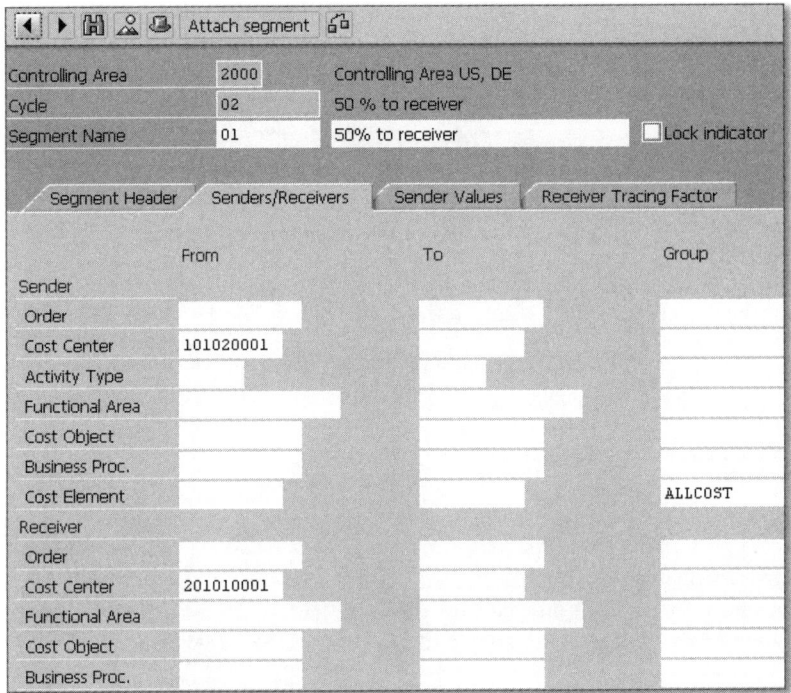

Figure 3.35 Senders/Receivers Definition

The next tabs in the cycle definition, SENDER VALUES, RECEIVING TRACING FACTOR, and RECEIVER WEIGHTING FACTORS will be different according to the definitions made on the SEGMENT HEADER tab. If the cycle will use statistical key figures as the base to allocate the costs, you must enter which statistical key figure will be used in the SENDER VALUES tab.

The next kind of allocation we'll discuss is the distribution.

Distributions

Distributions are very similar to periodic reposting. They use cycles to define the allocation, but in distributions, only cost centers or Activity-Based Costing (CO-ABC) processes can be considered senders. It's also possible to see the credit value on the total records. Table 3.3 summarizes the differences between a distribution and periodic reposting.

Distribution	Periodic Reposting
Sender can be a cost center or CO-ABC process.	Sender can be a cost center, CO-ABC process, internal order, or other cost object.
Total values are saved, so it's possible to see the credit on the sender side.	Total values are not saved, making it impossible to see the credit on the sender side.
It doesn't allocate activity-dependent costs.	It can allocate activity-dependent costs.

Table 3.3 Differences Between Distribution and Periodic Reposting

Note
Standard SAP ERP follows the rules for senders and receivers demonstrated in Table 3.3. You can change the standard SAP behavior by applying the SAP Note 605281 (Allocations: WBS Elements and Orders as Senders) and SAP Note 626134 (Allocations: Maintenance Orders as Receivers).

To customize the planning distribution, you can use Transaction KSV7 or follow the IMG menu path CONTROLLING • COST CENTER ACCOUNTING • PLANNING • ALLOCATIONS • DISTRIBUTION • DEFINE DISTRIBUTION.

Other than the differences we've just discussed, the process to customize distributions is the same as for periodic reposting, so we'll move on to discuss the next allocation type: the assessment.

Assessment

An assessment uses cycles to transfer primary and secondary costs from the sender to the receiver. The sender and receiver can be a cost center, ABC process, internal order, or cost object.

The difference in assessments from distributions and periodic reposting is that the assessment summarizes all of the costs in the sender and uses a secondary cost element with category 42 (Assessment) to create both the credit in the sender and the debit in the receiver. Periodic reposting and distributions both use the same (primary) cost element rather than allocating costs in secondary cost elements.

Additionally, in assessments, allocation structures can be used that allow for the creation of a group of accounts that will be settling to a secondary cost element category 42 (Assessment). For example, all of the labor-related costs from a cost center will be settled using a specific secondary cost element, while all of the maintenance costs will be settled using a different secondary cost element. That means you can split the costs between groups of costs. Allocation structures are also used for internal order settlements. Table 3.4 shows one allocation structure example.

Assignment	Source Cost Element	Assessment Cost Element
01 – Administrative	422006 – 422008	610001 – Administrative
02 – Product cost	463000 – 463006	610002 – Product Cost
03 – Depreciation	422450	610003 – Depreciation

Table 3.4 Allocation Structure Example

You can create an allocation structure by following the IMG menu path CONTROL-LING • COST CENTER ACCOUNTING • PLANNING • ALLOCATIONS • ASSESSMENT • DEFINE ALLOCATION STRUCTURES. Figure 3.36 shows the first customizing screen of the allocation structure.

Create a new allocation structure by clicking on NEW ENTRIES. Mark the allocation structure on the right side of the screen, and double-click on ASSIGNMENTS on the left side of the screen. This will bring you to the screen shown in Figure 3.37.

Click on NEW ENTRIES to create the assignment groups. Assignments are used to define groups of sender cost elements, and you will define the cost elements for each in the next step. At this point, you only need to create the groups. There is no limit to how many groups you can create. After creating the assignments, the overlap signal will be yellow, meaning that no cost elements have yet been assigned. A green overlap signal means that no overlap between cost elements in the groups was found in the customizing, while red means that there is an overlap in the cost elements, which must be corrected.

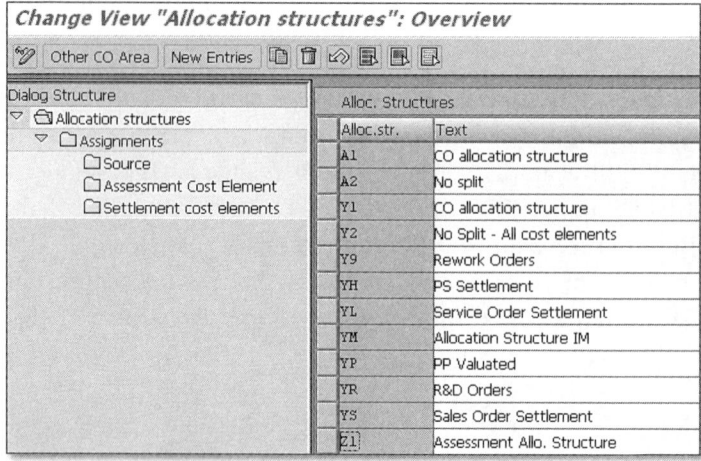

Figure 3.36 Allocation Structure

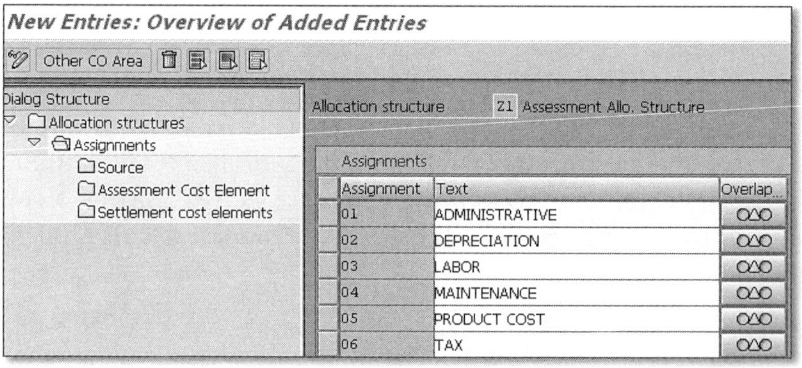

Figure 3.37 Allocation Structure Assignments

After creating the assignments, you should define which cost elements will be the source for each one. Mark the assignment on the right side of the screen, and double-click on SOURCE on the left side of the screen to define the cost elements. You can see in Figure 3.38 how the source cost elements are assigned.

Again, you can use the cost element group to define the cost elements instead of using a cost element range. The advantage to this approach is that you can maintain the cost element group in the production environment as master data without creating a transport request.

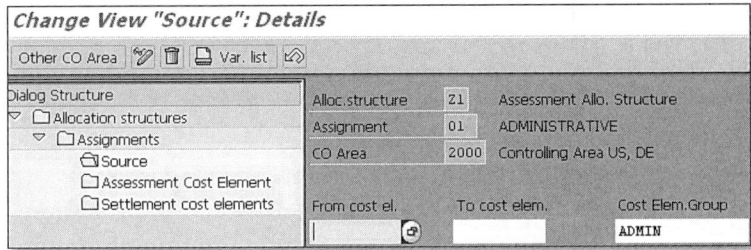

Figure 3.38 Allocation Structure, Source Definition

After you create the entry, it's time to set the assessment account for this assignment. On the left side of the screen, double-click on ASSESSMENT COST ELEMENT (see Figure 3.39).

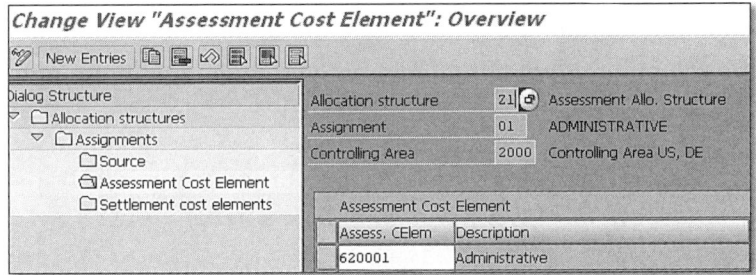

Figure 3.39 Allocation Structure, Assessment Cost Element

Click on NEW ENTRIES, and add the appropriate cost element. Only secondary cost elements with category 42 (Assessment) are allowed.

Now that you've assigned all source cost elements and the assessment cost element, you can return to the first screen. Now the overlap sign should be green, as shown in Figure 3.40.

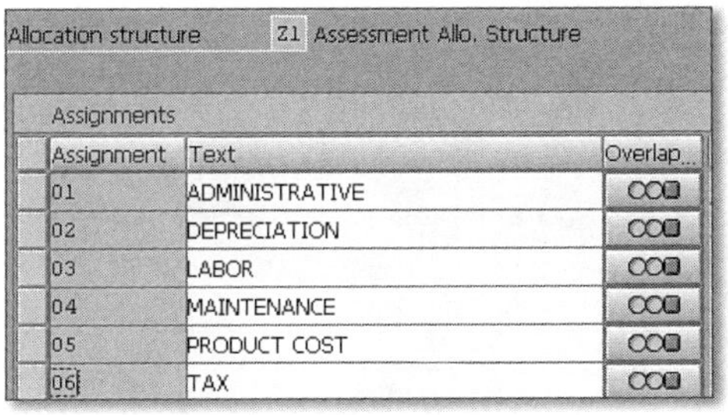

Allocation structure	Z1 Assessment Allo. Structure	
Assignments		
Assignment	Text	Overlap
01	ADMINISTRATIVE	⬤⬤▣
02	DEPRECIATION	⬤⬤▣
03	LABOR	⬤⬤▣
04	MAINTENANCE	⬤⬤▣
05	PRODUCT COST	⬤⬤▣
06	TAX	⬤⬤▣

Figure 3.40 Allocation Structure Status

Another view in an overview list format is available for the allocation structure, as shown in Figure 3.41. To get to this screen, select the OVERVIEW LIST option in the EXTRAS menu.

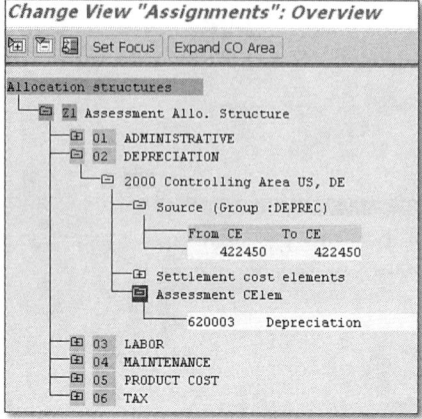

Figure 3.41 Allocation Structure Overview

After you define the allocation structure, you can create the assessment cycle. Use Transaction KSU7 or follow the IMG menu path CONTROLLING • COST CENTER ACCOUNTING • PLANNING • ALLOCATIONS • ASSESSMENT • DEFINE ASSESSMENT to create the assessment cycle. Figure 3.42 shows the first screen with the SEGMENT HEADER tab for the assessment cycle.

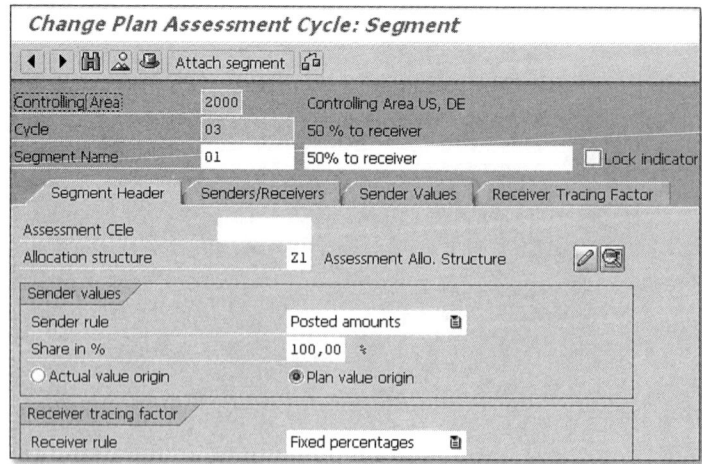

Figure 3.42 Assessment Cycle

Note that the main difference among assessments, distributions, and periodic reposting is the option to add the assessment cost element or allocation structure. The assessment uses a secondary cost element to allocate the costs.

To illustrate the differences between the three allocation types in cost center reports, we'll show one cost center allocation using the same rule for periodic reposting, distribution, and assessment, in all cases allocating 50% of the sender cost center to the receiver cost center. Figure 3.43 shows the results of the periodic reposting, Figure 3.44 shows the results using a distribution, and Figure 3.45 shows the results using an assessment. The report shown is Report S_ALR_87013611 – Cost Centers: Actual/Plan/Variance.

Cost Centers: Actual/Plan/Variance	Date: 10.07.2011		Page:	2 / 2
			Column:	1 / 2
Cost Center/Group	201010001	Finance		
Person responsible:	3001			
Reporting period:	1 to 12 2011			

Cost Elements	Act. Costs	Plan Costs	Var.(Abs.)	Var.(%)
422602 Municipal taxes		66.000,00	66.000,00-	100,00-
* Debit		66.000,00	66.000,00-	100,00-
** Over/Underabsorption		66.000,00	66.000,00-	100,00-

Figure 3.43 Periodic Reposting Results

Cost Centers: Actual/Plan/Variance	Date: 10.07.2011		Page:	2 / 2
			Column:	1 / 2
Cost Center/Group	201010001	Finance		
Person responsible:	3001			
Reporting period:	1 to 12 2011			

Cost Elements	Act. Costs	Plan Costs	Var.(Abs.)	Var.(%)
422602 Municipal taxes		132.000,00	132.000,00-	100,00-
* Debit		132.000,00	132.000,00-	100,00-
422602 Municipal taxes		66.000,00-	66.000,00	100,00-
* Credit		66.000,00-	66.000,00	100,00-
** Over/Underabsorption		66.000,00	66.000,00-	100,00-

Figure 3.44 Distribution Results

```
Cost Centers: Actual/Plan/Variance        Date: 10.07.2011              Page:    2 /   2

                                                                      Column:   1 /   2
Cost Center/Group         201010001              Finance
Person responsible:       3001
Reporting period:           1  to   12  2011


Cost Elements                     Act. Costs    Plan Costs    Var.(Abs.)      Var.(%)

    422602  Municipal taxes                      132.000,00   132.000,00-    100,00-
*   Debit                                        132.000,00   132.000,00-    100,00-

    422602  Municipal taxes
    620006  Tax Assessment                        66.000,00-   66.000,00     100,00-
*   Credit                                        66.000,00-   66.000,00     100,00-

**  Over/Underabsorption                          66.000,00    66.000,00-    100,00-
```

Figure 3.45 Assessment Results

Note that in the periodic reposting, you can't see the credit in the report but only the net result remaining, whereas in the distribution, you can see the credit in the same cost element but in a separate line in the report. The assessment uses a secondary cost element to allocate the costs, so the original amount is shown in the report, with the credit shown in the secondary cost element.

The most commonly used cycles to allocate costs are periodic reposting, distribution, and assessment. You also have the option to create an indirect activity allocation.

Indirect Activity Allocation

Indirect activity allocations can be used for activity type categories 02 (Indirect determination, indirect allocation) and 03 (Manual entry, indirect allocation).

Activity type category 02 (Indirect determination, indirect allocation) refers to a situation where the costs cannot be defined at the sender and instead the system needs information from the receivers to allocate the costs. A practical example of this is the allocation of a maintenance cost center to production cost centers without using a maintenance order, based on the hours of production in each production cost center. A relationship between the production hours and maintenance hours can be established, and through indirect activity allocation, the maintenance cost center is defined as the sender, and the production cost center is defined as a receiver using the production hours as the reference for the allocation.

Activity type category 03 (Manual entry, indirect allocation) is used when the sender quantity is entered manually in the sender, and the system uses the rule defined in the cycle to distribute the activity type quantities to the receivers. It uses a cycle definition in the same way as you saw for periodic reposting, distributions, and assessments.

To customize the planning for indirect activity allocation, you can use Transaction KSC7 or follow the IMG menu path CONTROLLING • COST CENTER ACCOUNTING • PLANNING • ALLOCATIONS • ACTIVITY ALLOCATION • INDIRECT ACTIVITY ALLOCATION • DEFINE INDIRECT ACTIVITY ALLOCATION.

At the end of the planning process or for actual posting at the end of the period, you can recalculate the activity price (actual and plan) using the planned values and activity quantities planned to create a new price.

Before activity price calculation can be done, you need to run the plan or actual cost splitting. This will split the planning or actual costs on the cost elements between the activity types planned in the cost center; then the system can divide the value for each activity type in a cost center by the quantity of this activity, creating the activity price. You customize the cost splitting using Transaction OKES or by following the IMG menu path CONTROLLING • COST CENTER ACCOUNTING • PLANNING • ALLOCATIONS • ACTIVITY ALLOCATION • SPLITTING • DEFINE SPLITTING STRUCTURE. You can see the first customizing screen for cost splitting in Figure 3.46.

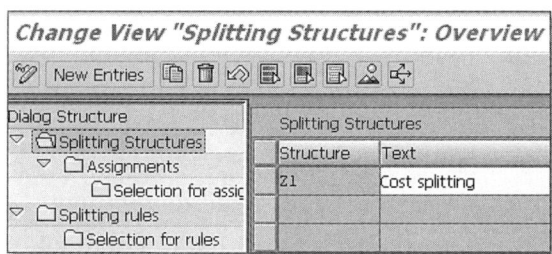

Figure 3.46 Cost Splitting Structures

Click on NEW ENTRIES, and create the splitting structure (in this case, Z1).

After creating the splitting structure, you must create the splitting rules. Double-click on SPLITTING RULES on the left side of the screen, and it will bring you to the screen shown in Figure 3.47. You define the method to be used by the system to create the cost splitting in the splitting rule.

Dialog Structure	Splitting rules				
	Rule	Text	Meth.	Text	Wt.
	0	No splitting	0	No splitting	☐
	12	Activity quantity	12	Activity quantity	☐
	21	Equivalence Numbers Planning	21	Equivalence Numbers Planning	☐
	22	Activity Quantity Planning	22	Activity Quantity Planning	☐
	23	Capacity Planning	23	Capacity Planning	☐
	24	Output Planning	24	Output Planning	☐
	25	Scheduled Activity Planning	25	Scheduled Activity Planning	☐
	41	Statistical key figure (qty)	41	Statistical key figure (qty)	☐
	51	Stat. key figure (plan. qty)	51	Stat. key figure (plan. qty)	☐

Figure 3.47 Splitting Rules

Splitting methods are assigned to the splitting rules. These methods specify how the costs are split. You can split plan costs according to the following criteria:

- 0: NO SPLITTING
- 12: ACTIVITY QUANTITY
- 21: EQUIVALENCE NUMBERS PLANNING
- 22: ACTIVITY QUANTITY PLANNING
- 23: CAPACITY PLANNING
- 24: OUTPUT PLANNING
- 25: SCHEDULED ACTIVITY PLANNING
- 41: STATISTICAL KEY FIGURE (QTY)
- 51: STAT. KEY FIGURE (PLAN. QTY)
- 52: STAT. KEY FIGURE (PLANMAXQTY)

The splitting rule is defined by the version. Mark the rule, and double-click on SELECTION FOR RULES on the left side of the screen. In Figure 3.48, you can see how to assign the version.

When splitting the costs between activity types with different units of measure, you can flag the field weighting indicator (WT.) shown in the far right column in

Figure 3.47. The system will use the equivalence number defined in the planning transaction to convert both activity type units to a common unit of measure. For example, for an activity type in hours and another in minutes, by selecting the field, you'll be able to maintain the equivalence number during planning.

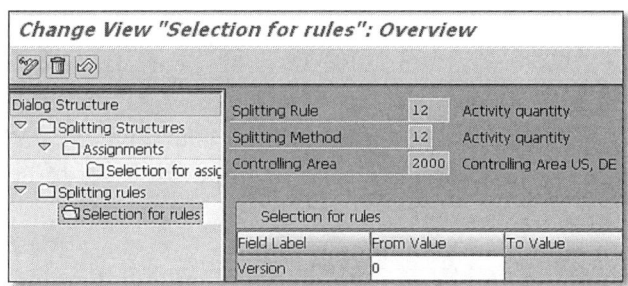

Figure 3.48 Selection for Rules, Version Definition

Now that you've created the splitting rules and assigned the rules to the planning version, you need to create the assignments for the splitting structure. Double-click on the left side of the screen on SPLITTING STRUCTURES, then mark the splitting structure (in our example, Z1), and on the left side of the screen, you can double-click on ASSIGNMENTS. In Figure 3.49, you can see how to create the assignments.

Change View "Assignments": Overview

Structure Name   Z1 Cost splitting

Assignments

Assgnmnt	Text	Rule	Text
DP	Depreciation	12	Activity quantity
EL	Electricity	12	Activity quantity
LB	Labor	12	Activity quantity
MA	Material	12	Activity quantity
MT	Maintenance	12	Activity quantity
OT	Others	12	Activity quantity
TX	Taxes	12	Activity quantity
WT	Water	12	Activity quantity

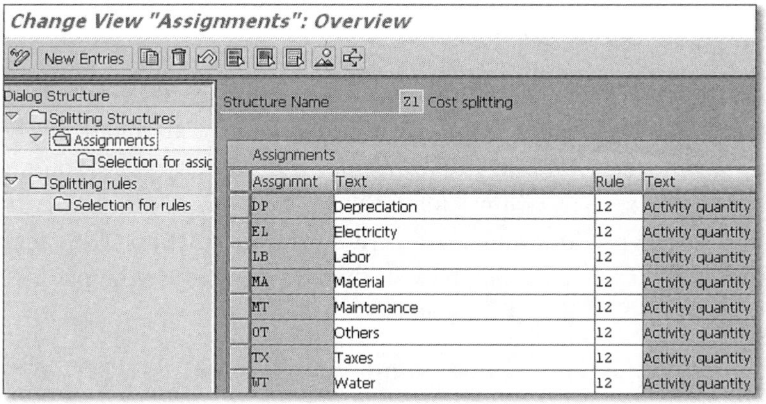

Figure 3.49 Splitting Structure Assignments

Click on NEW ENTRIES, and create the assignments for the splitting structure. Each assignment should be related to one rule recently created. (In our example, we used rule 12 – activity quantity.) Each rule should be assigned to a combination of cost elements and activity type. Mark the assignment, and double-click on SELECTION FOR ASSIGNMENT to create the combination between cost elements and activity type. The system will use this combination to split the cost and create the activity price. To illustrate this, we're using an example assignment called DEPRECIATION (DP). In this example, the system will split the cost from the cost element group depreciation, which contains all cost elements for depreciation, and divide by the activity type group PH (Production Hours). The resulting depreciation cost per production hour will then be available to use to distribute the total depreciation cost to the cost centers based on the planned production hours. Figure 3.50 shows this customizing screen, in which you can see the groups of cost objects used for the customizing.

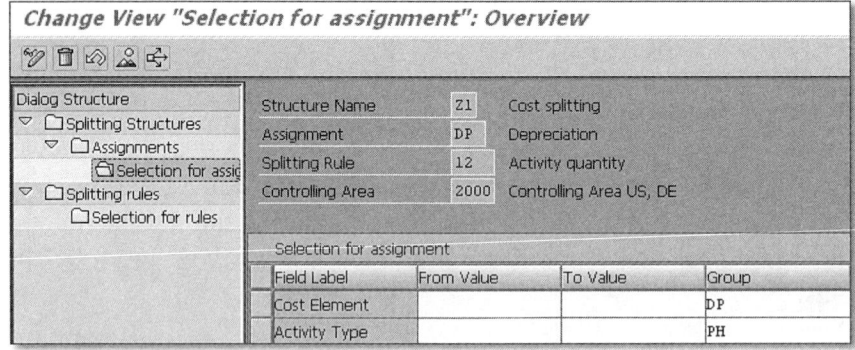

Figure 3.50 Cost Element and Activity Type Definition

Let's look at an example of cost splitting to see how it can be used. In our example, we'll show how planned values from four cost elements (Table 3.5) can be split based on two activity types (Table 3.6) to calculate two activity rates. You can see in Table 3.7 how the system will calculate the portion of the planned costs from each cost element to use in the planned activity rate calculation. The calculated amounts shown for each activity type will then be divided by the planned activity quantity to determine the planned activity rates.

Cost Element	Planned Value
414300 – Electric Power	$25,000
414202 – Maintenance/Repairs	$12,000

Table 3.5 Cost Center/Cost Element Planning Example

Cost Element	Planned Value
421101 – Salaries and fee	$17,000
422450 – Depreciation/Amortization	$7,000

Table 3.5 Cost Center/Cost Element Planning Example (Cont.)

Activity Type	Quantity Planned
PH – Production Hours	300
Deprec – Depreciation	100

Table 3.6 Activity Type Planning Example

Cost Element	Depreciation	Depreciation Splitting	PH	PH Splitting
414300	100/400	25,000 * 0,25 = $6,250	300/400	25,000 * 0,75 = $18,750
414202	100/400	12,000 * 0,25 = $3,000	300/400	12,000 * 0,75 = $9,000
421101	100/400	17,000 * 0,25 = $4,250	300/400	17,000 * 0,75 = $12,750
422450	100/400	7,000 * 0,25 = $1,750	300/400	7,000 * 0,75 = $5,250

Table 3.7 Activity Type Splitting Example

After creating the splitting structure, you must assign the structure to the cost centers that will send or receive the activity types. Most of the time, this means production and maintenance cost centers. You can see the first screen for assigning the splitting structure to cost centers in Figure 3.51. Use Transaction OKEW, or follow the IMG menu path CONTROLLING • COST CENTER ACCOUNTING • PLANNING • ALLOCATIONS • ACTIVITY ALLOCATION • SPLITTING • ASSIGN SPLITTING STRUCTURE TO COST CENTERS.

You can restrict the selection using a specific cost center, cost center group, or all cost centers, and customize for one or all CO versions. After indicating your selection, click on the CHANGE icon to bring you to the Change Splitting Assignment screen shown on the left side in Figure 3.52. On this screen, mark all of the cost centers that you want to add to the splitting structure, leave the cursor on the splitting structure, mark the second button on the screen, and the cost center will be assigned.

Splitting: Assignment of Cost Center to Splitting Structure
Cost center
to
Cost center group
01
Company Code US
Selection Variant
All Cost Centers
Parameters
Version
0
All versions
Fiscal Year
2011

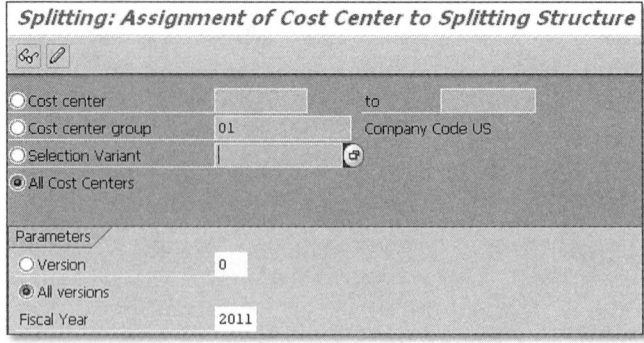

Figure 3.51 Assign Splitting Structure to Cost Center

The screen on the right side of Figure 3.52 shows the view after you have assigned the cost centers to the splitting structure.

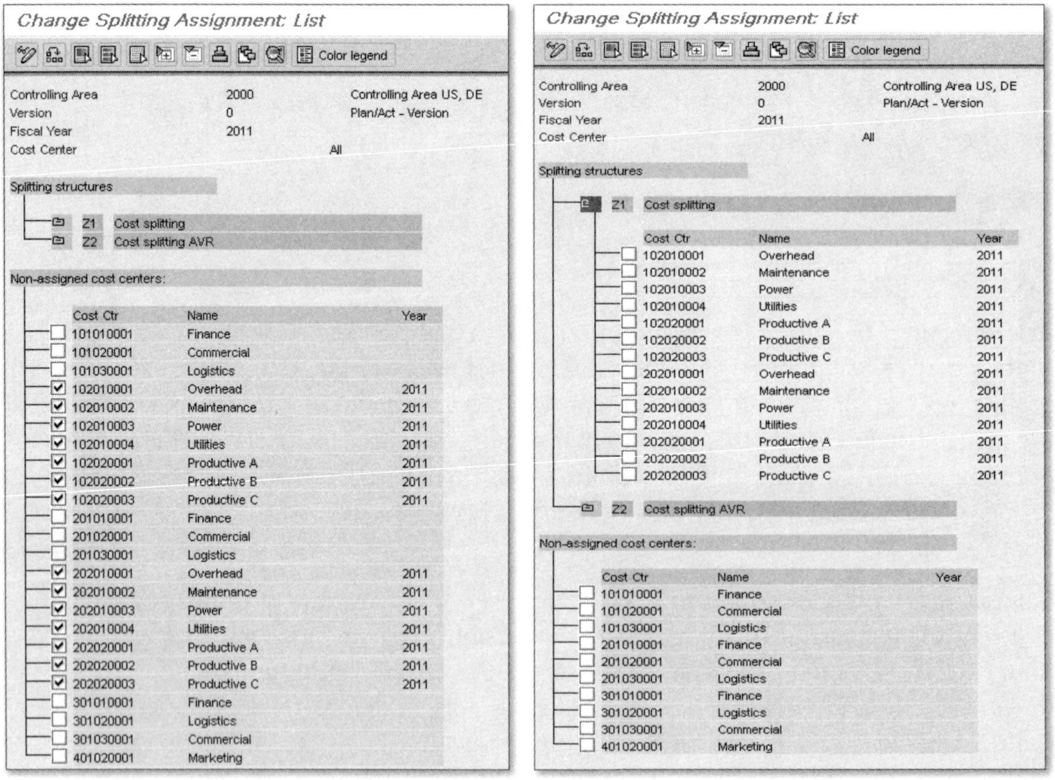

Change Splitting Assignment: List
Color legend
Controlling Area 2000 Controlling Area US, DE
Version 0 Plan/Act - Version
Fiscal Year 2011
Cost Center All
Splitting structures
Z1 Cost splitting
Z2 Cost splitting AVR
Non-assigned cost centers:
Cost Ctr Name Year
101010001 Finance
101020001 Commercial
101030001 Logistics
102010001 Overhead 2011
102010002 Maintenance 2011
102010003 Power 2011
102010004 Utilities 2011
102020001 Productive A 2011
102020002 Productive B 2011
102020003 Productive C 2011
201010001 Finance
201020001 Commercial
201030001 Logistics
202010001 Overhead 2011
202010002 Maintenance 2011
202010003 Power 2011
202010004 Utilities 2011
202020001 Productive A 2011
202020002 Productive B 2011
202020003 Productive C 2011
301010001 Finance
301020001 Logistics
301030001 Commercial
401020001 Marketing
Change Splitting Assignment: List
Color legend
Controlling Area 2000 Controlling Area US, DE
Version 0 Plan/Act - Version
Fiscal Year 2011
Cost Center All
Splitting structures
Z1 Cost splitting
Cost Ctr Name Year
102010001 Overhead 2011
102010002 Maintenance 2011
102010003 Power 2011
102010004 Utilities 2011
102020001 Productive A 2011
102020002 Productive B 2011
102020003 Productive C 2011
202010001 Overhead 2011
202010002 Maintenance 2011
202010003 Power 2011
202010004 Utilities 2011
202020001 Productive A 2011
202020002 Productive B 2011
202020003 Productive C 2011
Z2 Cost splitting AVR
Non-assigned cost centers:
Cost Ctr Name Year
101010001 Finance
101020001 Commercial
101030001 Logistics
201010001 Finance
201020001 Commercial
201030001 Logistics
301010001 Finance
301020001 Logistics
301030001 Commercial
401020001 Marketing

Figure 3.52 Cost Center Splitting Structure Assignment

> **Note**
>
> We advise that you create a splitting structure just for the cost centers involved in maintenance activities when you are using the Plant Maintenance (PM) component. Typically most organizations consider the costs in maintenance cost centers in total, rather than by a more detail-splitting level that would be desired for production cost centers.

The activity price calculation is the last step in customizing allocations. After performing the cost allocations (periodic reposting, distributions, and assessments) and running the cost splitting, the system is ready to calculate the activity price.

To calculate the activity price, the system will get the amount for each activity type as defined in the cost splitting and divide by the activity type quantity.

The customizing done in the version and the way that the activity type was created directly impacts how the system creates the activity price, as discussed previously in Section 3.1.2.

Now that we've talked about all of the processes involved in planning and how to customize the system to best suit your organization's planning requirements, we can move to the next topic: budget management.

3.3   Budget Management

Cost center budgeting provides one more method of planning in cost centers. Rather than primary and secondary cost planning, the budget can be set by cost center rather than by cost elements. To create the budget in this manner, you should first create the budget profile. The budget profile contains information for the following settings:

- ▶ Budgeting time frame
- ▶ Decimal places
- ▶ Scaling factor
- ▶ Distribution keys
- ▶ Fiscal year or period values

To customize the cost center budget profile, either use Transaction OKF1 or follow the IMG menu path CONTROLLING • COST CENTER ACCOUNTING • BUDGET

Management • Define Budget Planning Profiles. Figure 3.53 shows the budget profile customizing screen.

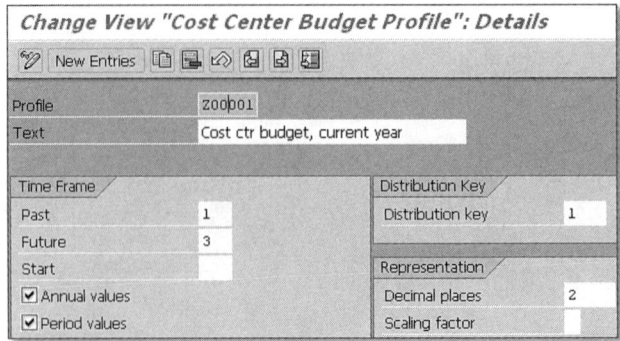

Figure 3.53 Cost Center Budget Profile

> **Note**
>
> Availability control is not available for cost center budgeting.

Figure 3.54 shows an example of budgeting using the standard Report S_ALR_87013648 – Range: Actual/Budget/Commitments.

Range: Actual/Budget/Commitments   Date: 10.07.2011   Page: 2 / 2

Column: 1 / 1

Cost Center Group 01   Company Code US
Responsible: 2001
Fiscal Year 2011

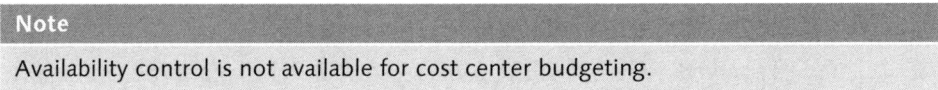

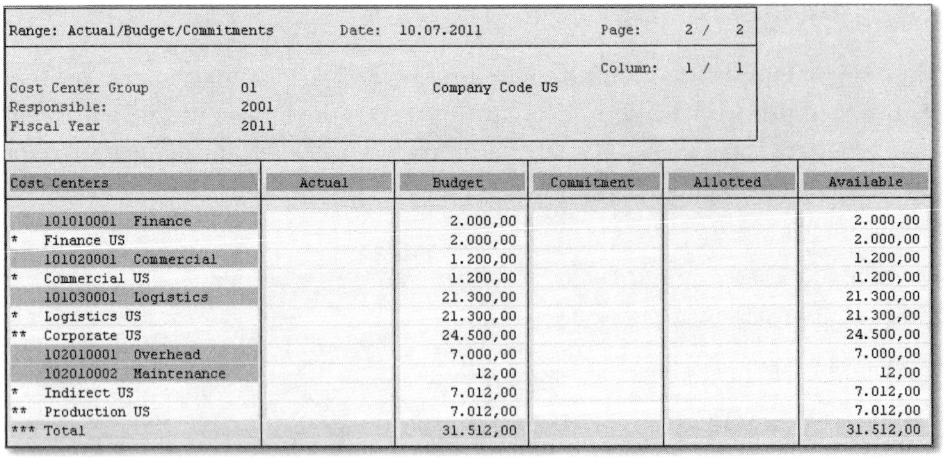

Cost Centers	Actual	Budget	Commitment	Allotted	Available
101010001 Finance		2.000,00			2.000,00
* Finance US		2.000,00			2.000,00
101020001 Commercial		1.200,00			1.200,00
* Commercial US		1.200,00			1.200,00
101030001 Logistics		21.300,00			21.300,00
* Logistics US		21.300,00			21.300,00
** Corporate US		24.500,00			24.500,00
102010001 Overhead		7.000,00			7.000,00
102010002 Maintenance		12,00			12,00
* Indirect US		7.012,00			7.012,00
** Production US		7.012,00			7.012,00
*** Total		31.512,00			31.512,00

Figure 3.54 Cost Center Budget Report Example

The budget process is very simple. For each cost center, you can budget by month or by year, depending on how the settings in the budget profile are set.

Now that we've explained cost center budgeting, and how to create the budget profile, let's move on to commitments.

3.4 Commitments and Funds Commitments

Commitments are payment obligations that are not entered into the accounts but that can lead to actual costs at a future date.

The commitment has its origin in the purchase requisition and purchase order. If you enter a CO object in the purchase requisition, it will show as a commitment on CO reports. If you use this purchase requisition to create the purchase order, the system will transfer the commitments from the purchase requisition to the purchase order automatically, and when you goods receipt and invoice receipt this purchase order, the system transfers the commitment to actual values. Commitments are not only useful for managing costs against plan or budget values by tracking both actual costs incurred but also for providing visibility to items already committed.

You activate commitments management in the controlling area settings in the same customizing screen that you used to activate the CO-CCA using Transaction OKKP. Notice the Commit. Management field in Figure 3.55. There are two options available: Components active or Components not active. With commitments management activated, the system will track the costs of commitments.

Controlling Area	2000 Controlling Area US, DE	
Fiscal Year	1992 to 9999	
Activate Components		
Cost Centers	Component active	
☐ AA: Activity Type		
Order Management	Component active	
Commit. Management	Components active	
ProfitAnalysis	Component not active	
Acty-Based Costing	Component Active for Parallel and Integrated Calculation	

Figure 3.55 Controlling Area Commitment Customizing

Additionally, the cost center master data must not be locked for commitments. In Figure 3.56, you can see the Lock indicator in a cost center master data example.

Now that you know the importance of commitments and how to activate them, we'll discuss actual postings in CO-CCA.

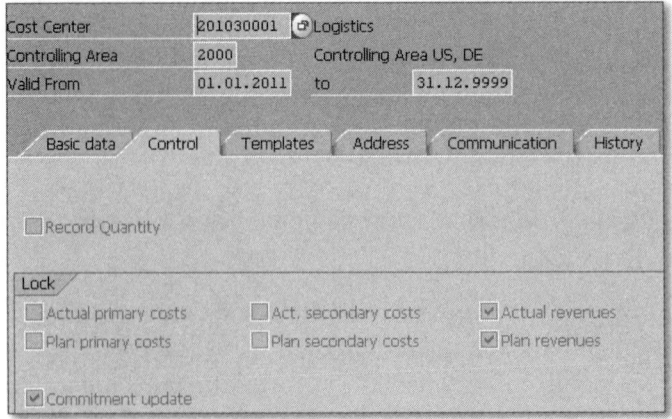

Figure 3.56 Cost Center Example with the Commitment Update Flagged

3.5 Actual Postings

Actual cost posting involves transferring cost amounts to CO from other components, such as FI, PP, HCM, and also from transactions performed within the CO component, such as assessments, distributions, and others.

The first area to look at is the manual actual postings, where you define automatic accounting assignment.

3.5.1 Manual Actual Postings

You can define automatic accounting assignment for controlling posting, which means that by default you can set cost centers, profit centers, or orders to be used when a posting occurs in a specific cost element and company code. You customize the automatic accounting assignment in Transaction OKB9 or by following the IMG menu path CONTROLLING • COST CENTER ACCOUNTING • ACTUAL POSTINGS • MANUAL ACTUAL POSTINGS • EDIT AUTOMATIC ACCOUNT ASSIGNMENT. In Figure 3.57, you can see the customizing screen. We'll discuss all of the elements of this screen and how to use it next.

In the first screen, you define the company code and cost element combination, and the cost object to be used in posting. Additionally, you can define the following extra options in the ACCT ASSIGNMT DETAIL column:

- 1: Valuation area is mandatory

- 2: Business area is mandatory

- 3: Profit center is mandatory

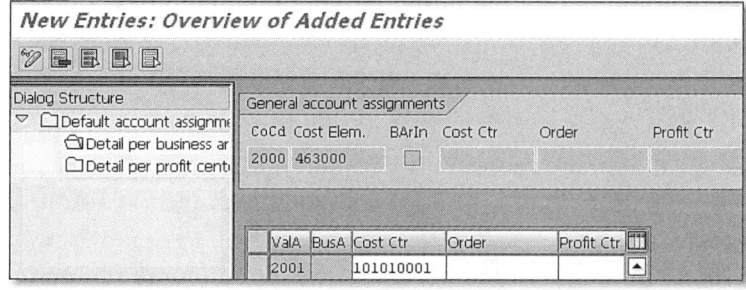

Change View "Default account assignment": Overview

New Entries | BC Set: Change Field Values

	CoCd	Cost Elem.	BA	Cost Ctr	Order	PrfS	Profit Ctr	A	Acct assignmt detail
Dialog Structure	1000	323100	☐			☐	YB999	3	Profit center is mandatory
▽ 🗀 Default account assignm	1000	421105	☐	1101		☐			
🗀 Detail per business ar	1000	422510	☐	1101		☐			
🗀 Detail per profit cent	1000	464001	☐	1602		☐			
	1010	323100	☐			☐	YB999		
	1010	421105	☐	YB1010		☐		1	Valuation area is mandat ...
	1010	422510	☐	YB1010		☐		1	Valuation area is mandat ...
	1010	464001	☐	YB1010		☐		1	Valuation area is mandat ...

Figure 3.57 Default Account Assignment

If you set one of these options in the Acct assignmt detail column, you can create one more breakdown for the automatic account assignment. For example, we
will set one line as Valuation area is mandatory, mark the line, and double-click
on Detail per business area/valuation area, as shown in Figure 3.58.

New Entries: Overview of Added Entries

Dialog Structure	General account assignments				
▽ 🗀 Default account assignm	CoCd	Cost Elem.	BArIn	Cost Ctr	Order	Profit Ctr
🗀 Detail per business ar	2000	463000	☐			
🗀 Detail per profit cent						

ValA	BusA	Cost Ctr	Order	Profit Ctr
2001		101010001		

Figure 3.58 Account Assignment Detail Example

The customizing shown in the example in Figure 3.58 means that all postings in
company code 2000, cost element 463000, and valuation area 2001 will have cost
center 101010001 as the default assignment. This can be useful if you need to
ensure that all postings to an account are reflected in a certain cost center. For
instance, you may want all electric power utility costs to be posted in one cost
center because you plan to use a distribution to allocate them to other cost centers
based on electric power consumption during the period-end processing.

After customizing the accounting assignments, you can now move on to the period-end closing customizing.

3.5.2 Period-End Closing

Period-end closing consists of making the values in CO understandable for users of the data. Here you can create manual postings to reclassify amounts posted in CO, and run accrual calculations, allocations, and activity prices.

The actual period-end closing is very similar to the planning process, but now we are talking about actual values. The company can use the following SAP ERP processes to precede the period-end closing:

▶ Periodic reposting

▶ Distribution

▶ Assessment

▶ Activity allocation

▶ Accrual calculation

The customizing for all of these processes follows the same principle as for the planning process. The only difference is the absence of the requirement for a version in the customizing. Because we've already covered the details of the cycles for planning periodic reposting, and the cycles for actual are much the same, we'll only show the transaction paths for the customizing to avoid repetitive information.

You customize the actual periodic reposting by using Transaction KSW1 or following the IMG menu path CONTROLLING • COST CENTER ACCOUNTING • ACTUAL POSTINGS • PERIOD-END CLOSING • PERIODIC REPOSTING • DEFINE PERIODIC REPOSTINGS. The actual periodic reposting cycle customizing follows the same options of the planning periodic reposting.

To customize actual distributions, either use Transaction KSV1 or follow the IMG menu path CONTROLLING • COST CENTER ACCOUNTING • ACTUAL POSTINGS • PERIOD-END CLOSING • DISTRIBUTION • DEFINE DISTRIBUTION. The actual distribution cycle customizing follows the same options as you saw for the planning distribution.

The next actual allocation to customize is the assessment. To customize the actual assessment, you can use Transaction KSU1 or follow the IMG menu path CONTROLLING • COST CENTER ACCOUNTING • ACTUAL POSTINGS • PERIOD-END CLOSING •

ASSESSMENT • MAINTAIN ASSESSMENT. The actual assessment cycle customizing follows the same options as in the planning assessment.

The last actual allocation to customize is activity allocation by using Transaction KSC1 or following the IMG menu path CONTROLLING • COST CENTER ACCOUNTING • ACTUAL POSTINGS • PERIOD-END CLOSING • INDIRECT ACTIVITY ALLOCATION • DEFINE INDIRECT ACTIVITY ALLOCATION. The actual activity allocation cycle customizing follows the same options as the planning assessment.

We've explained the accrual calculation in Chapter 2, Section 2.2, so we won't repeat that here.

After you customize the allocation cycles that you will use, you have the option to customize variance settings for cost centers.

3.5.3   Variances

Variances in CO help you to understand the difference between planning and actual costs (under-absorption/over-absorption), to analyze the reason for the differences, and to measure the efficiency and productivity of a company or a product line. Variances can have different causes. There are two kinds of variances: input variances and output variances.

Input variances are classified as follows:

▶ **Input price variance**
This is caused by a change in price of the material component or the price of the activity type. For example, the machine hours planned for a specific cost center were 15 hours with a price of $10, making a total of $150. The actual hours for the cost center were 15 hours, but the actual price is different, and in this case was $13, making the actual cost equal to $195. The difference in this case is caused by a price difference. No quantity difference exists in this example.

▶ **Input quantity variance**
This type of variance occurs if the plan quantity differs from the actual quantity consumed. For example, the machine hours planned for a specific cost center were 15 hours with a price of $10, making a total of $150. The machine worked in a capacity of 110%. The actual hours for the cost center were 20 hours, and the actual price was $13, making the actual cost equal to $260. The formula for the input quantity variance is = (Actual input quantity – Target input quantity) × Plan price or (20 – 16.5) × 10 = $35.

▶ **Resource usage variance**
No actual or target costs exist for a cost element. For example, the planning cost element is different from the actual cost element. The system can't assign the difference to input price or input quantity variance, so it classifies the input variance as resource usage variance.

▶ **Remaining input variances**
You choose not to calculate input quantity, input price, or resource-usage variances, or the system can't assign the variances in any of the preceding categories.

Output variances are classified as follows:

▶ **Output price variance**
This variance occurs when an activity price (such as cost per labor hour) was entered manually. Output price variance = (Planned price – Actual price) × Actual activity.

▶ **Output quantity variance**
This variance occurs when a quantity was posted manually for the activity type (e.g., number of labor hours), and it differs from the quantity planned. Output quantity variance = (Actual quantity – Manually entered actual quantity) × Actual price.

▶ **Fixed cost variance**
This is the difference between the actual fixed costs and the planned fixed costs.

SAP ERP calculates and posts the input price variances for primary postings. To customize it, either use Transaction OKA8 or follow the IMG menu path CONTROLLING • COST CENTER ACCOUNTING • ACTUAL POSTINGS • VARIANCES • DEFINE VARIANCE VARIANTS. You can see in Figure 3.59 that we have defined for controlling area 2000 and fiscal year 2011, and input price variances will post 100% to cost element 463000 for all periods.

After defining the cost element for primary price variances, define which kind of variance the system will calculate for the controlling area and version. To customize the variance variant, you can use Transaction OKVF, or follow the IMG menu path CONTROLLING • COST CENTER ACCOUNTING • ACTUAL POSTINGS • VARIANCES • DETERMINE PRIMARY DATA INPUT PRICE VARIANCES. You can see we've defined a variant for all of the variance categories already described in Figure 3.60.

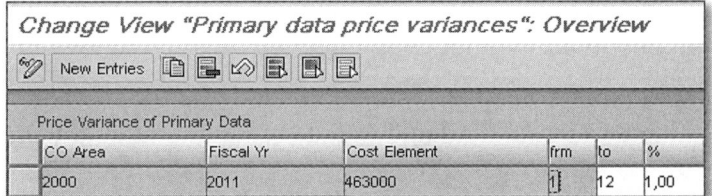

Figure 3.59 Primary Data Price Variances

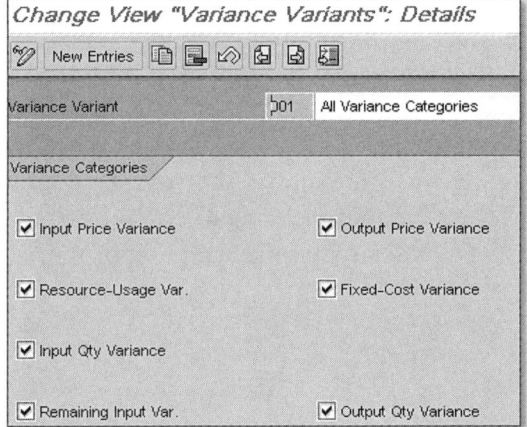

Figure 3.60 Variance Variants

Now you can assign the variance variant to the version and controlling area. To assign the variance variant to a target version, either use Transaction OKV5 or follow the IMG menu path Controlling • Cost Center Accounting • Actual Postings • Variances • Define Target Cost Versions. In Figure 3.61, we've assigned our example Variance Variant 001 to controlling area 2000 and version 0.

> **Note**
>
> Before assigning the variant to a version, you should first verify that the version customizing is set to calculate variances.

The process to calculate the variances will follow this sequence:

1. Calculate target costs.

2. Perform cost splitting.

3. Calculate variances.

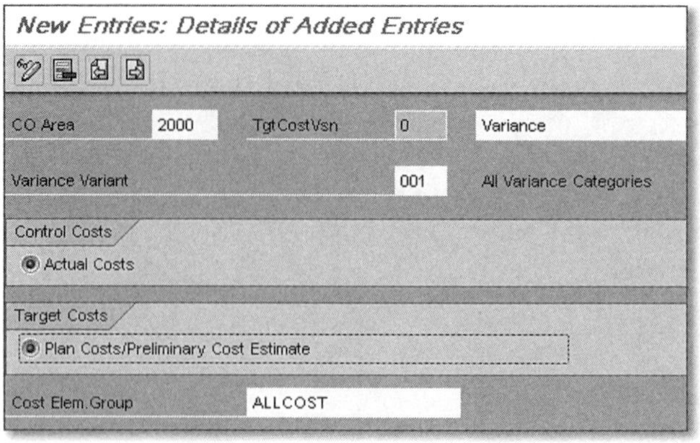

New Entries: Details of Added Entries

| CO Area | 2000 | TgtCostVsn | 0 | Variance |
| Variance Variant | | | 001 | All Variance Categories |

Control Costs
◉ Actual Costs

Target Costs
◉ Plan Costs/Preliminary Cost Estimate

Cost Elem.Group | ALLCOST

Figure 3.61 Assign Variance Variant to a Version

Now that you've learned about the options and how to set the customizing for cost center master data, planning, budgets, commitments, and actual postings, next we'll look at how all of these cost center areas are reflected in reporting.

3.6 Information System

All of the customizing steps we've covered up to this point are designed to help the company meet their reporting needs. So after you've considered all of these needs in determining the structure and options to select for your organization, you'll be able to use the cost center information from reports to aid in managing your business and meeting other organizational needs you have defined in your project blueprint. SAP ERP provides a large number of standard reports for CO-CCA. We'll show some examples of the most important reports for CO-CCA.

By following the user menu path ACCOUNTING • CONTROLLING • COST CENTER ACCOUNTING • INFORMATION SYSTEM • REPORTS FOR COST CENTER ACCOUNTING, you can see the following folders:

▸ Plan/Actual Comparisons

▸ Actual/Actual Comparisons

▸ Target/Actual Comparisons

▸ Planning Reports

▸ Prices

▸ Line Items

▶ Master Data Indexes

▶ More Reports

You can choose from several different reports inside each folder. By understanding how one of them works, you can apply the same idea for all and be able to choose the one that best fits your needs.

The most commonly used report is S_ALR_87013611 – Cost Centers: Actual/Plan/Variance (as shown in Figure 3.62). We've already used this report several times in this chapter to demonstrate the planning values and also to show the allocation results.

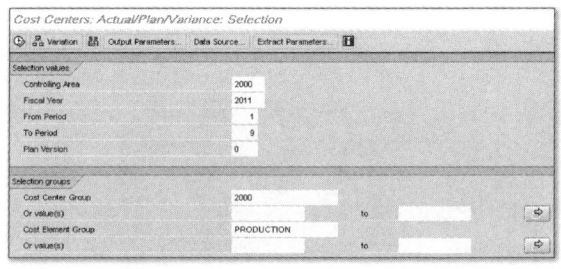

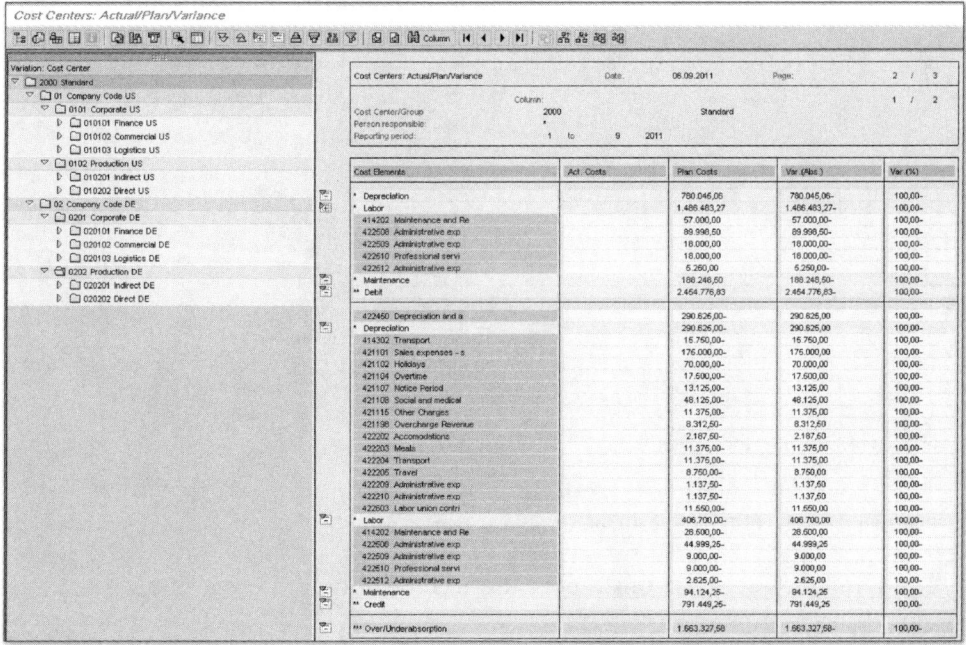

Figure 3.62 Report S_ALR_87013611 – Cost Centers: Actual/Plan/Variance

In the selection screen, you'll see the option to use either a cost center group or a cost element group, or both. By using the groups, the system will show the report output by creating the breakdown and summary lines according to the way that the groups were defined. In the left side of the report output in Figure 3.62, you can see the cost center groups; and in the right side, you can see the cost element groups. You can also navigate between the individual cost center groups by marking the desired group and then collapsing or expanding the values.

Another important report is KSBT – Cost Centers: Activity Prices, where you can see the planned and actual activity price for the selected cost center. It's very useful for comparing the planned and actual values after the month-end closing. Figure 3.63 shows the selection screen, and Figure 3.64 shows the report.

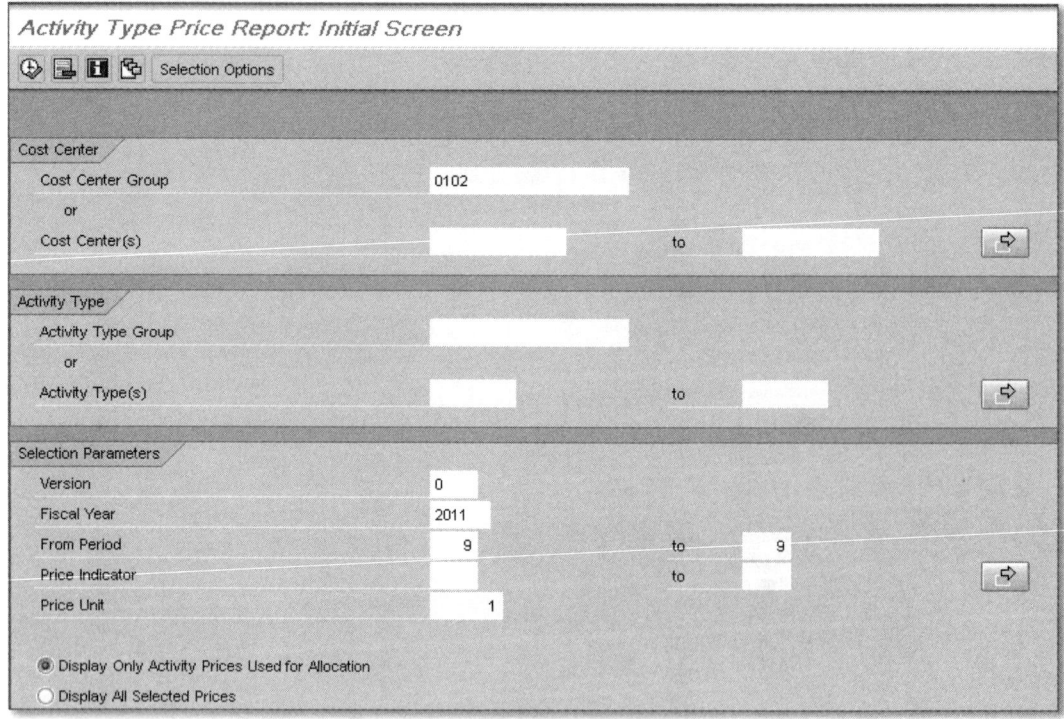

Figure 3.63 Activity Type Price Report: Initial Screen

The selection screen for this report also has the option to use groups.

```
Cost Center Group   0102
Activity Type
Version            0 Plan/Act - Version
Fiscal Year        2011
Period             9 To 9
Price unit         1
```

Cost Center	Acty Type	Cost ctr short text	Act. type short text	COCr	Total price	Variable price	Price (Fixed)	Pri	AUn	VT	A	ObCur	Fix+vbl price OCrcy	Vbl. price in OCrcy	Fxd Prices in OCrcy
102010001	DEPREC	Overhead	Depreciation	USD	0,45	0,00	0,45	1	H	1	P	USD	0,45	0,00	0,45
		Overhead	Depreciation	USD	0,00	0,00	0,00	5	H	4	A	USD	0,00	0,00	0,00
	PH	Overhead	Production hours	USD	0,36	0,00	0,36	1	H	1	P	USD	0,36	0,00	0,36
		Overhead	Production hours	USD	0,00	0,00	0,00	5	H	4	A	USD	0,00	0,00	0,00
102010002	DEPREC	Maintenance	Depreciation	USD	1,26	0,00	1,26	1	H	1	P	USD	1,26	0,00	1,26
		Maintenance	Depreciation	USD	0,00	0,00	0,00	5	H	4	A	USD	0,00	0,00	0,00
	PH	Maintenance	Production hours	USD	0,16	0,00	0,16	1	H	1	P	USD	0,16	0,00	0,16
		Maintenance	Production hours	USD	0,00	0,00	0,00	5	H	4	A	USD	0,00	0,00	0,00
102010003	DEPREC	Power	Depreciation	USD	0,50	0,00	0,50	1	H	1	P	USD	0,50	0,00	0,50
		Power	Depreciation	USD	0,00	0,00	0,00	5	H	4	A	USD	0,00	0,00	0,00
	PH	Power	Production hours	USD	0,44	0,00	0,44	1	H	1	P	USD	0,44	0,00	0,44
		Power	Production hours	USD	0,00	0,00	0,00	5	H	4	A	USD	0,00	0,00	0,00
102020001	DEPREC	Productive A	Depreciation	USD	0,37	0,00	0,37	1	H	1	P	USD	0,37	0,00	0,37
		Productive A	Depreciation	USD	1.868,25	0,00	1.868,25	5	H	4	A	USD	1.868,25	0,00	1.868,25
	PH	Productive A	Production hours	USD	0,17	0,00	0,17	1	H	1	P	USD	0,17	0,00	0,17
		Productive A	Production hours	USD	47.642,18	0,00	47.642,18	5	H	4	A	USD	47.642,18	0,00	47.642,18
102020002	DEPREC	Productive B	Depreciation	USD	2,03	0,00	2,03	1	H	1	P	USD	2,03	0,00	2,03
		Productive B	Depreciation	USD	9.853,95	0,00	9.853,95	5	H	4	A	USD	9.853,95	0,00	9.853,95
	PH	Productive B	Production hours	USD	1,21	0,00	1,21	1	H	1	P	USD	1,21	0,00	1,21
		Productive B	Production hours	USD	4.986,86	0,00	4.986,86	5	H	4	A	USD	4.986,86	0,00	4.986,86
102020003	DEPREC	Productive C	Depreciation	USD	0,86	0,00	0,86	1	H	1	P	USD	0,86	0,00	0,86
		Productive C	Depreciation	USD	5.101,29	0,00	5.101,29	5	H	4	A	USD	5.101,29	0,00	5.101,29
	PH	Productive C	Production hours	USD	0,57	0,00	0,57	1	H	1	P	USD	0,57	0,00	0,57
		Productive C	Production hours	USD	5.592,01	0,00	5.592,01	5	H	4	A	USD	5.592,01	0,00	5.592,01

Figure 3.64 Activity Type Price Report

In the output of this report, you can see two lines for each cost center, separately reporting the values for planning and actual. The way to identify which line is which is to look at the VT (value type) column in the report. An entry of 1 indicates plan values, and an entry of 4 designates actual values.

For a cost center line-item report, you can choose one from the following list:

► KSB1 – Cost Centers: Actual Line Items

► KSB2 – Cost Centers: Commitment Line Items

► KSBP – Cost Centers: Plan Line Items

► KSB5 – CO Documents: Actual Costs

► KABP – CO Plan Documents

We won't cover the details of how to create new reports using Report Painter or Report Writer in this book, but additional reports are available for CO-CCA that are accessed via Transaction GRR3, shown in Figure 3.65.

The most common library for CO-CCA is 1VK Cost Centers: Absorption Costing, where you can find most of the cost center reports. Select the desired report, and click on Execute on the top menu. You can also choose other libraries related to CO-CCA, depending on your needs.

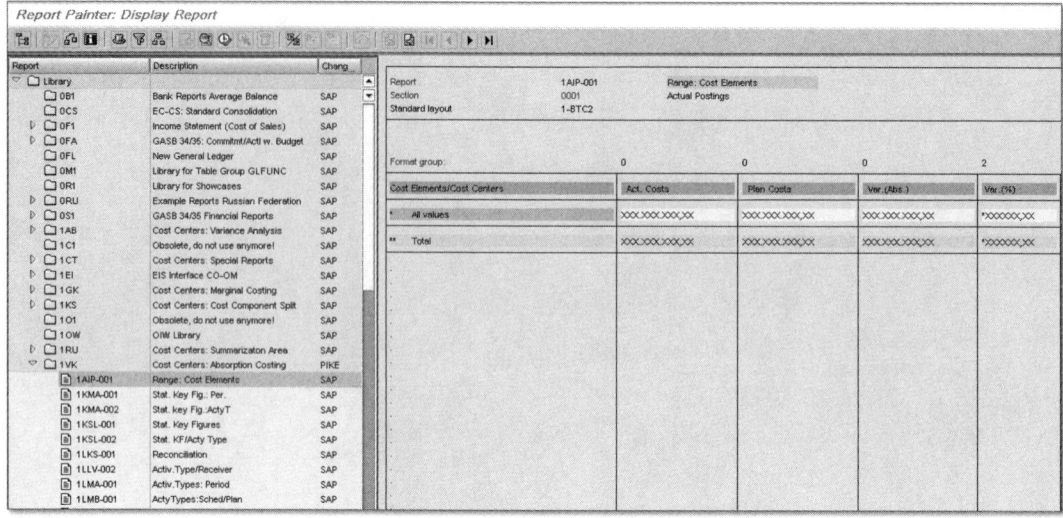

Figure 3.65 Report Painter Example

As we discussed in Chapter 2, sometimes you may need to import the standard reports from SAP ERP client 000. The procedure to import the standard reports is similar to that described for cost element reports. Use Transaction OKD3, or follow the IMG menu path CONTROLLING • COST CENTER ACCOUNTING • INFORMATION SYSTEM • STANDARD REPORTS • IMPORT STANDARD REPORTS. Figure 3.66 shows the customizing screen where you can select the report group to import.

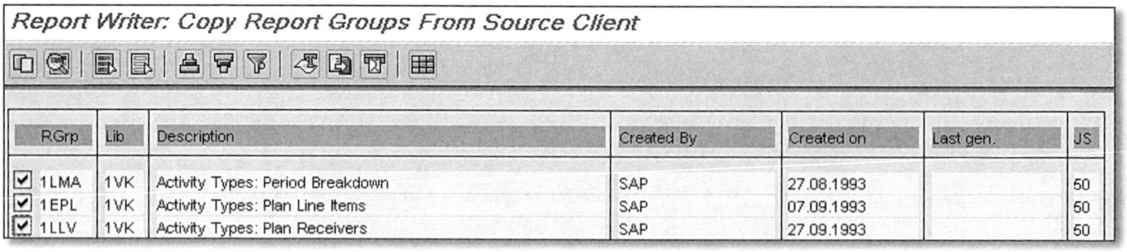

Report Writer: Copy Report Groups From Source Client

RGrp	Lib	Description	Created By	Created on	Last gen.	JS
☑ 1LMA	1VK	Activity Types: Period Breakdown	SAP	27.08.1993		50
☑ 1EPL	1VK	Activity Types: Plan Line Items	SAP	07.09.1993		50
☑ 1LLV	1VK	Activity Types: Plan Receivers	SAP	27.09.1993		50

Figure 3.66 Import Report Group from SAP ERP Client 000

After importing the reports, you need to generate them. To generate the reports, you can use Transaction OKB6 or follow the IMG menu path CONTROLLING • COST CENTER ACCOUNTING • INFORMATION SYSTEM • STANDARD REPORTS • GENERATE STANDARD REPORTS. In Figure 3.67, you can see the generate reports selection screen.

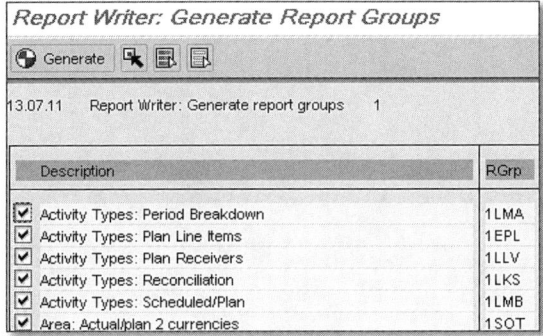

Figure 3.67 Generate Report Groups

Now that you've seen how to use the more common CO-CCA reports, and how to import and regenerate the standard cost center reports in SAP ERP, let's summarize what we've learned about CO-CCA in this chapter.

3.7 Summary

In this chapter, you've learned about SAP ERP Cost Center Accounting, and how to activate and customize it to obtain the best result for your organization.

You should now have a good understanding of the importance of cost centers as cost objects, and also about how to customize activity types, statistical key figures, and the other related master data for your organization.

We've also explained how you can customize the system to create the ideal planning environment to meet your organization's requirements, and you should now have a good understanding of the different types of allocations available in SAP ERP, including periodic reposting, distributions, and assessments, and know which combination will best meet your various needs.

CO-CCA is a very powerful and flexible tool for organizations to track, manage, and report on their cost information according to their individualized needs. You've seen in the customizing options the choices you have, and you can now determine the optimal structure and custom configuration for your organization. In the next chapter, Internal Orders, you'll learn about another type of CO cost collector that can be used with CO-CCA to provide even more flexibility to your cost tracking and control processes.

In this chapter, you'll learn about the importance of internal orders and how to customize them in SAP ERP for your organization.

4   Internal Orders

Internal orders are flexible tools that provide an auxiliary way to analyze and manage costs in SAP ERP Controlling (CO). An internal order is another type of cost collector that functions similarly to cost centers but has a transitory nature. All costs assigned to an internal order must be further settled to another object (such as a cost center), another internal order, a fixed asset, or a Financial Accounting (FI) account. Internal orders have a beginning and an end date, and they are typically used for only a temporary time and for a specific purpose, such as the duration of a defined activity or project.

This chapter explains the concepts behind using internal orders, customizing the master data, planning, budgeting and availability control, and all other necessary customizing for the internal order component (CO-OPA), including actual posting and period-end closing. We'll also review some of the most important and commonly used standard reports for internal orders, with examples so that you can see how the decisions you make in the customizing for internal orders will affect the information available for management reporting.

A common example of the use of internal orders can be demonstrated using the marketing department. Let's assume that the marketing department manages various customer events, seminars, and training programs all during the same time period, and it wants to know the cost of each event separately. One approach would be to create one cost center for each event, but this isn't the recommended approach because this cost center will be needed just for a period of time and would inflate the cost center hierarchy. An alternative and better solution for this situation is to create one internal order for each event and assign the costs to the appropriate internal order during the month. At the end of the month, the internal order costs would be settled to the marketing cost center. With this process, the managers are able to track the cost of each event by looking at internal order reports and to see the overall department costs in the marketing cost center by using cost center reports. All of the costs of the individual events will be reflected, along with other department costs in the marketing cost center. This method provides flexibility in the options available to analyze and manage costs, and satisfies multiple needs.

Internal orders can also be used to track overhead costs, investments, accruals, and revenues.

To use CO-OPA, you must first activate order management in the controlling area settings. This is the same customizing used to activate CO-CCA. Use Transaction OKKP, or go to Controlling • Organization • Maintain Controlling Area, which brings you to the controlling area basic data screen shown in Figure 4.1.

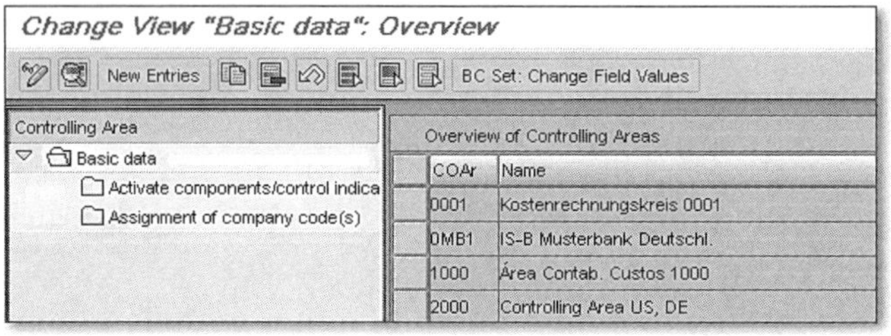

Figure 4.1 Maintain Controlling Area

In the overview screen, you'll see the available controlling areas in the right side of the screen, while the left side shows the activities that you can perform. Select the controlling area on the right side of the screen, and click on Activate components/control indicators. Figure 4.2 shows the next screen, which you may remember from Chapter 3. You can see whether the controlling area you selected already has cost centers activated. The two components you can activate here that relate to CO-OPA are order management and commitment management.

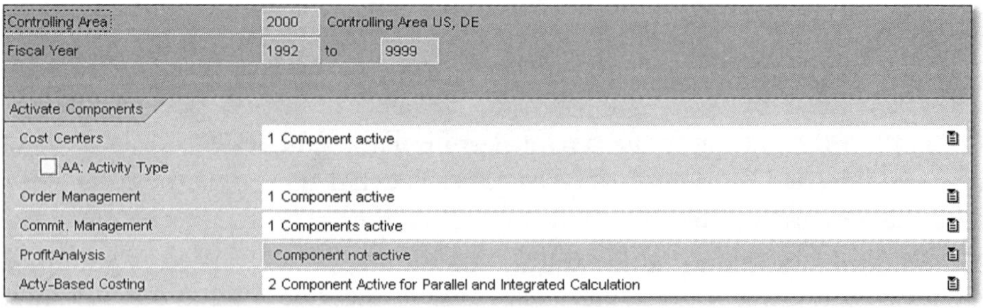

Figure 4.2 Activate Components for Controlling Area

To activate CO-OPA in SAP ERP, you must select one of the following options for the ORDER MANAGEMENT field:

▶ COMPONENT NOT ACTIVE
This the default setting in the controlling area, indicating that the component is not yet active.

▶ COMPONENT ACTIVE
The component is activated without restriction, internal orders will work as cost objects, and all CO functionality for CO-OPA will be available.

▶ ACTIVE FOR VALIDATIONS
The component is not active, and you can use internal orders as cost objects, but the CO component will not be updated. It is useful only to check and validate the postings.

▶ ACTIVE FOR EXISTENCE CHECKS
The component is not active and is used only for validation. In this case, the system will check only if the internal order master data exists or not.

The most common approach is to use the first option (COMPONENT NOT ACTIVE) or the second option (COMPONENT ACTIVE). You can create validations using the second option as well as with the third option, but with the second, the internal order functionality will be fully operational.

Now that you've learned how to activate the internal orders in SAP ERP, you'll learn how to customize the internal order master data.

4.1   Master Data

All definitions for the internal order master data (such as the order number range, settlement profile definition, planning profile, and budget profile) are stored in the order type. To create an internal order, you must first select the order type, which will define the behavior of the internal order master data, how the settlement is done, and how the planning and budget is executed.

4.1.1   Define Order Type

You can see the customizing screen for the order types in Figure 4.3. Use Transaction KOT2, or go to IMG menu path CONTROLLING • INTERNAL ORDERS • ORDER MASTER DATA • DEFINE ORDER TYPES.

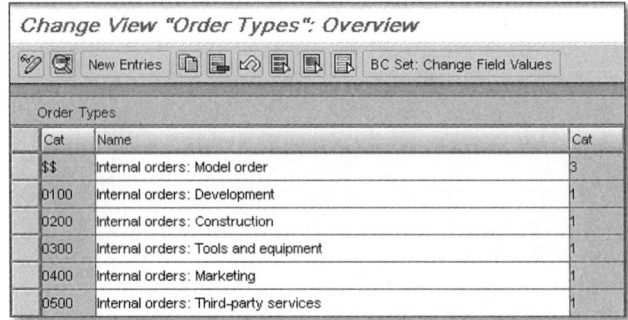

Figure 4.3 Order Types

You can either use the standard order types provided by SAP ERP or create your own order type. To create a new type, you can copy from an existing one or click on NEW ENTRIES to create a new order type from scratch. When you are creating a new one, SAP ERP will prompt you to select the order type category. The first field in the screen is the ORDER TYPE, followed by the order type name, and the ORDER CATEGORY. For internal orders, you must choose category 1 – INTERNAL ORDER (CONTROLLING).

You can customize six areas of settings for an order type, as shown in Figure 4.4:

▶ NUMBER RANGE INTERVAL

▶ GENERAL PARAMETERS

▶ CONTROL INDICATORS

▶ ARCHIVING

▶ STATUS MANAGEMENT

▶ MASTER DATA DISPLAY

Number Range Interval

The first step is to define which number range you'll assign to the order type. You can do this by clicking on the assign/change intervals icon (the pencil icon beside the NUMBER RANGE INTERVAL field). Figure 4.5 shows the next screen, which lists the available number ranges and the existing order types already assigned.

New Entries: Details of Added Entries

Order Type	Z001	Overhead Order Type
Order category		1 Internal Order (Controlling)

Number range interval	Not assigned

General parameters

Settlement prof.	
Strat seq. sett.rule	
Planning profile	
Execution Profile	
Budget Profile	
Object class	
Functional area	
Model Order	

Collective order without automatic goods movement

Control indicators

CO Partner Update	X Active

☐ Classification
☐ Commit. Management
☐ Revenue postings
☐ Integrated planning

Archiving

Residence Time 1		Months
Residence Time 2		Months

Status management

Status Profile	

☐ Release immediately
☐ Status dependent field select.

Master data display

Order layout	
Print form	

☐ Field selection

Figure 4.4 Order Type Settings

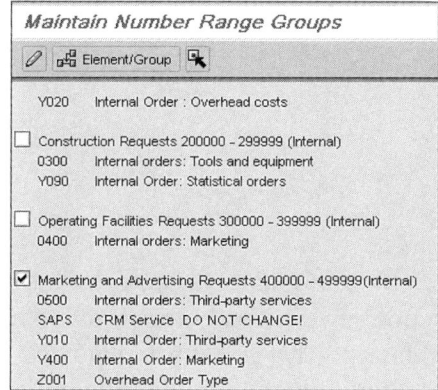

Maintain Number Range Groups

🖉 ⊞ Element/Group 🔍

Y020   Internal Order : Overhead costs

☐ Construction Requests 200000 – 299999 (Internal)
0300   Internal orders: Tools and equipment
Y090   Internal Order: Statistical orders

☐ Operating Facilities Requests 300000 – 399999 (Internal)
0400   Internal orders: Marketing

☑ Marketing and Advertising Requests 400000 – 499999 (Internal)
0500   Internal orders: Third-party services
SAPS   CRM Service DO NOT CHANGE!
Y010   Internal Order: Third-party services
Y400   Internal Order: Marketing
Z001   Overhead Order Type

Figure 4.5 Order Type Number Range Assignment

Assigning number ranges for internal orders is very similar to the CO number ranges. You have a list of standard number ranges available, and you can also create others. Leave the cursor on the order type you've created, click on SELECT, and then click on ELEMENT/GROUP to assign the order type to the number range.

General Parameters

In the GENERAL PARAMETERS section, you define the behavior for the values in the internal order. Some options selected here, such as OBJECT CLASS and FUNCTIONAL AREA, will define the values to be proposed when creating an internal order, and they can be changed by the user at time.

In the settlement profile, you define to which object you can settle the order and how the settlement will be performed. You'll see the detailed customizing for settlements in Section 4.2.3.

The planning profile and budget profile are where you define the parameters for the planning and budgeting for all internal orders created using this order type. You'll see this in depth in Section 4.2 and Section 4.3.

After defining the settlement profile, planning profile, and budget profile, you can assign the profiles to the order type.

In the GENERAL PARAMETERS section, you can also set a model order. The model order is very useful. For example, when you want to create orders with predefined fields, you create an internal order as a model and assign it to this field, and all orders that you create using this order type will copy the fields defined in the model order master data by default. These predefined fields can be changed when you are creating the order.

Control Indicators

In the CONTROL INDICATORS section, you can set the following options:

▶ CO PARTNER UPDATE
This selection will update the CO partner in the totals tables for all order business transactions. You can choose between not active, partially active, and fully active. The difference between partially and fully active is that partially means that only allocations between orders will create total records containing the relationship, and fully active will create them for all settlements.

▶ CLASSIFICATION
You set this indicator to classify the orders for summarization reports with system and user-defined fields. When selecting this option, you also need to select the characteristics to use to classify the orders. Additional customizing steps are required to activate classification, but we won't cover them in this book because the customization is mainly used to add additional fields in the order master data.

▶ COMMIT. MANAGEMENT
Set this flag to activate the commitments line items for internal orders. To use this function, you must have already activated commitment management in the controlling area settings.

▶ REVENUE POSTINGS
You must select this field if orders created under this order type are revenue orders.

▶ INTEGRATED PLANNING
Select this option to activate integrated planning between internal orders and cost centers. To use this function, integrated planning must also be activated in the version maintenance, as explained in Chapter 1, Section 1.1.3.

Archiving

Two fields are available in the ARCHIVING section:

▶ RESIDENCE TIME 1
Determines the minimum period in months to set the deletion indicator by the archiving program after the delete flag is set for the order master data.

▶ RESIDENCE TIME 2
Determines the minimum period in months before the deletion program (archiving) will perform the final deletion step after residence time 1 is met.

Both of these time periods should be specified here if you intend to archive order data.

Status Management

In this section of the dialog box, you'll set the STATUS PROFILE field and also define whether the orders created under this order type will have immediate release functionality (RELEASE IMMEDIATELY checkbox). The status profile will be explained in more detail in Section 4.1.2.

Master Data Display

You define in the MASTER DATA DISPLAY section the fields in the order master data that will be required, optional, displayed, or hidden. You also determine here if you want to highlight fields for the order master data, and define the order layout. Clicking on the FIELD SELECTION button opens another screen where you'll see all of the modifiable fields in order master data. You can select the fields by clicking the radio button indicators to determine how they will appear in orders using this type. You can see an example of the settings for hidden, input, required entry, and highlighted fields in Figure 4.6.

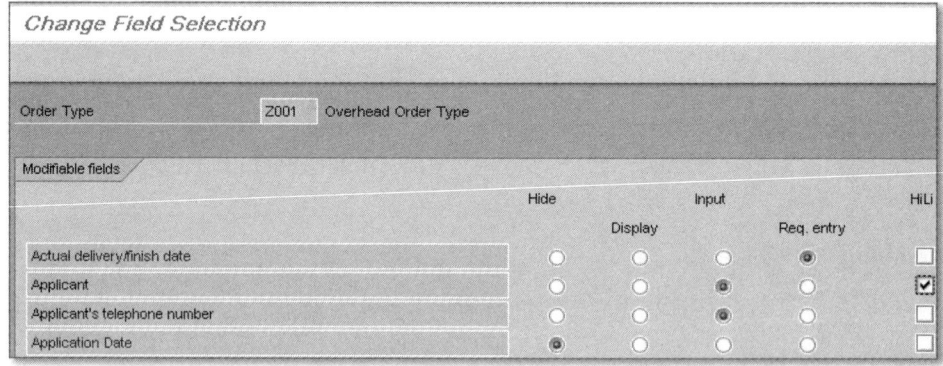

Figure 4.6 Order Type Field Selection

After determining the basic settings for the order type, you're ready to move to the next customizing step: status management.

4.1.2 Status Management

The available operations in the internal order are defined by one or more status indicators. A status is a code that tells you a certain state has been reached (e.g., "The order was released") and influences the number and type of transactions that can be performed for the object.

A status can be active or inactive. A status is currently active when it's set to an object. It's inactive when it was never activated or was active but has been disabled. A status may be configured to allow a transaction, to allow a transaction but with a warning, or to completely prohibit a transaction.

There are two kinds of status in SAP ERP—the system status and user status:

▶ System status is defined by the system to inform the user about performing a certain function on an object. You can only influence this status by performing another transaction that causes the change of status. When you release an order, for example, the system automatically sets the system status to "Released."

▶ With the user status it is possible to differentiate from the system status. The user status is defined in a status profile, and you can assign this profile to the order type. In the user statuses, you can set allowed transactions for the status and also assign the status line to the user rules, allowing you to create security authorizations for each step of the status.

The first step in creating a user status is to define the status profile. The status profile contains a number of user status and user-defined rules. You can assign the status profile to the order type. The status profile includes the following definitions:

▶ Set the user status, and assign a status number to determine the sequence of the expected flow of the user status.

▶ Set an initial status (done automatically when an object is created).

▶ Determine the rules for an automatic setting of the user status when executing a transaction.

▶ Allow or prohibit the execution of transactions if a status is active.

By assigning a number to a user status, you must set lower and upper limits by specifying the interval from which the user status can be selected later. Table 4.1 shows an example of a status profile; the columns will be explained in detail shortly.

Status Number	Status	Short Text	Lowest Status No.	Highest Status No.
10	INIT	Initial Screen	10	20
20	PLAN	Planning	10	30

Table 4.1 User Status Example

Status Number	Status	Short Text	Lowest Status No.	Highest Status No.
30	APRV	Approved	30	40
40	BUIL	Building	30	50
50	DELI	Delivered	50	60
60	CMPL	Complete	60	60
70	ALL	Full Access	70	10

Table 4.1 User Status Example (Cont.)

For each status number, you can select which business transactions can be performed. You can also restrict groups of users to only certain status numbers through security profiles.

To create the status profile, you can use Transaction OK02 or go to IMG menu path CONTROLLING • INTERNAL ORDERS • ORDER MASTER DATA • STATUS MANAGEMENT • DEFINE STATUS PROFILES. The initial screen for the status profile customizing is shown in Figure 4.7.

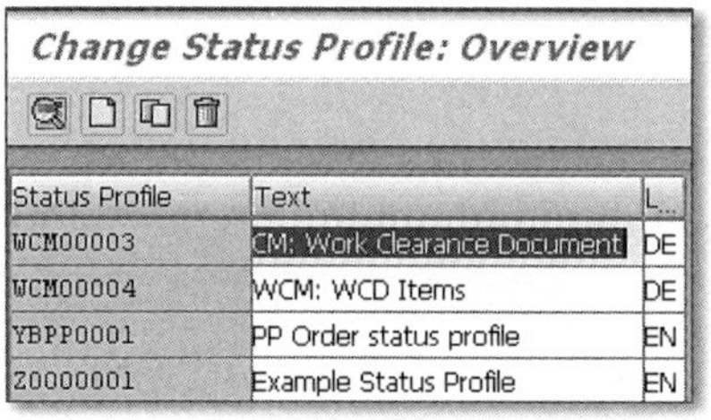

Figure 4.7 Status Profile Initial Screen

You can change an existing status profile or create a new one. After creating a status profile, double-click on the status to create the customizing. Figure 4.8 shows the second customizing screen.

In the first column, you assign the status number, followed by the four-digit definition for the status in the second column, and the short text description in the third column. The INIT. STATUS flag defines which status will be the first status when an internal order is created. The LOWEST and HIGHEST columns define from which status this line can go. For example, line 10 can change from INIT to PLAN, line 40 (BUIL) can go back to line 30 (APRV) or go to the next status, 50 (DELI).

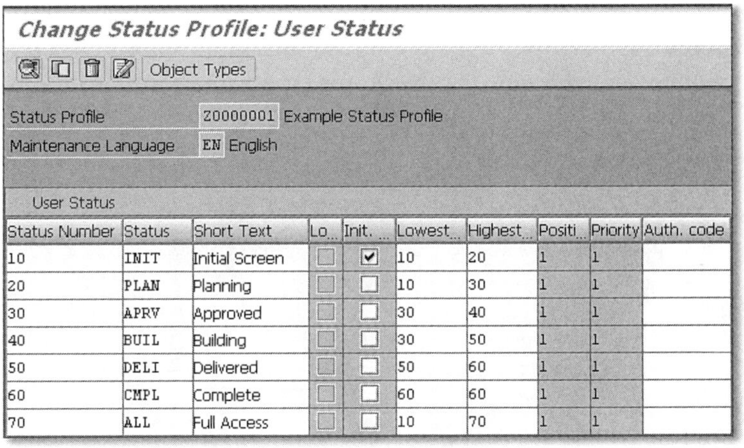

Figure 4.8 Status Profile Definition

The last field to assign is the authorization code for each status. You can then use the authorization codes in the user security role maintenance to define which types of actions a group of users may perform. For instance, you may want to have one group of users who can create new orders and attach the planning, but only another restricted group of users can approve the orders. This is very useful to establish and maintain a sound segregation of duties scheme for internal order transactions.

To use the new status profile in CO-OPA, you must assign it in object types. Click on the OBJECT TYPES button, and mark the item INTERNAL ORDER, as showed on Figure 4.9.

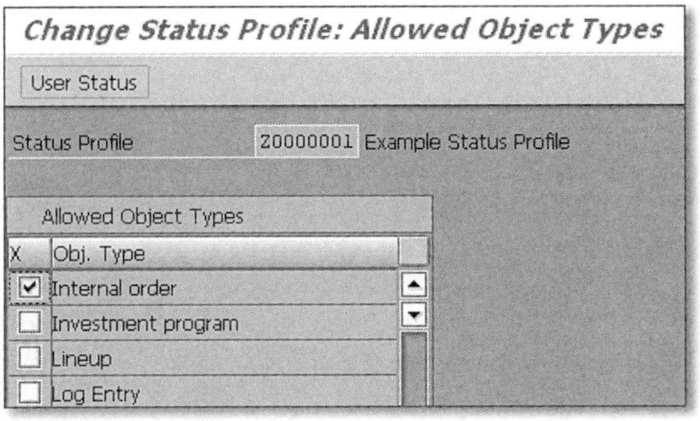

Figure 4.9 Change Status Profile: Allowed Object Types

Click on USER STATUS to return to the status profile definition screen. Now you must define the allowed business transactions for each line. Double-click on a line (e.g., line 10) to open the available options, as shown in Figure 4.10.

Change Status Profile: Transaction Control

Business Transaction	No influ.	Allowed	Warning	Forbidd.	No acti.	Set	Delete
Actual Overhead Assessment	◉	○	○	○			
Actual Overhead Distribution	◉	○	○	○			
Actual Periodic Repostings	◉	○	○	○			
Actual activity allocation	◉	○	○	○			
Actual cost center accrual	◉	○	○	○			
Actual inverse activity alloc.	◉	○	○	○			
Actual overhead (periodic)	◉	○	○	○			
Actual overhead (realtime)	◉	○	○	○			
Actual settlement	◉	○	○	○			
Automat. WIP/results analysis	◉	○	○	○	◉	○	
Availability control	◉	○	○	○			
Budget return	◉	○	○	○			
Budget supplement	◉	○	○	○	◉	○	
Budgeting	◉	○	○	○	◉	○	
Complete	◉	○	○	○	◉	○	

Figure 4.10 Status Profile: Transaction Control

In this screen, you can select which possible business transactions can influence, are allowed, will generate a warning, or are forbidden for the status. This definition must be done for each status line.

The next step is to create the authorization key to be used in each line of the status profile. You maintain these using Transaction BS52 or by going to IMG menu path CONTROLLING • INTERNAL ORDERS • ORDER MASTER DATA • STATUS MANAGEMENT • DEFINE STATUS PROFILES, which brings you to the screen shown in Figure 4.11.

To use the authorization key, you must assign it to user role maintenance with authorization object B_USERSTAT using Transaction PFCG, and you must also assign it to a line in the status profile. Figure 4.12 shows one example of the B_USERSTAT object in the user role maintenance. Figure 4.13 shows the assignment in the user status profile.

Change View "Authorization key": Overview

New Entries

AuthKey	Text
Z001	Initial
Z002	Planning
Z003	Execution
Z004	All access

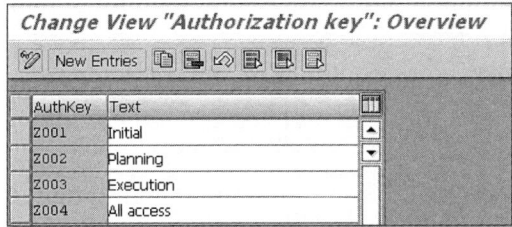

Figure 4.11 Authorization Key

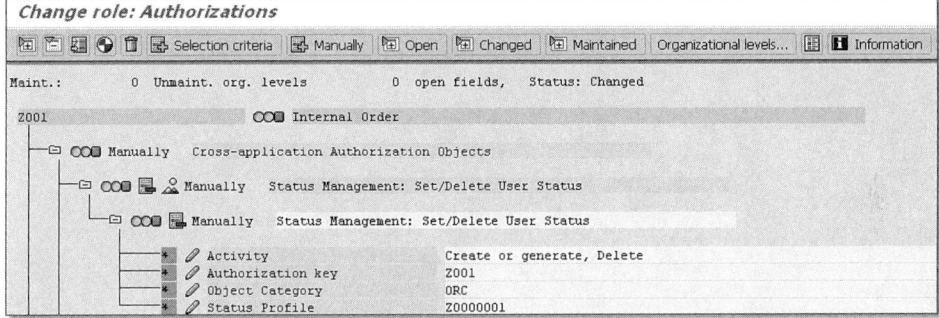

Figure 4.12 User Role Maintenance, Authorization Key Assignment

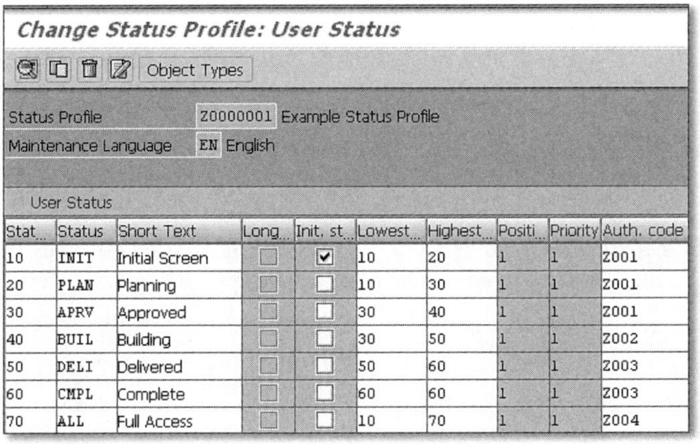

Change Status Profile: User Status

Object Types

Status Profile Z0000001 Example Status Profile

Maintenance Language EN English

User Status

Stat...	Status	Short Text	Long...	Init. st...	Lowest...	Highest...	Positi...	Priority	Auth. code
10	INIT	Initial Screen	☐	☑	10	20	1	1	Z001
20	PLAN	Planning	☐	☐	10	30	1	1	Z001
30	APRV	Approved	☐	☐	30	40	1	1	Z001
40	BUIL	Building	☐	☐	30	50	1	1	Z002
50	DELI	Delivered	☐	☐	50	60	1	1	Z003
60	CMPL	Complete	☐	☐	60	60	1	1	Z003
70	ALL	Full Access	☐	☐	10	70	1	1	Z004

Figure 4.13 Status Profile with Authorization Code

Now that you've created the status profiles, assigned the allowed business transactions for each status line, created the authorization codes, and assigned them to user role maintenance, you must assign the status profile to the order type in the STATUS MANAGEMENT section using Transaction KOT2, as shown in Figure 4.14.

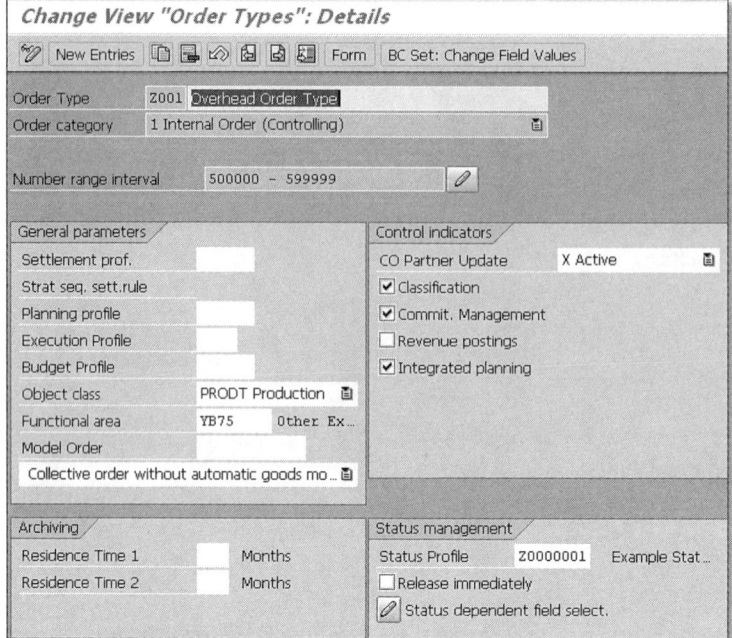

Figure 4.14 Status Management on Order Type

You can see one example of the user status in an internal order in Figure 4.15. This internal order was created using Transaction KO01, and the USER STATUS field entry is visible in the internal order CONTROL DATA tab.

You can see in the STATUS NUMBER and USER STATUS fields that the initial status of 10 – INIT was adopted from the status profile customizing.

Internal order master data grouping is also available. You can create, change, or display the groups using Transactions KOH1, KOH2, and KOH3, respectively. The groups are useful in order maintenance, executing settlements, and also in reporting, so you should consider your needs in these areas when establishing a structure of internal order groupings. For instance, you may have one group of internal orders that you want to settle on a weekly basis, compared to another that you want to only settle at the end of the month. Because order settlement can be executed or scheduled by group, this can be easily managed by groups rather than some other method such as variants.

Now that you know how to create order types and define the status management, we're ready to discuss CO-OPA planning.

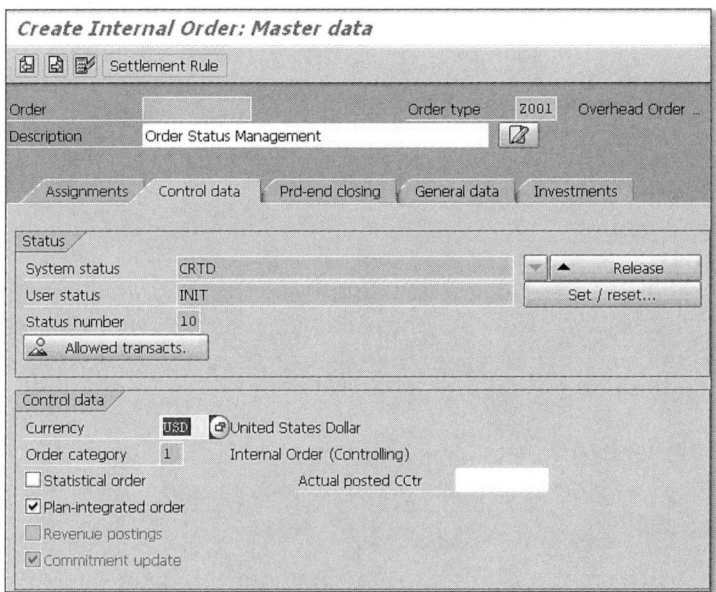

Figure 4.15 Internal Order User Status

4.2 Planning

CO-OPA planning customizing follows the same principle of CO-CCA planning customizing, where you have to establish the basic settings, manual planning, and planning aids. The difference is that for internal orders, there is a new step to customize—the settlement structure and settlement profile. We'll quickly review the steps that you've already seen and that should already be customized in previous areas and discuss the new steps in detail.

4.2.1 Basic Settings

You must establish some basic settings before you can move on to the customizing steps for CO-OPA planning. These have already been addressed in earlier steps of your CO customizing, but we'll review them briefly here.

The basic settings consist of the following:

▸ Define exchange rate types
▸ Maintain exchange rates

- Assign planning transactions to number ranges
- Maintain versions
- Set integrated planning in order types as default

The steps to define exchange rate types and maintain exchange rates are the same that we've already explained for CO-CCA planning in Chapter 3, Section 3.2.1, and there is no difference for CO-OPA planning.

We've discussed how to maintain number ranges for the controlling area in Chapter 1, Section 1.1.2, and because we've already defined number ranges for all business transactions, the planning number ranges have been defined; therefore, nothing further is required for internal orders.

No special treatment is required in version maintenance for CO-OPA planning. It follows the same options as already explained and defined for cost center planning in Chapter 3, Section 3.2.1.

The last option in the basic settings is to set the integrated planning in the order type as default, which was discussed in Chapter 1, Section 1.1.1.

Now that we've reviewed the basic settings, you can go on to manual planning.

4.2.2   Manual Planning

The manual planning process is the step where you define the planning layouts to assign to the planner profile. The functions and the process to define the planning layout and the planner profile is the same as those for cost center planning in Chapter 3, Section 3.2.2. You can use the same planner profiles for both cost centers and internal orders. The only additional step is to assign a planning layout to ORDERS: COST ELEMENT/ACTIVITY INPUTS and ORD: STATISTICAL KEY FIGURES, as shown in Figure 4.16 and Figure 4.17.

Another difference in manual planning between cost centers and internal orders is that for internal orders, you can create a planning profile for overall planning. Using overall planning, you can plan the internal order by year or by total values, and the planning is not divided by period. Figure 4.18 shows the planning profile. To customize the planning profile for overall planning, go to IMG menu path CONTROLLING • INTERNAL ORDERS • PLANNING • MANUAL PLANNING • MAINTAIN PLANNING PROFILES FOR OVERALL PLANNING.

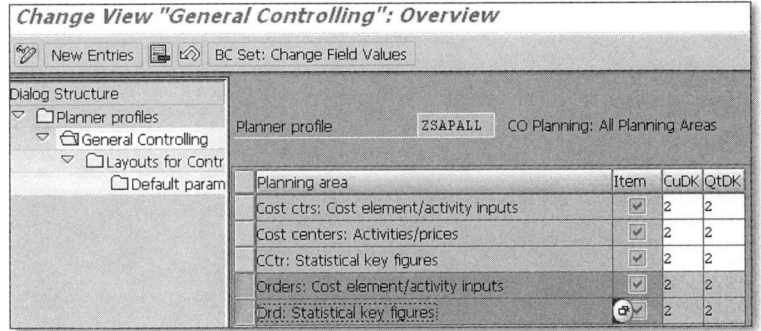

Figure 4.16 Planner Profile for Internal Orders

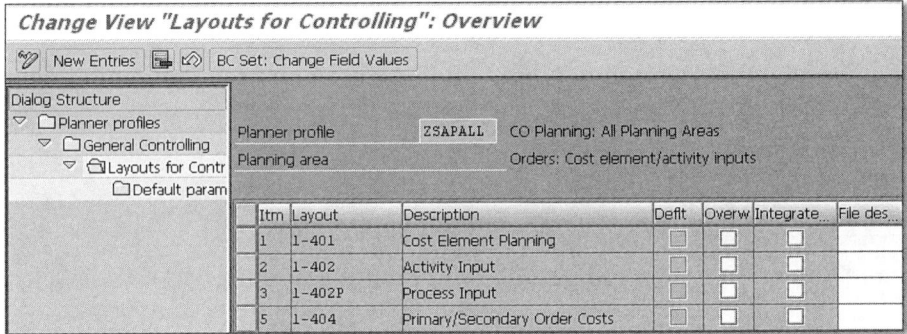

Figure 4.17 Layouts for CO-OPA Planning

As you can see in Figure 4.18, in the planner profile for overall planning, you define the time frame for the planning, for how many years in the past and how many years in the future you want to create the planning, and also whether your internal order planning will use total values or annual values. If the Annual Values option is flagged, then you can split the overall planning by year, as you can see in the example in Figure 4.19, where we have used Transaction KO12 to create an overall planning.

In the overall planning profile, you can also define the decimal places for the values; the scaling factor; whether the planning will be performed in controlling area currency, object currency, or transaction currency; the exchange rate type, and which cost elements you can plan in the detail planning.

After defining the overall planning profile, you must assign it to the order type using Transaction KOT2.

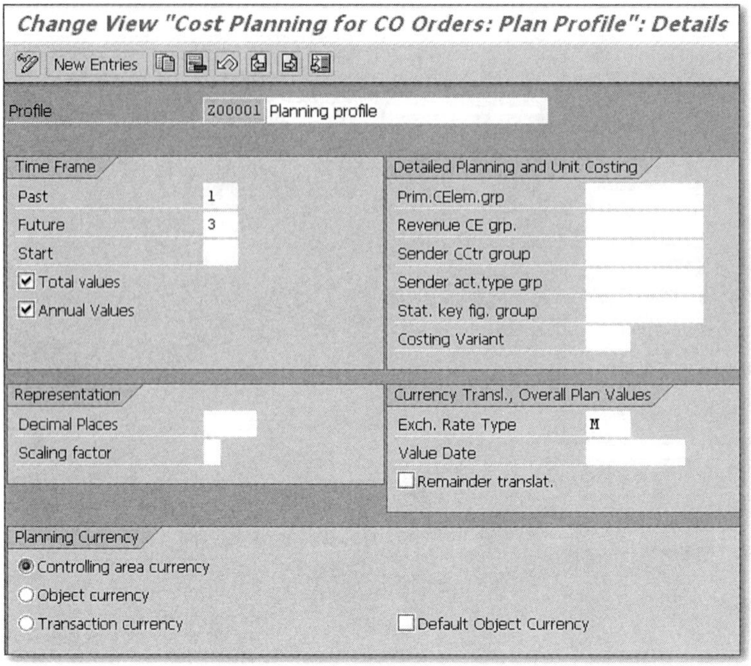

Figure 4.18 Overall Planning Profile

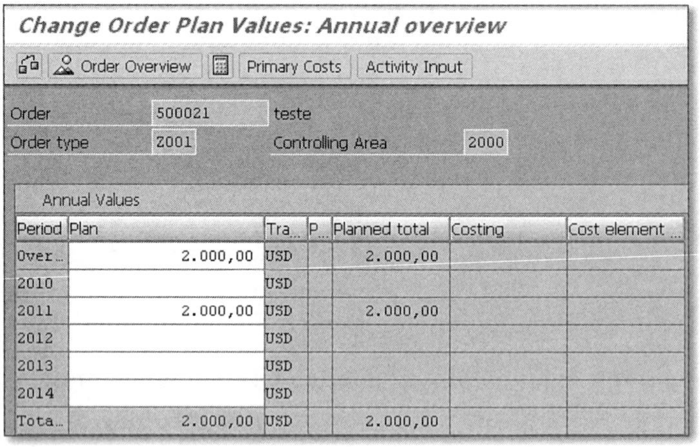

Figure 4.19 Overall Planning Example

After assigning the planning profiles, all of the customizing steps for CO=OAP planning are completed, and we're ready to move on to discuss order settlement and how to customize the SETTLEMENT PROFILE field, which is the final field remaining in the order type.

4.2.3 Maintain Settlement

As you already know, the internal order is another type of cost collector that functions similarly to a cost center but with a transitory nature. In the internal order master data, you must set a beginning and an end period. Internal orders must be settled to move the costs to another object at the end of the period or at the end of their life. The object definition and how it will be settled is maintained in the settlement structure and settlement profile. The customizing done here will affect both planning and actual values.

The settlement definition consists of the following steps:

▶ Maintain settlement structure

▶ Maintain source structure

▶ Define the CO-PA transfer structure

▶ Assign number range for settlement documents

▶ Maintain settlement profiles

Maintain Settlement Structure

Internal orders are settled using a secondary cost element with category 21 (Internal settlement) or by using the same account where the cost occurs. You can define the combination of accounts in the settlement structure in this step, except that for internal production orders, the account determination is established in the Materials Management (MM) account determination.

You define the settlement structure in the same transaction used to define the allocation structure for assessments that we discussed in Chapter 3. This time, however, instead of assigning a secondary cost element for an assessment, you'll assign a secondary settlement cost element. To define the settlement structure, go to IMG menu path CONTROLLING • INTERNAL ORDERS • PLANNING • MANUAL PLANNING • MAINTAIN SETTLEMENT. The initial screen is shown in Figure 4.20.

Double-click on MAINTAIN SETTLEMENT STRUCTURE to begin this step of the customizing using the screen shown in Figure 4.21.

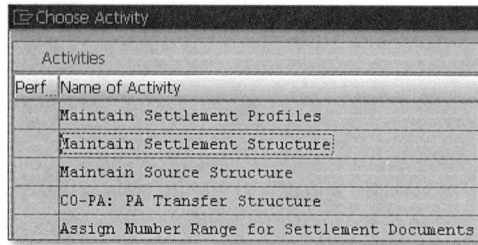

Figure 4.20 Internal Order Settlement Customizing

Change View "Allocation structures": Overview

Alloc.str.	Text
A1	CO allocation structure
A2	No split
Y1	CO allocation structure
Y2	No Split - All cost elements
Y9	Rework Orders
YH	PS Settlement
YL	Service Order Settlement
YM	Allocation Structure IM
YP	PP Valuated
YR	R&D Orders
YS	Sales Order Settlement
Z1	Assessment Allo. Structure

Dialog Structure
- Allocation structures
  - Assignments
    - Source
    - Assessment Cost Element
    - Settlement cost elements

Figure 4.21 Internal Order Settlement Structure

The definition here is the same as for assessments that you've seen in Chapter 3, where you had to define an allocation structure, the source cost elements, and the settlement cost elements. We'll use the same allocation structure used for the example for assessments, Z1 – ASSESSMENT ALLO. STRUCTURE. Mark the allocation structure on the right side of the screen, and double-click on ASSIGNMENTS on the left side of the screen. Figure 4.22 shows the next screen.

Because we've already defined the source for this allocation structure in the assessment customizing, we just need to define the SETTLEMENT COST ELEMENTS. Marking one assignment on the right side (e.g., ADMINISTRATIVE), and double-clicking on SETTLEMENT COST ELEMENTS will bring you to the screen shown in Figure 4.23.

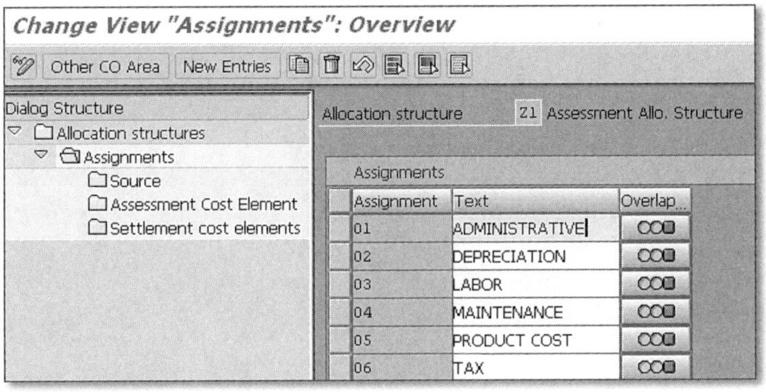

Figure 4.22 Internal Order Settlement Structure, Assignments

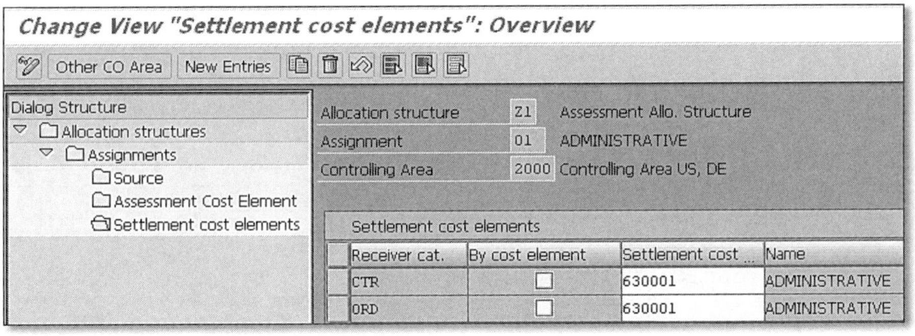

Figure 4.23 Settlement Cost Elements

Click on NEW ENTRIES, and select the receiver category from the list, either cost center, other internal order, fixed asset, or others. If you flag the field by cost element, the system will use the same primary cost element to settle the cost. If not, then you must enter the settlement secondary cost element. Table 4.2 shows the difference between using the same cost element and a secondary cost element.

Cost Element	Settlement Cost Element (by Cost Element Flagged)	Secondary Cost Element
414303 Indirect labor	414303 Indirect labor	630001 ADMINISTRATIVE
422200 Mail	422200 Mail	630001 ADMINISTRATIVE
422206 Office supply	422206 Office supply	630001 ADMINISTRATIVE

Table 4.2 Settlement by Cost Element vs Secondary Cost Element

If you flag the field, the costs from the cost element 414303 will be settled using the same cost element 414303. If it's not flagged, the system will use cost element 630001. You can choose just one for each receiver category.

> **Note**
>
> When using the setting to settle by cost element, you should consider that if the order has any values in a secondary cost element, the system won't settle these costs, and you'll get an error. This setting should only be used in cases where the orders will contain only postings in primary cost elements.

You can see the difference between these approaches in Figure 4.24, where the solution of a settlement cost element was used, and in Figure 4.25, where the settlement was done by the origin primary cost element. The internal order Report S_ALR_87012993 – Orders: Actual/Plan/Variance was used in these examples.

Cost Elements	Actual	Plan	Var.(Abs.)	Var.(%)
Orders: Actual/Plan/Variance Date: 06.11.2011 19:41:39 Page: 2 / 2				
Order/Group 500040 Internal Order				
Reporting period 11 – 11 2011				
414302 Transport		1.500,00	1.500,00-	100,00-
414303 Indirect labor - com		275,00	275,00-	100,00-
421101 Sales expenses - sel		16.666,66	16.666,66-	100,00-
421102 Holidays		6.666,66	6.666,66-	100,00-
421104 Overtime		1.666,66	1.666,66-	100,00-
421107 Notice Period		1.250,00	1.250,00-	100,00-
421108 Social and medical care		4.583,34	4.583,34-	100,00-
421115 Other Charges		1.083,34	1.083,34-	100,00-
421198 Overcharge Revenues		791,66	791,66-	100,00-
422200 Administrative expen		16,66	16,66-	100,00-
422202 Accomodations		208,34	208,34-	100,00-
422203 Meals		1.083,34	1.083,34-	100,00-
422204 Transport		1.083,34	1.083,34-	100,00-
422205 Travel		833,34	833,34-	100,00-
422206 Administrative expen		416,66	416,66-	100,00-
422207 Administrative expen		19,16	19,16-	100,00-
422209 Administrative expen		108,34	108,34-	100,00-
422210 Administrative expen		108,34	108,34-	100,00-
422450 Depreciation and amortization		3.166,66	3.166,66-	100,00-
422506 Taxes and Fees		1.500,00	1.500,00-	100,00-
422603 Labor union contribution		1.100,00	1.100,00-	100,00-
431101 Discounts granted		4,16	4,16-	100,00-
431200 Other operacional expenses		7,50	7,50-	100,00-
* Costs		44.139,16	44.139,16-	100,00-
630001 ADMINISTRATIVE		739,14-	739,14	100,00-
630003 DEPRECIATION		3.166,66-	3.166,66	100,00-
630004 LABOR		38.733,36-	38.733,36	100,00-
630006 TAX		1.500,00-	1.500,00	100,00-
* Settled Costs		44.139,16-	44.139,16	100,00-
** Balance				

Figure 4.24 Internal Order Report, Settlement Cost Element Solution

Orders: Actual/Plan/Variance

Orders: Actual/Plan/Variance		Date:	06.11.2011	19:44:33	Page:		2 / 2
Order/Group	500040	Internal Order					
Reporting period	11 - 11	2011					

Cost Elements	Actual	Plan	Var. (Abs.)	Var. (%)
414302 Transport		1.500,00	1.500,00-	100,00-
414303 Indirect labor - com		275,00	275,00-	100,00-
421101 Sales expenses - sal		16.666,66	16.666,66-	100,00-
421102 Holidays		6.666,66	6.666,66-	100,00-
421104 Overtime		1.666,66	1.666,66-	100,00-
421107 Notice Period		1.250,00	1.250,00-	100,00-
421108 Social and medical care		4.583,34	4.583,34-	100,00-
421115 Other Charges		1.083,34	1.083,34-	100,00-
421198 Overcharge Revenues		791,66	791,66-	100,00-
422200 Administrative expen		16,66	16,66-	100,00-
422202 Accomodations		208,34	208,34-	100,00-
422203 Meals		1.083,34	1.083,34-	100,00-
422204 Transport		1.083,34	1.083,34-	100,00-
422205 Travel		833,34	833,34-	100,00-
422206 Administrative expen		416,66	416,66-	100,00-
422207 Administrative expen		19,16	19,16-	100,00-
422209 Administrative expen		108,34	108,34-	100,00-
422210 Administrative expen		108,34	108,34-	100,00-
422450 Depreciation and amortization		3.166,66	3.166,66-	100,00-
422506 Taxes and Fees		1.500,00	1.500,00-	100,00-
422603 Labor union contribution		1.100,00	1.100,00-	100,00-
431101 Discounts granted		4,16	4,16-	100,00-
431200 Other operacional expenses		7,50	7,50-	100,00-
* Costs		44.139,16	44.139,16-	100,00-
414302 Transport		1.500,00-	1.500,00	100,00-
414303 Indirect labor - com		275,00-	275,00	100,00-
421101 Sales expenses - sal		16.666,66-	16.666,66	100,00-
421102 Holidays		6.666,66-	6.666,66	100,00-
421104 Overtime		1.666,66-	1.666,66	100,00-
421107 Notice Period		1.250,00-	1.250,00	100,00-
421108 Social and medical care		4.583,34-	4.583,34	100,00-
421115 Other Charges		1.083,34-	1.083,34	100,00-
421198 Overcharge Revenues		791,66-	791,66	100,00-
422200 Administrative expen		16,66-	16,66	100,00-
422202 Accomodations		208,34-	208,34	100,00-
422203 Meals		1.083,34-	1.083,34	100,00-
422204 Transport		1.083,34-	1.083,34	100,00-
422205 Travel		833,34-	833,34	100,00-
422206 Administrative expen		416,66-	416,66	100,00-
422207 Administrative expen		19,16-	19,16	100,00-
422209 Administrative expen		108,34-	108,34	100,00-

Figure 4.25 Internal Order Report, Origin Cost Element Solution

With settlement by secondary cost element, the settlement groups the costs into categories, providing a summary in internal order reports and segregating the costs from internal order settlements in cost centers from other costs from primary postings. However, with this option, planning is only possible by planning to orders and settling the planned orders.

With settlement by primary cost element, you won't see the summary by groups or categories in the internal order reports, or see the costs from order settlement in the receiving cost centers segregated from other primary postings, but planning *is* possible in the receiving cost centers as part of your overall cost center planning.

Both approaches have advantages and restrictions, so you'll need to weigh them according to your priorities to determine the best to use.

Now that you've learned the difference between both settlement approaches, we can move to customizing the source structure.

Maintain Source Structure

In the settlement structure, the system splits the costs equally from all cost elements to the receiver object considering the settlement rule in the internal order master data. You can use the source structure to create distribution rules for different groups of costs. For example, you may want to settle personnel costs to a specific cost center and maintenance costs to another cost center. You can do this by using the source structure. To customize the source structure, double-click on MAINTAIN SOURCE STRUCTURE as shown earlier in Figure 4.20, which will bring you to Figure 4.26.

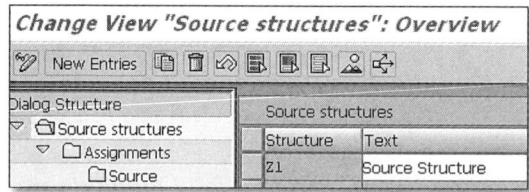

Figure 4.26 Source Structure

The customizing for the source structure is similar to that for the settlement structure, but, in this case, you don't need to define a settlement cost element, just the source cost elements. Create a new structure by clicking on NEW ENTRIES, mark the structure, and double-click on ASSIGNMENTS on the left side of the screen. This brings you to the Change View Assignments Overview screen shown in Figure 4.27.

To select the source cost elements, mark the assignment and double-click on SOURCE, which will open the screen shown in Figure 4.28.

On this screen, you can select one cost element, a range, or a cost element group. In our example, we've selected the cost element group ADMIN.

You maintain the source structure in the settlement profile.

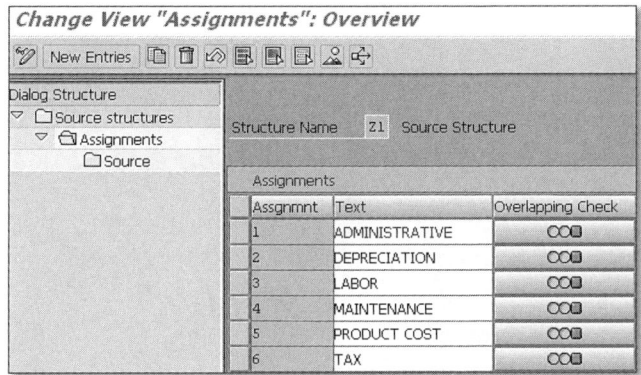

Figure 4.27 Source Structure, Assignments

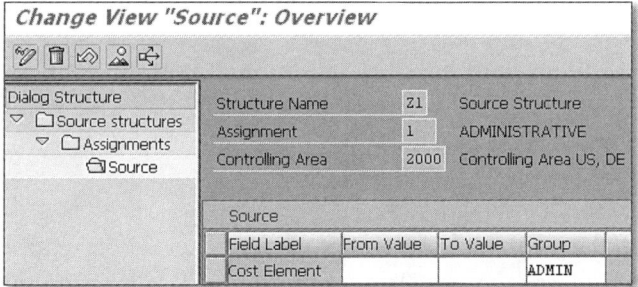

Figure 4.28 Source Structure, Cost Element Assignment

We'll discuss CO-PA transfer structure in Chapter 7, so let's move on to the next step: defining the number range for settlement documents.

Assign Number Range for Settlement Documents

The number range definition for order settlement documents follows the same principles as for CO number ranges. You choose a group, assign the controlling area to the group, and double-click on ASSIGN NUMBER RANGE FOR SETTLEMENT DOCUMENTS in the screen shown earlier in Figure 4.20. You can see the number range for settlement documents in Figure 4.29.

Mark the controlling area with the SELECT button, leave the cursor on the desired group, and click on ELEMENT/GROUP. That will assign the controlling area to the settlement number range group.

After creating the number range, it's time to customize the settlement profile.

```
┌──────────────────────────────────────────────────────────┐
│ Maintain Number Range Groups                             │
│ ┌────────────────────────────┐                           │
│ │ ✎ │ 🔲 Element/Group │ 🔍 │                             │
│ └────────────────────────────┘                           │
│ Number range object CO object Settlement                 │
│ Grouping.........                                        │
│                                                          │
│ ☐ Group Without Text                                     │
│    0001 1000 2000 4000 5000 RECO REOB SG01               │
│                                                          │
│ ☐ Ralf's group                                           │
│                                                          │
│ ☐ Ralf's group 2                                         │
│                                                          │
│ ☐ Hofmann group                                          │
│                                                          │
│ ☐ Ralf's group 4                                         │
│                                                          │
│ ☐ Group for cost element ledger test KoReKr KAL1         │
│                                                          │
│ ☐ mk group                                               │
│                                                          │
│ Not assigned                                             │
│    OMB1 BE01 CA01 CF11 CH01 CN01 C001 COPY CZ01 DE01 DE02 │
└──────────────────────────────────────────────────────────┘
```

Figure 4.29 Settlement Document Number Range

Maintain Settlement Profiles

You've already customized the settlement structure and the source structure. Now you must assign both structures to a settlement profile, and then assign the settlement profile to the order type.

The settlement profile maintains the customizing of all structures used to settle the internal order costs and also to the definition of which objects you can settle. It will also determine the settlement behavior of the internal orders. To customize the settlement profile, double-click on MAINTAIN SETTLEMENT PROFILES in Figure 4.20. You can create a new settlement profile or change an existing one. You can see the customizing screen for the settlement profile in Figure 4.30.

The following sections of the New Entries screen shown in Figure 4.30 contain options that you can define in the settlement profile:

- ACTUAL COST/COST OF SALES
- DEFAULT VALUES
- INDICATORS
- VALID RECEIVERS
- OTHER PARAMETERS

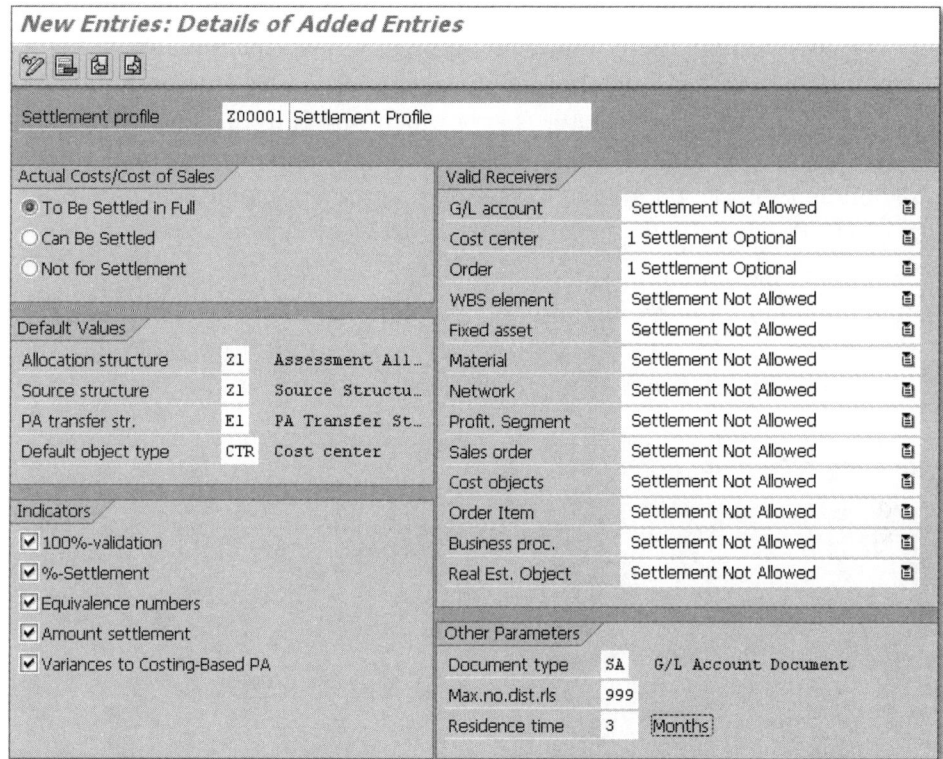

Figure 4.30 Settlement Profile definition

The following are descriptions of each section of the settlement profile:

▶ ACTUAL COST/COST OF SALES

In the ACTUAL COST/COST OF SALES section, you can select whether the internal order will settle in full, which means that all costs in the internal order will be settled to the receiver object. If the settlement profile has the TO BE SETTLED IN FULL flag marked, and you want to set the delete flag in the internal order, the internal order balance must be zero. If you mark CAN BE SETTLED, you are saying that you can set the delete flag in the internal order even if the order has a balance.

The NOT FOR SETTLEMENT option means that the costs in the internal order will never be settled even if you have defined a receiver object in the internal order settlement rule.

▶ DEFAULT VALUES

In the DEFAULT VALUES section, you'll assign the settlement structure, source structure, PA transfer structure, and the default object type to which the internal order will propose to settle if more than one is available. For example, referring to Figure 4.23, if you've customized cost center and internal order as the settlement rule, the system will propose first a cost center in the settlement rule, but you can also define an internal order as settlement object.

▶ INDICATORS/VALID RECEIVERS

To illustrate this how the options available in this section work, let's look at an example of an internal order settlement rule shown in Figure 4.31. We used Transaction KO03 to display the internal order settlement rule.

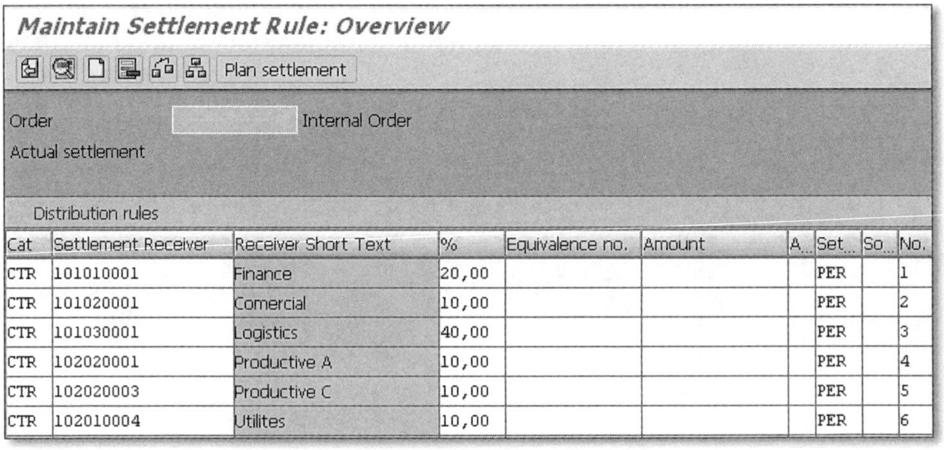

Maintain Settlement Rule: Overview

Order   Internal Order
Actual settlement

Distribution rules

Cat	Settlement Receiver	Receiver Short Text	%	Equivalence no.	Amount	A	Set	So	No.
CTR	101010001	Finance	20,00				PER		1
CTR	101020001	Comercial	10,00				PER		2
CTR	101030001	Logistics	40,00				PER		3
CTR	102020001	Productive A	10,00				PER		4
CTR	102020003	Productive C	10,00				PER		5
CTR	102010004	Utilites	10,00				PER		6

Figure 4.31 Settlement Rule Example

The customizing done in the settlement profile will impact which fields are available here. The first field shown is used to define the account assignment category for this settlement rule. You customize which will be valid categories in the VALID RECEIVERS section in the settlement profile. In the customizing, you can select from SETTLEMENT NOT ALLOWED, SETTLEMENT OPTIONAL, and SETTLEMENT REQUIRED. The options available in the account assignment are limited to those selected in the settlement profile customizing shown previously in Figure 4.30.

If you set the fields %-SETTLEMENT, EQUIVALENCE NUMBERS, and AMOUNT SETTLE-MENT in the settlement profile customizing, these fields become available to enter in the settlement rule as shown in Figure 4.31. If you select the 100%-VALIDATION flag, the system will check that the % field in the settlement rule has 100% distributed between the distribution rules. You can see the field source structure in Figure 4.31. If you want to use the source structure to separate groups of costs, you may enter the group here. The last field in the INDICATORS section in the settlement profile customizing is VARIANCES TO COST-ING-BASED PA, which means that you can settle this order to the Profitability Analysis (PA) component, as explained in Chapter 7.

▶ OTHER PARAMETERS

You can define here the document type used in the internal order settlement, when the internal order is going to be settled to a General Ledger (GL) account or a fixed asset. The MAX.NO.DIST.RLS (maximum number of distribution rules) field will define how many lines you can have in the settlement rule showed in Figure 4.31. The RESIDENCE TIME field contains the residence time in months for settlement documents; as these documents require storage, you can set how many months the documents should stay online before being archived.

Now that you've defined the settlement structure, source settlement, and the settlement profile, you must assign the settlement profile to the order type using Transaction KOT2. You can see the assignment in Figure 4.32.

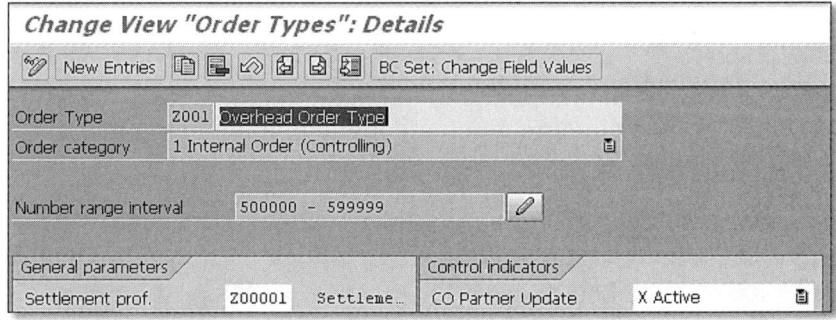

Figure 4.32 Order Type Settlement Profile Assignment

In CO-OPA, you can use a periodic reposting for both planning and actual values. The periodic reposting customizing was explained in Chapter 3, and you can simply specify an internal order (or internal order group) as the sender or as the receiver object in the periodic reposting.

You've now learned the planning customizing for CO-OPA and also seen the importance of the settlement structure and settlement profile. Now let's discuss budgeting and availability control, which is where you'll see the biggest difference between the cost center and internal order budget process and also understand one of the most important functions of CO-OPA.

4.3   Budgeting and Availability Control

The budget process for internal orders is similar to the process for cost centers, but for internal orders, you have the advantage of availability control. This is where the system can be set to check if there is budget available for the internal order before allowing the posting of costs. It doesn't mean that the system will check the budget for all internal order postings, but that it will check only the orders for which you've assigned a budget and activated the availability control.

The customizing of CO-OPA budgeting is made up of six sequential steps:

1. Maintain the budget profile.
2. Maintain number ranges for budgeting.
3. Define tolerance limits for the availability control.
4. Specify exempt cost elements from the availability control.
5. Set up the availability control again.
6. Maintain the budget manager.

Next, we'll walk through how to customize each step.

4.3.1   Maintain Budget Profile

In the budget profile, you customize the behavior of CO-OPA budgeting by defining parameters such as time frame, exchange rate type, and other parameters that you can see on the screen in Figure 4.33. To customize the budget profile, either use Transaction OKOB, or go to the IMG menu path Controlling • Internal Orders • Budgeting and Availability Control • Maintain Budget Profile. You can create a new one by clicking on New Entries, or you can change an existing one.

In the TIME FRAME section, you define for how many years in the past and how many years into the future you want to create the budget, and also whether the budget will be total values or annual values. If the ANNUAL VALUES indicator is flagged, you can split the overall budgeting by year.

By updating the EXCH. RATE TYPE field in the Currency TRANSLATION: OVERALL BUDGET section, you can define the exchange rate type to be used in the budgeting process if the budget currency is different from the controlling area currency. If no value date is defined, the system will adopt the currency of the first day of each period from the currency type assigned here.

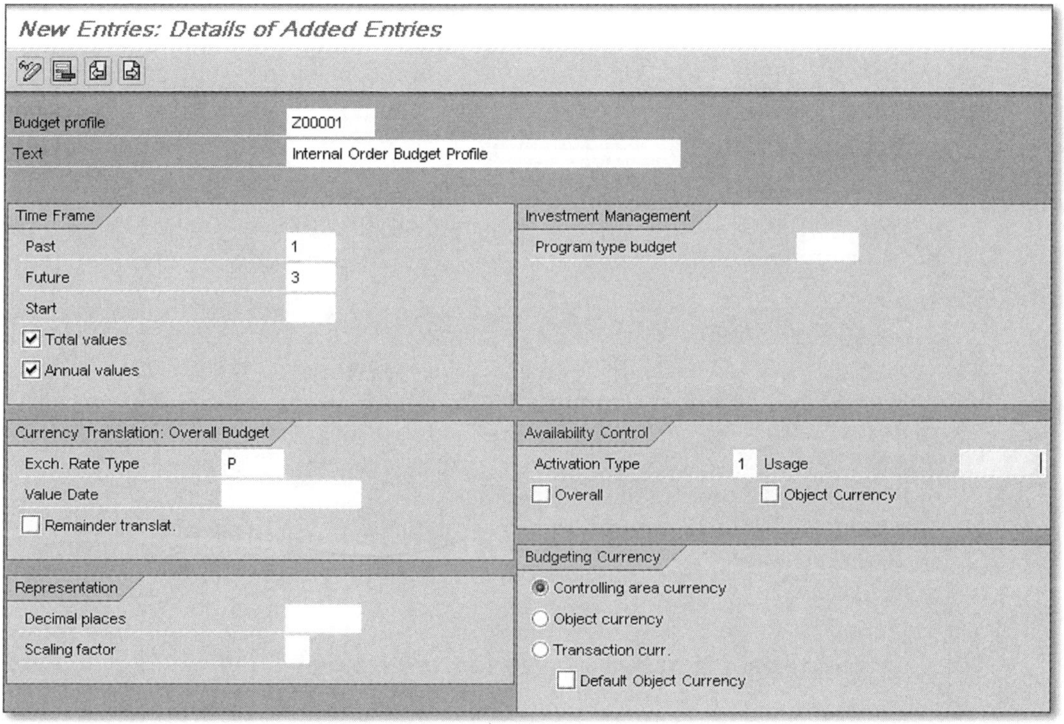

Figure 4.33 Maintain Budget Profile

The REPRESENTATION section allows you to define the decimal places for the budgeting amounts and also the scaling factor to be used.

The budget profile can be also be used in investment management, and if so, you can define the program type budget in the INVESTMENT MANAGEMENT section.

In the Availability Control section, you define how the system will consider the budget control. In the Activation Type field, you choose from the following three options:

- ▶ 0: Cannot be activated
- ▶ 1: Automatic activation during budget allocation
- ▶ 2: Background activation

You can also set whether the budget control should consider the overall budget or by year. Overall, in this case, means that the Total values option is flagged in the Time Frame section, and also whether the budget control will be performed in the object currency rather than in the controlling area currency.

In the last section, Budgeting Currency, you set the currency by choosing from the following options: Controlling area currency, Object currency, or Transaction curr. If you select Transaction curr, you then have the option to also check the Default object currency box, which means the system will always default the object currency (from the company code) as the budget currency at the time of planning.

> **Note**
>
> You can create the budget in the company code currency, but the availability control will always be performed in the controlling area currency. One example is a controlling area with USD as currency and a company code assigned to this controlling area with EUR as company code currency. You can create the budget in EUR, but the SAP system will convert the budget to USD and perform the availability control in USD, so if there is any difference in the exchange rate during the period it will compromise the availability of the budget in the internal order.

4.3.2 Maintain Number Ranges for Budgeting

The budget number range is not dependent on the controlling area. To define the internal order budget number range, you must define the number range 04 provided for order budgeting. To define the budgeting number range, either use Transaction OK11 or go to IMG menu path Controlling • Internal Orders • Budgeting and Availability Control • Maintain Number Ranges for Budgeting. Click on Change Intervals on the first screen, and you can see the intervals in Figure 4.34.

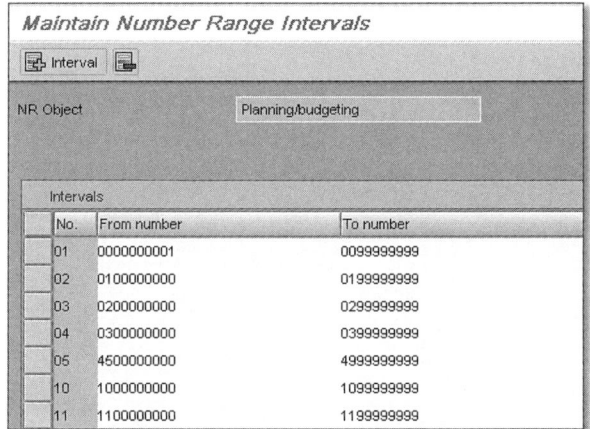

Figure 4.34 Budget Number Range

4.3.3 Define Tolerance Limits for Availability Control

If you want the SAP system to control the internal order budget, after defining the budget profile, you must create the tolerance limits for the budget profile. In the tolerance limits, you can define if any overspending should trigger a warning message or a hard error preventing posting of the transaction. If you don't define tolerance limits, the system won't check for budget availability when users create postings to the internal order. This would be the correct action if you want to define a budget for information reporting but not restrict users from creating transactions that would overspend the budget.

You create the tolerance limits for the budget profile by going to IMG menu path CONTROLLING • INTERNAL ORDERS • BUDGETING AND AVAILABILITY CONTROL • DEFINE TOLERANCE LIMITS FOR AVAILABILITY CONTROL.

Figure 4.35 shows the customizing screen for the tolerance limits. The definitions are made by controlling area, budget profile, and transaction group, where you can select for which kind of process you want to activate the tolerance limits. You can activate for all processes or for only selected ones, such as purchase requisitions. When the budget consumption reaches the amount specified in the USAGE IN % column, the system will perform the action assigned to the line. If you want to define an absolute variance amount for the action, you also have that option in this customizing screen.

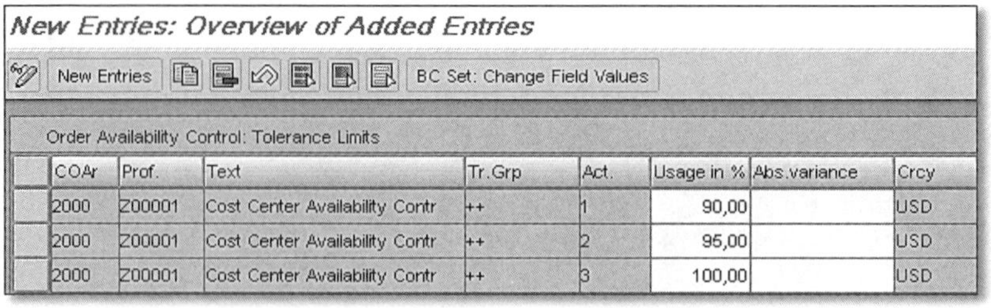

New Entries: Overview of Added Entries

New Entries | BC Set: Change Field Values

Order Availability Control: Tolerance Limits

COAr	Prof.	Text	Tr.Grp	Act.	Usage in %	Abs.variance	Crcy
2000	Z00001	Cost Center Availability Contr	++	1	90,00		USD
2000	Z00001	Cost Center Availability Contr	++	2	95,00		USD
2000	Z00001	Cost Center Availability Contr	++	3	100,00		USD

Figure 4.35 Tolerance Limits

Select one of three actions in the Act. column:

- 1: Warning
- 2: Warning with mail to person responsible
- 3: Error message

In the example shown in Figure 4.35, the system will consider postings from all transactional areas for the budget tolerance calculations and will issue a warning when the actual amounts reach 90% of the budget, will issue another warning message plus send an email to the person responsible (budget manager) when the amounts reach 95%, and will prevent postings that would exceed 100%.

Some business scenarios require flexibility for the tolerance limits by excluding some cost elements from the availability control. You can customize it further by specifying exempt cost elements from availability control.

4.3.4 Specify Exempt Cost Elements from Availability Control

You can define by controlling area which cost element you want to be ignored in the internal order availability control, as you can see in Figure 4.36. Use Transaction OPTK or go to IMG menu path Controlling • Internal Orders • Budgeting and Availability Control • Specify Exempt Cost Elements from Availability Control.

The definition of which cost elements are going to be exempt from the internal order budget control is by controlling area. Typically, organizations that want to use this exempting are excluding cost elements that are posted during a business process other than purchasing that they do not want to be interrupted, for instance, labor costs from payroll processing. In other circumstances, instead of setting up exempt cost elements, you may only have single-occurrence needs to remove the availability control temporarily.

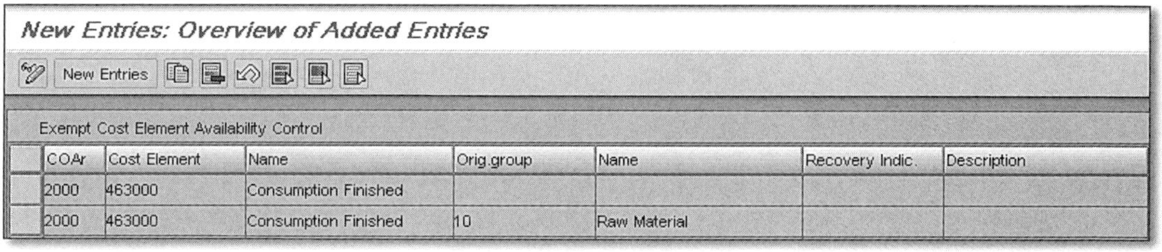

	COAr	Cost Element	Name	Orig.group	Name	Recovery Indic.	Description
New Entries: Overview of Added Entries							
Exempt Cost Element Availability Control							
	2000	463000	Consumption Finished				
	2000	463000	Consumption Finished	10	Raw Material		

Figure 4.36 Exempt Cost Elements

4.3.5 Set Up Availability Control Again

If for some reason you have to temporarily deactivate the availability control for an internal order (e.g., so that you can post a reclassification of values), you can activate the availability control again using this functionality, as long as the budget has not been exceeded for the internal order. To reactivate or reconstruct the availability control for orders, you can use Transaction KO31, or go to IMG menu path CONTROLLING • INTERNAL ORDERS • BUDGETING AND AVAILABILITY CONTROL • SET UP AVAILABILITY CONTROL AGAIN.

As you can see in Figure 4.37, you can perform the reconstruction of the availability control for a single order, for a range of orders, or by order types.

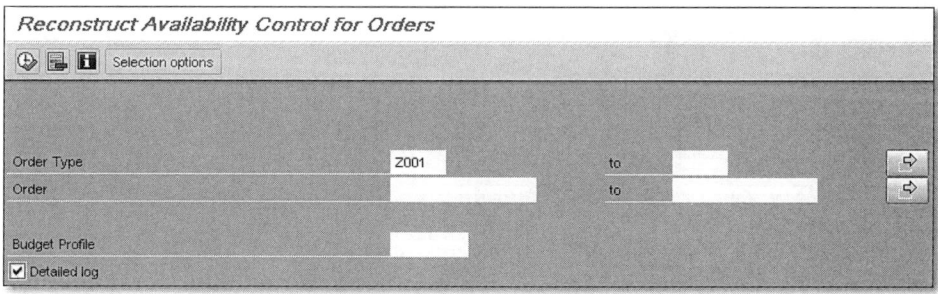

Figure 4.37 Reconstruct Availability Control

The last step in the budgeting and availability control for internal orders is to define the budgeting manager.

4.3.6 Maintain Budget Manager

The budget manager is the SAP user who will receive the email when specified tolerance levels are reached (if this option was selected in the availability control, as discussed in Section 4.3.3). Use Transaction OK14 or go to IMG menu path CONTROLLING • INTERNAL ORDERS • BUDGETING AND AVAILABILITY CONTROL • MAINTAIN BUDGET MANAGER.

You can define the budget manager by controlling area, order type, and object class, as shown in Figure 4.38. If you don't want to restrict by order type or order class and define just one budget manager, leave the ORDER TYPE and OBJCL fields blank.

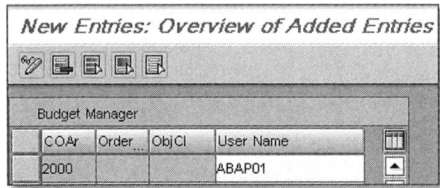

Figure 4.38 Budget Manager

> **Note**
>
> The budget manager user name must exist in all SAP ERP environments such as development, quality, and production. If the budget usage reaches the activity level where the system is supposed to send an email to the budget manager and the user doesn't exist, a system error will be received by the user entering the triggering transaction saying that the budget manager does not exist.

Now that you've defined all of the necessary customizing for the budgeting and availability, you must assign the budget profile to the order type using Transaction KOT2. You can see how the assignment is made in Figure 4.39.

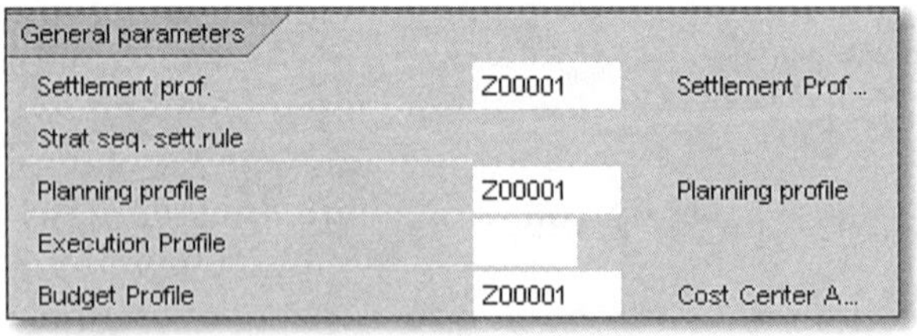

Figure 4.39 Budget Profile Order Type Assignment

Now that we've covered all of the steps in customizing availability control for CO-OPA, we'll now demonstrate how the availability control works by showing the entire process for an example internal order. We'll first create an internal order using Transaction KO01, assign a budget to the internal order using Transaction KO22, and then post actual values to the internal order using Transaction FB50 to see the behavior of the system when the budget is reached. You can see these steps in Figure 4.40, Figure 4.41, Figure 4.42, and Figure 4.43, respectively.

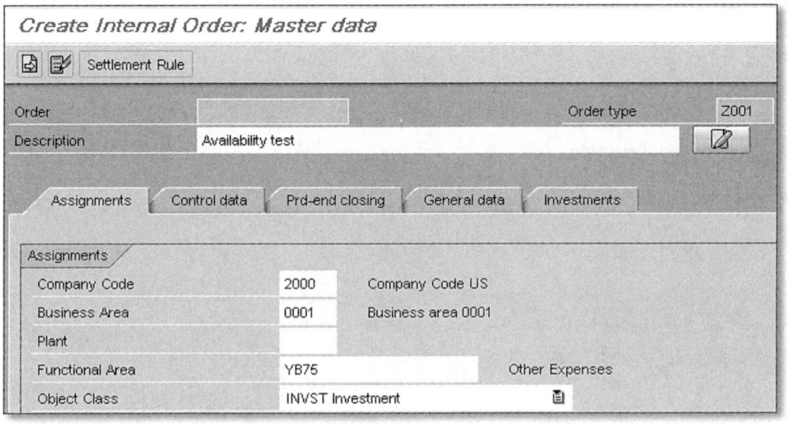

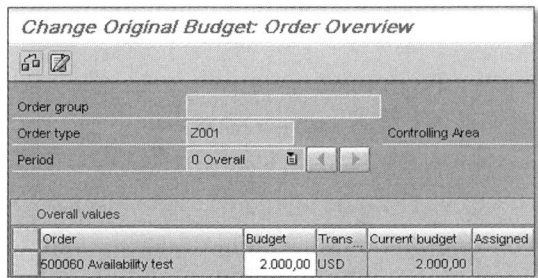

Figure 4.40 Create Internal Order

Figure 4.41 Define Budget for Internal Order

You can see in this example that the values posted in the first line of Figure 4.42 exceeded the budget value from Figure 4.41, and that the system issued an error as shown in Figure 4.43.

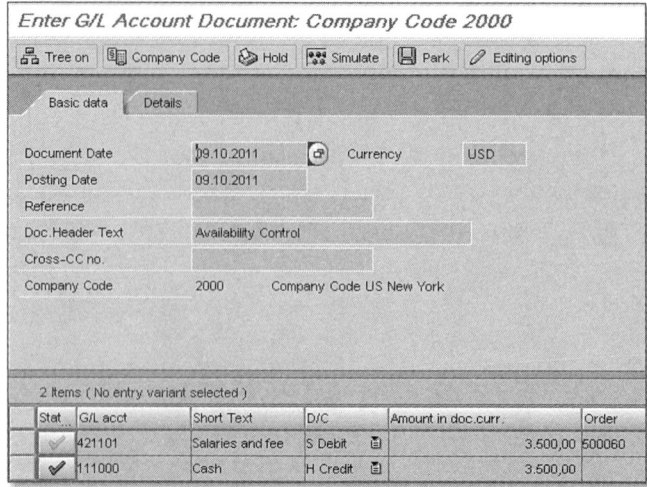

Figure 4.42 Actual Posting

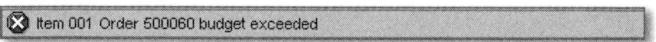

Figure 4.43 System Behavior When Budget Is Exceeded

Now that you know how to customize the budgeting and availability control for internal orders and understand how the budget and availability controls work, next you'll learn how to activate the commitments functionality for CO-OPA.

4.4 Commitments and Funds Commitments

The same functionality for commitments that you saw for CO-CCA is available for CO-OPA. Remember that commitments are payment obligations that have not yet occurred and therefore are not entered into the accounts but will lead to actual costs at a future date. Commitments can originate from either purchase requisitions or purchase orders. If an internal order is entered as the cost object in a purchase requisition or purchase order, and you have commitments activated, you can see the value in the internal order commitments reports. Commitments will also use the available budget for the internal order if the availability control is activated and can therefore be a good tool to manage the costs and to prevent overspending of budgeted amounts.

To use commitments in CO-OPA, first you need to activate commitment management in the controlling area settings using Transaction OKKP. You can see the COMMIT. MANAGEMENT field in Figure 4.44. There are two options available: COMPONENTS ACTIVE or COMPONENTS NOT ACTIVE.

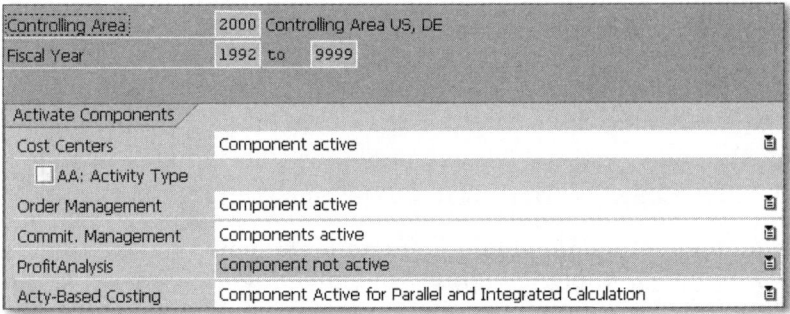

Figure 4.44 Controlling Area Commitment Customizing

You need to also set the commitment management to active by selecting the COMMIT. MANAGEMENT checkbox in the order type customizing using Transaction KOT2, as you can see in Figure 4.45.

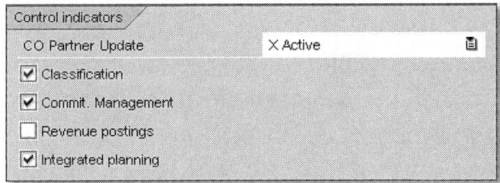

Figure 4.45 Commitment Management in Order Type Customizing

By selecting this checkbox, you are activating the commitments line items for internal orders assigned to this order type.

Note

If you activate commitments, we strongly recommend that you follow the practice of marking the final invoice indicator on the purchase order when all of the goods have been received for two reasons: to avoid showing commitments for remaining amounts in internal order commitments reports, and to avoid the available budget being committed by these remaining values. By marking the final invoice indicator on the purchase order, indicating that it is completely received and invoiced, you can clear any remaining commitments for this purchase order.

You now know and have created all customizing related to commitments for CO-OPA. The next area to cover in the internal order customizing is the actual posting.

4.5 Actual Postings

No additional customizing is necessary for the actual posting. When you customized the order type, planning, budgeting, and settlement profile, you also defined the customizing for actual postings. The definitions made for the settlement profile for planning purposes will also be used in managing actual postings.

The only thing to mention regarding actual posting is that when you are creating an internal order, you can propose a settlement rule for it. The settlement rule will define which object will receive the order values after it is settled. To define the automatic generation of the settlement rule, you must customize three steps:

1. Display strategies for automatic generation of settlement rules.

2. Create strategy sequences for automatic generation of settlement rules.

3. Assign a strategy sequence to the order type.

In the display strategies screen, you can see the available standard SAP ERP options to define the settlement rule, as shown in Figure 4.46. You can review the available options using this display transaction to determine in advance how you'll use them in your custom strategy sequence. Go to IMG menu path CONTROLLING • INTERNAL ORDERS • ACTUAL POSTINGS • SETTLEMENT • AUTOMATIC GENERATION OF SETTLEMENT RULES • DISPLAY STRATEGIES FOR AUTOMATIC GENERATION OF SETTLEMENT RULES.

Using the standard strategies provided by SAP ERP, you can create the strategy sequence for the automatic generation of the settlement rule, as you can see in Figure 4.47. You create the strategy sequence by going to IMG menu path CONTROLLING • INTERNAL ORDERS • ACTUAL POSTINGS • SETTLEMENT • AUTOMATIC GENERATION OF SETTLEMENT RULES • STRATEGY SEQUENCES FOR AUTOMATIC GENERATION OF SETTLEMENT RULES.

You can create your own strategy sequence or use one provided by SAP ERP. Select one strategy on the right side of the screen, and double-click on STRATEGIES on the left side, which brings you to Figure 4.48.

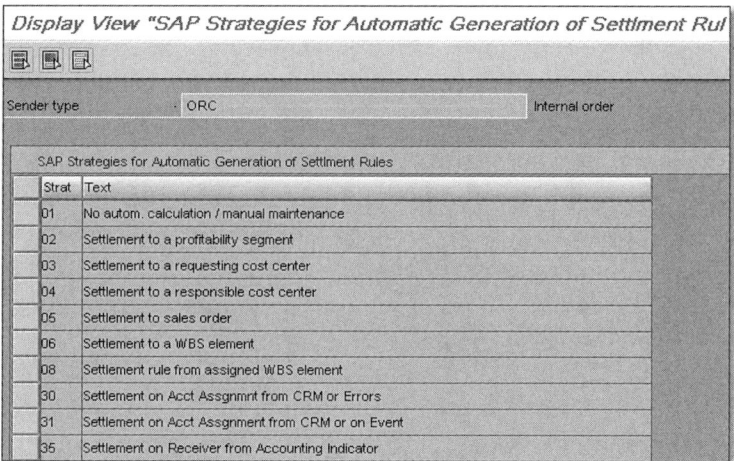

Figure 4.46 Strategies for Automatic Generation of Settlement Rule

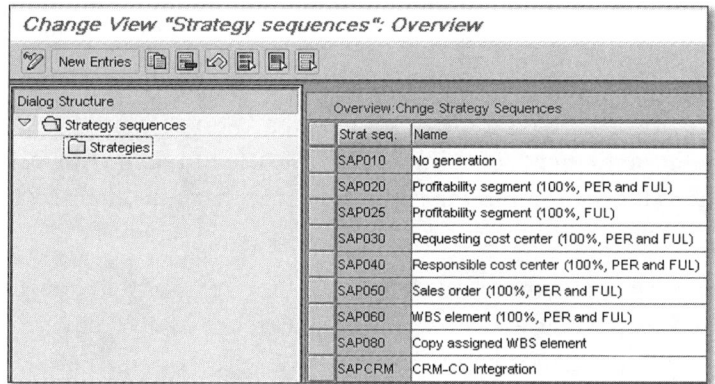

Figure 4.47 Strategy Sequence

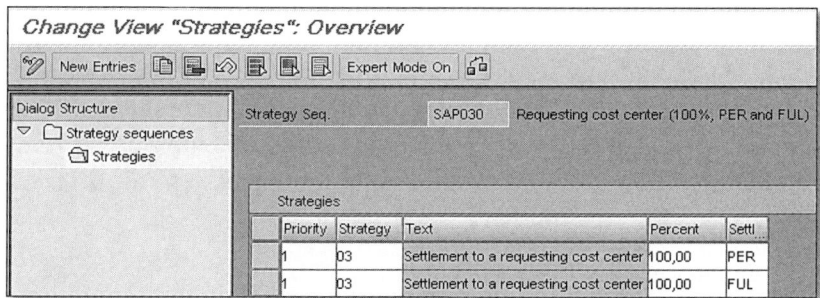

Figure 4.48 Strategies

You define the priority and enter the strategy that you selected by reviewing the list of those available in the screen shown earlier in Figure 4.46. In the example shown in Figure 4.48, the system will propose the settlement rule for both periodic and full settlement using the requesting cost center in the internal order master data. In this situation, you may want to define this field as a required field in the order type customizing (shown in Section 4.1.1), and then it will always have an entry. After creating the sequence, you need to assign the sequence to the order type by going to IMG menu path CONTROLLING • INTERNAL ORDERS • ACTUAL POSTINGS • SETTLEMENT • AUTOMATIC GENERATION OF SETTLEMENT RULES • ASSIGN STRATEGY SEQUENCE TO ORDER TYPE, as shown in Figure 4.49.

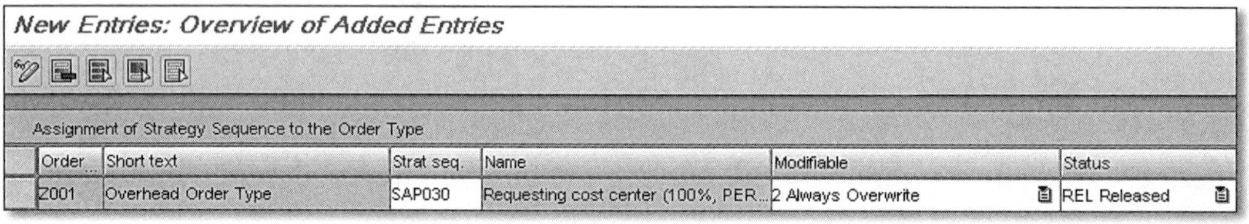

New Entries: Overview of Added Entries					
Assignment of Strategy Sequence to the Order Type					
Order	Short text	Strat seq.	Name	Modifiable	Status
Z001	Overhead Order Type	SAP030	Requesting cost center (100%, PER...	2 Always Overwrite	REL Released

Figure 4.49 Assign Strategy Sequence to Order Type

In this step, you define the order type strategy sequence and also determine if it's possible to overwrite the settlement rule. The last field is used to define the call point of the automatic determination of the settlement rule. It can be defined as at creation, release, or technical completion.

Now that you've learned all about internal orders—how they are used and how to customize the settings to control how they will behave in your SAP ERP environment—let's discuss the CO-OPA information system.

4.6 Information System

As it does with CO-CEL and CO-CCA, SAP ERP provides a large number of standard reports for internal orders that can be found in the user menu under information system for internal orders by following the user menu path ACCOUNTING • CONTROLLING • INTERNAL ORDERS • INFORMATION SYSTEM • REPORTS FOR INTERNAL ORDERS, where you can find the following reporting folders:

► Plan/actual comparisons
► Actual/actual comparisons

- ► Planning reports
- ► Line items
- ► Master data indexes
- ► Summarization reports
- ► More reports

You can choose from several different reports from inside each folder. The following are a few examples of some reports for internal orders. The first report example is using S_ALR_87012993 – Orders: Actual/Plan/Variance. See Figure 4.50 for the selection screen and Figure 4.51 for the report.

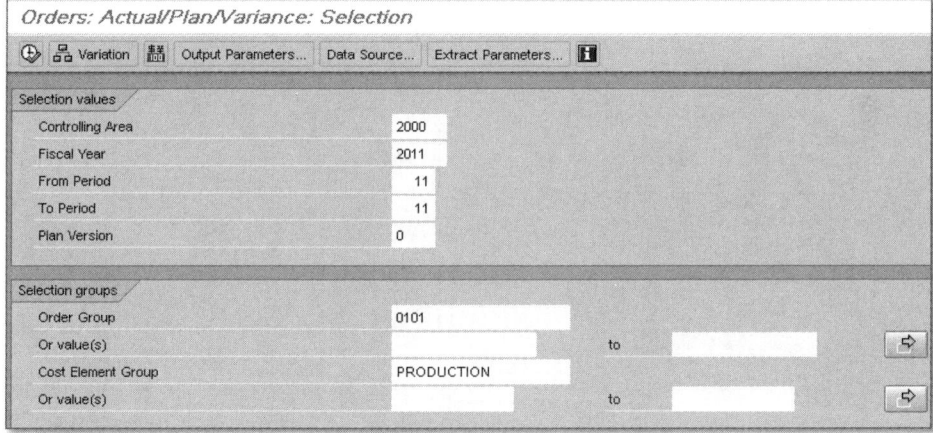

Figure 4.50 Internal Order Actual/Plan/Variance Report Selection Screen

The selection for this report can be for an individual order, multiple orders, or an order group.

As you can see in the report output, when you run it for an order group, you can either view the results in total or navigate among individual orders using the navigation pane on the left. This can save time in reviewing order data because you only need to execute the report once to see the group totals but can also see the individual order details in the same report.

Another important report is the S_ALR_87013019 – List: Budget/Actual/Commitments, where you can see the budget values for the internal order compared with the actual and the commitments. Consult the examples in Figure 4.52 and Figure 4.53, showing the selection screen and report, respectively.

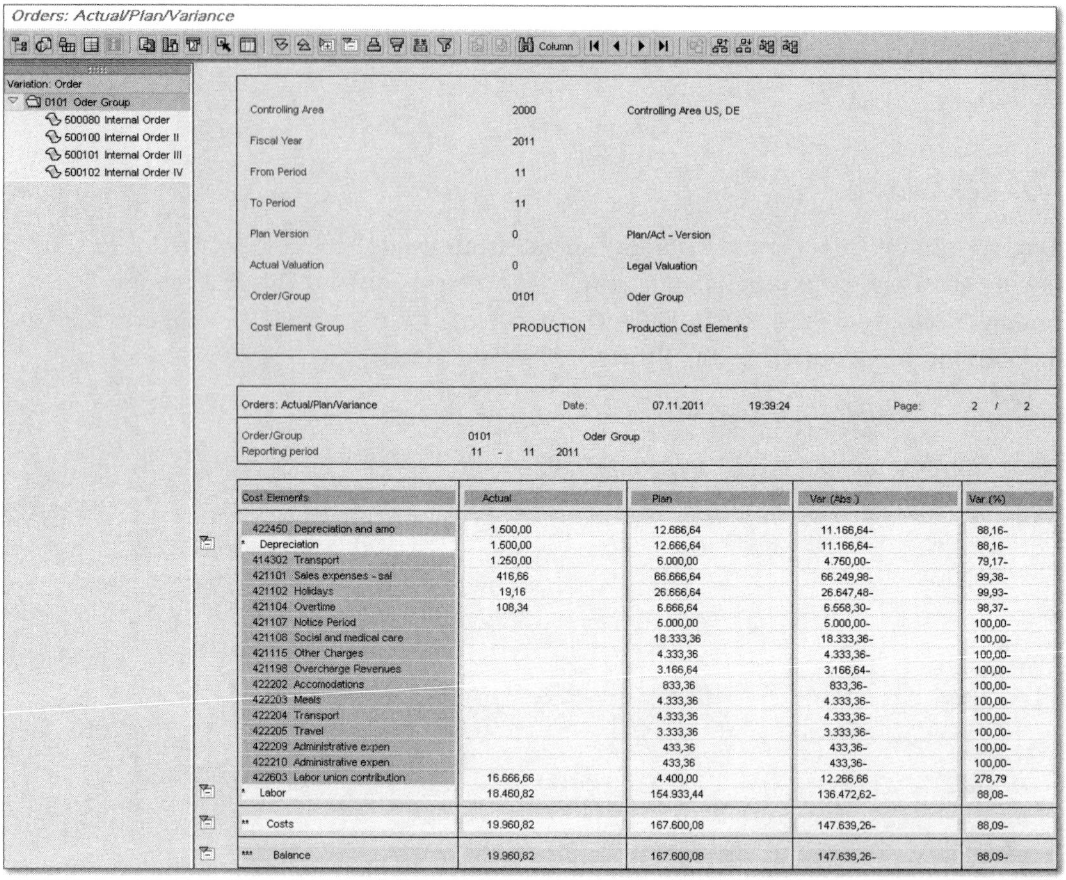

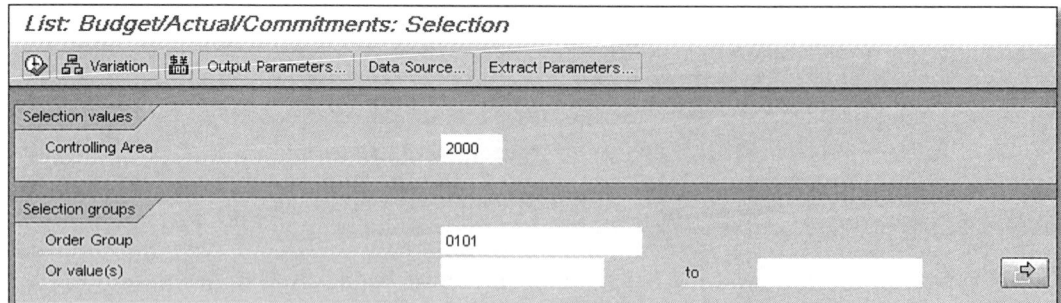

Orders: Actual/Plan/Variance
Column
Variation: Order
0101 Oder Group
500080 Internal Order
500100 Internal Order II
500101 Internal Order III
500102 Internal Order IV
Controlling Area 2000 Controlling Area US, DE
Fiscal Year 2011
From Period 11
To Period 11
Plan Version 0 Plan/Act - Version
Actual Valuation 0 Legal Valuation
Order/Group 0101 Oder Group
Cost Element Group PRODUCTION Production Cost Elements
Orders: Actual/Plan/Variance Date: 07.11.2011 19:39:24 Page: 2 / 2
Order/Group 0101 Oder Group
Reporting period 11 - 11 2011
Cost Elements Actual Plan Var (Abs.) Var (%)
422450 Depreciation and amo 1.500,00 12.666,64 11.166,64- 88,16-
* Depreciation 1.500,00 12.666,64 11.166,64- 88,16-
414302 Transport 1.250,00 6.000,00 4.750,00- 79,17-
421101 Sales expenses - sal 416,66 66.666,64 66.249,98- 99,38-
421102 Holidays 19,16 26.666,64 26.647,48- 99,93-
421104 Overtime 108,34 6.666,64 6.558,30- 98,37-
421107 Notice Period 5.000,00 5.000,00- 100,00-
421108 Social and medical care 18.333,36 18.333,36- 100,00-
421115 Other Charges 4.333,36 4.333,36- 100,00-
421198 Overcharge Revenues 3.166,64 3.166,64- 100,00-
422202 Accomodations 833,36 833,36- 100,00-
422203 Meals 4.333,36 4.333,36- 100,00-
422204 Transport 4.333,36 4.333,36- 100,00-
422205 Travel 3.333,36 3.333,36- 100,00-
422209 Administrative expen 433,36 433,36- 100,00-
422210 Administrative expen 433,36 433,36- 100,00-
422603 Labor union contribution 16.666,66 4.400,00 12.266,66 278,79
* Labor 18.460,82 154.933,44 136.472,62- 88,08-
** Costs 19.960,82 167.600,08 147.639,26- 88,09-
*** Balance 19.960,82 167.600,08 147.639,26- 88,09-

Figure 4.51 Internal Order Report Example

List: Budget/Actual/Commitments: Selection
Variation
Output Parameters...
Data Source...
Extract Parameters...
Selection values
Controlling Area
2000
Selection groups
Order Group
0101
Or value(s)
to

Figure 4.52 Internal Order Budget/Actual/Commitments Report Selection

Again, in this report example, you can see that order groups are important for report selections. If groups are not logically defined in a way to facilitate report selections, then users must maintain variants for the orders they want to see together.

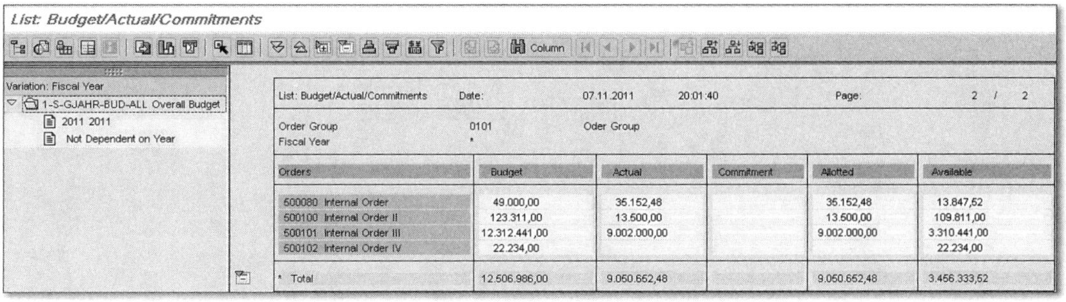

Figure 4.53 Internal Order Budget/Actual/Commitment Reports

In the report output, you can navigate through the levels of the group structure using the navigation pane on the left side. The right side displays a listing of order totals for budget, actual, commitments, allotted (actual plus commitments), and available (budget less allotted).

For internal order line-item reports, you can choose from the following transactions:

- KOB1: Orders: Actual Line Items
- KOB2: Orders: Commitment Line Items
- KOBP: Orders: Plan Line Items
- KOB4: Orders: Budget Line Items
- KSB5: CO Documents: Actual Costs
- KABP: CO Plan Documents
- KO2B: Display Budget Document

Additional reports are available for internal orders that are accessed by Transaction GRR3, shown in Figure 4.54.

The most common library for internal order Report Painter reports is 601 – Internal Orders, where you can find most of the internal orders reports. Select the desired report, and click on EXECUTE on the top menu.

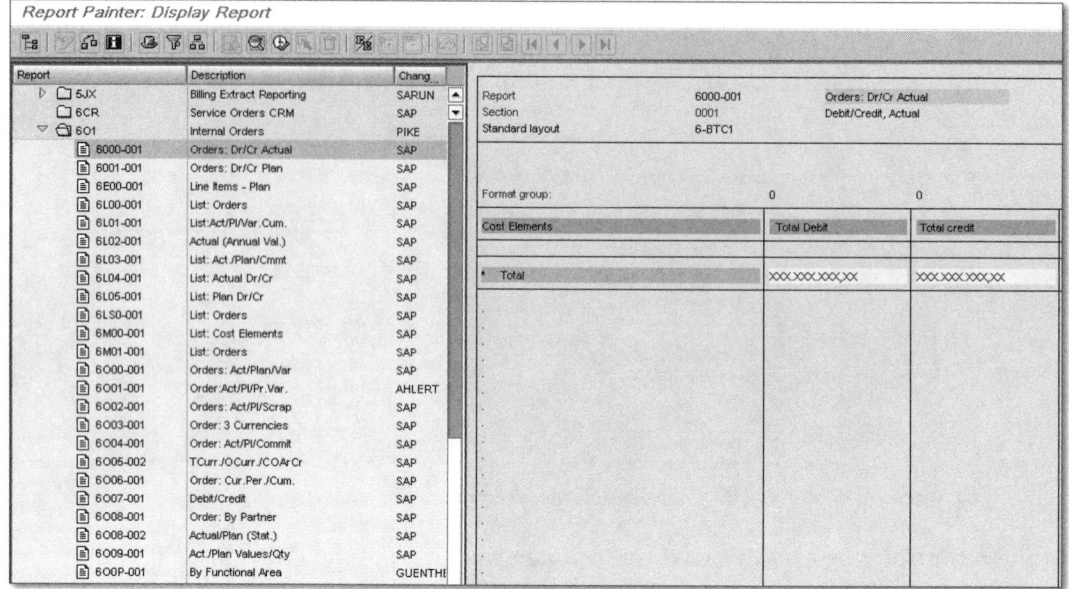

Figure 4.54 Internal Order Report Painter Example

In the same manner as for Cost Center Accounting reports, you can also import and generate SAP ERP standard reports from SAP ERP client 000 if for some reason the report stops working. The import process is the same as described in Chapter 3; use Transaction OKD6 to import them and Transaction OKSA to generate them.

4.7 Summary

By combining CO-CCA with CO-OPA, managers are able to track and distinguish costs in a variety of ways to meet different needs from the same transactional information.

The internal order can be viewed as a magnifier view of the organization's costs, allowing managers to see costs in both an overall and detailed manner. While CO-CCA allows visibility of cost information by functional area, internal orders facilitate another view of cost data and allow additional tracking by defined project, task, or other time-defined purpose. A thoughtful strategy in setting up internal order accounting (e.g., your decisions about how to use availability control and how you'll define groups) can provide an organization with virtually unlimited flexibility to track, budget, control, and report on cost information.

In this chapter, you've learned the principles of internal order master data by learning how to create the order type, control the internal orders by using status management, and define how the internal order costs will be settled. You also learned how to create the necessary customizing for CO-OPA planning.

When you learned about creating the customizing for the budget and availability control, you saw one of the most powerful functions of internal orders: the possibility to control and restrict further posting when the budget of an internal order is reached, which is different from cost center budgeting where you can't restrict the posting if the budget is exceeded.

Also, by customizing the commitments, you've learned how to enable tracking and to manage costs using internal order reporting allowing management to react proactively before they overspend or overcommit available funds.

Now that you have a good understanding of this amazing SAP ERP functionality, you are ready to move on to the next chapter, where we'll learn about Activity-Based Costing (CO-ABC) in SAP ERP.

5 Activity-Based Costing

Activity-Based Costing (CO-ABC) is used to bring to the business a more detailed level and a different view of cost allocations, increasing cost transparency. It provides an additional method to manage company overhead costs: the process-oriented method. It enhances CO-CCA and product costing coverage, allowing you to allocate costs with more accuracy by using cost drivers.

Let's begin by looking at some process examples using CO-ABC. To measure a procurement process, you can use the number of purchase orders created in the system. With this value, you can create a cost driver to measure the cost of each purchase order created, and then track the efficiency of the procurement cost center. The same idea can be applied for released purchase orders. Another example is to measure the master data maintenance process; you can create a cost driver to measure how many new materials were created, changed, or deleted.

You can see from these examples that basically you can create a cost driver for any process for which you want to measure and be able to report the cost.

You can distinguish between two approaches in CO-ABC: the "pull" method and the "push" method. The pull method uses a quantity input to trace the business process cost; the value will be defined by Input Quantity × Quantity Price, in the same manner as you saw for activity allocations in CO-CCA. The push method is called a direct distribution of costs, where you'll use an assessment or a distribution to evaluate the business process. The push method is the traditional approach to CO-ABC and is simple to implement, whereas the pull method is the more advanced CO-ABC implementation and requires more details and a more specific understanding of cost behavior.

The diagram in Figure 5.1 shows how cost center values can be settled to other cost objects.

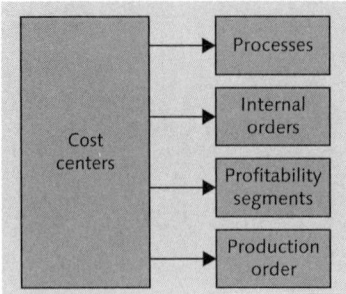

Figure 5.1 Cost Center Cost Allocation

To allocate costs from cost centers to other cost objects, you can use assessments, distributions, or activity allocations, which you saw in Chapter 3. When you use assessments and distributions to send cost center values to business processes, you are using the push method; if you use an activity type or a template to perform the allocation, you are using the pull method.

Figure 5.2 shows how the business processes can interact with other Controlling (CO) objects.

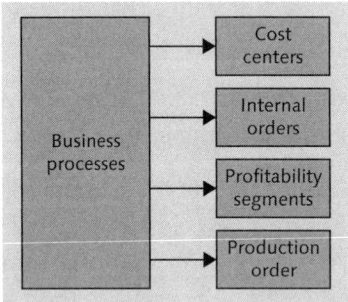

Figure 5.2 Business Process Cost Interaction

The business process also can return costs to cost centers or send them to other cost objects using assessments and distributions (push method), or quantity allocation (pull method). Template allocation is also available.

To use CO-ABC in SAP ERP, you must activate it in the controlling area settings using Transaction OKKP, as shown in Figure 5.3.

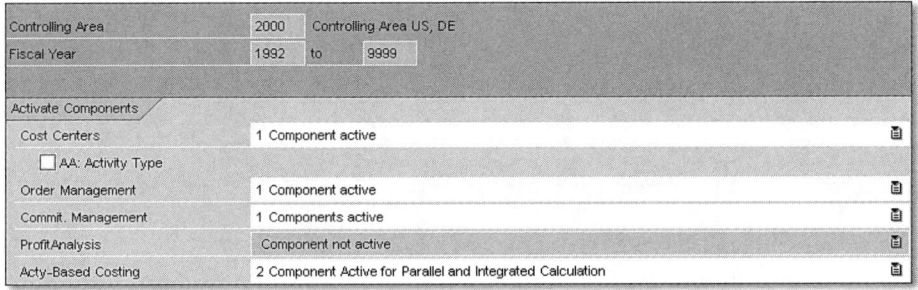

Figure 5.3 Controlling Area Settings, CO-ABC Activation

You can choose from three options for the ACTY-BASED COSTING field:

▶ COMPONENT NOT ACTIVE
The component is not activated. This is the default value when you establish the controlling area.

▶ COMPONENT ACTIVE FOR PARALLEL CALCULATION
The component is activated, but there are no actual postings in the version. All of the postings will be statistical in the delta version created for CO-ABC. The delta version is statistical. You can use this option to analyze your organization's subareas.

▶ COMPONENT ACTIVE FOR PARALLEL AND INTEGRATED CALCULATION
The component is activated without restriction. The business process will be credited with actual values in the version.

The next step in CO-ABC customizing is to establish the master data.

5.1   Master Data

CO-ABC master data customizing defines the basic structures for business processes, such as a standard hierarchy, attributes, business process groups, and others.

CO-ABC requires a standard hierarchy in the same way that CO-CCA does, but the way to create the first node for the standard hierarchy is different. In CO-CCA, you define the first node in the controlling area settings, as demonstrated in Chapter 3. For CO-ABC, you define the first node using Transaction 0KW1 or by going to CONTROLLING • ACTIVITY-BASED COSTING • MAINTAIN STANDARD HIERARCHY for Controlling Area. Either of these steps will bring you to the screen shown in Figure 5.4.

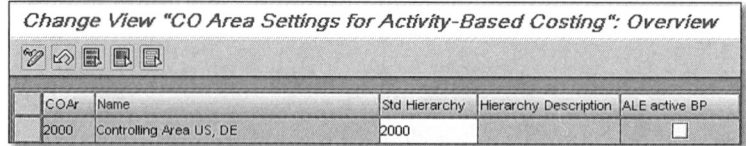

Figure 5.4 CO-ABC Standard Hierarchy First Node

In this step of the customizing, you define the first node for the standard hierarchy. You'll define the other nodes using a specific transaction for CO-ABC standard hierarchy that can be found in Controlling • Activity-Based Costing • Master Data • Business Processes • Maintain Standard Hierarchy of Business Processes. Figure 5.5 shows the standard hierarchy customizing screen.

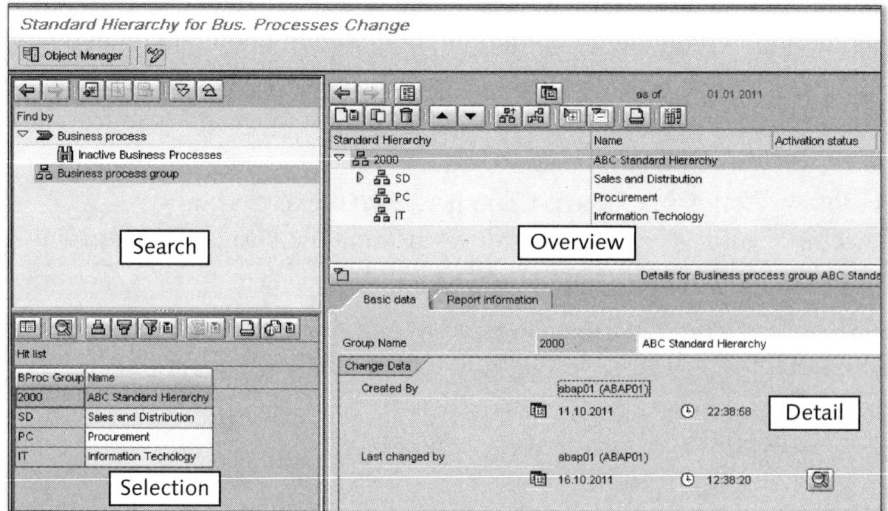

Figure 5.5 CO-ABC Standard Hierarchy

The standard hierarchy is divided into four areas:

► Search
► Selection
► Overview
► Details

In the search area, you'll create the search criteria for business processes, and the results will be displayed in the selection area. By selecting the business process or group in the selection area, you can see the overview of the results; if you select one group or business process in the overview, the detail is shown in the detail area.

In the overview area, you can maintain the nodes by creating new nodes or copying an existing node. You can also define a business process from the overview. The advantage of maintaining the standard hierarchy from this transaction is the drag-and-drop functionality, which lets you quickly move groups or business processes.

SAP ERP provides four additional groups of attributes to be added to business process master data that will be used to create reporting breakdowns. You can create as many attributes as you want inside each group. The following groups are available (and shown in Figure 5.6):

▶ BUSINESS PROCESS CATEGORIES

▶ COST BEHAVIOR

▶ VALUE ADDED RANKING

▶ ADDITIONAL ATTRIBUTES

To maintain the process categories for the groups, you can go to CONTROLLING • ACTIVITY-BASED COSTING • MASTER DATA • BUSINESS PROCESSES • DEFINE ATTRIBUTES. Figure 5.6 shows the Change View screen with some examples of process categories.

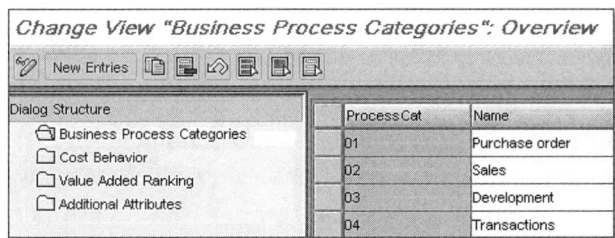

Figure 5.6 Attributes for Business Process

To customize the attributes for one group, select the group on the left side of the screen, and click on NEW ENTRIES. Add your defined process categories on the right side of the screen (e.g., see PURCHASE ORDER in Figure 5.6). Figure 5.7 shows an example of business process master data with the customized process category. The master data was created using Transaction CP01.

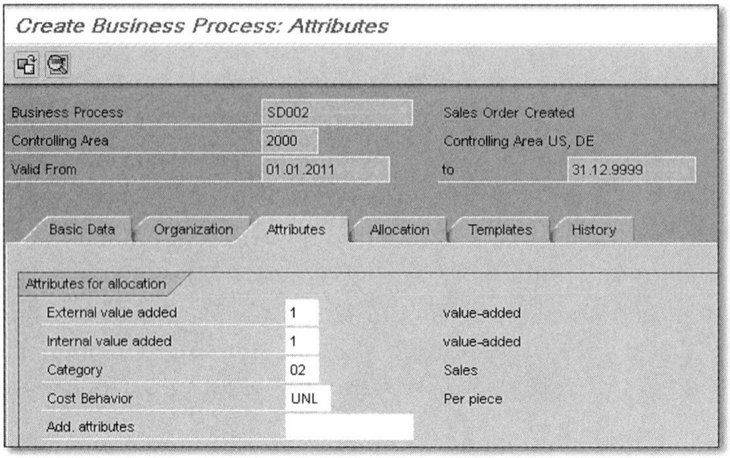

Create Business Process: Attributes

Business Process	SD002	Sales Order Created
Controlling Area	2000	Controlling Area US, DE
Valid From	01.01.2011	to 31.12.9999

Basic Data | Organization | Attributes | Allocation | Templates | History

Attributes for allocation

External value added	1	value-added
Internal value added	1	value-added
Category	02	Sales
Cost Behavior	UNL	Per piece
Add. attributes		

Figure 5.7 Attributes in Business Process Master Data

Business processes, as with other CO objects such as internal orders, cost centers, profit centers, and cost elements, can be grouped to streamline selections in reporting and also some customizing steps. Maintaining business process groups follows the same principle you've already seen for the others in previous chapters. You can create, modify, and display the groups using Transactions CPH1, CPH2, and CPH3, respectively.

Time-based fields are also available for business process master data, where you can determine whether SAP ERP will keep a record of the changes in the field's master data. Remember that you can only activate or deactivate some fields. You can't change the behavior, meaning that your options are recording the changes by day, period, or year, or not recording them at all. Use Transaction OKEZ, or go to CONTROLLING • ACTIVITY-BASED COSTING • MASTER DATA • BUSINESS PROCESSES • DETERMINE TIME-BASED FIELDS FOR BUSINESS PROCESSES. You can see the customizing screen in Figure 5.8.

It's easier to understand the business processes if you compare them to cost centers. Table 5.1 shows you the similarities and differences between business processes and cost centers. Note that only the last two rows are different, but it's important to understand these differences.

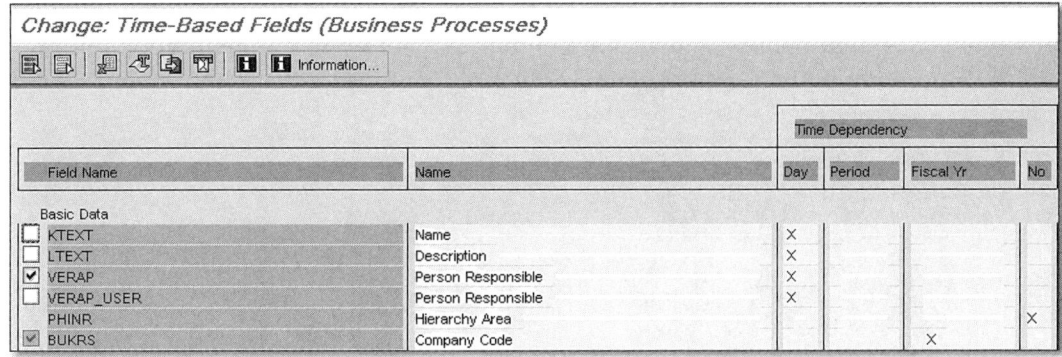

Figure 5.8 Time-Based Fields for Business Processes

	Business Process	Cost Center
Standard Hierarchy	Required	Required
Company Code	Required	Required
Profit Center	Optional	Optional
Grouping	Yes	Yes
Costs	Primary and secondary	Primary and secondary
Statistical Key Figure	Yes	Yes
Allocations	Yes	Yes
Output Measure	Yes (business process)	Yes (activity type)
Additional Attributes	Yes	No

Table 5.1 Business Process and Cost Center Comparison

One of the advantages of a CO-ABC process over a cost center is that CO-ABC can behave as a cost center and also as an activity type, meaning that it can be allocated by quantity to other cost objects. In Figure 5.2 earlier, you saw the available receiver cost objects from a sender business process. We've said that you can use assessments and distributions to perform the allocation, and you can also use the business process itself as an allocation object. In this case, the business process will behave as both a cost center and an activity type, and you must define a secondary cost element for allocation purposes. In Figure 5.9, on the ALLOCATION tab from the master data for a business process, you can see the definition of the allocation cost element and also how it must calculate the business process price in the PRICE INDICATOR field.

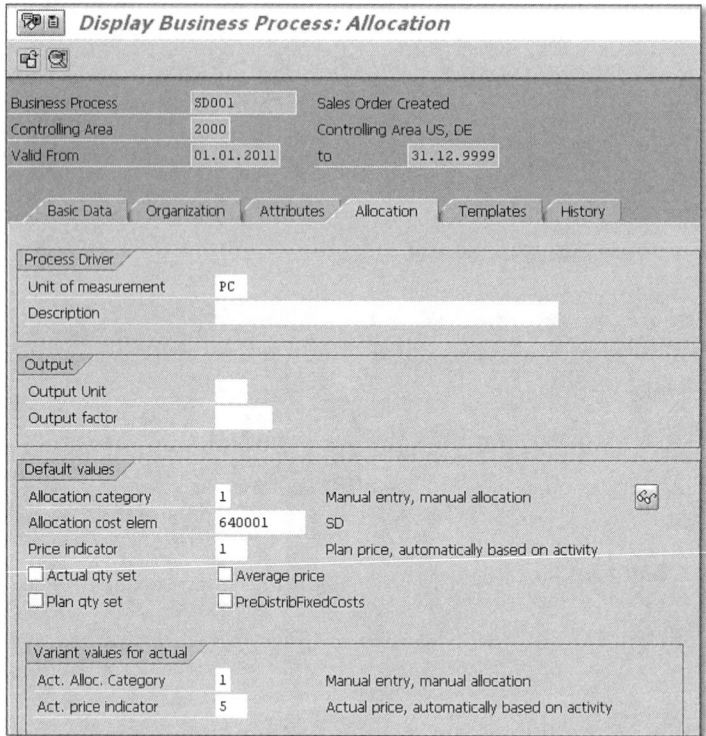

Figure 5.9 Business Process Allocation Tab

The secondary cost element used for allocation must be a category 43 (Internal activity allocation); its definition follows the same principles as the activity type definition already described in Chapter 3.

Now that you know how to establish the essential customizing to create business processes, let's move on to templates.

5.2   Templates

A template in CO-ABC is one of the available tools used to define the CO-ABC pull method, where an advanced CO-ABC can be implemented. With the pull method, you have a quantity structure and backflushing capability. Templates define the formulas to allocate costs. These formulas can use external sources, other SAP ERP sources, business processes, statistical key figures, or activity types as inputs to create the cost driver to be used to allocate the costs. The large number of possible inputs demonstrates how complex implementing CO-ABC using the pull method can be, but this complexity also provides significant flexibility to accommodate your business requirements.

To customize templates in CO-ABC, you must define the sender and receiver values and cost objects for the business process. To create a template, you also must select the environment for which the template will be available. Table 5.2 shows the most common template environments.

Environment	Description
001	Cost estimate/production orders
002	Reference and simulation costing
003	Cost estimate without quantity structure
004	Network
005	WBS element
006	General cost objects/CO hierarchy
007	Internal order
008	Sales order
009	Process order
010	Product cost collector
011	Service order
012	CO production order
PAC	Costing-based Profitability Analysis
PCA	Profit center planning
SBP	Business processes
SCD	Cost centers/activity types
SCI	Cost centers

Table 5.2 Templates Environment

To create a template, you can use Transaction CPT1, or go to CONTROLLING • ACTIVITY-BASED COSTING • TEMPLATES • MAINTAIN TEMPLATES. Figure 5.10 shows the first screen of template customizing you'll encounter.

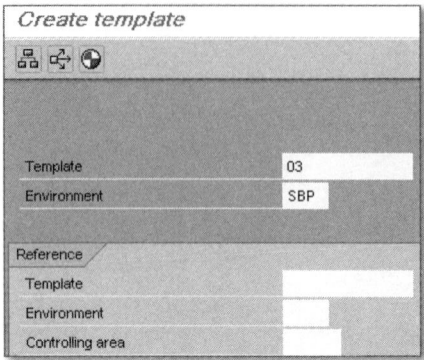

Figure 5.10 Maintain Template Initial Screen

You must define a template name and also select for which environment you want to create the template, remembering that the selected environment will define where you can use the template. You are ready to define the template itself after entering the template name and environment. You can see the next template customizing screen in Figure 5.11.

The first column in the template overview is TYPE. For this field, select from the following listed options:

▶ COMMENT ROW

▶ BUSINESS PROCESS

▶ SUB-TEMPLATE

▶ COST CENTER/ACTIVITY TYPE

▶ CALCULATION ROW (BUSINESS PROCESS)

▶ CALCULATION ROW (COST CENTER/ACTIVITY TYPE)

The template customizing can be simple as in the example in Figure 5.11, where a variable plan quantity was used to define the plan quantity, which is the sender business process. Another option is to add formulas to the quantities by using the available formulas on the lower-right side of the screen to create a complex template allocation. You can define how the template will work for both planning and actual values, using either fixed values or the available formulas.

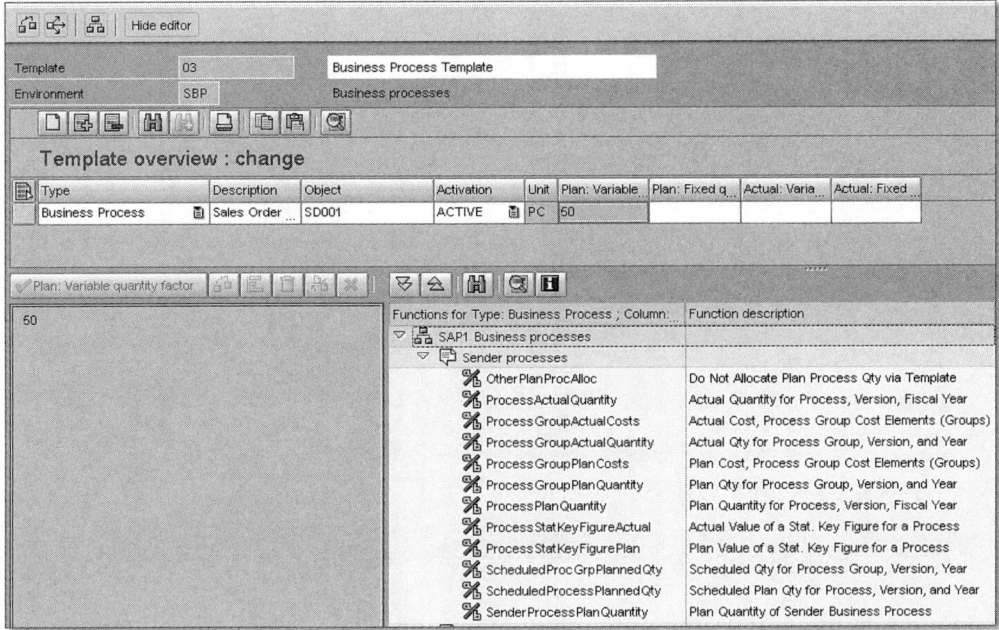

Figure 5.11 Template Customizing

You define the sender business process in the template definition. Next, you need to select which cost object will be the receiver. You can assign the template to either a business process or a cost center, remembering that only if you've selected the correct environment for the template customizing will it be available to be used in the selected cost object.

You define the template in the receiver cost object in the master data maintenance by using Transaction KS02 for a cost center and Transaction CP02 for a business process. Figure 5.12 shows an example of a template assignment to a cost center.

There are two definition options for formula planning:

▶ Activity-independent formula planning template (ACTY-INDEP. FORM.PLNG TEMP.)

▶ Activity-dependent formula planning template (ACTY-DEP. FORM.PLNG TEMP.)

For the activity-independent formula planning template, you must use environment CPI – ACTIVITY INDEP. COST CTR PLANNING, and for the activity-dependent formula planning template, you must use CPD – ACTIVITY DEP. COST CENTER PLANNING.

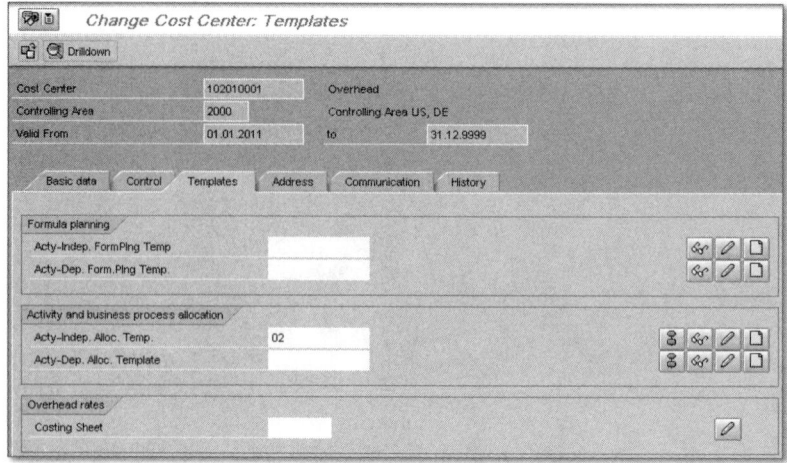

Figure 5.12 Cost Center Template Assignment

Similarly, you can also define two templates in activity and business process allocations:

- Activity-independent allocation template (ACTY-INDEP. ALLOC. TEMP.)
- Activity-dependent allocation template (ACTY-DEP. ALLOC. TEMPLATE)

For the activity-independent allocation template, you must use environment SCI – COST CENTER; for the activity dependent allocation template, you must use SCD – COST CENTERS/ACTIVITY TYPES.

Figure 5.13 shows an example of a template assignment to a business process.

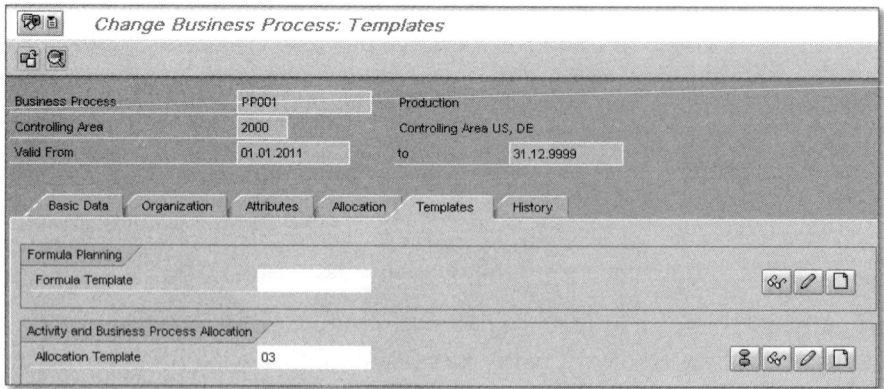

Figure 5.13 Business Process Template Assignment

There are two options for template assignments:

▶ Formula template

▶ Allocation template

In the Formula Template field, you must use environment BPP – Business pro-cess planning; in the Allocation Template field, you must use SBP – Business processes.

Next, you'll see an example of a planning template allocation for a cost center.

The process to create the example consists of two customizing steps and two transactional steps (normally performed by end users):

▶ Define the template.

▶ Assign the template.

▶ Run the template.

▶ Report.

To define a template to use in a cost center, use Transaction CPT1, and choose one of the following environments:

▶ CPI – Activity indep. cost ctr planning

▶ CPD – Activity dep. cost center planning

▶ SCI – Cost Center

▶ SCD – Cost centers/Activity types

We used SCI – Cost Centers in the example in Figure 5.14, which shows the tem-plate customizing screen.

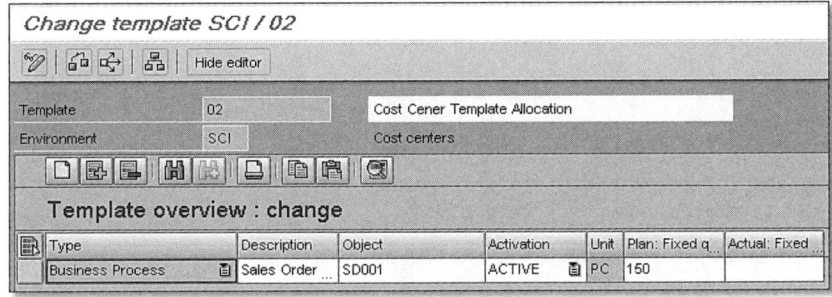

Figure 5.14 Template Definition – Cost Center Environment

In this template example, you can see that the sender is a business process (see the bottom left of the figure) and also that we used a fixed planning quantity (see the bottom right).

Because we've already assigned the template to a cost center in the step shown previously in Figure 5.12, the next step is to run the template allocation using Transaction CPPS, as shown in Figure 5.15.

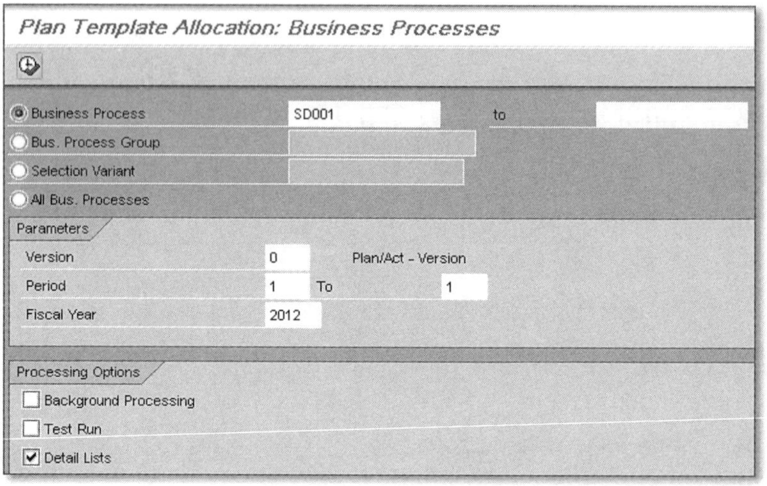

Figure 5.15 Template Allocation

On the selection screen, you choose the business process, version, period, and fiscal year that you want to run, and then execute.

After you run the template allocation, you can see the results in cost center reports and also in the business process reports. For a cost center report, we used Report S_ALR_87013611 – Cost Centers: Actual/Plan/Variance, shown in Figure 5.16.

By double-clicking in the planning value, you'll call up the planning line-item display, as shown in Figure 5.17.

In the listing, you can see the secondary cost element defined in the business process master data shown earlier in Figure 5.9, and the total quantity defined in the template customizing shown previously in Figure 5.14.

To see the business process side of the posting (see Figure 5.18), we used the Report S_ALR_87011761 – Process List: Plan/Actual Costs.

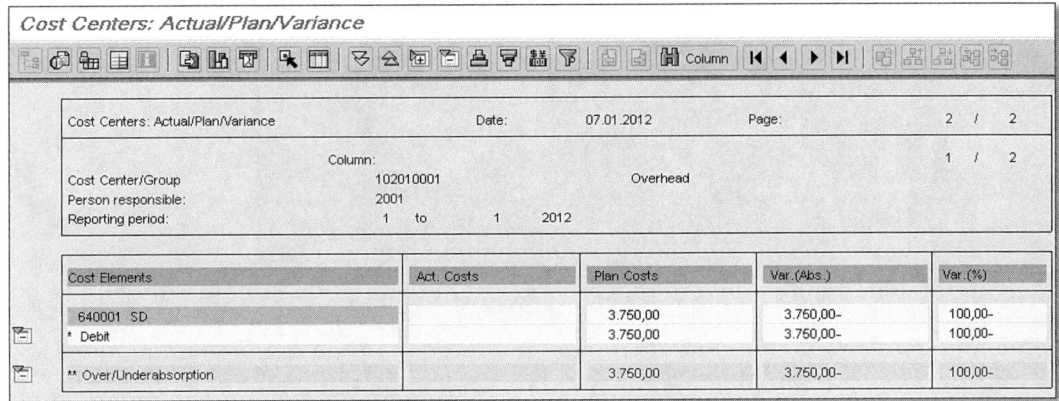

Figure 5.16 Cost Center Report

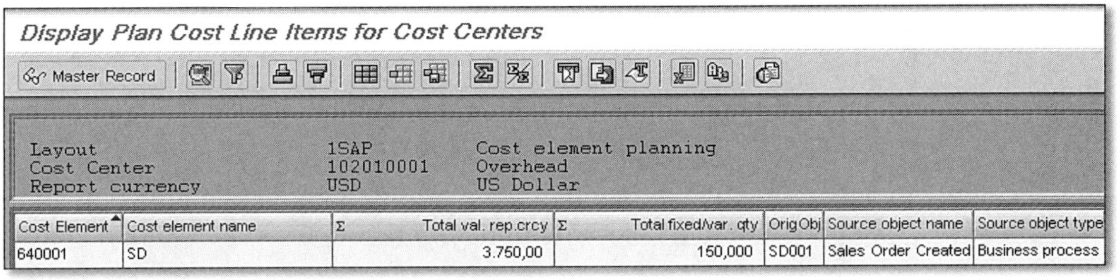

Figure 5.17 Cost Center Planning Line-Item Display

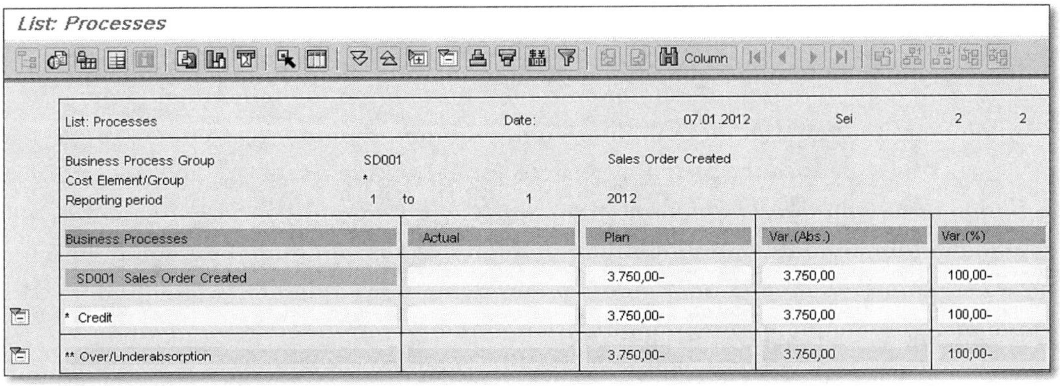

Figure 5.18 Business Process Report

By double-clicking in the planning values, you can see the planning line items, as shown in Figure 5.19.

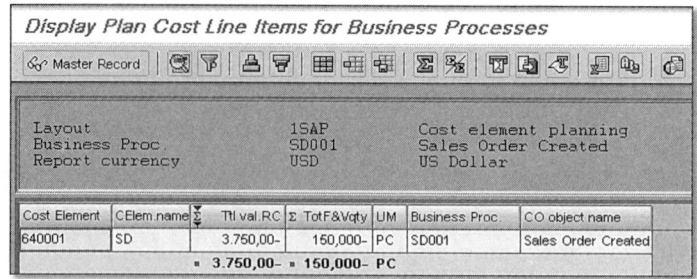

Figure 5.19 Business Process Planning Line-Item Report

Now that you know how to customize and use templates, you're ready to move to the next topic: CO-ABC planning.

5.3 Planning

CO-ABC planning is very similar to cost center planning. The customizing process is divided into the following steps, explored shortly:

1. Maintain the versions.

2. Perform group maintenance.

3. Define layouts and profiles for manual planning.

4. Define the templates for plan data transfer.

5. Define planning allocations.

5.3.1 Maintain Versions

You've defined the planning versions for CO-CCA in Chapter 3, and the same versions defined for CO-CCA are available to use in CO-ABC. You can use Transaction OKEQ to maintain versions.

5.3.2 Group Maintenance

The grouping functionality is available for business process master data. It works the same way as cost center and internal order groups and has the same benefits. Use Transactions CPH1, CPH2, and CPH3 to create, change, and display the business process groups, respectively.

5.3.3   Manual Planning

In the manual planning step, you'll define the planning layouts and planning profiles for CO-ABC planning. You've already created planning layouts for cost center planning in Chapter 3, and the process is similar in CO-ABC.

Use Transaction CP65 to create planning layouts for business process cost planning, Transaction CP75 for business process quantity/prices planning, and Transaction CP85 for business process statistical key figures planning.

5.3.4   Plan Data Transfer

Though transfer of quantities from SAP Production Planning (PP) is also available for CO-ABC, it works differently from CO-CCA , where you defined the scenarios to transfer from SAP PP to CO-CCA. In CO-ABC, you use a template to transfer quantities from SAP PP. In the template creation, you must use the SOP – Transfer Sales and Operations Plan environment.

5.3.5   Allocations

Planning allocations in CO-ABC are based on cycles (the same as in CO-CCA). The process to customize a cycle for CO-ABC is just like the process you saw in Chapter 3 for CO-CCA. The following planning allocations options are available for CO-ABC:

▶ Distribution

▶ Assessment

▶ Indirect activity allocation

Distributions and assessments follow the push method (the approach where you define a sender cost object and a receiver cost object for the costs without using a valuated quantity structure to perform the allocation). The customizing of distributions and assessments follows the same principle as for cost center distributions and assessments. Use Transactions CPV7, CPV8, and CPV9 to create, change, and display CO-ABC plan distributions, and use Transactions CPP7, CPP8, and CPP9 to create, change, and display CO-ABC plan assessments.

Together with templates, indirect activity allocations are used to create the pull method, where a complex allocation method based on quantity and formulas can be used to allocate the CO-ABC costs. Indirect activity allocation is also customized using allocation cycles, which have been already described in the Chapter 3. Use Transactions CPC7, CPC8, and CPC9 to create, change, and display CO-ABC indirect activity allocation.

Now that you've seen the CO-ABC planning customizing and its similarity with CO-CCA planning customizing, you're ready to move on to the next topic, actual posting.

5.4 Actual Postings

CO-ABC businesses processes are cost objects like cost centers and are integrated in SAP ERP. If a posting in SAP Materials Management (MM), SAP Financial Accounting (FI), or SAP Sales and Distribution (SD) is assigned to a business process, it will automatically be transferred to CO-ABC, not requiring a separate posting processing to integrate the values.

During the period-end closing, you can use actual allocations defined as distributions, assessments, and indirect activity allocations to manage CO-ABC by allocating the CO-ABC from a business process to another cost object, as shown earlier in Figure 5.2.

The CO-ABC actual allocations that are available are the same as CO-ABC planning allocations:

► Distribution

► Assessment

► Indirect activity allocation

The CO-ABC allocations use allocation cycles, and the customizing follows the same principle of cost center actual allocations described in Chapter 3. To create, change, or display actual CO-ABC distributions, use Transactions CPV1, CPV2, and CPV3, respectively; to create, change, or display actual CO-ABC assessments, use Transactions CPP1, CPP2, and CPP3, respectively; to create, change, or display actual CO-ABC indirect activity allocations, use Transactions CPC1, CPC2, and CPC3, respectively.

In CO-ABC, you use the business process itself to perform the quantity allocation; this is different from what you saw for cost center allocations, where you can use multiple activity types to create a quantity-based allocation. You don't need to create a splitting structure for CO-ABC as you did in CO-CCA because the only quantity available to split the cost is the business process quantity. To create the business process price, the system will simply divide the business process cost by business process quantity.

Now that you've learned the similarities and differences between managing actual postings in CO-ABC and CO-CCA, let's discuss the information system.

5.5   Information System

All of the CO-ABC customizing steps we've covered up to this point are designed to help the company meet its reporting needs. SAP ERP provides a large number of standard reports for CO-ABC. We'll show some examples of the most important reports for CO-ABC.

By following the user menu path ACCOUNTING • CONTROLLING • ACTIVITY-BASED COSTING • INFORMATION SYSTEM • REPORTS FOR ACTIVITY-BASED COSTING, you'll see the following report folders:

▶ PLAN/ACTUAL COMPARISONS

▶ TARGET/ACTUAL COMPARISONS

▶ PLANNING REPORTS

▶ PRICES

▶ LINE ITEMS

▶ MASTER DATA INDEXES

▶ PROCESS ATTRIBUTES

▶ MORE REPORTS

Inside of each folder, you'll find a large number of reports. We'll show some examples, and the same idea can be applied for other CO-ABC reports.

The first most commonly used report is S_ALR_87011761 – Process List: Plan/Actual Costs, shown in Figure 5.20.

In the selection screen, you'll see the option to use a business process group, a cost element group, or both. If you select the report by group, the system will create the breakdowns in the reporting following the group's nodes.

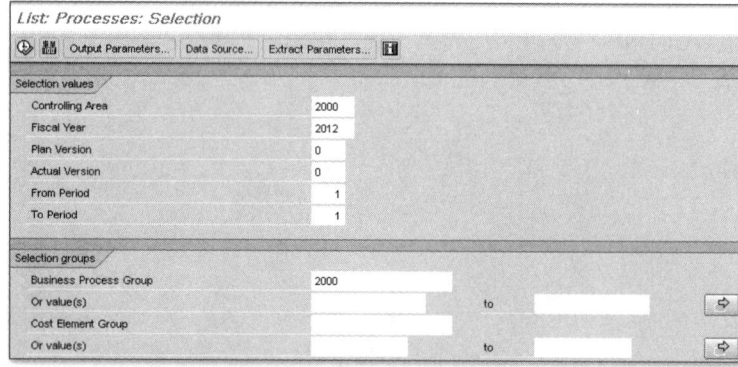

Figure 5.20 Process List: Plan/Actual Costs Report

You can see the same values in a different way using Report S_ALR_87011760 – Plan/Actual Comparison for Business Processes (by Cost Elements), where the result will be shown by cost element. See Figure 5.21 for an example.

The selection screen for the report is the same as the one shown in Figure 5.20, but the result is displayed using cost elements as the breakdown.

Notice the business process group structure in the left side of the report output in Figure 5.21. You can also navigate between the individual business process groups by marking the desired group and then collapsing or expanding the values.

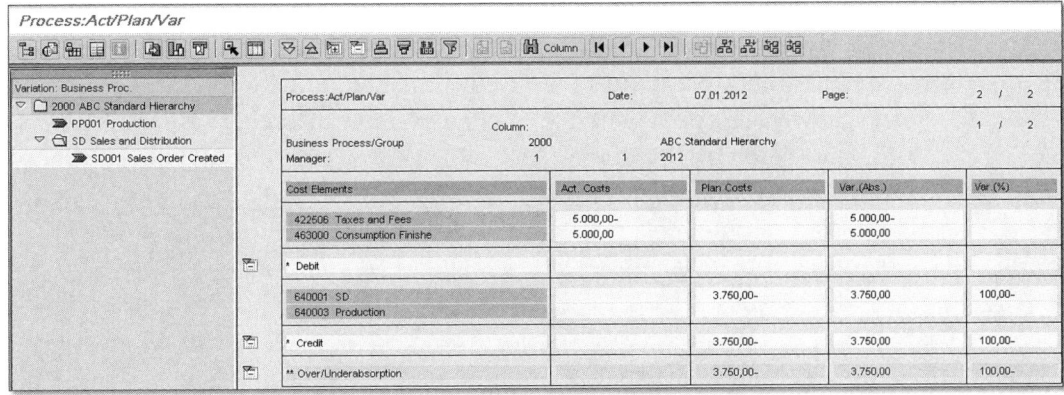

Figure 5.21 Plan/Actual Comparison for Business Processes Report

Because business processes can behave as activity types, another good report is the business process price report (CPBT – Price Report for Business Processes) shown in Figure 5.22. This report is useful for a quick overview of the fixed, variable, and total prices for business processes.

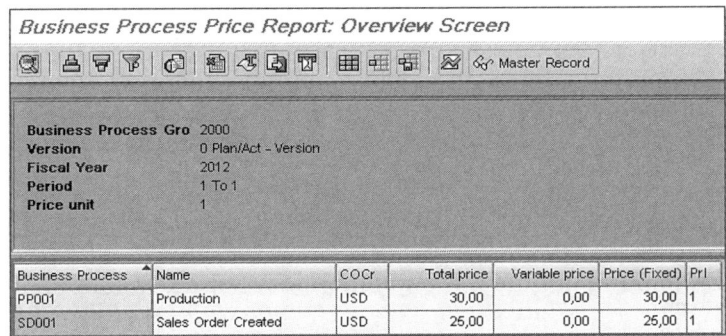

Figure 5.22 Business Process Price Report

Inside the line items report folder, you can choose between the following report options:

▸ CPB1 – Business Processes: Actual Line Items

▸ CPBP – Business Processes: Plan Line Items

▸ KSB5 – CO Documents: Actual Costs

▸ KABP – CO Plan Documents

One of the differences between cost centers and business processes is that for a business process, you can create process attributes to facilitate various reporting breakdowns. The process attributes are maintained in the business process master data shown earlier in Figure 5.7. A good example of a report using the process category breakdown is Report S_ALR_87011771 – List: Breakdown by Process Category, as shown in Figure 5.23.

9LCA-001		List: Process Category			
Data:		07.01.2012			
Strony:		2			
±dane przez:		ABAP01			
Controlling Area		2000	Controlling Area US, DE		
Fiscal Year		2012			
From Period		1			
To Period		1			
Actual Version		0			
Plan Version		0			
Business Process Group		2000	ABC Standard Hierarchy		
Cost Element Group		*	Cost Element Group		

List: Process Category		Data:	07.01.2012	Strona:	2 / 2
	Kolumna:				1 / 2
Business Process/Group	PP001,SD001,				
Okres sprawozdawczy:	1 do 1 2012				

Category/Processes	Actual	Plan	Var. (Abs)	Var. (%)
**	5.000,00		5.000,00	
** 02 Sales	5.000,00-		5.000,00-	
*** Debit				
**				
* Sales and Distribution		3.750,00-	3.750,00	100,00-
** 02 Sales		3.750,00-	3.750,00	100,00-
*** Credit		3.750,00-	3.750,00	100,00-
**** Over/Underabsorption		3.750,00-	3.750,00	100,00-

Figure 5.23 Breakdown by Process Category Report

In this report, you can see the cost displayed by process category. The process categories displayed in this report example are the ones customized in Figure 5.6 and maintained in the business process master data.

5.6   Summary

This chapter taught you about CO-ABC in SAP ERP, the benefits it can bring to a business, how to activate the subcomponent, and the difference between push and pull CO-ABC methods.

You've also learned the similarities and differences between CO-CCA and CO-ABC and how templates can be used to allocate costs in the different environments.

CO-ABC is a powerful and flexible component that provides one more tool to allocate, measure, and report costs, bringing added value to your business.

Now that you've learned about all of the subcomponents within the Overhead Management CO component, you are ready to move on to the next chapter, where you will learn about one of the most important CO subcomponents: Product Cost Controlling (CO-PC).

Customizing the system can help you meet your organization's objectives for managing production costs, from cost planning to actual costing.

6 Product Cost Controlling

Product Cost Controlling (CO-PC) is one of the main CO components. You'll now see how part of the costs from the overhead management component that you've learned about in the previous chapters can be absorbed and assigned to a product created in the manufacturing process.

In the same manner as with overhead management, the decisions you make in customizing the system for CO-PC will determine how deep you can go in the product cost analysis. Consequently, it's important for you to have a clear understanding of the business and management's requirements before you can determine the best structure for your organization.

CO-PC has two major areas of focus. You can use CO-PC to develop estimates of what it will cost to produce a product, and you can track the actual costs of production. It also provides extensive reporting tools to analyze and manage production costs.

A product cost is generally composed of the combination of a bill of material (BOM) and a routing. Together, you can think of these as a recipe, where the BOM is the list of ingredients (and respective quantities), and the routing is the list of processing steps that are needed. Product costing combines the information from the "recipe" with the costs associated with each ingredient and processing step to determine an overall cost of the product. Figure 6.1 illustrates how SAP ERP product cost is composed.

The BOM contains information about all of the material inputs (components) to manufacture the product, and the routing contains information about all of the processes and activity types used in production of the item. The combination of data from both the BOM and the routing results in the product costing.

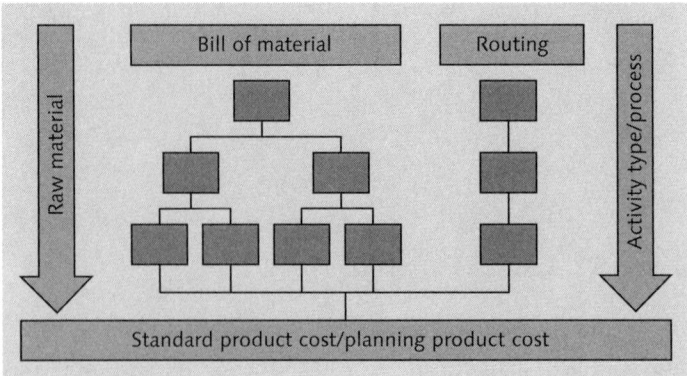

Figure 6.1 SAP ERP Product Cost Diagram

To better understand this diagram, let's look at an example using the manufacture of a strawberry cake.

The BOM would contain the ingredients for the cake: flour, baking powder, eggs, water, butter, cream cheese, sugar, and strawberries. The BOM would also contain the quantity requirement for each ingredient.

The routing would contain the activities or processes involved in production of the cake: preheat the oven; combine the flour and baking powder; blend the eggs, cream cheese, and sugar; mix all together; bake for 35 minutes; allow to cool; and top with strawberries.

If you translate this example to SAP ERP product costing accounting, you would see all of the material consumption and related costs from the BOM, and all of the activities with related costs from the routing, together creating what is called the *standard cost estimate*.

You could also see the multilevel costing, meaning the cost of each step of production.

You can create an additional planning product costing to test the impact on the overall cost of changing a raw material or a step in the routing. The advantage of this process is that you can simulate the product costing result without having to physically produce it. You can compare multiple planning costs to see which one is the best for the company in terms of value and material consumption before you begin.

Now you'll learn how to customize the system to best use product cost planning.

6.1 Product Cost Planning

With product cost planning, you can create cost estimates to address your company's needs. SAP ERP product cost planning is flexible and supports the product lifecycle, from the product idea with cost simulation, through the specification and design, and ending with the final product ready for manufacture.

Before starting the customizing of product cost planning, first you need to understand the relevant fields in material master data for CO-PC because the way you define the material master data will directly impact the product cost planning behavior.

6.1.1 Material Master Data

The material master data is divided into tabs, each related to one or more SAP ERP subcomponents. Because a definition made in one tab can affect the material behavior in all components, it's important to know which fields will affect the product costing.

The first relevant tab is MRP 1, shown in Figure 6.2, using Transaction MM03 to display a material master. The MRP tabs are most commonly updated by the production and procurement departments, since the settings must be made while considering the effects on product costing.

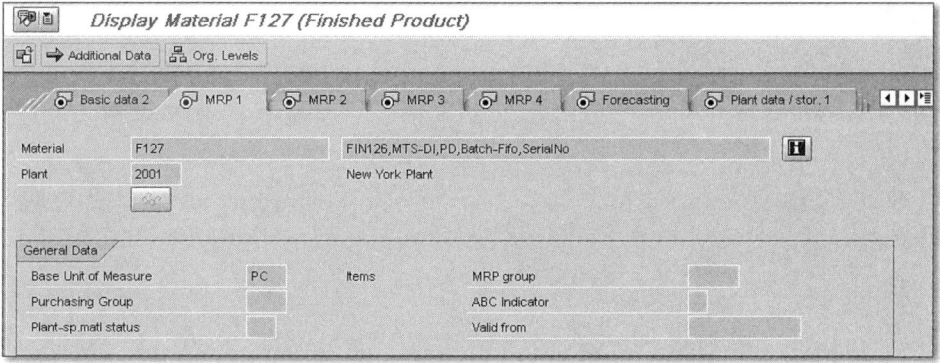

Figure 6.2 MRP 1 Material Master

BASE UNIT OF MEASURE and PLANT-SP.MATL STATUS are the relevant fields for CO-PC in this tab. BASE UNIT OF MEASURE will define the base unit for the material, which will be used by default in product costing.

In Plant-sp.matl status, you can define messages for specific SAP ERP processes. You can, for example, block the cost estimate creation for the material starting with a specific date. You can customize different statuses for different purposes. Figure 6.3 shows you the customizing screen for the plant-specific material status. To customize, you can either use Transaction OMS4 or go to Controlling • Product Cost Controlling • Product Cost Planning • Material Cost Estimate with Quantity Structure • Settings for Quantity Structure Control • Material Data • Check Material Status.

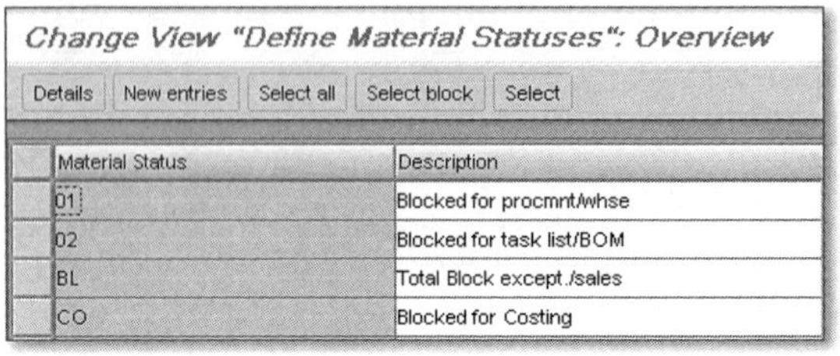

Material Status	Description
01	Blocked for procmnt/whse
02	Blocked for task list/BOM
BL	Total Block except ./sales
CO	Blocked for Costing

Figure 6.3 Define Material Statuses

You can create a new entry by clicking on New entries, or you can change an existing one by double-clicking on it, as you can see in Figure 6.4.

Transaction OMS4 is sometimes used, for example, when the material master data creation process is done by different departments to prevent the use of the material before all views are created. You can set the status in the material master, blocking some SAP ERP processes until you are ready for the material to be used in the processes.

For all processes, excluding the material cost estimate, there are three options available:

▶ No message

▶ Warning

▶ Error message

These options affect how the system will respond when the material is being used in the process. No message means that the material is freely available to use, while the warning and error messages will be issued to a user attempting to create a document or transaction using the material. The difference between a warning and an error is that a warning can be bypassed by the user and the process can proceed, whereas an error stops all further processing.

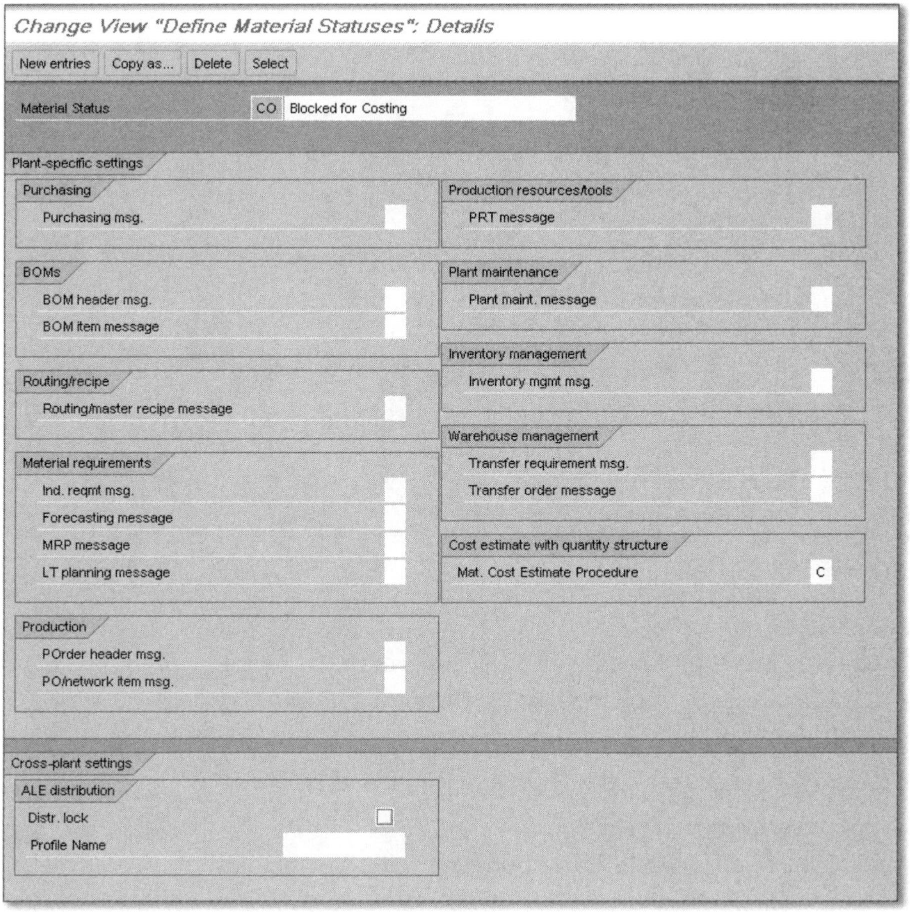

Figure 6.4 Define an Existing Material Status

For MAT. COST ESTIMATE PROCEDURE, you can choose from five options:

▶ COST MATERIAL

▶ COST MATERIAL; ISSUE WARNING IF MATERIAL COMPONENT

▶ COST MATERIAL; ISSUE ERROR IF MATERIAL COMPONENT

▶ DO NOT COST MATERIAL; ISSUE WARNING IF MATERIAL COMPONENT

▶ DO NOT COST MATERIAL; ISSUE ERROR IF MATERIAL COMPONENT

The next relevant tab for product costing in the material master data is MRP 2, shown in Figure 6.5.

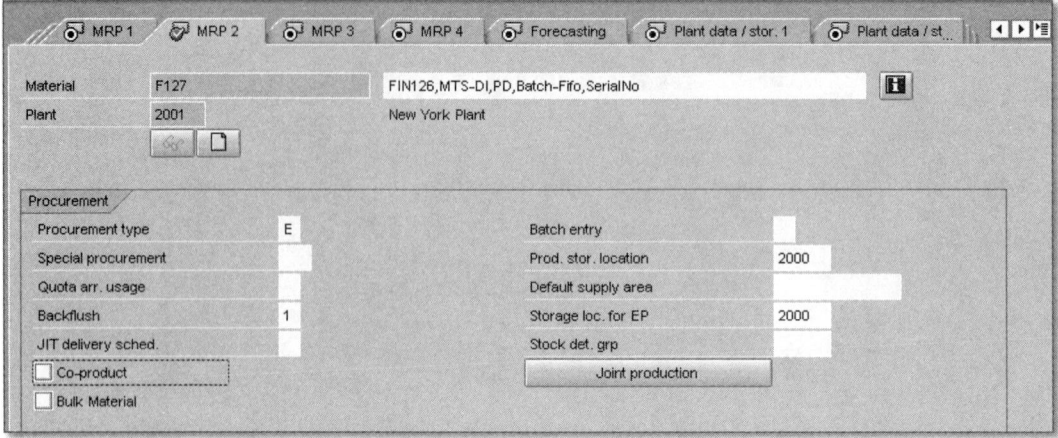

Figure 6.5 MRP 2 Material Master

The PROCUREMENT TYPE field defines how the material is procured. You can select from the following options:

▶ E: In-house production
Used for material produced with BOM and routing. SAP ERP will use the BOM and routing to determine the cost estimate for the material.

▶ F: External procurement
Defines if the material will be purchased rather than produced.

▶ X: Both procurement types
Material can either produced or purchased.

▶ No procurement
Material is not procured.

In the SPECIAL PROCUREMENT field, you define extra kinds of procurement (e.g., subcontracting, or if the material is produced in another plant or purchased from consignment). It's also a customized field in CO-PC. Use Transaction OMD9, or go to CONTROLLING • PRODUCT COST CONTROLLING • PRODUCT COST PLANNING • MATERIAL COST ESTIMATE WITH QUANTITY STRUCTURE • SETTINGS FOR QUANTITY STRUCTURE CONTROL • MATERIAL DATA • CHECK SPECIAL PROCUREMENT TYPES. You can see the customizing screen in Figure 6.6.

Click on NEW ENTRIES to create a new special procurement, as shown in Figure 6.7.

Plnt	Name 1	Sp.Pr.Type	Special procurement type description
2001	New York Pl...	10	Consignment
2001	New York Pl...	20	External procurement
2001	New York Pl...	30	Subcontracting
2001	New York Pl...	40	Stock transfer (proc.from alter.plant)
2001	New York Pl...	45	Stock transfer from plant to MRP area
2001	New York Pl...	50	Phantom assembly
2001	New York Pl...	52	Direct production / collective order

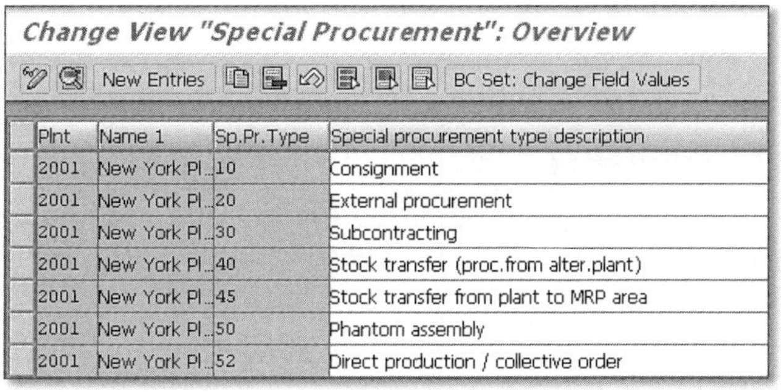

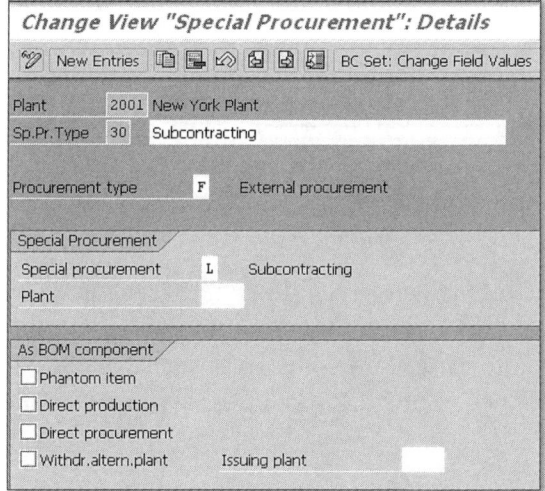

Figure 6.6 Special Procurement

Figure 6.7 Special Procurement Detail

You define the plant and special procurement type as a key combination. For the PROCUREMENT TYPE field, you can choose between two options:

- E: IN-HOUSE PRODUCTION
- F: EXTERNAL PROCUREMENT

If you select "E: IN-HOUSE PRODUCTION" in PROCUREMENT TYPE, the following options are available for special procurement.

- E: IN-HOUSE PRODUCTION
- P: PROD. OTHER PLANT

An example of a use for the production in other plant setting is when the material is produced in one plant and consumed in another plant. In this case, the system will calculate the cost estimate in the producing (other) plant and use that as the cost of the material in the main plant when consumed in a BOM.

If you select "F: EXTERNAL PROCUREMENT" in PROCUREMENT TYPE, the following options are available for special procurement:

► INIT. VALUE: EXTERNAL

► K: CONSIGNMENT

► L: SUBCONTRACTING

► U: STOCK TRANSFER

For stock transfer, you can define the supplier plant. In this case, for cost estimate purposes, where you have a material in a plant that is supplied by another plant, and the special procurement is defined as stock transfer, the system will calculate the cost estimate for the sending plant and adopt this cost estimate in the receiver plant because the material in the receiver plant doesn't have a quantity structure (i.e., isn't produced in that plant).

The BACKFLUSH field (refer to Figure 6.5) is where you determine if the material will be backflushed. Backflushing means that when you do the material production confirmation, the system will automatically withdraw the raw materials or other materials consumed in the production process from inventory based on the BOM.

The CO-PRODUCT field defines that this material will be produced at the same time as another material. If you check this field, then you now need to define in JOINT PRODUCTION the proportions for how the costs will be distributed between the co-products. You must use a source structure to define it. The source structure used in this situation is the same as you've already learned about in Chapter 4.

The BULK MATERIAL flag is used for materials that aren't relevant for product costing or that have an irrelevant cost. For bulk materials, you must set the flag both in the material master and also in the BOM.

The MRP 4 tab, which is shown in Figure 6.8, is also very important for product costing.

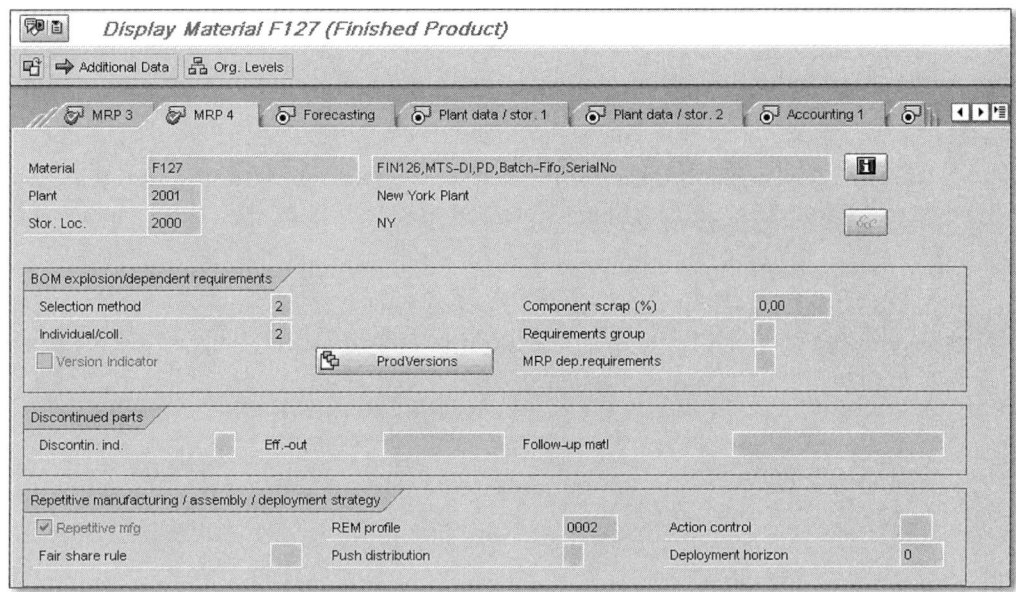

Figure 6.8 MRP 4 Material Master

This tab contains information about how the BOM will be selected, if the material has different production versions, and also whether it will use repetitive manufacturing.

In the SELECTION METHOD field, you can choose from four options:

▶ SELECTION BY ORDER QUANTITY
BOM selection will be based on the lot size range of the order quantity.

▶ SELECTION BY EXPLOSION DATE
The system will use the BOM valid for the order date.

▶ SELECTION BY PRODUCTION VERSION
BOM selection will be based on defined production versions.

▶ SELECTION ONLY BY PRODUCTION VERSION
Production order will only be created if a production version is found.

Also in the BOM EXPLOSION/DEPENDENT REQUIREMENTS section of the MRP 4 tab, you can define a COMPONENT SCRAP (%). This indicates the percentage of the material that will be considered as scrap during the production process. You can also set this indicator in the BOM. If defined differently in both places, the number defined in the BOM will override the one defined in the material master.

If the material has multiple production versions, you must do two things: mark the VERSION INDICATOR flag and define a production version (by clicking the PROD-VERSIONS button) for the material where you can choose a different lot size, BOM, or routing.

The last relevant field in the MRP 4 tab is the REPETITIVE MFG flag and REM PRO-FILE. Both of these fields will be explained in Section 6.2.

The next tabs in the material master that are important to discuss for costing are ACCOUNTING 1 and ACCOUNTING 2. These are often maintained by the financial accounting team in cooperation with the product cost team. You can see the available fields of ACCOUNTING 1 in Figure 6.9.

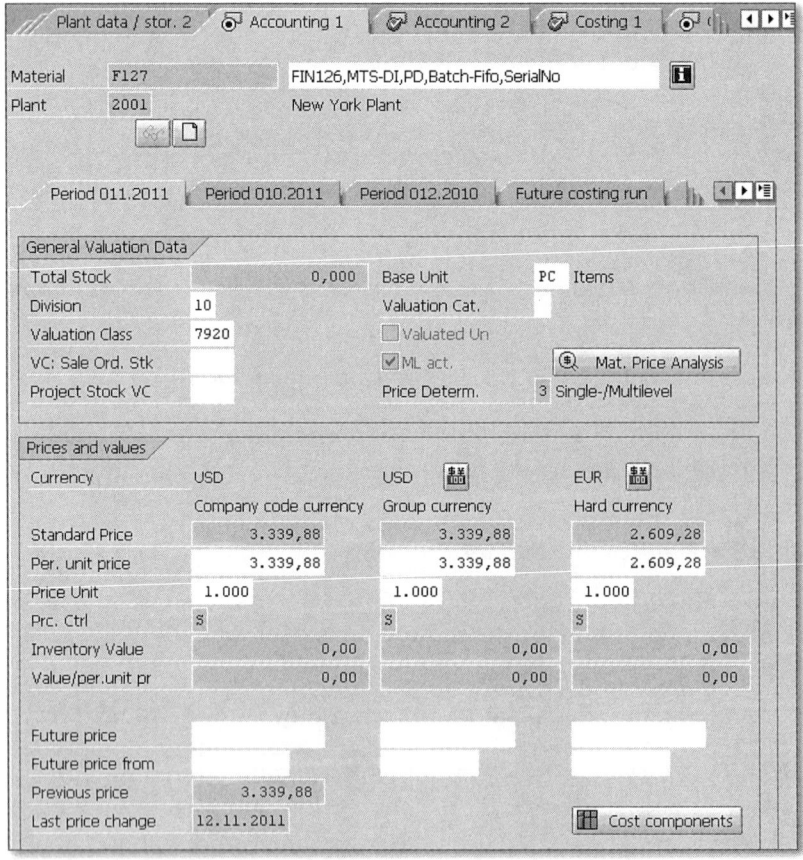

Figure 6.9 Material Master Accounting 1 Tab

We'll discuss only the fields that are important for product costing.

The field VALUATION CLASS determines the accounting behavior for the material, including the definition of the balance sheet account for the inventory and P&L accounts for all of the possible goods movements.

The fields PRC CTRL (price control), PRICE DETERM., STANDARD PRICE, PER. UNIT PRICE, and ML ACT. (Material Ledger activated) will be explained in Section 6.3.

PRICE UNIT defines the number of units of measure on which the price is based. For instance, because the price per unit can only contain two decimal places, if you have items with a per unit price of less than $0.01, you can maintain accuracy in the total valuation of the inventory by setting a price unit of 100 or 1000. This allows you to inventory the items as individuals while avoiding discrepancies in the total valuation due to rounding.

FUTURE PRICE and FUTURE PRICE FROM are used to set a standard price for the material when a cost estimate isn't available. You define a value and the starting date for this value to be valid.

The ACCOUNTING 2 tab shows the different kinds of prices that can be used to evaluate the inventory with a value other than the one set as the standard or the moving average price. Figure 6.10 shows the ACCOUNTING 2 tab.

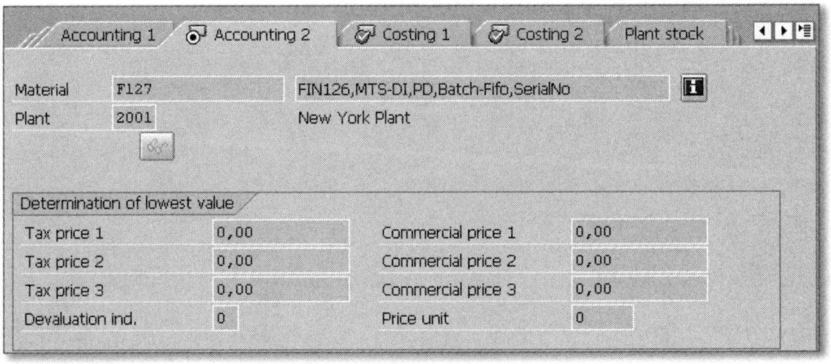

Figure 6.10 Material Master Accounting 2 Tab

The fields can be maintained by the user or can be populated automatically. One example of the use of these fields is when you are creating a cost estimate for the material. You'll see in the "Valuation Variants" subsection under Section 6.1.3, that you can select a strategy sequence to define which price the cost estimate will use to create the cost estimate. You can set the valuation variant to get one of the tax or commercial prices available in this screen. Also in the costing estimate, you can select which price the cost estimate will update (again you can select one of those available in this screen).

Next we'll discuss the COSTING 1 and COSTING 2 tabs, both of which are strictly related to product costing.

The COSTING 1 tab is shown in Figure 6.11.

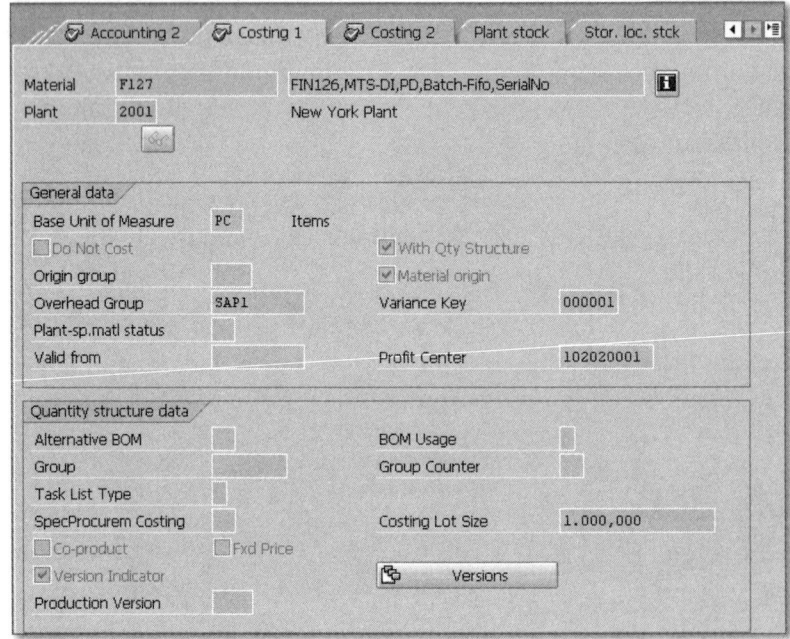

Figure 6.11 Material Master Costing 1 Tab

The screen has two sections: GENERAL DATA and QUANTITY STRUCTURE DATA.

In the GENERAL DATA section, the following fields and checkboxes are available:

▶ BASE UNIT OF MEASURE

▶ DO NOT COST

▶ ORIGIN GROUP

▶ OVERHEAD GROUP

▶ PLANT-SP.MTL STATUS

- VALID FROM
- WITH QTY STRUCTURE
- MATERIAL ORIGIN
- VARIANCE KEY
- PROFIT CENTER

You've already seen BASE UNIT OF MEASURE on the MRP 1 tab. If you haven't defined it yet, you can enter it here.

DO NOT COST indicates that SAP ERP will not cost this product when creating a cost estimate. If the material is used in a quantity structure, the system will determine the price using the sequence defined in the valuation variant.

You define to which origin group the material belongs in the ORIGIN GROUP field. You can see in detail how an origin group works in Section 6.1.2.

OVERHEAD GROUP is used when you want to apply an overhead percentage to the material. Instead of maintaining the percentage on each material, you can customize the overhead group and use it in one or more materials. This is also a way to define which material will be subject to a template calculation. Overhead and template calculations will be explained in more detail in Section 6.2.

PLANT-SP.MTL STATUS and VALID FROM are the same fields you've already seen on the MRP 1 tab. They can be maintained in either tab.

WITH QTY STRUCTURE is the indicator that the material has a BOM and a routing, and that you can create a cost estimate for the material. You can see an example of a cost estimate with quantity structure in Section 6.1.5.

MATERIAL ORIGIN is used when you want to update the CO line items table with the material number. This functionality makes it possible to see the material in controlling reports. It's very important to select this checkbox if your organization desires material-level detail visibility in the production cost variance reports.

> **Note**
>
> Updating the material origin will increase the database size, so we recommend that you evaluate the need for the detail down to the material number in the controlling reports. To update the field for materials in a collective way, you can run Program RKHKMATO in Transaction SE38 and select for which materials and plants you want to update the field.

VARIANCE KEY defines whether the variance will be calculated for the material. This is used only in product cost collectors or manufactured orders. If you activate the variances, the scrap value is calculated at the target value and is used to determine the actual costing.

The PROFIT CENTER is used to define the profit center for the material if you have activated EC-PCA in the controlling area. You can leave it blank, but if EC-PCA is activated, a warning message will be displayed suggesting that you update the material profit center.

In the QUANTITY STRUCTURE DATA section, you can define which BOM the system will use when creating the cost estimate. A fixed BOM entry here will override the definition made in the MRP 4 tab (refer to Figure 6.8) for the BOM explosion, and instead adopt the one defined here.

The SPEC PROCURM COSTING field can be used to establish special procurement information for costing purposes only. It's similar to the SPECIAL PROCUREMENT field that you saw previously on the MRP 2 tab, but here you can make an entry that will always be used for costing purposes, ignoring any definition made in the SPECIAL PROCUREMENT field.

The fields CO-PRODUCT and VERSION INDICATOR have already been defined on the MRP 2 and MRP 4 tabs, respectively. They can be maintained in either tab.

COSTING LOT SIZE will define the lot size to be used when creating the costing estimate.

In the COSTING 2 tab, shown in Figure 6.12, you can see the standard prices for the material and also other kinds of prices.

In the STANDARD COST ESTIMATE section, the system shows information for FUTURE, CURRENT, and PREVIOUS cost estimates for the material if you've created a cost estimate for the material. When you mark a cost estimate for the material, it will show as FUTURE with a period and year. After you release the cost, the cost estimate will move from FUTURE to CURRENT, and the cost estimate in the CURRENT field will move to the PREVIOUS one. This is a helpful reference because you can compare FUTURE versus CURRENT versus PREVIOUS cost estimates for the material in one screen. You'll see this process in detail in Section 6.1.5.

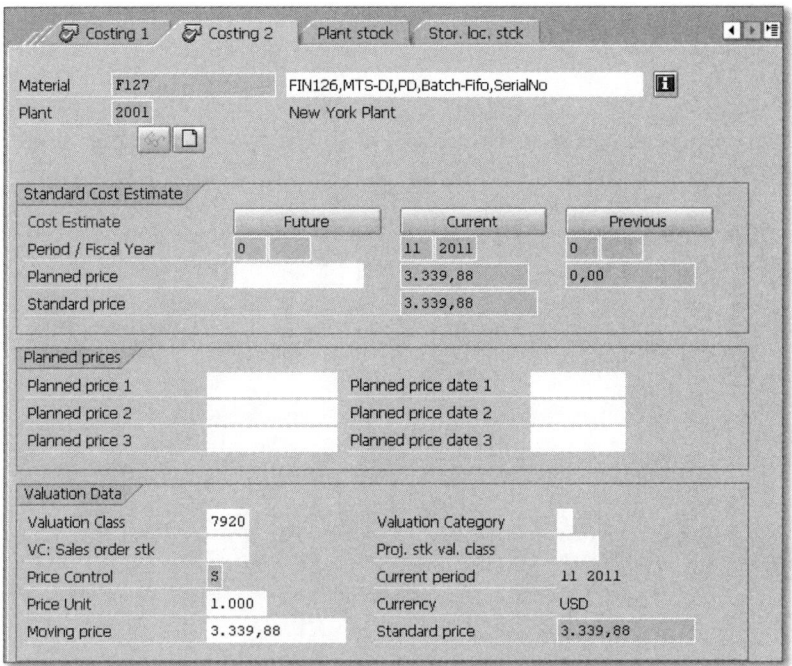

Figure 6.12 Material Master Costing 2 Tab

The PLANNED PRICES section is used to store prices. You define the price to be used for the material in the valuation variants in the same way as for the commercial and tax prices in the ACCOUNTING 2 tab. You must define the strategy sequence to get one of the planned prices.

The VALUATION DATA section shows the same information as on the ACCOUNTING 1 tab.

Now that we've reviewed the important material master data fields for product costing, let's move on to the basic settings for material costing.

6.1.2 Basic Settings for Material Costing

Two major definitions are made in the basic settings for product cost planning. The first is the origin group, and the second is the cost component structure.

When a raw material is used to produce a finished good, then from an accounting perspective, the posting will credit the raw material inventory account and debit an expense account. In CO, this debit will be reflected in a cost element assigned to a production order.

In SAP ERP product costing reporting, you can split the cost by cost element (shown in the production order report example in Figure 6.13) using Report S_ALR_87012993.

| Orders: Actual/Plan/Variance | | Date: | 22.10.2011 | 23:23:12 | Page: | | | 2 / 2 |

| Order/Group | 700040 | | Version 1 | | | | |
| Reporting period | 1 - 12 | 2011 | | | | | |

Cost Elements	Actual	Plan	Var.(Abs.)	Var.(%)
463006 Raw material - 3000	93.979,20		93.979,20	
810001 Depreciation Activi	15,34		15,34	
810002 Production Hours	32,41		32,41	
* Costs	94.026,95		94.026,95	
463008 Transf. Prod. Costs	414,53		414,53	
* Settled Costs	414,53		414,53	
463008 Transf. Prod. Costs	94.441,48-		94.441,48-	
* Deliveries to Stock	94.441,48-		94.441,48-	
** Balance				

Figure 6.13 Production Order Report Example

In the example shown in Figure 6.13, you can see that most of the costs are in the cost element 463006 RAW MATERIAL – 3000. If you need to do a full analysis of this cost element, and you have many production orders during the month, then the process to analyze the cost element can be difficult and almost impossible.

When you use the functionality of the cost component split, you can see the product costing split into components that you define in the customizing. Using Transaction CK13N, you can see in Figure 6.14 an example of a product with the cost component split activated.

The cost component split uses the cost element in the production order to define how to categorize costs in reporting when you have just one cost element for all raw material consumption, as in the example shown in Figure 6.13. To avoid creating a lot of cost elements and valuation classes, SAP ERP provides functionality for separating the costs posted in one cost element. To use cost component split, you must create an origin group and assign it to the material master in the COSTING 1 tab (review Figure 6.11). To customize the origin group, either use Transaction OKZ1, or go to CONTROLLING • PRODUCT COST CONTROLLING • PRODUCT COST PLANNING • BASIC SETTINGS FOR MATERIAL COSTING • DEFINE ORIGIN GROUPS. See Figure 6.15.

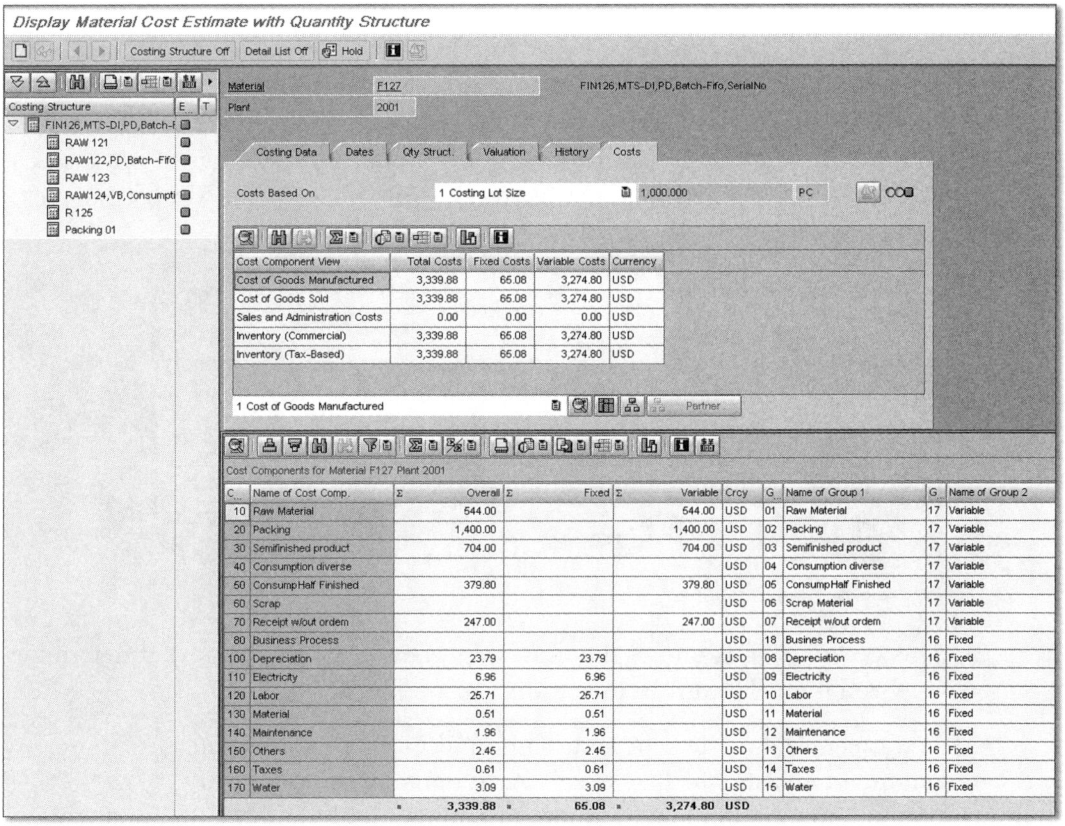

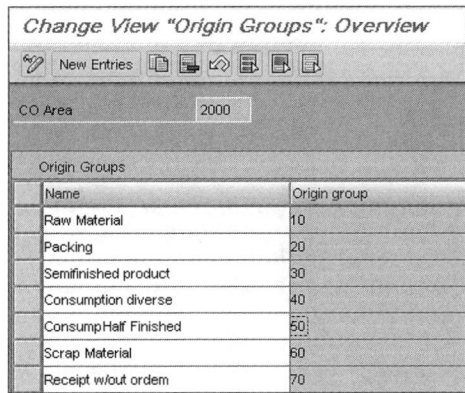

Display Material Cost Estimate with Quantity Structure

Costing Structure Off | Detail List Off | Hold

Material	F127	FIN126,MTS-DI,PD,Batch-Fifo,SerialNo
Plant	2001	

Costing Structure | E | T
FIN126,MTS-DI,PD,Batch-
- RAW 121
- RAW122,PD,Batch-Fifo
- RAW 123
- RAW124,VB,Consumpti
- R 125
- Packing 01

Costing Data | Dates | Qty Struct. | Valuation | History | **Costs**

Costs Based On   1 Costing Lot Size   1,000.000   PC

Cost Component View	Total Costs	Fixed Costs	Variable Costs	Currency
Cost of Goods Manufactured	3,339.88	65.08	3,274.80	USD
Cost of Goods Sold	3,339.88	65.08	3,274.80	USD
Sales and Administration Costs	0.00	0.00	0.00	USD
Inventory (Commercial)	3,339.88	65.08	3,274.80	USD
Inventory (Tax-Based)	3,339.88	65.08	3,274.80	USD

1 Cost of Goods Manufactured   Partner

Cost Components for Material F127 Plant 2001

C	Name of Cost Comp.	Σ	Overall Σ	Fixed Σ	Variable	Crcy	G	Name of Group 1	G	Name of Group 2
10	Raw Material		544.00		544.00	USD	01	Raw Material	17	Variable
20	Packing		1,400.00		1,400.00	USD	02	Packing	17	Variable
30	Semifinished product		704.00		704.00	USD	03	Semifinished product	17	Variable
40	Consumption diverse					USD	04	Consumption diverse	17	Variable
50	Consump Half Finished		379.80		379.80	USD	05	Consump Half Finished	17	Variable
60	Scrap					USD	06	Scrap Material	17	Variable
70	Receipt w/out ordern		247.00		247.00	USD	07	Receipt w/out ordern	17	Variable
80	Business Process					USD	18	Busines Process	16	Fixed
100	Depreciation		23.79	23.79		USD	08	Depreciation	16	Fixed
110	Electricity		6.96	6.96		USD	09	Electricity	16	Fixed
120	Labor		25.71	25.71		USD	10	Labor	16	Fixed
130	Material		0.51	0.51		USD	11	Material	16	Fixed
140	Maintenance		1.96	1.96		USD	12	Maintenance	16	Fixed
150	Others		2.45	2.45		USD	13	Others	16	Fixed
160	Taxes		0.61	0.61		USD	14	Taxes	16	Fixed
170	Water		3.09	3.09		USD	15	Water	16	Fixed
			3,339.88	65.08	3,274.80	USD				

Figure 6.14 Cost Component Report Example

Change View "Origin Groups": Overview

New Entries

CO Area	2000

Origin Groups

Name	Origin group
Raw Material	10
Packing	20
Semifinished product	30
Consumption diverse	40
Consump Half Finished	50
Scrap Material	60
Receipt w/out ordern	70

Figure 6.15 Origin Group Customizing

You can either create a new origin group or copy an existing one. You must also customize the cost component structure to define how the costs from all of the cost elements used in the production process will be categorized. Figure 6.16 shows the first customizing screen of the cost component structure. Use Transaction OKTZ, or go to CONTROLLING • PRODUCT COST CONTROLLING • PRODUCT COST PLANNING • BASIC SETTINGS FOR MATERIAL COSTING • DEFINE COST COMPONENT STRUCTURE.

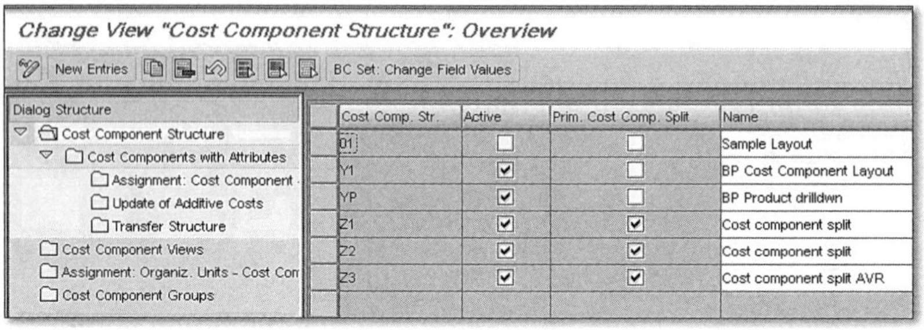

Figure 6.16 Cost Component Structure

This customizing is one of the most important in CO-PC because it determines how you'll see the costs in the product cost reports.

You can either create a new structure or copy an existing one. There are two important fields in the first screen: ACTIVE and PRIM. COST COMP. SPLIT.

The ACTIVE setting activates and deactivates the cost component split. To maintain an existing split, you must first deactivate, make the changes, and activate it again.

When you set the PRIM. COST COMP. SPLIT flag, it means that the cost component structure will use the primary cost elements as a reference to create the cost component split. This definition is used, for example, when you are using only a few activity types to allocate the costs from the cost center to the production order. An example is where you are using just two activities types, one for depreciation and the other for the remaining costs, but you want to see the remaining costs separated. If you activate the primary cost component split, the system will follow the primary cost element and not the secondary cost element to allocate the costs into the correct cost components.

By marking the cost component structure you just created and double-clicking on the left side of the screen on the COST COMPONENTS WITH ATTRIBUTES node, you'll see the customizing screen for the cost component, as shown in Figure 6.17.

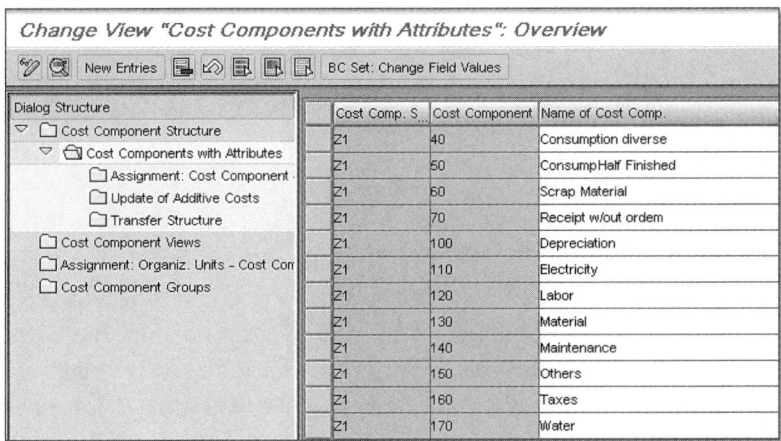

Figure 6.17 Cost Components with Attributes

You define the cost components in this customizing screen. Click on NEW ENTRIES to customize each one on the screen shown in Figure 6.18 and described in the following subsections.

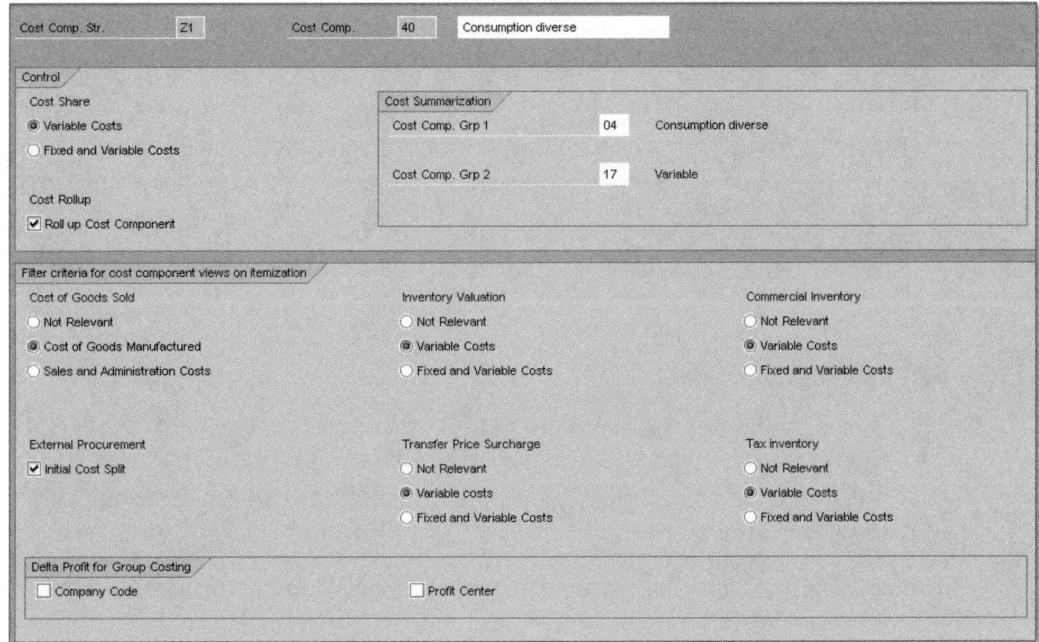

Figure 6.18 Cost Component Definition

In the CONTROL section of the screen, you define the following options:

▸ VARIABLE COSTS or FIXED AND VARIABLE COSTS

▸ ROLL UP COST COMPONENT

▸ COST SUMMARIZATION

Variable Costs or Fixed and Variable Costs

These fields will determine the behavior of the costs. SAP ERP provides up to 40 fields to be used in the cost component structure if you use only variable costs, and 20 fields if you use fixed and variable costs. It's common to always mark the costs as FIXED AND VARIABLE costs and only mark a field as variable if you need more than 20 fields on the cost component structure. If you mark a field as variable costs only and assign a cost element belonging to an activity type, you'll get an error when you try to create a cost estimate because costs from activity types are considered both fixed and variable. When planning an activity type using Transaction KP26, both FIXED AND VARIABLE PRICE fields are available, so even if both aren't used in the planning of activity types, the system requires both to be allowed in the settings.

> **Note**
>
> It's important to not change the definition of variable and fixed cost after you have activated and started to use it. If you change a cost component definition, it will cause inconsistencies in the cost component split, and the costs from previous periods will never report in the right way. If you want to change the definition of a cost component, you must create a new cost component structure, and create a valid date for the old and for the new cost component structure to avoid this type of inconsistency.

Roll Up Cost Component

Mark this field if you want to roll up the costs from one cost level to another cost level. For example, if you produce a semi-finished product, and it's used to produce a finished product, the cost component from the semi-finished will roll up to the finish product.

You can't unmark the field when the cost is relevant to cost of goods sold and inventory valuation, so the most common practice is to leave it marked.

Cost Summarization

There are two additional cost component groups available for each cost component. You can group cost components together to be used in the standard reports. For example, you can create a group for variable costs and another for fixed costs and use these to classify the cost components into fixed and variable in reports. The cost components group is also customized in the cost components structure, which we'll discuss in detail later in this section.

In the FILTER CRITERIA FOR COST COMPONENT VIEWS ON ITEMIZATION section, you define how this cost component should behave in different views of costing. It's also used for reporting. You should assign this where you want to see the cost component and later customize the cost components views.

The INITIAL COST SPLIT checkbox is used when you want to use cost component split (e.g., to split out freight costs).

In the DELTA PROFIT FOR GROUP COSTING section, you can mark two options. This is used to see the internal profits between company codes and profit centers. It can't be marked when the cost component is relevant for inventory valuation and the Material Ledger must be activated to use this functionality. To use it, you must create an auxiliary cost component structure without selecting inventory valuation, and assign the main cost component split to the auxiliary cost component split. You'll learn about the transfer price functionality in detail in Chapter 8.

The next customizing step is to assign cost elements to the cost components. Double-click on ASSIGNMENT: COST COMPONENT – COST ELEMENT INTERVAL, and you'll see the screen shown in Figure 6.19.

Change View "Assignment: Cost Component - Cost Element Interval": Over

New Entries | BC Set: Change Field Values

Dialog Structure	Cost Comp. Str.	Chart of Accts	From cost el.	Origin group	To cost elem.	Cost Component	Name of Cost Comp.
▽ ☐ Cost Component Structure	Z1	0050	463006		463006	10	Raw Material
▽ ☐ Cost Components with Attributes	Z1	0050	463006	10	463006	10	Raw Material
☐ Assignment: Cost Component ·	Z1	0050	463006	20	463006	20	Packing
☐ Update of Additive Costs	Z1	0050	463006	30	463006	30	Semifinished product
☐ Transfer Structure	Z1	0050	463006	40	463006	40	Consumption diverse
☐ Cost Component Views	Z1	0050	463006	50	463006	50	ConsumpHalf Finished
☐ Assignment: Organiz. Units – Cost Com	Z1	0050	463006	60	463006	60	Scrap
☐ Cost Component Groups	Z1	0050	463006	70	463006	70	Receipt w/out ordem

Figure 6.19 Cost Element Assignment

You can see in this example the uses of the origin group. This customizing shows, for example, that costs from materials that have the cost element 463006 as their consumption cost element and their origin group equal to 40 must be assigned to cost component 40. Cost from materials with cost element 463006 that do not have an origin group assigned will be assigned to cost component 10. The origin group must also be maintained in the material master data, as you've seen in Figure 6.11.

By double-clicking on UPDATE OF ADDITIVE COSTS, you can assign additive costs to different cost components. You can also define a transfer structure for the cost component, which is shown in Figure 6.20.

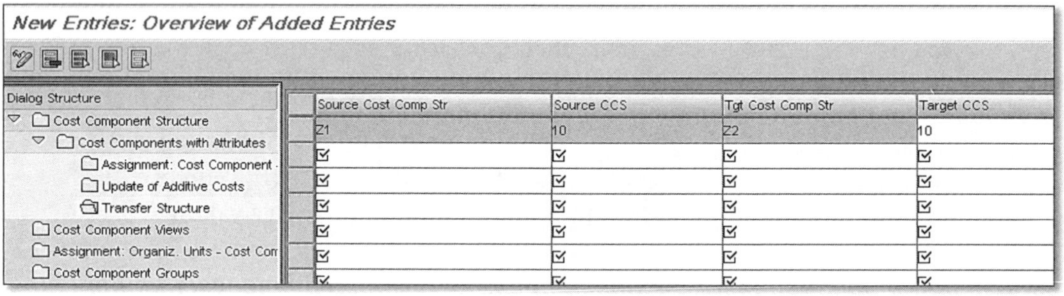

Figure 6.20 Transfer Structure

In the transfer structure, you define a source cost component structure and a source cost component, and assign them to a target cost component structure and a target cost component. By creating this relationship, you now have two views of cost components for each material. You must assign all senders' cost components to be able to activate the cost component split.

In the COST COMPONENT VIEWS folder, you'll define how many cost perspectives you want to see. You can see the SAP ERP default in Figure 6.21.

You can create the cost component views to be used in reports. The customizing you've already done for cost component definition (where you defined the relevance of the cost component for the different views) will affect the values here. You can create a new one or change an existing one. By double-clicking on the view, you can select which kind of cost you want to show in this view. Figure 6.22 shows an example.

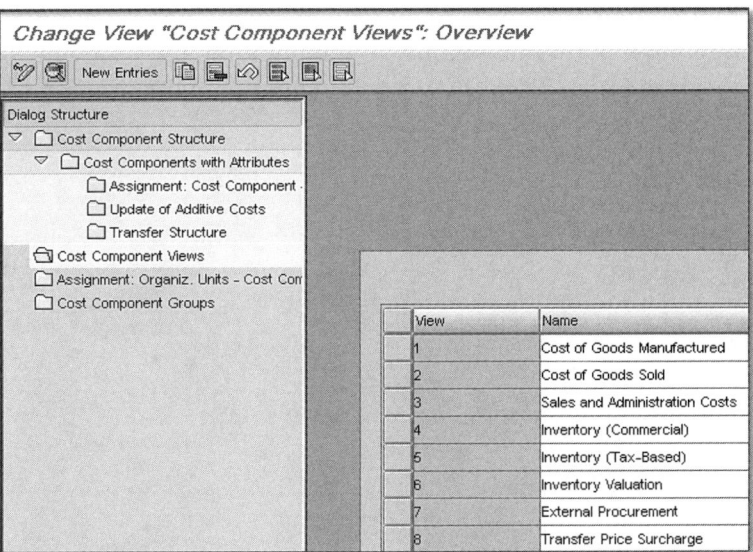

Figure 6.21 Cost Components Views

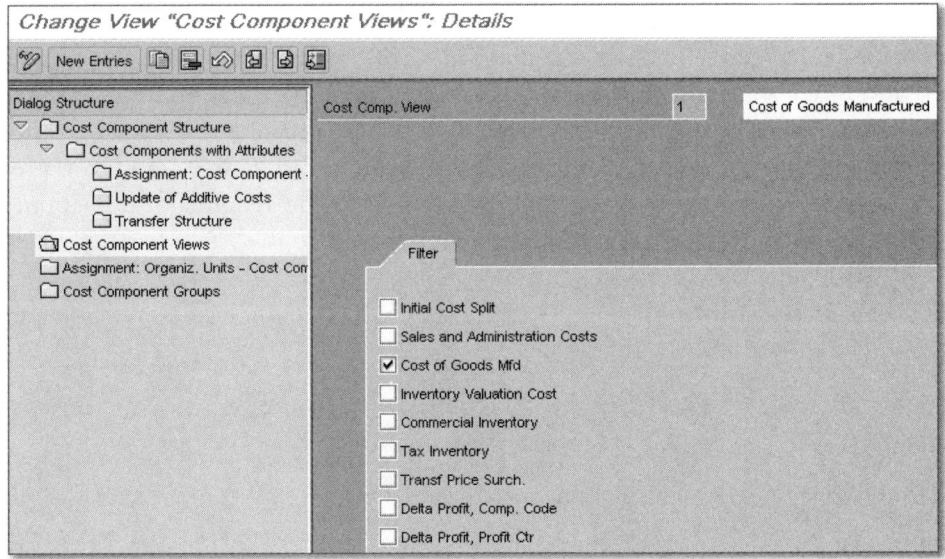

Figure 6.22 Cost Component View

You can see in this example that the fields available in the cost component customizing are displayed here. If, for example, you've selected all cost components relevant for commercial inventory, then you'll see the values of all cost components summarized in the report. The system will summarize the costs following the definition you've made here for the cost components.

The next step is to assign the cost component structure to organizational units, as you can see in Figure 6.23.

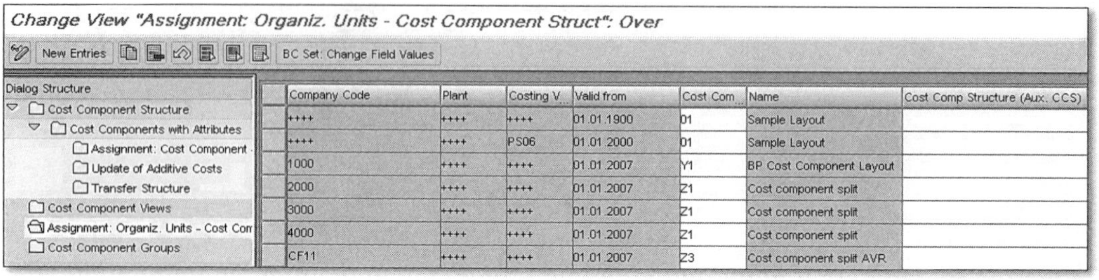

Company Code	Plant	Costing V...	Valid from	Cost Com...	Name	Cost Comp Structure (Aux. CCS)
++++	++++	++++	01.01.1900	01	Sample Layout	
++++	++++	PS06	01.01.2000	01	Sample Layout	
1000	++++	++++	01.01.2007	Y1	BP Cost Component Layout	
2000	++++	++++	01.01.2007	Z1	Cost component split	
3000	++++	++++	01.01.2007	Z1	Cost component split	
4000	++++	++++	01.01.2007	Z1	Cost component split	
CF11	++++	++++	01.01.2007	Z3	Cost component split AVR	

Figure 6.23 Organizational Units Assignment

You can define a cost component structure for the company code, plant, or costing variant, and also define a valid from date. You can also define an auxiliary cost component structure. When you are defining the assignments for cost components in this screen, entries are required in all of the COMPANY CODE, PLANT, and COSTING VARIANT fields. In the example shown in Figure 6.23, you can see that we've used masking in the definitions for some of the organization structures that we did not want to restrict. Masking means that you can enter "++++" to represent all possible values if you do not want to restrict the assignment to just one. In our example, we've assigned the cost component split Z1 to company codes 2000, 3000, and 4000 for all plants and costing variants. The last customizing in the cost component structure is the creation of cost component groups, shown in Figure 6.24.

In this customizing, you define the cost components groups to be used in the cost component customizing that you saw earlier in Figure 6.18.

If you defined the cost component structure as a primary cost component split in Figure 6.18, and you want to be able to easily reconcile the cost components between CO-CCA and CO-PC, then you can also assign the cost component structure to the controlling planning version using Transaction OKEQ, as you can see in Figure 6.25.

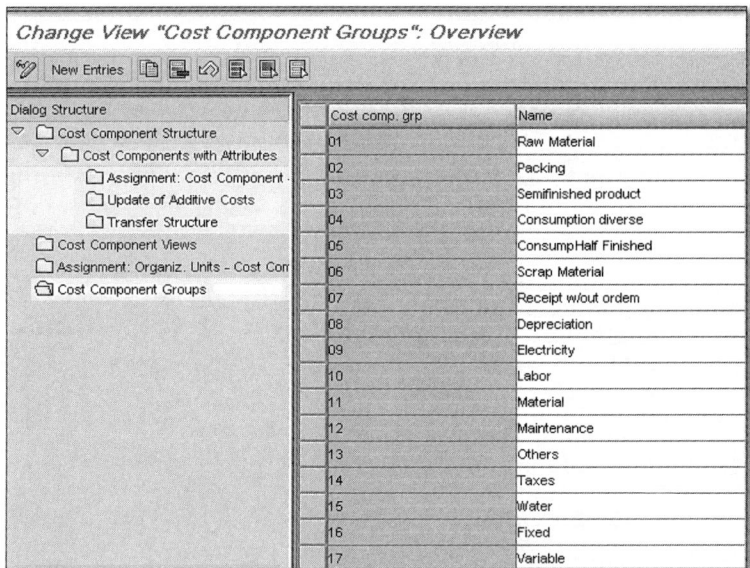

Figure 6.24 Cost Components Groups

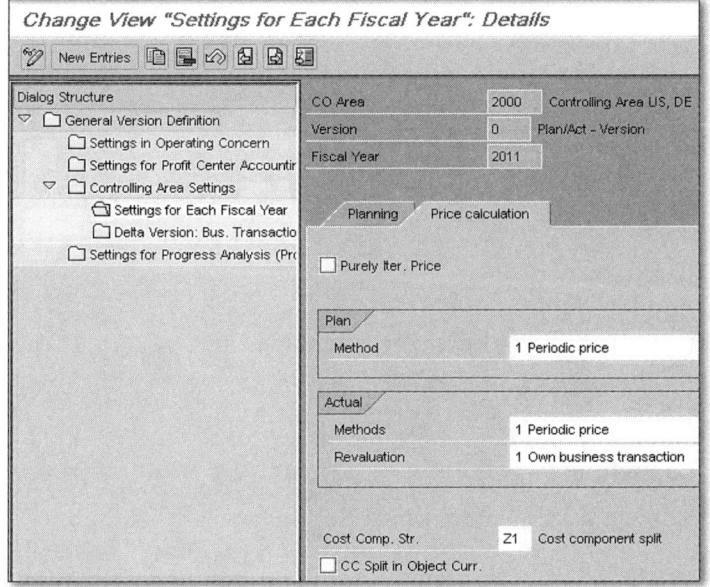

Figure 6.25 Cost Component Version Assignment

The definition in version maintenance is made under the controlling area settings by fiscal year and on the PRICE CALCULATION tab.

Now, so that you can see all of the customizing we've discussed for the basic settings and to illustrate how all of these steps work together, we'll show you one example of a cost estimate. Figure 6.26 shows an example of cost estimates using Transaction CK13N.

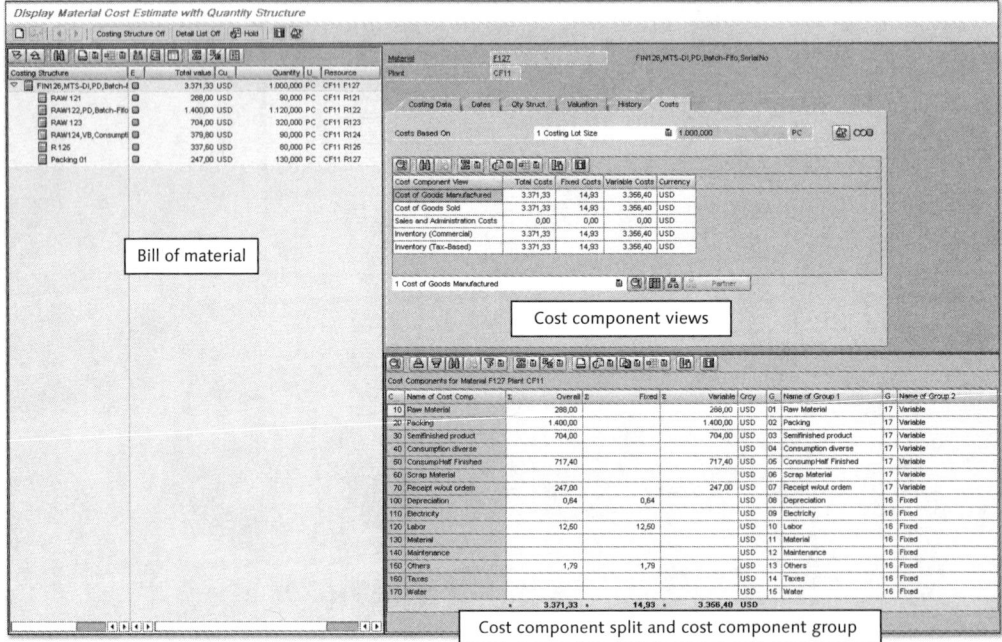

Figure 6.26 Cost Estimate Example

Now that you understand the basic settings for material costing, we can discuss material cost estimates with quantity structure.

6.1.3 Material Cost Estimate with Quantity Structure

When a material is said to be with quantity structure, this means that there is at least a BOM and a routing for the produced material. In this section, you'll customize the costing variant for materials with quantity structure.

To create a cost estimate for the material, you need a costing variant. The costing variant contains all of the parameters that the system will use to create the cost estimate (e.g., the validity of the costing estimate, which BOM will be used, currency, etc.).

The costing variant is composed of the following parameters:

▶ Costing Types

▶ Valuation Variants

▶ Date Control

▶ Quantity Structure Control

▶ Transfer Control

▶ Reference Variants

First you'll need to define the parameters. Then we'll discuss how to customize the costing variant.

Costing Types

The costing type defines which price in the material master data will be updated when a cost estimate is created and marked. Use Transaction OKKI, or go to Controlling • Product Cost Controlling • Product Cost Planning • Material Cost Estimate with Quantity Structure • Costing Variant: Components • Define Costing Types. You can see the first customizing screen in Figure 6.27.

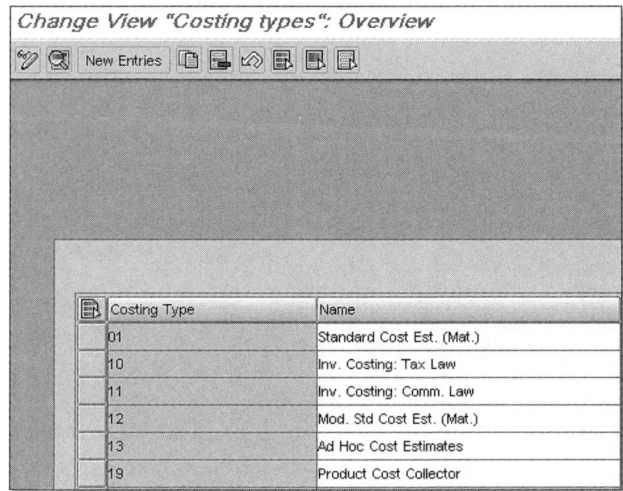

Change View "Costing types": Overview

New Entries

	Costing Type	Name
	01	Standard Cost Est. (Mat.)
	10	Inv. Costing: Tax Law
	11	Inv. Costing: Comm. Law
	12	Mod. Std Cost Est. (Mat.)
	13	Ad Hoc Cost Estimates
	19	Product Cost Collector

Figure 6.27 Costing Types Overview

SAP ERP provides some standard costing types, or you can create your own. Double-click on an existing costing type to access the definition, as shown in Figure 6.28.

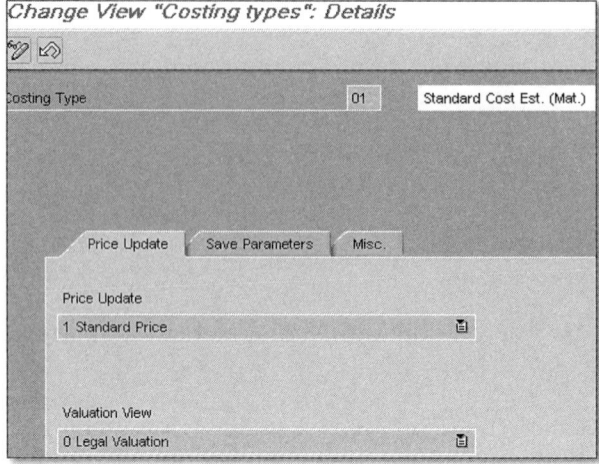

Figure 6.28 Costing Type Price Update Tab

The first tab, PRICE UPDATE, is where you define which price and valuation view of the material will be updated by the cost variant.

For the PRICE UPDATE field, you can choose from the following options:

- NO UPDATE
- STANDARD PRICE
- TAX-BASED PRICE
- COMMERCIAL PRICE
- PRICES OTHER THAN STANDARD PRICE

When using the costing type to update the standard price, you can create only one costing type for each valuation view.

For the VALUATION VIEW field, you can select from the following options:

- LEGAL VALUATION
- GROUP VALUATION
- PROFIT CENTER VALUATION

The next tab is SAVE PARAMETERS, where you define which date will be saved with the cost estimate for cost estimates with quantity structures and also for additive cost estimates (see Figure 6.29).

You can choose from three options:

▶ WITH A DATE

▶ WITHOUT A DATE

▶ WITH START OF PERIOD

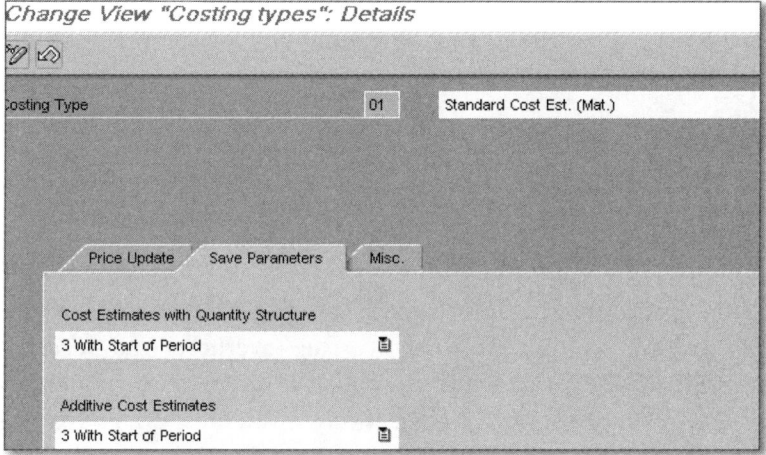

Figure 6.29 Costing Type Save Parameters Tab

For costing types that update standard costs, you can only choose one option: WITH START OF PERIOD.

The last tab in costing type is MISC., where you define the COST PORTION FOR OVERHEAD APPLICATION and the PARTNER COST ELEMENT SPLIT. See Figure 6.30 for a view of this tab.

You can use one of the costing views defined on the cost component split as the base for the overhead calculation. If you leave it blank, the system will adopt the cost of the material item assigned to stock valuation.

In PARTNER COST COMPONENT SPLIT, you'll select for which partner object you want to update the cost component split. This is relevant when you have parallel valuations.

Change View "Costing types": Details

Costing Type   01   Standard Cost Est. (Mat.)

Price Update   Save Parameters   Misc.

Cost Portion for Overhead Application

Calculation Base   1 Cost of Goods Manufactured

Partner Cost Component Splits

Partner Version   1

Figure 6.30 Costing Type Misc. Tab

Valuation Variants

In valuations variants, you are setting how the system will get the prices for materials, activity types, subcontracting, external processing, overhead, and miscellaneous, as shown in Figure 6.31. Use Transaction OKK4, or go to CONTROLLING • PRODUCT COST CONTROLLING • PRODUCT COST PLANNING • MATERIAL COST ESTIMATE WITH QUANTITY STRUCTURE • COSTING VARIANT: COMPONENTS • DEFINE VALUATION VARIANTS.

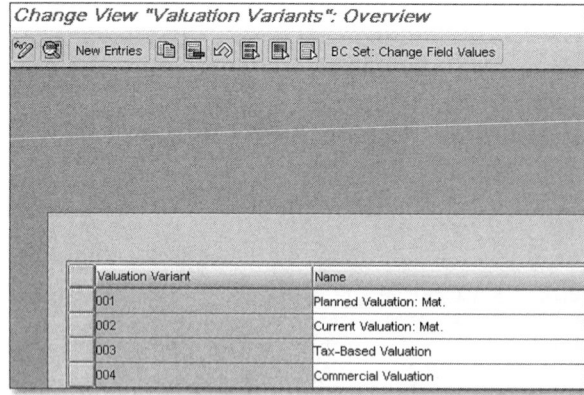

Change View "Valuation Variants": Overview

New Entries   BC Set: Change Field Values

Valuation Variant	Name
001	Planned Valuation: Mat.
002	Current Valuation: Mat.
003	Tax-Based Valuation
004	Commercial Valuation

Figure 6.31 Valuation Variants

You can either copy an existing variant or create a new one. By double-clicking in an existing valuation variant, you can see the options available. Figure 6.32 shows valuation variant 001 – PLANNED VALUATION: MAT.

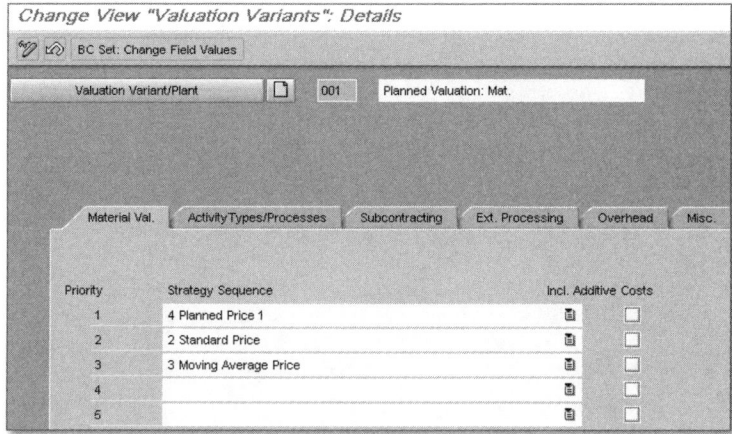

Figure 6.32 Valuation Variants Details

The valuation variants screen is divided into six tabs:

▸ MATERIAL VAL.

▸ ACTIVITY TYPES/PROCESSES

▸ SUBCONTRACTING

▸ EXT. PROCESSING

▸ OVERHEAD

▸ MISC.

In the MATERIAL VAL. tab, you'll define the sequence that the system must respect when searching for a price for a material when creating a cost estimate. You have up to five priority sequences to define. If the system doesn't find a price in the first priority, then it jumps to the second, and so on, until it finds a valid price. This is used, for example, to define which price the system will use to value a raw material used in a cost estimate for a finished good. You can also define the valuation using a user exit. There are several fields that can be referenced in the user exit in the material master data, as you've already seen.

The next tab, ACTIVITY TYPES/PROCESSES, follows the same principle as in the priority sequence for material prices, as you can see on Figure 6.33.

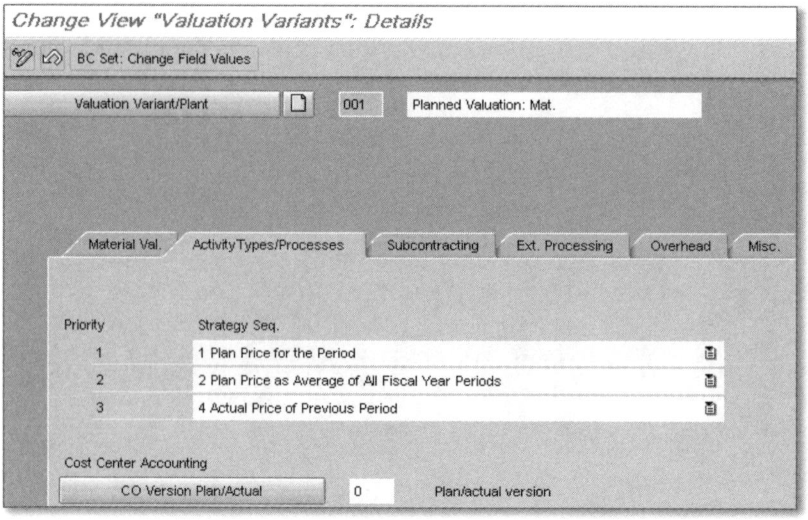

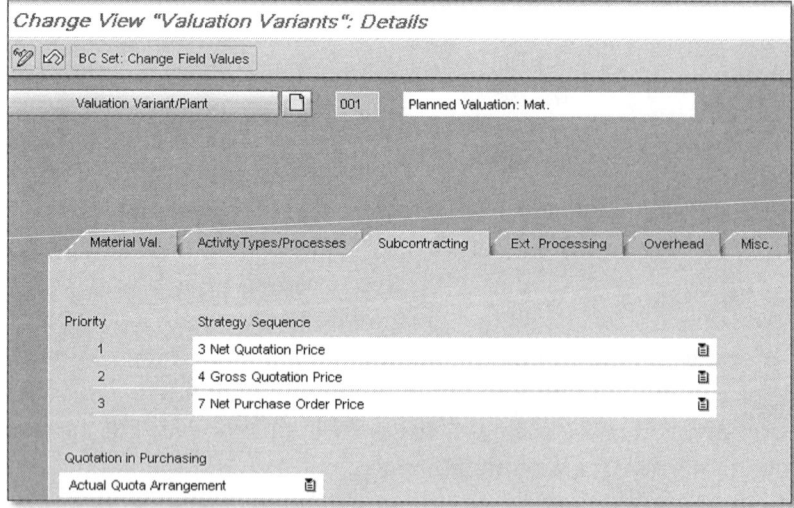

Figure 6.33 Valuation Variant Activity Types/Processes Tab

You can choose up to three strategies for the strategy sequence and also which version the system will use to search for the activity price.

In the SUBCONTRACTING tab shown in Figure 6.34, you can define up to three strategy sequences to determine in which order the system should search for prices.

Figure 6.34 Valuation Variant Subcontracting Tab

You also have three strategies available on the EXT. PROCESSING tab, as you can see in Figure 6.35.

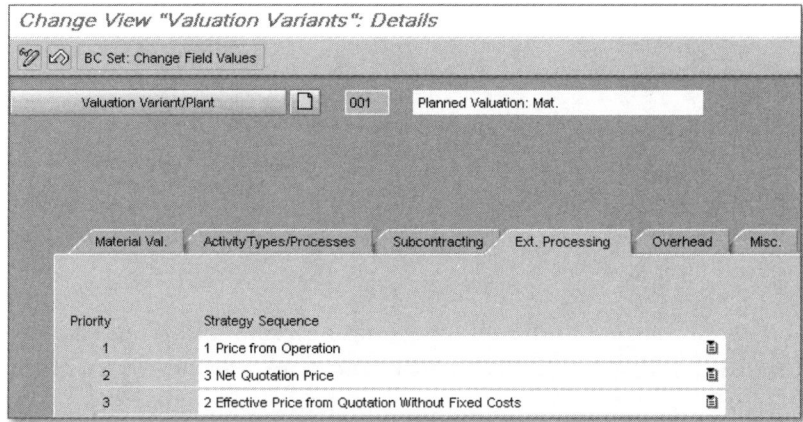

Figure 6.35 Valuation Variant Ext. Processing Tab

In the OVERHEAD tab, you'll define the costing sheet for semi-finished materials, finished materials, and material components, which is demonstrated in Figure 6.36.

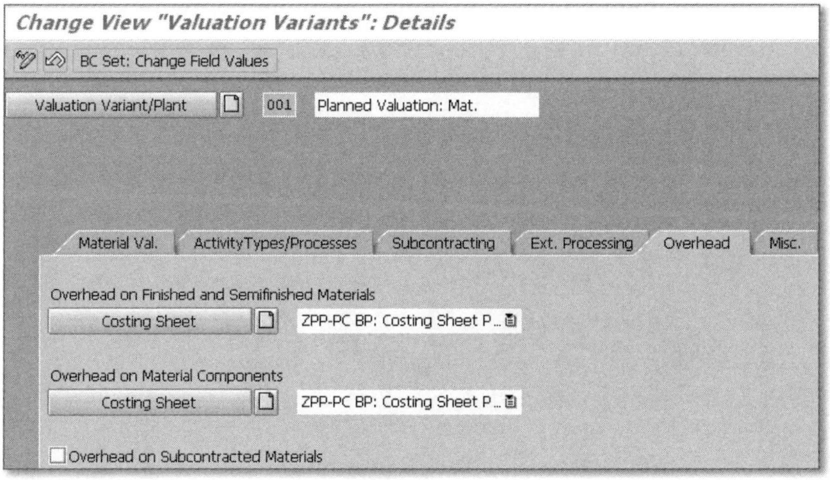

Figure 6.36 Valuation Variant Overhead Tab

The last tab for valuation variants is MISC. Here you assign price factors relevant for costing, as shown in Figure 6.37.

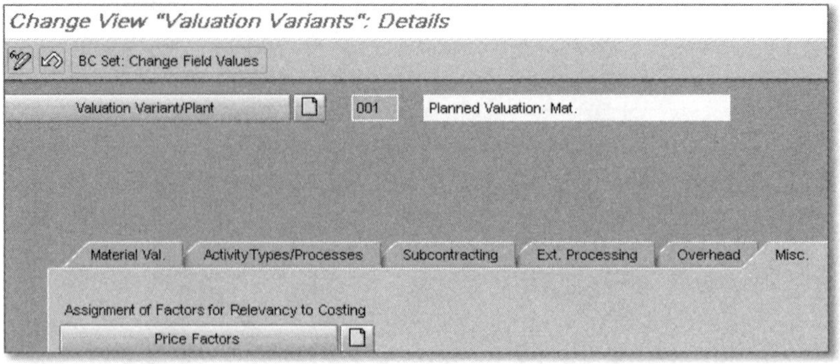

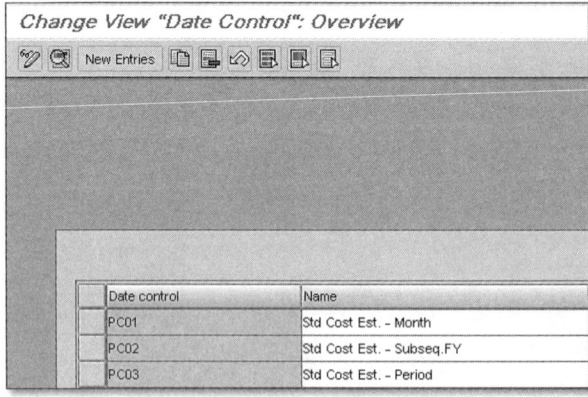

Figure 6.37 Valuation Variant Misc. Tab

Another good option available in the valuation variant customization is the possibility to create different strategies by plant in the same valuation variant. By clicking on VALUATION VARIANT/PLANT, you can define an entirely different sequence for any plants that should follow a different set of rules other than the main one you've customized.

Date Control

In the date control screen, you'll define the validity of the cost estimate and the date the system should select for the quantity structure and valuation. Figure 6.38 shows the customizing screen. Use Transaction OKK6, or go to CONTROLLING • PRODUCT COST CONTROLLING • PRODUCT COST PLANNING • MATERIAL COST ESTIMATE WITH QUANTITY STRUCTURE • COSTING VARIANT: COMPONENTS • DEFINE DATE CONTROL.

Figure 6.38 Date Control Overview

You can create a new date control or select an existing one. Double-clicking in one date control brings you to the screen shown in Figure 6.39.

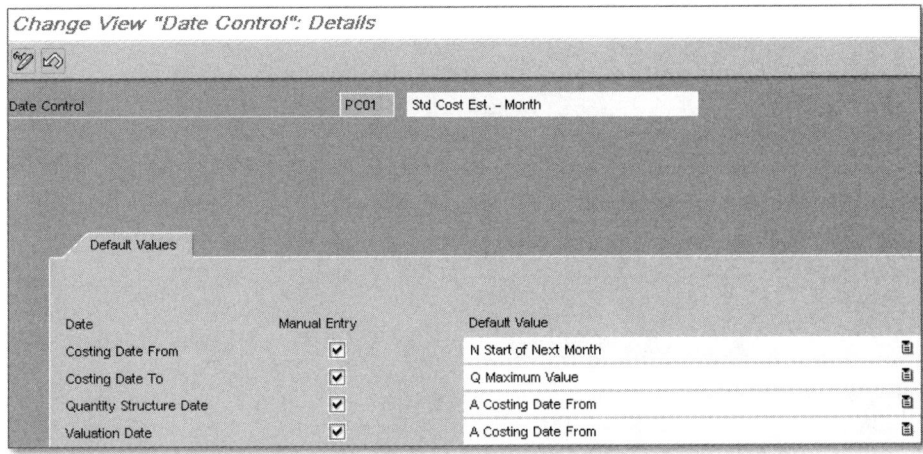

Figure 6.39 Date Control Details

When you create a cost estimate, the system will propose costing dates "from and to" according to the default values set in this step in the customizing.

The QUANTITY STRUCTURE DATE field is the date the system will use to get the BOM and routing to use in the cost estimate. The VALUATION DATE field is used by the system to get the valid price to value the materials. For example, if you've defined in the valuation variant the PLANNED PRICE 1 as the first in the strategy sequence, and entered a valid date for this price of 12/15/2011 though the cost estimate has a valuation date of 12/01/2011, the system won't use the PLANNED PRICE 1 and will instead jump to the next strategy in the sequence.

Quantity Structure Control

The quantity structure control defines which BOM and which routing should be used when creating a cost estimate. It's very useful, for example, if you have different BOMs for the same material (one for costing, one for engineering, and another for budget), in which case, you can create cost estimates for each case and compare the results. This also can be very useful when you want to test different raw material mixes to see the cost results in the finished product. You can see the first screen of the customizing in Figure 6.40. Use Transaction OKK5, or go to CONTROLLING • PRODUCT COST CONTROLLING • PRODUCT COST PLANNING • MATERIAL

COST ESTIMATE WITH QUANTITY STRUCTURE • COSTING VARIANT: COMPONENTS • DEFINE QUANTITY STRUCTURE CONTROL.

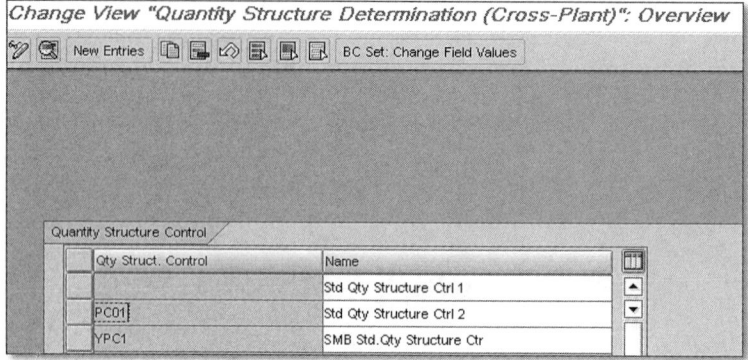

Figure 6.40 Quantity Structure Determination Overview

You can use an existing quantity structure control delivered by SAP ERP or create a new one. Double-click on an existing control to see the available options. Figure 6.41 shows an example with the details.

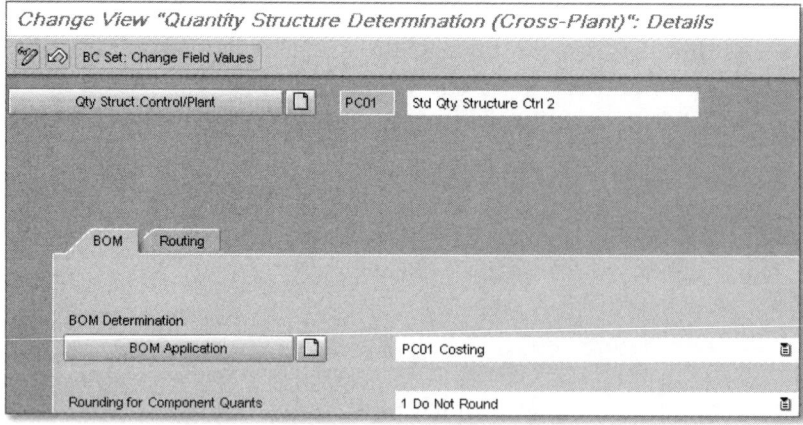

Figure 6.41 Quantity Structure Determination Detail BOM

You'll next see how to customize the BOM application.

The BOM APPLICATION field is defined in two customizing steps. The first will define the sequence of BOMs the system should search, and the next will define for what kind it is valid.

To customize the first step, either use Transaction OPJI, or go to CONTROLLING • PRODUCT COST CONTROLLING • PRODUCT COST PLANNING • MATERIAL COST ESTIMATE WITH QUANTITY STRUCTURE • SETTINGS FOR QUANTITY STRUCTURE CONTROL • BOM SELECTION • CHECK BOM SELECTION. See Figure 6.42 for an example of the transaction screen.

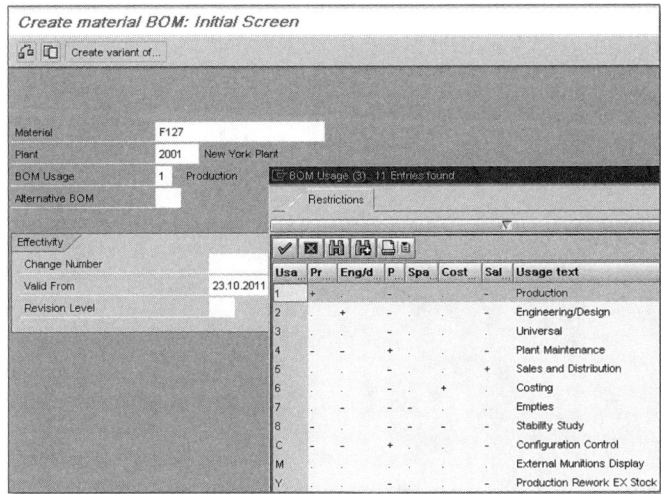

Figure 6.42 Order of Priority for BOM Usages

The first field you'll define is the selection ID (SELID); the second field is the selection priority (SELPR), and the third field is which BOM the system should use, by the BOM usage (BOMUSG). Each BOM contains an indicator for BOM usage, and you can use this classification here to help determine the order of priority for costing purposes.

Figure 6.43 shows an example of where the BOM usage is defined on the screen for Transaction CS01.

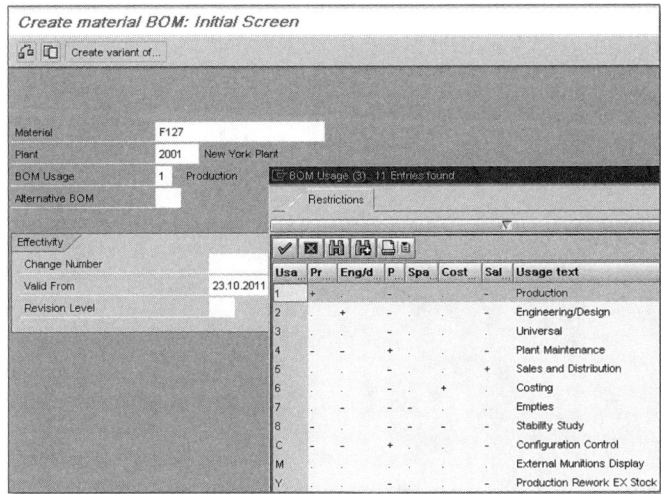

Figure 6.43 Bill of Material Creation

According to the example shown earlier in Figure 6.42, the system will search for the correct BOM in this order: 6 – Costing, 1 – Production, 3 – Universal, and 2 – Engineering/Design.

The second step is to customize the BOM application. Use Transaction OPJM, or go to CONTROLLING • PRODUCT COST CONTROLLING • PRODUCT COST PLANNING • MATE-RIAL COST ESTIMATE WITH QUANTITY STRUCTURE • SETTINGS FOR QUANTITY STRUCTURE CONTROL • BOM SELECTION • CHECK BOM APPLICATION. The result of this sequence is shown in Figure 6.44.

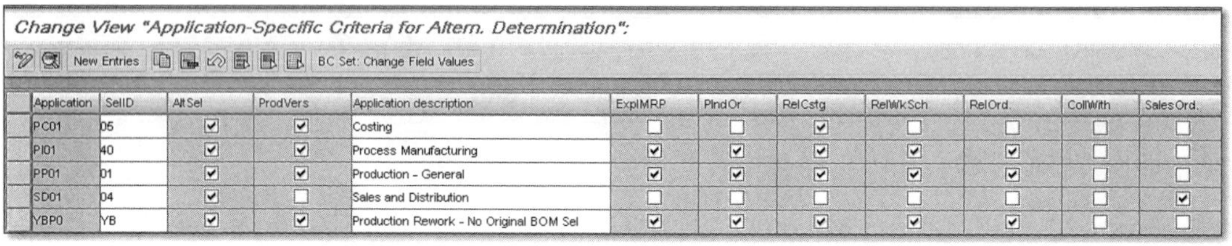

Change View "Application-Specific Criteria for Altern. Determination":

Application	SellD	AltSel	ProdVers	Application description	ExplMRP	PlndOr	RelCstg	RelWkSch	RelOrd.	CollWith	Sales Ord.
PC01	06	☑	☑	Costing	☐	☐	☑	☐	☐	☐	☐
PI01	40	☑	☑	Process Manufacturing	☑	☑	☑	☑	☑	☐	☐
PP01	01	☑	☑	Production - General	☑	☑	☑	☑	☑	☐	☐
SD01	04	☑	☐	Sales and Distribution	☐	☐	☐	☐	☐	☐	☑
YBP0	YB	☑	☑	Production Rework - No Original BOM Sel	☑	☑	☑	☑	☑	☐	☐

Figure 6.44 BOM Selection

In this step, you define the BOM application key, selection ID, and where it can be used. Now you can use the BOM application in the customizing of the quantity structure control.

As you can see in Figure 6.45, the next tab for the quantity structure control is ROUTING, where you'll define the routing selection.

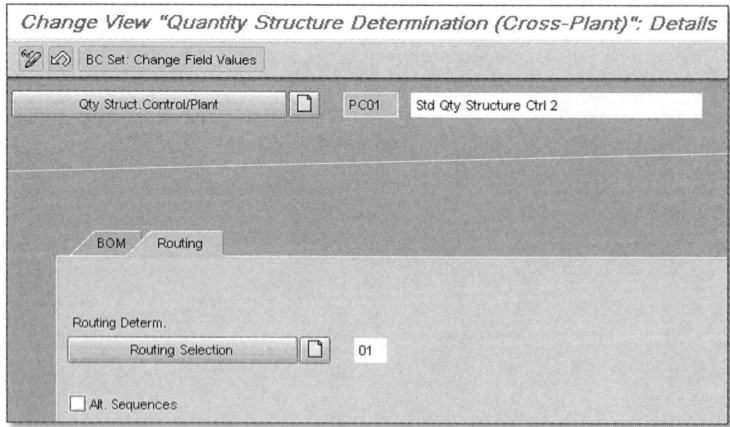

Figure 6.45 Quantity Structure Determination Detail Routing

The routing selection must also be customized here. Use Transaction OPJF, or go to CONTROLLING • PRODUCT COST CONTROLLING • PRODUCT COST PLANNING • MATERIAL COST ESTIMATE WITH QUANTITY STRUCTURE • SETTINGS FOR QUANTITY STRUCTURE CONTROL • ROUTING SELECTION • CHECK AUTOMATIC ROUTING SELECTION, which brings you to Figure 6.46.

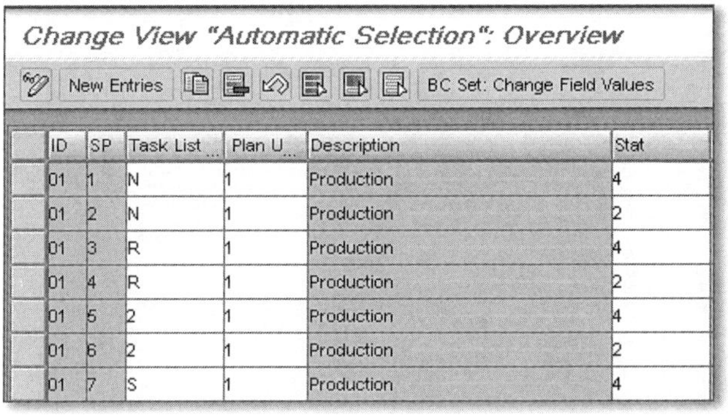

ID	SP	Task List ...	Plan U...	Description	Stat
01	1	N	1	Production	4
01	2	N	1	Production	2
01	3	R	1	Production	4
01	4	R	1	Production	2
01	5	2	1	Production	4
01	6	2	1	Production	2
01	7	S	1	Production	4

Figure 6.46 Routing Automatic Selection

You define in this screen the selection ID, selection priority, plan usage, and status for the routing. After setting this, you can assign the customized selection ID to the quantity structure control on the ROUTING tab.

You can also select different structures by plant by clicking on QTY STRUCT. CONTROL/PLANT in Figure 6.45.

Transfer Control

Transfer control is used to set controls to avoid changing the cost estimate for components that already have cost estimates when you want to create a cost estimate for a new material that will consume another with an already-existing valid cost estimate. For instance, you may have a semi-finished product that is used in the production of other finished materials, and you now want to set up a new finished product that will consume this semi-finished material. You may not want the system to recalculate the cost estimate for the semi-finished material when you cost the new finished product, but instead want to use the already-existing valid cost estimate for the semi-finished material. To avoid that situation, SAP ERP provides this functionality where you can consider the existing valid cost estimate for the component material instead of creating a new one. You can see

the first customizing screen in Figure 6.47. Use Transaction OKKM, or go to CON-
TROLLING • PRODUCT COST CONTROLLING • PRODUCT COST PLANNING • MATERIAL COST
ESTIMATE WITH QUANTITY STRUCTURE • COSTING VARIANT: COMPONENTS • DEFINE
TRANSFER CONTROL.

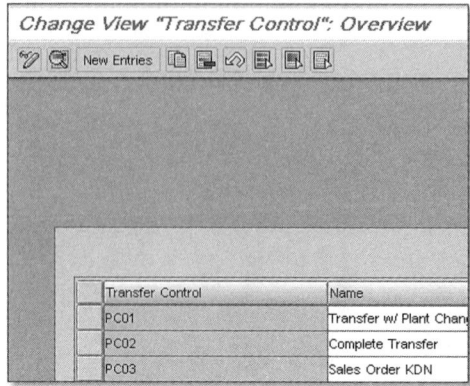

Figure 6.47 Transfer Control Overview

You can create a new transfer control or change an existing one by double-clicking
on it, as shown in Figure 6.48.

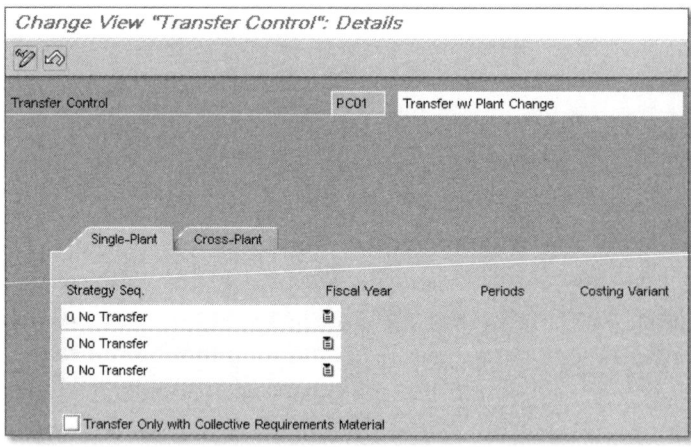

Figure 6.48 Transfer Control Single-Plant Detail

The SINGLE-PLANT tab is used to control material produced in the same plant. This
effectively prevents the creation of new cost estimates for the component materials that already have valid cost estimates.

The CROSS-PLANT tab is used when you are consuming a material directly from another plant, using a special procurement key you have defined in the material master MRP 2 tab.

You can choose up to three strategies on each tab. Figure 6.49 shows the options for the STRATEGY SEQ. field.

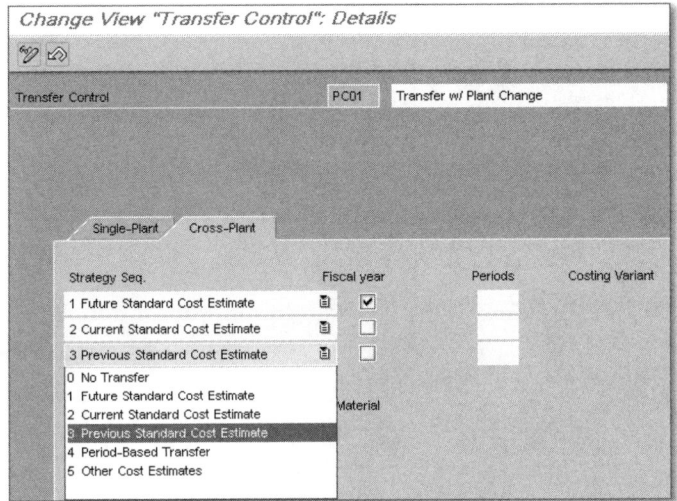

Figure 6.49 Transfer Control Cross-Plant Detail

In this example, the system will first check the future standard cost estimate valid for the fiscal year; if that doesn't exist, it will then search for the current standard cost estimate. If no current one exists, it will search for and use the previous standard cost estimate.

Now that we've discussed transfer control, we can move on to the last parameter for the costing variant: reference variants.

Reference Variants

You can create cost estimates by referencing another cost estimate that uses the same quantity structure. Figure 6.50 shows one example of referencing other cost estimates. You customize the reference variants by using Transaction OKYC or by going to CONTROLLING • PRODUCT COST CONTROLLING • PRODUCT COST PLANNING • MATERIAL COST ESTIMATE WITH QUANTITY STRUCTURE • COSTING VARIANT: COMPONENTS • DEFINE REFERENCE VARIANTS.

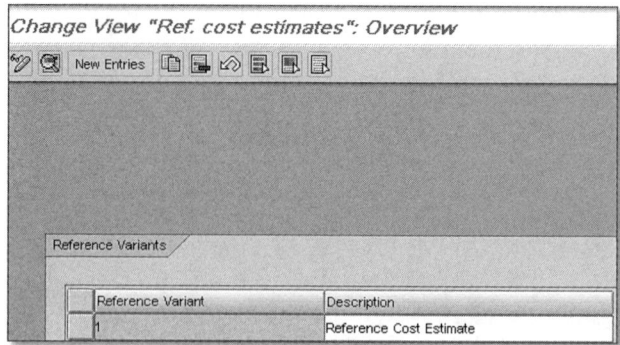

Figure 6.50 Reference Cost Estimates

You can either create a new reference variant or change an existing one by double-clicking on it. This brings you to Figure 6.51.

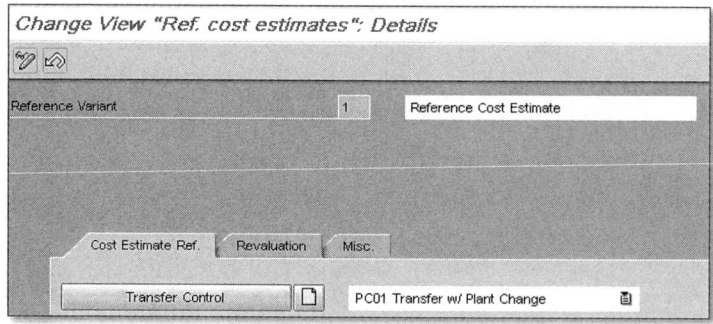

Figure 6.51 Reference Cost Estimate Details

In the first tab, you define the transfer control for the reference cost estimate. No cross-plant transfer is available—only single-plant transfer.

In the REVALUATION tab, you select which item for the cost estimate should be reevaluated. Figure 6.52 shows an example of MATERIAL COMPONENTS being selected for revaluation.

In the last tab, you define whether it will transfer the additive costs, shown in Figure 6.53.

Now that you've customized all of the necessary parameters for the cost estimate, it's time to combine all options to create the costing variant.

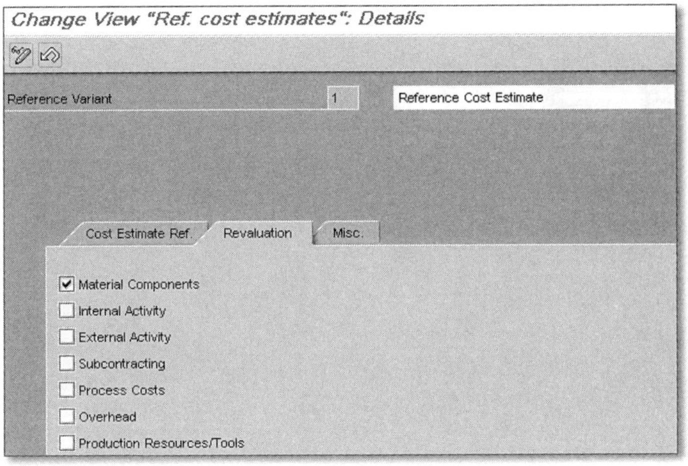

Figure 6.52 Reference Cost Estimates Revaluation Tab

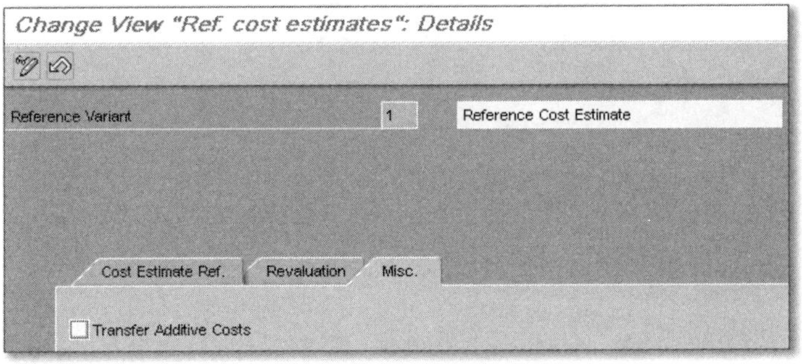

Figure 6.53 Reference Cost Estimates Misc. Tab

6.1.4 Costing Variant

Costing variants combine all of the previously defined parameters for the cost estimate and also include some others.

To customize the costing variant, you can use Transaction OKKN, or go to CONTROLLING • PRODUCT COST CONTROLLING • PRODUCT COST PLANNING • MATERIAL COST ESTIMATE WITH QUANTITY STRUCTURE • DEFINE COSTING VARIANTS. The costing variants overview screen is shown in Figure 6.54.

You can create, copy, or change an existing costing variant. By double-clicking on an existing variant, you access the customizing options for a costing variant (see Figure 6.55).

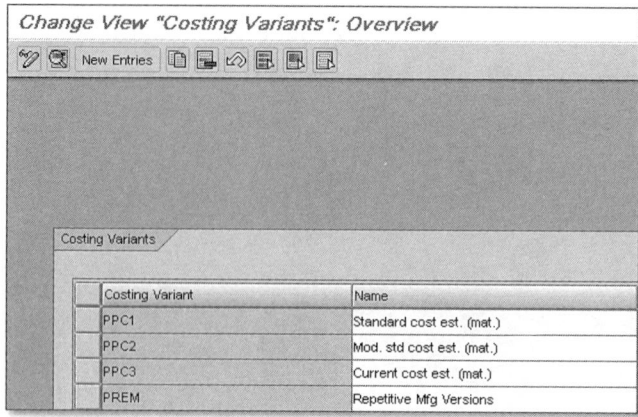

Figure 6.54 Costing Variant Overview

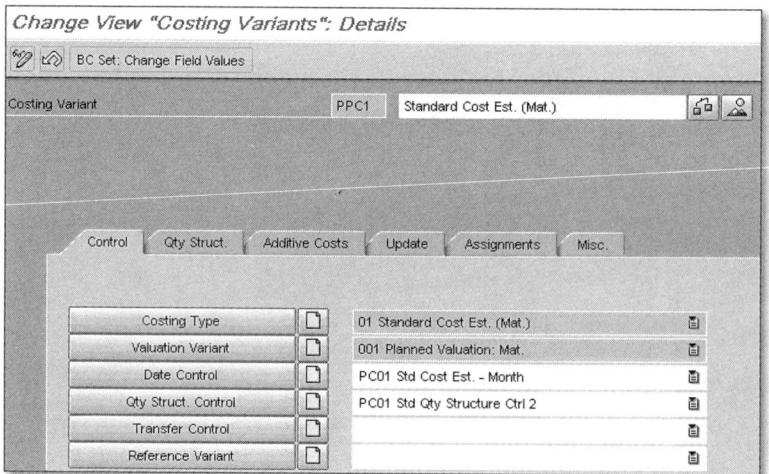

Figure 6.55 Costing Variant Details

The costing variant has six customizing tabs:

▶ CONTROL

▶ QTY STRUCT.

▶ ADDITIVE COSTS

▶ UPDATE

▶ ASSIGNMENTS

▶ MISC.

Control Tab

In the CONTROL tab you'll assign all of the parameters customized previously. TRANSFER CONTROL and REFERENCE VARIANT are optional.

Quantity Structure

You can see in Figure 6.56 the screen layout of the QTY STRUCT. tab.

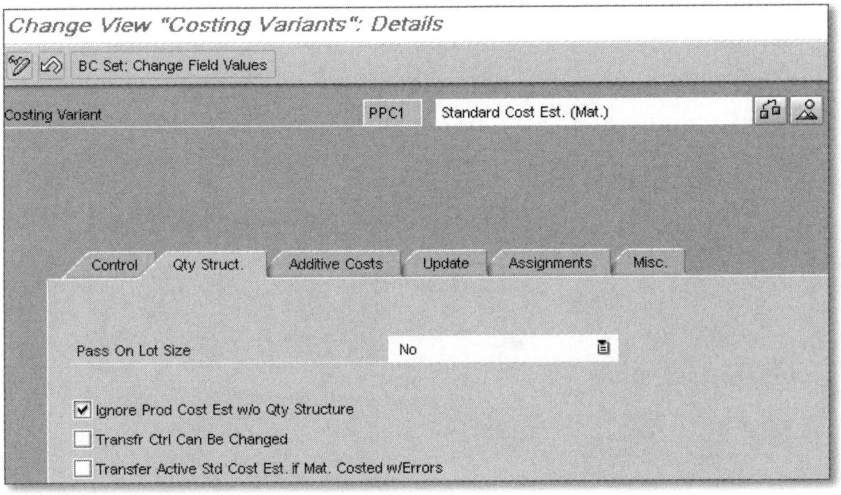

Figure 6.56 Costing Variant Qty Struct. Tab

PASS ON LOT SIZE will determine if the system will use the costing lot size of the highest material in the BOM, or the individual costing lot size from the material master on the COSTING 1 tab in the material master shown earlier in Figure 6.11.

You can also define whether the system should ignore the product cost estimate without a quantity structure. If you select the IGNORE PROD COST EST W/O QTY STRUCTURE checkbox, the system won't consider materials without a BOM and routing, decreasing the number of warning messages in the cost estimate process.

The next checkbox available is TRANSFER CTRL CAN BE CHANGED, where you can indicate if the transfer control can be changed while creating a cost estimate.

The last checkbox in the QTY STRUCTURE tab is TRANSFER ACTIVE STANDARD COST EST. IF MAT. COSTED W/ERRORS. Flagging this field means that if a cost estimate for a component in the BOM is costed with errors, the system will search for a valid cost for this component. If it can't determine a valid cost, then the system will use the material price for the component in accordance with the valuation variant.

Additive Costs

In Figure 6.57, you can see the customizing options for how the cost variant will consider the additive costs.

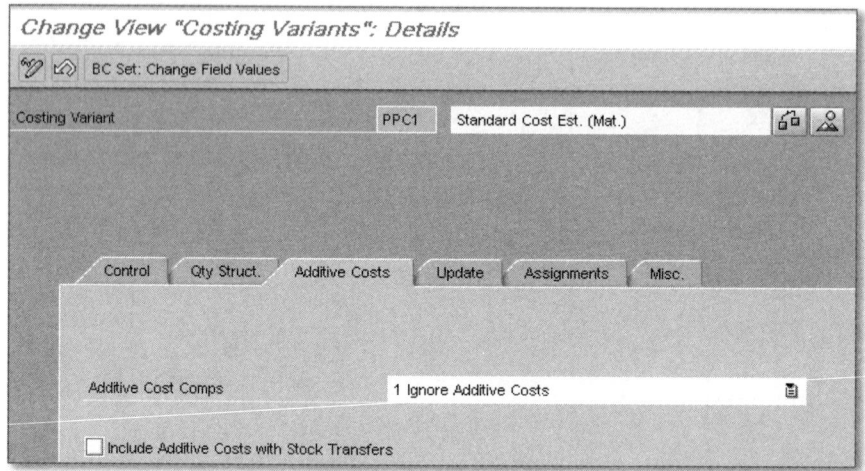

Figure 6.57 Costing Variant Additive Costs Tab

In this tab, you define the behavior of the additive costs in the costing variant. You can select from three options:

▶ IGNORE ADDITIVE COSTS

▶ INCLUDE ADDITIVE COSTS

▶ INCLUDE ADDITIVE COSTS AND APPLY OVERHEAD

You can also define if the additive costs will be considered in stock transfers.

Update

The UPDATE tab shown in Figure 6.58 is where you define how the system will update the cost estimate.

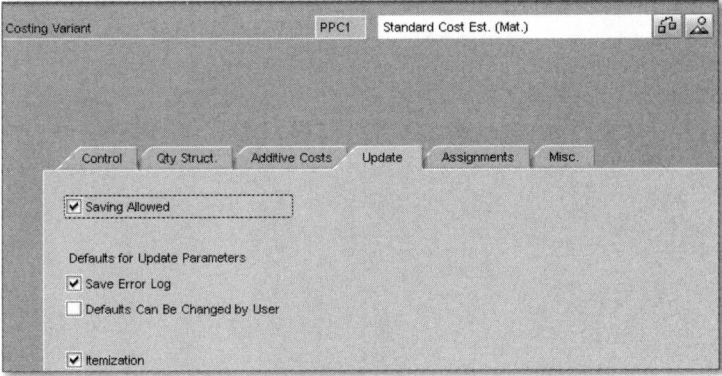

Figure 6.58 Costing Variant Update Tab

Saving Allowed is used when this cost estimate will be saved in the material master data. For costing variants used in the standard costing, you must mark this field. It's also used to save other prices in the material master.

Save Error Log will keep the log on the system for cost estimates created with errors so that you can analyze the cost estimate later. This field works together with the definition in the Misc. tab.

If you mark the Defaults Can Be Changed by User field, you have the option to change the default fields when saving a cost estimate.

If you flag the Itemization field, the cost estimate will save the itemization list when creating the cost estimate. Though it's used for costing analysis, you should also remember that the cost component split records the costs by components and that you can have this information summarized.

Assignments

The Assignments tab shows how the costing components are assigned to the costing variant. You can see the customizing screen in Figure 6.59.

Four assignments are checked in this screen:

▶ Cost Component Structure

▶ Costing Version

▶ Cost Comp. Split in Contr. Area Currency

▶ Cross-Company Costing

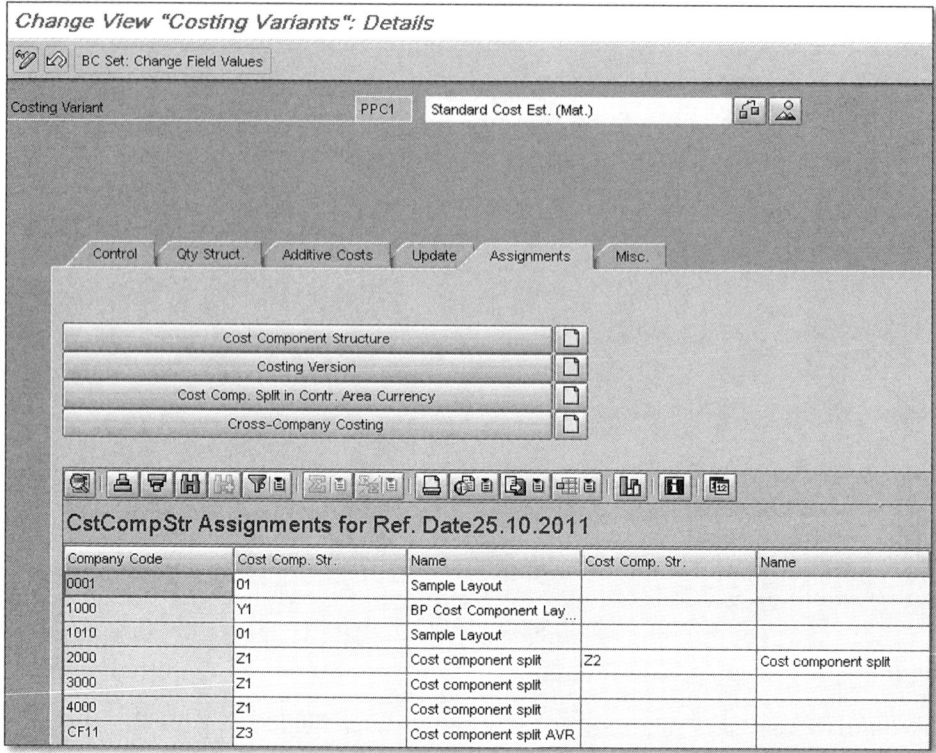

Figure 6.59 Costing Variant Assignments Tab

You've already defined Cost Component Structure in the basic settings for material costing using Transaction OKTZ. You can see the assignment overview by clicking on Cost Component Structure, as shown in Figure 6.59.

A new definition is shown if you click on Costing Version, as you can see in Figure 6.60.

This is a very useful customizing that lets you create up to 99 different cost estimate versions for the same costing variant using different combinations of costing type valuation variant, variant for costing price, and exchange rate type. By clicking on new entries for costing versions, you can customize the different costing versions (shown in Figure 6.61).

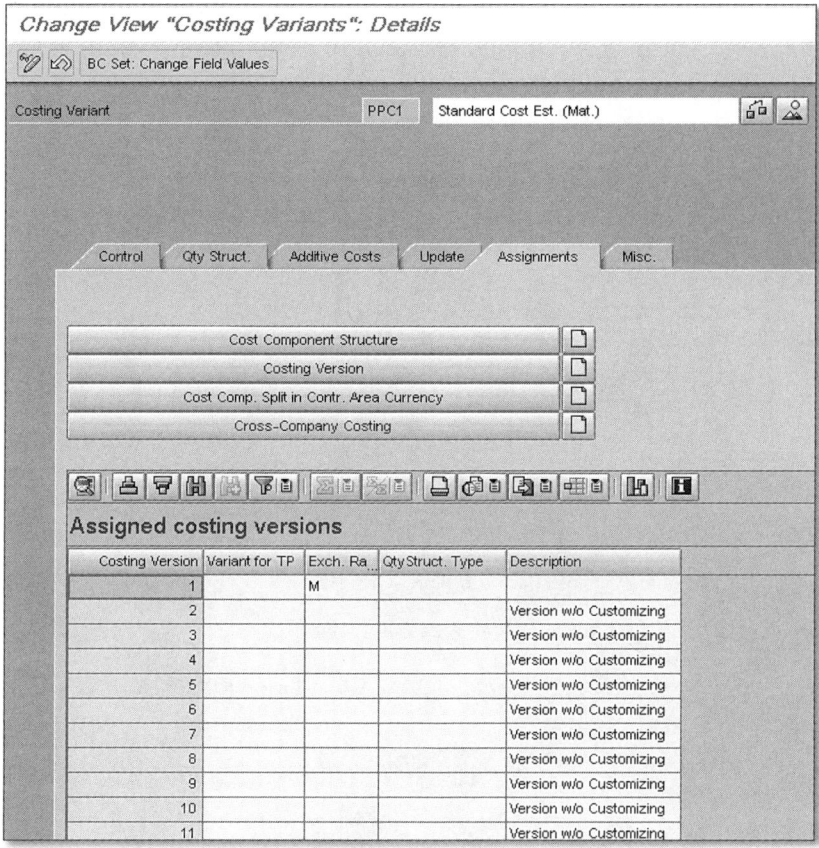

Figure 6.60 Costing Variant Assignments Tab (Costing Version)

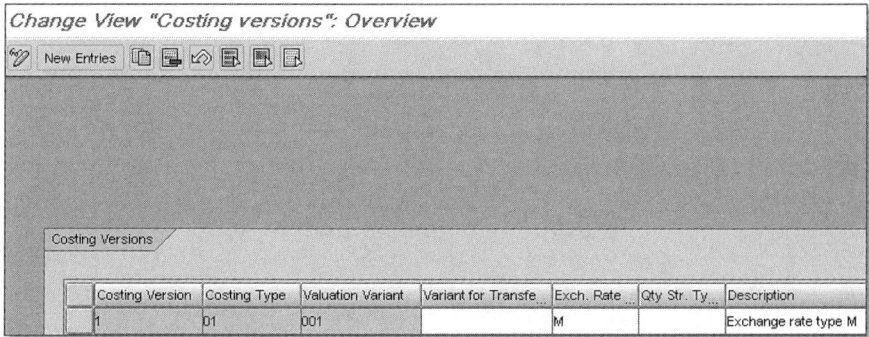

Figure 6.61 Costing Versions Overview

The next option, Cost Comp. Split in Contr. Area Currency, is also customized in the cost component structure definition in basic settings for material costing. Figure 6.62 shows an overview of the assignments, in which one company code has an additional cost component split defined.

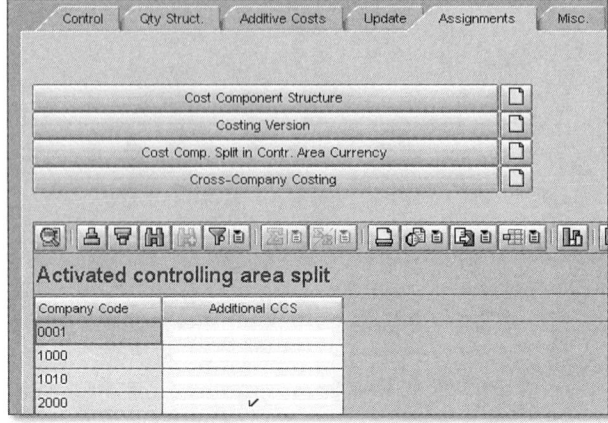

Figure 6.62 Cost Component Split in Controlling Area Currency

The last option is Cross-Company Costing, shown in Figure 6.63.

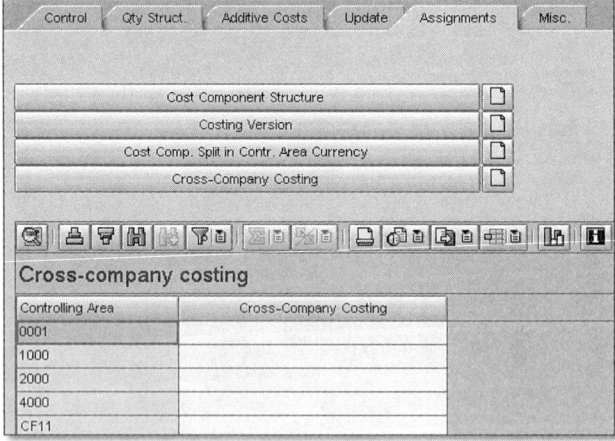

Figure 6.63 Cross-Company Costing

You can define whether a cost estimate with quantity structure will access information from plants in other company codes. An example of when this might be desirable is in a situation where there are stock transfers between plants located in different company codes. Click on new entries on cross-company costing to define for which kind of costing type and valuation variant the cross-company costing is valid. You can see an example in Figure 6.64.

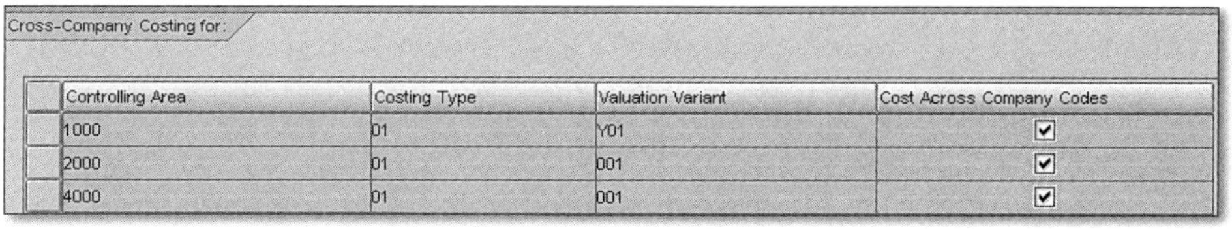

Cross-Company Costing for:			
Controlling Area	Costing Type	Valuation Variant	Cost Across Company Codes
1000	01	Y01	☑
2000	01	001	☑
4000	01	001	☑

Figure 6.64 Cross-Company Costing Detail

The last tab in the costing variant customizing is the MISC. tab.

Miscellaneous

In the MISC. tab, you define the behavior of the log errors for the cost estimate. You can see the options in Figure 6.65.

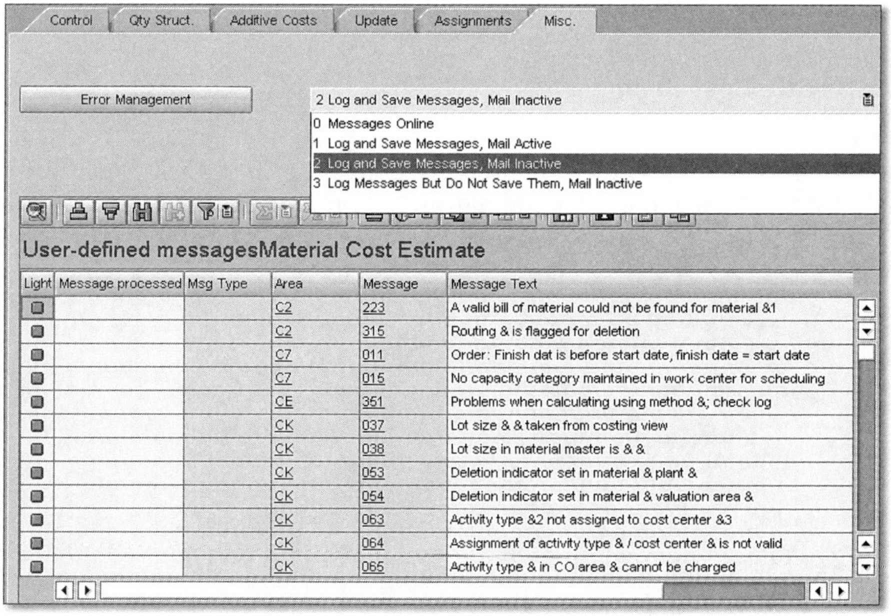

Figure 6.65 Costing Variant Misc. Tab

The following four options are available to define how the system will manage the error logs:

- ▶ 0: MESSAGES ONLINE
  The system will issue online messages for both errors and warnings. We recommend that you don't set this option because in a collective cost estimate creation, the system won't complete the cost estimate if an error message is reached.

- ▶ 1: LOG AND SAVE MESSAGES, MAIL ACTIVE
  The system will group and save the messages, additionally sending the messages to the person responsible for review and resolution of errors.

- ▶ 2: LOG AND SAVE MESSAGES, MAIL INACTIVE
  The system will group and save the messages. They can be viewed later so that you can print or manually send the messages to the person responsible.

- ▶ 3: LOG MESSAGES BUT DO NOT SAVE THEM, MAIL INACTIVE
  The system will group the messages, but you can't save or send the messages.

Now that you have customized the costing variant and all of its parameters, let's address the creation of a cost estimate.

6.1.5 Create Cost Estimate

You can now see in this example where each part of the costing variant customizing affects the cost estimate creation process. To create a cost estimate, use Transaction CK11N, which will result in the screen shown in Figure 6.66.

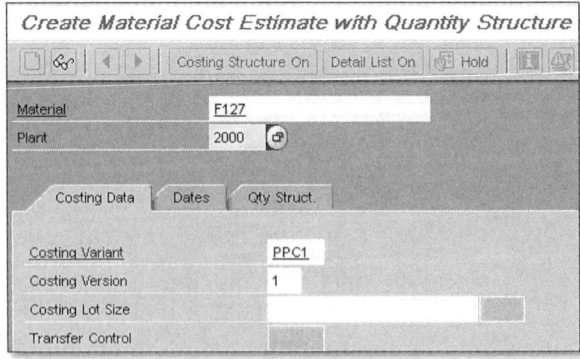

Figure 6.66 Create Cost Estimate Costing Data Tab

The first tab is Costing Data, where you can define the following:

▶ Costing Variant
Choose one of the costing variants you've customized.

▶ Costing Version
You defined the default version in the costing variant, in the Assignments tab shown earlier in Figure 6.59 and Figure 6.60.

▶ Costing Lot Size
You defined a costing lot size in the material master data on the Costing 1 tab. If you leave it blank on this screen, the system will use what is saved in the material; you can alternately specify a new costing lot size for this cost estimate.

▶ Transfer Control
This setting may be modifiable depending on the customizing done in the Control tab of the costing variant shown earlier in Figure 6.56.

The second tab contains the dates for the cost estimate (shown in Figure 6.67).

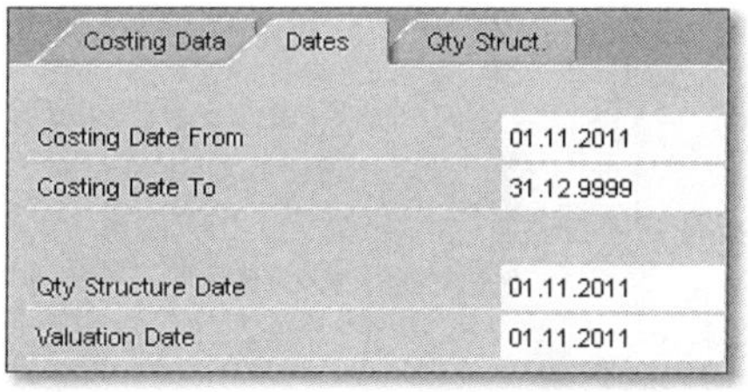

Figure 6.67 Create Cost Estimate Dates Tab

The cost estimate will propose the dates according to the customizing done in the date control (review Figure 6.39). You can also enter a new date for any of the fields.

The last tab on the first screen is Qty Struct., shown in Figure 6.68.

If you leave the fields blank, the system will use the customizing done in the quantity structure control to define which BOM and routing will be used in the costing estimate (refer to Figure 6.41 and Figure 6.45). You can override the settings from the customizing and choose either a specific BOM or a specific routing to be used instead.

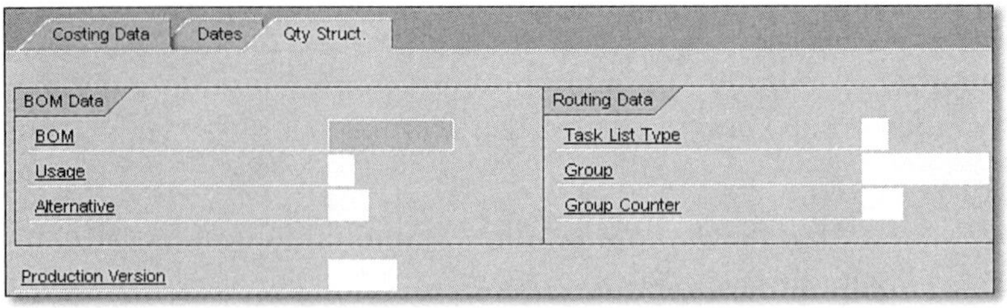

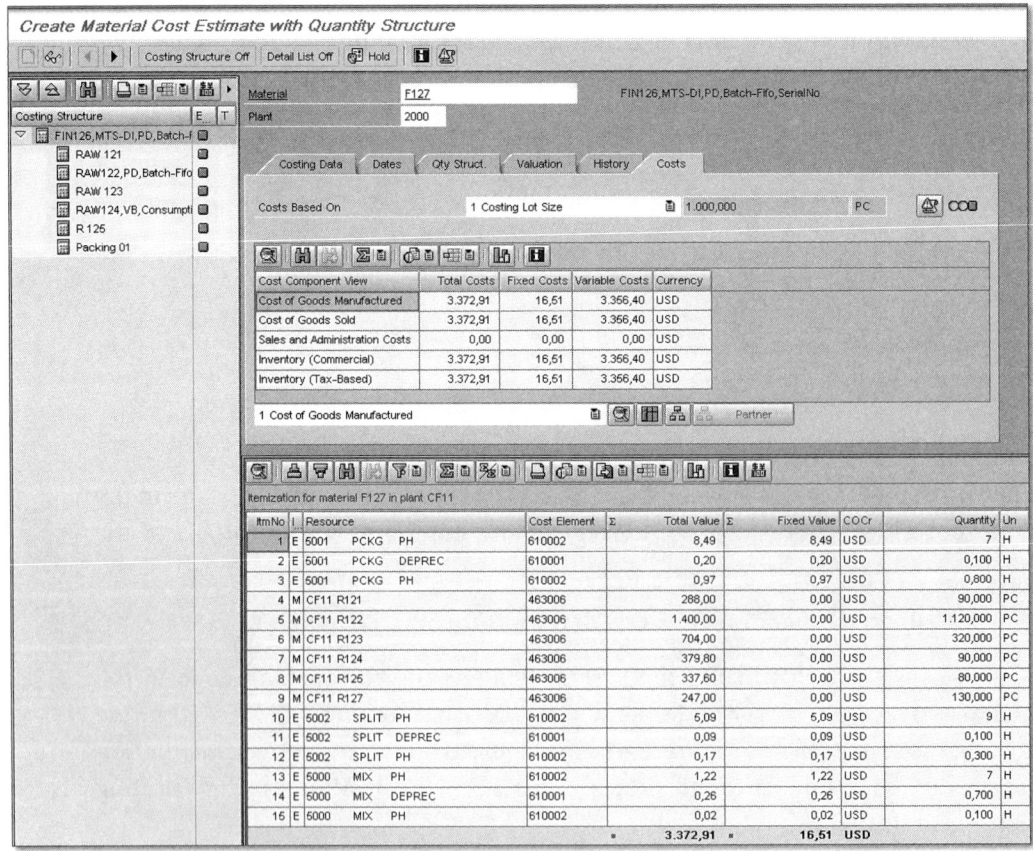

Figure 6.68 Create Cost Estimate Qty Struct. Tab

After completing the costing estimate parameters, the system will calculate the cost estimate for the material using the options customized in the costing variant. You can see the cost estimate result for our example in Figure 6.69.

Figure 6.69 Cost Estimate Example

You can see the BOM on the left side of the screen in Figure 6.69, as well as the parameters the system used to create the cost estimate by navigating between the tabs available on the top-right side of the screen. You can see the result with itemization, and you can save the itemization results by setting the flag on the UPDATE tab for the costing variant customizing (refer to Figure 6.58).

By changing the costing results view, you can see the cost component split for the cost estimate as shown in Figure 6.70.

C...	Name of Cost Comp.	Σ	Overall Σ	Fixed Σ	Variable	Crcy
10	Raw Material		288,00		288,00	USD
20	Packing		1.400,00		1.400,00	USD
30	Semifinished product		704,00		704,00	USD
40	Consumption diverse					USD
50	ConsumpHalf Finished		717,40		717,40	USD
60	Scrap Material					USD
70	Receipt w/out ordem		247,00		247,00	USD
100	Depreciation		0,25	0,25		USD
110	Electricity					USD
120	Labor		13,90	13,90		USD
130	Material					USD
140	Maintenance					USD
150	Others		2,36	2,36		USD
160	Taxes					USD
170	Water			.		USD
		▪	**3.372,91** ▪	**16,51** ▪	**3.356,40**	**USD**

Figure 6.70 Cost Component Split

The customizing for this structure was done in the basic settings for material costing, and you can see the assignment for the costing variant on the ASSIGNMENT tab in the costing variant customizing (review Figure 6.59).

The last step in the cost estimate is to save it, if you've defined the save option in the SAVE PARAMETERS tab in costing type customizing (refer to Figure 6.29).

When you save the cost estimate, the system will ask if you want to change the update parameters shown in Figure 6.71.

This option will only be available if you've defined it on the UPDATE tab in the costing variant customizing (refer to Figure 6.58).

If the recently created cost estimate used a costing variant that was customized to update the standard price (shown earlier in Figure 6.28), you now can mark the price as a future price and release it later.

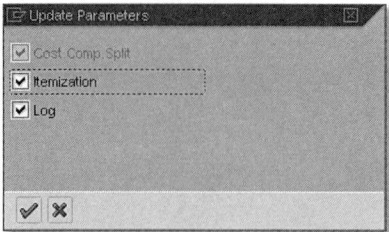

Figure 6.71 Update Parameters

6.1.6 Mark Standard Price

When we discussed the Costing 2 tab in the material master data back in Figure 6.12, we saw three fields related to cost estimate: Previous, Current, and Future.

When you mark a cost estimate as a standard price, the system will update the field Future cost estimate in the material master data with the cost estimate available for the period. To mark a cost estimate, use Transaction CK24. Figure 6.72 shows the transaction selection screen.

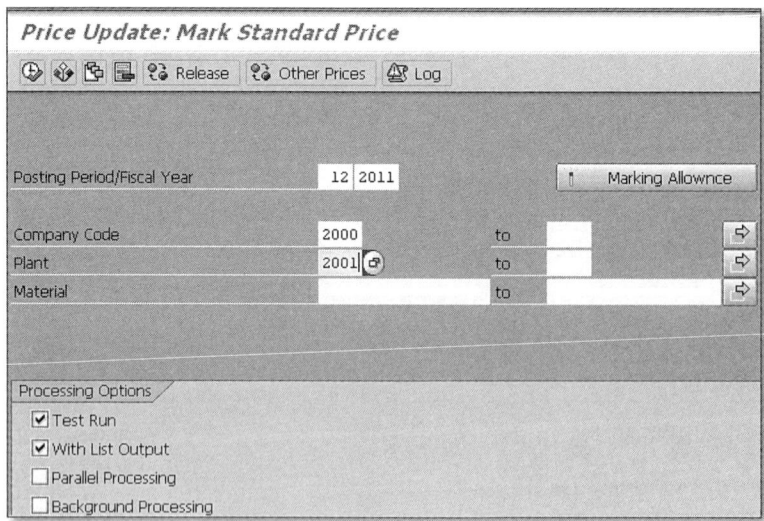

Figure 6.72 Price Update Mark Standard Price

Before marking the price, you must allow the period to be marked. Click on the Marking Allownce button, which brings you to Figure 6.73.

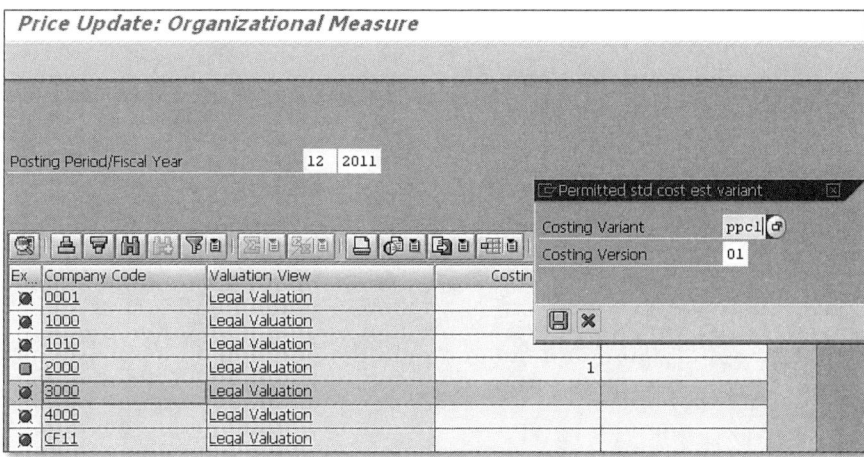

Figure 6.73 Price Update Organizational Measure

Mark the company code, and select the costing variant and the costing version. You can have only one combination that updates the standard cost for each company code for a period/year.

Having allowed the price marking, you are now ready to run the transaction. After marking, if you look at the material master data COSTING 2 tab, you can see the marked price in the FUTURE cost estimate field, as shown in Figure 6.74.

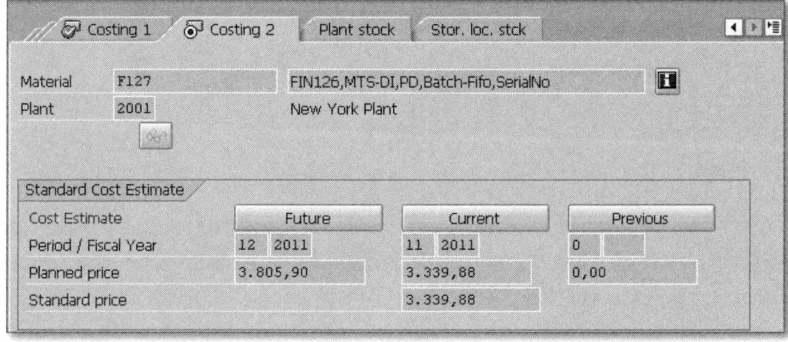

Figure 6.74 Material Master Data Costing 2 Tab, Cost Estimate

By clicking in other prices in Figure 6.72, you can mark other prices in the material master data, *if* the costing variant used to create the cost estimate was customized to mark other prices. See Figure 6.75 for more details on this price update.

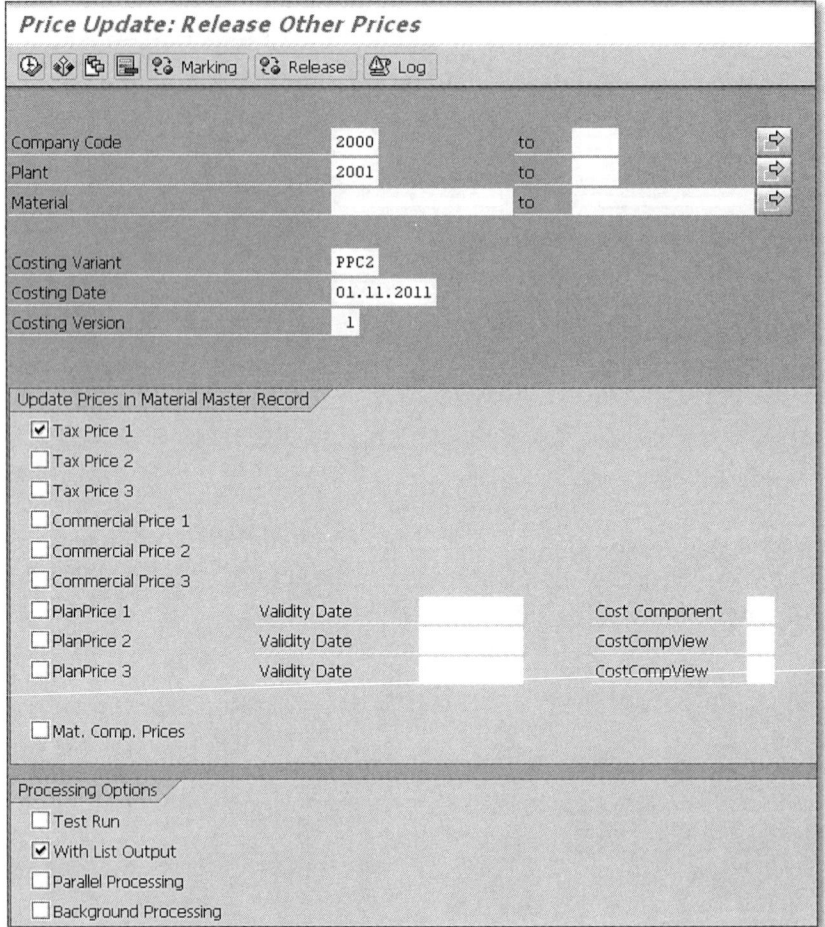

Figure 6.75 Price Update Release Other Prices

In this example, the costing variant PPC2 is customized to update one of the tax prices. If you mark any of the TAX PRICE fields available, the system will save the cost estimate result in the TAX PRICE field on the ACCOUNTING 2 tab, as you can see in Figure 6.76.

After marking the standard price, the last step is to release the cost estimate.

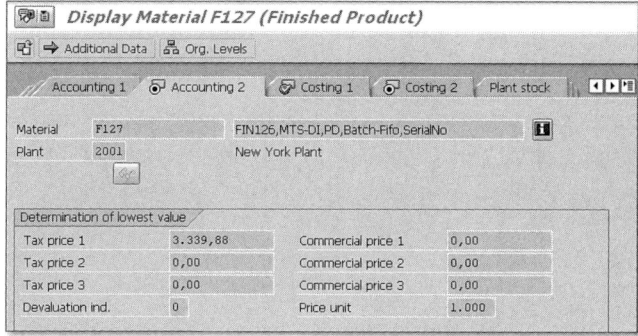

Figure 6.76 Material Master Accounting 2 Tab, Tax Price 1

6.1.7 Release Planned Price Changes

The release process is the final step in product costing. When you release a cost estimate, the cost estimate in the FUTURE cost estimate will move to the CURRENT cost estimate, and the CURRENT cost estimate will move to the PREVIOUS cost estimate. Use Transaction CKME to release the cost estimate. Figure 6.77 shows the transaction screen.

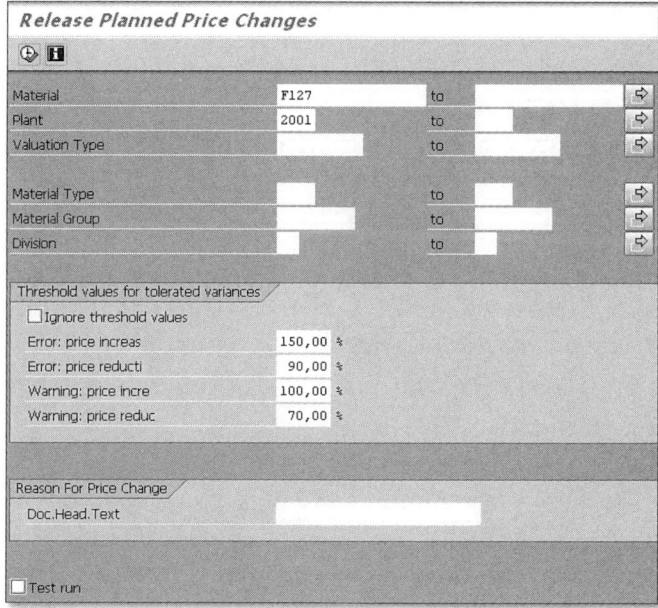

Figure 6.77 Release Planned Price Changes

The system provides a tool to prevent release of a price that differs too much from the current price. In the THRESHOLD VALUES FOR TOLERATED VARIANCES section, you can define percentage variances that can be accepted for the new price and issue an error or warning message. If you want to avoid the check, just mark the IGNORE THRESHOLD VALUES field, and the system will bypass the check. After releasing the price, the COSTING 2 tab in the material master data will look like Figure 6.78.

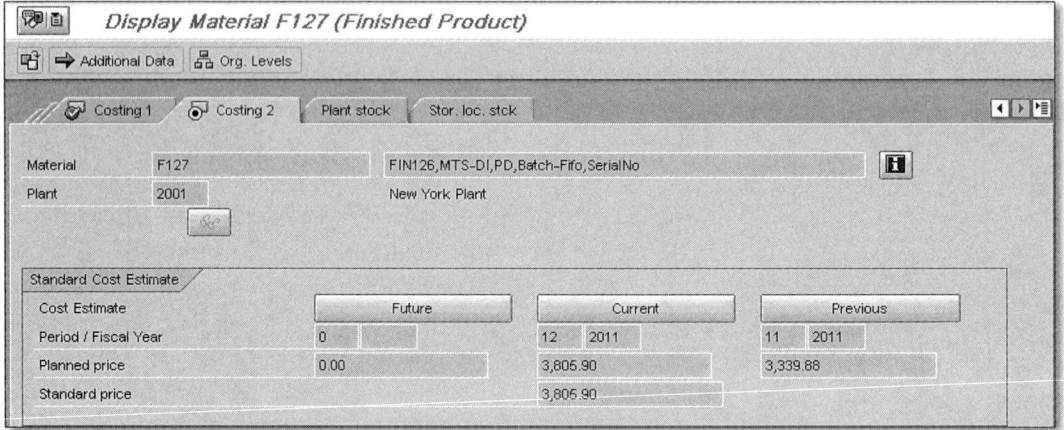

Figure 6.78 Material Master Data Costing 2 Tab, Cost Estimate

Compare Figure 6.78 with Figure 6.74. You can see that the FUTURE cost estimate, marked with Transaction CK24, was released with Transaction CKME, and the price moved from FUTURE to CURRENT.

The Transactions used to create and mark a cost estimate for a single material are CK11N and CK24, respectively. You can release a cost estimate for a single material using the release button in Transaction CK24 or by using Transaction CKME. SAP ERP also provides a Transaction CK40N, which allows you to do all of the steps in a single transaction in a collective way.

Now that you've learned about the product cost planning, let's proceed to the next topic, cost object controlling.

6.2 Cost Object Controlling

In cost object controlling, you define the cost behavior for the production process and establish the definitions related to production orders, process orders, and product cost collectors.

In product cost planning, you learned how to set the customizing to allow the creation of cost estimates for materials, and you learned the impacts of some key material master data fields on product costing.

Now you'll customize the cost behavior for the production process. The customizing is divided into two areas: product cost by period and product cost by order. We'll focus on the details of the customizing for product cost by period; where there are differences between product cost by period and by order, we'll illustrate how they differ.

6.2.1 Product Cost by Period

Product cost by period or the repetitive manufacturing process uses the product cost collector as a cost object. The customizing is divided into the following four topics:

▶ Basic settings for product cost by period
▶ Product cost collectors
▶ Simultaneous costing
▶ Period-end closing

Let's explore each one further.

Basic Settings for Product Cost by Period

The product cost estimate based on the combination of a BOM and a routing can have two additional components to add up costs: overhead costs and templates.

In the basic settings for product cost by period, you'll learn the overhead and template process in product costing. The overhead customizing uses a costing sheet to keep calculation information. A costing sheet is composed of a calculation base, percentage overhead rate, and a credit.

The process to customize the costing sheet is similar to the customizing of the accrual calculation percentage method that you learned in Chapter 2, Section 2.2.

To define the calculation base for the costing sheet, use Transaction KZB2, or go to Controlling • Product Cost Controlling • Cost Object Controlling • Product Cost by Period • Basic Settings for Product Cost by Period • Overhead • Costing Sheet: Components • Define Calculation Bases. You can see the screen in Figure 6.79.

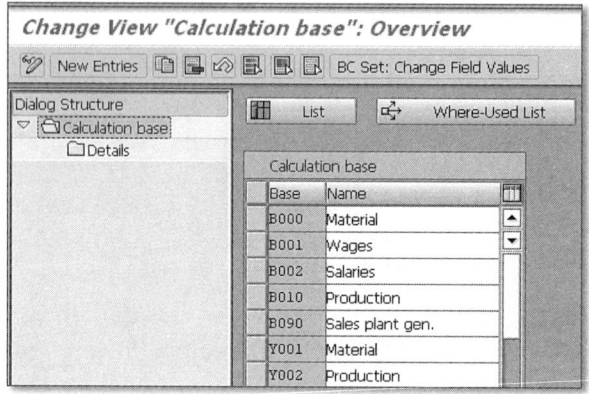

Figure 6.79 Costing Sheet Calculation Base Overview

By clicking on New Entries, you can create a new calculation or mark a base on the right side of the screen, and click on Details to change an existing one. Figure 6.80 shows you the Details screen.

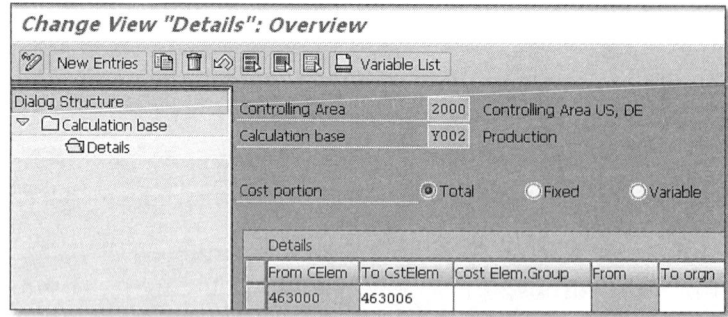

Figure 6.80 Costing Sheet, Calculation Base Definition

The calculation base is defined by either a single cost element or a group of cost elements. You can restrict the cost element selection by adding an origin group, and you can also select whether to apply it to the fixed, variable, or total cost. After creating the calculation base, you must create the percentage overhead rate using Transaction KZE2 or by going to CONTROLLING • PRODUCT COST CONTROLLING • COST OBJECT CONTROLLING • PRODUCT COST BY PERIOD • BASIC SETTINGS FOR PRODUCT COST BY PERIOD • OVERHEAD • COSTING SHEET: COMPONENTS • DEFINE PERCENTAGE OVERHEAD RATES. Figure 6.81 shows the percentage overhead overview screen.

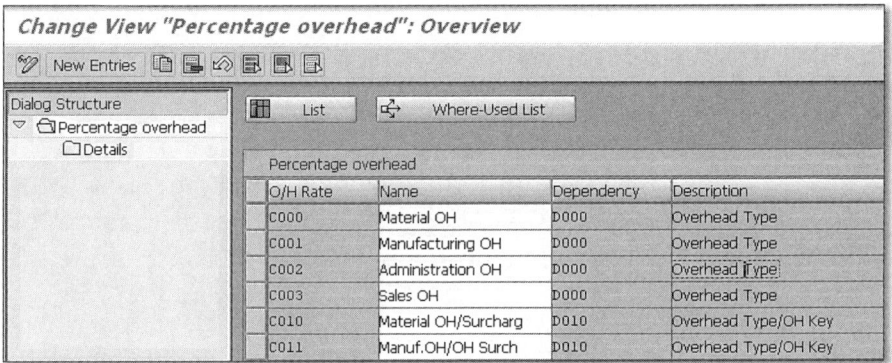

Figure 6.81 Costing Sheet, Percentage Overhead Overview

When you create an overhead rate, you must select a dependency. SAP ERP provides the following standard dependencies:

► D000: OVERHEAD TYPE

► D010: OVERHEAD TYPE/OH KEY

► D020: OVERHEAD TYPE/PLANT

► D030: OVERHEAD TYPE/COMPANY CODE

► D040: OVERHEAD TYPE/BUSINESS AREA

► D050: OVERHEAD TYPE/ORDER TYPE

► D060: OVERHEAD TYPE/ORDER CATG.

► D070: OVERHEAD TYPE/VERSION

► D080: SURCH. TYPE /PROFIT CENTER

The dependency is used to restrict the uses of the overhead rate even further. You can see one example of the overhead rate in Figure 6.82.

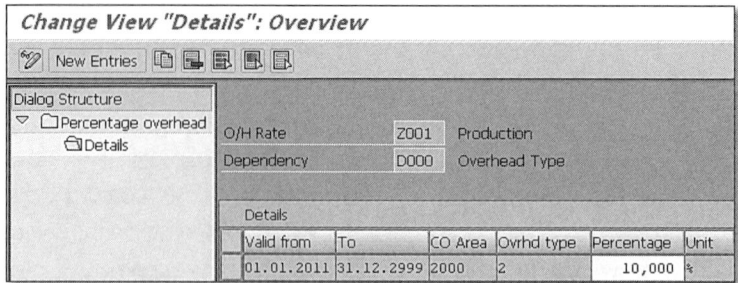

Figure 6.82 Costing Sheet, Overhead Rate Detail

You must define the VALID FROM and TO, CO AREA, DEPENDENCY, and the PERCENT-
AGE rate.

After defining the overhead rate, create the credit for the costing sheet using
Transaction KZE2 or by going to CONTROLLING • PRODUCT COST CONTROLLING • COST
OBJECT CONTROLLING • PRODUCT COST BY PERIOD • BASIC SETTINGS FOR PRODUCT COST
BY PERIOD • OVERHEAD • COSTING SHEET: COMPONENTS • DEFINE CREDITS. Figure 6.83
shows this screen.

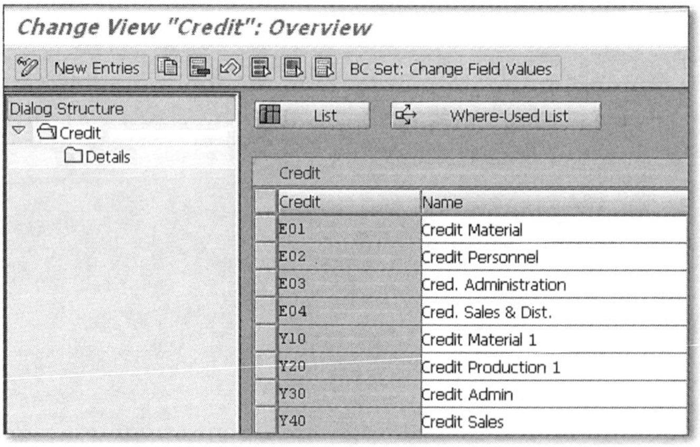

Figure 6.83 Costing Sheet, Credit Overview

You can change an existing credit or create a new one by clicking on NEW ENTRIES.
Figure 6.84 shows the options for the credit customizing.

Change View "Details": Overview

New Entries | BC Set: Change Field Values

Dialog Structure	
▽ ☐ Credit	
☐ Details	

Controlling Area	2000	Controlling Area US, DE
Credit	Y20	Credit Production 1

Details

Valid to	Cost Elem.	OrGp	Fxd %	Cost Center	Order	Business Proc.
31.12.2999	472000		100,00	102010001		

Figure 6.84 Costing Sheet, Credit Detail

In this screen, you define a VALID TO date and a secondary cost element (which must be category 41 – Overhead Rates). If the overhead costs will be split between fixed and variable, add the percentage belonging to fixed values and the credit object (a cost center, an internal order, or a business process).

Now that you've created the calculation base, the overhead rate, and the credit object, you can create the costing sheet by using Transaction KZS2 or by going to CONTROLLING • PRODUCT COST CONTROLLING • COST OBJECT CONTROLLING • PRODUCT COST BY PERIOD • BASIC SETTINGS FOR PRODUCT COST BY PERIOD • OVERHEAD • DEFINE COSTING SHEETS. See the costing sheet overview in Figure 6.85.

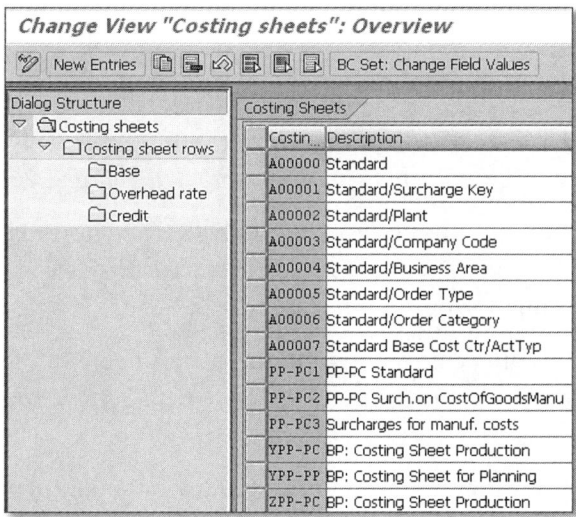

Change View "Costing sheets": Overview

New Entries | BC Set: Change Field Values

Dialog Structure	
▽ ☐ Costing sheets	
▽ ☐ Costing sheet rows	
☐ Base	
☐ Overhead rate	
☐ Credit	

Costing Sheets

Costin.	Description
A00000	Standard
A00001	Standard/Surcharge Key
A00002	Standard/Plant
A00003	Standard/Company Code
A00004	Standard/Business Area
A00005	Standard/Order Type
A00006	Standard/Order Category
A00007	Standard Base Cost Ctr/ActTyp
PP-PC1	PP-PC Standard
PP-PC2	PP-PC Surch.on CostOfGoodsManu
PP-PC3	Surcharges for manuf. costs
YPP-PC	BP: Costing Sheet Production
YPP-PP	BP: Costing Sheet for Planning
ZPP-PC	BP: Costing Sheet Production

Figure 6.85 Costing Sheet Overview

You can also define the BASE, OVERHEAD RATE, and CREDIT object in this transaction by navigating in the left side of the screen, but because we've already created those using the individual transactions, we'll next customize the COSTING SHEET ROWS directly. You can create a new costing sheet by clicking on NEW ENTRIES or mark one on the right side of the screen and double-click on COSTING SHEET ROWS on the left side. Figure 6.86 shows an example of a costing sheet that has been copied and modified.

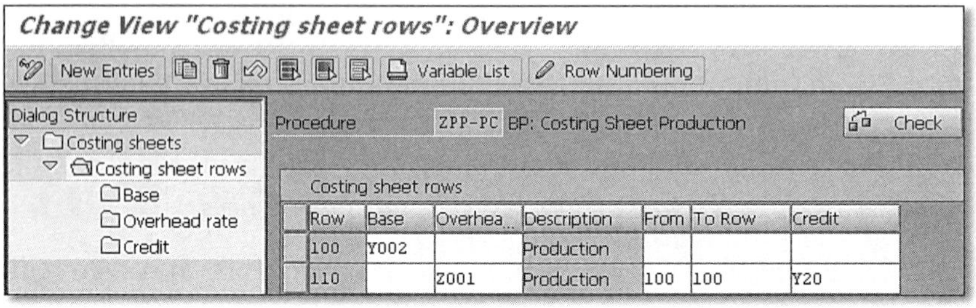

Figure 6.86 Costing Sheet Rows, Overview

Notice the base Y002 (defined earlier in Figure 6.80) is used in row 100 of Figure 6.86. Row 110 will apply the overhead rate Z001 (defined in Figure 6.82), from row 100 to row 100 and use the credit Y20 (defined in Figure 6.84). In other words, an overhead rate of 10% will be applied to the values from cost elements 463000 to 463006 and credit cost element 472000 in cost center 102010001. Reflect on the customizing that we've done in Figure 6.80, Figure 6.82, and Figure 6.84, where we defined the base, overhead rate, and the credit, respectively, and how they will act together in the costing sheet in our example in Figure 6.86.

To make the costing sheet operational in cost estimate calculation, you must define the costing sheet in the valuation variant to be used in the costing variant. Remember that you defined the valuation variant in Figure 6.36.

You can see how the system will use the costing sheet in the cost estimate in the example shown in Figure 6.87, where we created a cost estimate with Transaction CK11N.

Take notice of the result of the cost estimate for the material in Figure 6.87. On the bottom-right side of the screen, you can see the itemization for the material, showing a total of $3,594.80 for cost element 463006. The overhead rate of 10% was applied to this cost element, resulting in a $359.48 debit to cost element 472000, based on the customizing from the costing sheet.

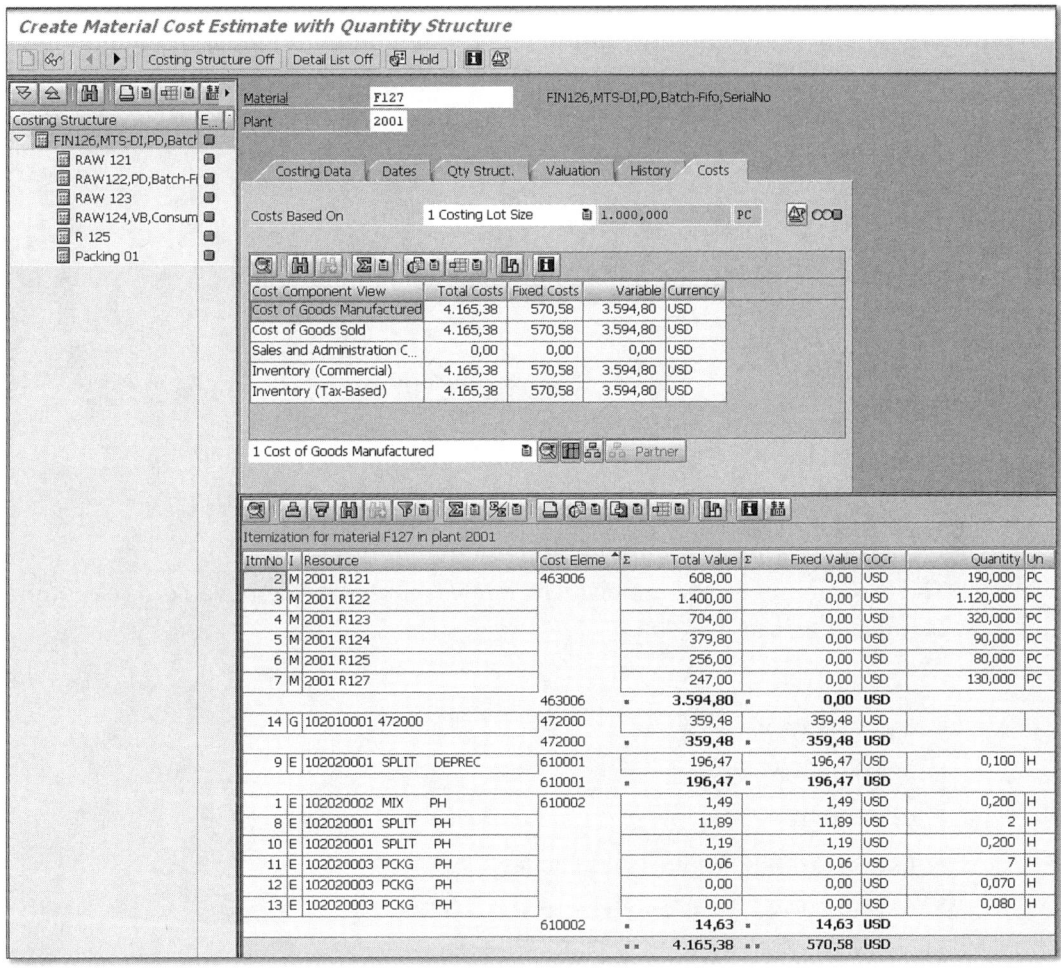

Figure 6.87 Cost Estimate Example, Costing Sheet

The next topic in the basic settings for product cost by period is the template. You've seen templates used in Chapter 5, Section 5.2 to define the sender and receiver values and cost objects for the business process. Because templates are defined by environment, you can now use one of the environments to add values to the cost estimate. The environment used for cost estimates is 001 – Cost estimate/production orders. You can see a template example in Figure 6.88. To create a template, go to CONTROLLING • PRODUCT COST CONTROLLING • COST OBJECT CONTROLLING • PRODUCT COST BY PERIOD • BASIC SETTINGS FOR PRODUCT COST BY PERIOD • TEMPLATES • MAINTAIN TEMPLATES.

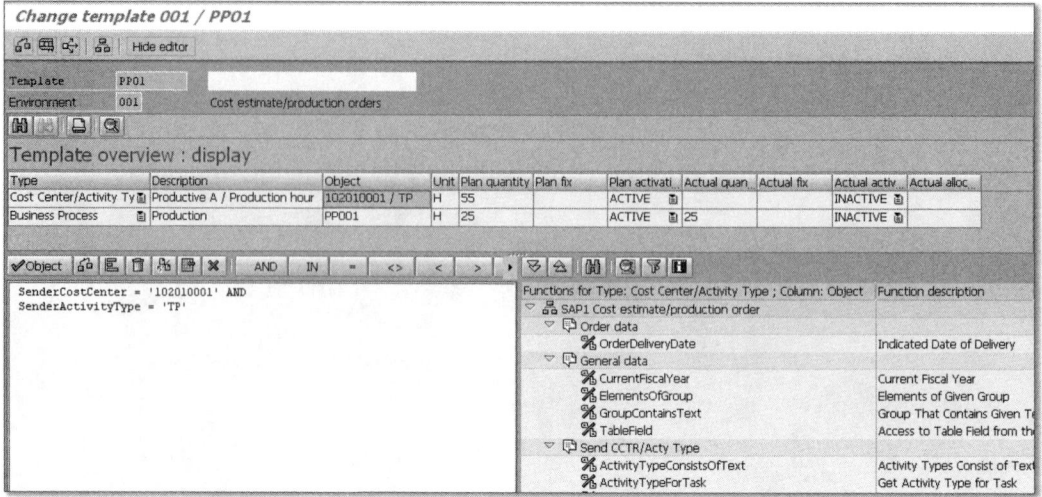

Figure 6.88 Template Example

The first column on the template overview is the TYPE, where you can select from the following listed options:

► COMMENT ROW

► BUSINESS PROCESS

► SUBTEMPLATE

► COST CENTER/ACTIVITY TYPE

► CALCULATION ROW (BUSINESS PROCESS)

► CALCULATION ROW (COST CENTER/ACTIVITY TYPE)

The template customizing can be as simple as the example in Figure 6.88, where a fixed plan quantity was used for the combination of a cost center/activity type in the first row, and in the second row, a fixed plan activity type was also used for the business process. You can establish more complex template definitions by adding formulas to the quantities using the available formulas on the lower-right side of the screen. You can also limit the uses of the template or create a quantity allocation based on formulas.

Templates for cost objects are dependent on materials and orders. Figure 6.89 shows the prerequisites to using templates in the costing planning process. All of the items starting from the left and moving toward the template in the diagram must be customized before you can establish a template.

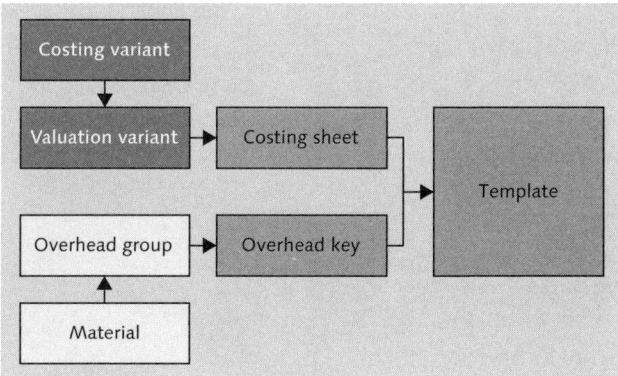

Figure 6.89 Template Selection Requirements

To select the correct template for material cost planning, SAP ERP uses a combination of the costing sheet and the overhead key.

Previously, we customized the costing sheet; to make it operational, we maintained the costing sheet definition in the valuation variant, and then we maintained the valuation variant definition in the costing variant. These steps have covered the first group of requirements to use a template, shown in the top section of the diagram in Figure 6.89. The second group of requirements to use the template in material cost planning is to create the overhead group with an overhead key and update the overhead group in the material master.

Figure 6.90 shows you the relevant fields for creating an overhead key. Use Transaction OKOG, or go to CONTROLLING • PRODUCT COST CONTROLLING • COST OBJECT CONTROLLING • PRODUCT COST BY PERIOD • BASIC SETTINGS FOR PRODUCT COST BY PERIOD • OVERHEAD • DEFINE OVERHEAD KEYS.

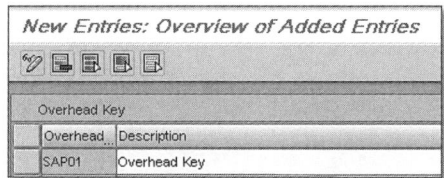

Figure 6.90 Maintain Overhead Key

The overhead key can also be used in the DEPENDENCY field for the percentage overhead rate in the costing sheet definition.

After creating the overhead key, you must assign it to an overhead group, as shown in Figure 6.91. To create the overhead group, you can use Transaction OKZ2, or go to CONTROLLING • PRODUCT COST CONTROLLING • COST OBJECT CONTROLLING • PRODUCT COST BY PERIOD • BASIC SETTINGS FOR PRODUCT COST BY PERIOD • OVERHEAD • DEFINE OVERHEAD GROUPS.

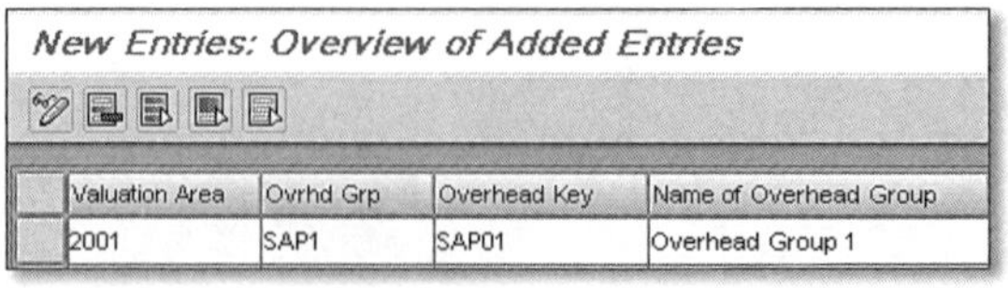

Valuation Area	Ovrhd Grp	Overhead Key	Name of Overhead Group
2001	SAP1	SAP01	Overhead Group 1

Figure 6.91 Maintain Overhead Group

The overhead group is defined by a combination of valuation area, overhead group, and overhead key.

Now that you've created the overhead group, overhead key, and the costing sheet, you are ready to define the combination of costing sheet and overhead key for the template. Do this by assigning the template to cost objects. Go to CONTROLLING • PRODUCT COST CONTROLLING • COST OBJECT CONTROLLING • PRODUCT COST BY PERIOD • BASIC SETTINGS FOR PRODUCT COST BY PERIOD • TEMPLATES • ASSIGN TEMPLATES TO COST OBJECTS. You can see the template determination customizing screen in Figure 6.92.

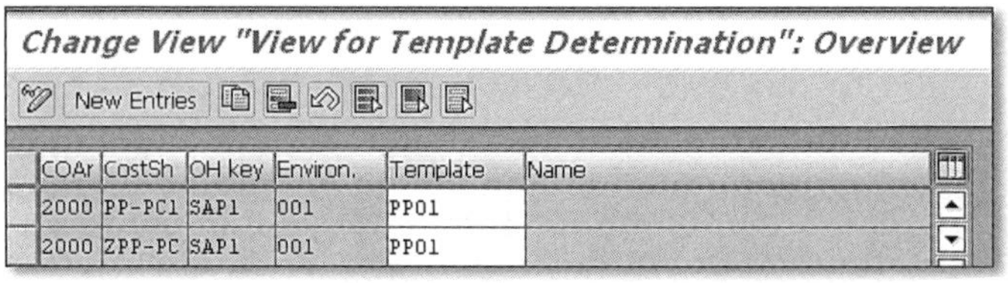

COAr	CostSh	OH key	Environ.	Template	Name
2000	PP–PC1	SAP1	001	PP01	
2000	ZPP–PC	SAP1	001	PP01	

Figure 6.92 Template Determination

The assignment is made by the controlling area, costing sheet, overhead key, environment, and template.

By assigning the template to this combination, the template is now ready to use. You now need to update the overhead group in the material master on the COSTING 1 tab using Transaction MM02, as Figure 6.93 shows.

You can see a new example of a cost estimate (created with Transaction CK11N) in Figure 6.94, but now with the costs added by the template and by the costing sheet.

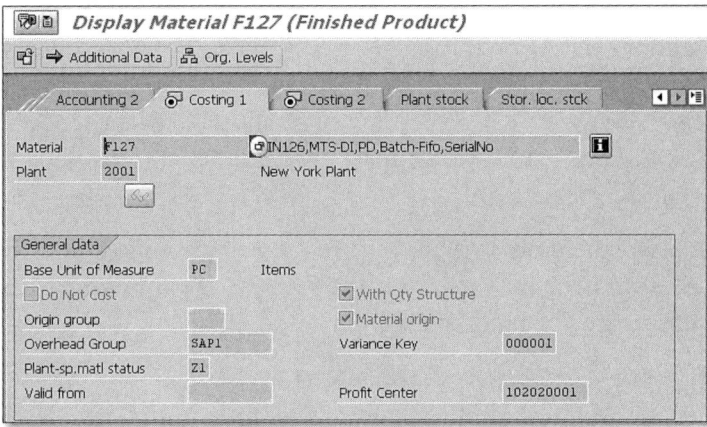

Figure 6.93 Material Master Data, Overhead Group Assignment

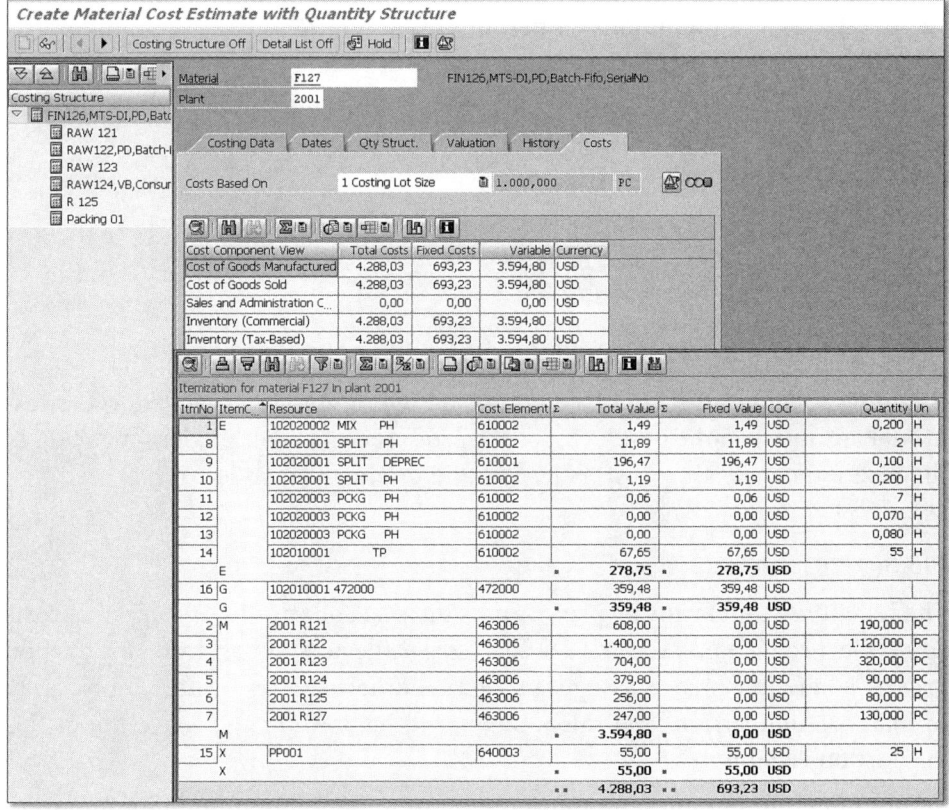

Figure 6.94 Cost Estimate, Costing Sheet and Template Example

In this example, you can see the result of the cost estimate, and, on the bottom-right side of the screen, the itemization for the material. On item number 14, you can see that the template allocates $67.65 to the cost estimate using the activity type TP. On item number 16, the overhead cost has been allocated in the amount of $359.48, and on item number 15, the template allocated $55.00 to the cost estimate using the business process PP001.

If you want to use the template in product costing, you must create the template, selecting the correct environment for each case. Table 6.1 shows the most common template environments for product costing.

Environment	Definition
001	Cost estimate/production orders
002	Reference and simulation costing
003	Cost estimate without quantity structure
006	General cost objects/CO hierarchy
009	Process order
010	Product cost collector
011	Service order
012	CO production order

Table 6.1 Environment Definition

Now that you've learned how templates and overheads can be added to the cost product planning in the basic settings for product cost by period, let's move on to the next topic in product cost by period: the product cost collector.

Product Cost Collectors

The repetitive manufacturing process uses the cost collector to collect actual costs from the production process. Product cost collectors differ from production orders because the system assigns an internal order number for the combination of material and version, and this number will be used for the active life of this production version.

Earlier in this chapter, when we walked through the customizing to create the product cost planning, we defined the behavior of the cost for the product cost simulation. Now we'll discuss the customizing to create the cost behavior for the product cost collector.

The way to define the cost is based on costing variants, which is similar to what we saw in product cost planning. The following general steps are used in the customizing of product cost collectors:

1. Define costing variants for product cost collectors.

2. Define valuation variants for product cost collectors.

3. Define order types.

4. Define default values that are relevant in cost accounting for order types and plants.

When customizing costing variants for product cost collectors, you need to define two different variants, one for planning values and another for actual values, which are defined as Costing Variants to Determine Activity Quantities and Costing Variants for Valuation of Internal Activities, respectively. To maintain the costing variant for product cost by period, go to Controlling • Product Cost Controlling • Cost Object Controlling • Product Cost by Period • Product Cost Collectors • Check Costing Variants for Product Cost Collectors. You can see both of these variants in Figure 6.95.

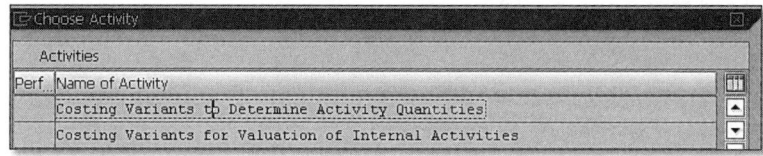

Figure 6.95 Costing Variants for Product Cost Collector

By clicking on Costing Variants to Determine Activity Quantities in the first line, you can see the available costing variants that fit this criterion, as shown in Figure 6.96.

You can see that this transaction called up the same customizing as for the costing variants for product costing planning already defined in Section 6.1.4.

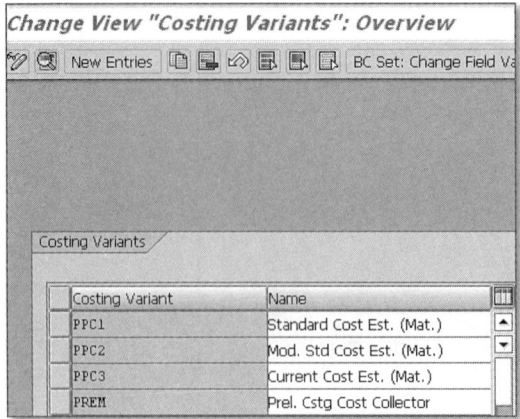

Figure 6.96 Costing Variants

What differentiates the costing variant for product cost planning from the product cost collector costing variant is that the costing type for the product cost collector costing variant can't update any price in the material master, and it also must be marked as preliminary costing. You'll be able to see the difference in the PREM costing variant example, shown in Figure 6.97.

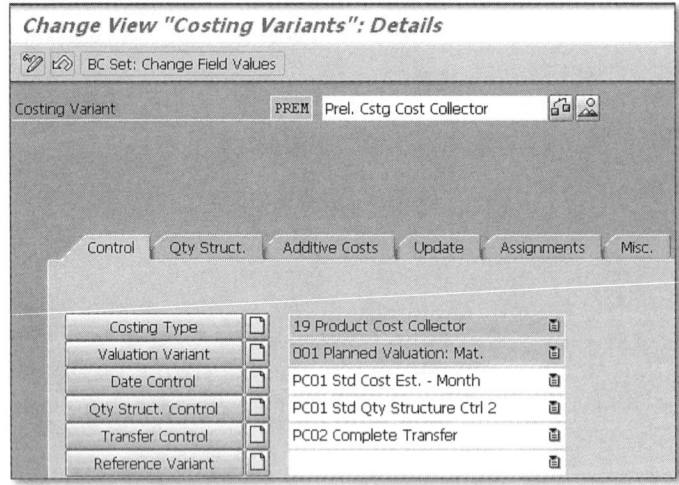

Figure 6.97 Product Cost Collector Costing Variant

If you click on COSTING TYPE, you can see its definition, as shown in Figure 6.98.

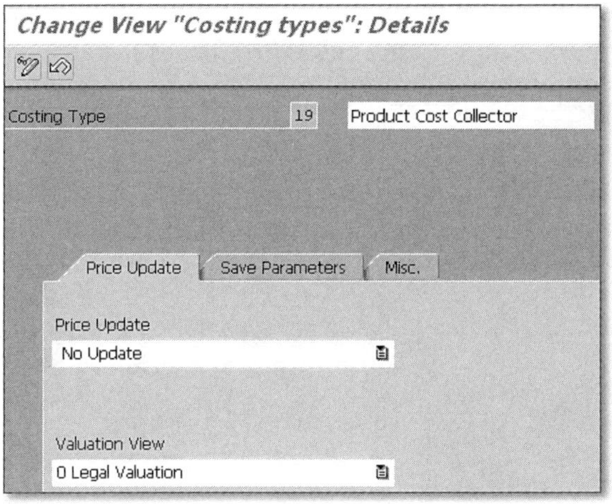

Figure 6.98 Product Cost Collector Costing Type

You can see in Figure 6.98 that the costing type isn't updating any price in the material master data. By selecting the Misc. tab (as in Figure 6.99), you can see where to update the costing type to use it as a preliminary costing for product cost collectors.

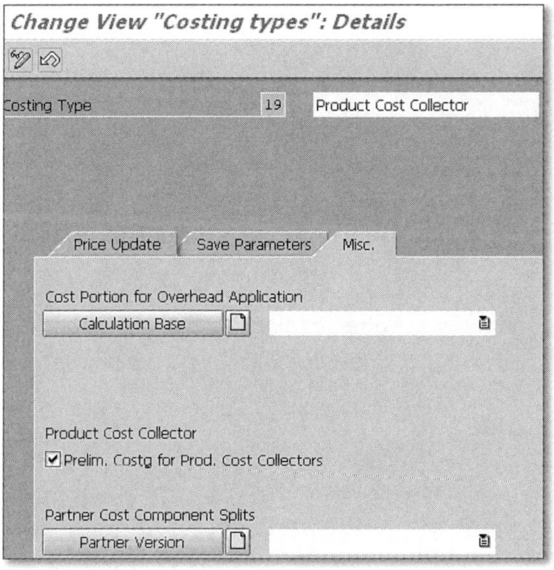

Figure 6.99 Costing Type Misc. Tab, Product Cost Collector

By flagging the PRELIM. COSTG FOR PROD. COST COLLECTOR field, you make this costing type available to be used in a costing variant for the product cost collector.

This costing variant can now be used as preliminary costing for the product cost collector; next you must define the actual costing variant. Double-click on the second line in the screen shown earlier in Figure 6.95 (COSTING VARIANTS FOR VALUATION OF INTERNAL ACTIVITIES), and you'll see the available variants (see Figure 6.100).

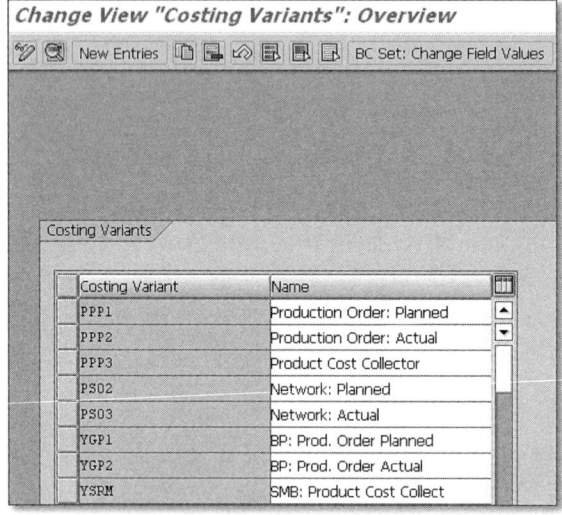

Figure 6.100 Costing Variants, Product Cost Collector Actual Costing

Again, the only difference from the planning costing variant is that for the actual, you define only the costing type and the valuation variant (as you can see in the example in Figure 6.101).

The next customizing step in the product cost collector is to define the valuation variant for product cost collectors. This is the same customizing you saw previously in Section 6.1.3.

After creating the costing variants and valuation variants for product cost collectors, you now can create the order type for the cost collectors. To define the order type, either use Transaction KOT2, or go to CONTROLLING • PRODUCT COST CONTROLLING • COST OBJECT CONTROLLING • PRODUCT COST BY PERIOD • PRODUCT COST COLLECTORS • CHECK ORDER TYPES, which brings you to the screen shown in Figure 6.102.

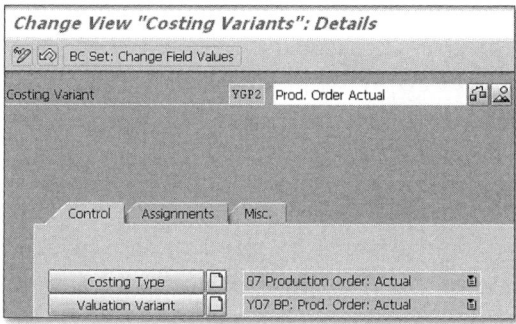

Figure 6.101 Costing Variants, Product Cost Collector Actual Costing Detail

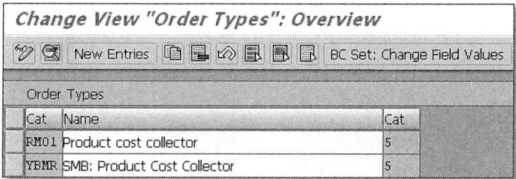

Figure 6.102 Product Cost Collector Order Type

You can create a new order type by clicking on NEW ENTRIES or by double-clicking on an existing order type to change it, as you can see in Figure 6.103.

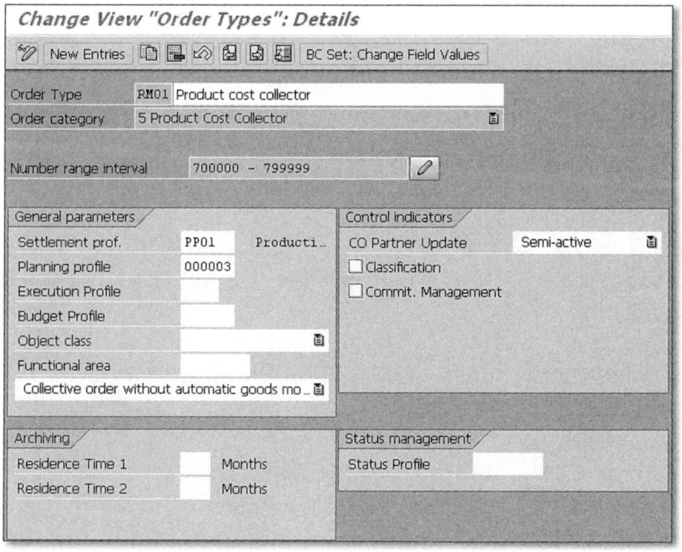

Figure 6.103 Product Cost Collector Order Type Detail

You'll notice that the product cost collector order type is similar to the definition you saw for order type in Chapter 4. The difference is that for product cost collectors, the order category used is 5 – PRODUCT COST COLLECTOR, and fewer fields can be customized. Because the definitions for each field in Figure 6.103 were already discussed in Chapter 4, Section 4.1.1, you should refer to that section if you want to review them.

Now that you know how to customize the variants for a product cost collector and also how to create the cost collector order type, the next step is to link the costing variants to the cost collector order type. The first screen is shown in Figure 6.104. Use Transaction OKZ3, or go to CONTROLLING • PRODUCT COST CONTROLLING • COST OBJECT CONTROLLING • PRODUCT COST BY PERIOD • PRODUCT COST COLLECTORS • DEFINE COST-ACCOUNTING-RELEVANT DEFAULT VALUES FOR ORDER TYPES AND PLANTS.

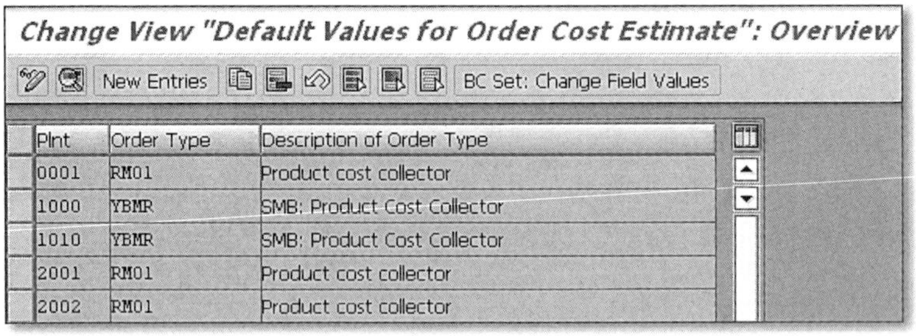

Figure 6.104 Default Values for Order Cost Estimate, Overview

By clicking on NEW ENTRIES, you can create the combination for a plant and order type or change an existing one by double-clicking. See the example for PLANT 2001 and ORDER TYPE RM01 in Figure 6.105.

In this screen, you must define two things for the combination of plant and order type: the costing variants to be used for planned costs and the costing variant for actual costs.

After assigning the costing variants to the plant and cost collector order type, you've finished the product cost collector customizing. You can now move on to the settings for simultaneous costing.

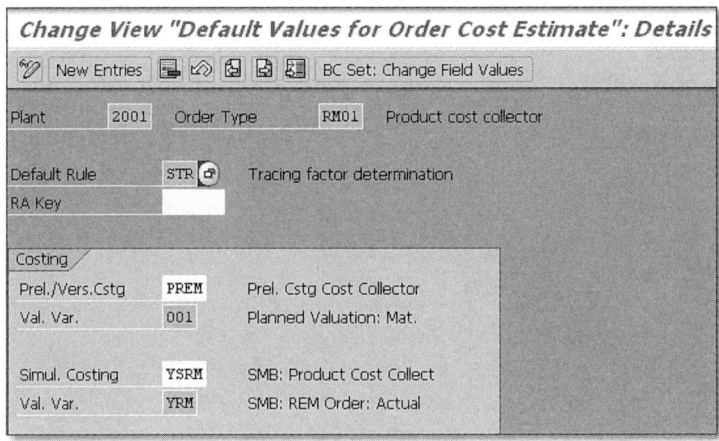

Figure 6.105 Default Values for Order Cost Estimate, Details

Simultaneous Costing

Simultaneous costing in SAP ERP means that the accounting side of the production confirmation is done automatically by the system. In SAP FI, when production of a finished good is confirmed, the system automatically credits the balance sheet account for the withdrawn materials, debits the P&L material consumption account, credits a stock transfer account (normally a P&L account for production credit), and debits the finished goods balance sheet account. At the same time, in CO, SAP ERP debits the material consumption primary cost element assigned to the production order of the finished good, credits the cost centers from the work centers in the routing using the secondary cost element assigned to the activity type, debits the same secondary cost element in the production order, and credits the production order with a stock transfer cost element.

The definition for the debit and credit accounts to be used in the SAP FI postings are maintained in the same transaction. Use Transaction OBYC, or go to CONTROLLING • PRODUCT COST CONTROLLING • COST OBJECT CONTROLLING • PRODUCT COST BY PERIOD • COST OBJECT HIERARCHIES • CHECK MATERIAL ACCOUNTS FOR SETTLEMENT. The result is shown in Figure 6.106.

The transaction key used to maintain the balance sheet (inventory) accounts is BSX, and the transaction to maintain the P&L accounts is GBB.

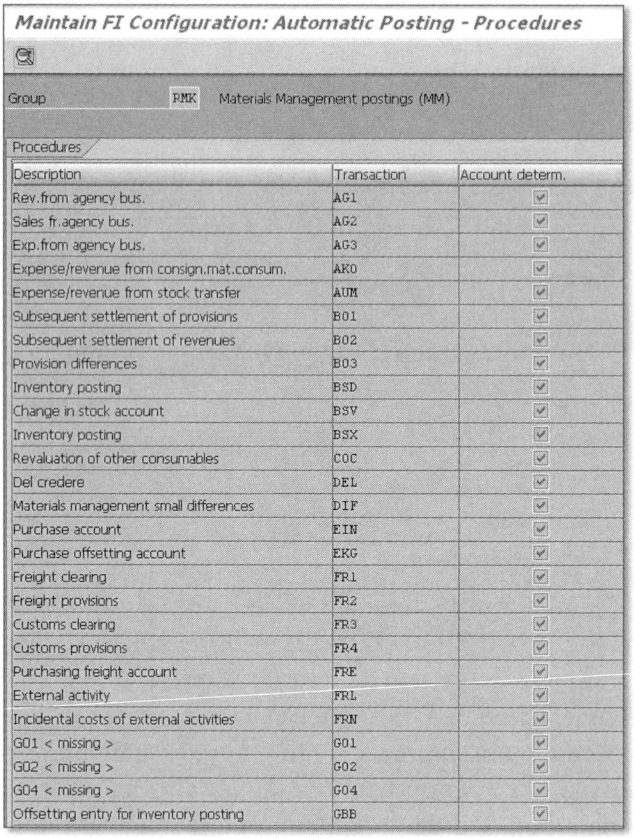

Description	Transaction	Account determ.
Rev.from agency bus.	AG1	☑
Sales fr.agency bus.	AG2	☑
Exp.from agency bus.	AG3	☑
Expense/revenue from consign.mat.consum.	AKO	☑
Expense/revenue from stock transfer	AUM	☑
Subsequent settlement of provisions	BO1	☑
Subsequent settlement of revenues	BO2	☑
Provision differences	BO3	☑
Inventory posting	BSD	☑
Change in stock account	BSV	☑
Inventory posting	BSX	☑
Revaluation of other consumables	COC	☑
Del credere	DEL	☑
Materials management small differences	DIF	☑
Purchase account	EIN	☑
Purchase offsetting account	EKG	☑
Freight clearing	FR1	☑
Freight provisions	FR2	☑
Customs clearing	FR3	☑
Customs provisions	FR4	☑
Purchasing freight account	FRE	☑
External activity	FRL	☑
Incidental costs of external activities	FRN	☑
G01 < missing >	G01	☑
G02 < missing >	G02	☑
G04 < missing >	G04	☑
Offsetting entry for inventory posting	GBB	☑

Figure 6.106 Maintain FI Automatic Posting

Let's first look at the BSX transaction key. Double-click in the BSX line to update the accounts. Figure 6.107 shows the customizing.

The BSX transaction key holds the balance sheet inventory accounts. In this case, the definitions of accounts are made by valuation group (in the VALUATION MODIF. column) and valuation class. Valuation group is used to group valuation areas (plants). You can have one account for a group of valuation areas, or, if you define one group for each valuation area, you can define a different account for each valuation area. By using the second approach, you can have separate inventory accounts by plant in the balance sheet. Valuation classes are assigned to materials in the material master data ACCOUNTING 1 tab. It's important to define in this step the accounts to be used for each possible valuation area and valuation class combination to avoid account determination errors during actual postings.

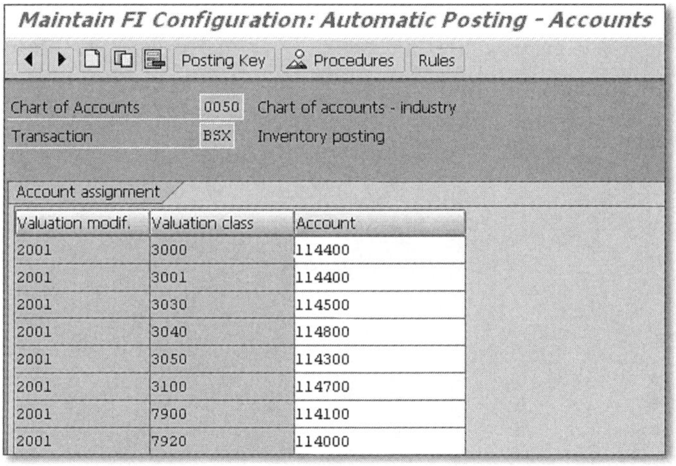

Maintain FI Configuration: Automatic Posting - Accounts

Posting Key | Procedures | Rules

Chart of Accounts 0050 Chart of accounts - industry

Transaction BSX Inventory posting

Account assignment

Valuation modif.	Valuation class	Account
2001	3000	114400
2001	3001	114400
2001	3030	114500
2001	3040	114800
2001	3050	114300
2001	3100	114700
2001	7900	114100
2001	7920	114000

Figure 6.107 Maintain FI Automatic Posting, BSX Transaction Key

Figure 6.108 shows the valuation group customizing, using Transaction OMWD to group the valuation areas.

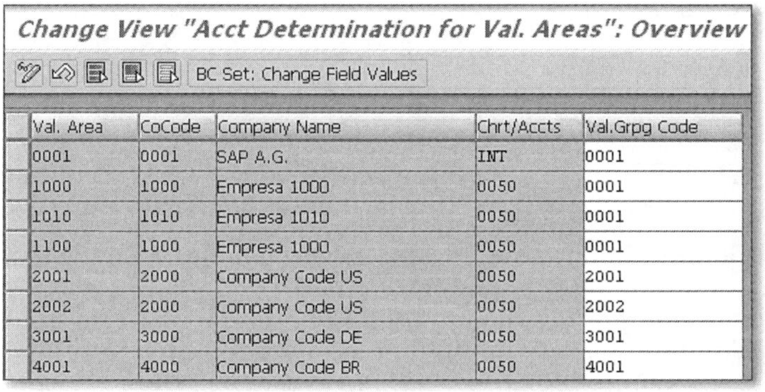

Change View "Acct Determination for Val. Areas": Overview

BC Set: Change Field Values

Val. Area	CoCode	Company Name	Chrt/Accts	Val.Grpg Code
0001	0001	SAP A.G.	INT	0001
1000	1000	Empresa 1000	0050	0001
1010	1010	Empresa 1010	0050	0001
1100	1000	Empresa 1000	0050	0001
2001	2000	Company Code US	0050	2001
2002	2000	Company Code US	0050	2002
3001	3000	Company Code DE	0050	3001
4001	4000	Company Code BR	0050	4001

Figure 6.108 Valuation Group Customizing

You can see in Figure 6.108 that both approaches were used in our example, where some valuation areas were grouped together and others were not. This grouping of the valuation areas allows for complete flexibility in your design of the accounting structure, simultaneously allowing for definitions to be consistent to simplify ongoing master data maintenance. For instance, if you decide to use the first approach and define different accounts for each valuation area, this will mean that each time you add a new plant to the system, you'll need to also set up a new valuation group, set up new FI accounts, and maintain the account determination. You should consider the implications to the long-term system maintenance when determining your approach to account determination. Now, let's look at the account determination for the GBB transaction key, shown in Figure 6.109.

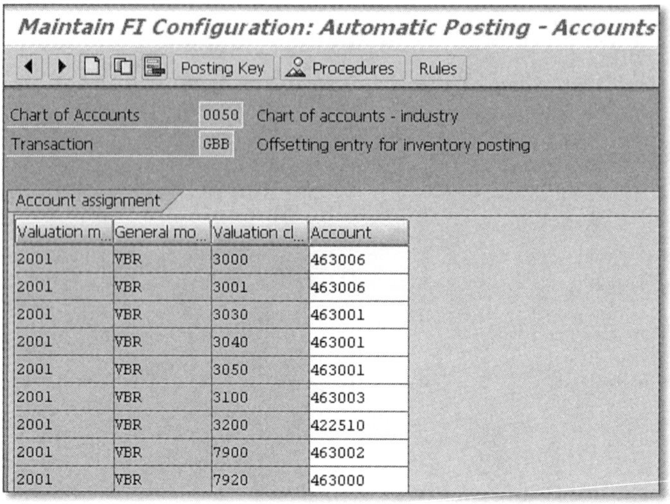

Figure 6.109 Maintain FI Automatic Posting, GBB Transaction Key

The GBB transaction key has an additional key to define the account. The GENERAL MODIFICATION field is used to identify the business transaction for the accounting posting. The important general modifications for the production process are both the VBR (used to identify the consumption P&L accounts) and the AUF (to identify the stock transfer accounts).

You can see in Figure 6.110 an example of the FI posting for a production order confirmation. Transaction FB03 was used to display the FI document.

This is the FI side of the posting, where SAP ERP has credited the raw material balance sheet account, debited the finished product balance sheet account, and updated the P&L based on the account determination set in the previous steps.

Now, let's look at the same example in the CO posting on the product cost collector order, shown in Figure 6.111. Transaction S_ALR_87012999 was used to display the order report.

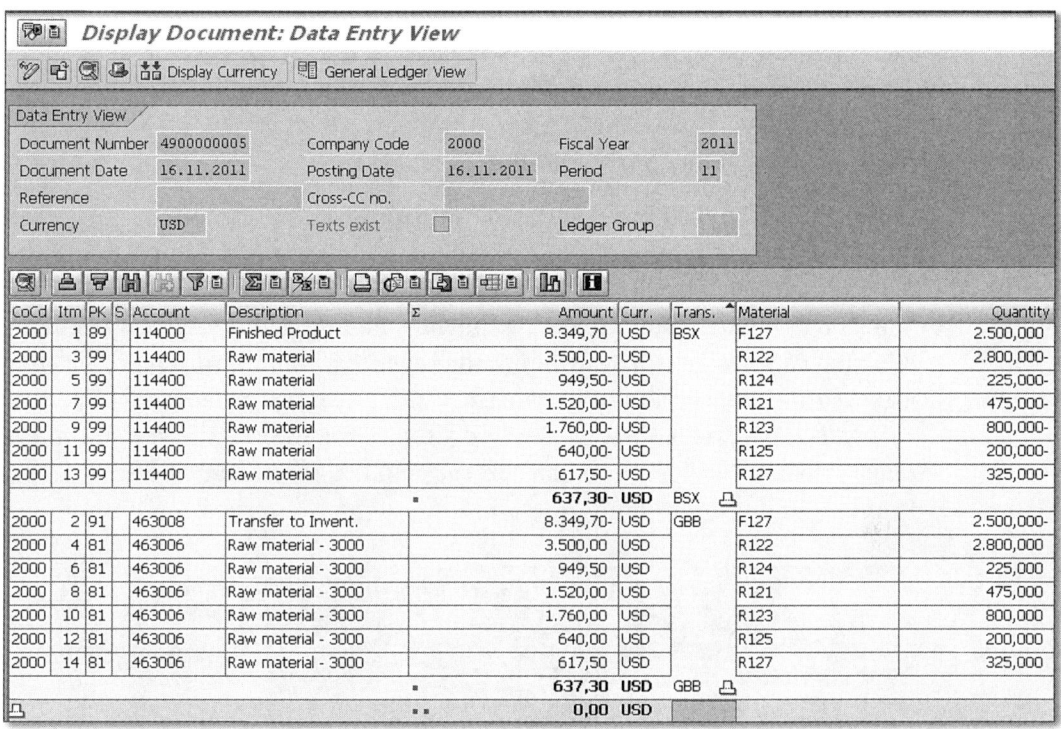

Figure 6.110 FI Document Display

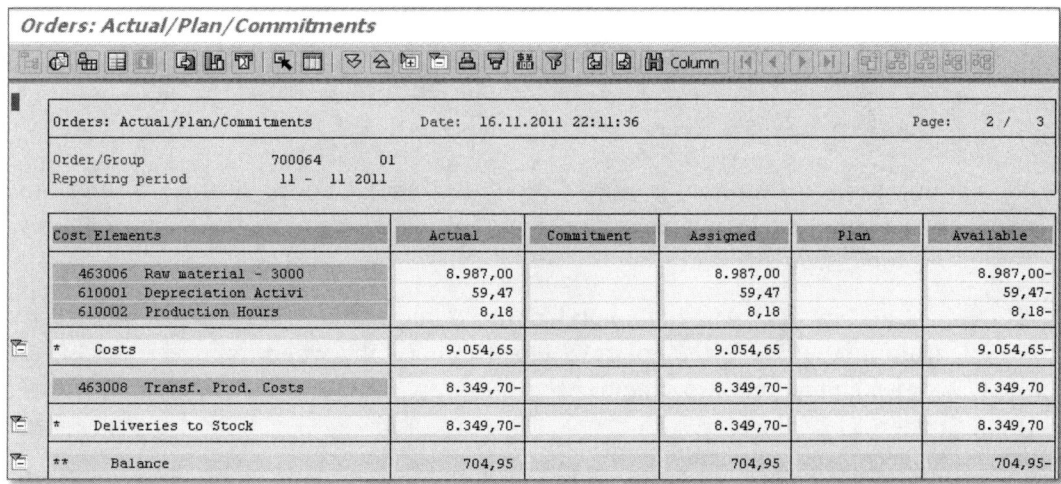

Figure 6.111 Product Cost Collector Order Report

You can see in the product cost collector order report a debit in the primary raw material cost element, a debit in the secondary activity type cost element, and a credit in the stock transfer primary cost element. The remaining balance in the order is called variance. The variance can be caused in several ways and is explained further in the next topic, period-end closing.

Another important customizing related to the product cost collector is the repetitive manufacturing profile. This is where you can determine how SAP ERP will create the material and activity type consumption, whether it will be backflushed or not, and also where you can define the movement type for each process in the production confirmation. To customize the repetitive manufacturing profile go to CONTROLLING • PRODUCT COST CONTROLLING • COST OBJECT CONTROLLING • PRODUCT COST BY PERIOD • SIMULTANEOUS COSTING • CHECK CONTROL DATA FOR REPETITIVE MANUFACTURING PROFILES. You can see the initial customizing screen in Figure 6.112.

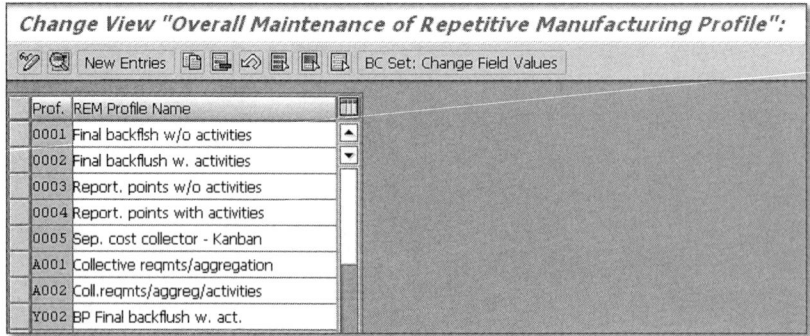

Figure 6.112 Repetitive Manufacturing Profile Overview

SAP ERP provides some standard repetitive manufacturing profiles. You can use one of these or create a new one. Figure 6.113 offers an example of a repetitive manufacturing profile.

On the CONTROL DATA 1 tab, you'll define whether the goods issue is to be posted at the same time as the goods receipt automatically when doing the production confirmation, and also whether the system will use a reporting point to do the material backflushing.

You'll also define the system behavior for cases when an error occurs during the backflushing process.

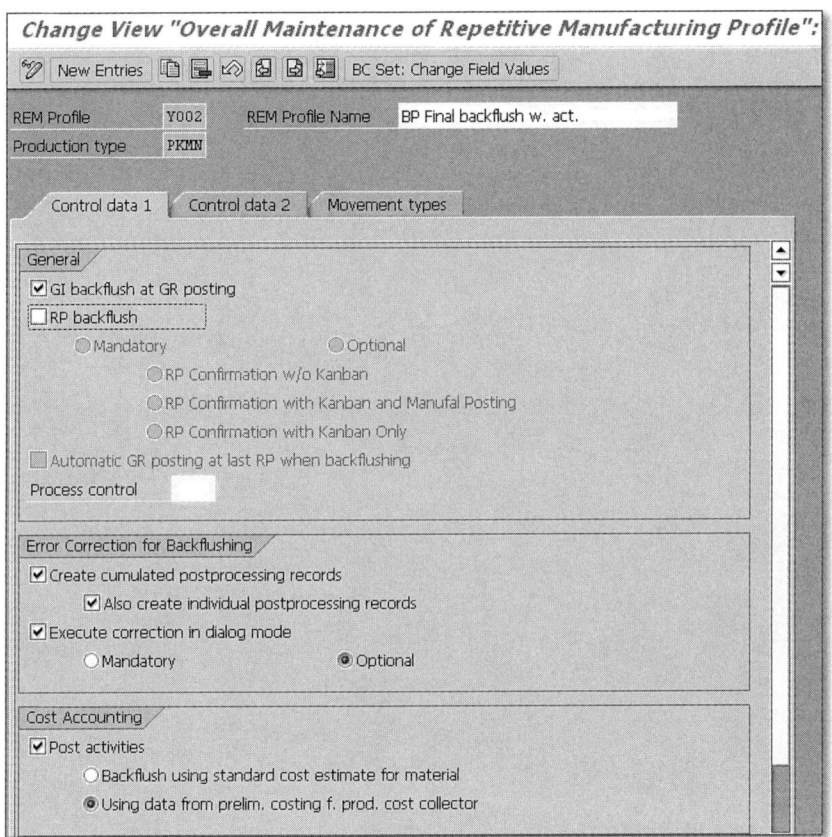

Figure 6.113 Repetitive Manufacturing Profile Control Tab 1 Detail

For the costing accounting, you can define whether the activity types are going to be backflushed and whether the system will use the standard cost for the material or the preliminary costing for the product cost collector for posting.

In the CONTROL DATA 2 tab, shown in Figure 6.114, you'll define how the system will consider the planned orders.

Movement types are used in Materials Management to identify and differentiate between types of inventory movements depending on the source, such as a goods receipt from a purchase order versus a goods receipt from a production order. In the MOVEMENT TYPES tab shown in Figure 6.115, you'll define the movement types for the production process.

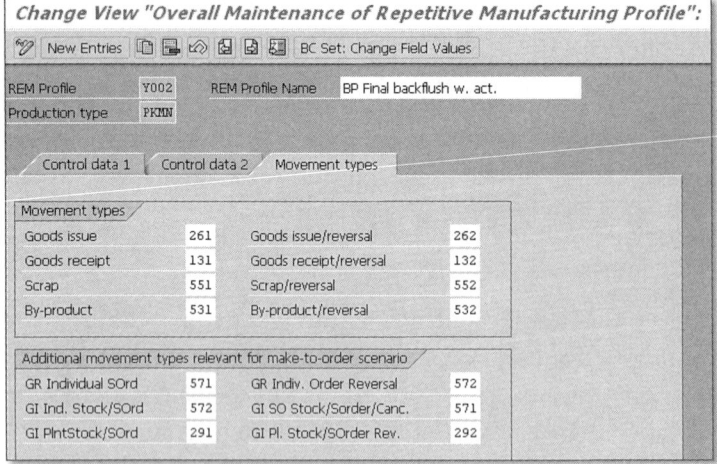

Change View "Overall Maintenance of Repetitive Manufacturing Profile":

🖉 New Entries 🗐 🔙 🖎 🔛 🔛 🔛 BC Set: Change Field Values

REM Profile Y002 REM Profile Name BP Final backflush w. act.
Production type PKMN

Control data 1 / Control data 2 / Movement types

Planned Orders

Planned Order Reduction
☑ Reduce planned orders assigned to version
    ☐ Plus planned orders not yet assigned
        ☐ Plus planned orders assigned to other versions
Reduction period 3 Days

Firming Logic
○ Do not firm   ◉ Always firm   ○ Firm within plng time fence

Creating Planned Orers when Reversing
☐ Create planned orders when reversing
    ○ For the GR amount of the current day
    ○ By requirement (asynchronous MRP run)

Material Requirements
Stock determation rule
Batch search procedure
☐ Aggregate reqmts
☑ Create reqmts for phantom assemblies

Figure 6.114 Repetitive Manufacturing Profile Control Tab 2 Details

Change View "Overall Maintenance of Repetitive Manufacturing Profile":

🖉 New Entries 🗐 🔙 🖎 🔛 🔛 🔛 BC Set: Change Field Values

REM Profile Y002 REM Profile Name BP Final backflush w. act.
Production type PKMN

Control data 1 / Control data 2 / Movement types

Movement types

Goods issue	261	Goods issue/reversal	262
Goods receipt	131	Goods receipt/reversal	132
Scrap	551	Scrap/reversal	552
By-product	531	By-product/reversal	532

Additional movement types relevant for make-to-order scenario

GR Individual SOrd	571	GR Indiv. Order Reversal	572
GI Ind. Stock/SOrd	572	GI SO Stock/Sorder/Canc.	571
GI PlntStock/SOrd	291	GI Pl. Stock/SOrder Rev.	292

Figure 6.115 Repetitive Manufacturing Profile Movement Type Tab Detail

After creating the repetitive manufacturing profile, you must assign it to the material master in the MRP 4 tab using Transaction MM02, as shown in Figure 6.116.

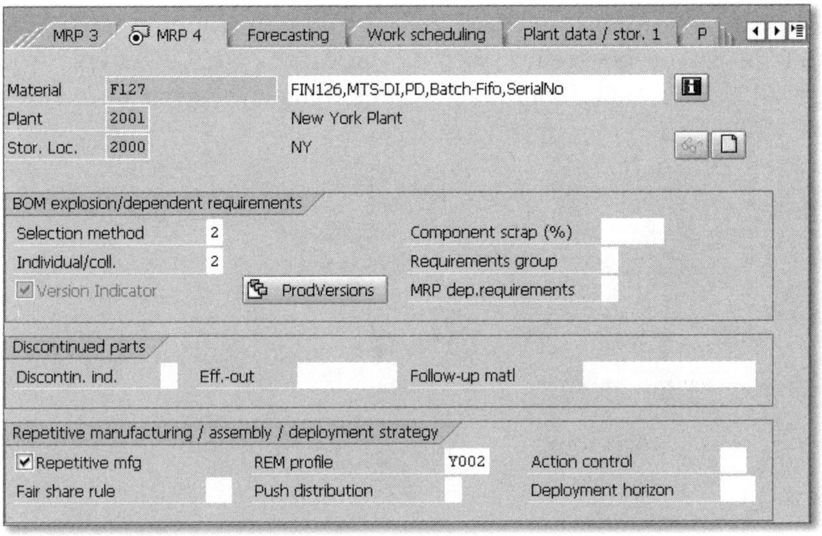

Figure 6.116 Material Master MRP 4 Tab, REM Profile

For additional analysis of the backflushing process, you can set the cost generation log for repetitive manufacturing by going to CONTROLLING • PRODUCT COST CONTROLLING • COST OBJECT CONTROLLING • PRODUCT COST BY PERIOD • SIMULTANEOUS COSTING • ACTIVATE GENERATION OF COST LOG IN REPETITIVE MANUFACTURING. This sequence brings you to Figure 6.117.

Figure 6.117 Repetitive Manufacturing Cost Log

With these settings, SAP ERP will create a log if an error occurs during the activity allocation.

The last customizing in simultaneous costing defines the cost behavior if the semi-finished or finished product has a price control of moving average instead of standard price. You must define which valuation variant should be used when the system posts the values in FI. To define the valuation variant go to CONTROLLING • PRODUCT COST CONTROLLING • COST OBJECT CONTROLLING • PRODUCT COST BY PERIOD • SIMULTANEOUS COSTING • DEFINE GOODS RECEIVED VALUATION FOR ORDER DELIVERY. You can see the customizing screen in Figure 6.118, where you must define the variants to be used by valuation area.

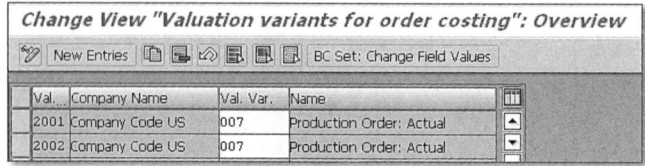

Figure 6.118 Valuation Variant Overview

We can now move to the last topic in the product cost by period: the period-end closing.

Period-End Closing

In the period-end closing, you'll customize how the variances in the product cost collector will be settled to Financial Accounting (FI) and Profitability Analysis (CO-PA).

In the example shown earlier in Figure 6.111, you saw a remaining balance in the product cost collector. This balance is called variance. You can identify the cause of the variance for reporting analysis and then settle the variances at a later time.

The product cost collector variances are divided into eight categories—five for input variance and three for output variances.

The following are the input variances:

▶ **Scrap variances**
These result from the difference between the planned and actual scrap.

▶ **Input price variance**
This occurs when there are differences between the planned prices and actual prices of the consumed materials, and also from the difference between actual and planned activity prices.

- **Resource usage variance**
  This results when a different component or activity type is used in the actual costs from the planned component or activity type.

- **Input quantity variance**
  This type of variance results from the difference between the planned and actual quantity for a material or activity type.

- **Remaining input variance**
  If the system cannot assign the input variances to any of the available ones, the balance is assigned as a remaining input variance.

The following are the output variances:

- **Mixed price variance**
  This type is caused by the difference of the standard price calculated in a mixed cost estimate with multiple procurement alternatives and the cost estimate with one procurement alternative.

- **Output price variance**
  These occur when the material price used to transfer values to inventory is different from the standard price calculated for the material. It typically indicates that the material price was changed in the middle of the production process.

- **Lot size variance**
  This is caused when the costing lot size used to create the cost estimate differs from the production cost collector or production order lot size.

Follow these steps to create the variances customizing for product cost collectors:

1. Define the variance keys.

2. Define the default variance keys for plants.

3. Define the variance variants.

4. Define the valuation variant for work in process (WIP) and scrap (target costs).

5. Define the target cost versions.

6. Define the primary data for the input price variances.

You set the variance key in the material master data. It's a prerequisite for the variance calculation in the product cost collector or manufacturing orders. Looking at Figure 6.119, you can see the customizing screen for the variance key.

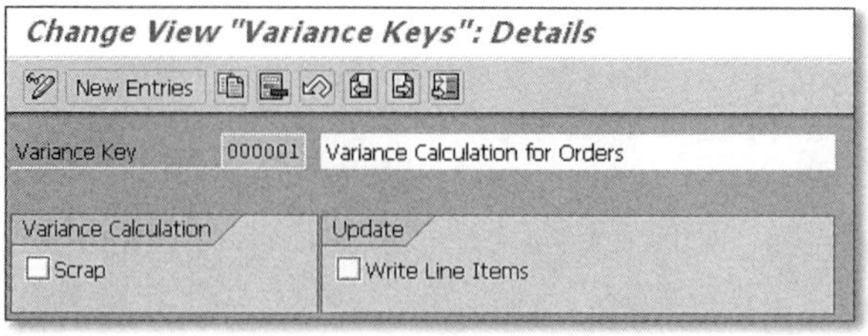

Figure 6.119 Variance Key Details

To customize the variance key, you can use Transaction OKV1 or go to CONTROL-LING • PRODUCT COST CONTROLLING • COST OBJECT CONTROLLING • PRODUCT COST BY PERIOD • PERIOD-END CLOSING • VARIANCE CALCULATION • DEFINE VARIANCE KEYS.

In this screen, you'll see the checkboxes SCRAP and WRITE LINE ITEMS, where you indicate whether you want the system to create scrap variances, and also whether you want to write the variance line items. If you select WRITE LINE ITEMS, the variance execution time will be longer.

After defining the variance key, next define the default variance key by plant, shown in Figure 6.120.

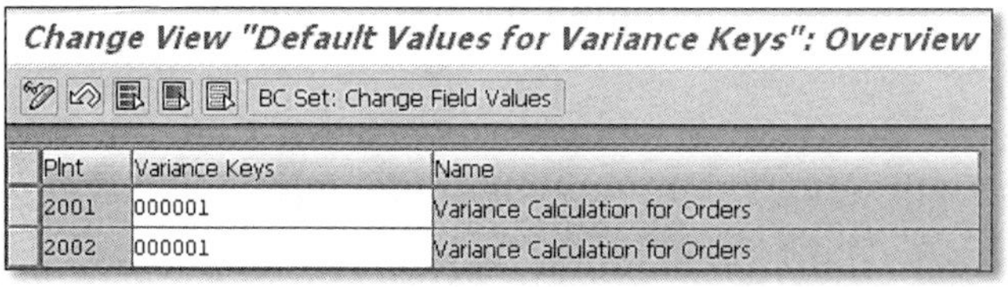

Figure 6.120 Default Variance Key by Plant

The system will propose the default variance key for every material created in the plant, but you can change the default variance key or remove it from the material master data. Customize the default variance key by plant by using Transaction OKVW or by going to CONTROLLING • PRODUCT COST CONTROLLING • COST OBJECT CONTROLLING • PRODUCT COST BY PERIOD • PERIOD-END CLOSING • VARIANCE CALCULATION • DEFINE DEFAULT VARIANCE KEYS FOR PLANTS.

Now that you've defined the default variance key to assign to the material master data, the next step is to create the variance variant, where you customize which variance categories will be used in the variance calculation. You can see in Figure 6.121 how to select the variances categories to be included in the variance variant.

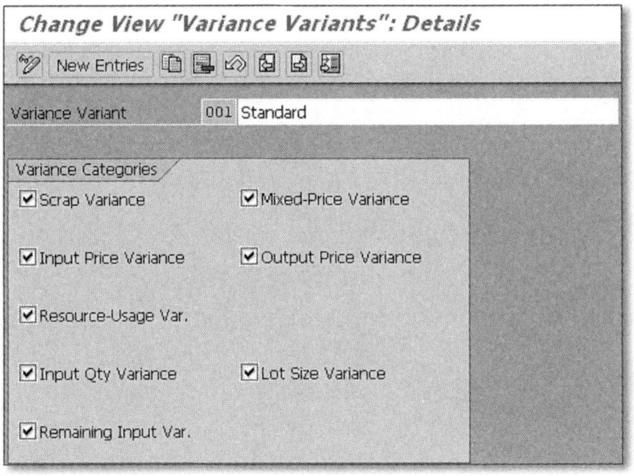

Figure 6.121 Variance Variants

Next, you select the fields of the variance categories you'll use in the variance calculation.

To customize the variance variant, you can use Transaction OKVG, or go to CONTROLLING • PRODUCT COST CONTROLLING • COST OBJECT CONTROLLING • PRODUCT COST BY PERIOD • PERIOD-END CLOSING • VARIANCE CALCULATION • DEFINE VARIANCE VARIANTS.

If you marked in the variance key that the system should calculate the scrap categories, you'll also need to create a valuation variance for scrap and WIP that will determine which values the system will use to calculate the scrap variances. You can see the available options for the valuation variance for scrap and WIP in Figure 6.122.

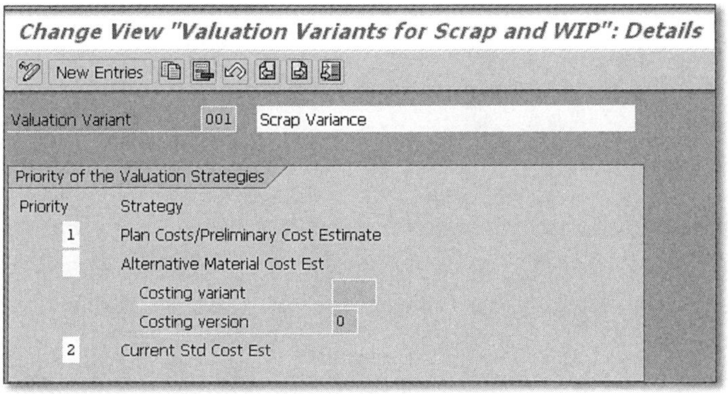

Figure 6.122 Valuation Variant for Scrap and WIP

In this customizing, you assign the priority of strategies the system will use to create the variance using numbers from 1 to 3. To customize the valuation variant for scrap and WIP, go to CONTROLLING • PRODUCT COST CONTROLLING • COST OBJECT CONTROLLING • PRODUCT COST BY PERIOD • PERIOD-END CLOSING • VARIANCE CALCULATION • DEFINE VALUATION VARIANT FOR WIP AND SCRAP (TARGET COSTS).

Now that you have the variance variant and the valuation variant for scrap and WIP, you must define for which CO target version you want to calculate the variance. By default, SAP ERP provides four target versions to calculate the variance:

▶ Target cost version 0 (total variance)

▶ Target cost version 1 (production variance)

▶ Target cost version 2 (planning variance)

▶ Target cost version 3 (production variance of the period)

Figure 6.123 shows an example of the customizing for target cost version 0.

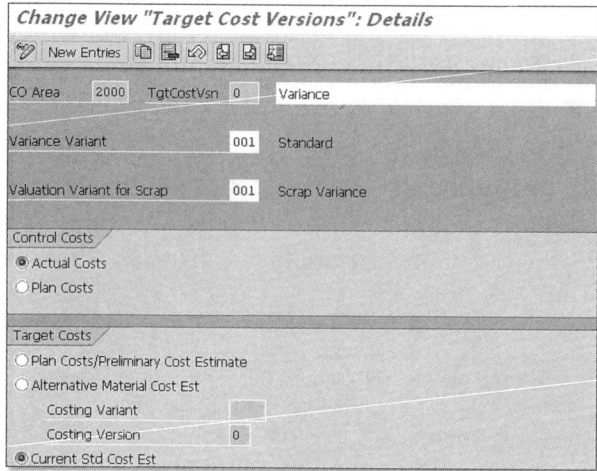

Figure 6.123 Target Cost Versions

To customize the target cost versions, either use Transaction OKV6, or go to CONTROLLING • PRODUCT COST CONTROLLING • COST OBJECT CONTROLLING • PRODUCT COST BY PERIOD • PERIOD-END CLOSING • VARIANCE CALCULATION • DEFINE TARGET COST VERSIONS.

You are defining in this customizing which costs the system will use to compare and calculate the variance, choosing between actual and planned for the control costs, and also defining which cost estimate will be used for the target cost. If scrap is to be calculated, you'll also choose which variance variant and valuation variant for scrap and WIP will be used for the target version.

In target version 0, the variance calculated will be posted in FI during the settlement process for the production orders. To create the total variance, mark ACTUAL COSTS in the CONTROL COSTS section, and mark CURRENT STD COST EST in the TARGET COSTS section for this version.

> **Note**
>
> Only variances calculated in target cost 0 can be settled to CO-PA, and only for this version can you define a valuation variant for scrap and WIP.

In target version 1 (production variance), select ACTUAL COSTS for control costs and PLAN COSTS/PRELIMINARY COST ESTIMATE for the target costs.

For target version 2 (planning variance), select PLAN COSTS for control costs and CURRENT STD COST EST for the target costs. The system will calculate the variance between the planned cost in the production order and the standard cost for the material. You can't use this option for product cost collectors.

To use version 3 (production variance of the period), where the system will calculate the variance between the actual costs and a selected cost estimate for a defined period, you must select ACTUAL COSTS for control costs, and choose which cost estimate you want to use in the alternative material cost estimate, defining a costing variant and a version.

If you've selected INPUT PRICE VARIANCE in the variance variant shown earlier in Figure 6.121, you must define the cost element and the percentage that the system will use to calculate the variance. You can see the primary data price variances customizing screen in Figure 6.124.

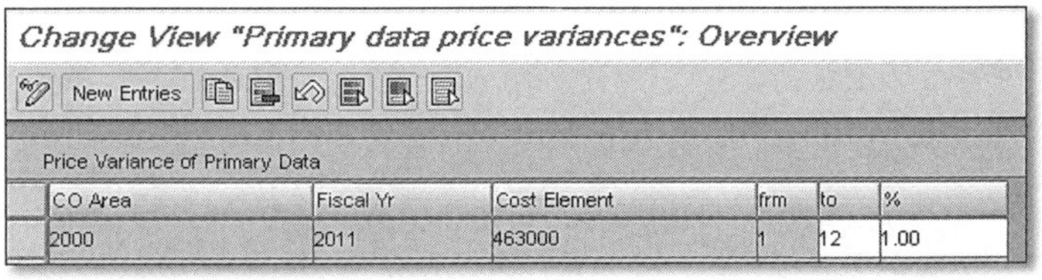

Figure 6.124 Primary Data Price Variances

In this example, the system will consider 1% of the value in the cost element 463000 as an input price variance. To customize the primary data price variances, you can use Transaction OKA8, or go to CONTROLLING • PRODUCT COST CONTROLLING • COST OBJECT CONTROLLING • PRODUCT COST BY PERIOD • PERIOD-END CLOSING • VARIANCE CALCULATION • DEFINE PRIMARY DATA FOR INPUT PRICE VARIANCES.

After finishing this customizing, you've now completed all of the necessary customizing for the variance in the product cost by period. Next, you can move on to settlement, the last topic in period-end closing.

The settlement customizing will define how the system will settle this variance. The settlement customizing for product cost by period and product cost by order are similar to the customizing you saw previously for settlement for internal order, and it has these same six steps:

1. Create the settlement profile.

2. Define the settlement cost elements.

3. Create an allocation structure.

4. Create a source structure.

5. Create the PA transfer structure.

6. Maintain number ranges for the settlement documents.

All six of these steps were covered in Chapter 4, Section 4.2.3, and you can refer back to that section to review.

After finishing the customizing for settlement in cost object controlling, your SAP ERP system is ready to use product costing as long as your company uses the standard cost approach to value inventory and cost of goods sold.

SAP ERP provides another excellent tool if you want to use a different cost model that includes actual costing, where you can define the absorption cost model for product costing. In the next section, you'll learn the advantages offered by this model and how to customize actual costing for CO-PC.

6.3   Actual Costing/Material Ledger

Material Ledger can add value to your product costing analysis in several ways. The following are some basic advantages that Material Ledger brings to your product costing:

▸ Material prices in multiple currencies

▸ Parallel valuations (e.g., USGAAP and IFRS)

▸ Actual costing

▸ Multilevel costing

▸ Reporting

With the Material Ledger activated, you can add two additional currency valuations instead of only the company code currency to inventory valuation. It also allows inventory valuations to be maintained based on different accounting rules. In a simpler implementation, it allows inventory balances to be valued at actual cost, while still maintaining the standard costing views. The actual costing has the capability to calculate the valuations in a multilevel manner, adding visibility to the effects on the costs of finished products of cost differences in raw materials and semi-finished materials. All of these additional features provide a much more robust reporting structure and can greatly enhance the analysis of inventory movements, as well as the analysis of the components of manufacturing costs.

The Material Ledger is activated by plant. Figure 6.125 illustrates one example of the product cost data contained in the material master with the Material Ledger activated in one plant and not activated in another plant. Transaction MM03 was used to display the material master data on the Accounting 1 tab.

On the left side (the plant with the Material Ledger activated), you can see the material prices are shown in three different valuations: Company code currency, Group currency, and Hard currency valuation.

On the right side, you can see the same material but in a plant without the Material Ledger activated. The material price is carried in only one currency valuation: the company code currency.

Before starting the customizing for the Material Ledger, it's necessary to understand the basic principles of the material prices, so we'll first review these.

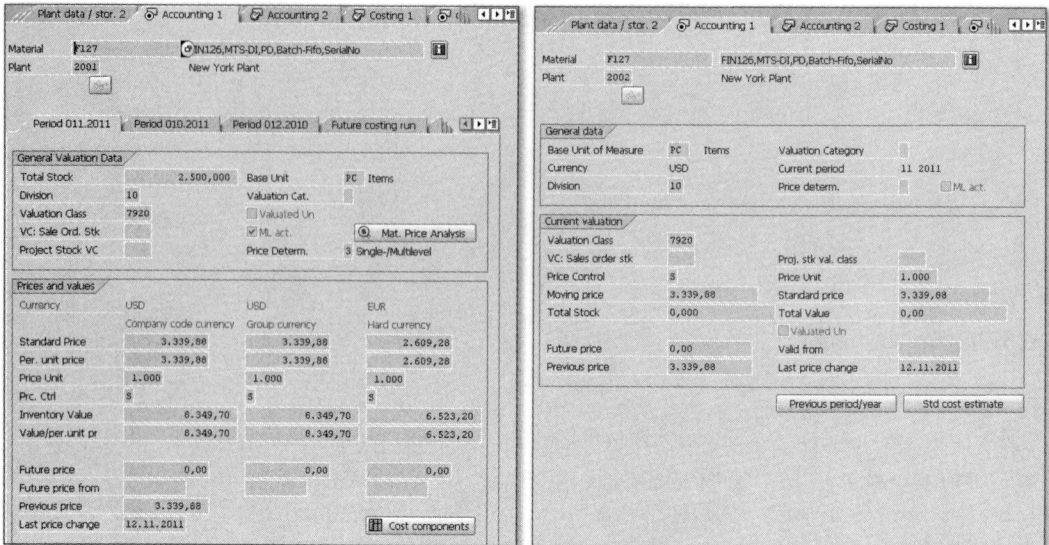

Figure 6.125 Material Ledger Plant versus Non-Material Ledger Plant

Materials in SAP ERP can be valued using either standard price or moving average price. For each material created, you can choose between these approaches in the material creation by maintaining the PRICE CONTROL field in the ACCOUNTING 1 tab (shown in Figure 6.125). Table 6.2 shows the main differences between the standard price and moving average price approach.

Moving Average Price (V)	Standard Price (S)
Adjusted for every material receipt	Constant during the period
Recommended for raw materials and other materials procured externally	Recommended for all produced and internally procured material types

Table 6.2 Moving Average Price versus Standard Price

When the Material Ledger is activated, a new field (PRICE DETERM.) will be available in the material master that you must address for both existing materials at activation and for the material creation process. You can see this field in the left side of Figure 6.125 in the GENERAL VALUATION DATA section. You can choose between two possibilities:

- ▶ 2: TRANSACTION-BASED
- ▶ 3: SINGLE-/MULTILEVEL

If you choose 2 – TRANSACTION-BASED price determination, either for materials with standard price control (S) or moving average price control (V), the material valuation won't reflect the Material Ledger. It will be the same as with the Material Ledger not activated for the plant. The advantage of this setting is that you can see the Material Ledger documents and also have multiple valuations for the material, but the multilevel costing isn't available for this material.

If you choose 3 – SINGLE-/MULTILEVEL, the Material Ledger features will be fully operational. Materials with standard price determination will keep the standard price unchanged during the period, and at the end of the period, an actual price will be calculated for this material considering all production of this material.

To activate the Material Ledger, either use Transaction OMX1, or go to CONTROLLING • PRODUCT COST CONTROLLING • ACTUAL COSTING/MATERIAL LEDGER • ACTIVATE VALUATION AREAS FOR MATERIAL LEDGER. The Material Ledger is activated by valuation area (plant), as you can see in Figure 6.126.

Change View "Activation of Material Ledger": Overview

BC Set: Change Field Values

Valuation Area	Company Code	ML Act.	Price Deter.	Price Det. Binding in Val Area
2001	2000	☑	3	☐
2002	2000	☐		☐

Figure 6.126 Material Ledger Activation

In this screen, flag the valuation areas that you want to have the Material Ledger activated by marking the ML ACT. checkbox.

For valuation areas for which the Material Ledger should be activated, you must also define the PRICE DETER. field default value to be proposed by the system when creating a material for this plant as either 2 or 3. You can change this field during the material creation process *unless* you also mark the field PRICE DET. BINDING IN VAL AREA, meaning that the price determination can't be changed by the user during the material creation process.

> **Note**
>
> If the price determination in the material master is defined as 3 – SINGLE-/MULTILEVEL, and you change it to 2 – TRANSACTION-BASED, all existing costing component history will be deleted, and any price differences in the material will remain in the P&L accounts and not be allocated back to the material.

After activating the Material Ledger, you must define which currency types you want to use in the Material Ledger. To maintain the currency types in the Material Ledger, use Transaction OMX2, or go to CONTROLLING • PRODUCT COST CONTROLLING • ACTUAL COSTING/MATERIAL LEDGER • ASSIGN CURRENCY TYPES TO MATERIAL LEDGER TYPE. Figure 6.127 shows how to define the currency types for the Material Ledger.

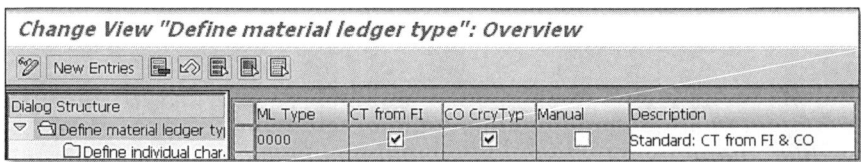

Figure 6.127 Material Ledger Currency Type

Click on NEW ENTRIES to define the Material Ledger type.

If you mark the CT FROM FI field (currency type from FI), the system will use the currency types defined for the company code when you defined the FI currency types in Chapter 1, Section 1.1.

If you mark CO CRCYTYPE, the system will use the currency type from the valuation profiles.

If you mark the MANUAL currency indicator, you must next define which will be the Material Ledger currency by double-clicking on DEFINE INDIVIDUAL CHAR. Figure 6.128 shows the next screen.

The company code currency type is defined by default, and you can't change this, but you can manually define up to two additional different currency types.

Now that you've defined the currency types for the Material Ledger, you must assign the Material Ledger type to the valuation area, as shown in Figure 6.129.

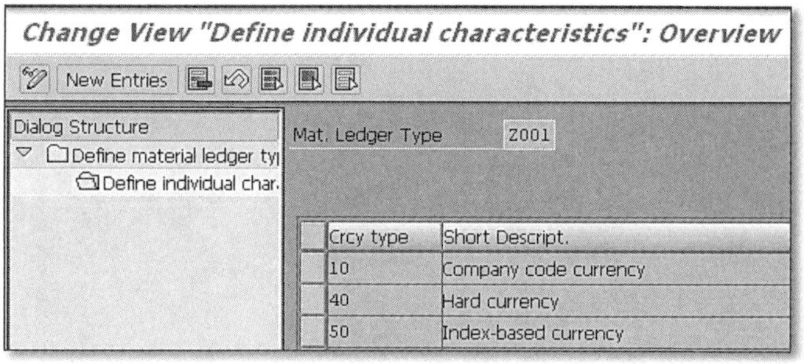

Figure 6.128 Define Individual Characteristics

Figure 6.129 Assignment of Material Ledger Types to Valuation Areas

To assign the Material Ledger type to a valuation area, you can use Transaction OMX3, or go to CONTROLLING • PRODUCT COST CONTROLLING • ACTUAL COSTING/ MATERIAL LEDGER • ASSIGN MATERIAL LEDGER TYPES TO VALUATION AREA.

You have defined the currencies for the Material Ledger, so now you need to define how the values will be structured for reporting purposes. This customizing is done in the material update.

6.3.1 Material Update

You'll now define how the system displays the values in the Material Ledger reports. You'll understand it better by looking at an example of a material price analysis that used Transaction CKM3N, shown in Figure 6.130.

The bottom part of the screen shown in Figure 6.130 shows the material history for the period. You can see several categories (e.g., RECEIPTS and CONSUMPTION), and inside of each category are the process categories (e.g., PRODUCTION inside RECEIPTS). You can customize how the material movements will be allocated to each of the process categories through a process called material update customizing.

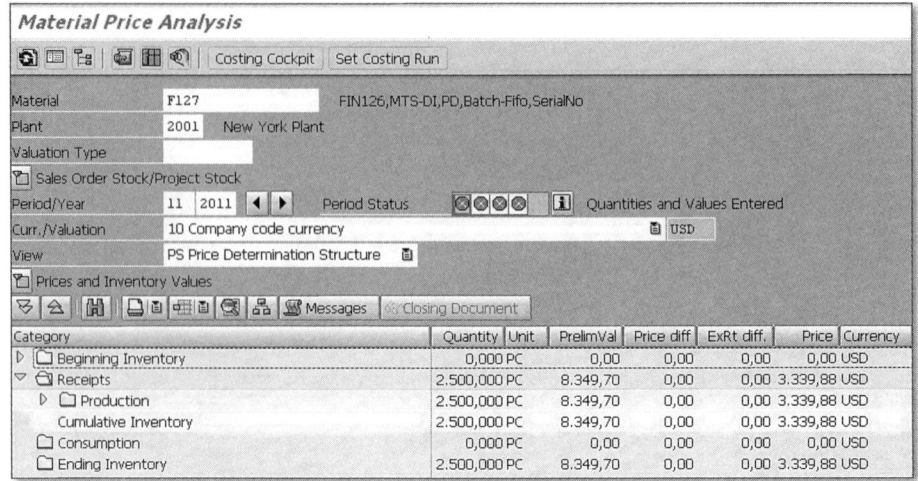

Figure 6.130 Material Price Analysis

The customizing for this area consists of the following four steps:

1. Define the movement type groups for the Material Ledger.

2. Assign the movement type groups of the Material Ledger.

3. Define the material update structure.

4. Assign the material update structure to a valuation area.

Define Movement Type Groups for the Material Ledger

In this step, you'll define the movement type groups to be assigned to the movement types. To define the movement type group for the Material Ledger update, either use Transaction OMX7, or go to CONTROLLING • PRODUCT COST CONTROLLING • ACTUAL COSTING/MATERIAL LEDGER • MATERIAL UPDATE • DEFINE MOVEMENT TYPE GROUPS OF MATERIAL LEDGER.

In Figure 6.131, you can see the customizing screen for the movement type group.

In the first columns, you define the movement type group (MTG) and the name. In the last column, you can define if the group is relevant for the revaluation of consumption step in the Material Ledger. Because one of the functions of the Material Ledger is to value the inventory at actual price, it also can be set to value consumption amounts at actual price. When, for example, a material is sold, it will credit the inventory account and debit the cost of goods sold account (based on the customizing for the valuation class belonging to the material) using the standard price defined for the material. When you run the Material Ledger period-end closing, it will update the inventory account with the difference between the standard price and the actual price. The system will also need to update the cost of goods sold. If you set the revaluation of consumption to 1 – Revaluation of GL Account, the system will post the difference in the same account of the cost of goods sold for the material. When you set it to 2 – Revaluation of GL Account and CO Account Assignment, the system will post the difference in the same account and also in the same cost object. This is used, for example, when the consumption is posted to a cost center. At the time of the inventory movement, it was posted using the standard price; at the end of period revaluation of consumption, the system posts the difference in the same account and same cost center. If you leave it blank, and there is a difference for revaluation of consumption, the system will post the difference in the account defined in Transaction OBYC for transaction key COC.

Change View "Define Movement Type Group for ML Update": Overview

New Entries | BC Set: Change Field Values

Define Movement Type Group for ML Update

MTG	Name	Reval. of Consu...
1	Initial Inventory Lo	
2	Procurement	
3	Plant transfers	
4	Inventory adjustment	
5	Internal consumption	
6	Sales	
7	External Procurement	
8	Sub Contracting	
CC	FI/CO Revaluation	2
CF	FI Revaluation	1

Figure 6.131 Movement Type Group for Material Ledger Update

After defining the movement type groups, you should assign the groups to the movement type.

Assign Movement Type Groups of the Material Ledger

Every material movement has a movement type assigned to the transaction (e.g., movement type 101 for goods receipt or 601 for goods issue). After defining the movement type group, you can group the movement types to be shown in different categories in the Material Ledger, as you can see in Figure 6.132.

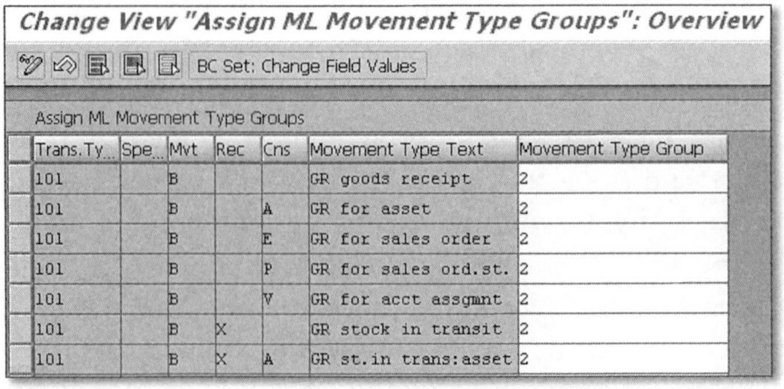
Change View "Assign ML Movement Type Groups": Overview

BC Set: Change Field Values

Assign ML Movement Type Groups

Trans.Ty...	Spe...	Mvt	Rec	Cns	Movement Type Text	Movement Type Group
101		B			GR goods receipt	2
101		B		A	GR for asset	2
101		B		E	GR for sales order	2
101		B		P	GR for sales ord.st.	2
101		B		V	GR for acct assgmnt	2
101		B	X		GR stock in transit	2
101		B	X	A	GR st.in trans:asset	2

Figure 6.132 Assign Movement Type Group to Movement Type

To create the customizing, you can use Transaction OMX0, or go to CONTROLLING • PRODUCT COST CONTROLLING • ACTUAL COSTING/MATERIAL LEDGER • MATERIAL UPDATE • ASSIGN MOVEMENT TYPE GROUPS OF MATERIAL LEDGER.

For each movement type that you want to categorize, assign the desired Material Ledger movement type group. You don't necessarily need to assign a group for every movement type. For movement types without a group, the system will use the standard definition to internally assign them to the Material Ledger process categories. Now that you've assigned the movement type groups to the movement types, you can go to the next customizing step: define the material update structure.

Define the Material Update Structure

As you've already seen, the system categorizes the values for the material transactions in different categories during the Material Ledger update. These include goods receipts or stock transfers. SAP ERP has default assignments for three categories:

- Receipts
- Consumption
- Other receipts/consumption

Receipts categories will always affect the valuation price, meaning that the differences between standard price and actual price will be considered during the Material Ledger closing to calculate the ending inventory price.

By default, consumption categories won't affect the material valuation price, but you can change this behavior by assigning the consumption process category to Other Receipts/Consumption.

You should carefully consider the implications to your inventory valuation before making a change in these assignments. It will change the system behavior and how the material is valued during the Material Ledger process. In most situations, the standard update structure proposed by SAP ERP is the best choice.

To maintain the update structure, either use Transaction OMX9, or go to CONTROLLING • PRODUCT COST CONTROLLING • ACTUAL COSTING/MATERIAL LEDGER • MATERIAL UPDATE • DEFINE MATERIAL UPDATE STRUCTURE. You can see the customizing screen in Figure 6.133.

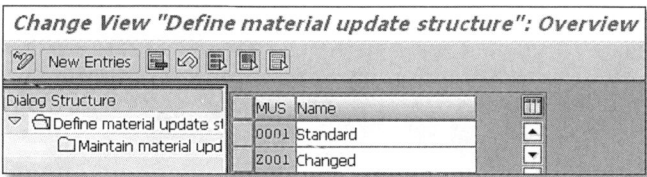

Figure 6.133 Material Update Structure

SAP ERP by default provides the structure 0001 – Standard, but you can also create a new one by clicking on NEW ENTRIES. By marking the available structures and double-clicking in MAINTAIN MATERIAL UPDATE STRUCTURE, you can see how to define the categories, as shown in Figure 6.134.

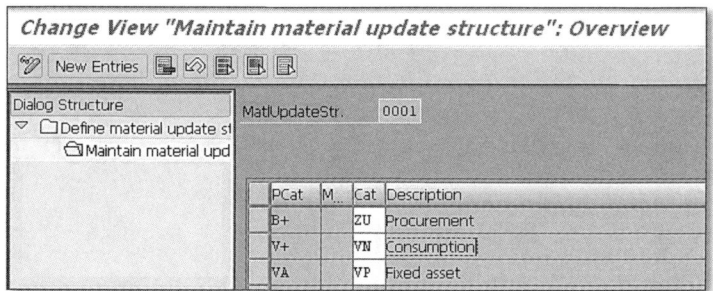

Figure 6.134 Maintain Material Update Structure

The process categories B+ and V+ are the default process categories proposed by SAP ERP. You can add a new process category for consumption and, instead of assigning it to the category CONSUMPTION you can assign it to the category OTHER RECEIPTS/CONSUMPTION. Figure 6.134 shows an example.

The process category FIXED ASSET is assigned to the category OTHER RECEIPTS/CONSUMPTION. Consumption of materials charged to a fixed asset will have influence in the material valuation price.

After creating the update structure, you must assign it to the valuation area.

Assign the Material Update Structure to a Valuation Area

The updated structure that you created in the previous step must be assigned to the valuation areas subject to the Material Ledger, as you can see in Figure 6.135.

Figure 6.135 Assign the Material Update Structure to the Valuation Area

In this step, you'll enter the recently created material update structure (or the standard one) for the valuation area by using Transaction OMX8 or by going to CONTROLLING • PRODUCT COST CONTROLLING • ACTUAL COSTING/MATERIAL LEDGER • MATERIAL UPDATE • ASSIGN MATERIAL UPDATE STRUCTURE TO A VALUATION AREA.

The next step in the customizing of the Material Ledger is to customize the actual costing.

6.3.2 Actual Costing

In this section, you'll define additional customizing for the Material Ledger by following these four new steps:

1. Activate actual costing.

2. Create user-defined names for receipts/consumption.

3. Assign user-defined names for receipts/consumption.

4. Activate actual cost component split.

The next several sections explore these steps in more detail.

Activate Actual Costing

In this customizing, you'll define whether the activity type consumption in the quantity structure should be valued at actual price. You can see the customizing screen in Figure 6.136. To activate the actual costing for a plant, go to Controlling • Product Cost Controlling • Actual Costing/Material Ledger • Actual Costing • Activate Actual Costing.

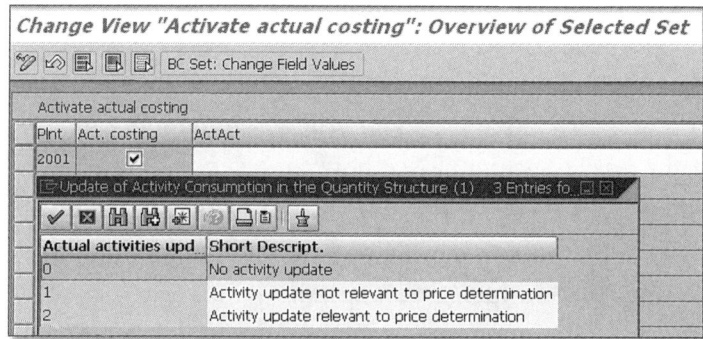

Figure 6.136 Activate Actual Costing

When you activate the actual costing for the plant, you must select the setting for the activity update in the quantity structure. You can choose from three options:

▶ 0: No activity update

▶ 1: Activity update not relevant to price determination

▶ 2: Activity update relevant to price determination

If it's set for No activity update, you must use the period-end closing step to revaluate the actual prices in the production orders. The system will update the cost center/activity and also the production order with the actual activity price.

If the update is active in a plant (i.e., you choose option 1 or 2), then all activity allocations to production orders are posted with a constant price in the period. If the activity isn't relevant for price determination (option 1), then an actual price for activity type isn't considered in the Material Ledger, and the activity type values in the material will be updated using the valid price defined in the strategy of the costing variant. By choosing option 2, the system will adopt the actual activity price and will update the material values with the actual price. The differences for the cost centers/processes are subsequently debited to the relevant material. The system will debit or credit the activity type sender cost center with the account customized in Transaction OBYC, transaction key GBB, and general modification AUI. When using this option, you can't use the period-end closing step to revalue the actual prices in the production orders because it will charge the material twice.

> **Note**
>
> Never change the activity update setting in the middle of the period. It will cause inconsistencies in the values. Always change it at the beginning of the period before any production activity has been entered.

In the Material Ledger reports, you can create and assign user-defined names for process categories. In the next topic, you'll see how to create the user-defined names for receipts/consumption transactions.

Create User-Defined Names for Receipts/Consumption

We'll explain one example of creating and assigning a user-defined name for receipts, and the process is the same for consumption. In the first customizing screen in Figure 6.137, you can see the option to create user names for receipts and consumption. Let's look at the receipts option. To create the user-defined names for receipts and consumption, go to CONTROLLING • PRODUCT COST CONTROLLING • ACTUAL COSTING/MATERIAL LEDGER • ACTUAL COSTING • CREATE USER-DEFINED NAMES FOR RECEIPTS/CONSUMPTIONS.

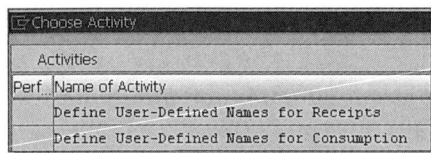

Figure 6.137 Define User-Defined Names for Receipts/Consumption

By double-clicking in the DEFINE USER-DEFINED NAMES FOR RECEIPTS line, you'll come to the customizing screen shown in Figure 6.138.

Create a new entry, and define a controlling level, a user-defined name, and the text for the controlling level.

After creating the controlling level, you must assign it to the desired process category.

Change View "User-defined names for receipts": Overview

New Entries

ControlLvl	User-defined name	Text
Z001	INITIAL INVENTORY LOAD	Initial Inventory Load
Z002	PRODUCTION	Production

Figure 6.138 User-Defined Names for Receipts

Assign User-Defined Names for Receipts/Consumption

The recently created controlling level must be assigned to a process category to be used in the Material Ledger reporting. You can see in Figure 6.139 the first customizing screen of how to assign the user-defined names to the process categories. To assign the user defined names for receipts and consumption to the process categories, go to CONTROLLING • PRODUCT COST CONTROLLING • ACTUAL COSTING/MATERIAL LEDGER • ACTUAL COSTING • ASSIGN USER-DEFINED NAMES FOR RECEIPTS/CONSUMPTIONS.

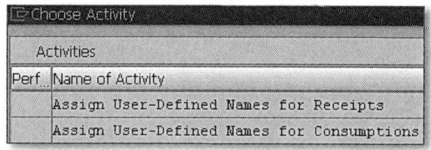

Choose Activity

Activities

Perf	Name of Activity
	Assign User-Defined Names for Receipts
	Assign User-Defined Names for Consumptions

Figure 6.139 Assign User-Defined Names for Receipts/Consumption

Double-click on ASSIGN USER-DEFINED NAMES FOR RECEIPTS to see one example of how to assign the names. Figure 6.140 shows the customizing screen.

Change View "Assign User-Defined Names for Receipts": Overview

New Entries

PCat	Description	MTG	ControlLvl	Text
B+	Procurement	1	Z001	Initial Inventory Load
B+	Procurement	9	Z002	Production

Figure 6.140 Assign User-Defined Names for Receipts

By clicking on NEW ENTRIES, you can select the process category and also the movement type group for the controlling level. This means that you can create a user-defined name for each movement type group that you've defined in Section 6.3.1. You can see in Figure 6.141 one example where we've assigned the movement type 561 to the movement type group INITIAL INVENTORY LOAD, and then assigned this movement type group to the controlling level Z001, INITIAL INVENTORY LOAD.

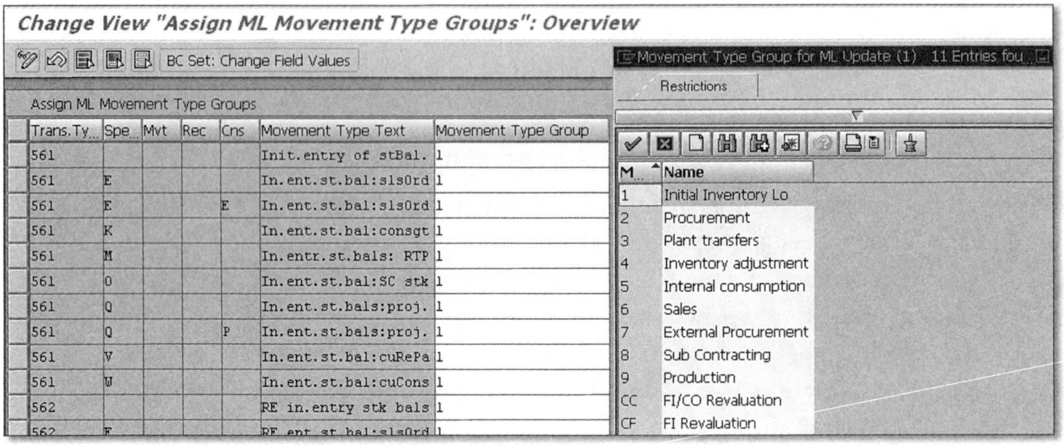

Trans.Ty..	Spe..	Mvt	Rec	Cns	Movement Type Text	Movement Type Group
561					Init.entry of stBal.	1
561	E				In.ent.st.bal:slsOrd	1
561	E			E	In.ent.st.bal:slsOrd	1
561	K				In.ent.st.bal:consgt	1
561	M				In.entr.st.bals: RTP	1
561	O				In.ent.st.bal:SC stk	1
561	Q				In.ent.st.bals:proj.	1
561	Q			P	In.ent.st.bals:proj.	1
561	V				In.ent.st.bal:cuRePa	1
561	W				In.ent.st.bal:cuCons	1
562					RE in.entry stk bals	1
562	E				RE ent.st.bal:slsOrd	1

M..	Name
1	Initial Inventory Lo
2	Procurement
3	Plant transfers
4	Inventory adjustment
5	Internal consumption
6	Sales
7	External Procurement
8	Sub Contracting
9	Production
CC	FI/CO Revaluation
CF	FI Revaluation

Figure 6.141 Assign Material Ledger Movement Type Groups

You can see the results of this customizing in Transaction CKM3N in the example shown in Figure 6.142.

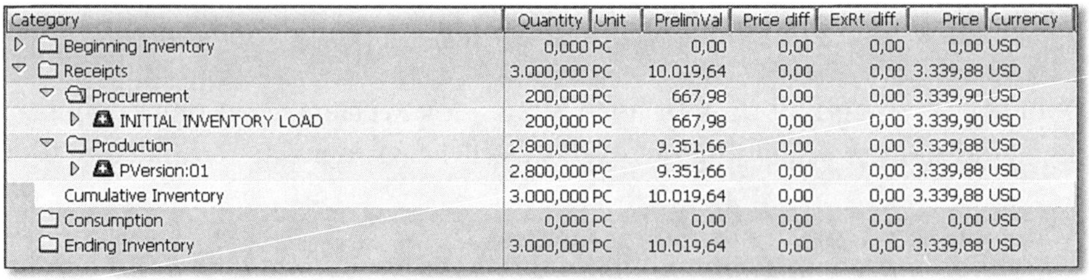

Category	Quantity	Unit	PrelimVal	Price diff	ExRt diff.	Price	Currency
Beginning Inventory	0,000	PC	0,00	0,00	0,00	0,00	USD
Receipts	3.000,000	PC	10.019,64	0,00	0,00	3.339,88	USD
Procurement	200,000	PC	667,98	0,00	0,00	3.339,90	USD
INITIAL INVENTORY LOAD	200,000	PC	667,98	0,00	0,00	3.339,90	USD
Production	2.800,000	PC	9.351,66	0,00	0,00	3.339,88	USD
PVersion:01	2.800,000	PC	9.351,66	0,00	0,00	3.339,88	USD
Cumulative Inventory	3.000,000	PC	10.019,64	0,00	0,00	3.339,88	USD
Consumption	0,000	PC	0,00	0,00	0,00	0,00	USD
Ending Inventory	3.000,000	PC	10.019,64	0,00	0,00	3.339,88	USD

Figure 6.142 Receipts User-Defined Name Example

You can see in Figure 6.142 that inside the PROCUREMENT category, the system is now showing the user-defined name for the movement type associated to the movement type group.

The last important customization in the Material Ledger is to activate the actual cost component split.

Activate Actual Cost Component Split

You've already seen the cost component split for product cost planning, and the Material Ledger allows you to use the cost component split for actual costing as well. Figure 6.143 shows the customizing screen to activate the actual cost component split. To activate go to CONTROLLING • PRODUCT COST CONTROLLING • ACTUAL COSTING/MATERIAL LEDGER • ACTUAL COSTING • ACTIVATE ACTUAL COST COMPONENT SPLIT.

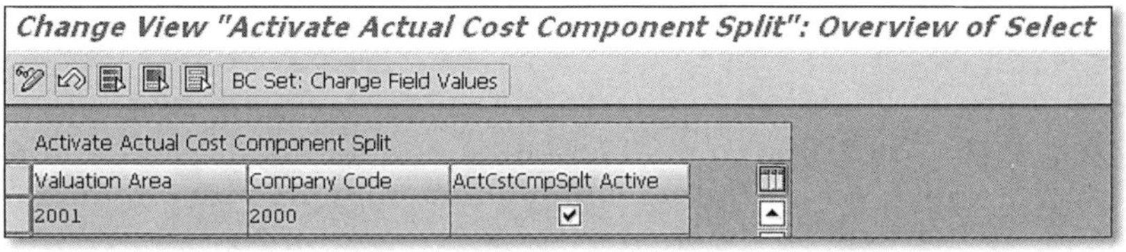

Figure 6.143 Activate Actual Cost Component Split

Mark the valuation areas for which you want to activate the actual cost component split. Figure 6.144 shows an example report showing the actual cost component split.

> **Note**
>
> After finishing the Material Ledger customizing, use Transaction CKMSTART to set it as productive for the valuation area.

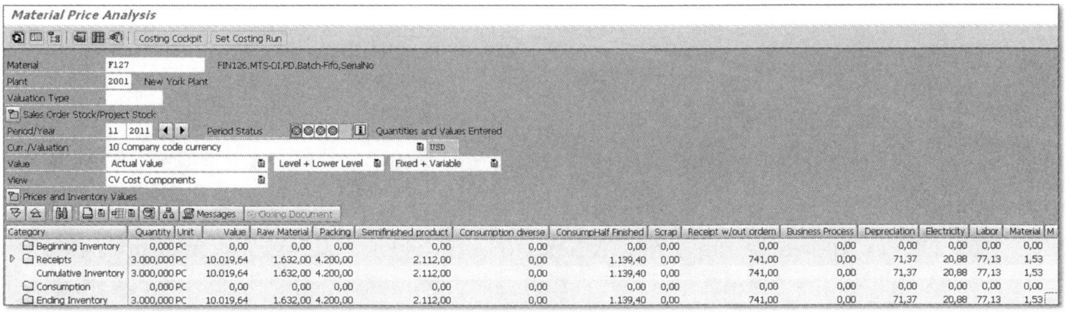

Figure 6.144 Material Price Analysis, Actual Cost Component Split

> **Note**
>
> If you are already using the Material Ledger, and you decide later to activate the cost component split, execute the Program MLCCS_STARTUP to create the actual cost component split for the previous period.

Now that you've finished all customizing related to product costing, you can turn your attention to the information system, where you'll see some important reports for product costing.

6.4   Information System

As we've progressed through the different areas of CO in this book, you've seen how each area increases the number of available reports and how the customizing decisions you make will affect the way you can see the information.

For CO-PC, as with other areas you have seen, SAP ERP provides a large number of standard reports, which are grouped into three main areas:

▶ Product cost planning

▶ Cost object controlling

▶ Actual costing/Material Ledger

You'll now see some examples of the most important reports in each area.

6.4.1   Product Cost Planning

In product cost planning, you can find the reports under the user menu path CONTROLLING • PRODUCT COST CONTROLLING • PRODUCT COST PLANNING • INFORMATION SYSTEM.

One of the most important reports in product cost planning is Report CK13N, which displays a material cost estimate. We've been using this report in the chapter to explain and show the impacts of the customizing decisions on CO-PC. In Figure 6.145, you can see the selection screen for the report.

You choose the material and plant. For the costing data, you can choose between the available costing variants and costing versions, and you select a date when the cost estimate was valid. You can see the results in Figure 6.146.

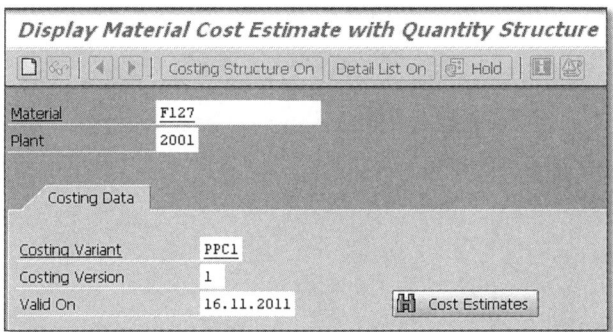

Figure 6.145 Display Material Cost Estimate Selection Screen

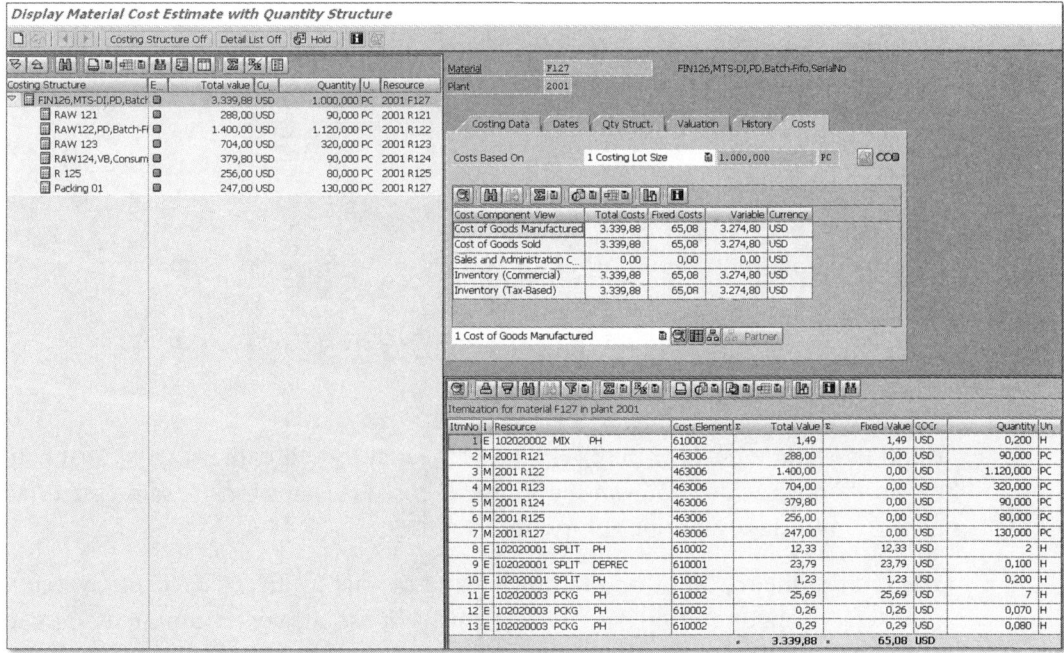

Figure 6.146 Display Material Cost Estimate with Quantity Structure

Notice the BOM usage for the cost estimate lot size on the left side of the screen. On the upper-right side, you can see the cost estimate result. You can navigate between the costing views defined in the cost component structure. This example shows the cost of goods manufactured.

On the bottom-right side of Figure 6.146, you can see the itemization result of the cost estimate, where all of the details of the material and activity type consumption are shown. You can also add more fields to the display list by changing the layout. By clicking on the COST COMPONENT button (icon to the right of the magnifying glass in the middle of the right side of the screen), you can display the cost estimate by cost component in front of the costing views, as shown in Figure 6.147.

Cost Components for Material F127 Plant 2001

CC	Name of Cost Comp.	Σ	Overall	Σ	Fixed	Σ	Variable	Crcy
10	Raw Material		544,00				544,00	USD
20	Packing		1.400,00				1.400,00	USD
30	Semifinished product		704,00				704,00	USD
40	Consumption diverse							USD
50	ConsumpHalf Finished		379,80				379,80	USD
60	Scrap							USD
70	Receipt w/out ordem		247,00				247,00	USD
80	Business Process							USD
100	Depreciation		23,79		23,79			USD
110	Electricity		6,96		6,96			USD
120	Labor		25,71		25,71			USD
130	Material		0,51		0,51			USD
140	Maintenance		1,96		1,96			USD
150	Others		2,45		2,45			USD
160	Taxes		0,61		0,61			USD
170	Water		3,09		3,09			USD
		▪	3.339,88	▪	65,08	▪	3.274,80	USD

Figure 6.147 Cost Estimate, Cost Component View

Another useful report is S_P99_41000111 – Analyze/Compare Material Cost Estimates, through which you can see different cost estimates for the same material. Figure 6.148 shows the selection screen.

You can run the report by plant or plants and restrict by material, costing variant, costing version, or costing date. You can also choose the cost component view to display. Figure 6.149 displays the report result.

In the report, you can see a list of the available cost estimates for the material in the lower portion of the screen. You can also add more fields to the report by changing the layout and selecting the additional fields to be displayed.

Additional reports are available for product cost planning in the INFORMATION SYSTEM folder, where you can navigate between the different kinds of reports.

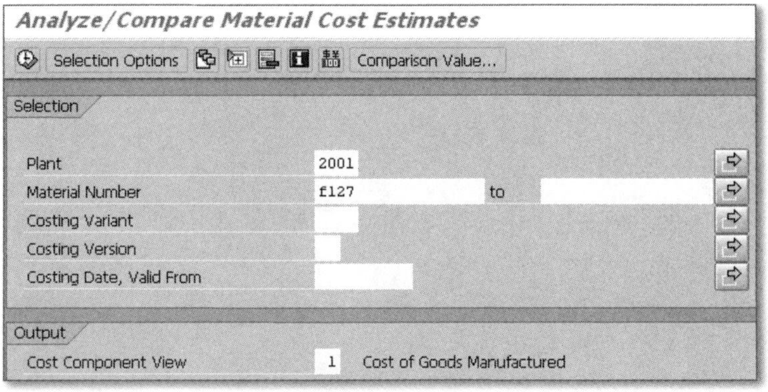

Figure 6.148 Analyze/Compare Material Cost Estimates Selection Screen

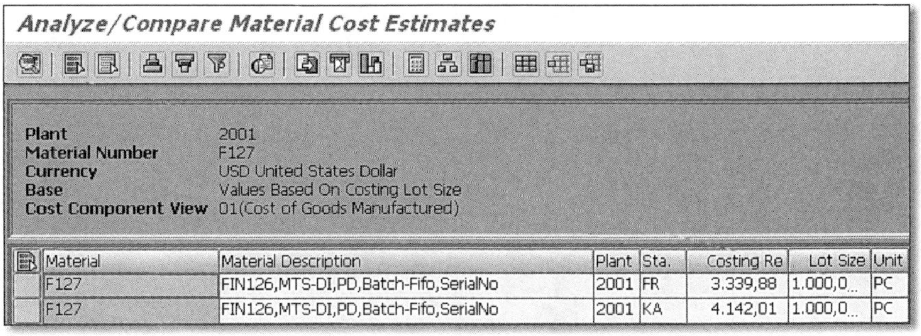

Figure 6.149 Analyze/Compare Material Cost Estimates.

6.4.2 Cost Object Controlling

The advantage in cost object controlling reports is that you can use the specific reports for cost object controlling and also all the available reports for internal orders because cost object controlling is based on orders (production orders, process orders, and product cost collector orders). You can also use the available features for internal orders such as order grouping to display the results grouped by a user definition. You can see how we used internal order reporting to show information from cost object controlling using Report S_ALR_87012993 – Orders: Actual/Plan/Variance in Figure 6.150.

This report works the same as you already saw in Chapter 4. You can see the order group in the selection screen, and Figure 6.151 displays the report result.

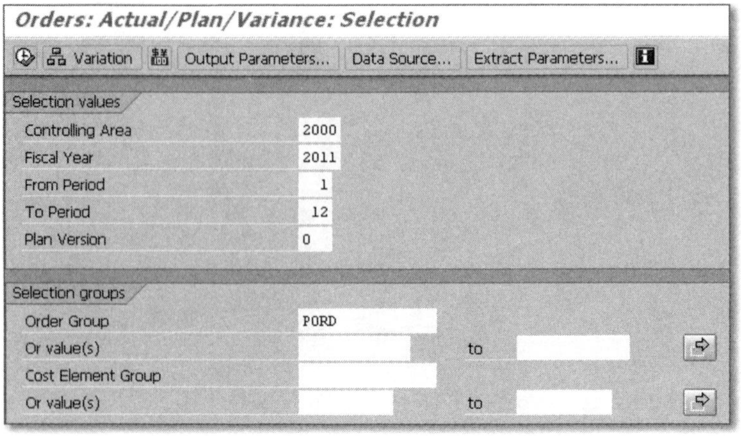

Figure 6.150 Actual/Plan/Variant Order Report Selection Screen

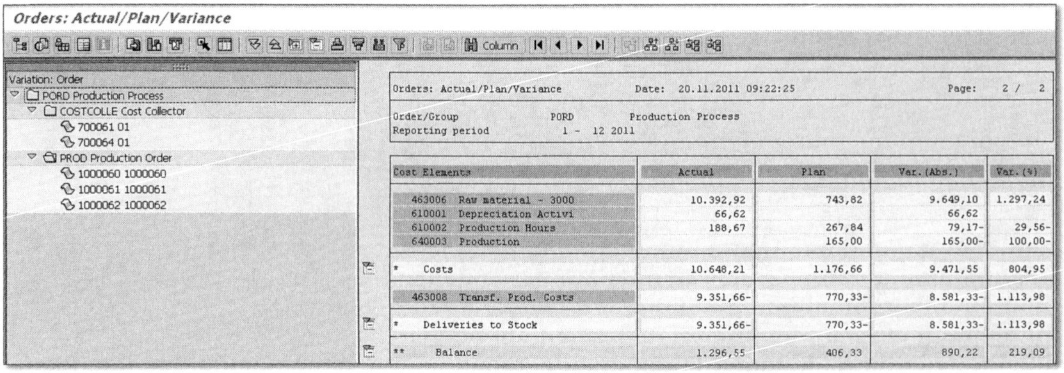

Cost Elements	Actual	Plan	Var. (Abs.)	Var. (%)
463006 Raw material - 3000	10.392,92	743,82	9.649,10	1.297,24
610001 Depreciation Activi	66,62		66,62	
610002 Production Hours	188,67	267,84	79,17-	29,56-
640003 Production		165,00	165,00-	100,00-
* Costs	10.648,21	1.176,66	9.471,55	804,95
463008 Transf. Prod. Costs	9.351,66-	770,33-	8.581,33-	1.113,98
* Deliveries to Stock	9.351,66-	770,33-	8.581,33-	1.113,98
** Balance	1.296,55	406,33	890,22	219,09

Figure 6.151 Actual/Plan/Variant Order Report

You can navigate between the groups and also select an individual order in the navigation section on the left side of the screen. For this example, two groups were created: one for product cost collectors and another for production orders.

Two other important reports for cost object controlling are Report KKBC_PKO – For Product Cost Collectors and Report KKBC_ORD – For Orders. Both have the same functionality, but one is to be used for product cost collectors and the other for production orders. If you know the product cost collector order number, you can use the order report easily. Figure 6.152 shows the selection screen for Report KKBC_ORD – For Orders.

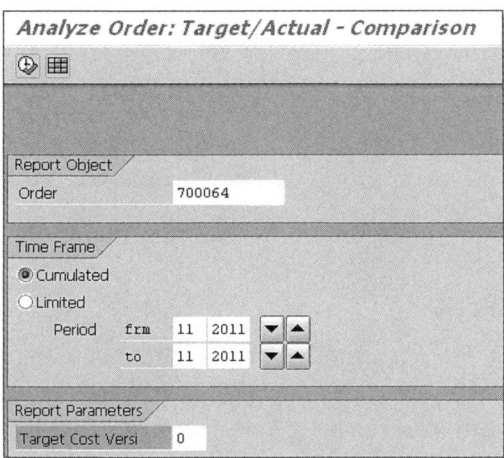

Figure 6.152 Analyze Order Target/Actual – Comparison

Enter the production order number, and select whether the analysis should be performed cumulatively or restricted by period/year. You can also select the version to use to display the variances. Figure 6.153 shows the report result.

Target/Actual - Comparison

Order 700064 01
Plant 2001 New York Plant
Material F127 FIN126,MTS-DI,PD,Batch-Fifo,SerialNo
Production Process PVersion:01
Actual Quantity 2.800,000 PC Items
Target Cost Version 0 Variance

Cumulative Data
Legal Valuation
Company Code Currency/Object Currency

Cost Element	Cost Element (Text)	Origin	Σ Total target costs	Σ Total actual costs	Σ Target/actual var.	T/I var(%)	Currency
463006	Raw material - 3000		716,80	716,80	0,00		USD
463006	Raw material - 3000	2001/R121	806,40	1.702,40	896,00	111,11	USD
463006	Raw material - 3000	2001/R122	3.920,00	3.920,00	0,00		USD
463006	Raw material - 3000	2001/R123	1.971,20	1.971,20	0,00		USD
463006	Raw material - 3000	2001/R124	1.063,44	1.063,44	0,00		USD
463006	Raw material - 3000	2001/R127	691,60	691,60	0,00		USD
463008	Transf. Prod. Costs to Inventory	2001/F127	0,00	9.351,66-	9.351,66-		USD
610001	Depreciation Activity allocation	102020001/DEPREC	66,61	66,61	0,00		USD
610002	Production Hours	102020001/PH	15,77	3,45	12,32-	78,12-	USD
610002	Production Hours	102020002/PH	4,17	4,18	0,01	0,24	USD
610002	Production Hours	102020003/PH	27,23	1,54	25,69-	94,34-	USD
			9.283,22	789,56	8.493,66-		USD
			9.283,22	789,56	8.493,66-		USD

Figure 6.153 Target/Actual Comparison

Access the available reports for product cost by period by following the user menu path CONTROLLING • PRODUCT COST CONTROLLING • COST OBJECT CONTROLLING • PRODUCT COST BY PERIOD • INFORMATION SYSTEM.

Access the available reports for product cost by order by following the user menu path CONTROLLING • PRODUCT COST CONTROLLING • COST OBJECT CONTROLLING • PRODUCT COST BY ORDER • INFORMATION SYSTEM.

6.4.3 Actual Costing/Material Ledger

We used one report, CKM3N – Material Price Analysis, in all our earlier examples to show the value flows in the Material Ledger. This report is considered to be one of the most important reports for the Material Ledger and provides a variety of different analysis views all in one transaction. Figure 6.154 shows the report example.

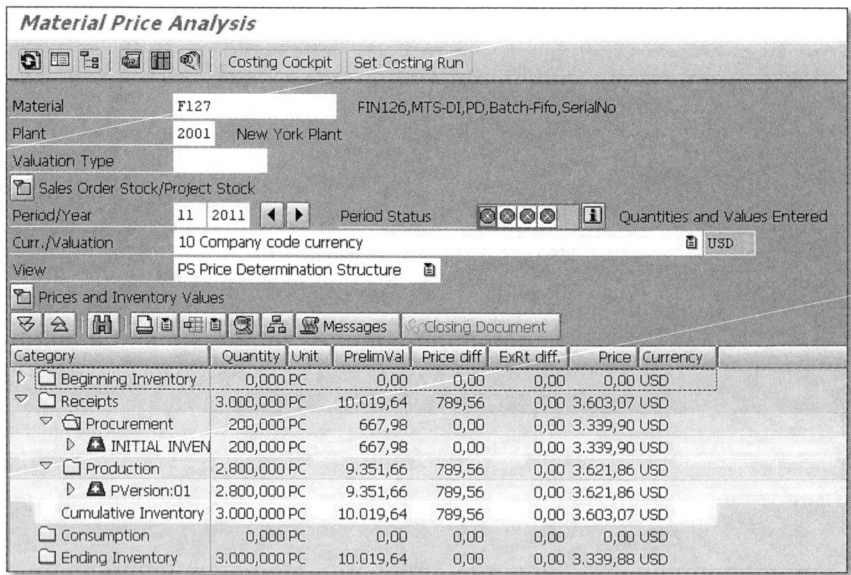

Figure 6.154 Material Price Analysis

Enter the selection by material and plant only, and then navigate between the periods to see the material analysis for the selected period/year. In the bottom portion of the screen, you can see the material analysis according to the view selected. This example shows the PS PRICE DETERMINATION STRUCTURE view with the breakdown by categories. In this view, you can see the quantity assigned to each category, the preliminary value (which is the quantity valued at standard price), the price difference (the difference between standard and actual), the exchange rate difference (if the material is subject to an exchange rate difference such as for imported material), and the actual price for the category.

In CURR./VALUATION, you can choose from the three currencies customized for the Material Ledger.

In VIEW, you can select different display views of the report. You can see another view in Figure 6.155 where the cost components for each category are displayed.

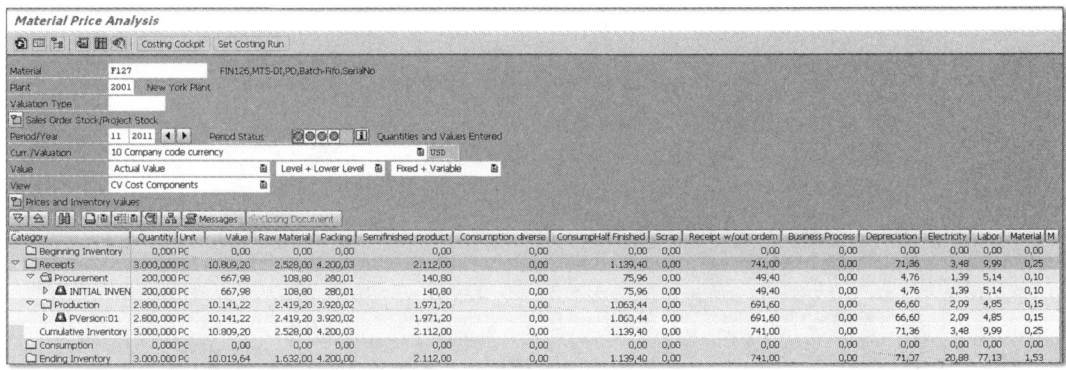

Figure 6.155 Material Price Analysis with Cost Components Displayed

Another important report in the Material Ledger is S_P99_41000062 – Prices and Inventory Values, where you can see a list of material prices and do a comparison between the actual cost and the standard cost for the material. You can see the selection screen in Figure 6.156.

You can restrict the selection by material and plant, and you can also select a period and year for the report. Because you can have multiple currency valuations in the Material Ledger, you can also select one of the available currencies. An example of the report results are shown in Figure 6.157.

You can see the list of materials with the standard price and also the periodic unit price. You can change the layout by adding additional fields to the report.

The reports related to the Material Ledger can be found under the user menu path CONTROLLING • PRODUCT COST CONTROLLING • COST OBJECT CONTROLLING • ACTUAL COSTING/MATERIAL LEDGER • INFORMATION SYSTEM.

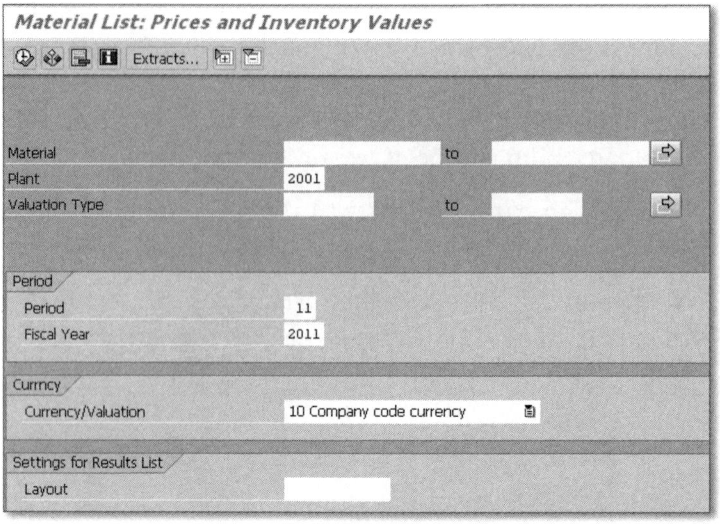

Figure 6.156 Material List Prices and Inventory Values Selection Screen

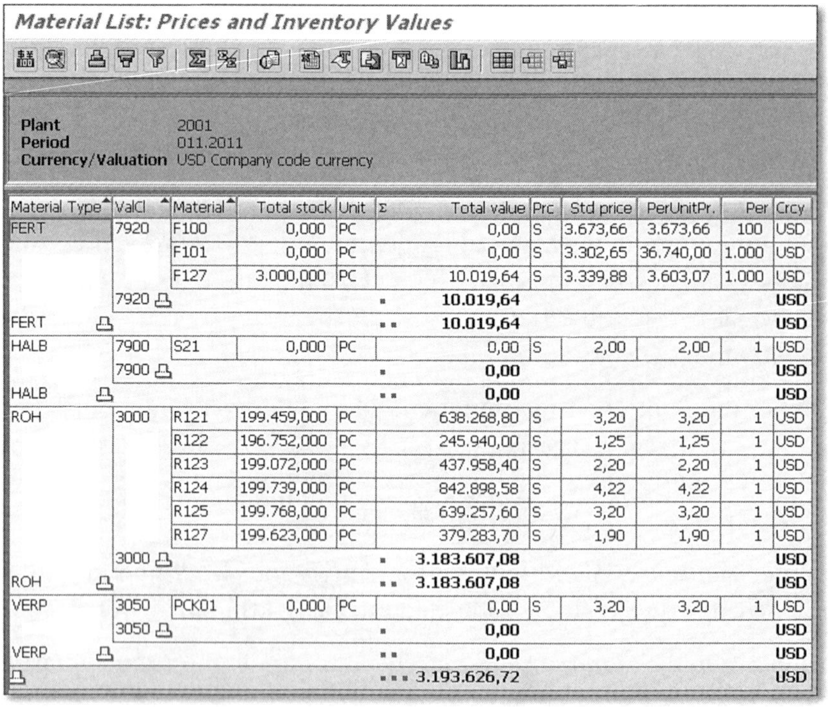

Material List: Prices and Inventory Values

Plant 2001
Period 011.2011
Currency/Valuation USD Company code currency

Material Type	ValCl	Material	Total stock	Unit	Σ	Total value	Prc	Std price	PerUnitPr.	Per	Crcy
FERT	7920	F100	0,000	PC		0,00	S	3.673,66	3.673,66	100	USD
		F101	0,000	PC		0,00	S	3.302,65	36.740,00	1.000	USD
		F127	3.000,000	PC		10.019,64	S	3.339,88	3.603,07	1.000	USD
	7920				•	**10.019,64**					**USD**
FERT					••	**10.019,64**					**USD**
HALB	7900	S21	0,000	PC		0,00	S	2,00	2,00	1	USD
	7900				•	**0,00**					**USD**
HALB					••	**0,00**					**USD**
ROH	3000	R121	199.459,000	PC		638.268,80	S	3,20	3,20	1	USD
		R122	196.752,000	PC		245.940,00	S	1,25	1,25	1	USD
		R123	199.072,000	PC		437.958,40	S	2,20	2,20	1	USD
		R124	199.739,000	PC		842.898,58	S	4,22	4,22	1	USD
		R125	199.768,000	PC		639.257,60	S	3,20	3,20	1	USD
		R127	199.623,000	PC		379.283,70	S	1,90	1,90	1	USD
	3000				•	**3.183.607,08**					**USD**
ROH					••	**3.183.607,08**					**USD**
VERP	3050	PCK01	0,000	PC		0,00	S	3,20	3,20	1	USD
	3050				•	**0,00**					**USD**
VERP					••	**0,00**					**USD**
					•••	**3.193.626,72**					**USD**

Figure 6.157 Material List Prices and Inventory Values

Now that you've learned the concepts of CO-PC and discovered how to customize the subcomponent to achieve the best results to meet your company's needs, let's review the main concepts covered in this chapter.

6.5   Summary

CO-PC is one of the most important subcomponents in SAP ERP Controlling.

It combines information from all of the areas that you've customized in previous chapters of this book, from CO-CEL (where you defined the primary and secondary cost elements), CO-CCA (where you defined the cost center structure), CO-OPA (where you defined the settlement rules for internal and production orders), and from CO-ABC (where you learned about templates).

This chapter about CO-PC showed you how this powerful tool can be used to simulate costs in product cost planning and manage the product lifecycle, and how changes in the material master data can affect the costing results.

You've learned how to create costing variants to create cost estimates for different purposes, both for standard prices and also for simulating product costing. You've seen how to add more variables to your cost estimates by using costing sheets and templates. We demonstrated how to implement actual costing by activating the Material Ledger, and how to customize the Material Ledger to add even more flexibility and visibility to manufacturing costs to meet your company's specific needs.

Last, this chapter reviewed a sample of the large number of reporting options available for these areas in the information system, showing how all of the decisions made in the customizing of the CO-PC areas affect the information available to you in reporting.

You are now ready to jump to the next exciting chapter: Profitability Analysis (CO-PA). In that chapter, you'll learn about the benefits this component can bring to your company and how to customize it to best meet your profitability analysis reporting needs.

Profitability Analysis in SAP ERP can bring value to your organization for both flexible analysis and planning. Customizing the CO-PA subcomponent can help you meet your specific business needs.

7   Profitability Analysis

This chapter explains the main concepts of the Profitability Analysis (CO-PA) subcomponent, the differences between account-based and cost-based CO-PA, and how to customize the subcomponent to obtain accurate reports using both planning and actual values. You'll first learn about the CO-PA structures and how they are the most important definitions you'll make in your customization. Then we'll look at the master data requirements, how to use CO-PA in your planning, how you can customize the ways that actual values flow into CO-PA, and the options you have for creating your customized multidimensional profitability analysis reports.

CO-PA provides the ability to analyze the profitability of your business by market segments, products, divisions, product hierarchies, or profit centers. It combines information from Sales and Distribution (SD), Product Cost Controlling (CO-PC), Materials Management (MM), Cost Center Accounting (CO-CCA), and Profit Center Accounting (EC-PCA), and allows you to create multidimensional reports using information from all of these SAP ERP areas.

The CO-PA subcomponent can provide real-time profitability information combined from these areas for managers in operations, sales, marketing, or planning to use in both strategic and day-to-day decision making.

There are two kinds of CO-PA:

► **Costing-based**
Revenues and costs are stored in CO-PA based on value fields. For example, from SD, pricing conditions relevant for analyses; from CO-PC, cost estimate and cost component split data; and from CO-CCA, the overhead costs can all be transferred to CO-PA value fields.

▶ **Account-based**
Revenues and costs are transferred to CO-PA based on postings in the accounts relevant for CO-PA, such as revenues, sales deductions, cost of goods sold (COGS), and overhead costs. The account-based approach easily reconciles with Financial Accounting (FI).

Figure 7.1 shows how both approaches can be used to reach the same results.

Costing-based			Account-based	
Sales quantity	3000.00		311000 - Sales quantity	3000.00
Revenues	25,000.00		311000 - Product sales	25,000.00
Discounts	2,000.00		322000 - Discounts	2,000.00
Tax	3,000.00	Vs.	323000 - Tax	3,000.00
COGS	17,000.00		341000 - COGS	17,000.00
Gross margin	3,000.00		Gross margin	3,000.00
Overhead	1,500.00		422200-Administrative expenses 422450-Depreciation 414202-Labor	1,500.00
Profit/loss	1,500.00		Profit/loss	1,500.00

Figure 7.1 Costing-Based vs. Account-Based CO-PA

In the next section, you'll learn about the CO-PA structures and how to create them to initiate the subcomponent in SAP ERP.

7.1 Structures

The CO-PA functionality is built around some new structural elements that are unique to this subcomponent, and that define the dimensions of your business that will be available for multidimensional analysis. Because the structural definitions are the limiting factors in your CO-PA capability, and you define them entirely according to your needs, you'll need to have a clear understanding of the analysis requirements of your organization to determine the optimal strategy to use.

We'll discuss the structures now so that you can learn how they can be used and then how to customize them in SAP ERP. These structures are composed of the following three elements:

▶ Characteristics

▶ Value fields

▶ Operating concern

Either the characteristics or value fields must first exist in the CO-PA field catalog to be used in the operating concern. By default, SAP ERP provides some characteristics and value fields in the field catalog, and you can also create your own characteristics and value fields.

7.1.1 Characteristics

Characteristics are the dimensions that you'll report in CO-PA (for example, customers, distribution channels, or divisions). Table 7.1 shows some examples of characteristics.

Characteristics	Value
Region	East
Profit center	100101
Plant	2001
Sales organization	2001
Fiscal year	2012

Table 7.1 CO-PA Characteristic Example

Some essential characteristics are created by default by SAP ERP when you are creating an operating concern, such as plant, cost element, customer, sales organization, distribution channel, division, and profit center. These characteristics are called fixed characteristics. You can also define additional characteristics to be added to the characteristic list.

Figure 7.2 gives a good overview of how characteristics are established in CO-PA.

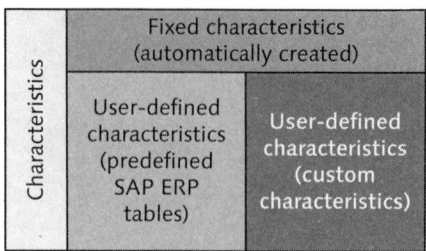

Figure 7.2 CO-PA Characteristics Origin

To create a CO-PA characteristic, you can either use Transaction KEA5 or go to CONTROLLING • PROFITABILITY ANALYSIS • STRUCTURES • DEFINE OPERATING CONCERN • MAINTAIN CHARACTERISTICS. Figure 7.3 shows the first customizing screen.

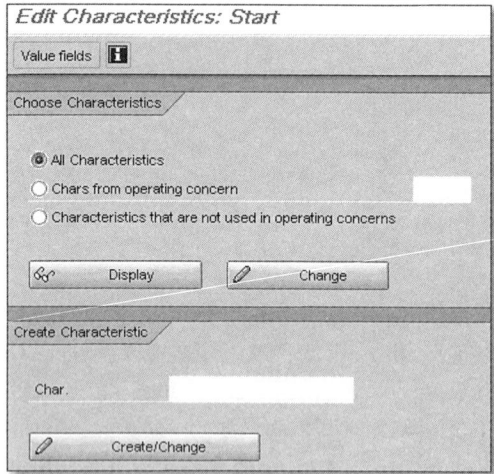

Figure 7.3 Edit Characteristics

By clicking on CREATE/CHANGE, you can define new characteristics to be used in the operating concern. Figure 7.4 shows the characteristics creation screen.

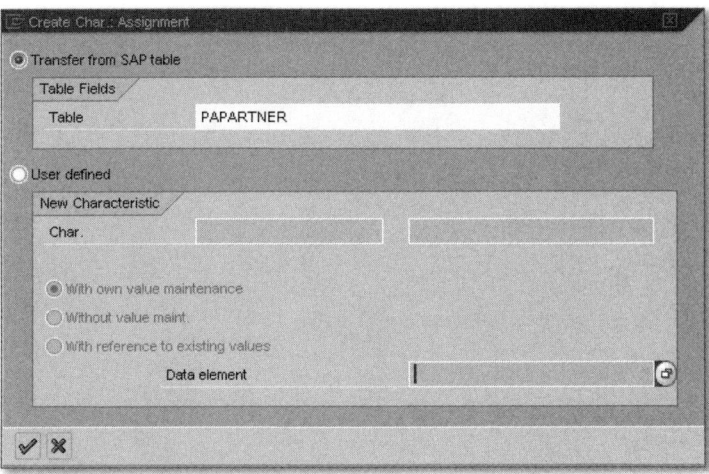

Figure 7.4 Create Characteristic Screen

As you've already seen, there are two types of characteristics that you can create. You can import characteristics from predefined SAP ERP tables, or you can create custom characteristics. Let's first look at the characteristics that can be transferred from SAP ERP tables. Table 7.2 shows the tables from which you can import predefined characteristics.

Table	Description
KNA1	General Data in Customer Master
KNB1	Customer Master (Company Code)
KNVV	Customer Master Sales Data
MARA	General Material Data
MARC	Plant Data for Material
MVKE	Sales Data for Material
PACPROJECT	Characteristics from Projects That Can Be Used in CO-PA
PACRMIPM	Characteristics from CRM IPM That Can Be Used in CO-PA
PACRMSLS	Attributes of CRM Sales That Can Be Used in PA
PACRMSRV	Attributes of CRM Service That Can Be Used in PA

Table 7.2 Predefined SAP ERP Tables for CO-PA Characteristics

Table	Description
PAPARTNER	SD Partner That Can Be Used in CO-PA
PARETAIL	Retail Fields That Can Be Used in CO-PA
PRPS	WBS (Work Breakdown Structure) Element Master Data
T001W	Plants/Branches
VBAK	Sales Document: Header Data
VBAP	Sales Document: Item Data
VBKD	Sales Document: Business Data
VIAUFKST	Generated Table for View VIAUFKST

Table 7.2 Predefined SAP ERP Tables for CO-PA Characteristics (Cont.)

We'll use Table PAPARTNER – SD PARTNER to create one characteristic as an example. After you enter the table name in the TABLE field shown in Figure 7.4, the system will then show the available table fields to be created as characteristics, as you can see in Figure 7.5.

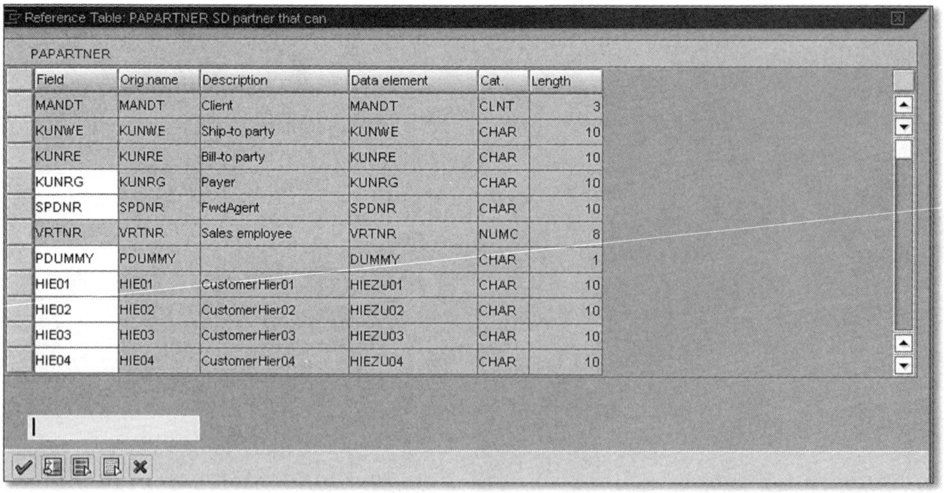

Field	Orig.name	Description	Data element	Cat.	Length
MANDT	MANDT	Client	MANDT	CLNT	3
KUNWE	KUNWE	Ship-to party	KUNWE	CHAR	10
KUNRE	KUNRE	Bill-to party	KUNRE	CHAR	10
KUNRG	KUNRG	Payer	KUNRG	CHAR	10
SPDNR	SPDNR	FwdAgent	SPDNR	CHAR	10
VRTNR	VRTNR	Sales employee	VRTNR	NUMC	8
PDUMMY	PDUMMY		DUMMY	CHAR	1
HIE01	HIE01	CustomerHier01	HIEZU01	CHAR	10
HIE02	HIE02	CustomerHier02	HIEZU02	CHAR	10
HIE03	HIE03	CustomerHier03	HIEZU03	CHAR	10
HIE04	HIE04	CustomerHier04	HIEZU04	CHAR	10

Figure 7.5 Predefined SAP ERP CO-PA Characteristics

The fields shown in white are the fields that you can create as characteristics, whereas the ones shown in gray are the fields that have already been created as characteristics. Mark the field that you want to create and confirm. A new screen will be shown where you'll need to activate the field as you can see in Figure 7.6. You must do this step for each characteristic you create.

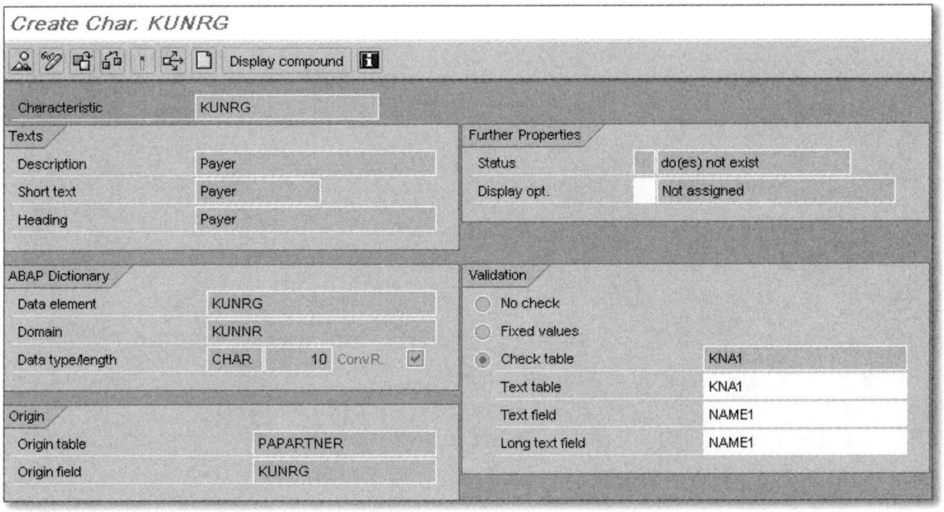

Figure 7.6 Create Characteristic, Activation Screen

When you click the ACTIVATE button, the field is created in the field catalog and can be assigned to an operating concern.

The second option in the screen in Figure 7.4 is to create user-defined characteristics. All user-defined characteristics must start with "WW," followed by two or three more characters.

You can select from three kinds of user-defined characteristics:

▶ WITH OWN VALUE MAINTENANCE

▶ WITHOUT VALUE MAINT.

▶ WITH REFERENCE TO EXISTING VALUES

With Own Value Maintenance

By choosing the WITH OWN VALUE MAINTENANCE option, you create the characteristic by defining the field length and whether it will be numerical or alphanumeric, as you can see in Figure 7.7 in the DATA TYPE/LENGTH FIELD.

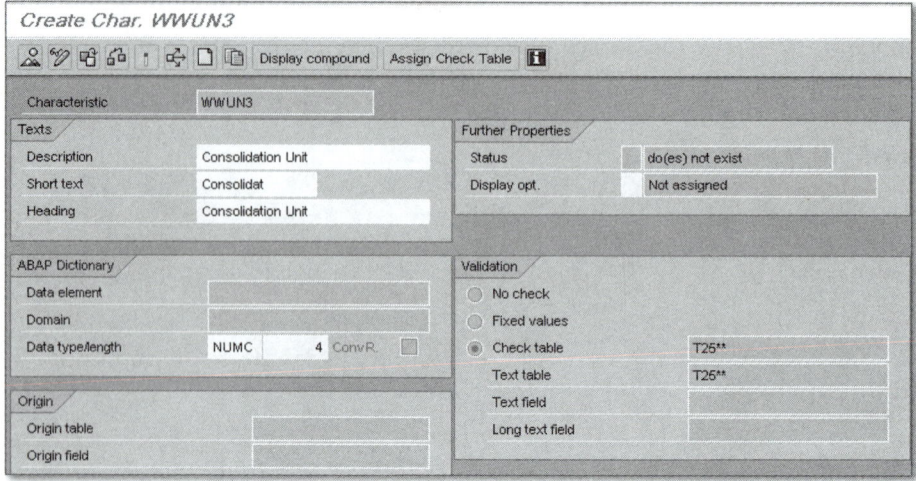

Figure 7.7 Characteristics Creation, User-Defined

SAP ERP automatically creates the table where the characteristics will be maintained. This method is used when you want to assign to the document an external characteristic that isn't already present in SAP ERP. You must use a derivation rule to fill the field with the available values you defined in the characteristics maintenance.

You also need to activate the characteristic to make it available to be assigned to an operating concern.

Without Value Maintenance

In this option, the creation process follows the same principle as in the WITH OWN VALUE MAINTENANCE option. You define the field length and whether it will be alphanumerical or numeric, but in this case, SAP ERP doesn't create a reference table to be maintained, and, consequently, you can't select the characteristic values from the values in the reference table. You must use a derivation process for each value you want to assign to the characteristic. SAP ERP will not validate what is in the derivation against values in a maintained table.

With Reference to Existing Values

In this option, you define a reference data element for the characteristic, and you can then select in the derivation the values from the reference data element. For example, if you use data element BUKRS – Company Code, then you can use as characteristics only company code values that are valid in the system.

7.1.2 Value Fields

In costing-based CO-PA, the reporting values are stored in value fields. Value fields are divided into two categories: amount and quantity.

Examples of amount value fields are revenue, cost of goods sold, and freight. For the quantity value field, a good example is sales quantity. Table 7.3 shows an example of some value fields in CO-PA.

Value Field	Value
Sales quantity	35
Revenue	3500
Discounts	200
Freight	30

Table 7.3 CO-PA Value Field Examples

Similar to CO-PA characteristics, SAP ERP also provides some default value fields in the field catalog. Value fields are not automatically assigned to the operating concern when you create it, meaning that there are no fixed value fields for CO-PA. You can choose to use the proposed value fields or to create your own value fields.

When creating your own value fields, the field name must begin with "VV," followed by two or three additional characters, and you then must identify it as either an amount or quantity value field. Figure 7.8 illustrates how the value fields are established in CO-PA.

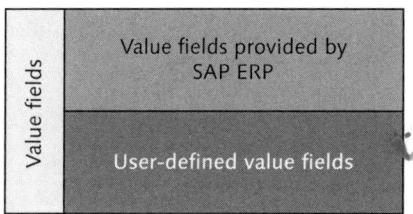

Figure 7.8 CO-PA Value Fields

To create a CO-PA value field, you can either use Transaction KEA6 or go to CONTROLLING • PROFITABILITY ANALYSIS • STRUCTURES • DEFINE OPERATING CONCERN • MAINTAIN VALUE FIELDS. Figure 7.9 shows the first customizing screen, which features both the CHOOSE VALUE FIELDS and CREATE VALUE FIELD sections.

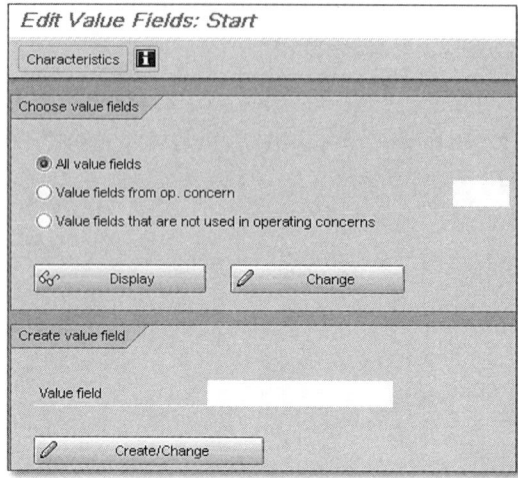

Figure 7.9 Edit CO-PA Value Fields

By clicking on CREATE/CHANGE, you can define new value fields. The following screen is shown in Figure 7.10.

Figure 7.10 Create CO-PA Value Field

You must select the radio button for either AMOUNT or QUANTITY for the value field. After confirming, the system will open the value field definition, shown in Figure 7.11.

You must select in the aggregation based on time field—AGG. (TIME)—if it will be summarized, average, or last value. You need to activate the value field to make it available in the CO-PA field catalog.

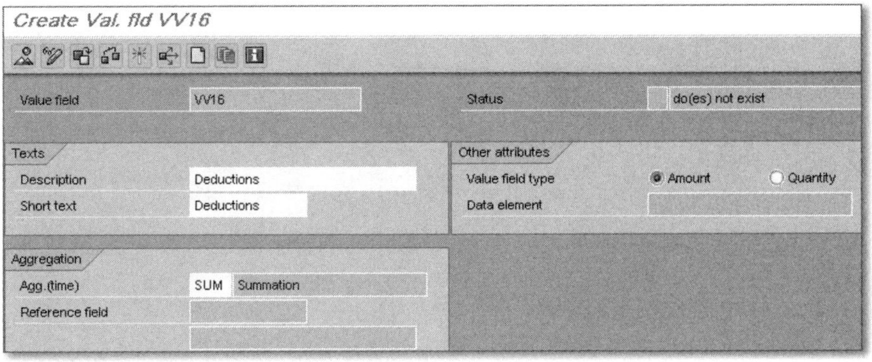

```
Create Val. fld VV16

[toolbar icons]

Value field          VV16                        Status              do(es) not exist

Texts                                            Other attributes
Description          Deductions                  Value field type    ● Amount        ○ Quantity
Short text           Deductions                  Data element

Aggregation
Agg.(time)           SUM   Summation
Reference field
```

Figure 7.11 CO-PA Value Field Definition

> **Note**
>
> For calculated reporting amounts such as gross margin, profit/loss, or net sales, you don't need to create a value field. These values are created in the report formulas.

7.1.3   Operating Concern

The operating concern is the main organizational unit in CO-PA, just as the plant is for MM, the company code for FI, and the controlling area for CO.

When you learned about the controlling area, you saw that you can have one controlling area for multiple company codes or one controlling area for each company code.

The operating concern has a higher organization level than the controlling area; you can have an operating concern that combines multiple controlling areas or just one controlling area, as you can see in Figure 7.12.

You've seen that your choice for the controlling area assignment can directly impact cost reporting. If you've chosen one controlling area for each company code, it's impossible to consolidate cost reports at a higher level, combining more than one company code. The operating concern can consolidate multiple controlling areas. In Figure 7.12, you can see examples of both approaches for operating concerns: one controlling area for one company code and one operating concern (B), and another with two controlling areas, one with two company codes and one with only one company code assigned to another operating concern (A). In the case of operating concern (A), you can have consolidated profitability reports that combine two different controlling areas and three company codes.

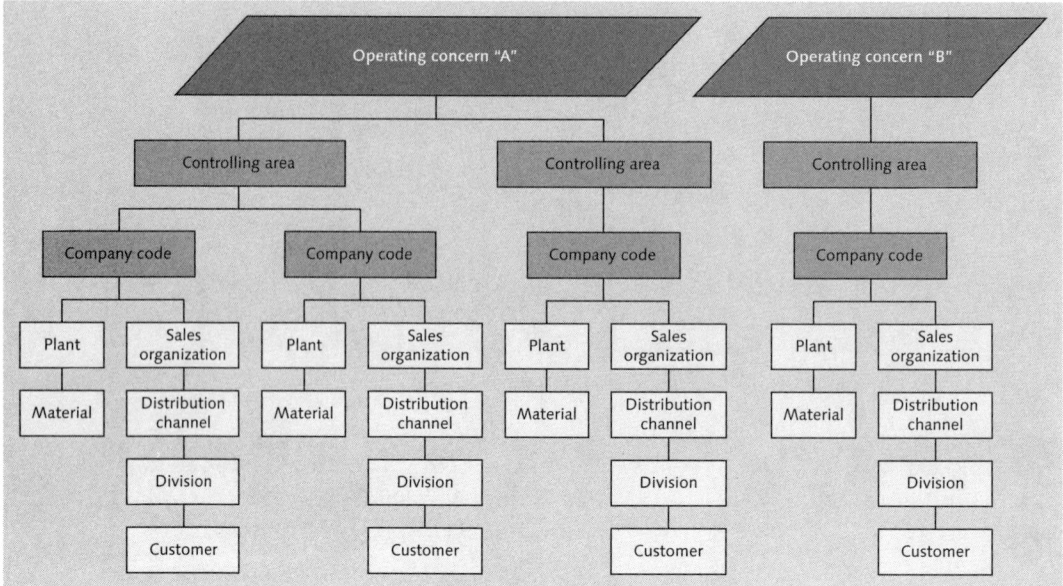

Figure 7.12 Operating Concern Assignment

You can see in Figure 7.13 how the combination of characteristics and value fields creates the profitability segments and gives CO-PA the ability to have multidimensional reports.

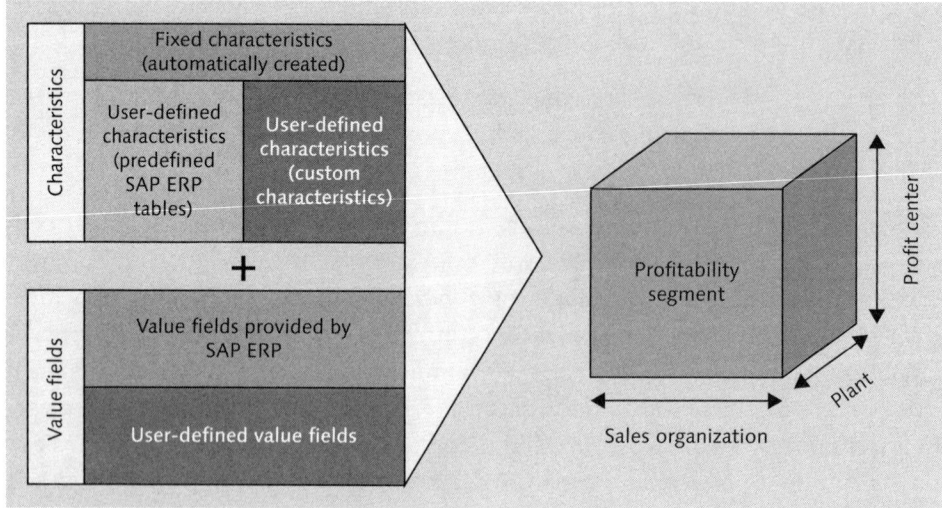

Figure 7.13 CO-PA Multidimensional Report

In CO-PA reports, you can create report definitions and navigate in the reports by any of the characteristics in the profitability segments, creating multidimensional reports. Figure 7.14 shows one example of how multidimensional analysis can be used in a CO-PA report.

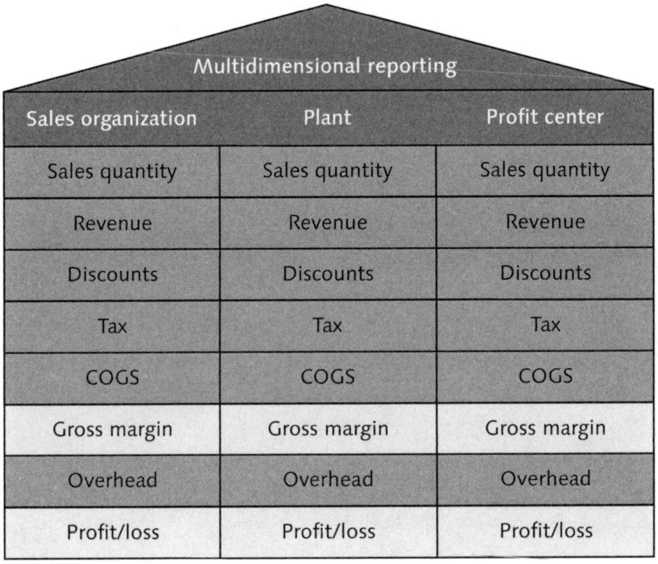

Multidimensional reporting		
Sales organization	Plant	Profit center
Sales quantity	Sales quantity	Sales quantity
Revenue	Revenue	Revenue
Discounts	Discounts	Discounts
Tax	Tax	Tax
COGS	COGS	COGS
Gross margin	Gross margin	Gross margin
Overhead	Overhead	Overhead
Profit/loss	Profit/loss	Profit/loss

Figure 7.14 Multidimensional CO-PA Report

You can navigate between the characteristics, and the same data will be available in the report for the chosen characteristic. In the example in Figure 7.14, you can navigate by sales organization, plant, and profit center.

Now that you've created the field catalogs for characteristics and value fields, you must define the operating concern and assign the characteristics and value fields to the operating concern.

To create an operating concern, either use Transaction KEA0, or go to CONTROLLING • PROFITABILITY ANALYSIS • STRUCTURES • DEFINE OPERATING CONCERN • MAINTAIN OPERATING CONCERN. Figure 7.15 shows the first customizing screen, opened to the DATA STRUCTURE tab.

In this screen, define the operating concern as a four-character alphanumeric field, give it a description, and indicate whether it is costing-based or account-based operating concern. You must first define its attributes before creating the data structure for the operating concern. You can see the ATTRIBUTES tab in Figure 7.16.

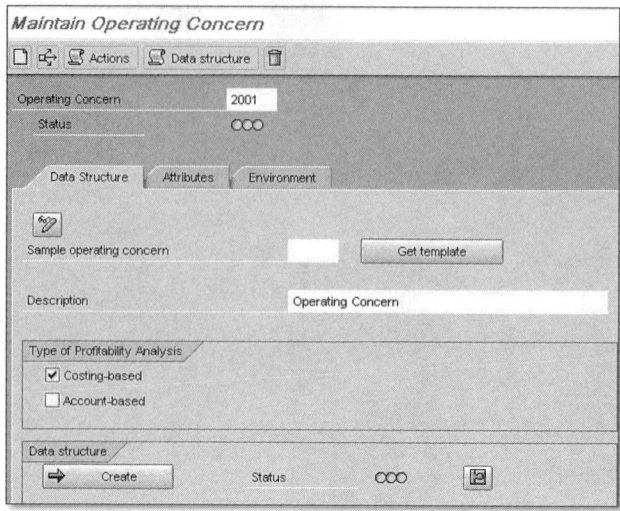

Figure 7.15 Maintain Operating Concern, Data Structure Tab

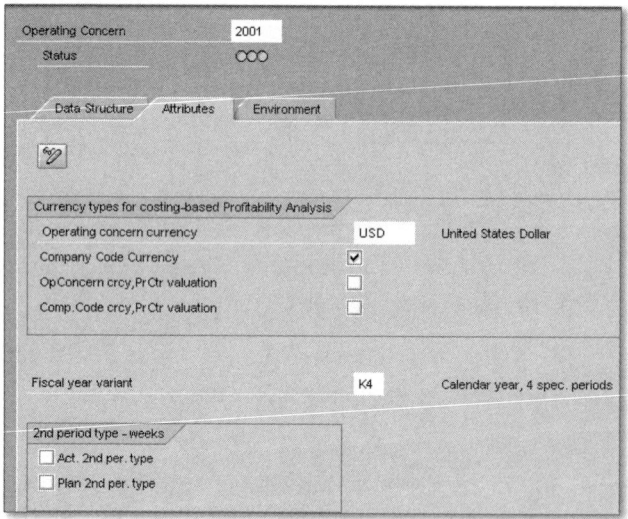

Figure 7.16 Operating Concern, Attributes Tab

In the ATTRIBUTES tab, you'll define the operating concern currency. (Here, the input is "USD".) You can also add different currencies to the operating concern, such as company code currency and profit center valuation currencies. The company code currency is important to add if the organization has operations in different countries; by updating the company code currency, you can run any

CO-PA report in the controlling area currency and also in the company code currency. You can also select to store profit center valuation currency; this currency will then be available in the CO-PA reports.

Note

By selecting additional currencies to be available in your operating concern, you are considerably increasing the database size. Before selecting all currencies for your operating concern, be sure that analysis in different currencies is truly necessary for your organization.

In the ATTRIBUTES tab, you also define the fiscal year variant and if the system will store the actual and plan data by week as well. The weekly period selection will also increase the database size.

After defining the ATTRIBUTES tab, return to the DATA STRUCTURE tab, save the operating concern, and click on the CREATE DATA STRUCTURE button (refer to Figure 7.15). This will bring you to the characteristics and value fields operating concern assignment, as shown in Figure 7.17.

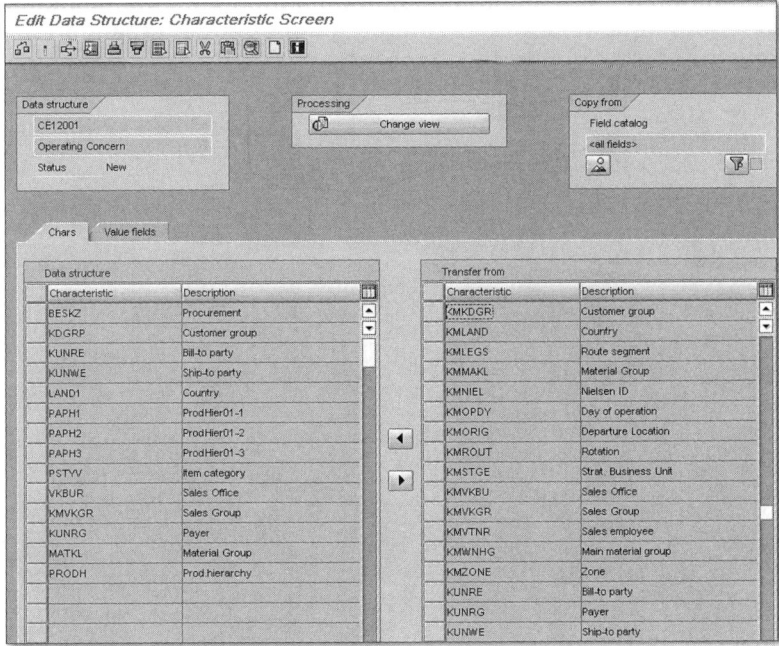

Figure 7.17 Operating Concern Data Structure, Characteristics

The characteristics that you've added to the field catalogs are shown on the right side of the screen and are therefore available to be added to the operating concern. On the left side of the screen, you'll find the characteristics you've added to your operating concern. Mark an available characteristic on the right side of the screen, click on the arrow to send to the left side, and repeat for each characteristic you want to add. Remember that the fixed characteristics will be automatically attached to your operating concern and won't show here.

You may also define the value fields for your operating concern in this screen. Move to the VALUE FIELDS tab to select which value fields you want to add in the same way as you did for the characteristics. Figure 7.18 shows the options.

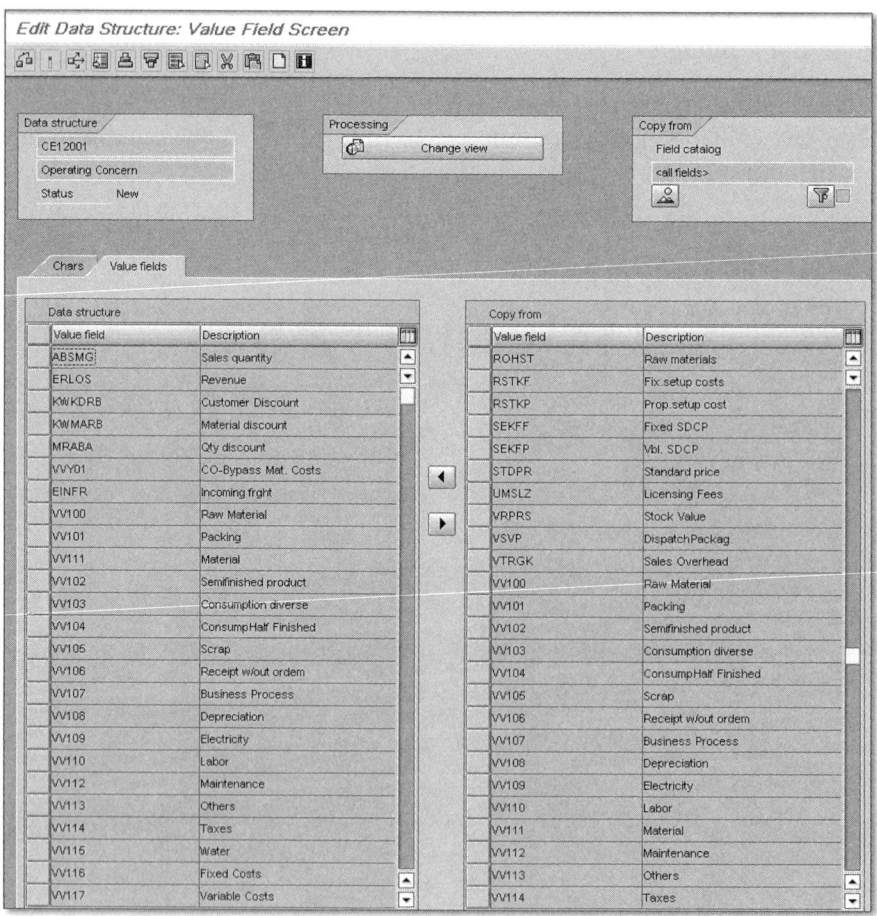

Figure 7.18 Operating Concern Data Structure, Value Fields

Because there are no fixed value fields for the operating concern, you must define all of the value fields.

After adding the characteristics and the value fields to your operating concern, you will need to activate the operating concern on the last tab in the operating concern maintenance (the ENVIRONMENT tab), as shown in Figure 7.19. This will cause the system to create all of the tables for the operating concern.

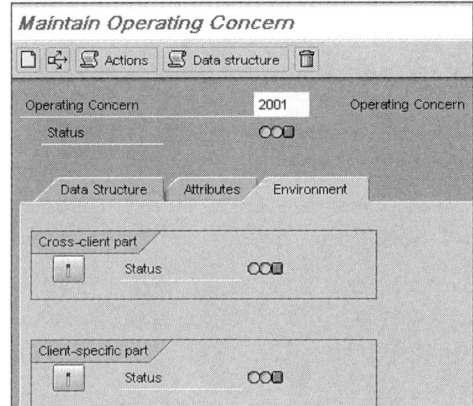

Figure 7.19 Operating Concern, Environment Tab

You activate the operating concern by clicking on ACTIVATE (the icon with the picture of a match) in both the CROSS-CLIENT PART and CLIENT-SPECIFIC PART sections on the ENVIRONMENT tab, as shown in Figure 7.19.

When you activate the operating concern, the system creates the necessary tables for the operating concern. These tables will vary depending on whether you selected costing-based or account-based CO-PA. Table 7.4 shows the tables where the system stores the data for each type.

Data Type	Costing-Based CO-PA	Account-Based CO-PA
Actual line items	CE1XXXX	COEJ
Plan line items	CE2XXXX	COEP
Totals	CE3XXXX	COSS+COSP
Profitability segments	CE4XXXX	CE4XXXX

Table 7.4 CO-PA Tables Definition

As you can see in Table 7.4, the account-based CO-PA uses the same tables used for controlling accounting data, which will consequently increase the response time for controlling reports. The "XXXX" in the table name represents the operating concern.

Every time you change the operating concern, you must activate it again in both these sections on the ENVIRONMENT tab. This will regenerate the operating concern and modify the related tables in light of the new changes.

You've learned how to create the field catalogs for characteristics and value fields, and how to create and assign them to the operating concern. Next you need to assign the controlling areas to the operating concern and activate the operating concern in each controlling area.

7.1.4 Assign Controlling Area to an Operating Concern

You saw in Figure 7.11 that an operating concern can have either one controlling area or multiple controlling areas assigned to it. Now you'll learn how to assign controlling areas to an operating concern in SAP ERP.

To assign a controlling area to an operating concern, use Transaction KEKK, or go to ENTERPRISE STRUCTURE • ASSIGNMENT • CONTROLLING • ASSIGN CONTROLLING AREA TO OPERATING CONCERN. Figure 7.20 shows the assignment screen.

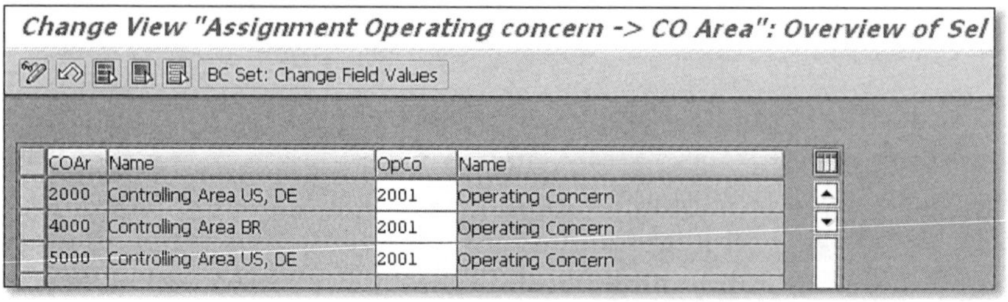

Figure 7.20 Assignment Controlling Area to Operating Concern

In this example, you can see that we've assigned multiple controlling areas to the came operating concern. But only assigning the controlling areas doesn't make the operating concern operational. You also need to activate the CO-PA in the controlling areas.

7.2   Activate CO-PA for a Controlling Area

So far in this book, you've had to activate the subcomponents in the controlling area customizing for all of the CO subcomponents that you've encountered. For CO-PA, there is a different process for the activation in the controlling area.

The CO-PA activation must be in accordance with the kind of operating concern you've defined, whether it is a costing-based or account-based operating concern. You can choose from four options:

- ▶ 1 COMPONENT NOT ACTIVE
- ▶ 2 COMPONENT ACTIVE FOR COSTING-BASED PROFITABILITY ANALYSIS
- ▶ 3 COMPONENT ACTIVE FOR ACCOUNT-BASED PROFITABILITY ANALYSIS
- ▶ 4 COMPONENT ACTIVE FOR BOTH TYPES OF PROFITABILITY ANALYSIS

To activate the CO-PA for the controlling area, you can either use Transaction KEKE, or go to CONTROLLING • PROFITABILITY ANALYSIS • FLOWS OF ACTUAL VALUES • ACTIVATE PROFITABILITY ANALYSIS. Figure 7.21 illustrates the activation screen.

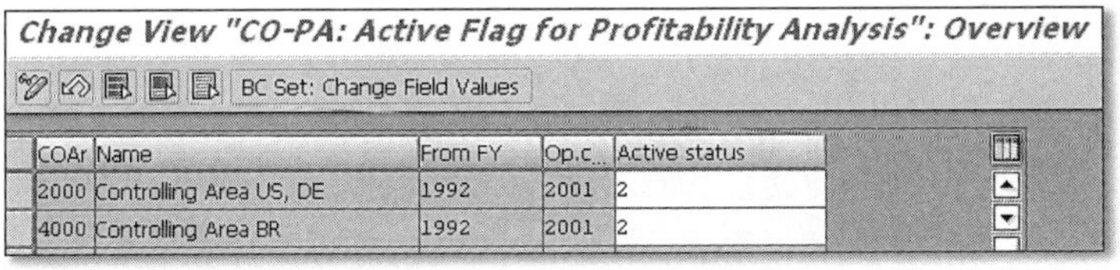

COAr	Name	From FY	Op.c	Active status
2000	Controlling Area US, DE	1992	2001	2
4000	Controlling Area BR	1992	2001	2

Change View "CO-PA: Active Flag for Profitability Analysis": Overview

Figure 7.21 CO-PA Activation

After saving, you may want to check the operating concern activation in the controlling area customizing. Use Transaction OKKP as shown in Figure 7.22.

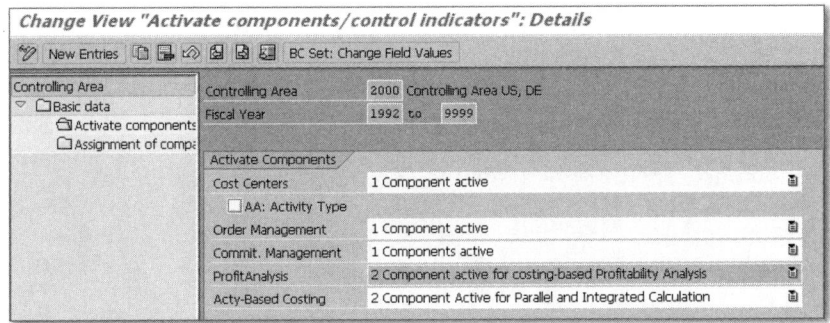

Figure 7.22 Controlling Area Activate Components

The CO-PA is grayed out because you can't change it from here; you can only view the activation information.

Now that you've finished the operating concern structure customizing and have learned how to assign controlling areas and how to activate the CO-PA, let's move on to the next CO-PA customizing topic: master data.

7.3 Master Data

When a value flows from SD, MM, CO, and FI to CO-PA, it will create a line item in the CO-PA tables. The way you customize the master data will directly impact how the characteristics and value fields are populated in the line items. Figure 7.23 shows one example of a CO-PA line item.

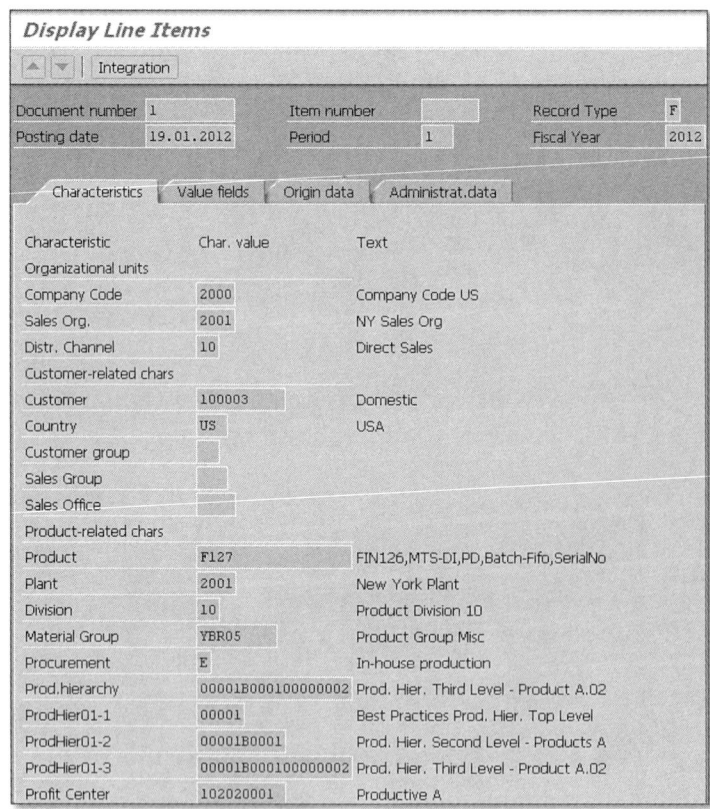

Figure 7.23 CO-PA Line Item

You can see that the characteristics were populated automatically by the system in Figure 7.23. You can change the behavior of the assignments and also complete the missing ones. It's very important to have all characteristics filled for each posting so that the CO-PA reports you run for any characteristic are complete.

In master data you'll customize three important definitions:

▶ Characteristic values

▶ Characteristic derivation

▶ Valuation

We'll explore these in the following sections.

7.3.1 Characteristic Values

When you created the field catalogs for characteristics, if you defined any fields as custom characteristics with own value maintenance, you now need to create the values for these characteristics to be used in CO-PA. This means that the values for the characteristics will be selected from values in a table you define. In the example shown earlier in Figure 7.7, we created the characteristic WWUN3 – CONSOLIDATION UNIT. Now we'll define the possible values for the consolidation unit. To maintain characteristic values for the characteristics you've defined, use Transaction KES1, or go to CONTROLLING • PROFITABILITY ANALYSIS • MASTER DATA • CHARACTERISTIC VALUES • MAINTAIN CHARACTERISTIC VALUES. You can see the first maintenance screen in Figure 7.24.

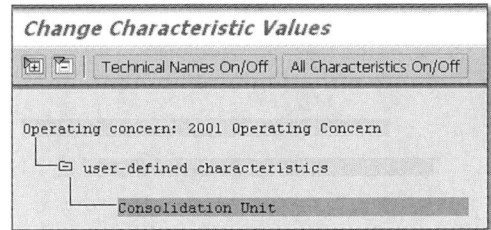

Figure 7.24 Change Characteristic Values

If you click on the characteristic, the system will open the corresponding table maintenance screen, as shown in Figure 7.25.

You can add or remove table entries.

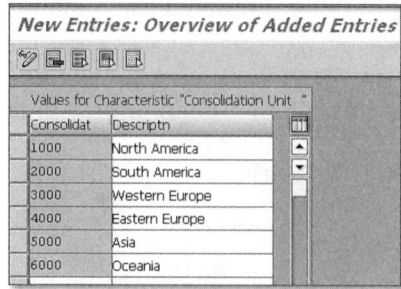

Figure 7.25 Maintain Characteristic

> **Note**
>
> If you've already assigned a value for a characteristic in one CO-PA line item, do not remove it from the list of characteristics. This could cause reporting inconsistencies, which you should avoid.

In CO-PA you can group single characteristics to create a user hierarchy for the characteristic, which allows you to see reports both at the detailed level and also according to the hierarchy you created.

We'll now create a hierarchy for the values defined for the consolidation unit in Figure 7.25. To define the characteristic hierarchy, either use Transaction KES3, or go to Controlling • Profitability Analysis • Master Data • Characteristic Values • Define Characteristics Hierarchy. You can see in Figure 7.26 the first customizing screen.

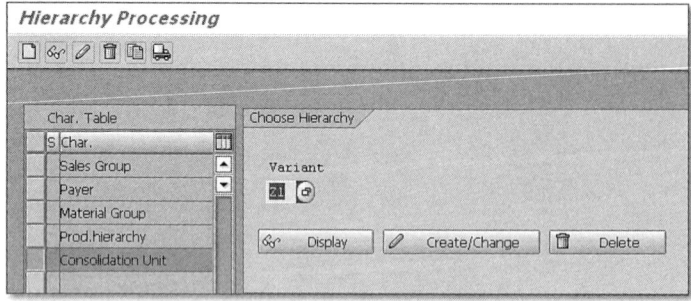

Figure 7.26 Maintain Characteristic Hierarchy

Find and mark in the left side of the screen the characteristic for which you want to create the hierarchy, enter the first node for the hierarchy, and click on the

CREATE/CHANGE button. This will bring you to the hierarchy attribute maintenance screen, shown in Figure 7.27, where you can enter the name for the first node of the hierarchy.

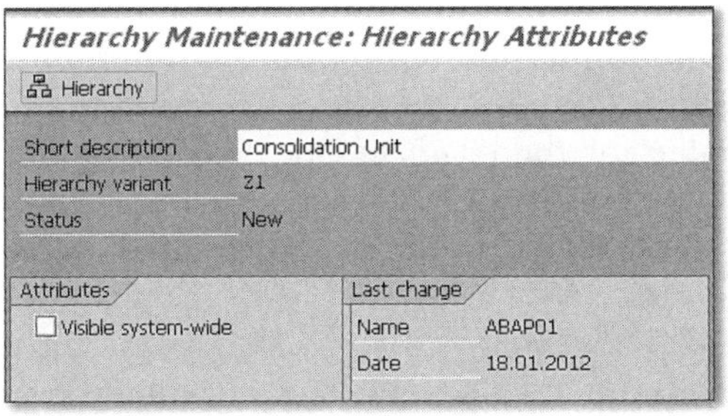

Hierarchy Maintenance: Hierarchy Attributes

品 Hierarchy	

Short description	Consolidation Unit
Hierarchy variant	Z1
Status	New

Attributes	Last change	
☐ Visible system-wide	Name	ABAP01
	Date	18.01.2012

Figure 7.27 Hierarchy Maintenance, Short Description

Enter a short description for the hierarchy, and then click on the HIERARCHY button. The next screen allows you to enter or create the hierarchy structure, as shown in Figure 7.28.

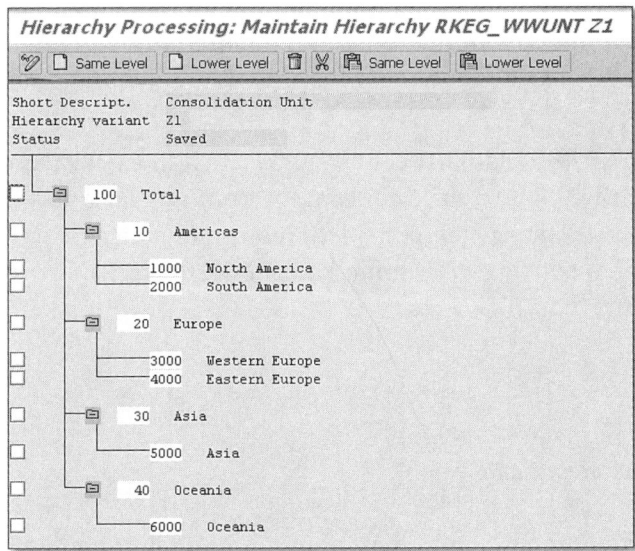

Figure 7.28 Hierarchy Processing

You can define the lower levels and same levels by clicking on the corresponding button. When you reach the last desired level, enter the characteristic value, and the system will automatically bring in the characteristic name. In this example, we'll be able to see analysis by the consolidation units themselves and also by groupings corresponding to the hierarchy nodes in the CO-PA reports.

Next, you'll customize the characteristic derivation in the master data section.

7.3.2 Characteristic Derivation

When the system can't determine a value for the characteristic, or if in certain cases, you want to override what has been defined by the system, you can create a derivation step to determine the characteristic values during posting of the CO-PA documents.

> **Note**
>
> Derivations are used only for characteristics. You can't modify value fields using derivations.

The CO-PA derivations are defined by five different types of derivation steps:

▶ DERIVATION RULE
  This rule is based on an "if-then" where you define a condition and a derivation to use if the condition is met.

▶ TABLE LOOKUP
  The system will read a specified table that contains a key that must exist as a characteristic, and then it will derive the field content from this table to the characteristic if the characteristic has the same definition as the table field. It can be used, for example, to derive a value from the material master table that is not present in the posting document.

▶ MOVE
  This step will move a characteristic value or a constant to a target field.

▶ CLEAR
  This step will delete the characteristic value.

▶ ENHANCEMENT
  If you want to create a custom program to define the characteristic derivation, use COPA0001.

To create a characteristic derivation, you can use Transaction KEDR, or go to CONTROLLING • PROFITABILITY ANALYSIS • MASTER DATA • DEFINE CHARACTERISTIC DERIVATION. You can see in Figure 7.29 the first customizing screen.

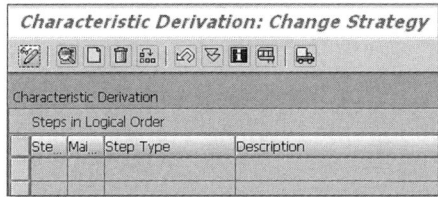

Figure 7.29 Characteristic Derivation

In the first customizing screen, select the kind of derivation step you want to create. We'll illustrate a derivation rule step in the next example. Click on the NEW ENTRIES button, and select from the types of steps available, as you can see in Figure 7.30.

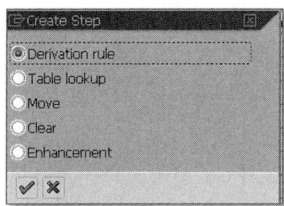

Figure 7.30 Derivation Step

After selecting the type, you'll come to the screen shown in Figure 7.31.

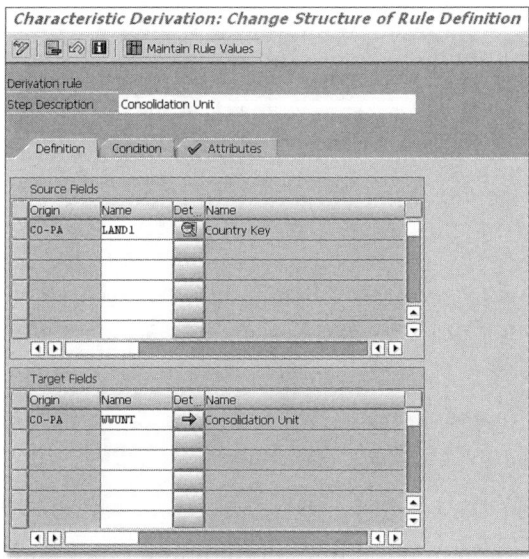

Figure 7.31 Characteristic Derivation

In this screen, you'll enter the step description and then build the derivation rule. In the SOURCE FIELDS area, you select the "If" condition for the derivation, and in the TARGET FIELDS area, you select the "Then" field.

If you click the magnifying glass button in front of the source field, you can define whether an initial value for the field is allowed.

If you click the arrow button in front of the target field, you can chose from the following options:

- DO NOT OVERWRITE WITH A NEW VALUE IF THE FIELD IS ALREADY FILLED
- OVERWRITE WITH A NEW VALUE EVEN IF THE FIELD IS ALREADY FILLED
- OVERWRITE WITH A NEW VALUE ONLY IF THE IS FIELD ALREADY FILLED

After defining the "If and Then" for the derivation rule, click on MAINTAIN RULE VALUES to update the values for the SOURCE FIELDS and TARGET FIELDS. You can see the assignments for our example in Figure 7.32.

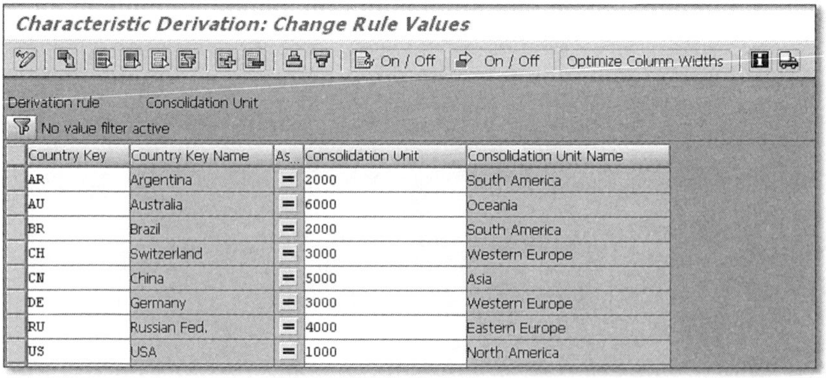

Country Key	Country Key Name	As..	Consolidation Unit	Consolidation Unit Name
AR	Argentina	=	2000	South America
AU	Australia	=	6000	Oceania
BR	Brazil	=	2000	South America
CH	Switzerland	=	3000	Western Europe
CN	China	=	5000	Asia
DE	Germany	=	3000	Western Europe
RU	Russian Fed.	=	4000	Eastern Europe
US	USA	=	1000	North America

Figure 7.32 Derivation Rule, Assignments

You can see in the example shown in Figure 7.31 that a derivation based on COUNTRY KEY was created to determine the CONSOLIDATION UNIT, depending on the relationships defined in Figure 7.32.

Returning to the first customizing screen, two more tabs are left to discuss: CONDITION and ATTRIBUTES. Figure 7.33 shows the CONDITION tab.

In this tab, you can further restrict the derivation rule by defining user filters for the derivation selection. The last tab, ATTRIBUTES, shows additional options for the derivation rule, as you can see in Figure 7.34.

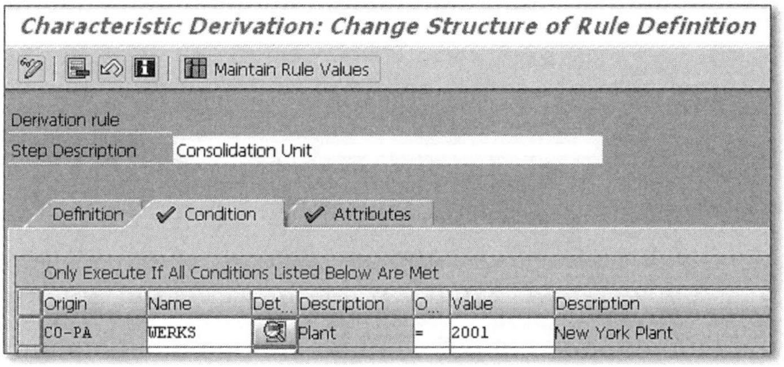

Figure 7.33 Characteristics Derivation, Condition Tab

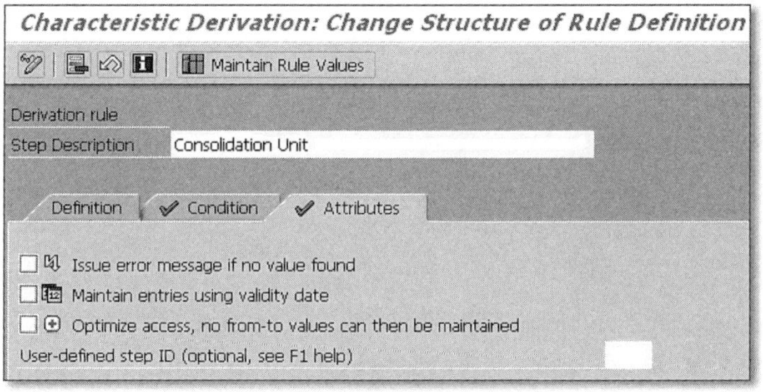

Figure 7.34 Characteristics Derivation, Attributes Tab

In the ATTRIBUTES tab, you can define whether the system will issue an error when the derivation doesn't find a value to derive, define if the validation will have a starting date, and restrict the validation by removing the from-to option.

> **Note**
>
> If you indicate that an error will be issued when no value is found for the derivation, it will block the creation of the CO-PA document, and consequently the FI document. Make sure this is the desired outcome before choosing this option.

Up to this point in this section, you've learned how to maintain the user-created characteristics, how to create the characteristic hierarchy and also how to customize the characteristic derivation. Now let's discuss valuation customizing.

7.3.3 Valuation

In costing-based CO-PA, you can define valuation methods to add more information to your reporting analysis.

From billing documents, the system will automatically add the values that have an accounting posting in FI, such as revenues, discounts, and quantities, to CO-PA. In valuation, you determine which cost estimate the system will use for value fields that can't be directly obtained from SD. If it is not present in the cost estimate, you can also determine the value using a costing sheet.

Figure 7.35 illustrates a CO-PA document with the origins of the values fields.

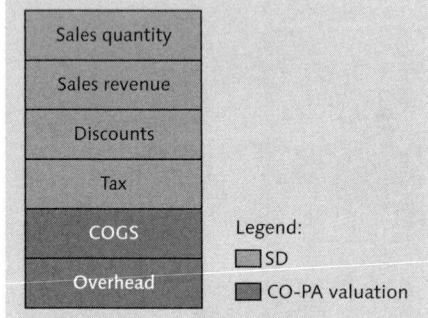

Figure 7.35 CO-PA Values, Origin

To access the valuation for CO-PA, you must create a valuation strategy and define the time of valuation, whether it will be real-time or periodic, for which record type and if a CO-PA version is defined for planning.

Figure 7.36 illustrates how SAP ERP accesses the valuation values in CO-PA.

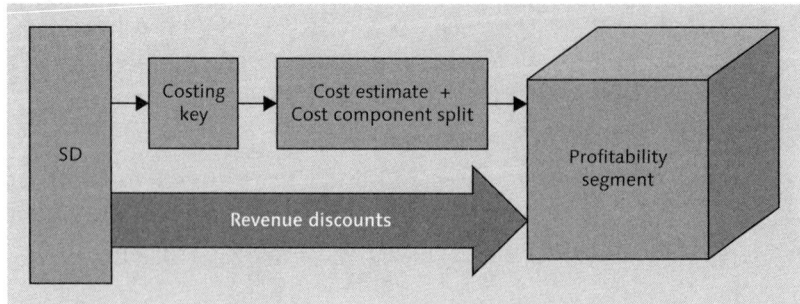

Figure 7.36 Valuation Strategy

Before you define the valuation strategy, you must first set up whether the valuation will use a material cost estimate or a costing sheet.

Valuation Using a Material Cost Estimate

In product cost planning, you've seen that you can create costing variants for different purposes, such as standard costs, simulated new costs, new production lines, new BOMs, and so on. In CO-PA, you can bring these costs to your profitability reports. To determine COGS, for example, the system will use Sales Quantity × Cost Estimate; if you've defined the cost component split, you can also add that to the CO-PA. In Figure 7.37, you can see a CO-PA document with the valuation for the cost estimate and cost component split.

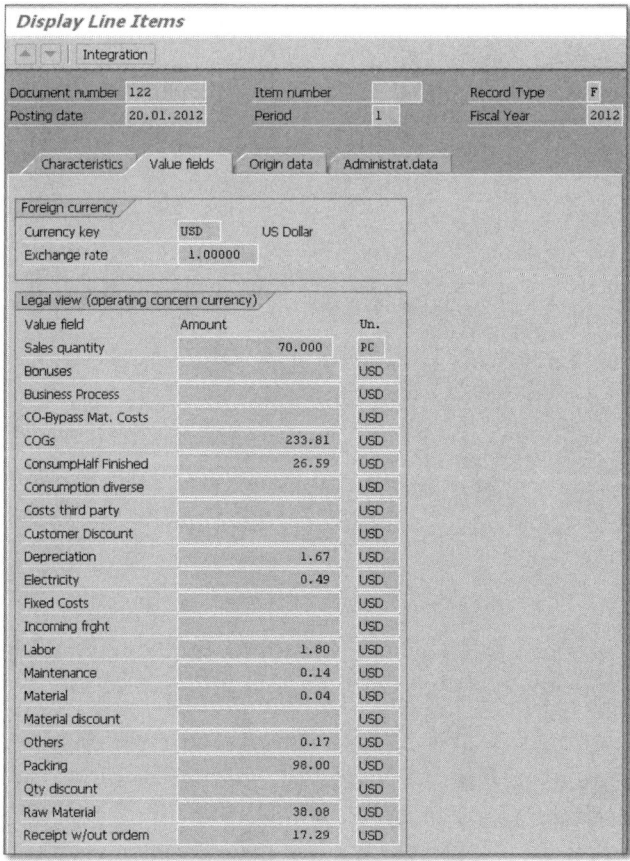

Figure 7.37 CO-PA Cost Estimate Valuation

To access the material cost estimate and the cost component split, you need to create a costing key (refer to Figure 7.36) and define which cost variant this costing key will access. To create the costing key, either use Transaction KE40, or go to CONTROLLING • PROFITABILITY ANALYSIS • MASTER DATA • VALUATION • SET UP VALUATION USING MATERIAL COST ESTIMATE • DEFINE ACCESS TO STANDARD COST ESTIMATES, as shown in Figure 7.38.

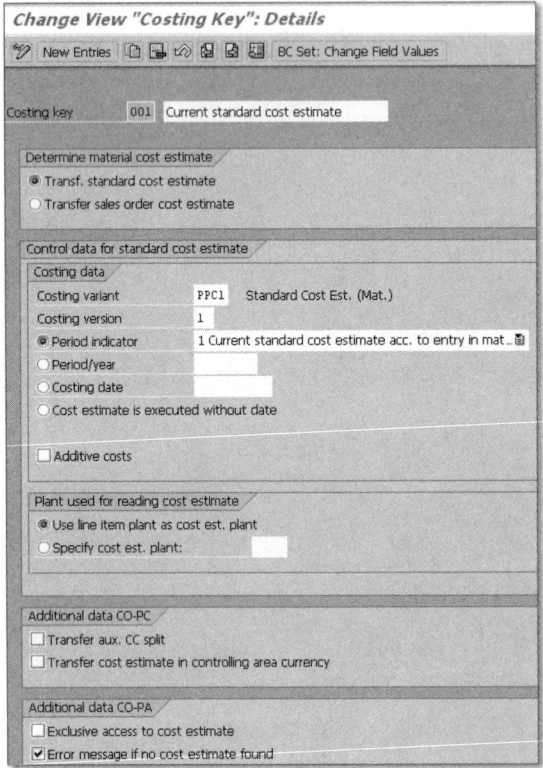

Figure 7.38 Costing Key

In this customizing screen, you can select which cost estimate the system will transfer: the standard cost estimate or the sales order cost estimate.

In the CONTROL DATA FOR STANDARD COST ESTIMATE section, you can define the costing variant, costing version, and, if it's to bring cost from the material standard cost estimate, you can choose from previous, actual, and future cost estimates for the material. The system will use the cost estimate from the material master data, shown in Figure 7.39.

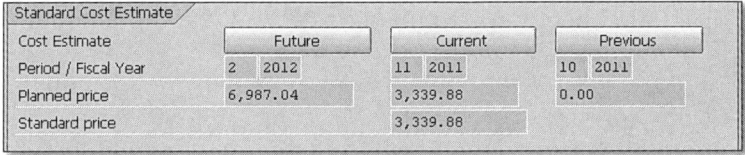

Figure 7.39 Material Cost Estimate

You can also select the released cost estimate effective for the goods issue posting date, the valid cost estimate for the posting date, or the cost estimate valid for a specific period or date. Alternatively, you can set in the costing key to read the cost estimate from a different plant than the plant in the posting.

> **Note**
>
> If you are using a costing variant that is different from the standard cost costing variant, the strategy to bring the costs from the material master data won't work because only the variant for standard cost estimate updates the material master data. In this case, you must select the material cost estimate valid on the posting date or define the period/ year you want to use.

In the ADDITIONAL DATA CO-PC section, you can transfer the auxiliary cost component split, if you've defined one, and also indicate if the cost should be in the controlling area currency.

In ADDITIONAL DATA CO-PA, you can define if it will exclusively use the cost estimate (meaning if the system finds a valid cost estimate, it won't search for another strategy) and also indicate if you want the system to issue an error if no cost estimate is found for the material.

> **Note**
>
> If you flag the field ERROR MESSAGE IF NO COST ESTIMATE FOUND, and the system can't determine a valid cost estimate in the strategy for a material in a billing document, it will issue a hard error and not create the FI document for the billing document. This will require further action to be taken to complete the posting of this billing document, such as creating a cost estimate for the material and then releasing the billing document. To help prevent this error, we recommend that you create one strategy to use the current cost estimate and another strategy to use, for example, the future cost estimate.

If you've activated the Material Ledger and also want to transfer the actual cost to CO-PA, you must create a costing key for actual costing. To create the actual costing key, go to CONTROLLING • PROFITABILITY ANALYSIS • MASTER DATA • VALUATION • SET UP VALUATION USING MATERIAL COST ESTIMATE • DEFINE ACCESS TO ACTUAL COSTING/MATERIAL LEDGER, as shown in Figure 7.40.

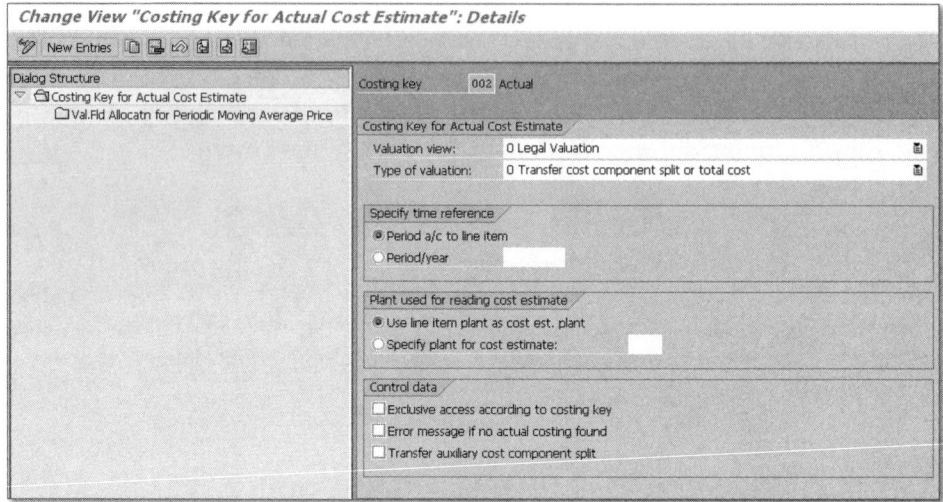

Figure 7.40 Costing Key for Actual Costing

The definition is similar to the one we've already covered for the costing key for cost estimate. The difference is that you can select the valuation view, LEGAL VALUATION, GROUP VALUATION, or PROFIT CENTER VALUATION, and in TYPE OF VALUATION, you select whether or not to transfer the actual cost component split. You also need to define the value field for the periodic moving average price. Double-click on the left side of the screen to define the value field, as you can see in Figure 7.41.

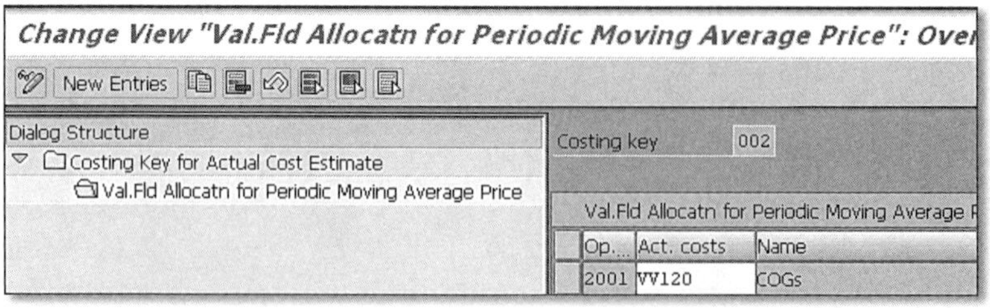

Figure 7.41 Value Field for the Periodic Moving Average Price

The value field for the periodic moving average price is defined by the operating concern.

Now that you've created the costing key to access the cost estimate and also for the Material Ledger, you must now define how the material cost estimate will be accessed by the system. You have three options to define the assignment:

▸ Assign costing keys to products

▸ Assign costing keys to material types

▸ Assign costing keys to any characteristics

In the first option, assign costing keys to products, you'll make the assignment material by material. This is mostly used when you need to define a different costing key for a specific material. We recommend that you avoid using this option for all materials because you need to maintain the customizing every time a new material is created. Use Transaction KE4H to assign the costing key to individual materials.

The second option, assign costing keys to material types, is most commonly used. We'll describe how to make the assignment using this option.

In CO-PA, there are four different point of valuation:

▸ 01: Real-time valuation of actual data

▸ 02: Periodic revaluation of actual data

▸ 03: Manual planning

▸ 04: Automatic planning

You must define how the system will access the costing key for each point of valuation. To assign the costing key to material types, either use Transaction KE4J, or go to Controlling • Profitability Analysis • Master Data • Valuation • Set Up Valuation Using Material Cost Estimate • Assign Costing Keys to Material Types. Figure 7.42 shows the assignment screen.

Assigning the costing key to material types makes the process easier and eliminates the need to maintain the customizing every time you create a new material (as is the case where you assign the costing key to a material).

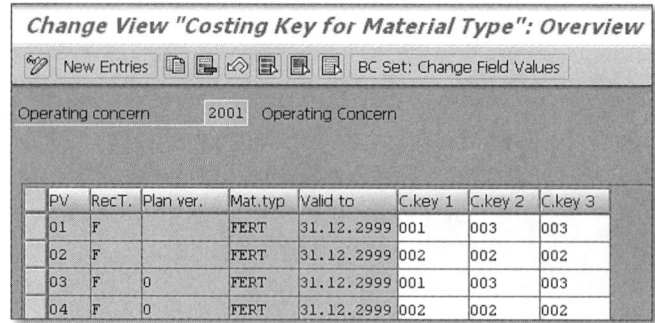

Figure 7.42 Assign Costing Key to Material Type

You must enter the point of valuation for actual and planning, choose the record type, material type, a valid date, and define costing keys 1, 2, and 3. The reason for three costing keys is that if the system doesn't find a cost estimate in the first costing key, it tries the second, and then the third. You can use, for example, the first key to select the current cost estimate, the second key to access the future cost estimate, and the third key to access the previous cost estimate in the material master data.

For the record type, the following options are available:

- A: INCOMING SALES ORDER
- B: DIR.POSTING FROM FI
- C: ORDER/PROJ.SETTLEMNT
- E: SINGLE TRANS COSTING
- F: BILLING DATA
- I: ORDER-REL. PROJECT.

When none of the options are appropriate to access the valuation for the cost estimate, you can also use the third option: assign costing keys to any characteristics. This is mostly used when you want to set up a strategy to use an enhancement. For a custom program in this situation, use enhancement COPA0002. To customize it, use Transaction KEPC.

After defining the costing key and how the cost estimate will be accessed, and assigning the costing key to a material type, you now need to define which value fields will receive the cost components split in the example in Figure 7.42.

To use the cost component split, you must have created a value field for each cost component. To assign the cost component to the value fields, either use Transaction KE4R, or go to CONTROLLING • PROFITABILITY ANALYSIS • MASTER DATA • VALUATION • SET UP VALUATION USING MATERIAL COST ESTIMATE • ASSIGN VALUE FIELDS. In the first screen, define which operating concern and cost component structure will be used in the definition, as shown in Figure 7.43.

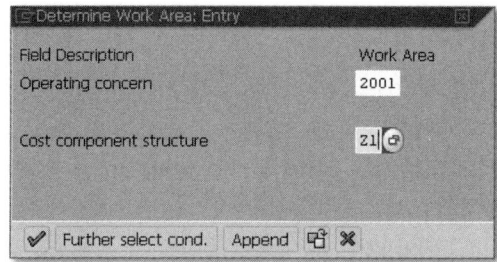

Figure 7.43 Determine Work Area

After defining the operating concern and the cost component split, the next screen will allow you create the assignment between cost components and value fields, as shown in Figure 7.44.

Change View "Assign Costing Elements to Value Fields": Overview

📝 New Entries 🗋 🖫 🖉 🖫 🖫 🖫 BC Set: Change Field Values

Op. concern 2001 Operating Concern
Cost comp. stru Z1 Cost component split

PV	CCo	Name of Cost Comp.	F/V	Fld name 1	Fld name 2	Fld name 3	
01	10	Raw Material	3	VV100	VV120	VV100	
01	20	Packing	3	VV101	VV120	VV101	
01	30	Semifinished product	3	VV102	VV120	VV102	
01	40	Consumption diverse	3	VV103	VV120	VV103	
01	50	ConsumpHalf Finished	3	VV104	VV120	VV104	
01	60	Scrap	3	VV105	VV120	VV105	
01	70	Receipt w/out ordem	3	VV106	VV120	VV106	
01	80	Business Process	3	VV107	VV120	VV107	
01	100	Depreciation	3	VV108	VV120	VV108	
01	110	Electricity	3	VV109	VV120	VV109	
01	120	Labor	3	VV110	VV120	VV110	

Figure 7.44 Assign Costing Elements to Value Fields

In the first column, you define the point of value; in the second column, you define the cost component. You can split the fixed and variable costs from the cost components in different value fields if you want, by selecting 1 – FIXED AMOUNTS, 2 – VARIABLE AMOUNTS, or 3 – SUM OF FIXED AND VARIABLE AMOUNTS, and then maintaining the value field.

You can add in this customizing up to three value fields for the same line. This customizing must be in accordance with what you've defined for the assignment of costing variant for materials.

In the example in Figure 7.42, for point of valuation = 1 (Real-time valuation of actual data), document type = F (Billing data), material type = FERT (Finished product), three costing keys were defined: 001, 003, and 003, respectively. Now looking in the customizing in Figure 7.44, for the first line, point of value 01 (Real-time valuation of actual data), cost component 10 (RAW MATERIAL), fixed or variable = 3 (Sum of fixed and variable amounts), three value fields were assigned: VV100, VV120, and VV100, respectively. The system will send the values for the value field VV100 from the costing key 001, and it will send the values for the value fields VV120 and VV100 from costing key 003.

> **Note**
>
> In the preceding example, you can see that there are two combinations with the same costing key and value field. In this case, the system will not duplicate the values in the value field.

You've now seen how to use the valuation to bring cost estimates to CO-PA. In addition to that, you can use calculated methods to add additional information to CO-PA, information that is not directly available from other SAP ERP components, such as overhead costs, surcharges, and cash discounts. The calculated method uses a costing sheet. We'll now review how to customize your CO-PA to bring in this additional information.

Set Up Conditions and Costing Sheets

Using conditions and costing sheets, you can create statistical values inside CO-PA to project values that are not yet available at the time the sales document is created and include them in the reports. One good example is overhead costs. The actual company overhead costs remain unknown until the end of the period, but you have a projection of these costs, and you can use the costing sheet to create an accrual of the overhead costs in CO-PA. The system will create an accrual for the overhead in the CO-PA document for every document in CO-PA, if the costing sheet requirement is met.

The customizing process is divided into four steps:

1. Define the condition tables.

2. Define the access sequences.

3. Create the condition types and costing sheets.

4. Assign the value fields.

You'll learn how to perform each one of these steps.

Define Condition Tables

In the same manner as in SD, condition tables are used to store the prices and also to define how the prices will be stored. You can create a condition table to store prices by material, material/plant, material/plant/customer, or material/price list, or you can use the characteristics assigned to the operating concern to create the condition table.

To create the condition table, either use Transaction KE4A, or go to CONTROLLING • PROFITABILITY ANALYSIS • MASTER DATA • VALUATION • SET UP CONDITIONS AND COSTING SHEETS • DEFINE CONDITION TABLES. Figure 7.45 shows the first customizing screen where you define the condition table.

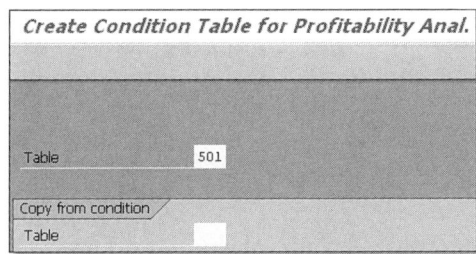

Figure 7.45 Create Condition Table

Define the condition table number, which must be between 501 and 999. If you have defined one condition table, you can use it as reference for the new one. Figure 7.46 shows the screen where you can select the characteristics to compose the condition table.

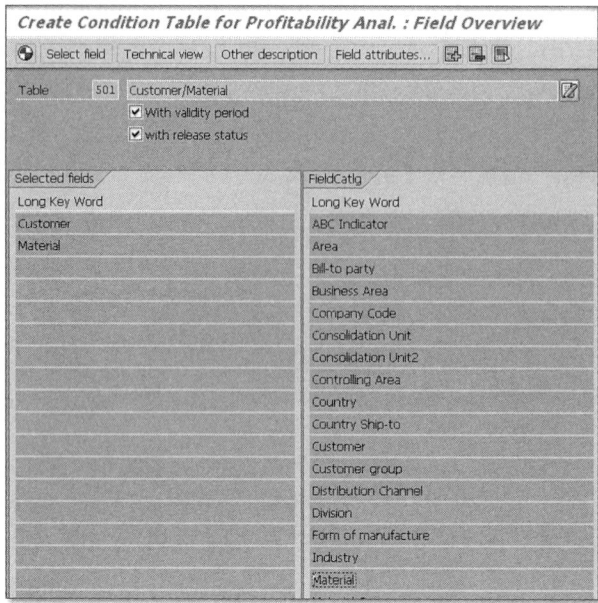

Figure 7.46 Condition Table Definition

The right side of the screen shows the available fields to use in the condition table. Select the fields you want to include by double-clicking on them, and they will be automatically transferred to the left side and included in the condition table. After defining the relevant fields for the condition table, you must activate the table by clicking on the ACTIVATE button (the icon on the far left of the button row before the SELECT FIELD button).

By clicking on TECHNICAL VIEW, you can change the behavior of the table maintenance when entering values in the table. Figure 7.47 shows the table technical view.

Change Condition Table for Profitability Anal. : Technical View

| Dictionary elements | Other description | Field attributes... |

| Table | 501 | Customer/Material |

☑ With validity period
☑ with release status

Selected fields

Short Description	Key	Footer fld	Text field	Field Na	Data element	Domain name
Customer	☑	☐	○	KUNNR	KUNNR_V	KUNNR
Material	☑	☑	◉	MATNR	MATNR	MATNR

Figure 7.47 Condition Table, Technical View

By checking the FOOTER FLD checkbox, you define whether the field is part of the header or will be maintained as a fast entry. You can see the difference in Figure 7.48.

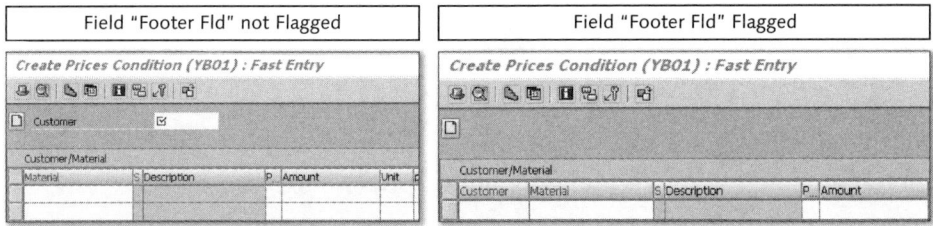

Figure 7.48 Difference Between the Field Footer Fld Flagged and Not Flagged

The advantage of having the field flagged as fast entry is that you can, for example, copy and paste a table from a spreadsheet and update all at the same time, instead of having to make separate entries by customer.

The next step in the customizing is to define the access sequence for the condition table.

Define Access Sequences

In the access sequences, you define which table condition must have priority over other table conditions, so that if the system can't determine a price for the combination in the first table condition, it will search the second, third, and so on until it finds a valid combination.

To define access sequences, you can use Transaction KE48, or go to CONTROLLING • PROFITABILITY ANALYSIS • MASTER DATA • VALUATION • SET UP CONDITIONS AND COSTING SHEETS • DEFINE ACCESS SEQUENCES. In Figure 7.49, you can see how to define the access sequence.

In the right side of the screen, you define the access sequences. After creating the access sequences, mark the access sequence, and double-click on ACCESSES on the left side of the screen, which brings you to Figure 7.50.

Click NEW ENTRIES, and then enter a sequence number and the table conditions. If you mark the condition as EXCLUSIVE, the system won't search for new conditions in the sequence after it finds one valid.

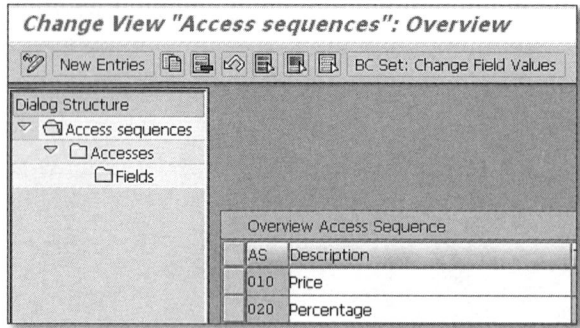

Figure 7.49 Access Sequences

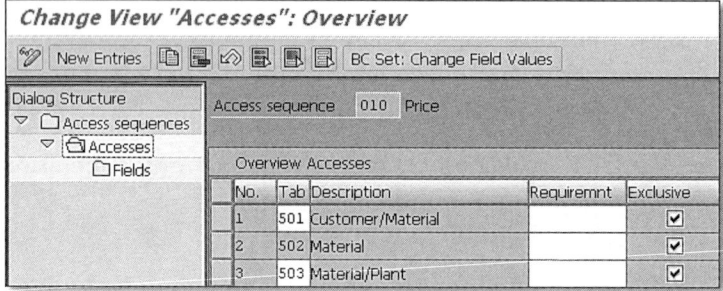

Figure 7.50 Overview Accesses, Table Condition Assignment

Now that you've defined the condition tables and the access sequence, you can create the condition types and also create the costing sheet.

Create Condition Types and Costing Sheets

The condition type acts like the pricing conditions in SD. You can create condition types for price, surcharge, overhead, tax, or any value you want to view in CO-PA.

The customizing screen for condition types is in the same customizing screen as the costing sheet. You'll first learn how to create the condition types and then how to assign them in the costing sheet. To create the condition types and create the costing sheet, either use Transaction 8KEV, or go to CONTROLLING • PROFITABILITY ANALYSIS • MASTER DATA • VALUATION • SET UP CONDITIONS AND COSTING SHEETS • CREATE CONDITION TYPES AND COSTING SHEETS. You can see the screen in Figure 7.51.

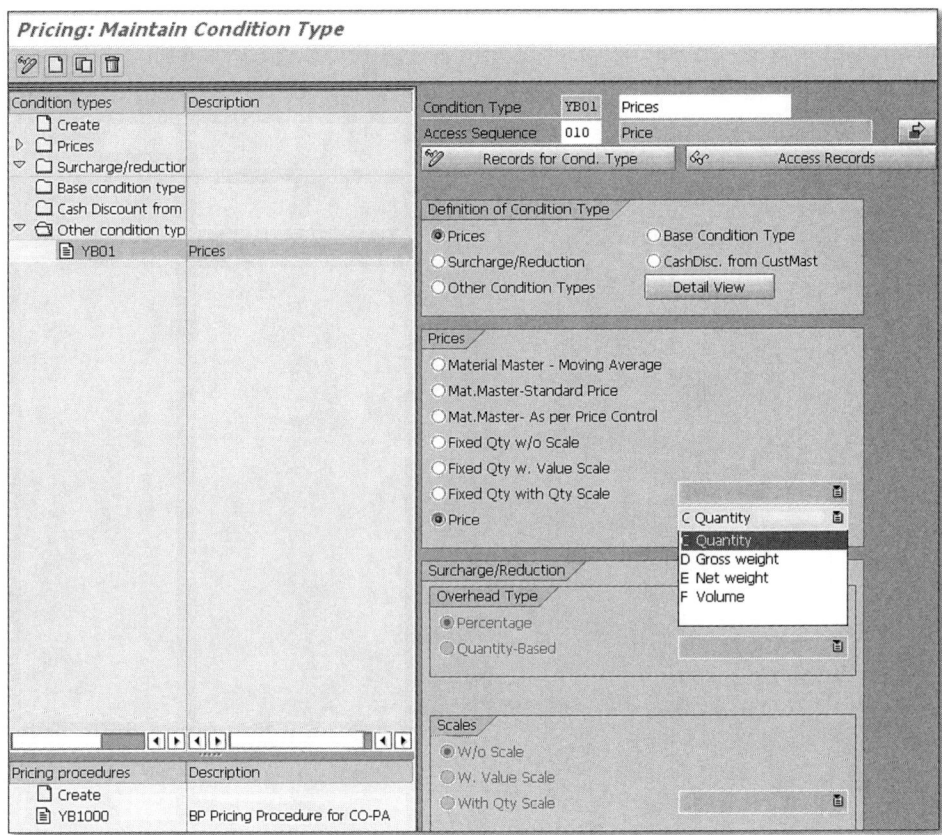

Figure 7.51 Maintain Condition Type

To create a condition type, click on NEW ENTRIES, and then enter the condition type name and the access sequence. Then choose in the right side of the screen what kind of condition type it will be from the following options:

▶ PRICES

▶ SURCHARGE/REDUCTION

▶ OTHER CONDITION TYPE

▶ BASE CONDITION TYPE

▶ CASHDISC. FROM CUSTMAST

If the condition is price related, you can choose whether the system will use values stored in material master data. The example in Figure 7.51 shows a price-related condition. For surcharges, you may choose whether it will be percentage or quantity-based. Additional condition type customizing is available if you click DETAIL VIEW in the DEFINITION OF CONDITION TYPE section, as you can see in Figure 7.52.

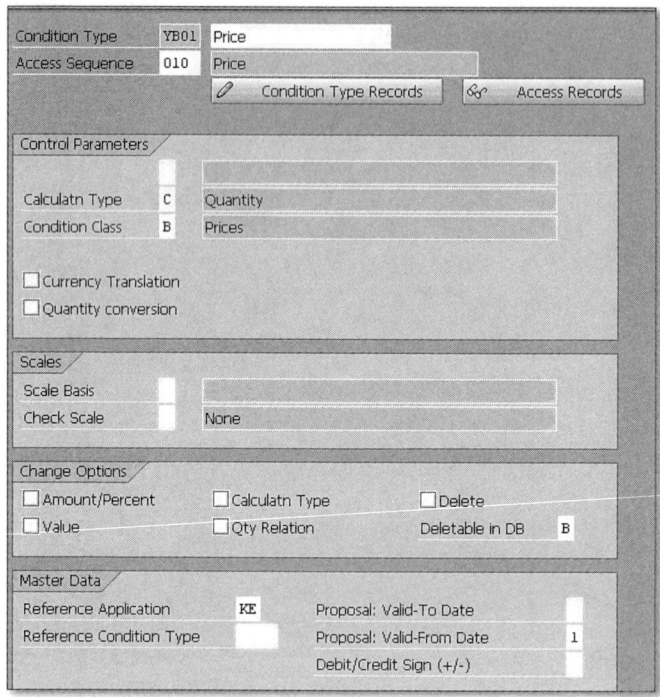

Figure 7.52 Additional Customizing for Condition Type

In this screen, you can set up additional information for the condition type, such as change control where you can define whether a change in the condition is allowed, define scales, and also define the proposed valid date.

Return to the first screen (Figure 7.51); now you can create the costing sheet. In the bottom-left side of the screen, click on CREATE to define a new costing sheet as shown in Figure 7.53.

We described the costing sheet functionality previously when we talked about accrual calculation in Chapter 2 and overhead definition for cost estimates in Chapter 6.

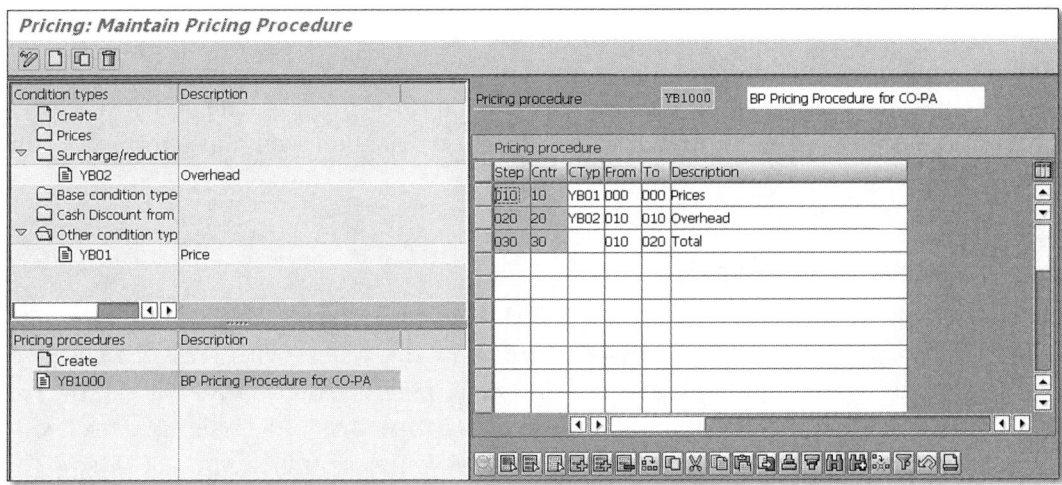

Figure 7.53 Pricing Procedure, Costing Sheet

In CO-PA, the way to customize the costing sheet is similar. You define the first row of the costing sheet, choose which condition type will receive the value, and select the line from and to. You can also create total lines. In the example in Figure 7.53, the system will add up the values from lines 010 to 020 in line 030.

The costing sheet is also used to create automatic planning in CO-PA.

Now that you've created the condition types and the costing sheet, you need to assign the condition types to CO-PA value fields.

Assign Value Fields

To send the values calculated by the costing sheet, you must assign the condition types to CO-PA value fields, and then the system will update the CO-PA document with the values from the costing sheet. Use Transaction KE45, or go to CONTROLLING • PROFITABILITY ANALYSIS • MASTER DATA • VALUATION • SET UP CONDITIONS AND COSTING SHEETS • ASSIGN VALUE FIELDS. You can see the screen in Figure 7.54.

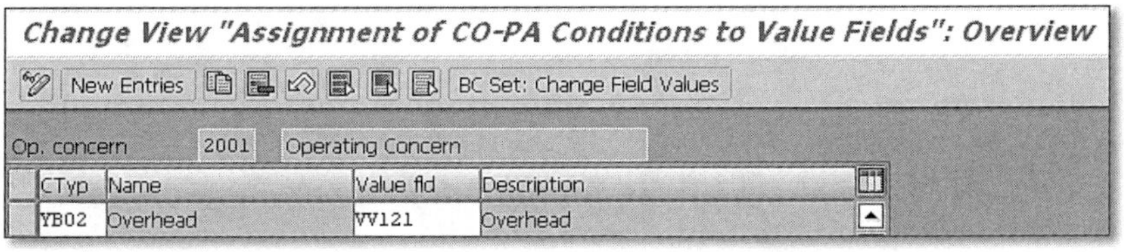

Figure 7.54 Assignment of CO-PA Condition Types to Value Fields

In this screen, you select the condition type and define which value field will receive the condition type value.

For the last step, after creating the valuations for cost estimate and cost component split, and performing the costing sheet valuation, you must create the valuation strategy.

Valuation Strategies

In the valuation strategy, you'll define the methods by which a costing-based CO-PA will update the value fields, define how the system will access the cost estimate and the costing sheet, and also determine whether to use a user exit. Use Transaction KE4U, or go to CONTROLLING • PROFITABILITY ANALYSIS • MASTER DATA • VALUATION • VALUATION STRATEGIES • DEFINE AND ASSIGN VALUATION STRATEGY. The customizing screen is shown in Figure 7.55.

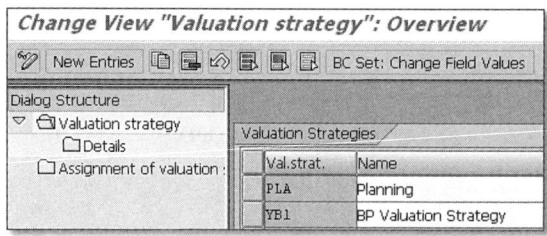

Figure 7.55 Valuation Strategy

First, click on NEW ENTRIES, and define the valuation strategy on the right side of the screen. Mark the created valuation strategy, and double-click on DETAILS on the left side of the screen. Figure 7.56 shows the details.

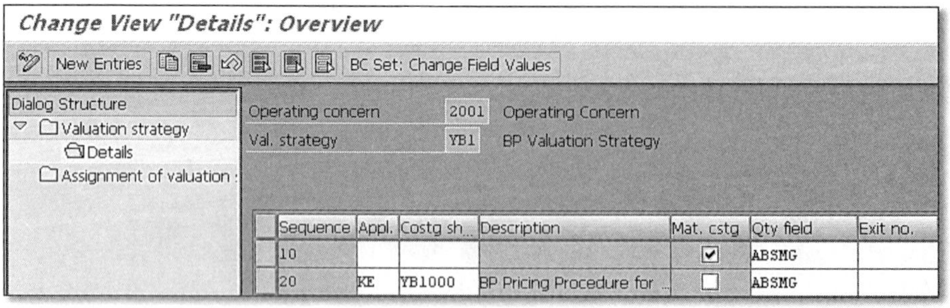

Change View "Details": Overview

Dialog Structure							
Operating concern	2001	Operating Concern					
Val. strategy	YB1	BP Valuation Strategy					

Sequence	Appl.	Costg sh	Description	Mat. cstg	Qty field	Exit no.
10				☑	ABSMG	
20	KE	YB1000	BP Pricing Procedure for ...	☐	ABSMG	

Figure 7.56 Valuation Strategy Details

Two sequences were created for the strategy in Figure 7.56. The first sequence will access the cost estimate because the MAT. CSTG flag is marked, and also indicates which field the system will use as reference for the quantity to calculate the COGS (remembering that COGS = Sold Quantity × Cost Estimate).

After determining the cost estimate for the material according to the customizing done earlier, the system will jump to the next sequence number where it will use the costing sheet to create the values for overhead using the same quantity field as a reference. You can create more sequences if you like, and you can also use a user exit that must be defined in enhancement COPA0002.

After saving the valuation strategy, you must assign the valuation strategy to a point of valuation and to a record type. Double-click on ASSIGNMENT OF VALUA-TION STRATEGY on the left side of the screen, and a new screen will be shown (see Figure 7.57).

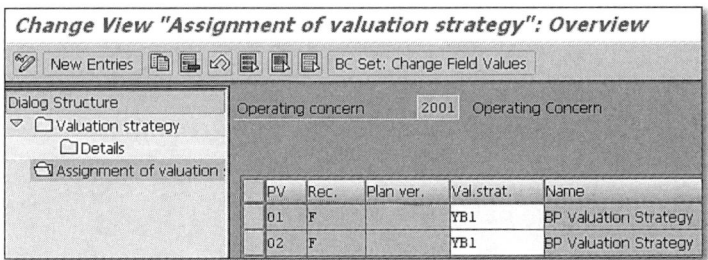

Figure 7.57 Assignment Valuation Strategy

The diagram in Figure 7.58 illustrates the valuation process in CO-PA.

Now you should understand all of the master data elements required for your CO-PA, have defined the characteristics values (including using derivations to populate customized characteristics), and determined the valuation options and strategies. You are ready to move on to the next topic in CO-PA customizing where you'll see how to define the way that actual values flow into CO-PA.

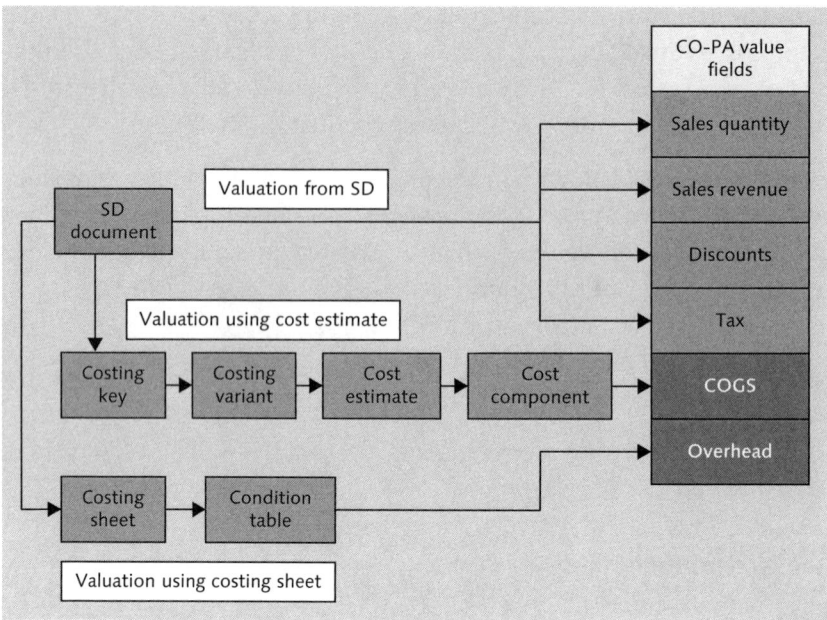

Figure 7.58 CO-PA Valuation Process

7.4 Flows of Actual Values

In the preceding section, we discussed how to customize CO-PA to obtain values from cost estimates and also how to use a costing sheet to create additional values. Now you'll see how to customize CO-PA to directly import actual values from other SAP ERP components, such as SD, FI, and CO.

In Chapter 1, you saw how values flow from FI, MM, SD, and PP to CO and to CO-PA. Figure 7.59 shows this value flow diagram again so that you can see how all of these areas can send information to CO-PA.

In CO-PA, we need to customize the following areas to transfer actual values from other components or other CO subcomponents:

▶ Transfer of incoming sales orders (optional)

▶ Transfer of billing documents (standard)

▶ Order and project settlement

▶ Direct posting from FI/MM

▶ Settlement of production variances

▶ Transfer of overhead

We'll examine these areas in the next subsections.

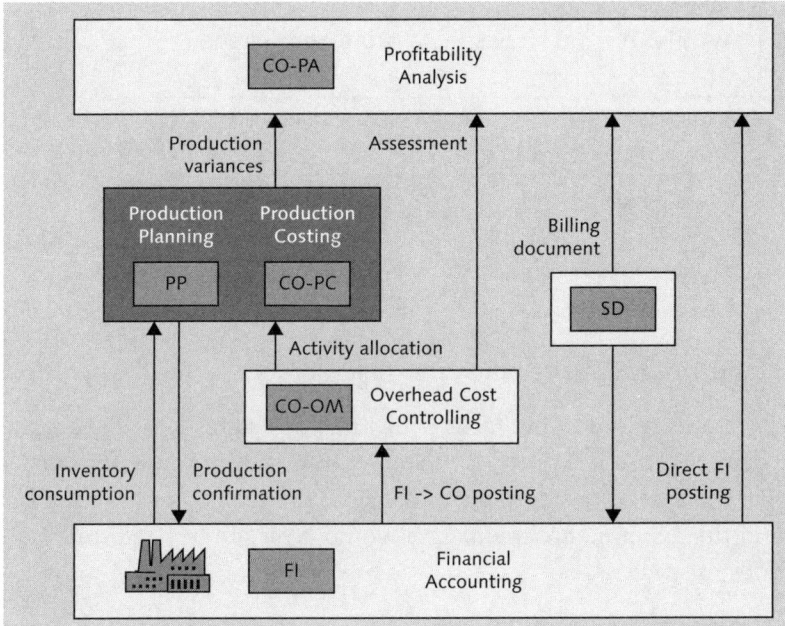

Figure 7.59 CO Values Flow

7.4.1 Transfer of Incoming Sales Orders

You can transfer values from sales orders to CO-PA in the same way as you transfer them to the billing documents. These will update the CO-PA tables with record type = A (Incoming sales order). This is used if you want to create reports from sales orders to compare with the reports from billing documents.

You'll need to define three steps to allow CO-PA to receive values from sales orders:

1. Assign value fields.

2. Assign quantity fields.

3. Activate the transfer of incoming sales orders.

Assign Value Fields

In this step of the customizing, you'll assign the value field in CO-PA with the pricing condition in the pricing procedure used for sales orders. To assign the values fields, either use Transaction KE4I, or go to CONTROLLING • PROFITABILITY ANALYSIS • FLOWS OF ACTUAL VALUES • TRANSFER OF INCOMING SALES ORDERS • ASSIGN VALUE FIELDS. Figure 7.60 shows the customizing screen.

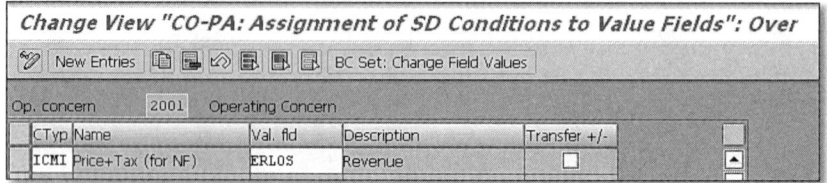

Figure 7.60 CO-PA Value Fields Assignment, SD Conditions

Select the condition type, and assign the value field.

Generally CO-PA stores values in the table with a positive sign, leaving the negative sign to be declared in the report form. Sometimes, it's necessary to transfer the sign from SD. If it's necessary to transfer the sign, use the indicator in the last column shown in the assignment screen. This would typically be used for reversals, credit memos, or returns.

The next step is to assign the quantity fields.

Assign Quantity Fields

To bring quantities from the sales order to CO-PA, you'll need to assign the CO-PA quantity value field to the respective quantity field from the sales order. Use Transaction KE4M, or go to CONTROLLING • PROFITABILITY ANALYSIS • FLOWS OF ACTUAL VALUES • TRANSFER OF INCOMING SALES ORDERS • ASSIGN QUANTITY FIELDS. Figure 7.61 shows the customizing screen.

From SD, you can choose from the following options for quantity:

▶ ABSMG: SALES QUANTITY

▶ BRGEW: GROSS WEIGHT

▶ FKIMG: BILLED QUANTITY

▶ FKLMG: BILLING QTY IN SKU

- KBMENG: Cumulative confirmed quantity in sales unit
- KLMENG: Cumulative confirmed quantity in base
- KWMENG: Order Quantity
- LSMENG: Required deliv. qty
- NTGEW: Net weight
- VOLUM: Volume

After defining which field you want to transfer as the sales quantity, you can then assign the CO-PA field for the sales quantity.

The last step to transfer values from sales orders to CO-PA is to activate the transfer functionality for sales orders.

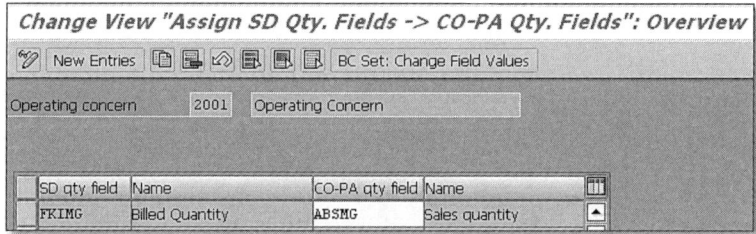

Figure 7.61 CO-PA Quantity Fields Assignment, SD Quantity Field

Activate Transfer of Incoming Sales Orders

To bring sales order information to CO-PA, you need to activate the transfer functionality. Use Transaction KEKF, or go to Controlling • Profitability Analysis • Flows of Actual Values • Transfer of Incoming Sales Orders • Activate Transfer of Incoming Sales Orders. Figure 7.62 shows the customizing screen.

COAr	Name	From FY	Op.c	Inc.SO
2000	Controlling Area US, DE	1992	2001	1
4000	Controlling Area BR	1992	2001	1

Figure 7.62 Activate Transfer to CO-PA from Incoming Sales Order

For the activation, you can choose from four options:

- INACTIVE
- 1: ACTIVE WITH DATE OF ENTRY
- 2: ACTIVE WITH DELIV.DATE/BILLING PLAN DEADLINE (USING KWMENG)
- 3: ACTIVE WITH DELIV.DATE/BILLING PLAN DEADLINE (USING KBMENG)

> **Note**
>
> If you activate the transfer for sales orders to your CO-PA, it will considerably increase the database size, so you should determine if this area is one that your business management considers necessary.

7.4.2 Transfer of Billing Documents

The transfer of values from billing documents to CO-PA doesn't require activation. The values will automatically be transferred online after you've activated the operating concern in the controlling area. The record type for billing documents is F (Billing data).

When working with transfers of data from other components to CO-PA that involve FI, all values will be transferred to CO-PA using cost elements. This means that the FI P&L account related to the value being transferred must be created as a cost element so that values can flow between FI and CO-PA, such as for revenues from billing documents.

Because, in most cases, CO-PA updates values in the CO-PA tables with positive signs, one way to distinguish debits and credits is to use different cost element categories. Two cost element categories are available to use in CO-PA:

- 11: Revenues
- 12: Sales deductions

By selecting the correct cost element category according to the account nature, CO-PA can determine if the value should be treated as having a positive or negative sign (i.e., a debit or credit value).

The process to customize the transfer of billing documents to CO-PA has three steps:

1. Assign value fields.

2. Assign quantity fields.

3. Reset the value/quantity fields.

The first and second steps are the same as we just saw for the process to set up a transfer from incoming sales orders. In case you elected not to use the transfer from sales orders, you'll need to perform those steps to assign the value and quantity fields from SD to CO-PA.

Reset Value/Quantity Fields

In some situations, you may need to reset value fields in CO-PA for certain billing document types, for example, return freight or cost estimate. Use Transaction KE4W, or go to CONTROLLING • PROFITABILITY ANALYSIS • FLOWS OF ACTUAL VALUES • TRANSFER OF BILLING DOCUMENTS • RESET VALUE/QUANTITY FIELDS. Figure 7.63 shows the customizing screen.

New Entries: Overview of Added Entries

Op. concern 2001 Operating Concern

BillT	Description	Value fld	Description	Reset
RE	Credit for Returns	ABSMG	Sales quantity	☑
RE	Credit for Returns	VV100	Raw Material	☑
RE	Credit for Returns	VV101	Packing	☑
RE	Credit for Returns	VV102	Semifinished product	☑
RE	Credit for Returns	VV103	Consumption diverse	☑
RE	Credit for Returns	VV104	ConsumpHalf Finished	☑
RE	Credit for Returns	VV105	Scrap	☑
RE	Credit for Returns	VV106	Receipt w/out ordem	☑
RE	Credit for Returns	VV107	Business Process	☑
RE	Credit for Returns	VV108	Depreciation	☑
RE	Credit for Returns	VV109	Electricity	☑
RE	Credit for Returns	VV110	Labor	☑
RE	Credit for Returns	VV111	Material	☑
RE	Credit for Returns	VV112	Maintenance	☑
RE	Credit for Returns	VV113	Others	☑
RE	Credit for Returns	VV114	Taxes	☑
RE	Credit for Returns	VV115	Water	☑

Figure 7.63 Reset CO-PA Value Fields

The reset is done by billing document type and also value field.

Next in CO-PA customizing, you'll see how to set up the transfer of values from orders and project settlements.

7.4.3 Order and Project Settlement

In Chapter 4 and in Chapter 6, we mentioned that you can settle orders and product cost variances to CO-PA. Now you'll see how to customize the transfer of these settlements to CO-PA.

The steps we'll now cover apply to order and project settlement, direct posting to FI/MM, and settlement of production variances.

To customize these transfers, you need to create a PA transfer structure, which is very similar to the process you saw for customizing allocation structures in Chapter 3, Chapter 4, and Chapter 6.

To create the PA transfer structure, you can either use Transaction KEI2 or go to CONTROLLING • PROFITABILITY ANALYSIS • FLOWS OF ACTUAL VALUES • ORDER AND PROJECT SETTLEMENT • DEFINE PA TRANSFER STRUCTURE FOR SETTLEMENT. Figure 7.64 shows the first customizing screen.

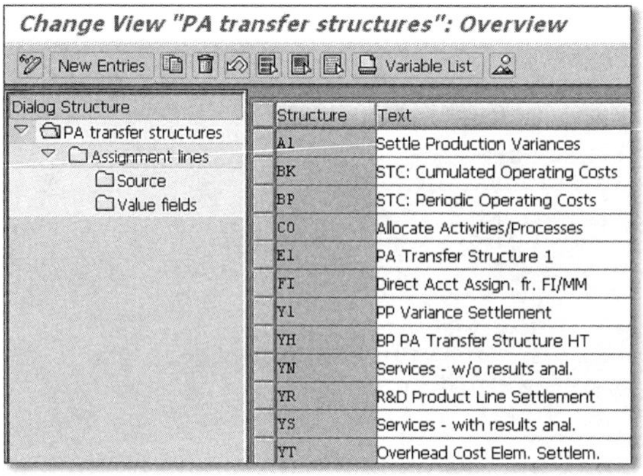

Figure 7.64 PA Transfer Structure

For the PA transfer structure, you must define the transfer structure, the source cost elements, and the receiver CO-PA value field.

To create a new PA transfer structure, click on NEW ENTRIES, and, in the right side of the screen, enter the definition and a name for the PA transfer structure.

After creating the PA transfer structure, mark the recently created one, and double-click on ASSIGNMENT LINES in the left side of the screen to create the lines of assignment, as shown in Figure 7.65. We are using E1 – PA TRANSFER STRUCTURE 1 as our example.

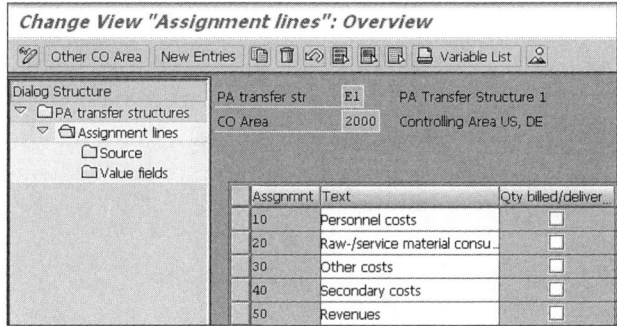

Figure 7.65 PA Transfer Structure, Assignment Lines

If you want to split the source costs to different value fields in CO-PA, you can create assignments for each cost element or use groups of cost elements.

If you mark the field Qty billed/delivered, you can transfer production quantities to a quantity value field in CO-PA.

Select one line in the right side of the screen, and double-click on source in the left side of the screen, which will then bring you to the screen to define the source cost elements, as shown in Figure 7.66.

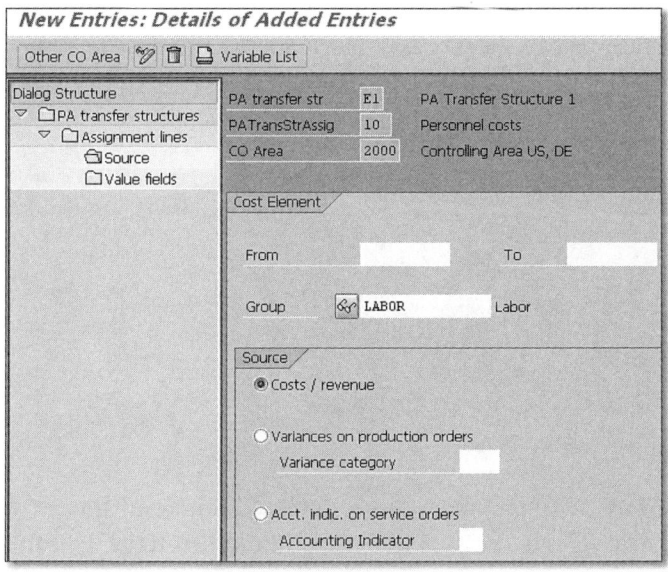

Figure 7.66 PA Transfer Structure, Source

In this screen, you define the range of cost elements or a cost element group to be the source of the amounts to be transferred.

You may also define if it will transfer all costs/revenues or variances on production orders. If you mark to transfer variances on production orders, you must also define the variance category you want to transfer by choosing from the following options:

▶ PRIV: Input Price Variance

▶ QTYV: Input Quantity Variance

▶ RSUV: Resource-Usage Variance

▶ INPV: Remaining Input Variance

▶ MXPV: Mixed-Price Variance

▶ OPPV: Output Price Variance

▶ LSFV: Lot Size Variance/Fixed-Cost Variance

▶ REMV: Remaining Variance

▶ SCRP: Scrap

These are the same variance categories that we discussed in Chapter 6.

After defining the source cost elements, double-click on VALUE FIELDS on the left side of the screen to define the receiver value fields in CO-PA on the screen shown in Figure 7.67.

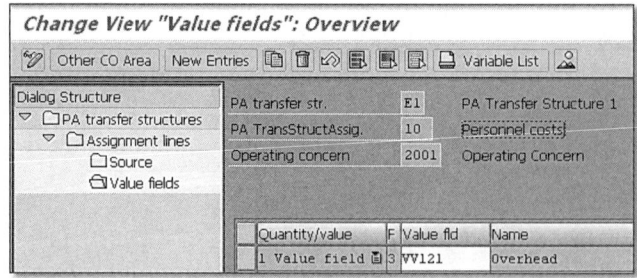

Figure 7.67 PA Transfer Structure, Receiver Value Field

Click on NEW ENTRIES, and in the right side of the screen, add the new value field. You can add up to three value fields for each assignment: one for fixed amounts (1), one for variable amounts (2), and one for the sum of fixed and variable amounts (3). If you use (3), only one value field is needed.

You must repeat this process until you've filled all assignment lines with a source and a value field.

Now that you've created the PA allocation structure, you'll need to assign it to a settlement profile when you want to settle from orders, projects, or production orders. To assign the PA transfer structure to a settlement profile, either use Transaction OKO7, or go to CONTROLLING • PROFITABILITY ANALYSIS • FLOWS OF ACTUAL VALUES • ORDER AND PROJECT SETTLEMENT • ASSIGN PA TRANSFER STRUCTURE TO SETTLEMENT PROFILE. Figure 7.68 shows the customizing screen.

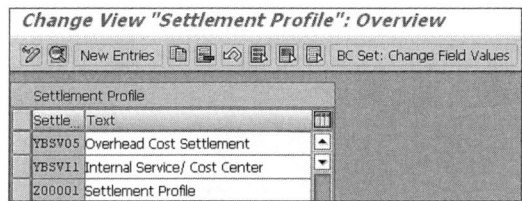

Figure 7.68 Maintain Settlement Profile

Double-click on the settlement profile you want to assign to the PA transfer structure, and the customizing screen will be shown, as in Figure 7.69.

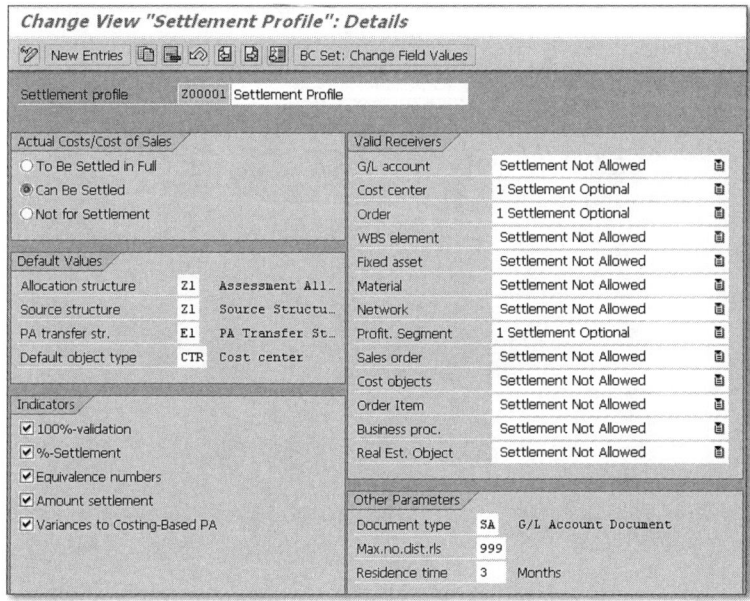

Figure 7.69 Settlement Profile

We've already covered this screen in detail in Chapter 4, but there are two additional fields here that we now need to talk about: the assignment of the PA transfer structure to the settlement profile and the flag to send variances to costing-based PA.

As you saw earlier in the transfer of billing documents, you need to create the P&L account used for settlements as a cost element with a cost element category 11 or 12 to work in CO-PA. There can be manual entries posted in these accounts in FI, so to ensure consistency between FI and CO-PA these values need to be transferred. Therefore, these cost elements must be maintained in the automatic account assignment as CO-PA accounts. Use Transaction OKB9, or go to CONTROLLING • PROFITABILITY ANALYSIS • FLOWS OF ACTUAL VALUES • DIRECT POSTING FROM FI/MM • AUTOMATIC ACCOUNT ASSIGNMENT. Figure 7.70 shows the customizing screen.

Change View "Default account assignment": Overview					

New Entries	BC Set: Change Field Values					

Dialog Structure	CoCd	Cost Elem.	BA	Cost Ctr	Order	PrfS
▽ ☐ Default account assignment	2000	311000	☐			☑
☐ Detail per business area/valuation area	2000	312000	☐			☑
☐ Detail per profit center	2000	313000	☐			☑
	2000	321000	☐			☑
	2000	322000	☐			☑
	2000	323000	☐			☑
	2000	323100	☐			☑
	2000	323200	☐			☑
	2000	323300	☐			☑
	2000	323400	☐			☑
	2000	331101	☐			☑
	2000	331102	☐			☑
	2000	331103	☐			☑
	2000	331200	☐			☑
	2000	341000	☐			☑
	2000	342000	☐			☑
	2000	350000	☐			☑

Figure 7.70 Default Account Assignment

Enter the company code and cost element, and mark the field profitability segment (PRFS).

> **Note**
>
> Any manual posting in FI to an account that is related to a cost element with cost element category 11 or 12 will require a CO-PA object and a value field. Maintenance of the relationship between the cost elements and value fields is done in the PA transfer structure. You must maintain the PA transfer structure FI – DIRECT ACCT ASSIGN. FR. FI/ MM creating the relationship between cost elements and value fields; otherwise, the missing relationship will cause a hard error when posting to the account in FI.

7.4.4 Transfer of Overhead

When we previously discussed costing sheets, you saw that you can create a costing sheet to allocate overhead values, so that for every CO-PA document, the system will accrue a value for overhead. As an alternative to this approach, you can also transfer using an allocation from CO-CCA to CO-PA. You've already learned how to use cost center allocations in Chapter 3. The philosophy of CO-PA allocations is the same and is based on cycles. The most commonly used allocation is the assessment from CO-CCA to CO-PA. Use Transaction KEU1, or go to CONTROLLING • PROFITABILITY ANALYSIS • FLOWS OF ACTUAL VALUES • TRANSFER OF OVERHEAD • ASSESS COST CENTER COSTS/PROCESS COSTS • DEFINE STRUCTURE OF COST CENTER ASSESSMENT/PROCESS COST ASSESSMENT. You'll now see the difference between cost center assessments and CO-PA assessments. You can see the first customizing screen in Figure 7.71.

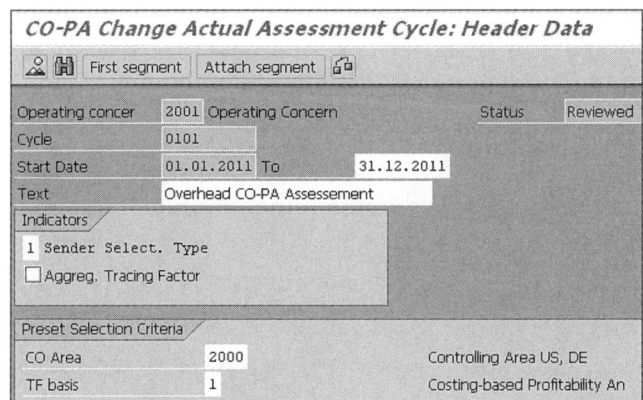

Figure 7.71 CO-PA Assessment

In this screen, you need to define in the INDICATORS section if you want to split the costs into fixed and variable or not (overall costs) by selecting either 1 – UNSPLIT COSTS (OVERALL COSTS) or 2 – SPLIT COSTS (SEPARATED IN FIXED AND VARIABLE COSTS) for the SENDER SELECT. TYPE. In the PRESET SELECTION CRITERIA section, you must also select the CO AREA to identify whether the assessment is for costing-based or account-based CO-PA. Click the FIRST SEGMENT button to see the screen shown in Figure 7.72.

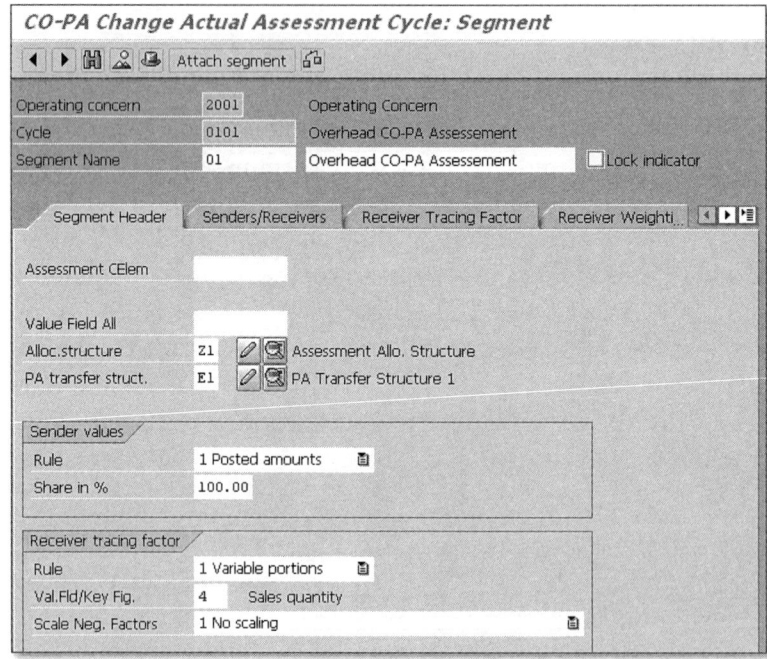

Figure 7.72 CO-PA Actual Assessment, First Segment

You can choose to either use a secondary cost element for assessment (category 42) or use an allocation structure, where you can define assessment cost elements for a group of sender cost elements in the same manner as you saw previously in Chapter 3.

You have the option to define the receiver value field or use a PA transfer structure to create a complex scheme of allocation by grouping sender cost elements to specific value fields, as shown earlier in this chapter when we created the PA transfer structure.

The other options in the cycle creation are similar to cost center account assessment.

Now that you've learned how to set up the actual values flows to CO-PA, let's look at how to customize CO-PA planning.

7.5   Planning

Planning in CO-PA is a powerful tool where you plan sales quantities, revenues, COGS, and overhead costs at either a very detailed level (such as by material/customer) or at a higher level (such as by company code).

The same structure available for actual CO-PA values is also available for CO-PA planning. This makes planning CO-PA comparable with actual CO-PA in the same characteristics level.

Because the planning process is not restricted to only one area of the company, you can also split responsibilities in the CO-PA planning process. For example, the marketing area can plan the sales quantities, the accounting department can plan the overhead costs, and the production department can plan the product costs. CO-PA can then combine all of these areas for a detailed plan.

CO-PA planning, like CO-CCA, is based on planning versions, so that you can have multiple planning scenarios, such as forecast, budget, price simulation, and margin simulation.

In Chapter 1, you learned how to maintain versions. For CO-PA planning, you can expand the versions you already created for CO-CCA. Use the same Transaction OKEQ to activate the version in CO-PA. Figure 7.73 shows the version maintenance screen.

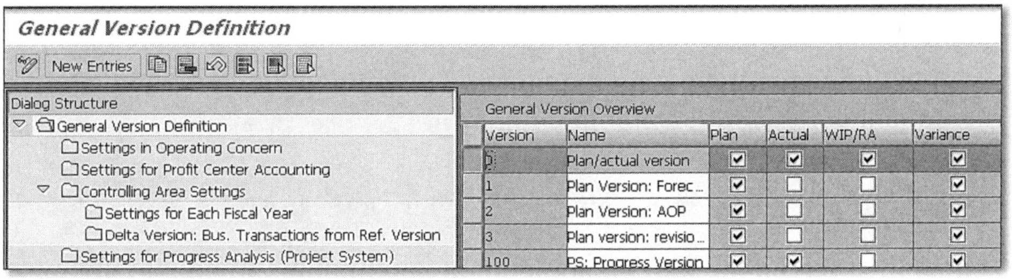

Figure 7.73 CO-PA Version Maintenance

Select the version you want to activate for CO-PA in the right side of the screen, and double-click on Settings in Operating Concern on the left side of the screen, which brings you to Figure 7.74.

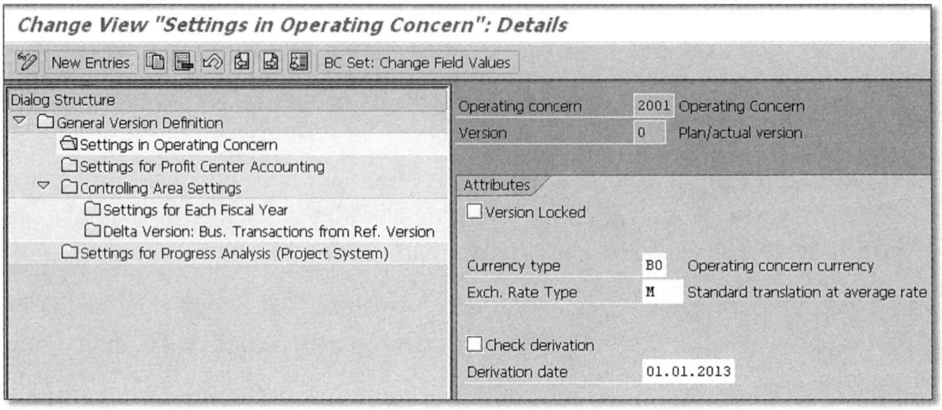

Figure 7.74 Version Maintenance, Operating Concern Settings

In this screen, you can define whether the version is locked for the operating concern.

For actual values, you saw that you can set the CO-PA to be updated in up to four different currencies (operating concern, company code, operating concern/profit center valuation, and company code/profit center valuation). In CO-PA planning, the system will update the operating concern using just one currency, which is defined in the version during this step of the customizing. You also need to define the exchange rate type.

If you flag the field Check derivation, the system will check if the characteristics you are planning are consistent with the derivation rules created for actual values.

Most of the planning customizing in CO-PA can be done in a tool called the planning framework.

The planning framework contains the settings to build the planning structure. To access the planning framework, use Transaction KEPM, or go to Controlling • Profitability Analysis • Planning • Planning Framework • Set Up Planning Framework. You can see the planning framework in Figure 7.75.

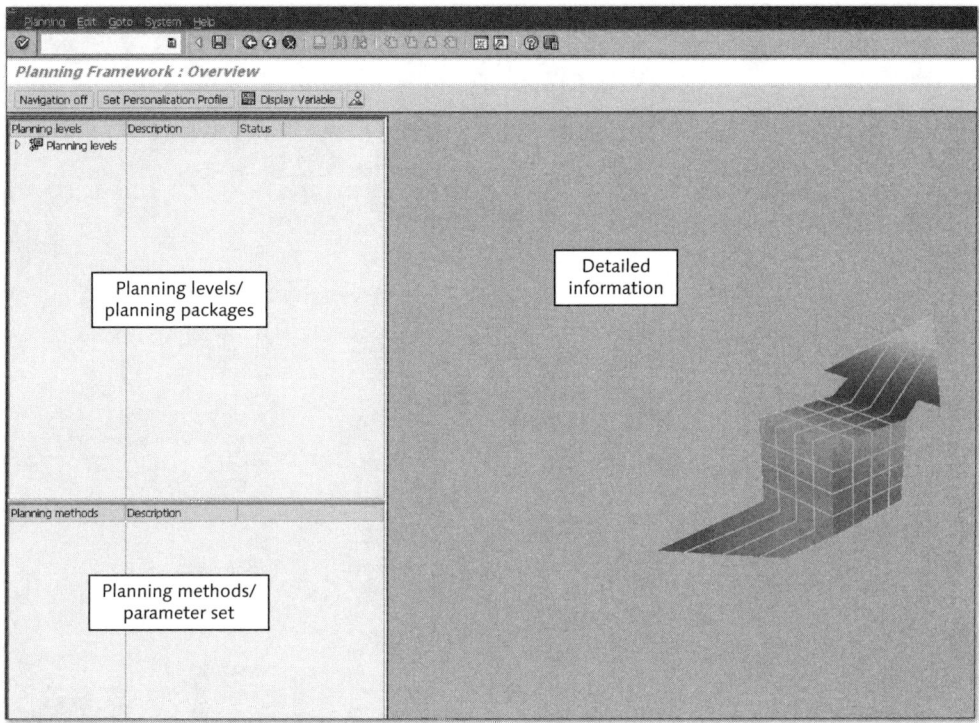

Figure 7.75 CO-PA Planning Framework

The planning framework consists of several areas:

- Planning level
- Planning package
- Planning method
- Parameter set

Planning Level

This is used to select the characteristics you want to plan in CO-PA. To create the planning level, go to EDIT on the top menu, and then go to PLANNING LEVEL – CREATE, which brings you to the screen shown in Figure 7.76.

Mark in the right side the characteristic you want to plan, and then click the arrow to send to the left side. Change to the SELECTION tab, and you can create a higher level filter for your planning level, as shown in Figure 7.77.

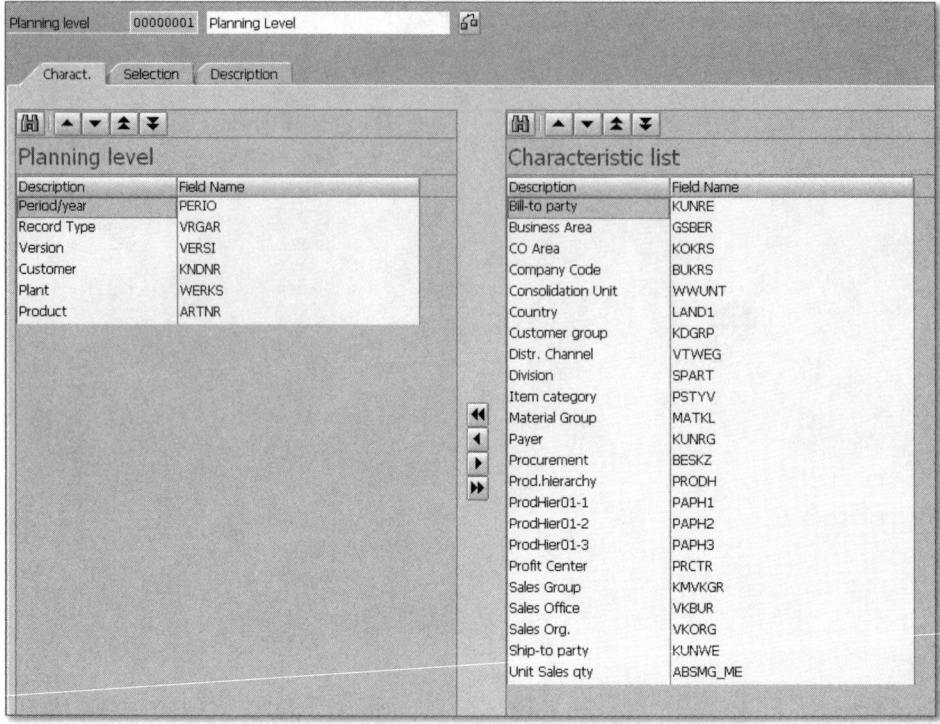

Figure 7.76 CO-PA Framework, Planning Level

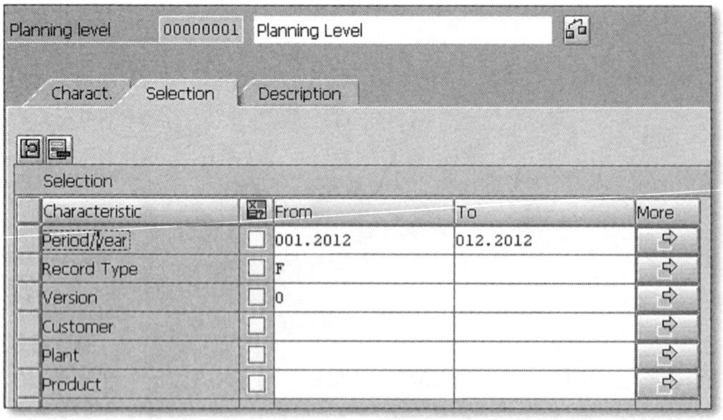

Figure 7.77 CO-PA Framework, Planning Level – Selection Tab

You can also restrict the planning using filters at the higher level as you can see in Figure 7.77. Save the planning level; now you can see the planning level in the left side of the screen under PLANNING LEVELS, as shown in Figure 7.78.

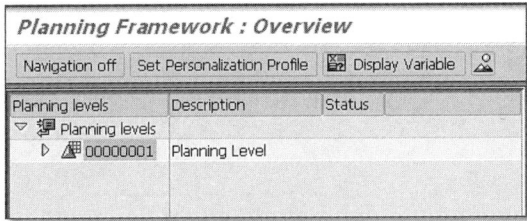

Figure 7.78 CO-PA Framework, Planning Level

The next step in the planning framework is to create the planning package.

Planning Package

In the planning package, you can create breakdowns in the characteristics that aren't fixed in the planning level. In the example from Figure 7.77, you can create planning packages to split the characteristic plant. To create the planning package, mark the planning level, go to EDIT on the top menu, and then go to PLANNING PACKAGE – CREATE. You can see the screen in Figure 7.79.

| Plan. package | 00000001 | Plant 2001 | | |

| Selection | Description |

Characteristic		From	To	More
Company Code	☐	2000		⇨
Customer	☐	#	ZZZZZZZZZZ	⇨
Period/year	☐	001.2012		⇨
Plant	☐	2001		⇨
Product	☐	#	ZZZZZZZZZZZZZZZZZZ	⇨
Record Type	☐	F		⇨
Version	☐	0		⇨

Figure 7.79 CO-PA Framework, Planning Package

You can see in Figure 7.79 that the characteristics you've defined in a higher level are gray in this screen indicating that you can't change them here. For the characteristics not shown in gray, some entry is required. Enter the values for the characteristic you want to restrict (the plant, in our example). An entry is required for all characteristics. If you want to include all possible values for a characteristic in the planning package, enter from "#" to "ZZZZZZZ" when the field is alphanumeric or from "#" to "99999999" if the field is numeric.

When you save the planning package, it will appear in the left side of the screen, as shown in Figure 7.80.

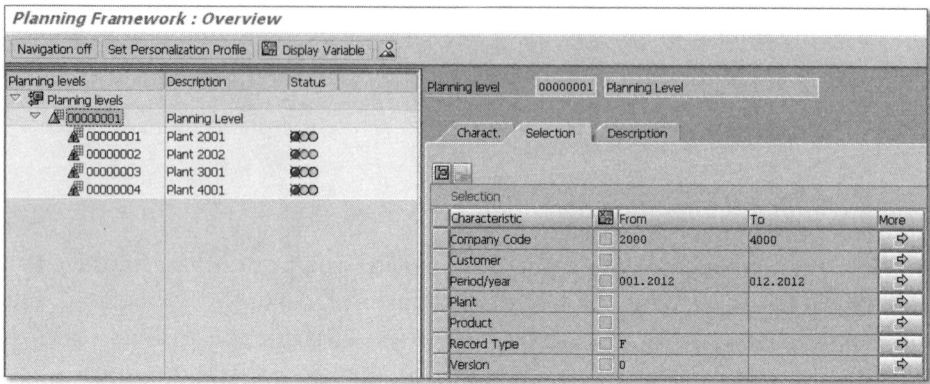

Figure 7.80 CO-PA Framework, Planning Package

You can see in our example in Figure 7.80 that four planning packages were created, one for each plant available. After finishing the planning package definition, double-click on the planning package you want to plan, and you can see the options for the planning method.

Planning Method

The planning methods are the options available to be used for planning (as shown in the bottom-left side of Figure 7.81).

You must choose at least one planning method for each planning package you created. These are the available planning methods:

► ENTER PLANNING DATA

► DISPLAY PLANNING DATA

► COPY

► FORECAST

► TOP-DOWN DISTRIBUTION

► RATIOS

▶ VALUATION

▶ REVALUATION

▶ EVENT

▶ PERIOD DISTRIBUTION

▶ DELETE

▶ CUSTOMER ENHANCEMENT

▶ PLANNING SEQUENCE

We'll show the details of all of the steps using the ENTER PLANNING DATA method as an example. The process is the same for the other methods.

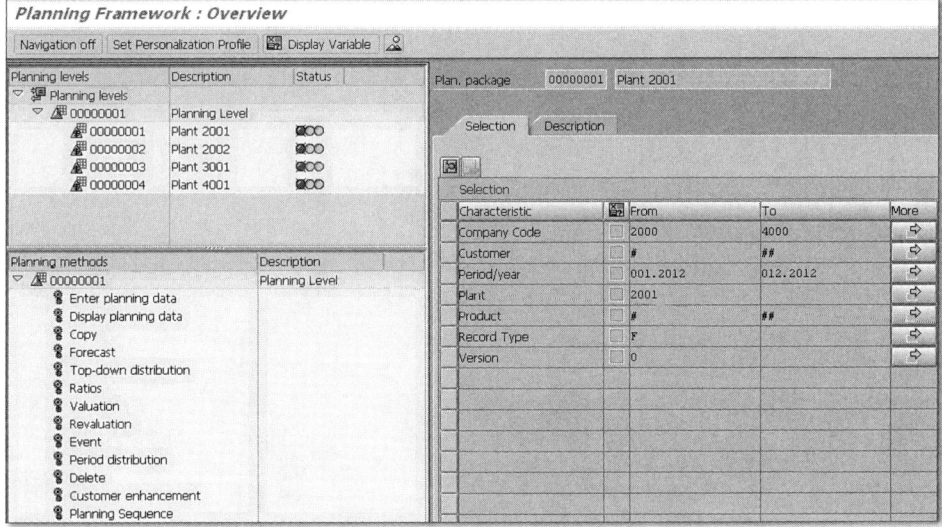

Figure 7.81 CO-PA Framework, Planning Method

Parameter Set

Select the planning method for which you want to create a parameter, right-click, and select CREATE PARAMETER SET. Figure 7.82 shows the customizing.

You must define a planning layout to plan. To create the planning layout, click on the CREATE button next to the LAYOUT field, which will bring you to the layout creation screen shown in Figure 7.83.

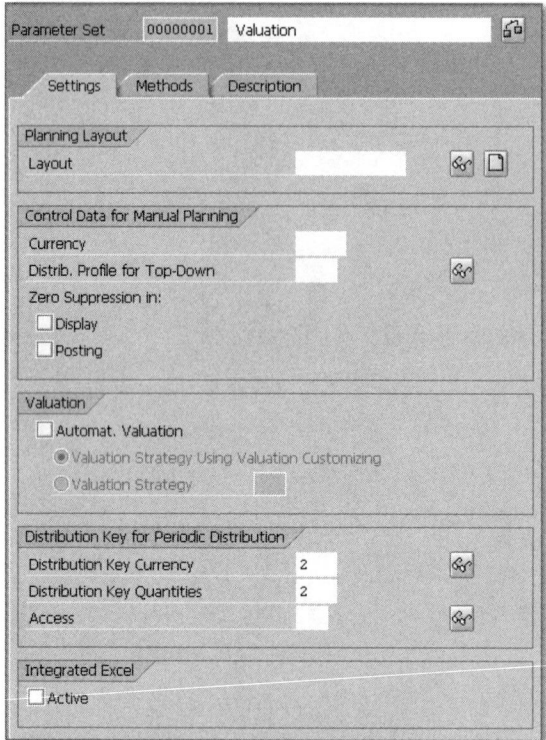

Figure 7.82 CO-PA Framework, Planning Set

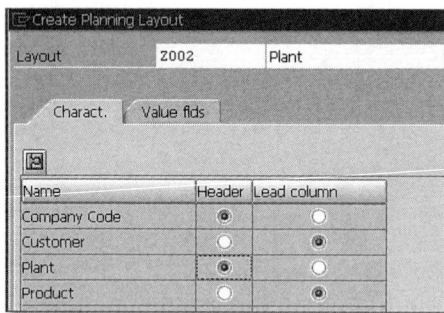

Figure 7.83 Planning Layout

Select the field you want to be in the header in the planning layout and the characteristics you want to include in manual planning. Usually, you set the characteristics that have been restricted to only one value (the plant, in our example) as the header.

Select the VALUE FLDS tab, and choose which value fields you'll plan, as shown in Figure 7.84.

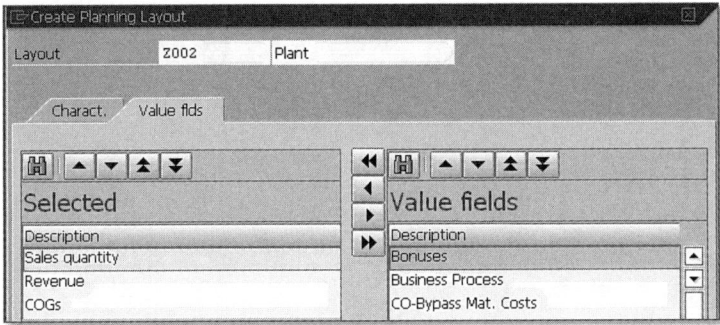

Figure 7.84 Planning Layout, Value Flds Tab

Usually, you just select the fields that don't belong to the automatic valuation. You'll see the planning valuation in more depth when we discuss the planning valuation method. Save the layout, and return to the parameter set screen (refer to Figure 7.82).

In the CONTROL DATA FOR MANUAL PLANNING section on the parameter set screen, you can define which currency you want to plan. The system will translate the planning currency to the version currency, using the exchange rate type defined in the version maintenance.

You can select the top-down distribution profile and automatic valuation.

In the DISTRIBUTION KEY FOR PERIODIC POSTING section, you define how the system will distribute quantities and values within the period range you defined for the planning level.

The last option that can be very useful is the INTEGRATED EXCEL flag. If you flag this option, the system will open Microsoft Excel to use as the interface to create the plan, instead of using the SAP ERP screen. After you save the parameter set, you're ready to plan in CO-PA.

Double-click in the newly created parameter set; the system will open the planning screen, as shown in Figure 7.85.

If you've created a valuation strategy for the planning version, you'll only need to plan the quantity and the remaining fields not included in the valuation strategy.

Figure 7.85 CO-PA Planning

Next in the customizing, we'll look at the parameter set for valuation.

Before creating the parameter set, however, let's recap how the system will assign values to the costs and revenues for the planning version. You've already been through the steps in the customizing for actual values. To review these settings, first go to Transaction KE4U to see the valuation strategy, as shown in Figure 7.86.

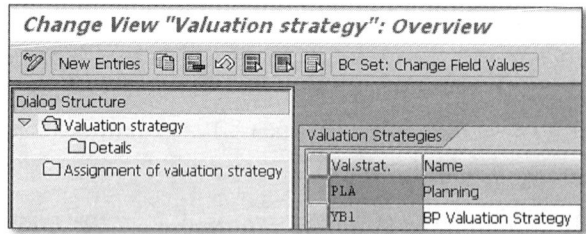

Figure 7.86 Valuation Strategy, Planning

Mark the valuation strategy and double-click on DETAILS on the right side of the screen. The strategy sequence is shown in Figure 7.87.

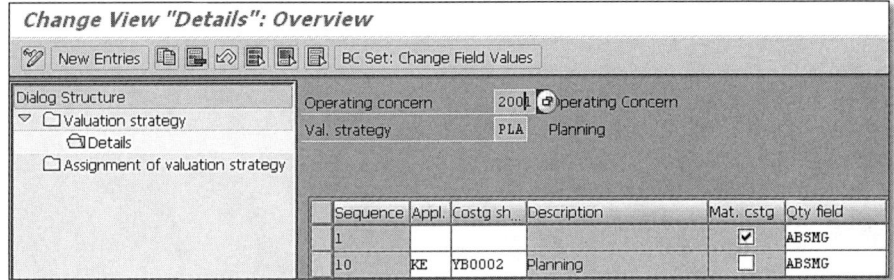

Figure 7.87 Valuation Strategy Sequence, Planning

You can see in this screen the sequence line "1"; the system will evaluate the material cost estimate using a quantity field as a reference.

In sequence line "10", the system will make the valuation using a costing sheet and also using a quantity field as a reference.

Double-click in the ASSIGNMENT OF VALUATION STRATEGY on the left side of the screen to see the version assignment, as shown in Figure 7.88.

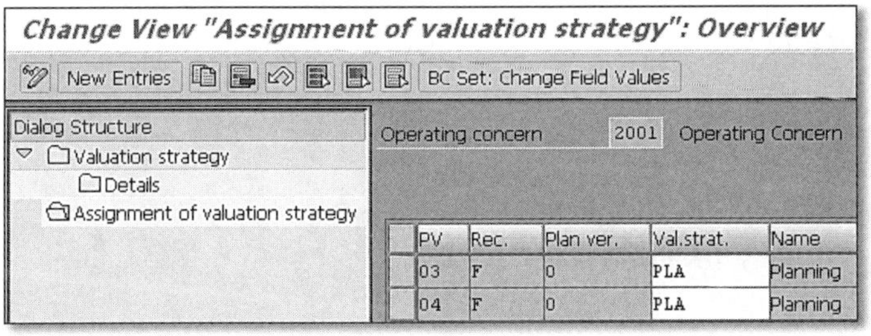

Figure 7.88 Assignment of Valuation Strategy, Planning

In this screen, we've assigned the valuation strategy to the point of valuation 03 (Manual planning) and 04 (Automatic planning), and also to version 0.

After reviewing that the valuation strategy for planning purposes is correct, next you'll see the assignment of costing keys to material types for planning purposes. Use Transaction KE4J, and you can see the assignment as shown in Figure 7.89.

We've defined the point of valuation, record type, planning version, material type, and which costing key the system will access to bring the cost estimate to CO-PA planning.

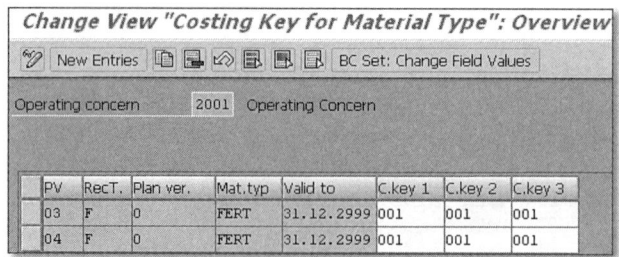

Figure 7.89 Costing Key for Material Type, Planning

The last step for the first sequence line in the valuation strategy (refer to Figure 7.87) is to assign the cost component split to the value fields. Use Transaction KE4R to assign, as in Figure 7.90.

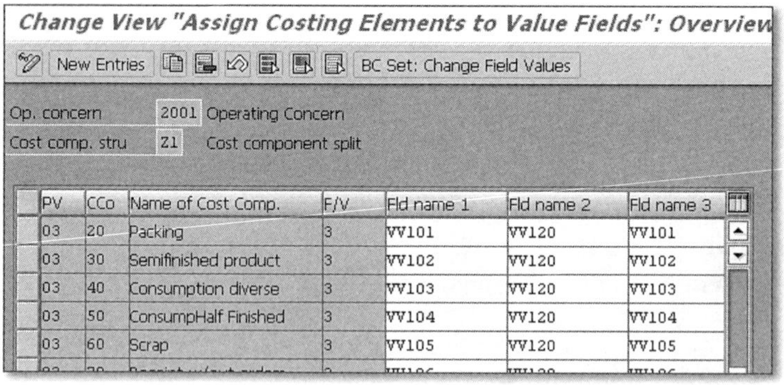

PV	CCo	Name of Cost Comp.	F/V	Fld name 1	Fld name 2	Fld name 3
03	20	Packing	3	VV101	VV120	VV101
03	30	Semifinished product	3	VV102	VV120	VV102
03	40	Consumption diverse	3	VV103	VV120	VV103
03	50	ConsumpHalf Finished	3	VV104	VV120	VV104
03	60	Scrap	3	VV105	VV120	VV105

Figure 7.90 Assign Costing Elements to Value Fields, Planning

You must assign the value fields for the point of valuation 03 and 04.

The next line of the strategy sequence is the costing sheet. Use Transaction 8KEV to check the customizing. Figure 7.91 shows the customizing screen.

You can see in Figure 7.91 that for the costing sheet YB0002, price condition YB03 was used to define the price. The last step is to check the assignment of the price condition to a value field. Use Transaction KE45, which is shown in Figure 7.92.

Now that all of the valuation customizing for planning purposes is complete, you can return to the parameter set in the planning framework (refer to Figure 7.85). Right-click, and create a parameter set for valuation, as shown in Figure 7.93.

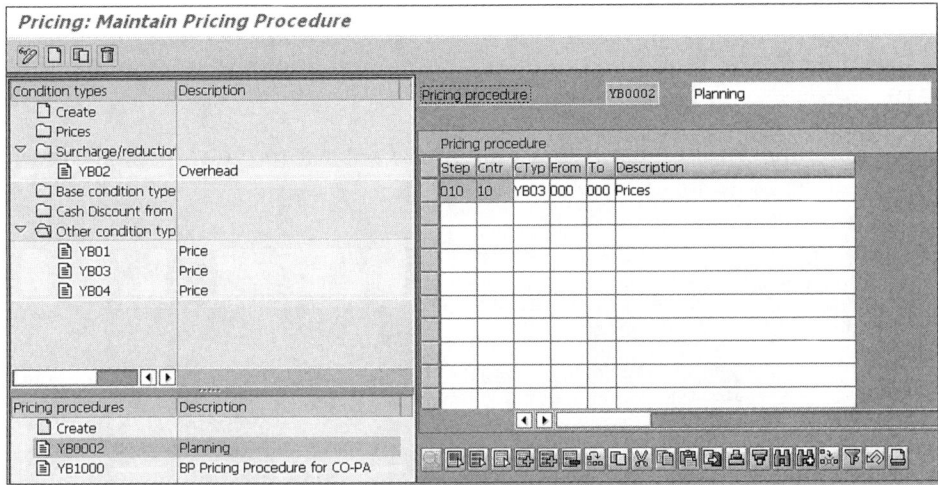

Figure 7.91 CO-PA Costing Sheet, Planning

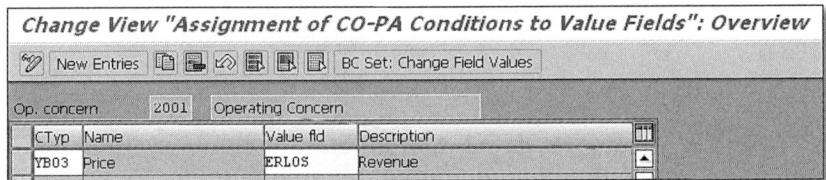

Figure 7.92 Assignment of CO-PA Conditions to Value Fields, Planning

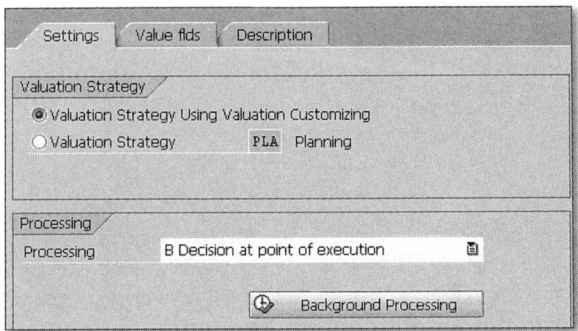

Figure 7.93 Valuation, Parameter Set, Settings Tab

You can choose in this screen whether the system will use the customizing to create the valuation for the planning values or use some other valuation strategy. You can also define what kind of processing will be used:

▶ TEST RUN

▶ UPDATE RUN

▶ DECISION AT POINT OF EXECUTION

Move to the next tab to select which fields are subject to the valuation. See the VALUE tab shown in Figure 7.94.

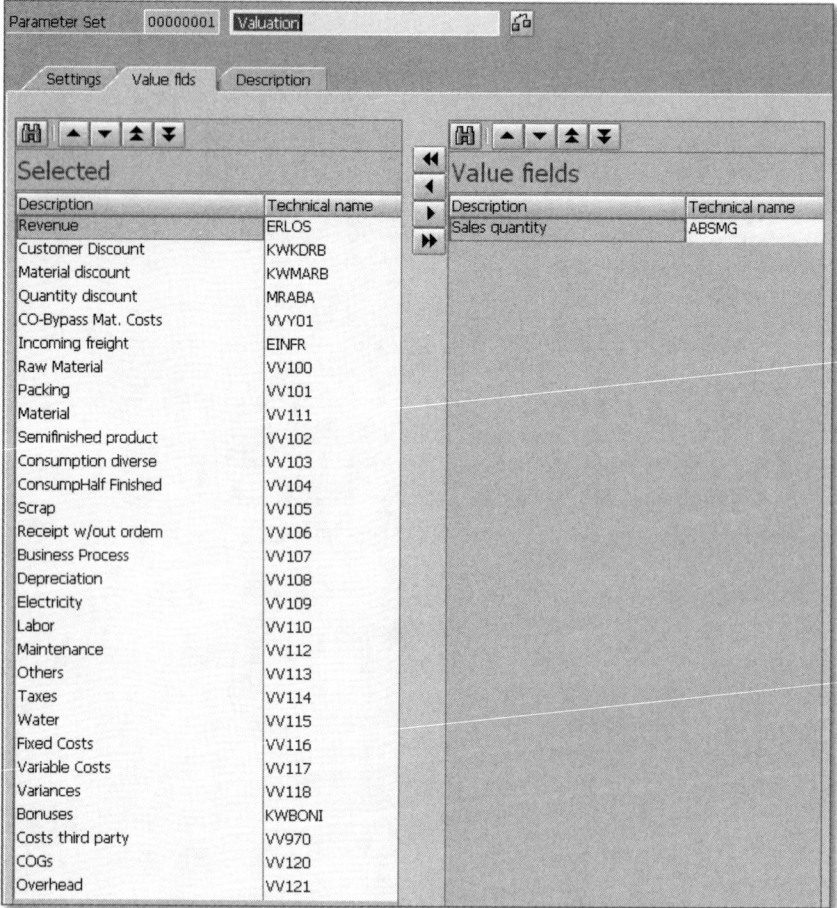

Figure 7.94 Valuation, Parameter Set, Value Fields

Save the valuation parameter set, and then open the data plan maintenance screen by double-clicking in the line created when you saved, as shown in Figure 7.95.

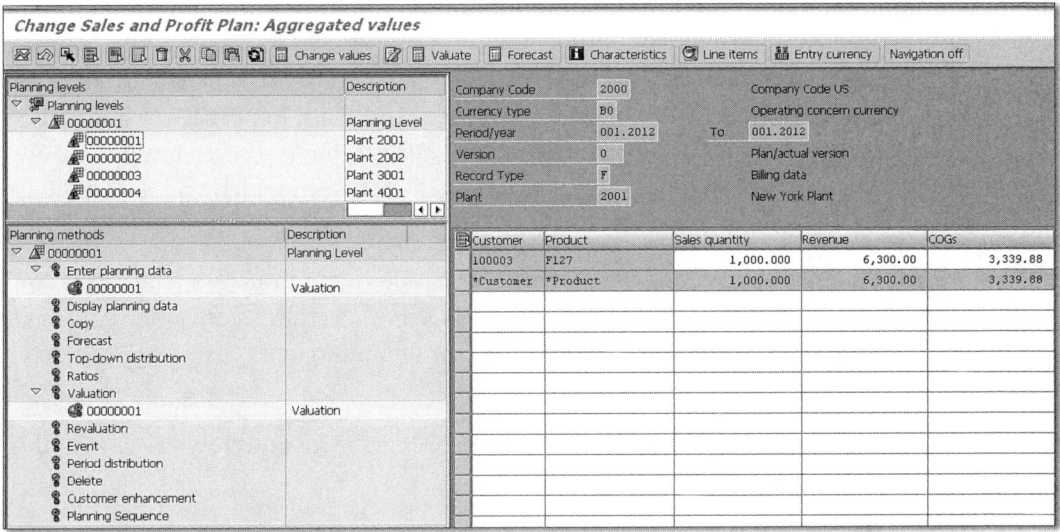

Figure 7.95 CO-PA Planning, Valuation Results

Comparing Figure 7.95 with Figure 7.85, you can see that the valuation has filled the fields SALES QUANTITY, REVENUE, and COGS. It evaluated all of the value fields selected in the valuation parameter set, but in the figure, you can only see these three because, in our example, the planning layout was not defined to show all values fields due to length limitations.

Now that you've learned how to customize the most important tool in CO-PA planning, the planning framework, you can see how all of the necessary parameters for CO-PA planning are controlled in one place.

In actual values, you were able to send overhead costs from cost centers to CO-PA using an assessment; the same functionality is available for planning purposes. The assessment customizing for planning is similar to the actual assessment. To create the CO-PA plan assessment, use Transaction KEU7, or go to CONTROLLING • PROFITABILITY ANALYSIS • PLANNING • INTEGRATED PLANNING • ASSESS COST CENTER COSTS/PROCESS COSTS • DEFINE STRUCTURE OF COST CENTER ASSESSMENT/PROCESS COST ASSESSMENT.

Now that you're familiar with all of the options available to you in CO-PA planning and can determine how to customize it for your needs, let's look at the reporting available to you from CO-PA.

7.6 Information System

The CO-PA information system is mainly created by the user. SAP ERP provides one standard line item report each for actual and plan, Report KE24 and Report KE25, respectively. For all other reporting needs, you'll need to build your own CO-PA reports using the Report Painter functionality, in which you define a form and use it to create a report.

The advantage of creating your own reports is that you can create the result analysis lines as you wish, depending on your needs. These custom reports provide multidimensional analysis of both actual and planning data, using the characteristics you've defined in your CO-PA.

In this section, you'll learn how to create a report form and how to create a flexible report using this form.

7.6.1 Define Forms for a Profitability Report

The report form for CO-PA reports is a combination of characteristics, values fields, and formulas. To create a report form, use Transaction KE34, or go to CONTROLLING • PROFITABILITY ANALYSIS • PLANNING • INFORMATION SYSTEM • REPORT COMPONENTS • DEFINE FORMS • DEFINE FORMS FOR PROFITABILITY REPORTS. The first definition screen is shown in Figure 7.96.

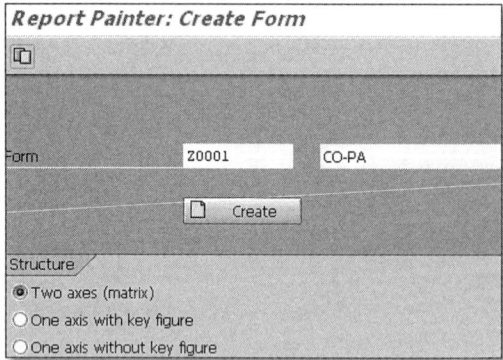

Figure 7.96 CO-PA Form Report

Define a report name, and click on CREATE. The form definition screen is shown on Figure 7.97.

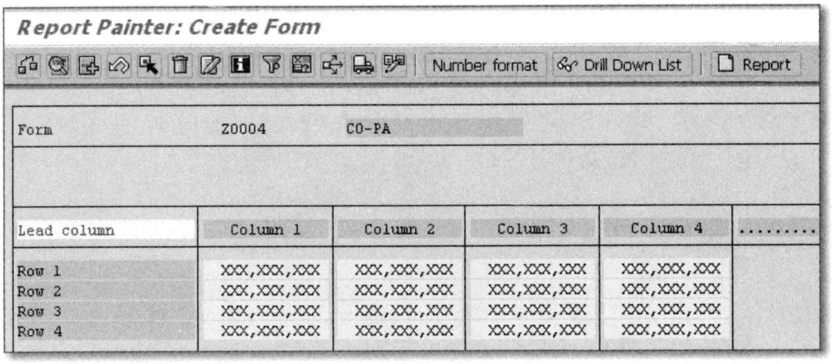

Report Painter: Create Form

Form	Z0004	CO-PA			

Lead column	Column 1	Column 2	Column 3	Column 4	....
Row 1	XXX,XXX,XXX	XXX,XXX,XXX	XXX,XXX,XXX	XXX,XXX,XXX	
Row 2	XXX,XXX,XXX	XXX,XXX,XXX	XXX,XXX,XXX	XXX,XXX,XXX	
Row 3	XXX,XXX,XXX	XXX,XXX,XXX	XXX,XXX,XXX	XXX,XXX,XXX	
Row 4	XXX,XXX,XXX	XXX,XXX,XXX	XXX,XXX,XXX	XXX,XXX,XXX	

Figure 7.97 Report Painter, Create Form

The values will be displayed in the intersection of the columns and the rows. Double-click on the column you want to define. The system will prompt you to select what kind of value you'll define for the column in a new screen (see Figure 7.98).

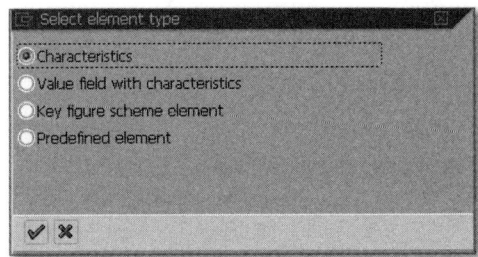

Figure 7.98 Select Element Type

After selecting characteristic for the column, you can restrict what will be displayed in the column by selecting filters for the characteristics in the screen shown in Figure 7.99.

After defining the column, double-click in the line to choose what will be displayed by the line. Figure 7.100 shows the selection.

If you select VALUE FIELD WITH CHARACTERISTICS, you can choose between the value fields available in the operating concern, as shown in Figure 7.101.

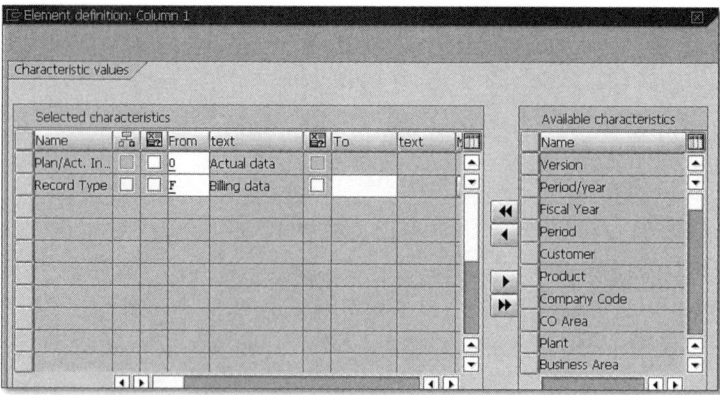

Figure 7.99 Element Definition, Characteristic Filter

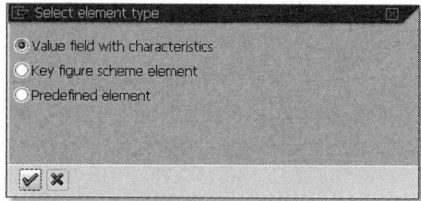

Figure 7.100 Select Element Type

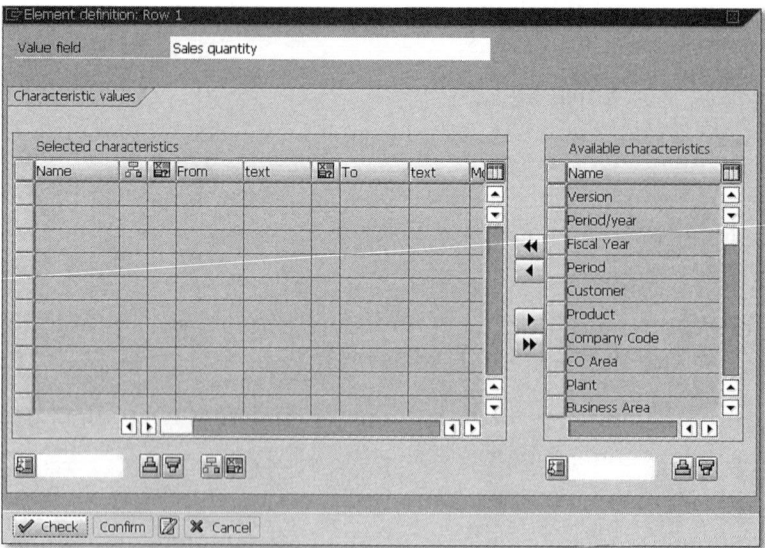

Figure 7.101 Row Definition

In VALUE FIELD, you can select which value field you want to display and also restrict the selection by applying characteristics filters. A finished report form for a sample margin statement is shown in Figure 7.102.

Form	Z0004	CO-PA	
Lead column	Actual dat	Planning d	Diff
Sales quantity	XXX,XXX,XXX	XXX,XXX,XXX	XXX,XXX,XXX
Revenue	XXX,XXX,XXX	XXX,XXX,XXX	XXX,XXX,XXX
COGs	XXX,XXX,XXX	XXX,XXX,XXX	XXX,XXX,XXX
Raw Material	XXX,XXX,XXX	XXX,XXX,XXX	XXX,XXX,XXX
Packing	XXX,XXX,XXX	XXX,XXX,XXX	XXX,XXX,XXX
Semifinished product	XXX,XXX,XXX	XXX,XXX,XXX	XXX,XXX,XXX
Consumption diverse	XXX,XXX,XXX	XXX,XXX,XXX	XXX,XXX,XXX
ConsumpHalf Finished	XXX,XXX,XXX	XXX,XXX,XXX	XXX,XXX,XXX
Scrap	XXX,XXX,XXX	XXX,XXX,XXX	XXX,XXX,XXX
Receipt w/out order	XXX,XXX,XXX	XXX,XXX,XXX	XXX,XXX,XXX
Business Process	XXX,XXX,XXX	XXX,XXX,XXX	XXX,XXX,XXX
Depreciation	XXX,XXX,XXX	XXX,XXX,XXX	XXX,XXX,XXX
Electricity	XXX,XXX,XXX	XXX,XXX,XXX	XXX,XXX,XXX
Labor	XXX,XXX,XXX	XXX,XXX,XXX	XXX,XXX,XXX
Material	XXX,XXX,XXX	XXX,XXX,XXX	XXX,XXX,XXX
Maintenance	XXX,XXX,XXX	XXX,XXX,XXX	XXX,XXX,XXX
Others	XXX,XXX,XXX	XXX,XXX,XXX	XXX,XXX,XXX
Taxes	XXX,XXX,XXX	XXX,XXX,XXX	XXX,XXX,XXX
Water	XXX,XXX,XXX	XXX,XXX,XXX	XXX,XXX,XXX
Margin	XXX,XXX,XXX	XXX,XXX,XXX	XXX,XXX,XXX

Figure 7.102 CO-PA Report Form

After creating the columns and rows, you can add additional columns and rows as formulas based on the ones you've created. In the example shown in Figure 7.102, the column DIFF and the line MARGIN are calculated based on formulas.

After creating the report form, you can now use the form to define a CO-PA report.

7.6.2 Create a Profitability Report

To create multidimensional CO-PA reports, use Transaction KE31, or go to CONTROLLING • PROFITABILITY ANALYSIS • PLANNING • INFORMATION SYSTEM • REPORT COMPONENTS • CREATE PROFITABILITY REPORT. The first definition screen is shown in Figure 7.103.

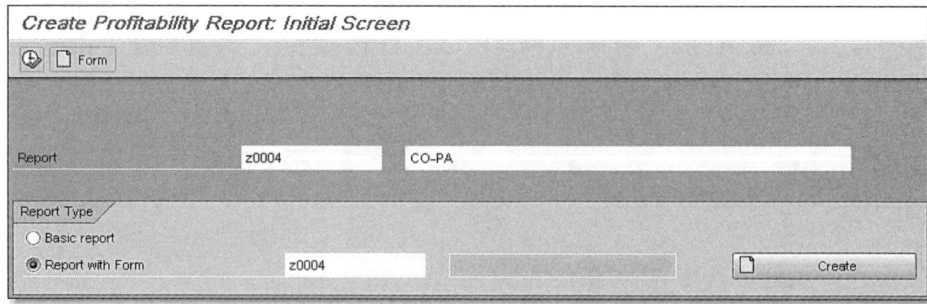

Figure 7.103 Create CO-PA Report

Define a name for the report, and choose a form you've created previously. Click on CREATE, which will bring you to a new screen to select which characteristics you want to see in the report (see Figure 7.104).

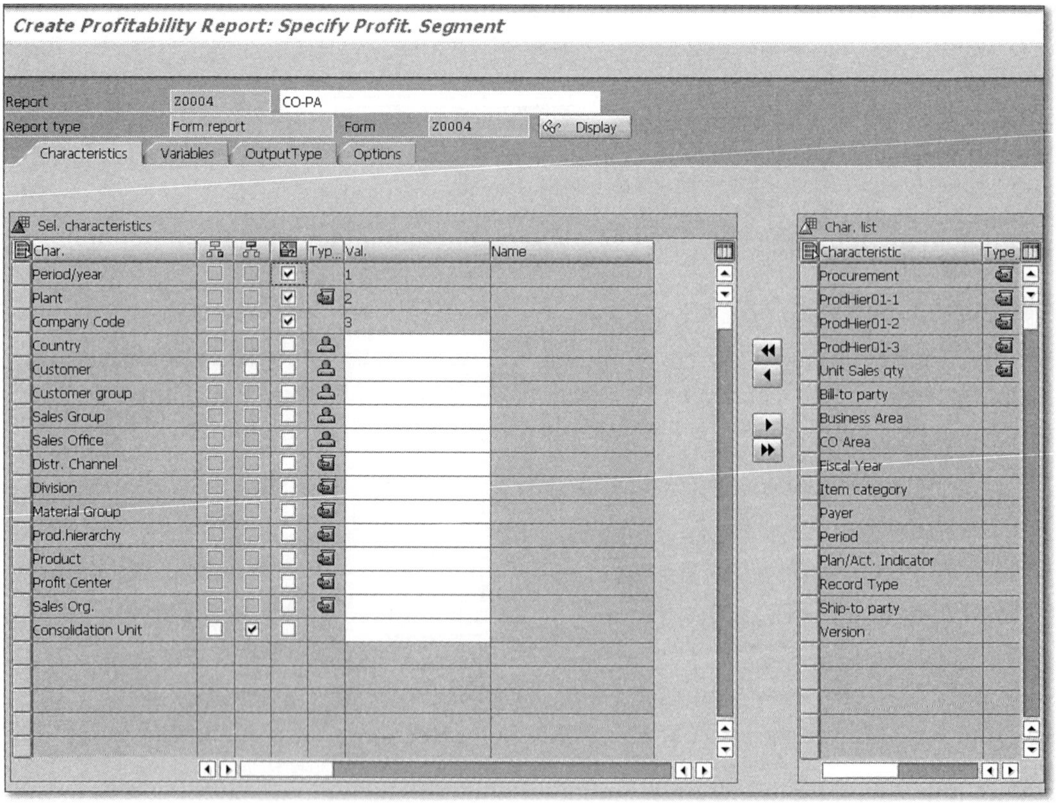

Create Profitability Report: Specify Profit. Segment									

Report: Z0004 CO-PA
Report type: Form report   Form: Z0004   Display

Characteristics | Variables | OutputType | Options

Sel. characteristics

Char.				Typ.	Val.	Name	
Period/year	☐	☐	☑		1		
Plant	☐	☐	☑	🔲	2		
Company Code	☐	☐	☑		3		
Country	☐	☐	☐	👤			
Customer	☐	☐	☐	👤			
Customer group	☐	☐	☐	👤			
Sales Group	☐	☐	☐	👤			
Sales Office	☐	☐	☐	👤			
Distr. Channel	☐	☐	☐	🔲			
Division	☐	☐	☐	🔲			
Material Group	☐	☐	☐	🔲			
Prod.hierarchy	☐	☐	☐	🔲			
Product	☐	☐	☐	🔲			
Profit Center	☐	☐	☐	🔲			
Sales Org.	☐	☐	☐	🔲			
Consolidation Unit	☐	☑	☐				

Char. list

Characteristic	Type
Procurement	🔲
ProdHier01-1	🔲
ProdHier01-2	🔲
ProdHier01-3	🔲
Unit Sales qty	🔲
Bill-to party	
Business Area	
CO Area	
Fiscal Year	
Item category	
Payer	
Period	
Plan/Act. Indicator	
Record Type	
Ship-to party	
Version	

Figure 7.104 CO-PA Report Definition

In the right side of the screen, you can see the characteristics available for the operating concern. Mark the characteristics you want available for navigation in the report, and click on the arrow to send them to the left side of the screen.

You can also mark the fields you want to be available as variables, meaning that they will be available on the selection screen. In the example shown in Figure 7.104, we've chosen PERIOD/YEAR, PLANT, and COMPANY CODE as variables.

If you look at the characteristic consolidation unit in Figure 7.104, you can see a new available option—to select the characteristic hierarchy that you've already defined. Figure 7.105 shows the selection option.

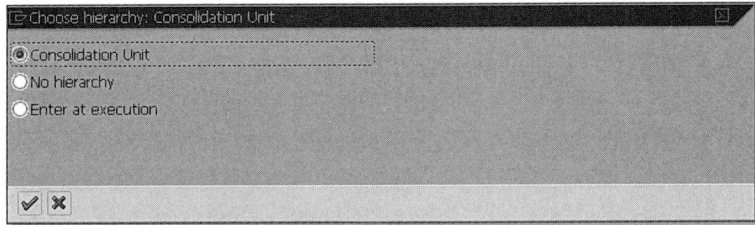

Figure 7.105 CO-PA Report, Choose Hierarchy

If you select to use the defined hierarchy, you can summarize and navigate in the report using the hierarchy nodes.

If you've selected characteristics to be variables, you can see those in the VARIABLES tab shown in Figure 7.106.

Create Profitability Report: Variables

Report	Z0004	CO-PA			
Report type	Form report		Form	Z0004	Display

Characteristics / Variables / OutputType / Options

Variable Name	Variable Value	Name	Entry at Execution
Company Code			☑
Plant			☑
Period/year			☑

Figure 7.106 CO-PA Report, Variables Tab

If you leave the field VARIABLE VALUE blank, the system will ask for the input when running the report; alternatively, you can define it as a fixed value in this screen. The next tab on the CO-PA report creation screen is OUTPUT TYPE, as shown in Figure 7.107.

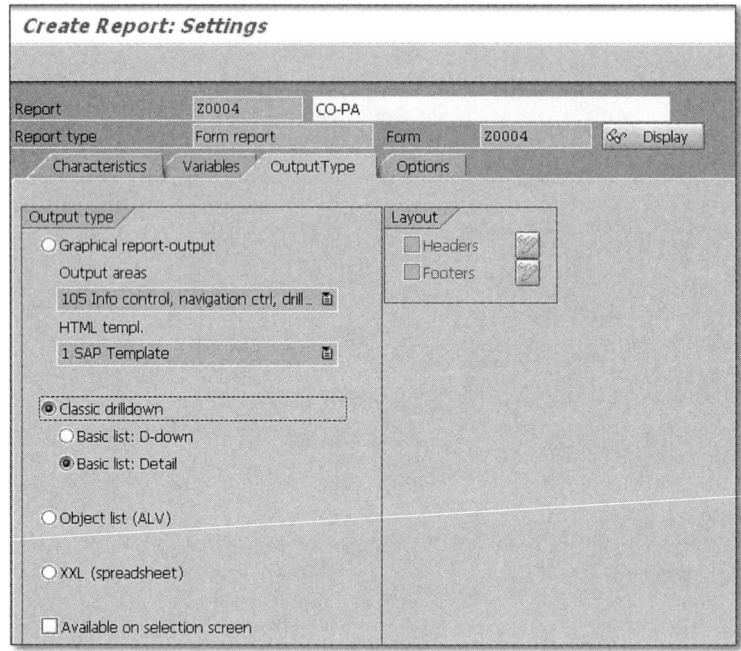

Figure 7.107 CO-PA Report, Output Type Tab

In OUTPUT TYPE, you select how the report will be displayed. We've chosen CLASSIC DRILLDOWN/BASIC LIST: DETAIL. This option only affects the way the user will see the report output; it has no effect on the information that will be included in the report.

After saving the report definition, you can then run it by using Transaction KE30. Figure 7.108 shows the selection screen for the report.

You can see in Figure 7.108 that the fields we've selected as variables are available on the REPORT SELECTION area of the screen. Figure 7.109 shows the report result.

Figure 7.109 shows another example of a CO-PA multidimensional report, where the report values change according to the filters you apply during the navigation.

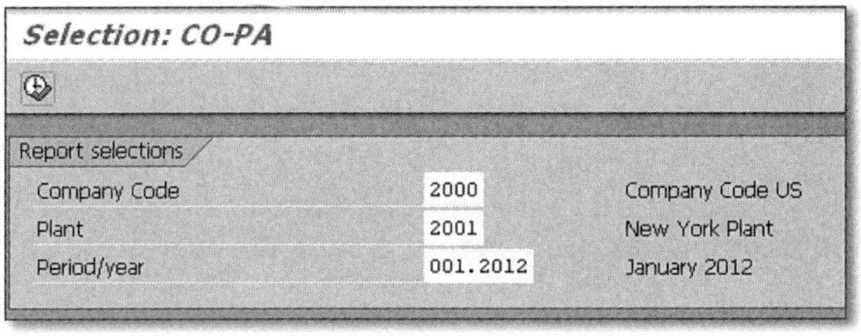

Figure 7.108 CO-PA Report, Selection Screen

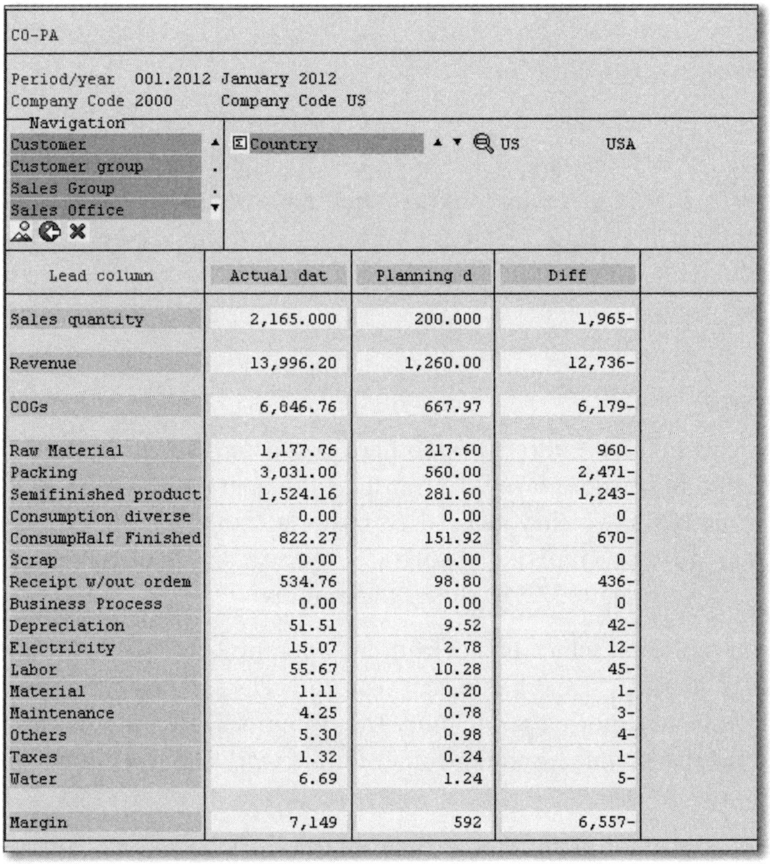

Lead column	Actual dat	Planning d	Diff
Sales quantity	2,165.000	200.000	1,965-
Revenue	13,996.20	1,260.00	12,736-
COGs	6,846.76	667.97	6,179-
Raw Material	1,177.76	217.60	960-
Packing	3,031.00	560.00	2,471-
Semifinished product	1,524.16	281.60	1,243-
Consumption diverse	0.00	0.00	0
ConsumpHalf Finished	822.27	151.92	670-
Scrap	0.00	0.00	0
Receipt w/out ordem	534.76	98.80	436-
Business Process	0.00	0.00	0
Depreciation	51.51	9.52	42-
Electricity	15.07	2.78	12-
Labor	55.67	10.28	45-
Material	1.11	0.20	1-
Maintenance	4.25	0.78	3-
Others	5.30	0.98	4-
Taxes	1.32	0.24	1-
Water	6.69	1.24	5-
Margin	7,149	592	6,557-

Figure 7.109 CO-PA Report

Click on the NAVIGATION pane, and select an available characteristic to add as a breakdown in the report. We chose in our example the characteristic COUNTRY. Use the arrow to change between the characteristics. To remove a characteristic from the filter, click on the "SUM" sign in front of the characteristic name. On the Navigation pane, you can add more characteristics to your report by clicking on the desired characteristic.

As you can see from these brief examples, the reporting tool in CO-PA has virtually unlimited flexibility to allow you to define your own reports to address the needs of your company.

Finally, you should know about some of the important technical tools available for CO-PA, which we'll discuss in the next topic.

7.7   Tools

When customizing the different areas for CO-PA you'll notice that for some, the system creates a transport request and for others not. For example, in the operating concern definition, the system won't ask for a transport request, but for the section valuation, it will. Next, you'll see how to transport the operating concern settings.

7.7.1   Transport

The transport process in CO-PA differs from other CO subcomponents because it requires a user action to be transported. To transport the operating concern definition and other areas for which you need to create a transport request, use Transaction KE3I, or go to Controlling • Profitability Analysis • Tools • Production Startup • Transport. Figure 7.110 shows the options.

In this screen, you can select which object from the operating concern you want to transport. If you mark Operating concern, you can select all operating concern customizing to be transported at one time. The system will ask for two transport requests—one for customizing and the other for the workbench, as shown in Figure 7.111.

After defining the transport requests, you must select which operating concern you want to transport, as shown in Figure 7.112.

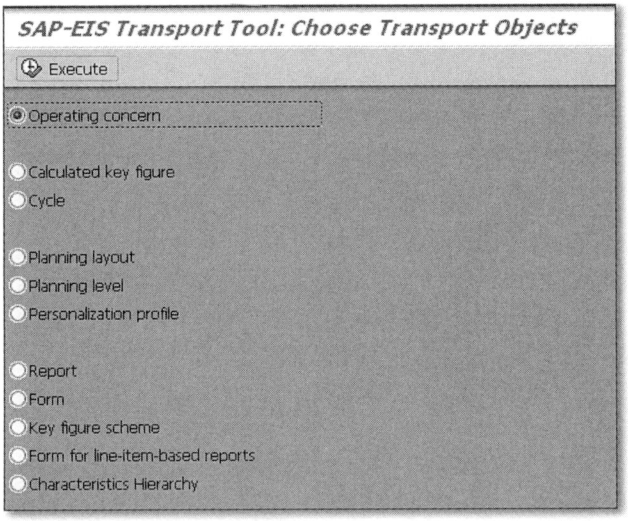

Figure 7.110 CO-PA, Transport Tool

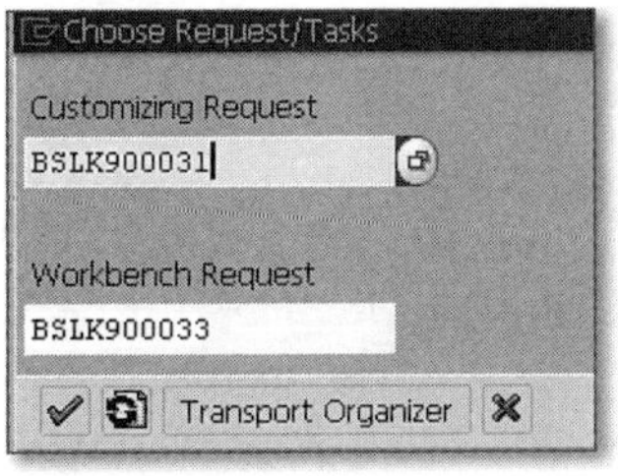

Figure 7.111 CO-PA, Transport Request

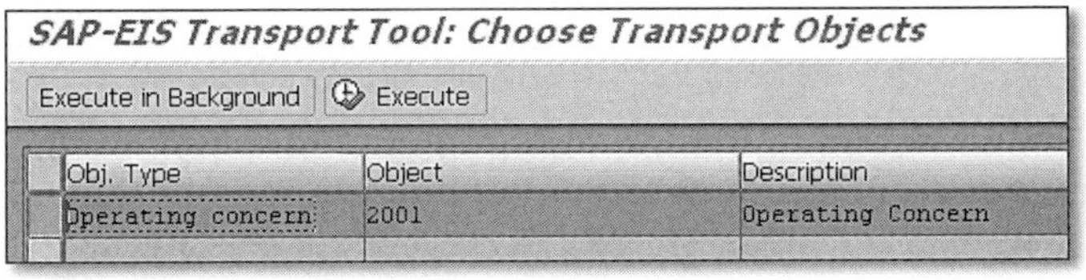

Figure 7.112 CO-PA, Operating Concern Transport

Select the operating concern you want to transport, and then click on EXECUTE. The system will prompt a screen to define which operating concern customizing option you want to be included in the transport request, as shown in Figure 7.113.

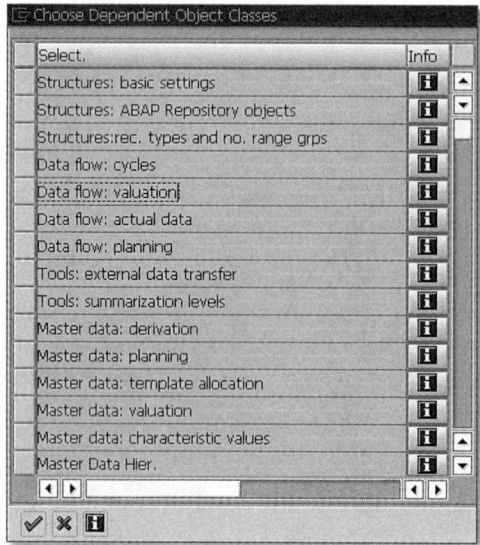

Figure 7.113 CO-PA, Transport Options

Select the customizing areas you want to transport, and then save.

If you've activated CO-PA in a production environment with data already in it, it's possible to import the old data to the newly activated CO-PA component.

7.7.2 Subsequent Posting of SD Documents

SAP ERP provides a tool that you can use to bring existing SD documents to the CO-PA tables even if they were created before the CO-PA activation. The system will import SD data according to the current CO-PA customizing using the valuation strategy defined in the CO-PA customizing. To import existing SD documents to CO-PA, either use Transaction KE4S, or go to CONTROLLING • PROFITABILITY ANALYSIS • TOOLS • PRODUCTION STARTUP • SUBSEQUENT POSTING OF SD DOCUMENTS • POST BILLING DOCUMENTS SUBSEQUENTLY. Figure 7.114 shows the options for importing SD data.

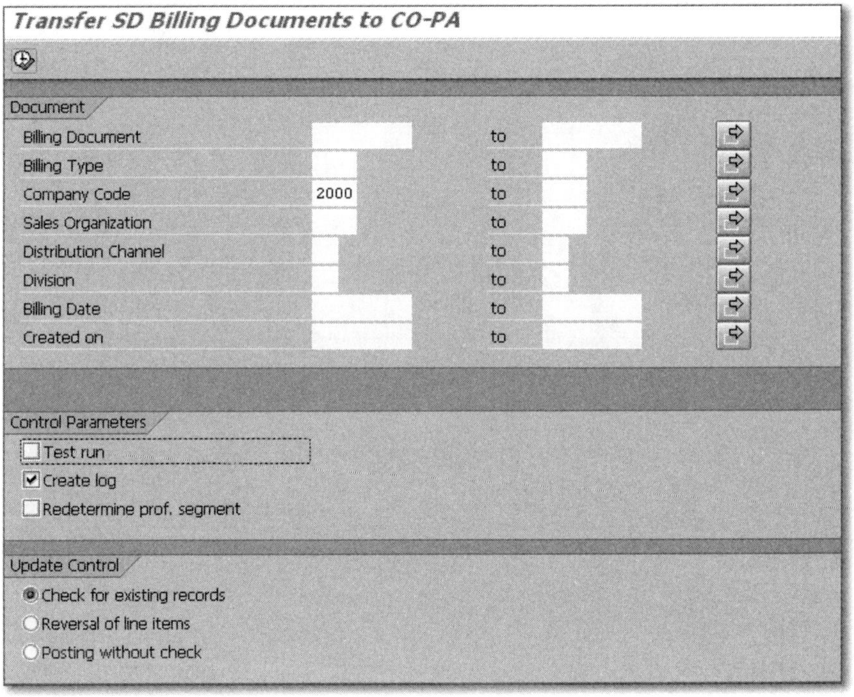

Figure 7.114 Transfer SD Billing Documents to CO-PA

Enter the selection options for the documents you want to import and run. You can see the results in Figure 7.115.

If you defined a range where the system had already posted documents to CO-PA, it will post only the documents that are not already posted in the component, as you can see in Figure 7.115.

Now that you've seen the customizing and concepts of CO-PA, and the tools available to use during start-up, let's review the key areas this chapter emphasized.

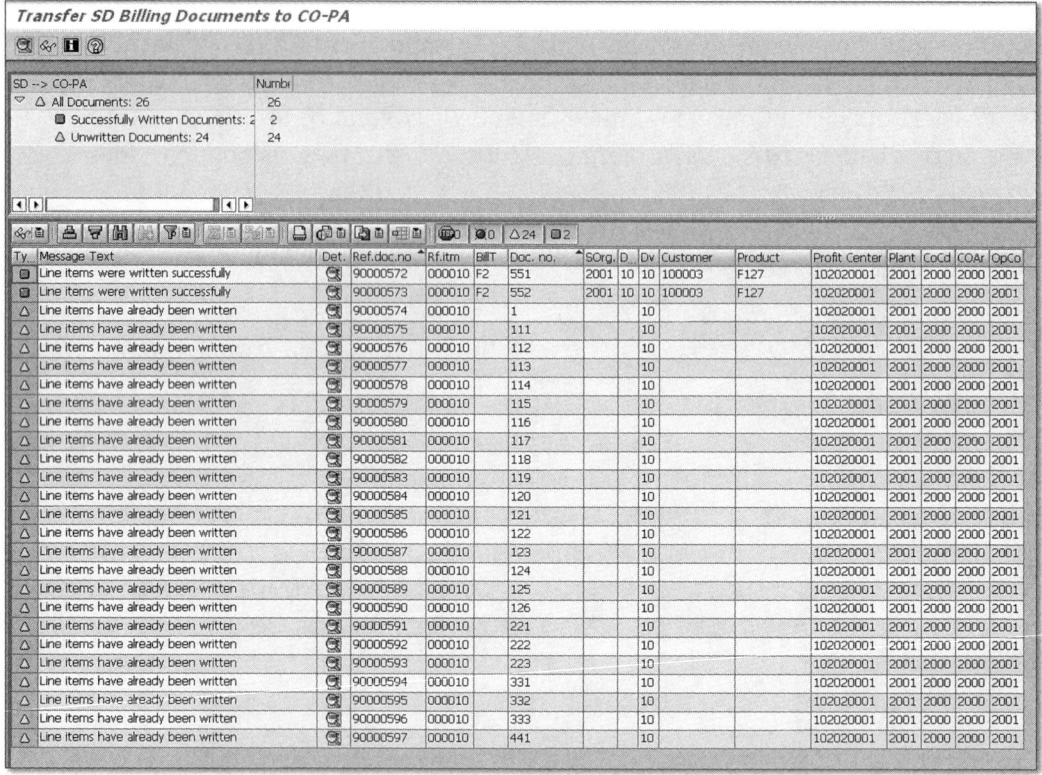

Figure 7.115 Transfer SD Billing Documents to CO-PA, Results

7.8 Summary

In this chapter, you saw that CO-PA has the ability to combine information from different components to obtain online customized multidimensional profitability reports.

When you define the characteristics and value fields and assign them to the operating concern, you are creating the reporting structure for CO-PA according to your business requirements.

With the created structure, you can customize how the values flow from other SAP ERP components to CO-PA, define how to access the cost estimates, and create costing sheets and condition types to add values to your analysis that aren't available to be imported from other SAP ERP components.

Using the CO-PA planning, you've seen how the planning framework can be used to create different planning scenarios such as budget, forecast, sales simulations, and cost simulations, and also how the planning framework can be set to automatically calculate planning values from defined user inputs (such as calculating revenues) based on input quantities and defined pricing conditions.

In the information system, you saw how you can create multidimensional reports by defining forms and reports to use for different business analysis purposes.

You learned that the method used to transport CO-PA customized settings is different from other components because you must use a specific transaction to transport the CO-PA structure. You also learned how you can import data from existing SD documents at the time of activation of your CO-PA.

Now you know the benefits this powerful subcomponent can bring to your business, and you can define all of the custom settings to implement it in your SAP ERP system.

You are now ready to move on to the next chapter, Profit Center Accounting (EC-PCA).

Profit Center Accounting in SAP ERP can work together with all other Controlling subcomponents that you have learned about so far. With it, you can help complete the management reporting environment to meet your organization's information objectives.

8 Profit Center Accounting

Profit Center Accounting (EC-PCA) provides a focus on internal areas of a company that have responsibility for achieving certain profit or productivity goals. This chapter will describe the most common business purposes for using EC-PCA. You'll learn to identify which information can be obtained from the component and how to customize EC-PCA to meet your organization's business information objectives. We'll start by explaining the basic settings that will determine how your EC-PCA will behave, and then we'll talk about the master data you'll need to establish for your EC-PCA structure. Then you'll learn about an important function in EC-PCA: transfer pricing. We'll talk about how to set up your planning structures, some tools you can customize to help manage the actual postings and period-end closing process, and how to prepare for consolidation. You'll learn about the most important standard EC-PCA reports, and you'll see examples of how your EC-PCA customization can affect the reporting information available. Finally, you'll discover some tools to help you manage changes in your environment and tips to avoid some common mistakes.

EC-PCA allows you to determine profit and loss of internal areas of your company. A profit center is the smallest organizational unit where your company wants to measure profits by tracking both revenues and expenses.

In Chapter 3, you learned how to define cost centers as cost objects containing only cost elements. EC-PCA is different because a profit center can be assigned for each kind of posting in accounting: fixed assets, materials, cost centers, internal orders, payables, receivables, and so on. This means you can have both a balance sheet and a P&L by profit center, and it creates another level that can be used to measure and analyze your business results. This level of information is used primarily for management reporting and allows you to define a management information structure that is independent of the legal entity (company code) view used for statutory reporting. This structure can be both at a lower level than the legal entity and also can cross legal entities.

At this point, you might be wondering why you would need to use EC-PCA if you plan to use Profitability Analysis (which you learned about in the previous chapter).

CO-PA is also a way to measure profits and losses in SAP ERP, but you can't analyze balance sheet items in CO-PA. You can customize CO-PA to meet specific profitability reporting needs from a business perspective (e.g., by region, by customer, sales organization, or material). Remember that profit centers can be used in CO-PA as characteristics in your profitability structure, but that many other characteristics from SD are also available.

EC-PCA is also a way to measure profit and loss but only by areas of responsibility, not by SD characteristics such as customer or material, and it isn't only restricted to the P&L information. You can also use EC-PCA to analyze your balance sheet by profit center, allowing you to determine working capital and other key measures related to the balance sheet by areas of responsibility.

Now let's look at the basic settings to activate EC-PCA.

8.1 Basic Settings

As you've seen in previous chapters for all of the CO subcomponents, EC-PCA needs to be activated in the controlling area settings in Transaction OKKP, as shown in Figure 8.1.

Flag the PROFIT CENTER ACCTG field to activate the EC-PCA controlling area. Now that you have activated EC-PCA in the controlling area settings, you must maintain specific settings for the EC-PCA in the controlling area.

Use Transaction OKE5, or go to PROFIT CENTER ACCOUNTING • BASIC SETTINGS • CONTROLLING AREA SETTINGS • MAINTAIN CONTROLLING AREA SETTINGS, which brings you to the screen shown in Figure 8.2. In this customizing, you define the first node of the standard hierarchy for EC-PCA.

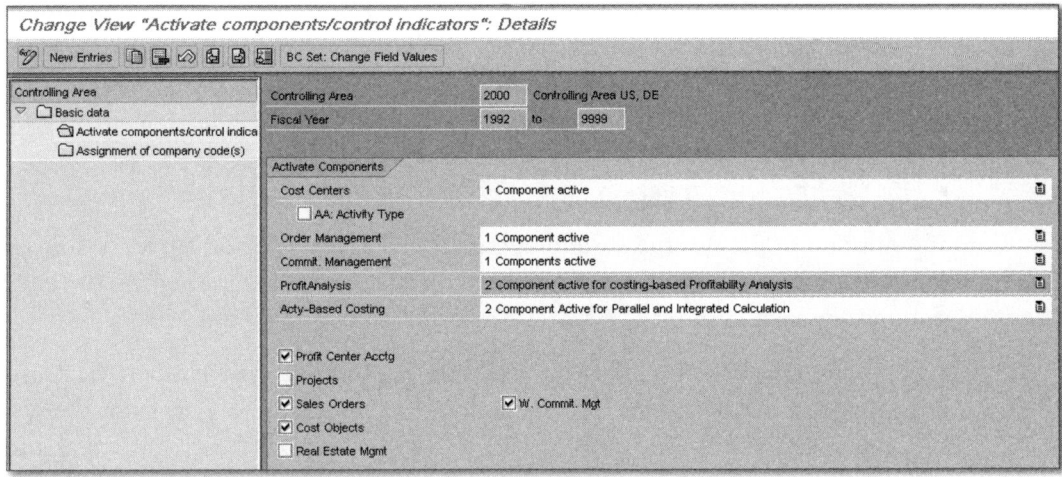

Figure 8.1 Controlling Area Settings, Profit Center Accounting Activation

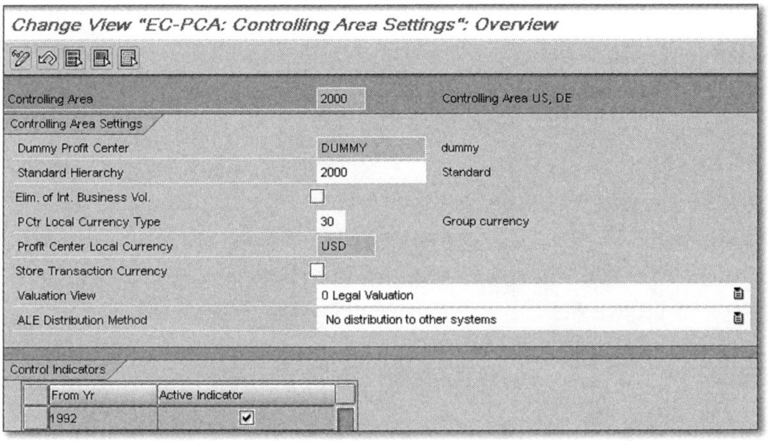

Figure 8.2 EC-PCA Controlling Area Settings

The dummy profit center isn't defined in this transaction—it's only displayed here. You'll see how to create the dummy profit center later in Section 8.3.

If you flag the field ELIMIN. OF INT. BUSINESS VOLUME, the system won't create entries for business transactions within the same profit center. For example, if an internal order with profit center "A" is going to be settled to a cost center assigned to the same profit center, the system won't create a line item for this posting in the EC-PCA. This helps to reduce the database size.

The next available field is the PCTR LOCAL CURRENCY TYPE. You can choose from three options:

▶ 20: CONTROLLING AREA CURRENCY

▶ 30: GROUP CURRENCY

▶ 90: PROFIT CENTER CURRENCY

If you select 20 or 30, the system automatically assigns a local currency for the EC-PCA, using either the currency defined for the controlling area or the currency defined as group currency.

If you select 90, the LOCAL CURRENCY field opens, and you can maintain the profit center local currency. If you mark the field STORE TRANSACTION CURRENCY, the system will also update the EC-PCA with the transaction currency for actual and planning values. If selected, this will increase the size of the database.

The VALUATION VIEW field is used in the transfer price functionality, which we'll cover in detail in Section 8.5. In the controlling area settings for EC-PCA, you can select the option 0 LEGAL VALUATION.

In the CONTROL INDICATORS section, you need to mark ACTIVE INDICATOR for the year selected.

Next in the basic settings, you'll need to activate the direct postings. Use Transaction 1KEF, or go to PROFIT CENTER ACCOUNTING • BASIC SETTINGS • CONTROLLING AREA SETTINGS • ACTIVATE DIRECT POSTINGS • SET CONTROL PARAMETERS FOR ACTUAL DATA, as you can see in Figure 8.3.

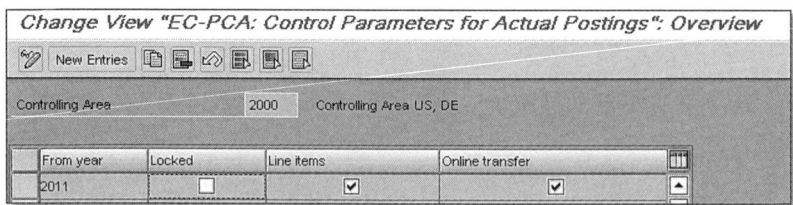

Figure 8.3 EC-PCA Control Parameters for Actual Posting

You define in this transaction whether the system will do two things: write the line items and perform an online transfer. Note that these settings are by year. For example, when the year changes, you'll create a new line for the new year and block the previous year for actual postings.

You also need to set up a version for EC-PCA. Use the same Transaction OKKP that you used to maintain the versions for Cost Center Accounting (CO-CCA), as shown in Figure 8.4.

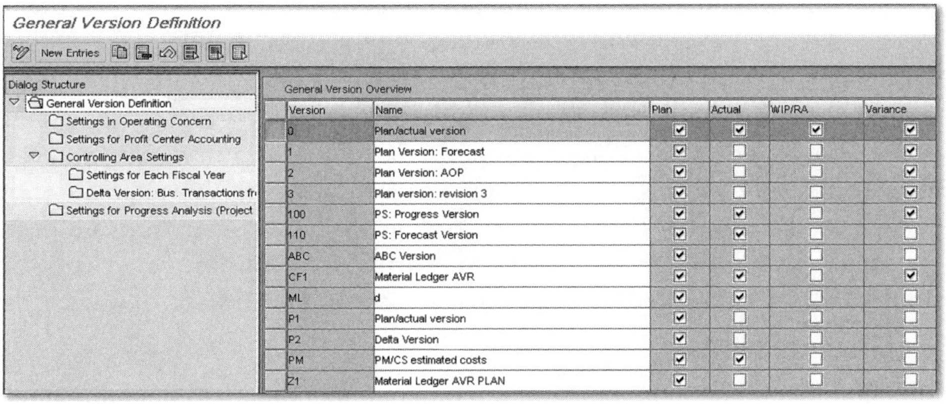

Figure 8.4 Version Maintenance

Mark the VERSION column entry you want to activate for EC-PCA, and double-click on the left side of the screen on SETTINGS FOR PROFIT CENTER ACCOUNTING, which brings you to the screen shown in Figure 8.5.

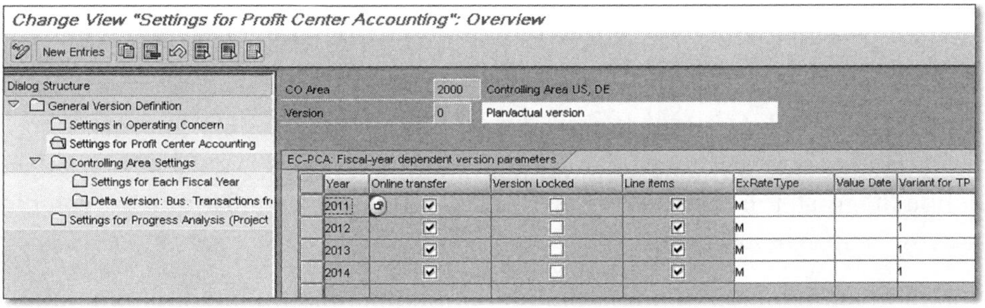

Figure 8.5 EC-PCA Version Maintenance

Click on NEW ENTRIES, and define the year for the EC-PCA version. You then can indicate if it will have online transfer, version locked, and line items, and also define the exchange rate type for the currency conversion. If you are using transfer price, you must define the variant for the transfer price.

> **Note**
>
> If you uncheck the ONLINE TRANSFER field, then planning done at the cost center level, for example, won't be transferred to EC-PCA online, demanding a program execution to transfer theses values.

Finally, in the basic settings for EC-PCA, you have the option to activate the balance carry-forward for balance sheet accounts in the same way that it happens for Financial Accounting (FI). This means at the beginning of a new year, you can transfer the end-of-year EC-PCA account balances for balance sheet accounts to the opening balances for the new year. To allow the balance carry-forward posting, either use Transaction 2KET, or go to PROFIT CENTER ACCOUNTING • BASIC SETTINGS • BALANCE CARRYFORWARD • ALLOW BALANCES TO BE CARRIED FORWARD. You can see the definition screen in Figure 8.6.

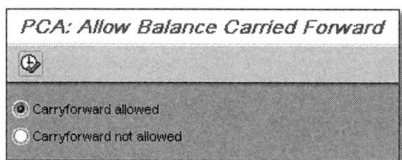

Figure 8.6 Allow Balance Carryforward

You can choose between CARRYFORWARD ALLOWED or CARRYFORWARD NOT ALLOWED.

Now that you've learned the basic settings for EC-PCA, including currencies, control parameters, versions, and the carry-forward settings, you'll next need to define the master data structures. As you'll see, these are similar to what you did for cost center master data.

8.2 Master Data

In EC-PCA master data customizing, you'll define the master data structures (including the profit center standard hierarchy and profit center group) and specify time-dependent fields for profit center master data.

The definition of profit center master data is in many ways similar to cost center master data. Due to this similarity, SAP ERP provides tools to import the cost center definitions and create a mirror of the cost centers as profit centers. In this case, you just need to update the fields you want to be different from the cost center master data.

The first definition for the profit center master data is the standard hierarchy. You've already seen this process in Chapter 3 and Chapter 5. The standard hierarchy is used to group the profit center master data in a logical multi-level structure. All profit centers must be assigned to the standard hierarchy, and you can create summarization levels to appear in EC-PCA reports.

You've already defined the first node of the profit center standard hierarchy in the controlling area settings in Figure 8.2. Now maintain the summarization nodes, and create or change the profit centers. To change the profit center standard hierarchy, use Transaction KCH5N, or go to PROFIT CENTER ACCOUNTING • MASTER DATA • PROFIT CENTER • DEFINE STANDARD HIERARCHY, as you can see in Figure 8.7.

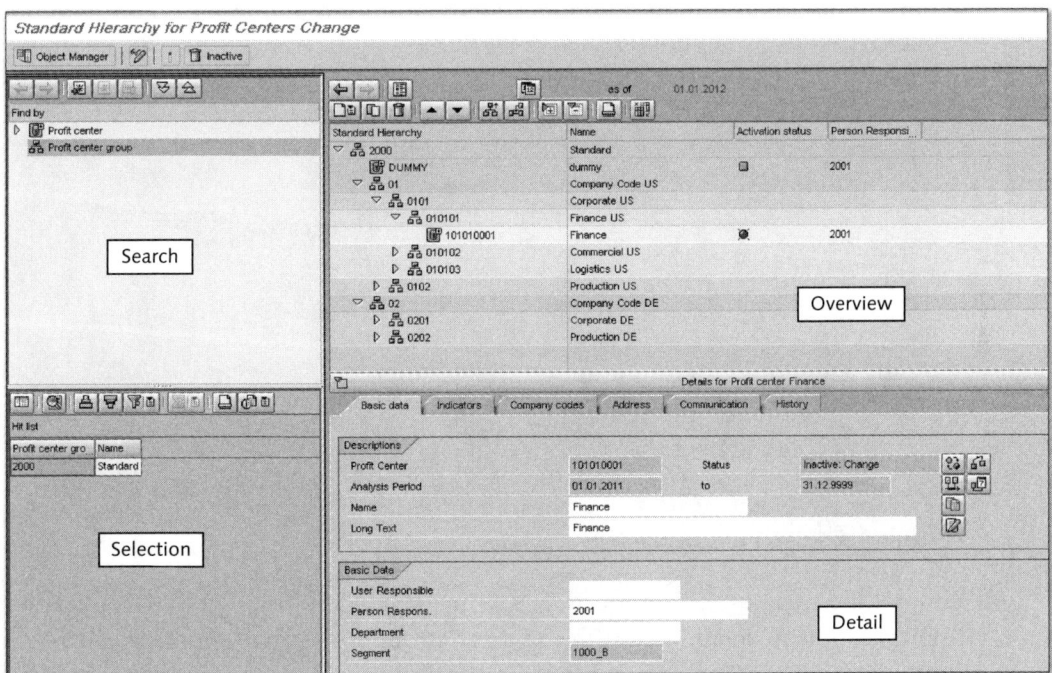

Figure 8.7 Profit Center Standard Hierarchy

The profit center standard hierarchy screen is divided into four sections:

- Search
- Selection
- Overview
- Detail

You can see the screen is similar to the one you used to define the cost center standard hierarchy, and the functionalities are the same. We'll explain how the profit center standard hierarchy differs from the cost center standard hierarchy.

When maintaining a profit center in the detail section of the screen, you can see a field called SEGMENT. With the New General Ledger, the segment is also a consolidation field. Used in combination with the profit center, it increases the FI reporting consolidation flexibility.

A major difference from cost center and business process master data is that you can assign a profit center to one or more company codes, as shown in the COMPANY CODES tab in Figure 8.8.

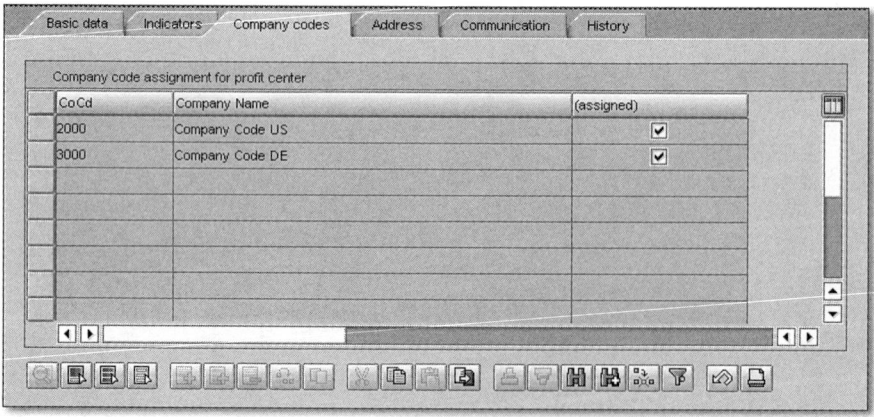

Figure 8.8 Profit Center Master Data, Company Code Assignment

Select the company code (or codes) to which you want to assign the profit center. Only company codes within the same controlling area will be displayed in the selection screen. Remember that the controlling area is the highest level that you can use in a CO reporting structure, so the profit center hierarchy is limited to companies contained within one controlling area.

After changing or creating a profit center, you must activate it. For example, if you change the segment in a profit center account and don't activate the profit center, a posting in the profit center will carry the old segment definition; the new definition will only be valid after you activate the profit center.

If your company profit center standard hierarchy is similar to the cost center standard hierarchy, you can copy from the cost center hierarchy as an alternative way to quickly create the profit center standard hierarchy. In the same transaction, you can copy the cost center groups. Use Transaction 2KEU, or go to PROFIT CENTER ACCOUNTING • MASTER DATA • PROFIT CENTER • COPY COST CENTER GROUPS. Figure 8.9 shows the selection screen.

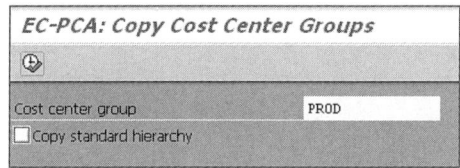

Figure 8.9 EC-PCA Copy Cost Center Group

Enter the group you want to be copied and then execute. If you flag the COPY STANDARD HIERARCHY checkbox, you can enter only the first node of the cost center standard hierarchy; the system will copy the complete cost center standard hierarchy.

The profit center standard hierarchy can't be overwritten, meaning that if you've already defined a standard hierarchy, you are no longer able to copy from the cost center standard hierarchy.

The standard hierarchy is copied empty, with only the summarization nodes. After copying, you can maintain the profit center standard hierarchy to fit your company needs, and then add the individual profit center nodes.

You saw in the profit center basic settings for controlling area in Figure 8.2, that you couldn't create or change the dummy profit center. It's created separately from the EC-PCA basic settings definition. Let's focus on the purpose for the dummy profit center, and then you can see how to maintain it.

For every posting relevant for EC-PCA without a profit center, the system will automatically assign the dummy profit center to that posting; during the period-end closing, you can create an allocation to clear the balance from the dummy profit center and allocate to other profit centers. To create the dummy profit center, either use Transaction KE59, or go to PROFIT CENTER ACCOUNTING • MASTER DATA • PROFIT CENTER • CREATE DUMMY PROFIT CENTER. Figure 8.10 shows the dummy profit center creation screen.

Figure 8.10 Create Dummy Profit Center

After defining a name for the dummy profit center, the system will show the maintenance screen where you can enter the profit center detail, as shown in Figure 8.11.

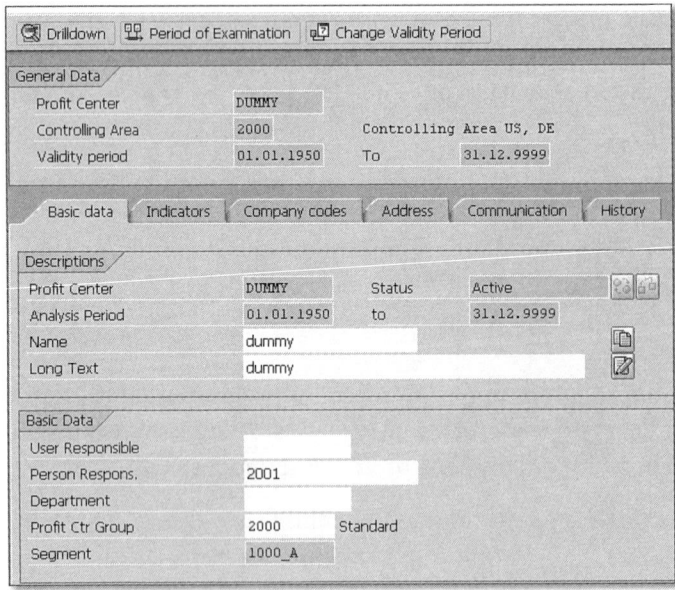

Figure 8.11 Create Dummy Profit Center, Maintenance Screen

When creating a dummy profit center, the system automatically assigns it to all company codes in the controlling area. You can see the company assignment in Figure 8.12.

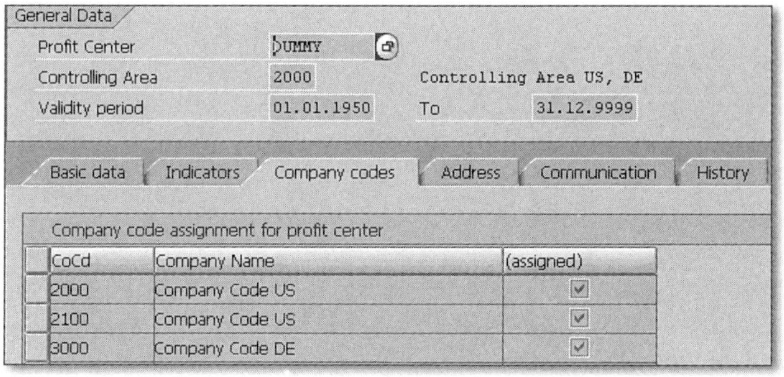

Profit Center	]UMMY	
Controlling Area	2000	Controlling Area US, DE
Validity period	01.01.1950	To 31.12.9999

| Basic data | Indicators | Company codes | Address | Communication | History |

Company code assignment for profit center

CoCd	Company Name	(assigned)
2000	Company Code US	✓
2100	Company Code US	✓
3000	Company Code DE	✓

Figure 8.12 Dummy Profit Center, Company Codes Assignment

You can see that the company code assignment is locked, and you can't change the definition.

You've learned that when you change or create a profit center, it needs to be activated in EC-PCA. If you aren't creating the profit center within the profit center standard hierarchy, or if you want to activate profit centers separately from the hierarchy maintenance, you can activate inactive profit centers using a specific transaction. Use Transaction KEOA2, or go to PROFIT CENTER ACCOUNTING • MASTER DATA • PROFIT CENTER • ACTIVATE INACTIVE PROFIT CENTERS. Figure 8.13 shows the selection screen.

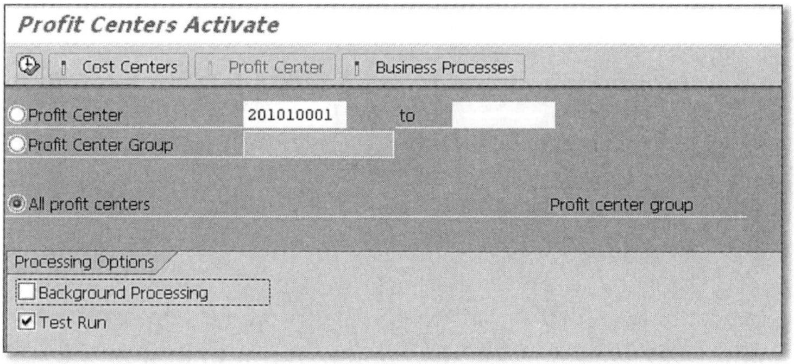

Profit Centers Activate

| Cost Centers | Profit Center | Business Processes |

○ Profit Center 201010001 to
○ Profit Center Group

⦿ All profit centers   Profit center group

Processing Options

☐ Background Processing
☑ Test Run

Figure 8.13 Profit Centers Activate

You can select an individual profit center, a range of profit centers, or a group of profit centers. Options are also available for background processing and test mode. After running the transaction, the system will show which profit centers have been activated, as you can see in the example in Figure 8.14.

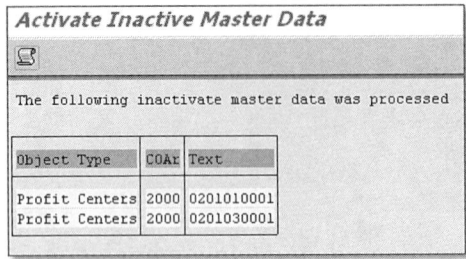

Figure 8.14 Activate Inactive Profit Center Master Data

Every time you make a change in a profit center, the system creates a new version of this profit center, and it will be operational only after you activate it. If for any reason you made a change and want to delete this profit center master data version before you activate it, SAP ERP provides a transaction to perform the deletion. Use Transaction KEOD2, or go to PROFIT CENTER ACCOUNTING • MASTER DATA • PROFIT CENTER • DELETE INACTIVE PROFIT CENTERS. Figure 8.15 shows the selection screen.

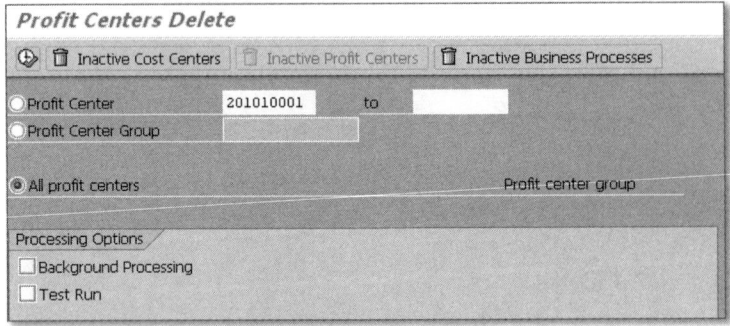

Figure 8.15 Delete Inactive Profit Center

You can enter an individual profit center, a range, or a group, or you can run for all profit inactive centers. After running the transaction, the system shows which profit centers were deleted and the tables involved, as shown in Figure 8.16.

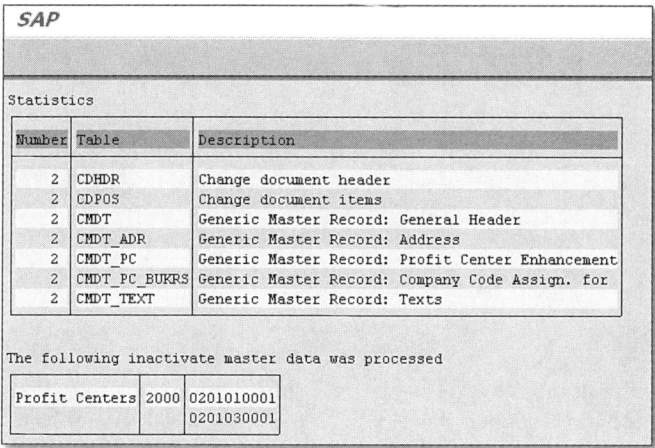

Figure 8.16 Delete Inactive Profit Center, Log

Another helpful tool provided by SAP ERP is to copy a cost center and create it as a profit center. It's used by many organizations where the managers need to view the profit center results in a similar summarization as the cost centers. Use Transaction 2KEV, or go to PROFIT CENTER ACCOUNTING • MASTER DATA • PROFIT CENTER • COPY COST CENTERS, as shown in Figure 8.17.

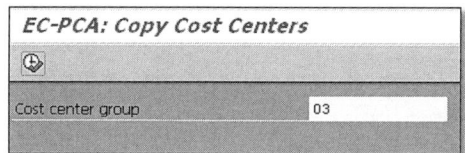

Figure 8.17 EC-PCA Copy Cost Centers

Enter the cost center group, and execute the transaction. Figure 8.18 shows the result.

The system will copy the fields that it finds as reference in the cost center master data. You'll need to maintain fields that are specific to the profit center after the copy. In Figure 8.18, you can see a warning message indicating that the field segment in the profit center master data must be defined.

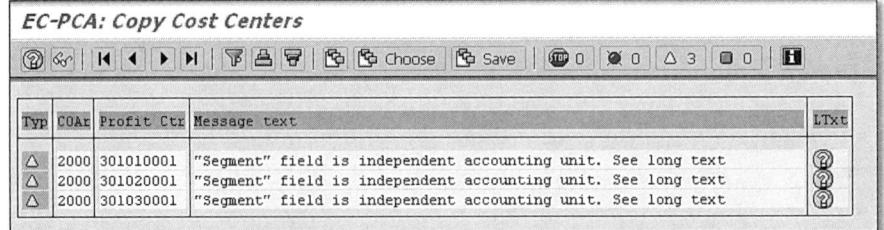

Figure 8.18 EC-PCA Copy Cost Centers, Log

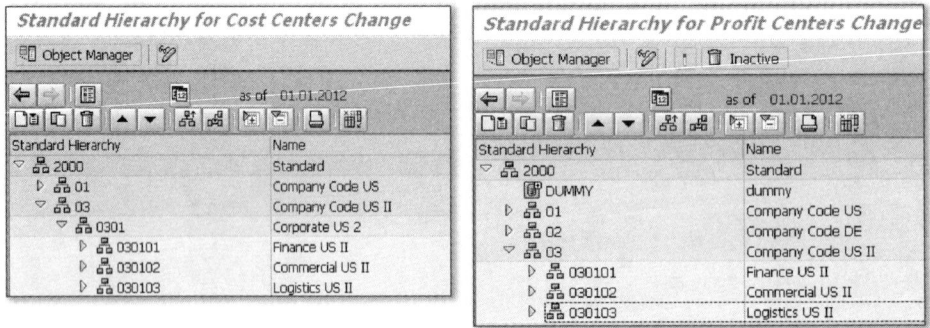

Figure 8.19 Cost Center and Profit Center Standard Hierarchy

In the example in Figure 8.19, the cost center within group 030103 – LOGISTICS US II can be copied as a profit center within the group 030103 – LOGISTICS US II.

In EC-PCA, statistical key figures are available for the same purpose as in CO-CCA. They add information to your profit center analysis in quantities based on a unit you define. Statistical key figures can be used, for instance, to track the number of employees, payroll hours, computers, machine hours, or kilowatt hours (KWH). The statistical key figure definition steps were already described in Chapter 3.

When you post a statistical key figure in a cost center or internal order, for example, it isn't automatically transferred to EC-PCA like the costs are. You must set up the system to automatically transfer the statistical key figures, if desired, and select which ones you want to be transferred. To activate the automatic transfer of statistical key figures from other components to EC-PCA, either use Transaction 3KEG, or go to Profit Center Accounting • Master Data • Statistical Key Figures • Choose Statistical Key Figures. You can see the customizing screen in Figure 8.20.

Figure 8.20 EC-PCA Statistical Key Figure, Transfer Setup

You can either copy or create a new entry. You must select the object type, the statistical key figure, or range of statistical key figures. The following are the available object types:

► HP: Cost Object

► KS: Cost Center

► NP: Network

► NV: Network Activity

► OR: Order

► PR: WBS Element

► VB: Sales Document

► BP: Business Process

► IW: Business Entity

► IV: Lease-Out

► IS: General Lease-Out

► IM: Rental Unit

► IG: Property

▶ IC: MANAGEMENT CONTRACT

▶ IB: BUILDINGS

▶ IA: SETTLEMENT UNIT

The customizing example shown in Figure 8.20 means that for every posting in the statistical key figure HEAD, the system will also post in EC-PCA in the profit center assigned to the cost center.

You've learned how to set up and maintain the profit center master data, so now you can move on to the next topic: assignments of account assignment objects to profit centers.

8.3 Assignments of Account Assignment Objects to Profit Centers

The assignment of a profit center to objects of profit, such as cost centers, materials, internal orders, production orders, or fixed assets, ensures that postings containing these objects will be transferred to EC-PCA in the correct profit center. A posting without a profit center in an account relevant for EC-PCA will be transferred to EC-PCA in the dummy profit center, requiring further action to clear the dummy profit center balance.

Figure 8.21 shows which objects can be assigned to a profit center.

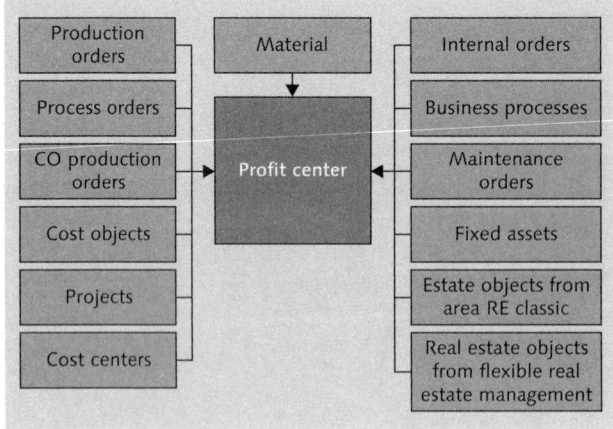

Figure 8.21 Profit Center Object Assignments

When you assign a profit center to a material in the master data, all movements related to this material will carry this profit center, and it will also derive the profit center for the production orders, process orders, CO production orders, and cost objects that contain this material. Other assignments, for example in fixed assets, are determined indirectly and the system determines the profit center by looking to the profit center assigned to the cost center in the asset master data.

The profit center assignments in these objects are maintained in the master data change transactions. The following list offers change transactions for each case:

- CO02: Assign PP Production Orders
- COR2: Assign Process Orders
- COR3: Assign CO Production Orders
- KKP2: Assign Cost Objects
- CJ07: Assign Projects
- KS02: Assign Cost Center
- KO02: Assign Internal Orders
- CP02: Assign Business Processes
- IW32: Assign Maintenance Orders
- AS02: Assign Fixed Assets
- FO62: Assign Real Estate Objects from Area RE Classic

> **Note**
>
> Most of the assignments can be made only at the time of the creation of the master data, or if the master data has no balance. For example, you can't change a profit center for a material that has an inventory balance. You first need to remove the inventory, clear all open purchase orders, and close all production orders for this material to be able to change the profit center assignment in the master data.

8.4 Transfer Prices

The transfer price is probably one of the most important functionalities of EC-PCA. Combined with the ability to create balance sheet and P&L statements by business, the transfer price allows you to measure profit between businesses inside the same organization.

For example, when a product from profit center A is transferred to profit center B, it should show as a transfer for statutory accounting purposes; a profit should normally not be shown as an increase in value in the balance sheet. However, from a business management perspective, profit center A and profit center B may be in different business units and therefore may need to show the profit of the internal transfer in the P&L statement. Transfer price functionality can bridge this gap, by automatically adding the cost and revenues between businesses for management reporting. In this way, you can have both types of financial analysis available within the system and meet both management and statutory reporting needs.

EC-PCA provides up to three different valuation perspectives:

▶ **Legal valuation**
Transfer of products between different profit centers can be valued based on sale prices defined between the trading partners. A profit and loss can be distributed between the trading partners and not seen only in the last profit center of the chain.

▶ **Group valuation**
Transfer of products between different profit centers will use the product cost, so no profit is measured between businesses, and it isn't possible to change the transfer price.

▶ **Profit center valuation**
Transfer of products between different profit centers can be done using a transfer price defined for the profit centers, and a profit and loss between the profit centers can be recorded.

These valuation perspectives are illustrated in Figure 8.22.

These are the steps to establish the multiple valuations in your environment:

1. Maintain the currency and valuation profile.
2. Create valuation versions.
3. Activate the Material Ledger.
4. Set up the EC-PCA transfer price.
5. Create the costing variant for EC-PCA.
6. Activate a multiple valuation approach.

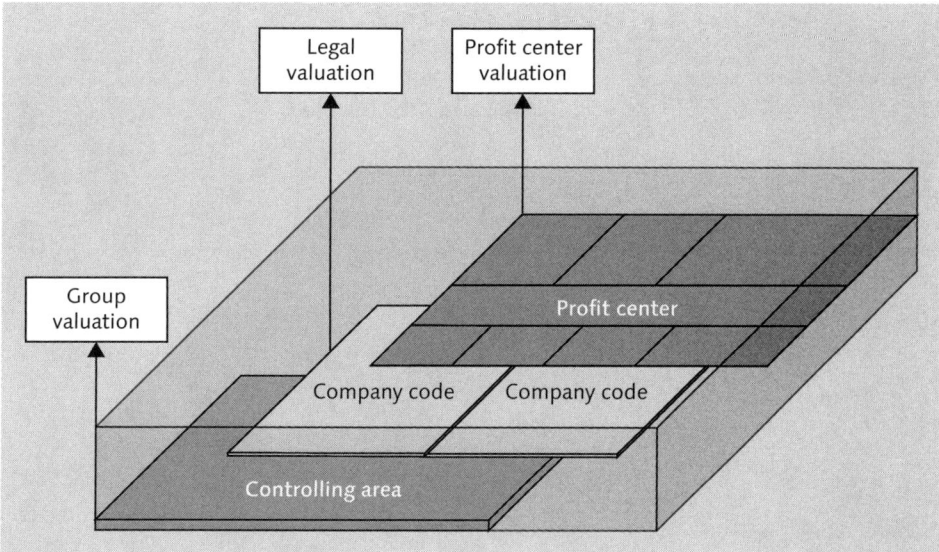

Figure 8.22 EC-PCA Valuation View

Next, you'll see each of the steps in detail.

8.4.1 Maintain Currency and Valuation Profile

In this step, you'll define which currencies and which valuation method you want to be used by the system in the valuation profile. Use Transaction 8KEM, or go to CONTROLLING • GENERAL CONTROLLING • MULTIPLE VALUATION APPROACHES/TRANSFER PRICES • BASIC SETTINGS • MAINTAIN CURRENCY AND VALUATION PROFILE. You can see the customizing screen in Figure 8.23.

Click on NEW ENTRIES, and define the valuation profile. After creating the valuation profile, mark the valuation profile (in the C+V PROF. column) on the right side of the screen, and double-click on DETAILS on the left side of the screen. Figure 8.24 shows the screen to define the currencies and the valuation methods.

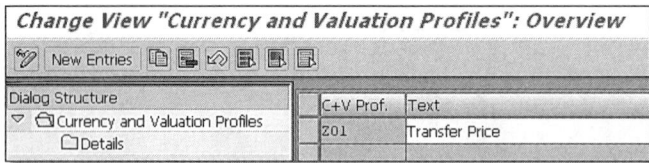

Figure 8.23 Currency and Valuation Profile

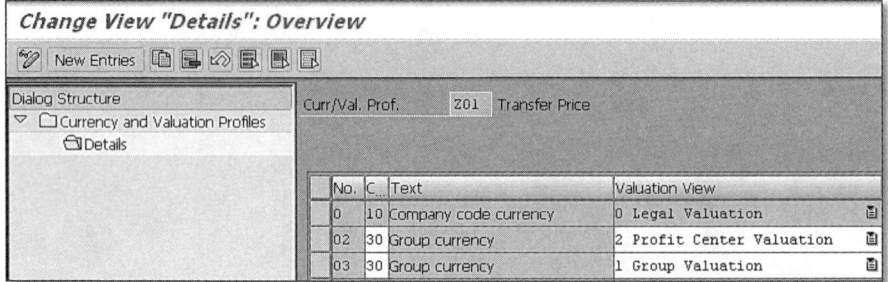

Figure 8.24 Currency and Valuation Profile, Currency Assignment

You can create up to three valuation views (LEGAL VALUATION, PROFIT CENTER VALUATION, and GROUP VALUATION) and use up to two different currencies. Our focus is in the PROFIT CENTER VALUATION.

> **Note**
>
> Depending on the currency settings you defined in the controlling area, you may not be able to activate multiple valuations. Only two currency types are permitted: currency types 10 and 30. The problem with using currency type 10 is that it's impossible to add to your controlling area a new company from another country with a different currency type 10. For this reason, it's strongly advised to use currency type 30 in the controlling area, EC-PCA, and profit center valuation.

After creating the valuation profile, you must assign it to the controlling area by using Transaction 8KEQ or by going to CONTROLLING • GENERAL CONTROLLING • MULTIPLE VALUATION APPROACHES/TRANSFER PRICES • BASIC SETTINGS PRICES • ASSIGN CURRENCY AND VALUATION PROFILE TO CONTROLLING AREA (see Figure 8.25).

In Figure 8.25, you can see that valuation profile Z01 had been assigned to controlling area TP01 – TRANSFER PRICE, which we created just for this example.

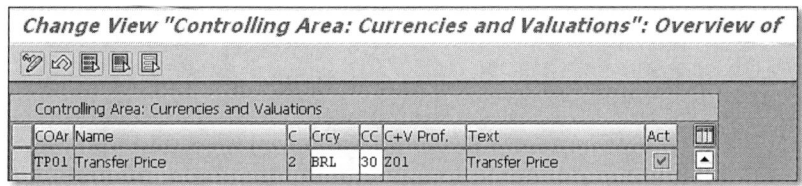

Figure 8.25 Valuation Profile, Controlling Area Assignment

After assigning the valuation profile to the controlling area, you must change the valuation view in EC-PCA basic settings. In Figure 8.2, it had been set as 0 – LEGAL VALUATION; you must change to 2 – PROFIT CENTER VALUATION, as you can see in Figure 8.26. Use Transaction 0KE5 to change the EC-PCA controlling area basic settings.

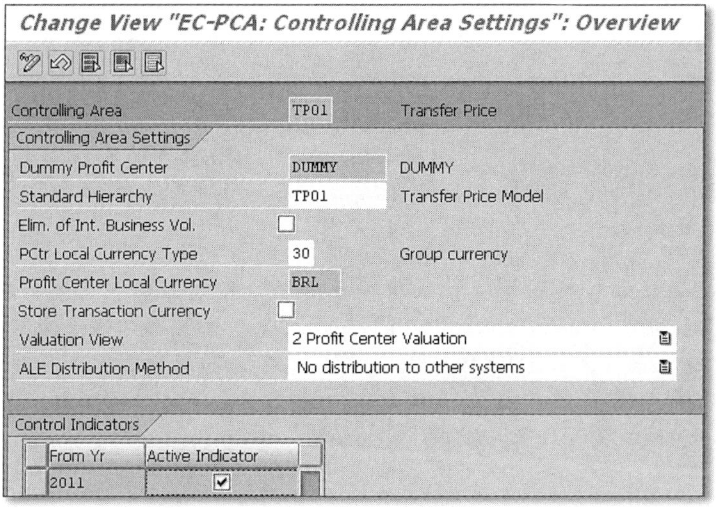

Figure 8.26 EC-PCA Controlling Area Settings

The next step in EC-PCA transfer price customizing is to define a version for the valuation approaches.

8.4.2 Create Versions for Valuation Methods

The parallel valuation approaches are saved in controlling versions. You must create a version for each valuation approach you want to activate.

> **Note**
>
> SAP ERP saves the legal valuation as version 000 by default, and you shouldn't change this. You should instead create a new version for each valuation approach you want to activate.

To create valuation versions, you can use Transaction OKEQ, or go to CONTROLLING • GENERAL CONTROLLING • MULTIPLE VALUATION APPROACHES/TRANSFER PRICES • BASIC SETTINGS PRICES • CREATE VERSIONS FOR VALUATION METHODS. Figure 8.27 shows the screen.

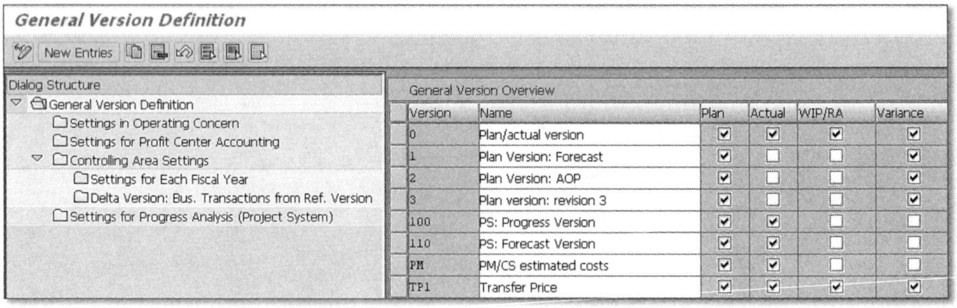

Figure 8.27 Version Maintenance

Create a new version for each valuation view for group or profit center. Remember that version 000 automatically contains the legal view. Mark the version in the right side of the screen, and double-click on SETTINGS FOR PROFIT CENTER ACCOUNTING on the left side of the screen. You'll see the new screen shown in Figure 8.28. We used version TP01 – TRANSFER PRICE for this example.

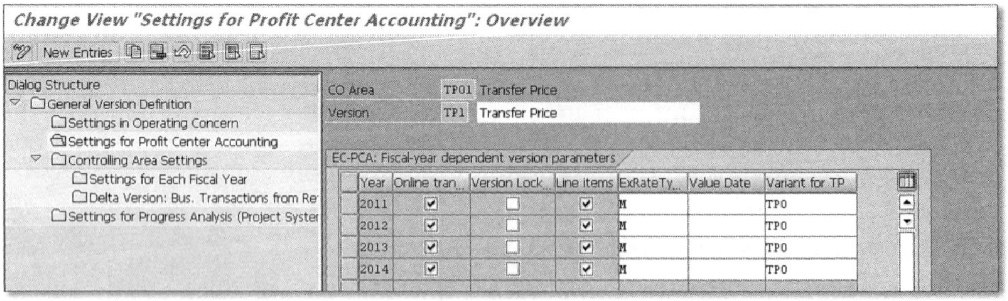

Figure 8.28 Version, Settings for Profit Center Accounting

470

Create an entry for each year, and indicate if it will be online transfer and if it should transfer line items. An important new field to be defined here is the variant for transfer price. To use transfer price functionality, you must select the variant you'll use to value the transfer price. You'll see how to define the variant for transfer price in Section 8.4.4.

You need to create this version in the CONTROLLING AREA SETTINGS. Return to the first screen by clicking on GENERAL VERSION DEFINITION, mark the version, and double-click in CONTROLLING AREA SETTINGS on the left side of the screen. Figure 8.29 shows the screen.

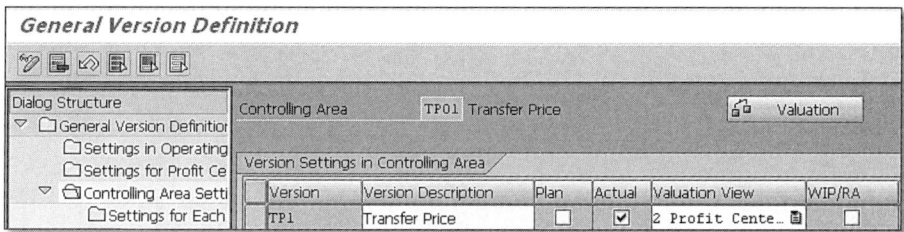

Figure 8.29 Version, Controlling Area Settings

In the VALUATION VIEW field, select 2 PROFIT CENTER VALUATION, mark the version, and expand it for each year by clicking on settings for each year on the left side of the screen (see Figure 8.30).

Change View "Settings for Each Fiscal Year": Overview

Dialog Structure	Controlling Area	TP01	Transfer Price		
▽ General Version Definition	Version	TP1	Transfer Price		
Settings in Operating					
Settings for Profit Ce					
▽ Controlling Area Setti	Version Settings for Each Fiscal Year				
Settings for Each	Year	Version Locked		Integrated Planning	Copying Allowed
Delta Version: Bu	2011	☐		☐	☐
Settings for Progress	2012	☐		☐	☐
	2013	☐		☐	☐
	2014	☐		☐	☐

Figure 8.30 Version, Controlling Area Settings, Year Definition

Click on NEW ENTRIES, and create the version for the year.

The next topic in the valuation approaches is the Material Ledger.

8.4.3 Activate the Material Ledger

You've seen the Material Ledger in Chapter 6, and how it increases your product cost analysis by adding the actual costing functionality.

The Material Ledger is mandatory for the transfer price functionality. You need to activate the Material Ledger for all valuation areas for which you want to use the transfer price.

The Material Ledger will record the inventory values in the legal valuation and also in the profit center valuation. The first step is to activate the Material Ledger for the valuation areas. To activate the Material Ledger, either use Transaction OMX1, or go to CONTROLLING • GENERAL CONTROLLING • MULTIPLE VALUATION APPROACHES/TRANSFER PRICES • BASIC SETTINGS PRICES • CHECK MATERIAL LEDGER SETTINGS • ACTIVATE VALUATION AREAS FOR MATERIAL LEDGER. Figure 8.31 shows the screen.

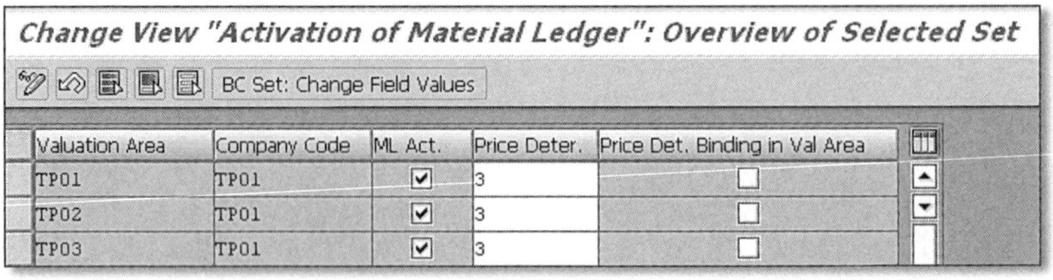

Figure 8.31 Material Ledger Activation Screen

Flag the valuation areas for which you want to activate the Material Ledger. You've already seen the other options for Material Ledger customizing in Chapter 6.

You also need to define the currency type for the Material Ledger. The currency type used for the valuation profile must be the same currency type as used for the Material Ledger. If you've defined only two currency types for the valuation profile, you can add a third currency type to the Material Ledger. To create the currency type for the Material Ledger, either use Transaction OMX2, or go to CONTROLLING • GENERAL CONTROLLING • MULTIPLE VALUATION APPROACHES/TRANSFER PRICES • BASIC SETTINGS PRICES • CHECK MATERIAL LEDGER SETTINGS • ASSIGN CURRENCY TYPES TO MATERIAL LEDGER TYPE. The first customizing screen is shown in Figure 8.32.

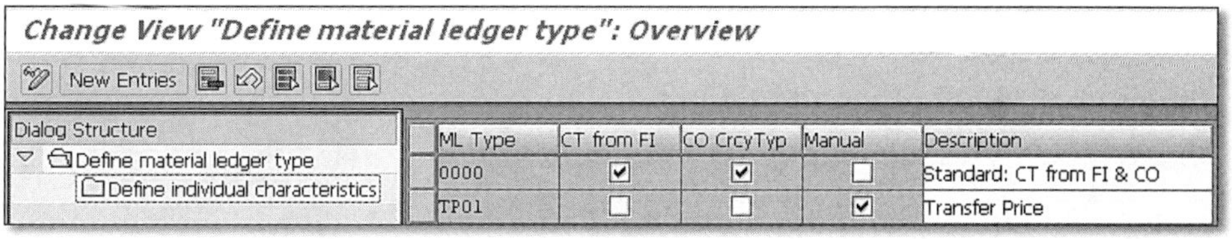

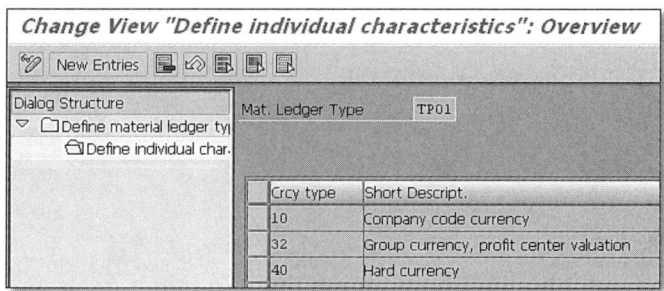

Figure 8.32 Material Ledger Currency Types

Because we've used only two currency types for the valuation profile, we'll define the Material Ledger currency type manually, to demonstrate the possibility to add a third currency to the Material Ledger. We've created the Material Ledger type TP01 marked as MANUAL. By entering "TP01" in the MAT. LEDGER TYPE field and double-clicking in DEFINE INDIVIDUAL CHAR., you can define the currency type for the Material Ledger type, as shown in Figure 8.33.

Figure 8.33 Define Currency Type for Material Ledger Type

SAP ERP brings by default the currency type 10 – COMPANY CODE CURRENCY, and you can't change this setting. You can only define the currency type 32 – GROUP CURRENCY, PROFIT CENTER VALUATION, and a third currency. We've chosen 40 – HARD CURRENCY. Using this customizing, the Material Ledger will be able to show three different currencies.

After defining the currency type in the Material Ledger type, you must assign the valuation areas. To assign the Material Ledger type to the valuation areas, you can use Transaction OMX3, or go to CONTROLLING • GENERAL CONTROLLING • MULTIPLE VALUATION APPROACHES/TRANSFER PRICES • BASIC SETTINGS PRICES • CHECK MATERIAL LEDGER SETTINGS • ASSIGN MATERIAL LEDGER TYPES TO VALUATION AREA. Figure 8.34 shows the customizing screen.

Figure 8.34 Assignment of Material Ledger Types to Valuation Area

After assigning the Material Ledger type to the valuation areas, you've finished the Material Ledger customizing for the multiple valuations approach.

The next step is to set up the transfer price in EC-PCA.

8.4.4 Set Up EC-PCA Transfer Price

In this step, you'll define the basic settings for transfer prices, the accounts for profit and loss between businesses (profit centers), and which movement types should be excluded from the transfer price. This customizing is also mandatory to activate the transfer price.

Basic Settings for Pricing

In the basic settings for transfer pricing, you'll define the conditions types, the pricing procedures, and the transfer price variants. To create the basic settings for transfer price, either use Transaction 8KEZ, or go to CONTROLLING • PROFIT CENTER ACCOUNTING • TRANSFER PRICES • BASIC SETTINGS FOR PRICING, which brings you to Figure 8.35.

You customize three basic settings for the transfer price based on conditions in the screen shown in Figure 8.35:

► CONDITION TYPES

► PRICING PROCEDURES

► TRANSFER PRICE VARIANTS

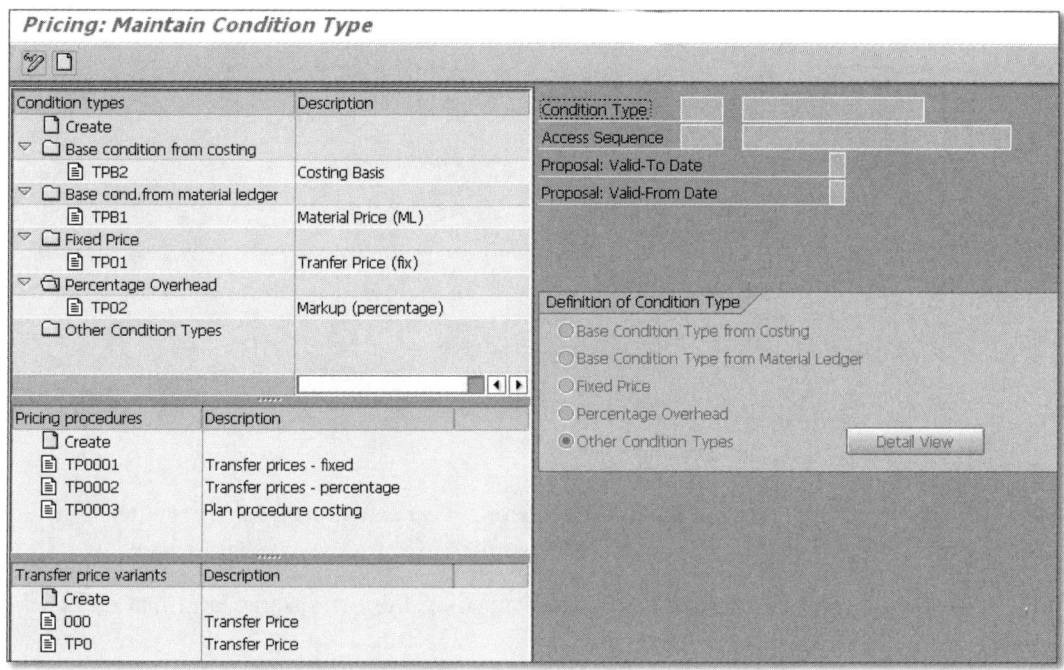

Figure 8.35 Transfer Price Basic Settings

Condition Types

In the CONDITION TYPES section, you define the dependencies for the transfer price. You can choose from five different condition types:

▶ BASE CONDITION FROM COSTING

▶ BASE COND. FROM MATERIAL LEDGER

▶ FIXED PRICE

▶ PERCENTAGE OVERHEAD

▶ OTHER CONDITION TYPES

SAP ERP provides four predefined condition types, and you can also define your own by clicking on CREATE in the CONDITION TYPES section on the left side of the screen, which brings you to the condition definition screen shown in Figure 8.36.

Choose which will be the access sequence for the condition and which kind of condition in the CONDITION TYPE field.

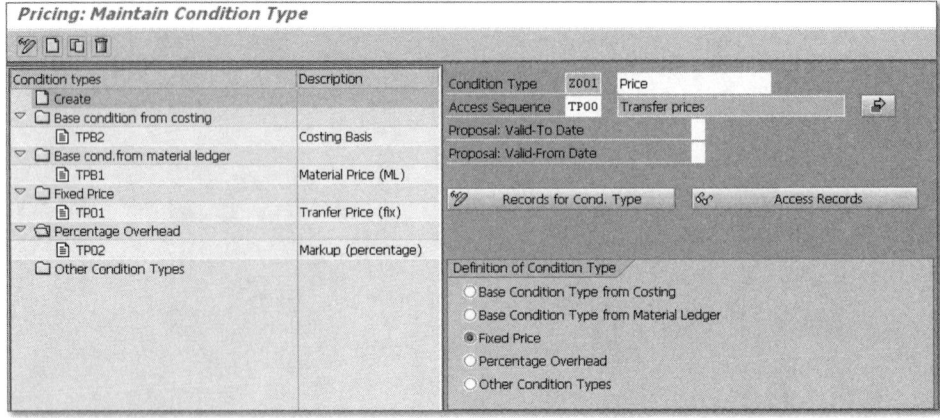

Figure 8.36 Maintain Condition Type

For the conditions set as base conditions, you can't maintain the values, and the system will pick up the cost from costing or from the Material Ledger.

For the other condition types, after defining the condition, you must create the pricing procedures.

Pricing Procedures

SAP ERP provides three predefined pricing procedures. To create a new one, click on CREATE in PRICE PROCEDURES on the left side of the screen. The definition screen is shown in Figure 8.37.

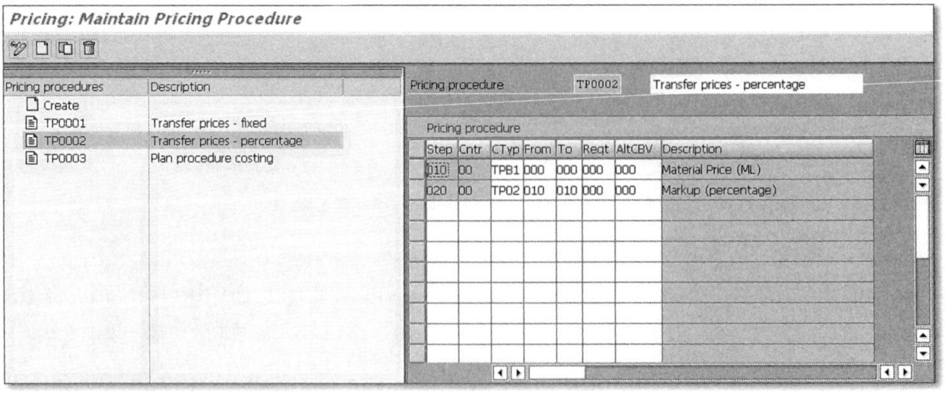

Figure 8.37 Pricing Procedures

The pricing procedure creation process is similar to the costing sheet definition you learned about in CO-PA planning in Chapter 7. You define the first line, which condition type will be applied, and, if there are more lines to be added, you continue to add referencing in the FROM and TO fields to determine to which line the condition should be applied. For each line in the pricing procedure, the system will create a value to be added to the transfer price.

Price Variant

The last definition in the basic settings for transfer price is to create the transfer price variant. Click on CREATE in the TRANSFER PRICE VARIANTS section on the left side the screen to create the variant. You can see the customizing screen in Figure 8.38.

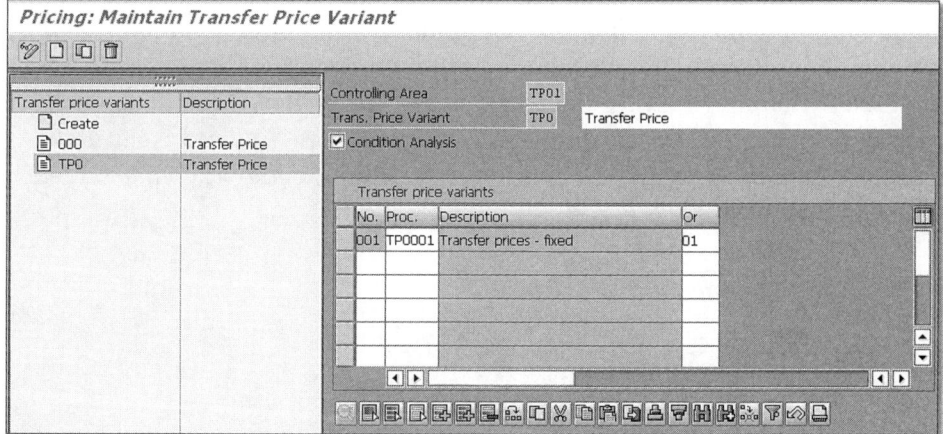

Figure 8.38 Maintain Transfer Price Variant

Define the transfer price variant, and enter which pricing procedure is to be used in the price variant. If you enter more than one, you can enter the sequence in the last field called OR (order).

Note

By flagging the CONDITION ANALYSIS field, the system will open a screen for every posting where the transfer price is called showing how the condition was accessed. It's used only for analysis.

Now that you've defined the price variant, you can add it to the valuation version in the same way as you've already seen in version for valuation methods in Figure 8.28.

Some advanced options for transfer price are also available in SAP ERP, such as creating condition tables, access sequence, and condition exclusion.

Define Price Dependencies (Condition Tables)

Condition tables are used to store the transfer price. In this customizing, you'll define the combination of fields to use to define the price. It can be stored by material, material/plant, or material/plant/profit center, for example. To create the basic settings for transfer price, either use Transaction 8KEA, or go to CONTROLLING • PROFIT CENTER ACCOUNTING • TRANSFER PRICES • ADVANCED SETTINGS FOR PRICING • DEFINE PRICE DEPENDENCIES (CONDITION TABLES). The first screen is shown in Figure 8.39.

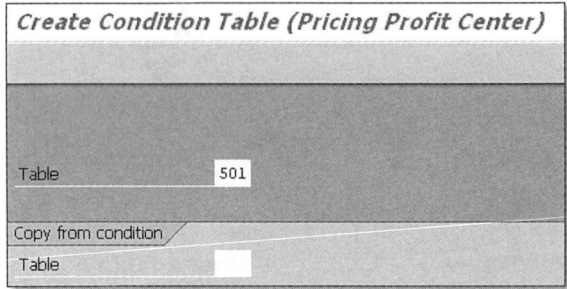

Figure 8.39 Create Condition Table (Transfer Price)

Define the condition table number. It must be in the range from 501 – 999. If you've already defined one condition table, you can use it as a reference for the new one. After you define the table number, the system will open the screen to define which fields are relevant for the table, as shown in Figure 8.40.

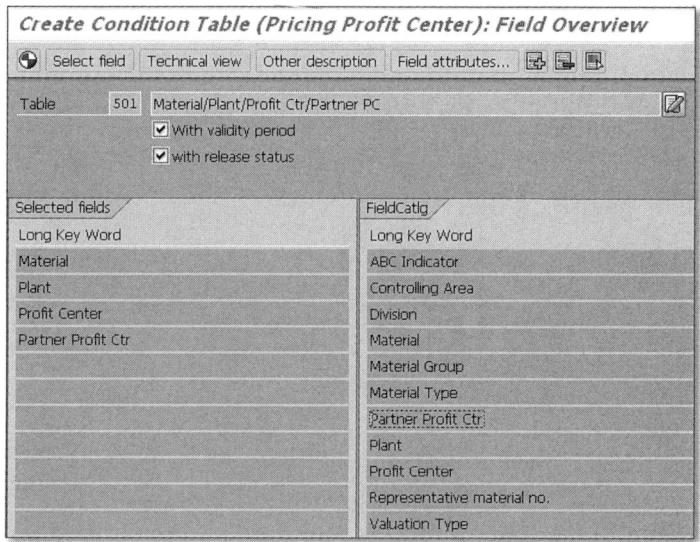

Figure 8.40 Create Condition Table (Transfer Price), Field Overview

In the right side of the screen, you can see the available fields; double-clicking in one of the fields moves it to the left side, indicating now that this field will be used in the condition table. Click on Technical view to define whether the fields selected will be the header or lines when entering values for a price condition that uses this table. The technical view is show in Figure 8.41.

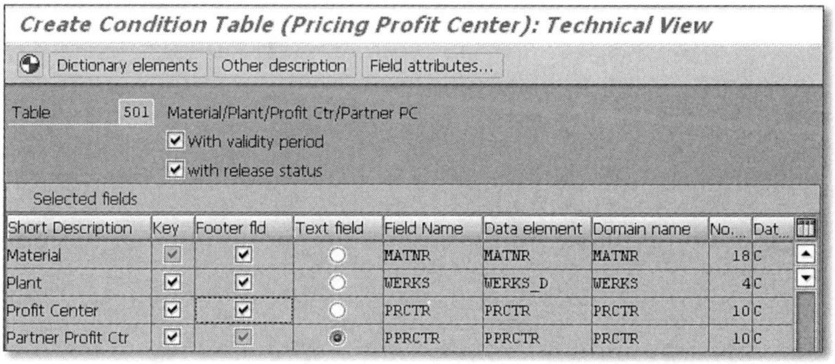

Short Description	Key	Footer fld	Text field	Field Name	Data element	Domain name	No.	Dat.
Material	☑	☑	○	MATNR	MATNR	MATNR	18	C
Plant	☑	☑	○	WERKS	WERKS_D	WERKS	4	C
Profit Center	☑	☑	○	PRCTR	PRCTR	PRCTR	10	C
Partner Profit Ctr	☑	☑	◉	PPRCTR	PPRCTR	PRCTR	10	C

Figure 8.41 Create Condition Table, Technical View

If you mark the FOOTER FLD field, the field will be in the line; if you don't mark it, the field will be in the header.

Activate the condition table, and it's ready to be assigned to an access sequence.

Define Access Sequences

In the access sequences, you'll define which will be the available tables to store the values for a condition type. To define the access sequence, either use Transaction 8KED, or go to CONTROLLING • PROFIT CENTER ACCOUNTING • TRANSFER PRICES • ADVANCED SETTINGS FOR PRICING • DEFINE ACCESS SEQUENCES. The customizing screen is shown in Figure 8.42.

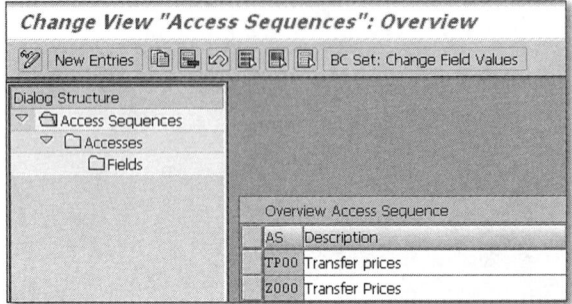

Figure 8.42 Define Access Sequence

Create the access sequence by clicking on NEW ENTRIES, or copy an existing one. SAP ERP provides the access sequence TP00 – TRANSFER PRICES as a default, and we've created a custom one as an example, Z000 – TRANSFER PRICES. After creating the access sequence, mark the access sequence, and double-click on ACCESSES in the left side of the screen, which brings you to Figure 8.43.

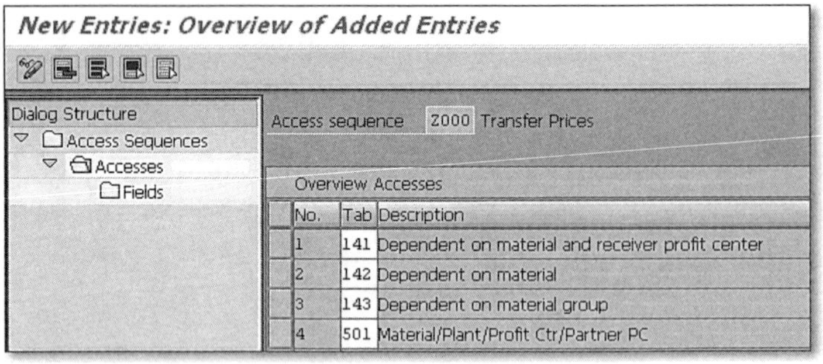

Figure 8.43 Define Access Sequence, Table Assignment

Enter the sequence number and the condition table. After creating the access sequence, you can use it in the condition type definition shown earlier in Figure 8.36.

Next in advanced settings for transfer price, we'll discuss the condition exclusion.

Define Condition Exclusion for Groups of Conditions

You can create a condition exclusion to prevent the system from getting the wrong value for the condition in case more than one record is valid for the document. You need to define an exclusion group, assign the condition type to the exclusion group, and then assign the exclusion group to the pricing procedure. All three steps of the customizing are defined from one screen. Go to CONTROLLING • PROFIT CENTER ACCOUNTING • TRANSFER PRICES • ADVANCED SETTINGS FOR PRICING • DEFINE CONDITION EXCLUSION FOR GROUPS OF CONDITIONS. The selection screen is shown in Figure 8.44.

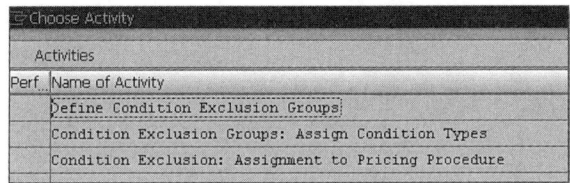

Figure 8.44 Condition Exclusion, Step Definition

First, you need to create the condition exclusion group. Double-click in DEFINE CONDITION EXCLUSION GROUPS, and the customizing screen is shown in Figure 8.45.

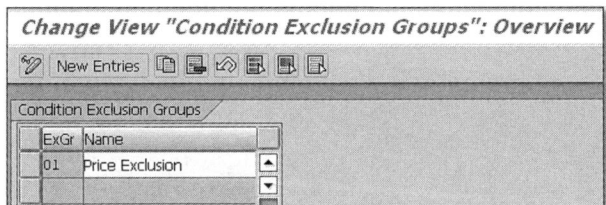

Figure 8.45 Condition Exclusion Groups

Click on NEW ENTRIES, and create the condition exclusion group. After creating the group, return to the screen shown previously in Figure 8.44. For the next step, double-click on CONDITION EXCLUSION GROUPS, ASSIGN CONDITION TYPES. The screen is shown in Figure 8.46.

Enter the condition group and which condition type should be excluded. After saving the assignment, return to the screen in Figure 8.44, and then double-click on CONDITION EXCLUSION: ASSIGNMENT TO PRICING PROCEDURE. You can see the screen in Figure 8.47.

New Entries: Overview of Added Entries
ExGr
Cond.exclusion group
CTyp
Condition Type
01
TPB2

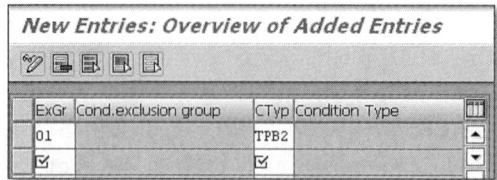

Figure 8.46 Condition Exclusion Groups: Assign Condition Types

Change View "Procedures": Overview
Dialog Structure
Procedures
Exclusion
Procedures
Proc.
ExPrc
Description
TP0001
Transfer prices - fixed
TP0002
Transfer prices - percentage
TP0003
Plan procedure costing

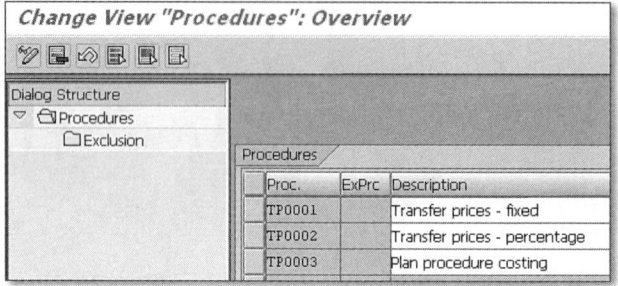

Figure 8.47 Condition Exclusion Assignment to Pricing Procedure

Mark the pricing procedure (Proc.) in the right side of the screen, and double-click on Exclusion in the left side of the screen, as shown in Figure 8.48.

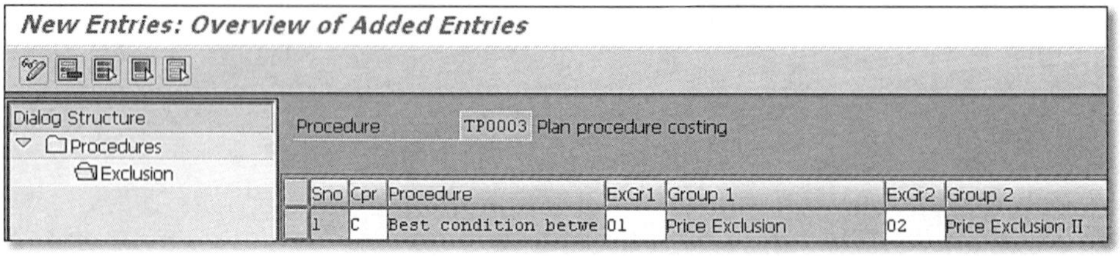

New Entries: Overview of Added Entries
Dialog Structure
Procedures
Exclusion
Procedure
TP0003
Plan procedure costing
Sno
Cpr
Procedure
ExGr1
Group 1
ExGr2
Group 2
1
C
Best condition betwe
01
Price Exclusion
02
Price Exclusion II

Figure 8.48 Condition Exclusion

Enter a sequence number (Sno), the condition exclusion procedure (Cpr), the exclusion group 1, and the exclusion group 2. You can choose from the following options for the condition exclusion procedure:

- A: Best condition between condition types
- B: Best condition within the condition type
- C: Best condition between the two exclusion groups
- D: Exclusive

▸ E: LEAST FAVORABLE WITHIN THE CONDITION TYPE

▸ F: LEAST FAVORABLE BETWEEN THE TWO EXCLUSION GROUPS

▸ L: LEAST FAVORABLE BETWEEN CONDITIONS TYPES

If the system finds one condition type in the document that belongs to the first group, it will remove all conditions from the second group, following the exclusion procedure you defined.

In EC-PCA transfer price, you also need to define the posting logic and the account determination for profit and loss in the transfer price.

Define Account Determination for Internal Goods Movements

When a transfer between profit centers occurs, a sale is made by the sender profit center, and a goods receipt is made by the receiving profit center. You need to define the accounts to be used in the customizing so that is possible to see the value flows in EC-PCA. The original document posting in FI will be unchanged by this definition. Only the EC-PCA values are updated.

You must define three P&L accounts:

▸ Internal revenues

▸ Internal change in stock

▸ Deliveries from profit centers

To define the accounts for EC-PCA internal goods movements, use Transaction 0KEK, or go to CONTROLLING • PROFIT CENTER ACCOUNTING • TRANSFER PRICES • SETTINGS FOR INTERNAL GOODS MOVEMENTS • DEFINE ACCOUNT DETERMINATION FOR INTERNAL GOODS MOVEMENTS. The customizing screen is shown in Figure 8.49.

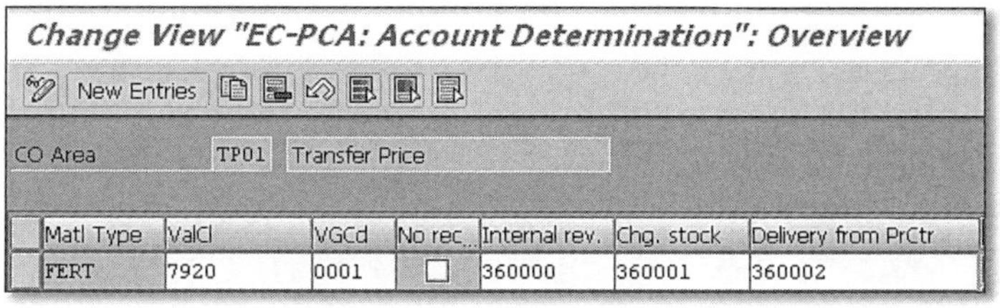

Figure 8.49 EC-PCA Account Determination

483

You can set up the account determination by combinations of these attributes from the material master:

- Material type
- Valuation class
- Valuation group

The first account defined is internal revenues, the second is the change in stock, and the third is delivery from another profit center.

> **Note**
>
> Accounts used in this customizing must be defined as only posting automatically in the account master data.

The same idea is applied to production variances. When a material is produced in one profit center that uses material from different profit centers, you need to define one account to settle the production variances. With this definition, the system will settle the variances to the sender profit center instead of to the receiver. To customize the account determination for production variances for EC-PCA internal goods movements, use Transaction 3KEL, or go to CONTROLLING • PROFIT CENTER ACCOUNTING • TRANSFER PRICES • SETTINGS FOR INTERNAL GOODS MOVEMENTS • DEFINE ACCT DETERMINATION FOR PRODUCTION VARIANCES IN DELIVS TO OTHER PCTRS. The customizing screen is shown in Figure 8.50.

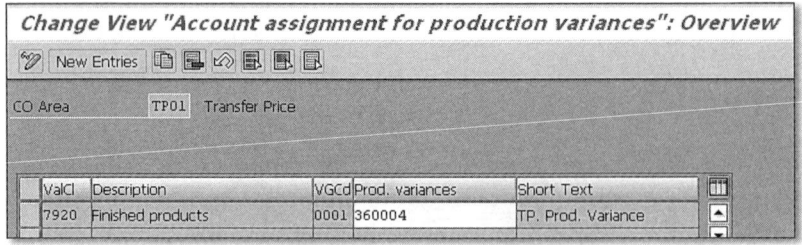

Figure 8.50 Account Determination for Production Variances

The accounts are defined by valuation class and valuation group.

Not all product movements should create a transfer price (for example, a goods transfer within the same profit center). To avoid creating a transfer price for certain movement types, you can create a special handling instruction.

Define Special Handling for Internal Goods Movements

In special handling for internal goods movements, you'll define which movement types aren't relevant for the transfer pricing. To define special handling for internal goods movements, either use Transaction OKEN, or go to CONTROLLING • PROFIT CENTER ACCOUNTING • TRANSFER PRICES • SETTINGS FOR INTERNAL GOODS MOVEMENTS • DEFINE ACCT DETERMINATION FOR DEFINE SPECIAL HANDLING FOR INTERNAL GOODS MOVEMENTS, as shown in Figure 8.51.

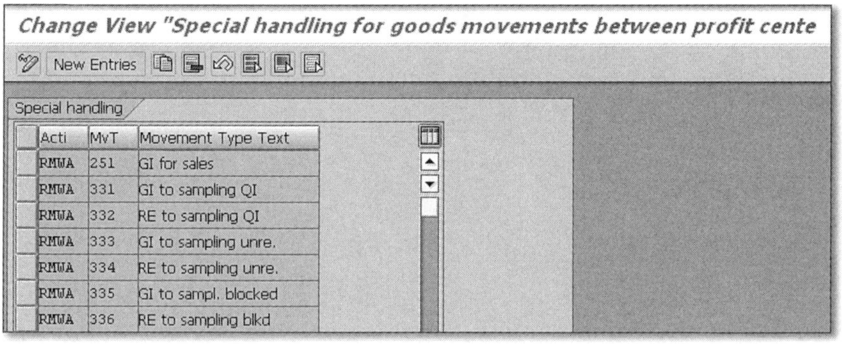

Figure 8.51 Special Handling for Internal Goods Movements

SAP ERP by default delivers the table with all movements that are normally considered not relevant for transfer pricing. You only need to review them, and then you can remove or add new movement types, if needed.

All customizing you've seen up to now relating to EC-PCA transfer price are mandatory to establish the transfer pricing process. In addition to these, you can also customize a different costing variant for the profit center valuation.

8.4.5 Create Costing Variant for EC-PCA

You'll remember from Chapter 6 that it's possible to maintain the costing variant for the three valuation views available: legal, group, and profit center. You've already customized the costing variant for legal valuation purposes. By using a different costing variant for transfer pricing, you can determine a different cost for the profit center valuation, and the Material Ledger will track all movements for the material considering the cost created using this costing variant.

Because you've already created all of the steps for the costing variant in Chapter 6, you'll see here only the difference between the costing variant for legal valuation and for profit center valuation.

First, create a different costing type for profit center valuation. Use Transaction OKKI to create the costing type, as you can see in Figure 8.52.

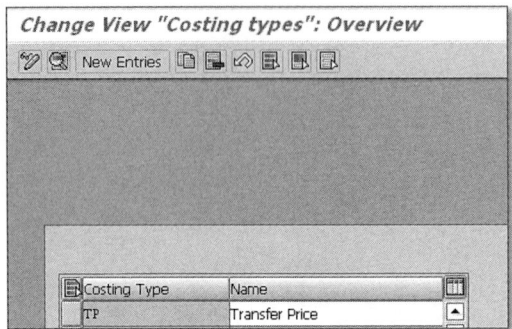

Figure 8.52 EC-PCA Costing Type Definition

Click on NEW ENTRIES to create the new costing type. The definition screen is shown in Figure 8.53.

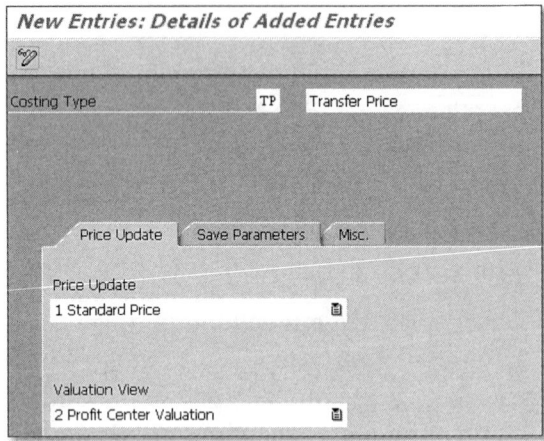

Figure 8.53 EC-PCA Costing Type, Details

Choose to update the STANDARD PRICE, and select PROFIT CENTER VALUATION in the VALUATION VIEW of the costing type details. The other definitions are the same as when you created the standard costing type.

After creating the costing type, you must create a new costing variant, using Transaction OKKN, as shown in Figure 8.54.

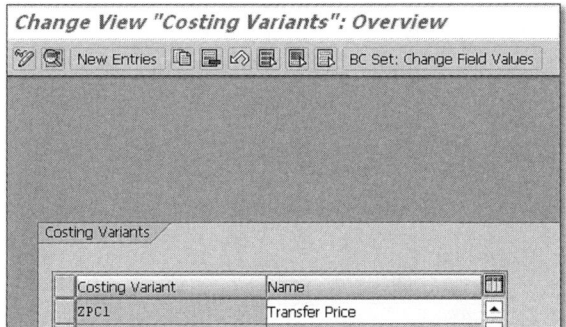

Figure 8.54 EC-PCA Costing Variant

Create a new costing variant by clicking on NEW ENTRIES, which brings you to Figure 8.55.

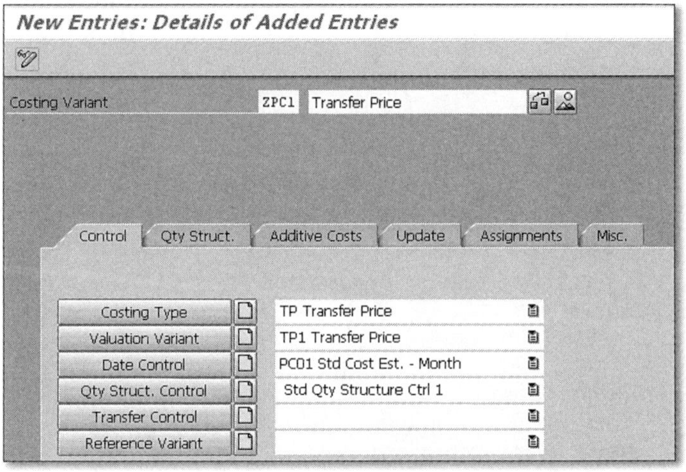

Figure 8.55 EC-PCA Costing Variant, Control Tab

Select the costing type you created for the transfer price, and then move to the UPDATE tab, and make sure the field SAVING ALLOWED is marked as shown in Figure 8.56.

The other tabs are the same as you learned how to customize in Chapter 6, and there is no difference for the transfer price costing variant.

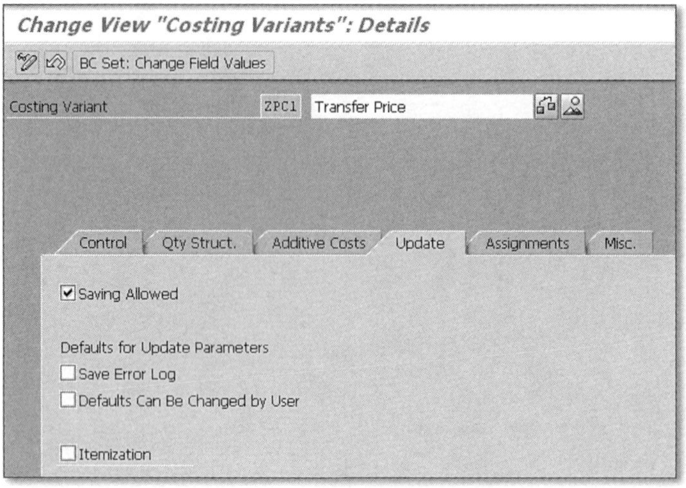

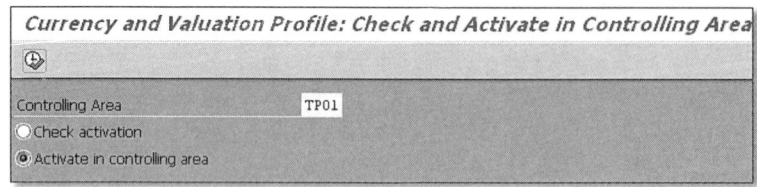

Figure 8.56 EC-PCA Costing Variant, Update Tab

Now that you've created the valuation profiles, defined the currency types, created the version, created the basic and advanced settings for transfer price, and created the costing variant for transfer pricing, it's time to activate the multiple valuation approach in the controlling area.

8.4.6 Activate Multiple Valuation Approach

The activation process is simple. Use Transaction 8KEP, or go to CONTROLLING • GENERAL CONTROLLING • ORGANIZATION • MULTIPLE VALUATION APPROACHES/TRANSFER PRICES • ACTIVATION • MULTIPLE VALUATION APPROACHES: CHECK/EXECUTE ACTIVATION, as shown in Figure 8.57.

Figure 8.57 Activate Multiples Valuation Profile

We recommend that you check the activation to see if there is some missing customizing before activating it in the controlling area. The resulting screen is shown in Figure 8.58.

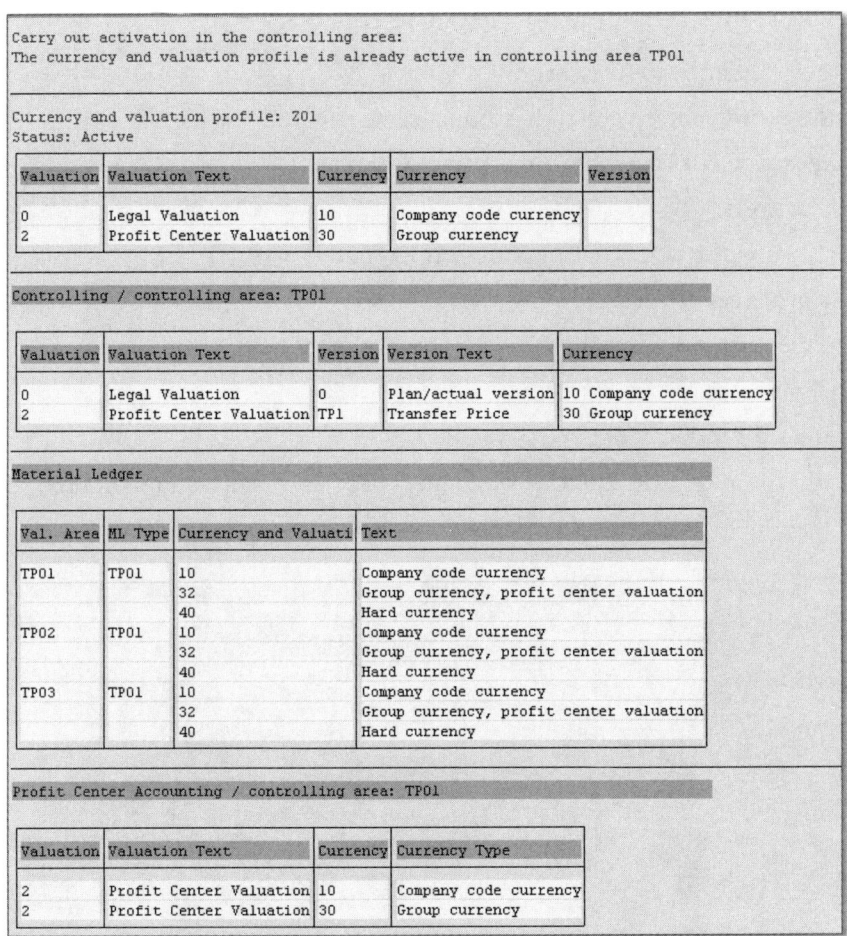

```
Carry out activation in the controlling area:
The currency and valuation profile is already active in controlling area TP01

Currency and valuation profile: Z01
Status: Active
```

Valuation	Valuation Text	Currency	Currency	Version
0	Legal Valuation	10	Company code currency	
2	Profit Center Valuation	30	Group currency	

Controlling / controlling area: TP01

Valuation	Valuation Text	Version	Version Text	Currency
0	Legal Valuation	0	Plan/actual version	10 Company code currency
2	Profit Center Valuation	TP1	Transfer Price	30 Group currency

Material Ledger

Val. Area	ML Type	Currency and Valuati	Text
TP01	TP01	10	Company code currency
		32	Group currency, profit center valuation
		40	Hard currency
TP02	TP01	10	Company code currency
		32	Group currency, profit center valuation
		40	Hard currency
TP03	TP01	10	Company code currency
		32	Group currency, profit center valuation
		40	Hard currency

Profit Center Accounting / controlling area: TP01

Valuation	Valuation Text	Currency	Currency Type
2	Profit Center Valuation	10	Company code currency
2	Profit Center Valuation	30	Group currency

Figure 8.58 Multiple Valuation Approach, Activation Log

You've now completed all of the steps required and activated the multiple valuation approach for the controlling area. Next, let's recap by walking through an example of how the system will now handle the transfer price in a product transfer between two different profit centers.

8.4.7 Transfer Price Example

To help you visualize how all of the customization for transfer pricing works together, we'll now walk through how to create the transaction example and then look at how the results appear in reporting.

The following are the steps to create the example:

1. Create the standard product cost.

2. Create the profit center valuation product cost.

3. Mark the standard and profit center valuation costs.

4. Release the costs.

5. Update the transfer prices for material/profit center.

6. Transfer products between profit centers.

7. Analyze the results.

Create Standard Product Cost

To create the product cost for the standard price, use Transaction CK11N, as shown in Figure 8.59.

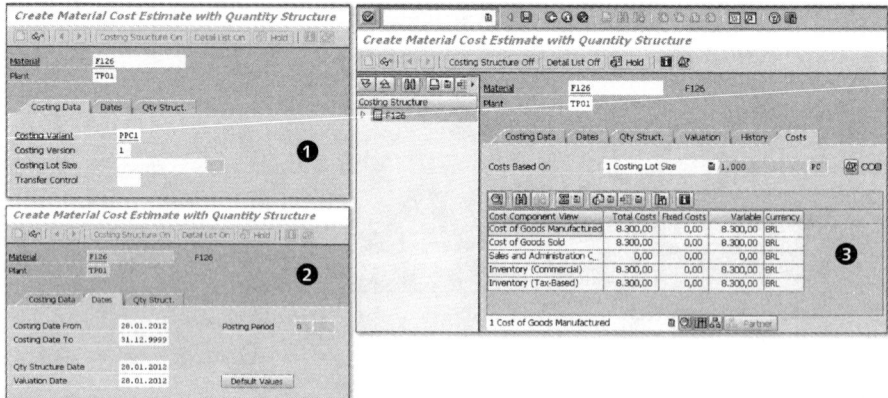

Figure 8.59 Create Standard Cost

In Figure 8.59, you can see that the standard costing variant (❶) was used, and you can see the cost estimate result (❸). This costing variant is used for the legal valuation.

Create Profit Center Valuation Product Cost

Employing the same Transaction CK11N, but now using the costing variant for the profit center valuation, creates the profit center valuation, shown in Figure 8.60.

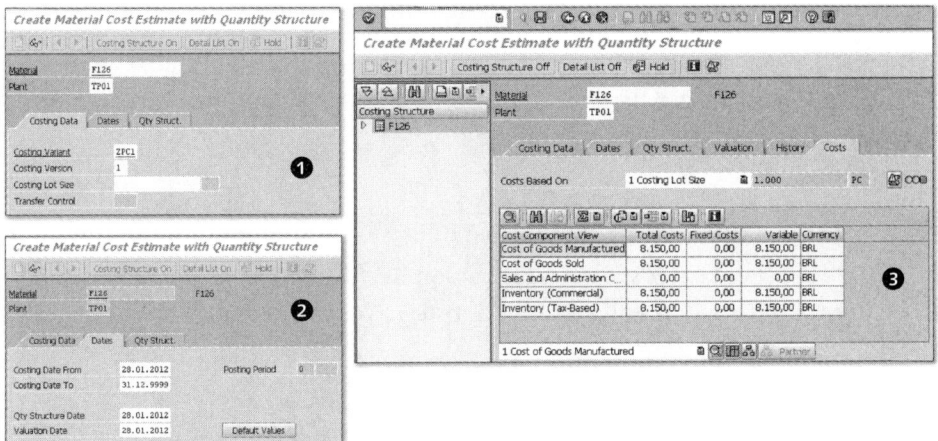

Figure 8.60 Create Profit Center Valuation Costs

In Figure 8.60, you can see that the costing variant for profit center valuation was used (❶), and you can see the cost estimate result (❸). This costing variant is used for the profit center valuation.

Mark Standard and Profit Center Valuation Costs

To mark the costs, use Transaction CK24. The selection screen is shown in Figure 8.61.

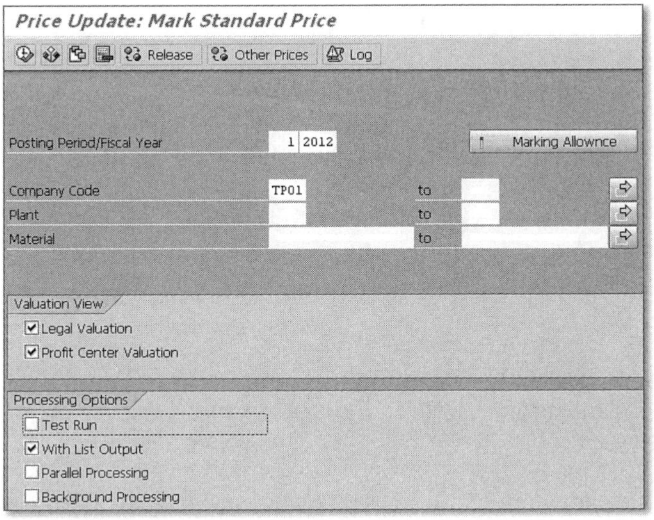

Figure 8.61 Mark Standard Price

Select both valuation views for Legal Valuation and Profit Center Valuation, and execute the transaction.

You've now marked the standard cost for both the legal and profit center valuations, and the next step is to release the costs.

Release Costs

To release the standard costs, use Transaction CKME; its selection screen is shown in Figure 8.62. This step will release the prices from both valuations at the same time.

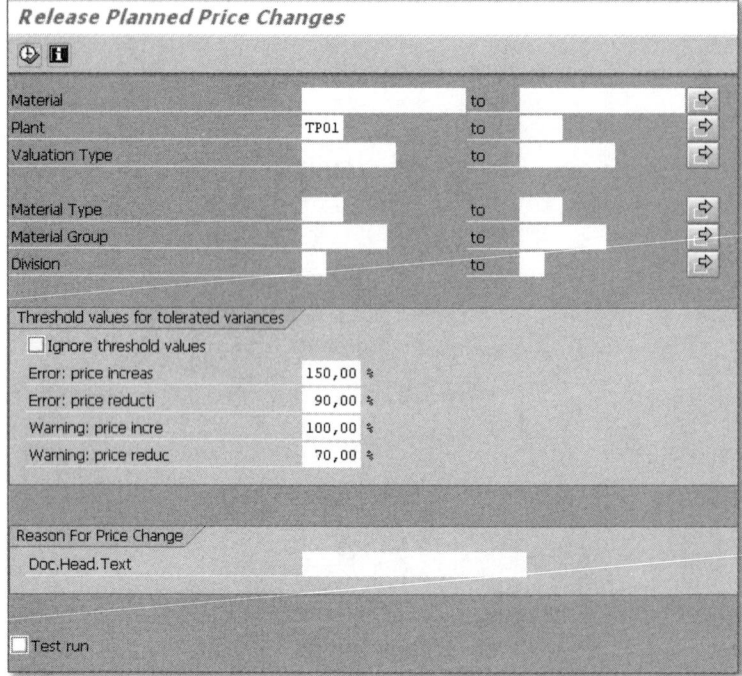

Figure 8.62 Release Planned Prices

Now you can see the prices in the material master data. Use Transaction MM03 to display the material master data, and navigate to the Accounting 1 tab, as shown in Figure 8.63.

You can see in the Accounting 1 tab the three currencies used in the Material Ledger and, consequently, for the multiple valuation approach.

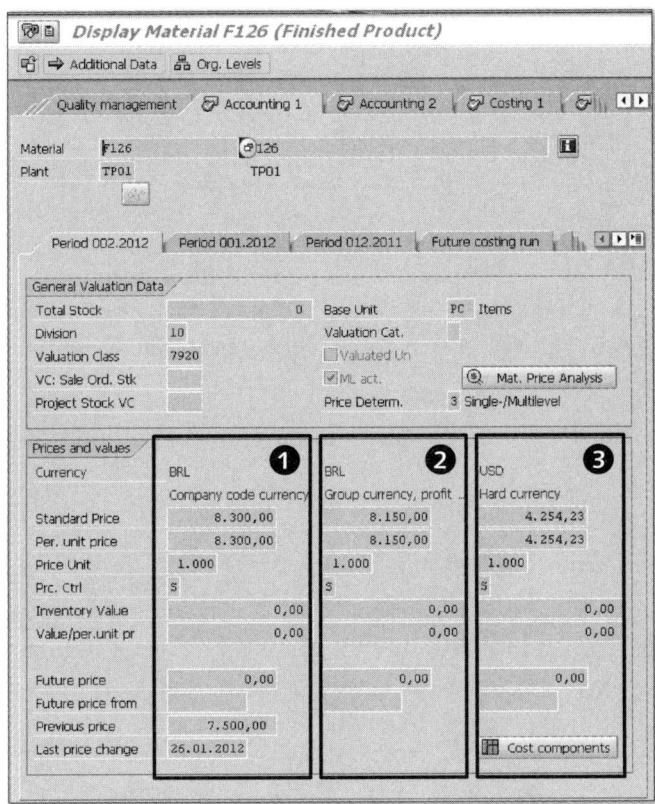

Figure 8.63 Display Material Master Data, Accounting 1 Tab

The legal valuation is represented in (❶); its price had been defined in the standard product cost in Figure 8.59, shown earlier.

The profit center valuation is represented in (❷); its price had been defined in the profit center valuation product cost in Figure 8.60.

The third valuation (which is also legal, but in a hard currency) is represented in (❸) with USD as currency. It's the standard cost (❶) divided by the currency conversion rate.

Next, you'll see how to update the prices for the transfer price.

Update Transfer Prices for Material/Profit Center

To create the transfer prices, use Transaction AKE5, as shown in Figure 8.64.

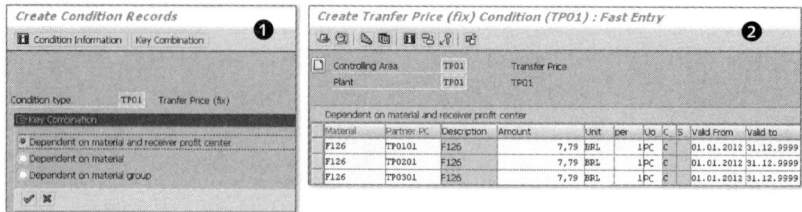

Figure 8.64 Create Transfer Price for Material

In panel (❶) of Figure 8.64, you can see the access sequence for the condition type that you defined earlier in Figure 8.42. In panel (❷), you can see the transfer price entered for the valuation class.

Now you've completed all of the necessary steps to be able to create a goods transfer.

Transfer Products Between Profit Centers

We are using Transaction MB1B and movement type 301. This movement type was not defined in the special handling for internal goods movements in Figure 8.51. Recall that movement types defined for special handling will not result in transfer pricing. You can see the transfer transaction in Figure 8.65.

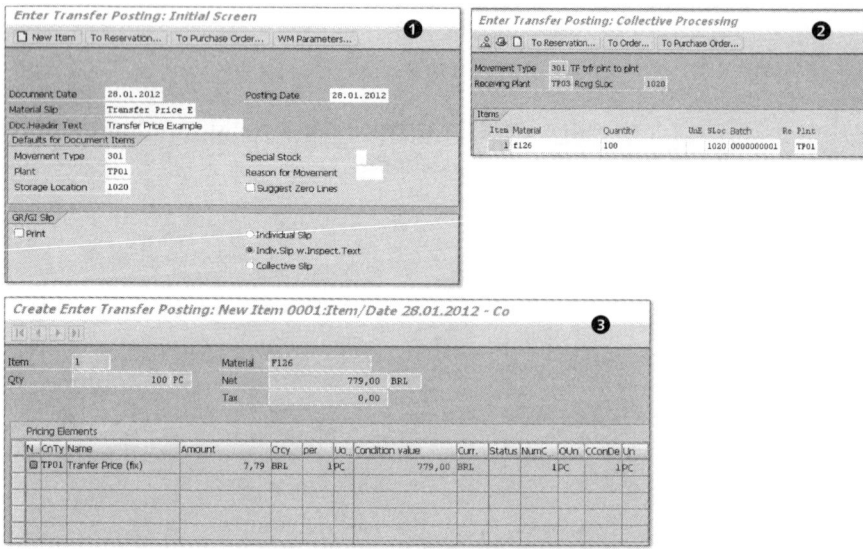

Figure 8.65 Product Transfer

In panel (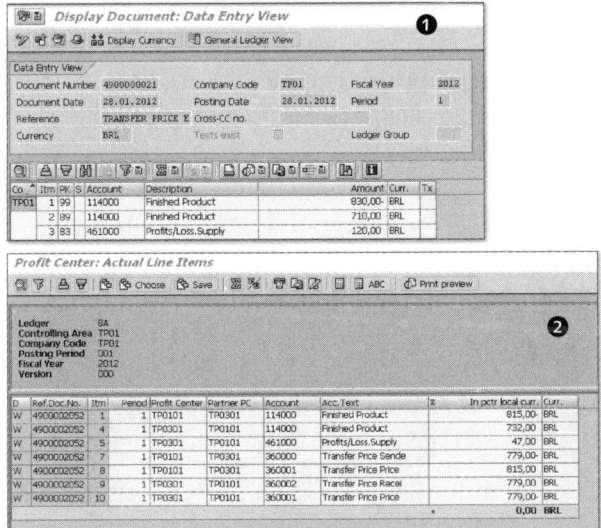❶) of Figure 8.65, you can see the selection screen of Transaction MB1B, where you define the movement type, plant, and storage location for the source of the transfer. In panel (❷), you define the receiver plant, the material to be transferred, and the quantity.

When you defined the price variant previously in Figure 8.38, the field condition analysis was available to select. If you marked the field, the screen in panel (❸) will be displayed during the posting that shows which condition was accessed by the system and its values.

After you save, all valuation views are updated by the system. Now let's look at the analysis.

Analyze the Results

First, let's view both the FI document and the EC-PCA document for the transfer that we just posted. Figure 8.66 shows both documents.

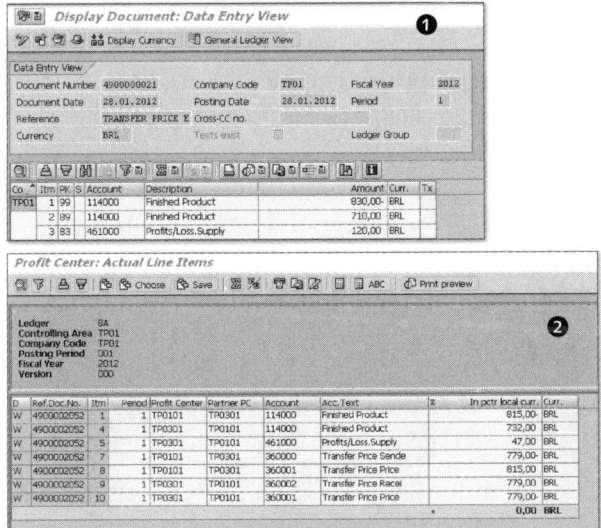

Figure 8.66 FI versus EC-PCA Document, Transfer Price

Panel (❶) shows the FI document using the legal valuation approach, where the transfer of products was made considering the standard price for the material in both plants, and the difference between the standard prices posts to the profit/loss supply account.

Panel (❷) shows the EC-PCA document using the profit center valuation approach. By comparing both documents, you can see that the system didn't use the legal valuation to perform the transfer. Also, the EC-PCA document posted in some additional accounts not included in the FI document.

In the first three lines, the postings are the same accounts as in the FI document, but you can see that the amounts are based on the profit center valuation cost estimate.

In ACCOUNT 360000 – TRANSFER PRICE SENDER, the system posted the internal revenue in the sender profit center using the transfer pricing determined in the customizing.

In ACCOUNT 360001 – TRANSFER PRICE, the system posted a debit in the sender profit center (representing the COGS) and a credit in the receiver profit center using the values from the transfer price determination.

In ACCOUNT 360002 – TRANSFER PRICE RECEIVER, the system posted the values in the receiver profit center for deliveries from other profit centers valued at the transfer price.

Another excellent analysis is the material price analysis (Transaction CKM3N) where you can see the value flows from the materials in the Material Ledger.

The legal valuation is shown in Figure 8.67.

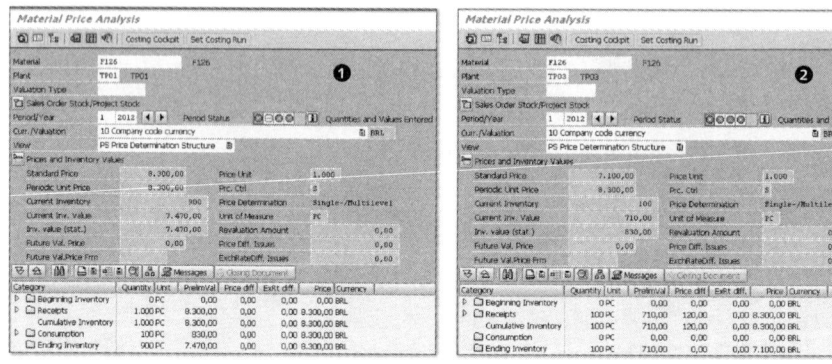

Figure 8.67 Material Price Analysis, Legal Valuation

Panel (❶) represents the sender plant. On the CONSUMPTION line, you can see consumption of 100 PC valuated at BRL 830.00 (standard price in company code currency, which is the Brazilian real).

Panel (❷) represents the receiver plant. The RECEIPTS line shows a 100 PC valuated as BRL 710.00 (standard price) + 120.00 (price difference), totaling BRL 830.00. In this case, a legal valuation approach had been used where a transfer was valued the same in both plants.

The profit center valuation is shown in Figure 8.68.

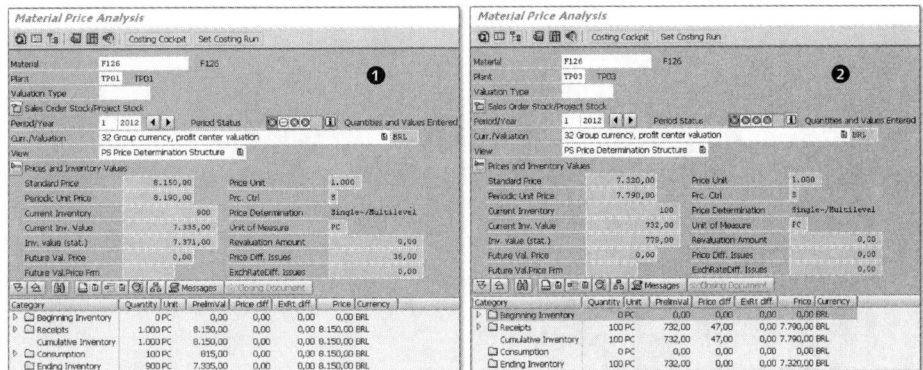

Figure 8.68 Material Price Analysis, Profit Center Valuation

Panel (❶) represents the sender plant. On the CONSUMPTION line, you can see consumption of 100 PC valuated as BRL 815.00 (profit center valuation product cost).

Panel (❷) represents the receiver plant. The RECEIPTS line shows 100 PC valuated as BRL 732.00 (profit center valuation product cost) + 47.00 (price difference), totaling BRL 779.00, the transfer price value. In this case, a profit center valuation was been used, and you can see that the product cost behaves as a sale.

> **Note**
>
> Before activating a transfer price in a live system, you need to analyze the possible effects to your system and carefully consider all of the existing customizations in your system. Also check for applicability in your situation, and consider the available information in SAP Note 120380 (Subsequent activation of multiple valuation approach), SAP Note 119428 (Controlling area: Currency type 20 or 30), SAP Note 120826 (Assignment of new company codes for currency type 10), SAP Note 122902 (TP: Assignment valuation to version), and SAP Note 122008 (Activate transfer prices/mult. valuation approaches). Additionally, because transfer pricing can be very difficult to deactivate after it's activated, the decision to activate this functionality should be carefully considered.

Next in EC-PCA, you'll learn how about the planning customizing.

8.5   Planning

The planning customizing in EC-PCA is very similar to the CO-OM-CCA planning customizing. EC-PCA planning can be transferred from other components in the same manner as the actual data, or you can manually plan the revenues/expenses.

Figure 8.69 shows how the planning in other components can be integrated with EC-PCA planning.

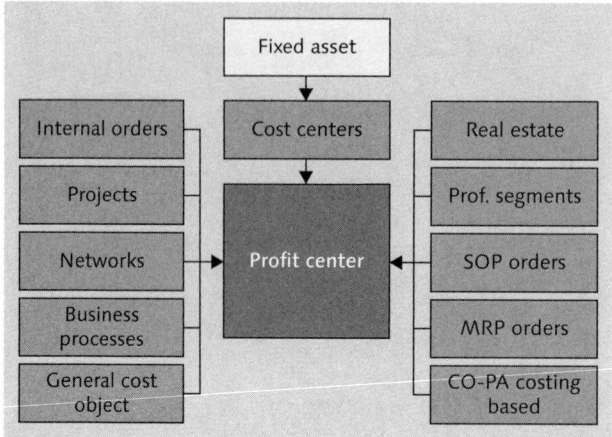

Figure 8.69 EC-PCA Automatic Planning

All objects assigned to a profit center can have their planning transferred to EC-PCA. The fixed asset depreciation planning is not automatically transferred to EC-PCA, but since the fixed asset master data is linked to a cost center, after you've planned the depreciation in the cost centers, you can transfer the depreciation planning to EC-PCA from CO-CCA.

The following are the areas to customize for EC-PCA planning:

1. Define the basic settings for planning.
2. Define the planning layouts and planning profiles for manual planning.
3. Establish the settings for formula planning.
4. Define the settings for plan data transfer from other SAP ERP areas.
5. Customize planning allocations.

Because these are the same areas you've already addressed to customize planning in other CO subcomponents, we'll review those that you've already seen, and only cover in detail the additional items in these areas that need to be customized specifically for EC-PCA.

8.5.1 Basic Settings for Planning

The definitions to be made in the basic settings for EC-PCA planning are the same as you've already done in Chapter 3 and also previously in this chapter.

In Chapter 3, you defined the exchange rate type and the exchange rates for planning. You also learned how to create a planning version to be used in CO-CCA. In this chapter, you've already learned how to extend the planning version to EC-PCA (review Figure 8.4 and Figure 8.5).

If, by mistake, you change the LINE ITEMS flag in Figure 8.5 in the version maintenance, and you have part of the planning recorded with line items and part without line items, you can check the consistency of the total and line items planning tables by using the Transaction KEE0 or by going to CONTROLLING • PROFIT CENTER ACCOUNTING • PLANNING • PLAN VERSIONS • ADJUST LINE ITEMS AND TOTALS RECORDS. The outcome of these steps is shown in Figure 8.70.

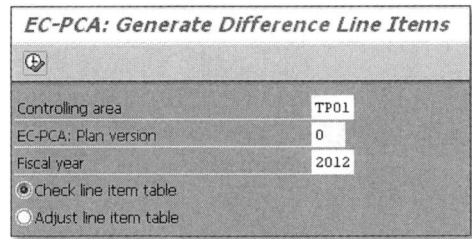

Figure 8.70 Generate Difference Line Items

You can either check or correct the table from this screen. Enter the controlling area, EC-PCA planning version, and the fiscal year. You can see the result in Figure 8.71.

If the system finds an error in the check, run the program again to fix the line item table.

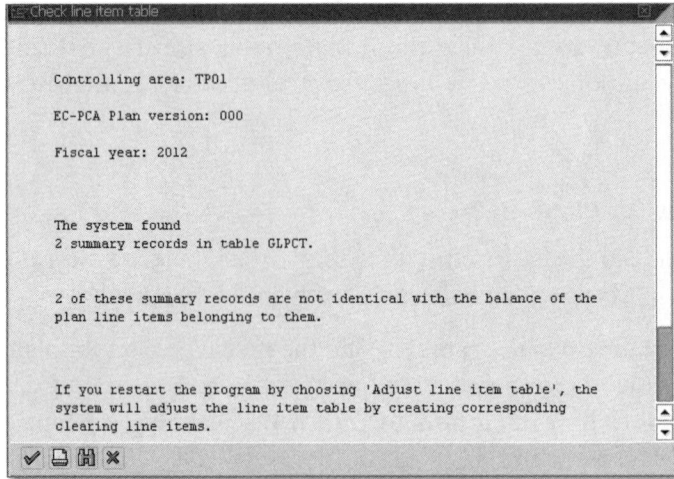

Figure 8.71 Generate Difference Line Items, Log

8.5.2 Manual Planning

In the manual planning step, you'll define the planning layouts and planning profiles for EC-PCA planning. You've already created planning layouts in Chapter 3, and the process is similar in EC-PCA.

Use Transaction 7KEA to create planning layouts for EC-PCA cost and revenues planning, use Transaction 7KEF to create planning layouts for balance sheet accounts, and use Transaction 7KEK for EC-PCA statistical key figures planning. To maintain the planning profiles for EC-PCA, use Transaction KP34.

8.5.3 Formula Planning

Template allocation is also available for EC-PCA planning. You've seen how to maintain the templates in Chapter 5 and Chapter 6. The template definition process is the same for EC-PCA; you only need to select the PCA – PROFIT CENTER planning environment.

8.5.4 Plan Data Transfer

For plan data transfer, you can customize how planned values in CO-PA will be transferred to EC-PCA and also which data you want to transfer from other objects to EC-PCA.

The first customizing step to link the CO-PA planning to EC-PCA planning is to define which CO-PA value fields should be transferred to EC-PCA with an opposite sign from what it has in CO-PA. Use Transaction KESF, or go to CONTROLLING • PROFIT CENTER ACCOUNTING • PLANNING • PLAN DATA TRANSFER • TRANSFER OF PLAN DATA FROM COSTING-BASED CO-PA • MAINTAIN +/− SIGN RULES, as shown in Figure 8.72.

Figure 8.72 EC-PCA Sign Changes for CO-PA Planning Integration

Click on NEW ENTRIES, and enter the CO-PA value field that you want to change the sign for when transferring to EC-PCA.

The next customizing step for EC-PCA and CO-PA planning integration is to assign the accounts to the CO-PA value fields. Use Transaction KEDP, or go to CONTROLLING • PROFIT CENTER ACCOUNTING • PLANNING • PLAN DATA TRANSFER • TRANSFER OF PLAN DATA FROM COSTING-BASED CO-PA • MAINTAIN ACCOUNT DETERMINATION, as shown in Figure 8.73.

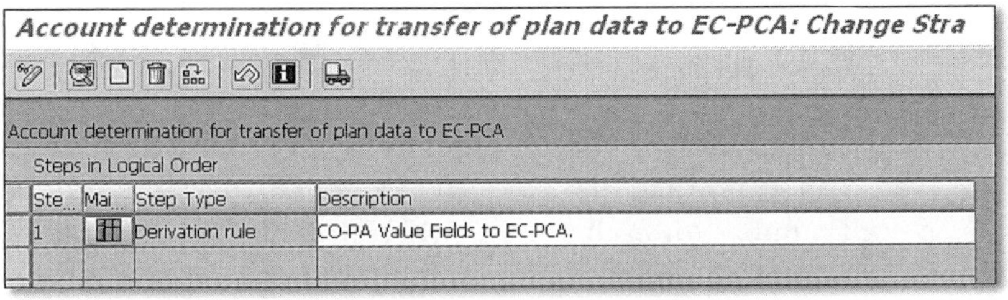

Account determination for transfer of plan data to EC-PCA: Change Stra			
Account determination for transfer of plan data to EC-PCA			
Steps in Logical Order			
Ste...	Mai...	Step Type	Description
1		Derivation rule	CO-PA Value Fields to EC-PCA.

Figure 8.73 Account Determination for EC-PCA Transfer from CO-PA

The account determination is defined by a derivation process, similar to derivations in CO-PA. Click on NEW ENTRIES to define a new derivation rule, which brings you to Figure 8.74.

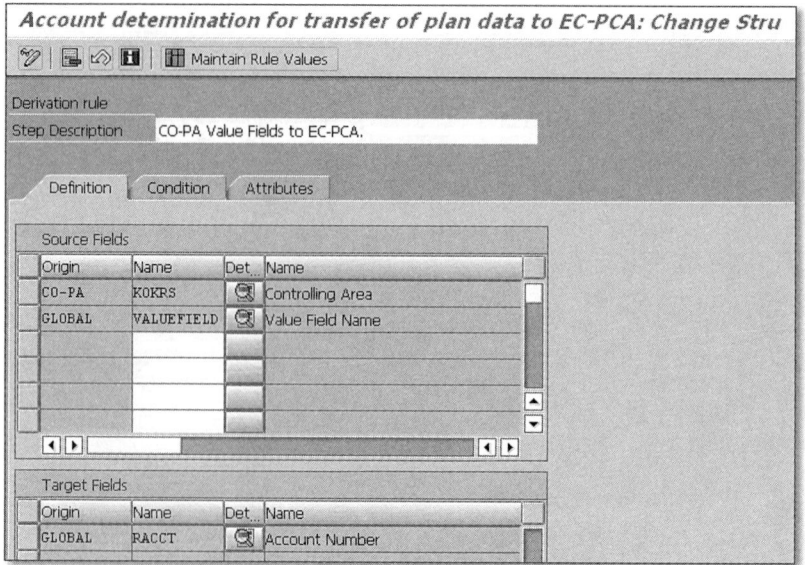

Figure 8.74 Account Determination for EC-PCA Transfer from CO-PA

Select the source value field, and click on MAINTAIN RULES VALUES. Figure 8.75 shows the assignment.

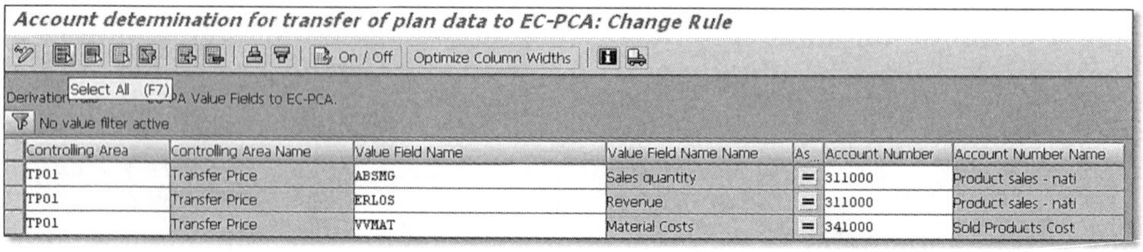

Figure 8.75 EC-PCA Transfer from CO-PA, Change Rule

Fill in the value fields you've selected in the screen in Figure 8.74 as sources, and then fill in the account number for each to be transferred to in EC-PCA. This list of value fields will be the selection criteria for the CO-PA plan data transfer.

After finishing this step, the customizing for transfer CO-PA values to EC-PCA is complete. You can see one report example in Figure 8.76 after a CO-PA planning transfer to EC-PCA. Report S_ALR_87009712 – Profit Center List: Plan/Actual was used to display the planning results.

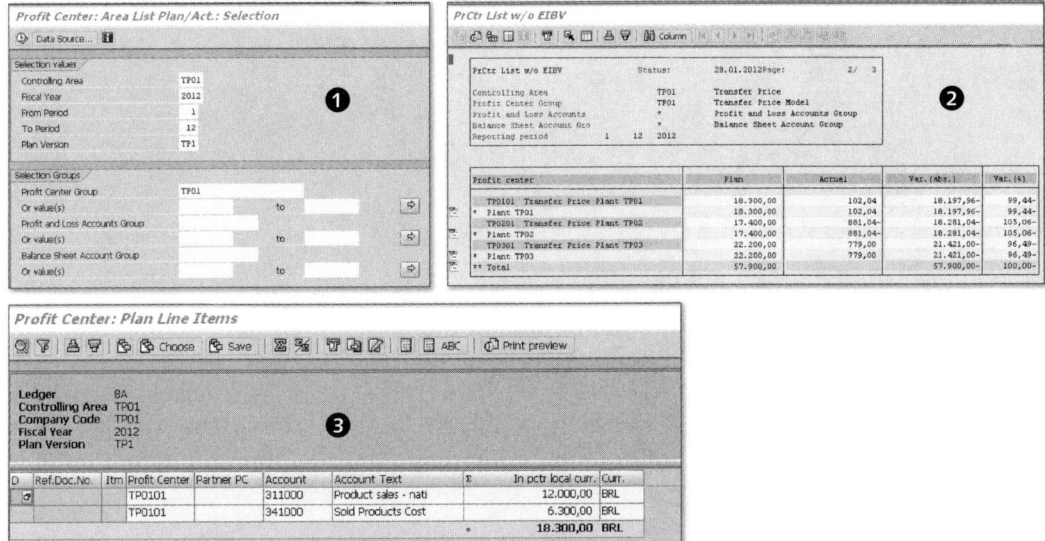

Figure 8.76 Plan/Actual EC-PCA Report

In panel (**❶**) you can see the selection screen for the report, where you define the controlling area, fiscal year, period, and version. The result screen is shown in panel (**❷**). You can see in this screen the planning values but not yet by account; by selecting planning line items for one line, you can see the planning line items by account. Notice both accounts that we defined in the account determination step in Figure 8.75.

To transfer planning values from other objects to EC-PCA, you don't need to customize. You just need to select for which object you want to transfer the planning by using Transaction 1KE0 or by going to CONTROLLING • PROFIT CENTER ACCOUNTING • PLANNING • PLAN DATA TRANSFER • TRANSFER CO PLAN DATA, as shown in Figure 8.77.

Select the plan version and the fiscal year and which data you want to transfer. You can see the result screen in Figure 8.78.

The last step in the plan data transfer is to transfer the statistical key figures from other components by using Transaction 1KEE or by going to CONTROLLING • PROFIT CENTER ACCOUNTING • PLANNING • PLAN DATA TRANSFER • STATISTICAL KEY FIGURES: TRANSFER PLAN OPENING BALANCE, as shown in Figure 8.79.

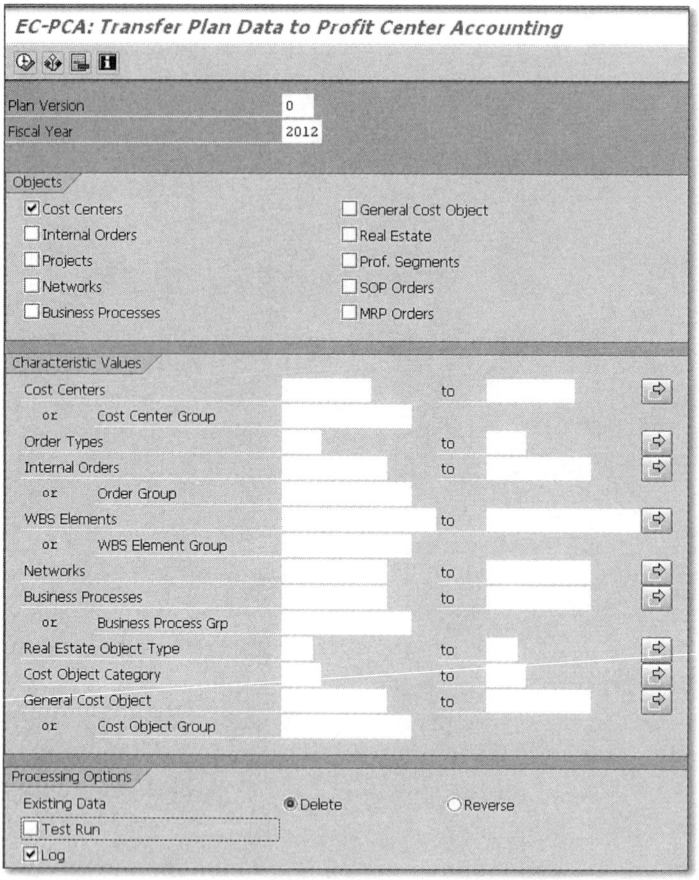

Figure 8.77 Transfer Plan Data to EC-PCA

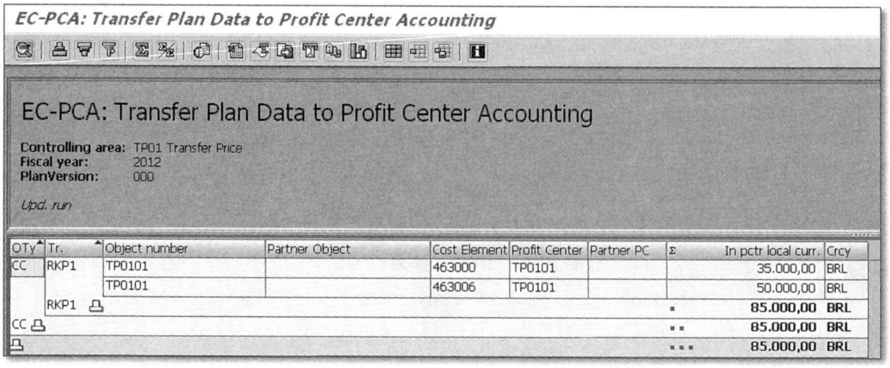

Figure 8.78 Transfer Plan Data to EC-PCA, Results

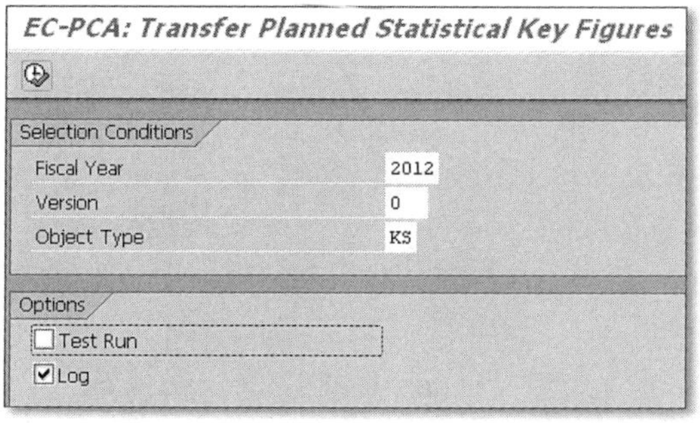

Figure 8.79 EC-PCA Transfer Planned Statistical Key Figure

Enter the fiscal year, version, and one of the following object types:

► HP: Cost Object

► KS: Cost Center

► NP: Network

► NV: Network Activity

► OR: Order

► PR: WBS Element

► VB: Sales Document

► BP: Business Process

► IW: Business Entity

► IV: Lease-Out

► IS: General Lease-Out

► IM: Rental Unit

► IG: Property

► IC: Management Contract

► IB: Buildings

► IA: Settlement Unit IA: Settlement Unit

Allocations are also available for use in the planning process.

8.5.5 Allocations

Planning allocations in EC-PCA are based on cycles, the same as in CO-CCA. You've seen how to customize a cycle in Chapter 3, and the process is the same for EC-PCA. The following planning allocations options are available for EC-PCA:

▶ Distribution

▶ Assessment

To create EC-PCA planning distributions, use Transaction 4KE7; to create EC-PCA planning assessments, use Transaction 3KE7.

You've now finished the EC-PCA planning customizing, so let's move on to actual postings.

8.6 Actual Postings

All postings from other SAP ERP components that have a profit center assigned will be automatically transferred to EC-PCA. In this section, you'll learn how to customize EC-PCA to also bring other postings in accounts not relevant for EC-PCA. You'll also see how to transfer actual data from other components and what tools are available for the period-end closing. Figure 8.80 illustrates how the actual values flow to and from EC-PCA.

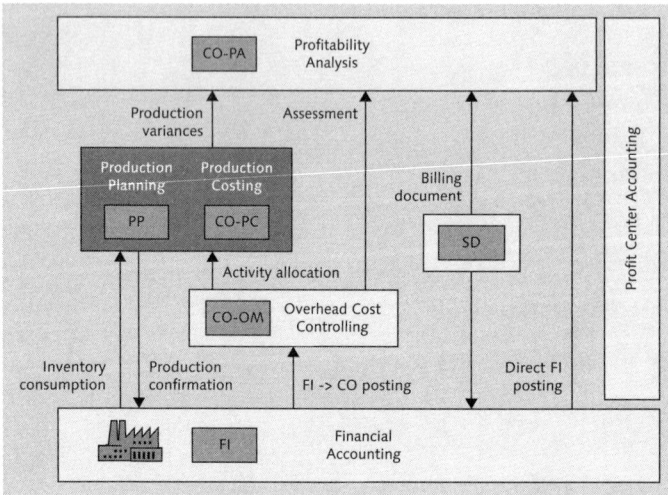

Figure 8.80 Value Flow to EC-PCA

You've seen this diagram before in Chapter 1, but without EC-PCA. Now you can see that EC-PCA is linked to all of the processes and postings we've discussed throughout this book.

The first definition for EC-PCA actual postings is the basic settings.

8.6.1 Basic Settings

In basic settings, you'll customize EC-PCA document types and document number ranges.

Define Document Type

To customize EC-PCA document types, use Transaction GCBA, or go to CONTROL-LING • PROFIT CENTER ACCOUNTING • ACTUAL POSTINGS • BASIC SETTINGS: ACTUAL • MAINTAIN DOCUMENT TYPES, as shown in Figure 8.81.

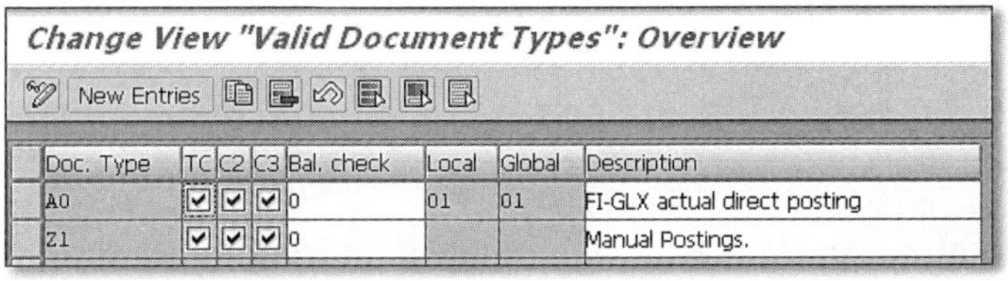

Doc. Type	TC	C2	C3	Bal. check	Local	Global	Description
A0	☑	☑	☑	0	01	01	FI-GLX actual direct posting
Z1	☑	☑	☑	0			Manual Postings.

Figure 8.81 EC-PCA Document Type

SAP ERP provides document type A0 – FI-GLX ACTUAL DIRECT POSTING by default. You can copy the existing one or create a new one.

When creating a document type, you can choose whether it will record currencies 1, 2, 3, or a combination of these.

Another important definition for the document type is the balance check (BAL. CHECK column), where you choose from the following options:

▸ 0: Error if balance is not zero

▸ 1: Warning if balance is not zero

▸ 2: No balance check

You can create a document type where the balance 0 is not checked. It's sometimes helpful to adjust a posting when an account in the posting was not defined in EC-PCA, so that its balance is not direct transferred to the component.

After creating the document type, you must maintain the document number range for the document type.

Define Number Ranges for Local Documents

You've seen how to maintain document number ranges in Chapter 1. EC-PCA document number ranges are maintained in the same way as the number ranges for controlling documents. Use Transaction GB02, or go to CONTROLLING • PROFIT CENTER ACCOUNTING • ACTUAL POSTINGS • BASIC SETTINGS: ACTUAL • DEFINE NUMBER RANGES FOR LOCAL DOCUMENTS. The EC-PCA number ranges are shown in Figure 8.82.

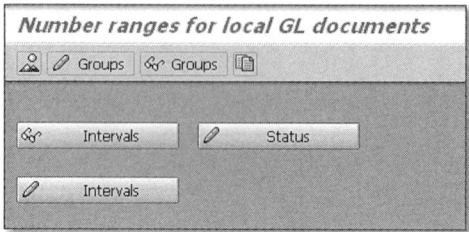

Figure 8.82 EC-PCA Number Ranges

Click on the GROUPS (with the pencil icon) button to add the recently created document type to a number range group, as shown in Figure 8.83.

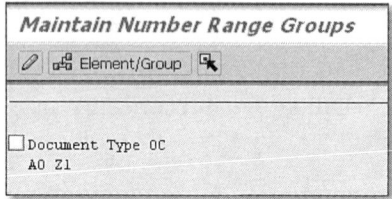

Figure 8.83 EC-PCA Number Ranges, Group Assignment

Find the document type without number range at the bottom of the screen, mark the DOCUMENT TYPE checkbox, then leave the cursor on the group that you want the document type to be, and click ELEMENT/GROUP.

You've completed the EC-PCA basic settings customizing. Now you'll see how to add accounts to EC-PCA that aren't automatically transferred to the component.

8.6.2 Choose Additional Balance Sheet and P&L Accounts

Some accounts, both balance sheet and P&L, aren't transferred to EC-PCA because either the accounts were created specifically to receive manual postings, or they aren't assigned to any profit center (e.g., cash accounts or down payments).

To add these accounts to EC-PCA, you must customize the account to be relevant to the component. Use Transaction 3KEH, or go to CONTROLLING • PROFIT CENTER ACCOUNTING • ACTUAL POSTINGS • CHOOSE ADDITIONAL BALANCE SHEET AND P&L ACCOUNTS • CHOOSE ACCOUNTS, as shown in Figure 8.84.

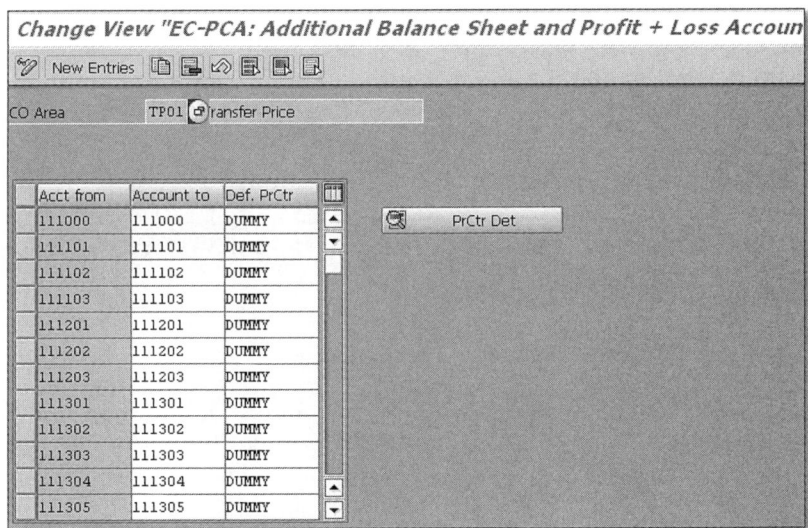

Figure 8.84 EC-PCA Additional Accounts Assignment

You choose the ACCOUNT FROM and ACCOUNT TO here and define a default profit center (DEF. PRCTR) for the account. Because the system can't automatically determine a profit center for these accounts, all posting will be done in the profit center assigned in this transaction (normally the dummy profit center), requiring a further processing step to clear the dummy profit center. You can use an assessment, distribution, or even a manual entry in EC-PCA to do this clearing.

Note
All accounts that you want to add to EC-PCA that aren't automatically transferred to EC-PCA must be maintained in this transaction.

If, for example, you've defined an account relevant for EC-PCA, and there is a rule to determine the profit center (for example, by company code), you can create a derivation rule for the account, and the profit center will be determined for the account based on the rule. To create the profit center derivation, either use Transaction 3KEI, or go to CONTROLLING • PROFIT CENTER ACCOUNTING • ACTUAL POSTINGS • CHOOSE ADDITIONAL BALANCE SHEET AND P&L ACCOUNTS • DERIVATION RULES FOR FINDING THE PROFIT CENTER, as shown in Figure 8.85.

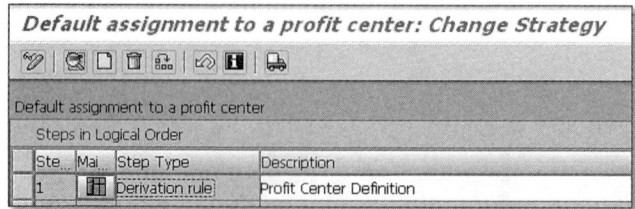

Figure 8.85 Derivation Rule for EC-PCA Profit Center

Click on NEW ENTRIES to create a new derivation rule, and a new screen to define the derivation appears, as shown in Figure 8.86.

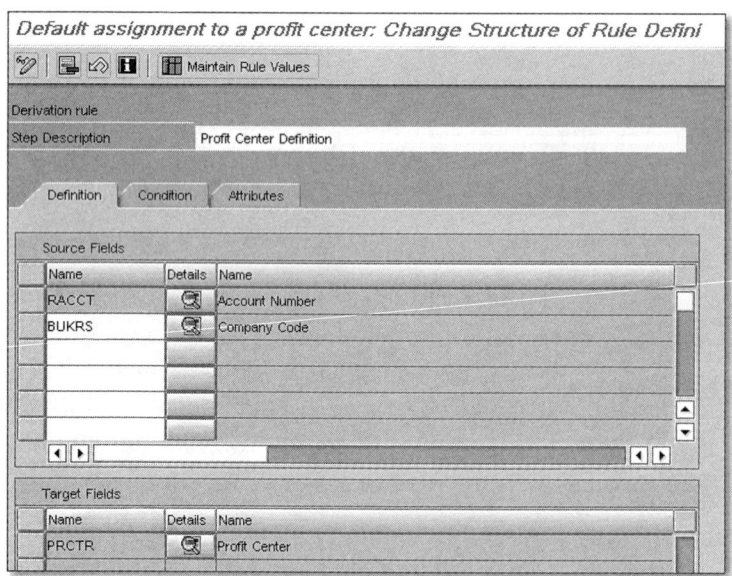

Figure 8.86 Derivation Rule for EC-PCA Profit Center, Definition

In the SOURCE FIELDS section, you can add the company code or valuation area. After defining which field you want to use as a source, click on MAINTAIN RULE VALUES, as shown in Figure 8.87.

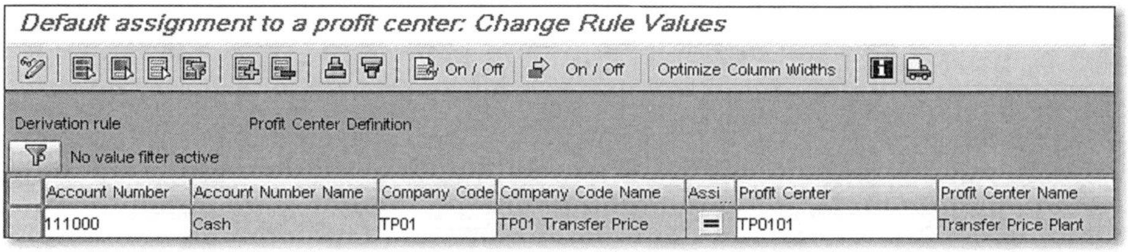

Figure 8.87 Derivation Rule for EC-PCA Profit Center, Assignment

In our example, because we defined the source fields account number and company code in Figure 8.86, the breakdown will be done by these source fields in the maintenance screen of Figure 8.87. Enter the combination of possible values, and save the derivation.

You can see one example of a derivation in Figure 8.88, where Report KE5Z – Profit Center: Actual Line Items was used to display the posting.

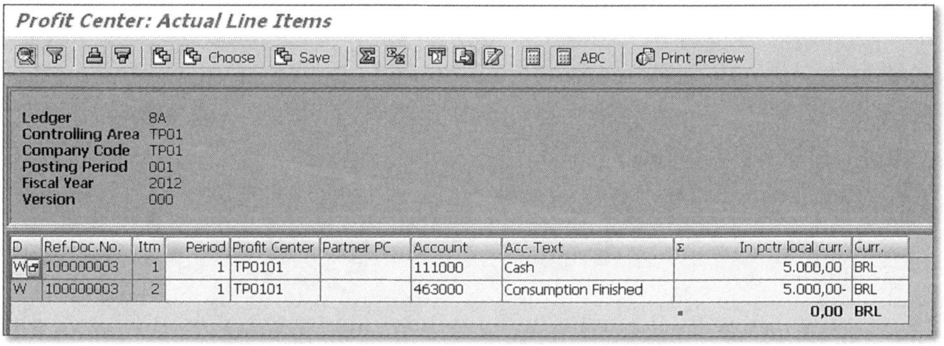

Figure 8.88 Actual Line Items Report

If you look back to Figure 8.84, you can see that for the account 111000 – Cash, a DUMMY profit center had been assigned making this account relevant to EC-PCA. In Figure 8.86 and Figure 8.87, a derivation rule was created for this account, defining a fixed profit center for the combination account/company code. In the report shown in Figure 8.88, you can see that the derivation rule was accessed and the profit center was changed during the posting.

Next in actual posting customizing for EC-PCA, we'll look at the period-end closing.

8.6.3 Period-End Closing

For the customizing for period-end closing in EC-PCA, you'll define the allocations for profit centers.

When you run an allocation in CO-CCA, it will automatically be transferred to EC-PCA, but there are some EC-PCA accounts that are either not created as cost elements and therefore are not included in any CO-CCA allocations, or they aren't P&L accounts but still need to be allocated to other profit centers.

Assessments and distributions are both available for EC-PCA, but there are restrictions by account type:

- Costs (assessment and/or distribution)
- Revenues and sales deductions (assessment and/or distribution)
- Balance sheet items (distribution only)

Assessments and distributions for actual costs are based on cycles, the same as the ones for planning. You've already seen in detail how to customize the cycles in Chapter 3.

To create an actual EC-PCA assessment, either use Transaction 3KE1, or go to CONTROLLING • PROFIT CENTER ACCOUNTING • ACTUAL POSTINGS • PERIOD-END CLOSING • DEFINE ASSESSMENT. The cost element category used for EC-PCA assessments is 42 – Assessment, which is the same cost element category used for CO-CCA assessments.

To create an actual EC-PCA distribution, either use Transaction 4KE1, or go to CONTROLLING • PROFIT CENTER ACCOUNTING • ACTUAL POSTINGS • PERIOD-END CLOSING • DEFINE DISTRIBUTION.

When first activating EC-PCA in the system, you'll need to generate the open balance for the balance sheet accounts.

8.6.4 Transferring Selected Balance Sheet Items

The following options are available to create the opening balance for balance sheet accounts:

- Generate opening balance for material stocks
- Generate opening balance for WIP
- Generate opening balance for assets
- Generate opening balance for payables and receivables

Generate Opening Balance for Material Stocks

In this customizing step, you'll transfer the opening balance for materials balance sheet accounts in EC-PCA. You can transfer only the current or previous period balance to a specified period. To transfer the material stock accounts' opening balances to EC-PCA, either use Transaction 1KEH, or go to CONTROLLING • PROFIT CENTER ACCOUNTING • ACTUAL POSTINGS • TRANSFERRING SELECTED BALANCE SHEET ITEMS • GENERATE OPENING BALANCE FOR MATERIAL STOCKS. You can see the selection screen in Figure 8.89.

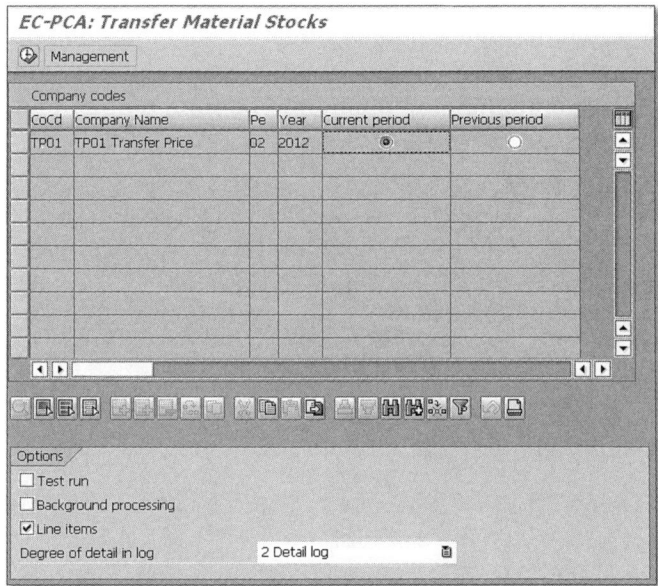

Figure 8.89 EC-PCA Transfer, Material Stocks

To transfer the material stocks balance to EC-PCA, you must select a company code (CoCd), select CURRENT PERIOD or PREVIOUS PERIOD, select TEST RUN or BACKGROUND PROCESSING, and indicate if the system should also create the line items by checking the LINE ITEMS checkbox.

> **Note**
>
> Because the material stocks accounts are automatically transferred online to EC-PCA, we recommend that you run the transaction only to create the opening balance. The system will then transfer all future material postings to EC-PCA online, keeping the amounts in balance.

Generate Opening Balance for Work in Process

If the WIP has been activated in your company, you can transfer the opening balance to EC-PCA. To transfer the opening balance for WIP to EC-PCA, you can use Transaction 1KEJ, or go to CONTROLLING • PROFIT CENTER ACCOUNTING • ACTUAL POSTINGS • TRANSFERRING SELECTED BALANCE SHEET ITEMS • GENERATE OPENING BALANCE FOR WORK IN PROCESS. You can see the selection screen in Figure 8.90.

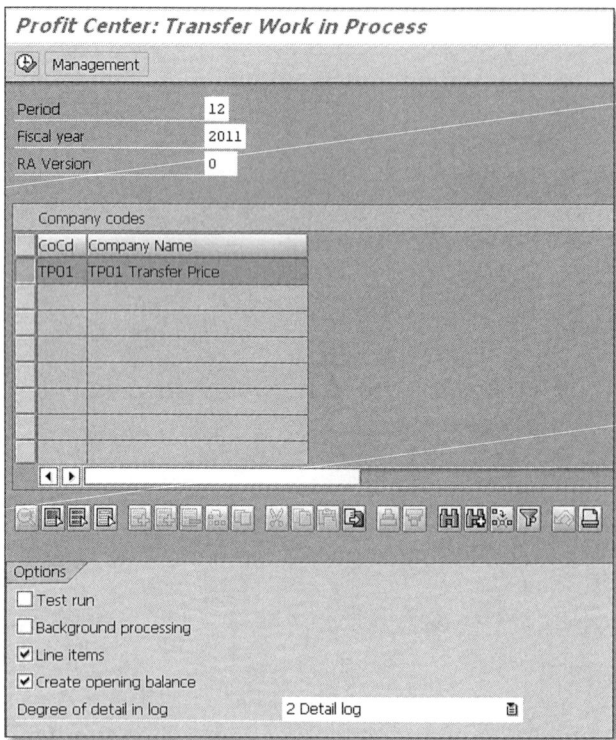

Figure 8.90 EC-PCA Transfer, WIP Opening Balance

Choose the FISCAL YEAR, PERIOD, and RA VERSION (results analysis), and then mark the company code (CoCd). In the OPTIONS section, you can choose TEST RUN and BACKGROUND PROCESSING, LINE ITEMS, and CREATE OPENING BALANCE.

In the same way as for material stocks, it's recommended to transfer the opening balance one time only; the system will update future postings online to EC-PCA.

Generate Opening Balance for Assets

You must also create the opening balances for Asset Accounting (AA). Use Transaction 1KEI, or go to CONTROLLING • PROFIT CENTER ACCOUNTING • ACTUAL POSTINGS • TRANSFERRING SELECTED BALANCE SHEET ITEMS • GENERATE OPENING BALANCE FOR ASSETS. You can see the selection screen in Figure 8.91.

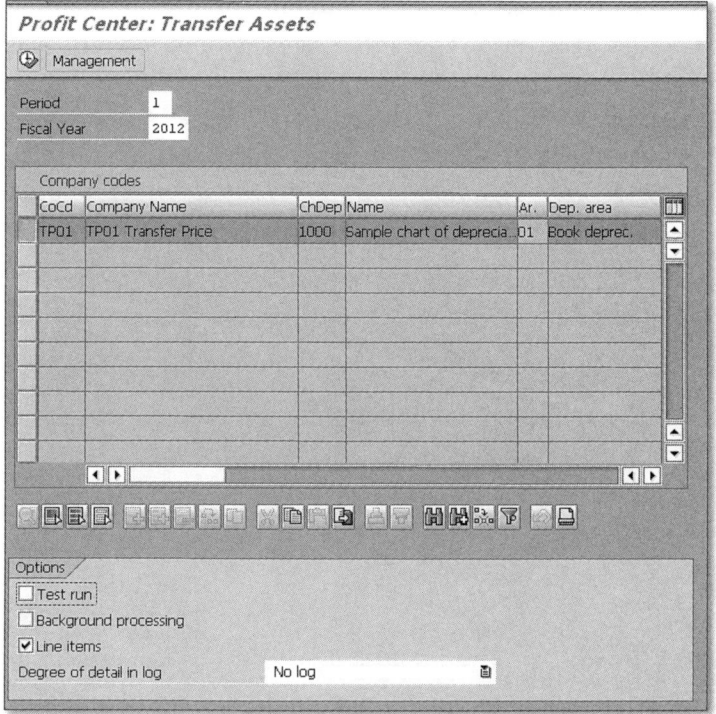

Figure 8.91 EC-PCA Transfer, Asset Opening Balance

Select the period and fiscal year. Mark the company code, and choose the depreciation area you want to transfer.

> **Note**
>
> If you've set the asset reconciliation account as relevant to EC-PCA, as reflected in Figure 8.84, you don't need to run this transaction on a monthly basis; instead, the system will post online the asset movements and transfer to EC-PCA. If you run this transaction after you've created the opening balances and in a system with postings in the depreciation area, the system will delete the posted line items and create opening balances again, losing the history of the past postings.

Generate Opening Balance for Payables and Receivables

The management of opening balances for account payables and receivables is different from open balances for other areas. Instead of just creating the open balance one time and letting the system update changes online, for account payables and receivables, you need to run the transfer transaction on a regular basis to transfer the account changes to EC-PCA. To transfer payables and receivables to EC-PCA, either use Transaction 1KEK, or go to CONTROLLING • PROFIT CENTER ACCOUNTING • ACTUAL POSTINGS • TRANSFERRING SELECTED BALANCE SHEET ITEMS • GENERATE OPENING BALANCE FOR PAYABLES AND RECEIVABLES. You can see the selection screen in Figure 8.92.

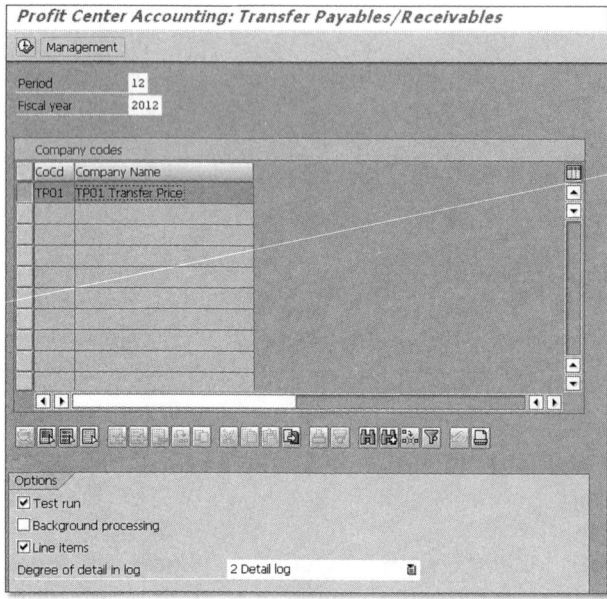

Figure 8.92 EC-PCA Transfer, Payables and Receivables

Select the period and fiscal year, mark the company code, select the available options, and execute.

In EC-PCA actual posting, you can also import values from other components relating to the period before the EC-PCA was activated.

8.6.5 Actual Data Transfer

You can transfer values to EC-PCA from the following different areas:

▸ Transfer CO actual data periodically

▸ Select and transfer CO actual data

▸ Transfer FI actual data

▸ Transfer MM actual data

▸ Transfer SD billing documents

▸ Transfer actual opening balance for statistical key figures

We'll now explore these areas individually.

> **Note**
>
> The transactions in this section are used to transfer values from before the EC-PCA component was activated. They aren't intended to run on a regular basis because the system will transfer the documents online to EC-PCA.

Transfer CO Actual Data Periodically

This activity will transfer all of the secondary postings in CO to EC-PCA. To Transfer CO documents to EC-PCA, use Transaction 0KE0, or go to CONTROLLING • PROFIT CENTER ACCOUNTING • ACTUAL POSTINGS • ACTUAL DATA TRANSFER • TRANSFER CO ACTUAL DATA PERIODICALLY. The selection screen is shown in Figure 8.93.

Choose the fiscal year and the period. In the OPTIONS section, you can choose to run in test mode, to post only documents with errors in the last transfer, and to write line items.

> **Note**
>
> When running the transfer from CO to EC-PCA, the system will delete the existing postings for that object and create a new entry in EC-PCA.

Therefore, we recommend that the manual transfer program only be used for cases where the online transfer was not turned on, or if there is a special situation that a document needs to be transferred again (this is rare).

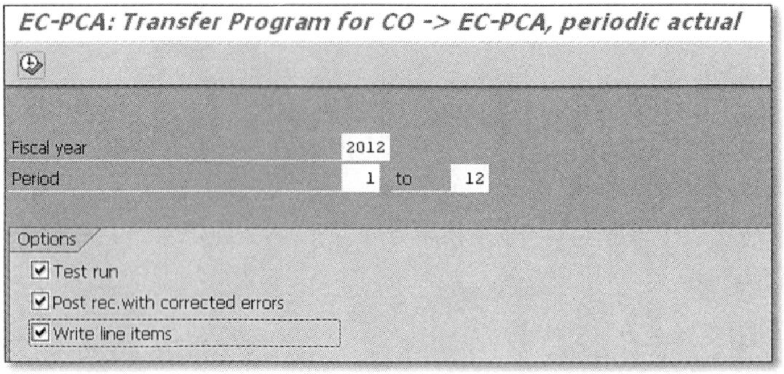

Figure 8.93 Transfer CO Documents to EC-PCA

Select and Transfer CO Actual Data

This activity is similar to transferring CO actual data periodically, but you can choose which activities and document numbers are to be transferred to EC-PCA. To transfer selected CO documents to EC-PCA, either use Transaction 1KEA, or go to CONTROLLING • PROFIT CENTER ACCOUNTING • ACTUAL POSTINGS • ACTUAL DATA TRANSFER • SELECT AND TRANSFER CO ACTUAL DATA. Figure 8.94 shows the selection screen.

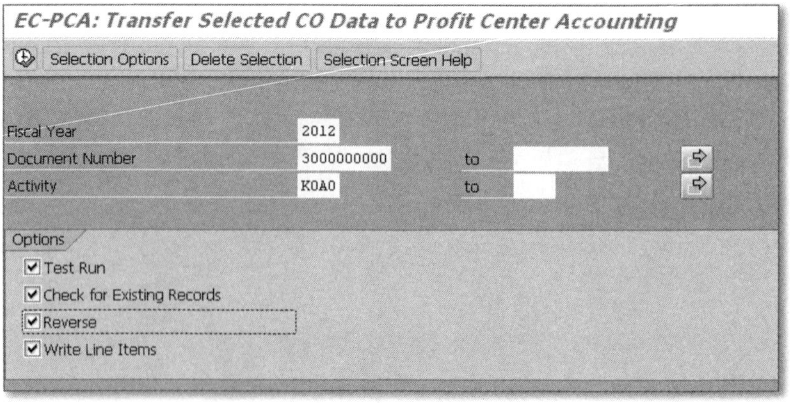

Figure 8.94 Transfer Selected CO Documents to EC-PCA

Enter the FISCAL YEAR, the DOCUMENT NUMBER, and which CO ACTIVITY you want to transfer. In OPTIONS, there are two new fields: CHECK FOR EXISTING RECORDS and REVERSE. If you mark CHECK FOR EXISTING RECORDS, the system will search for the record in the EC-PCA table. If the record already exists, it won't overwrite the existing one. If you unmark this field, the system won't check for existing records and will post the document anyway.

Transfer FI Actual Data

This functionality allows you to import documents from FI to EC-PCA. Use Transaction 1KE8, or go to CONTROLLING • PROFIT CENTER ACCOUNTING • ACTUAL POSTINGS • ACTUAL DATA TRANSFER • TRANSFER FI ACTUAL DATA. You can see the selection screen in Figure 8.95.

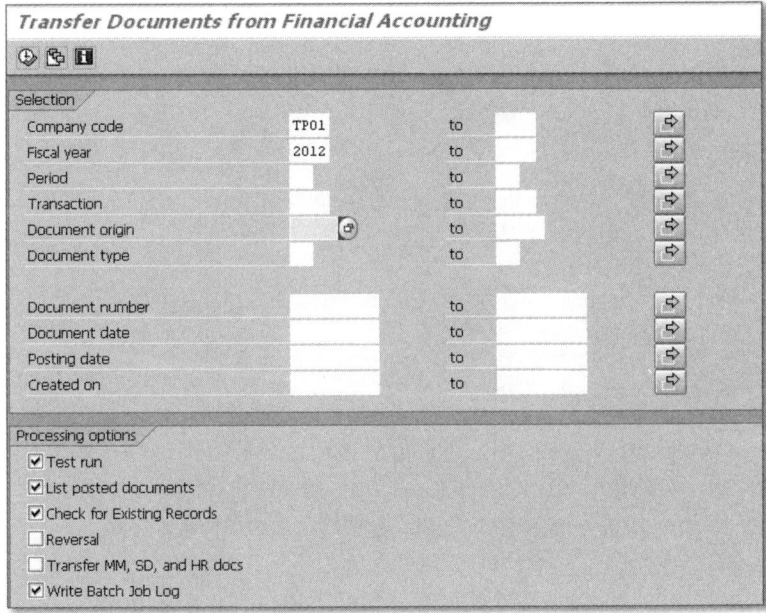

Figure 8.95 Transfer FI Documents to EC-PCA

You can select the fiscal year, period, and transaction documents. Using the selection filters, you can restrict the data you want to transfer. In the PROCESSING OPTIONS section, you also have the option available to check existing records and to transfer from MM, SD, and HCM docs. All FI postings relevant to EC-PCA will be transferred using this transaction.

Transfer MM Actual Data

In this transaction, the system will post documents from MM that couldn't be posted in the FI transfer, such as documents subject to transfer price. Use Transaction 1KEC, or go to CONTROLLING • PROFIT CENTER ACCOUNTING • ACTUAL POSTINGS • ACTUAL DATA TRANSFER • TRANSFER MM ACTUAL DATA. Figure 8.96 shows the selection screen.

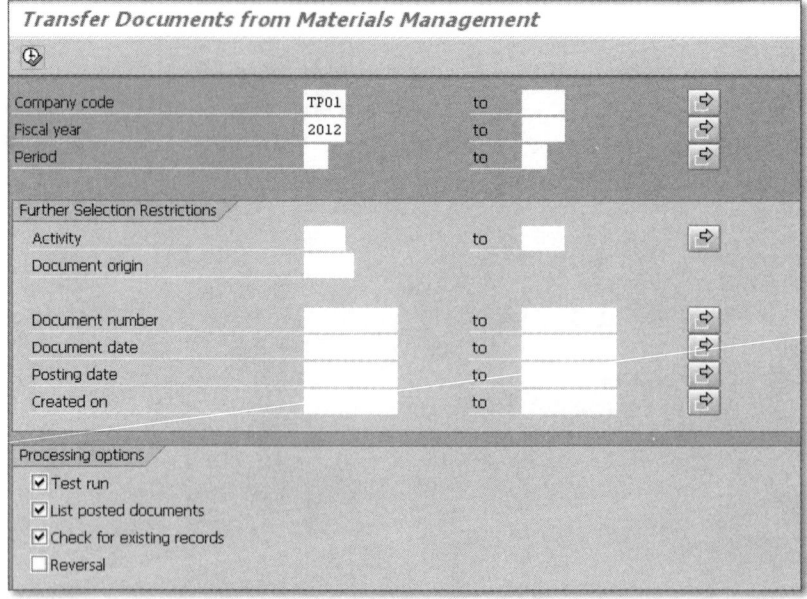

Figure 8.96 Transfer MM Documents to EC-PCA

You may choose the company code, fiscal year, and the period. If you want to restrict the selection, you can add filters in the FURTHER SELECTION RESTRICTIONS section and choose additional options in the PROCESSING OPTIONS section.

Transfer SD Billing Documents

In this transaction, the system will transfer the billing documents to EC-PCA. Use Transaction 1KE9, or go to CONTROLLING • PROFIT CENTER ACCOUNTING • ACTUAL POSTINGS • ACTUAL DATA TRANSFER • TRANSFER SD BILLING DOCUMENTS. You can see the selection screen in Figure 8.97.

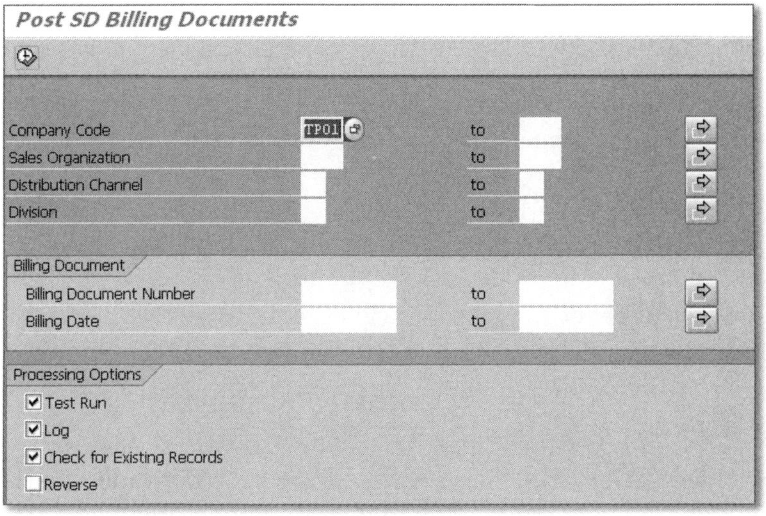

Figure 8.97 Transfer SD Documents to EC-PCA

You can restrict by company code, sales organization, distribution channel, and division. If you want additional filters, you can filter by billing document number and billing date. The PROCESSING OPTIONS checkboxes are also available.

Statistical Key Figures: Transfer Actual Opening Balance

You can also transfer the actual statistical key figures from the other components. Use Transaction 1KED, or go to CONTROLLING • PROFIT CENTER ACCOUNTING • ACTUAL POSTINGS • ACTUAL DATA TRANSFER • STATISTICAL KEY FIGURES: TRANSFER ACTUAL OPENING BALANCE. The selection screen is shown in Figure 8.98.

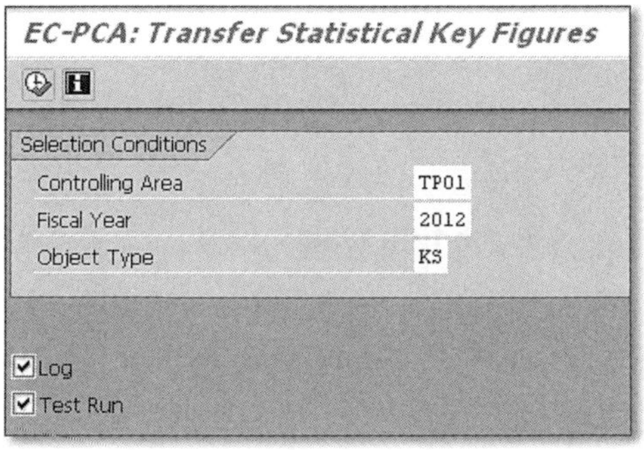

Figure 8.98 Transfer Statistical Key Figures to EC-PCA

The transfer works in the same manner as the plan data transfer, where you have to select the controlling area, fiscal year, and which object type you want to transfer.

You've now created the necessary customizing for EC-PCA actual postings. In the next section, you'll learn about the preparation for consolidation.

8.7 Preparation for Consolidation

In this customizing, you'll define the basic principles to derive the partner profit center for consolidation purposes. In some transactions, SAP ERP is unable to determine the partner profit center; in these cases, you can use a derivation process to fill the field.

SAP ERP has provided the capability for you to customize a derivation where you'll establish the rules for the system to determine the partner profit center for purchasing and sales transactions.

8.7.1 Derivation: Partner Profit Center in Purchasing and Sales

To create the partner profit center derivation for purchasing, use Transaction 8KES, or go to CONTROLLING • PROFIT CENTER ACCOUNTING • PREPARATION FOR CONSOLIDATION • DERIVATION: PARTNER PROFIT CENTER IN PURCHASING AND SALES • DERIVE PARTNER PROFIT CENTER IN PURCHASING, as shown in Figure 8.99.

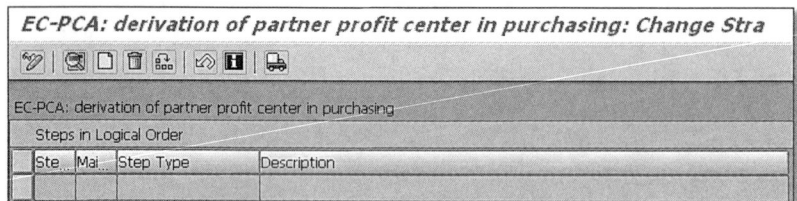

Figure 8.99 EC-PCA Partner Profit Center Derivation

Create a new derivation step by choosing one of the following:

▶ **Derivation rule**
Create a logical sequence to determine the partner profit center.

▶ **Move**
Move a value to a partner profit center when a condition is met.

▶ **Enhancement**

Write a custom program to do the determination. For an enhancement, use Derive PCA00003 – Partner Profit Center for External Deliveries.

Figure 8.100 shows the customizing screen of one example derivation step.

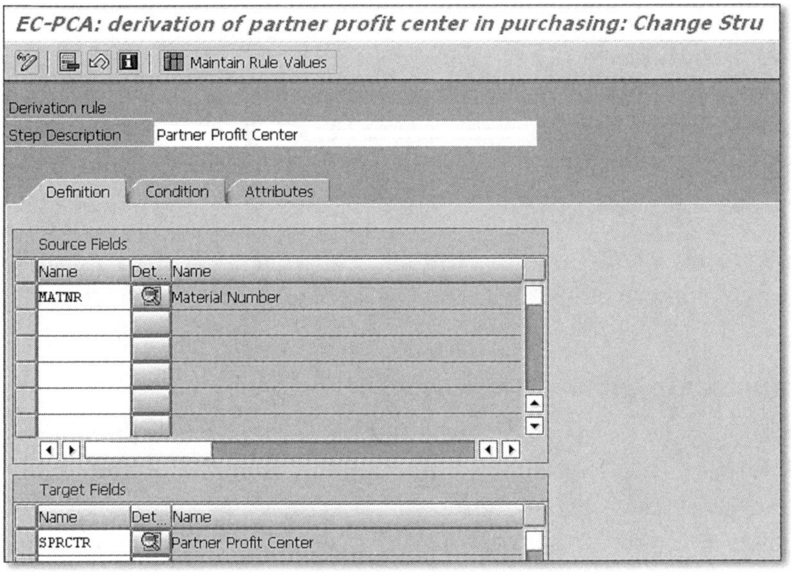

Figure 8.100 EC-PCA Trading Partner Derivation, Details

You've already learned about customizing derivations for CO-PA and also for other areas of EC-PCA. The partner profit center derivation works in the same manner. Choose the source field and the target field for the derivation, and click on MAINTAIN RULE VALUES to assign the partner profit center to the source you've defined, as shown in Figure 8.101.

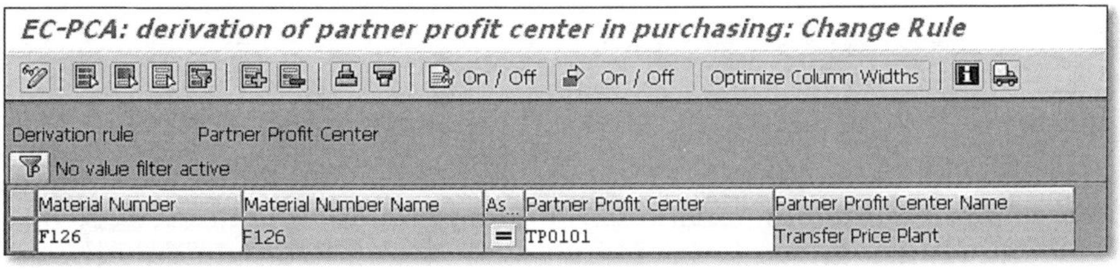

Figure 8.101 EC-PCA Trading Partner Derivation, Maintain Rule

Enter the source definition, which you defined in the previous step and which will be the partner profit center for the source. In our example, we have defined material number as the source, so we entered a specific material number and the specific partner profit center that should be used for that material number.

The derivation for sales is almost the same as for purchasing documents. The difference is that for sales, the source fields available belong to the SD component. We aren't going to customize the derivation for sales because you've already seen how to create a purchasing partner profit center derivation. Use Transaction 8KER, or go to CONTROLLING • PROFIT CENTER ACCOUNTING • PREPARATION FOR CONSOLIDATION • DERIVATION: PARTNER PROFIT CENTER IN PURCHASING AND SALES • DERIVE PARTNER PROFIT CENTER IN SALES.

In preparation for consolidation, you can also select for which affiliated companies the system must read information for trading partner and partner profit center.

8.7.2 Read Purchase Orders/Sales Orders

In this customizing, you'll define when SAP ERP will read the sales order and purchase order information to identify the partner profit center. Use Transaction OCCL, or go to CONTROLLING • PROFIT CENTER ACCOUNTING • PREPARATION FOR CONSOLIDATION • READ PURCHASE ORDERS/SALES ORDERS • IDENTIFY AFFILIATED COMPANIES. The customizing screen is shown in Figure 8.102.

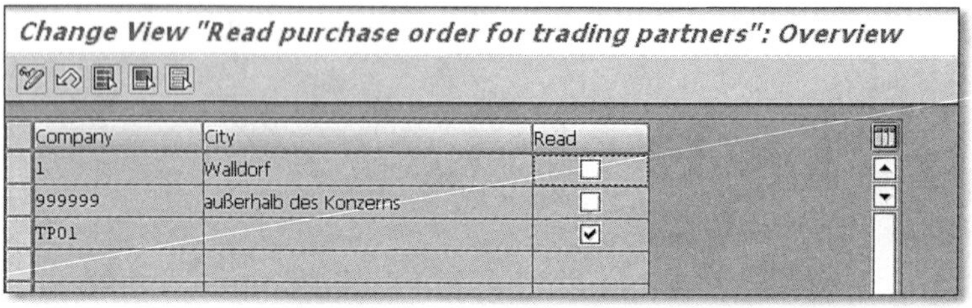

Figure 8.102 Read Purchase Order for Trading Partner

If a company code is selling a product to another company code in the same organization within SAP ERP, the system can fill the partner profit center by reading the purchasing order and sales order information between the affiliated companies.

Now that you have completed the customization for the EC-PCA in SAP-ERP, let's look at the information system.

8.8   Information System

The customizing done in EC-PCA in this chapter will help your company identify the profits for different businesses and also identify profits between them. SAP ERP provides a large number of standard reports for EC-PCA. You can also define your own reports using the Report Painter tools. We don't cover how to create reports with Report Painter in this book, but you'll see some of the most important standard reports for EC-PCA.

The report tree for EC-PCA is located under the menu path ACCOUNTING • CONTROLLING • PROFIT CENTER ACCOUNTING • INFORMATION SYSTEM • REPORTS FOR PROFIT CENTER ACCOUNTING and it's divided into the following folders:

▶ Interactive Reporting

▶ List-Oriented Reports

▶ Line Item Reports

▶ Special Functions

Inside the INTERACTIVE REPORTING folder, you'll see Report S_ALR_87013326 – Profit Center Group: Plan/Actual/Variance, as shown in Figure 8.103.

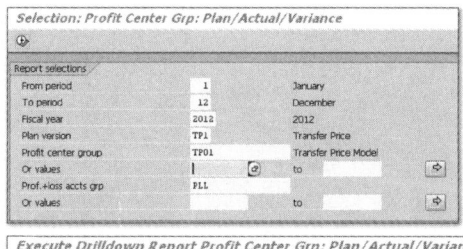

Figure 8.103 Profit Center Group Plan/Actual/Variance Report

In the selection screen of the report, you can choose the period, fiscal year, and plan version. For the profit center selection, you can either choose a profit center or a profit center group, and the same is true for P&L accounts. By choosing groups, you can see the group breakdown in the report.

In the report result, you can navigate between the characteristics for EC-PCA. This report will show only P&L accounts.

To view a similar report for balance sheet accounts, use Report S_ALR_87013336 – Profit Center Group: Balance Sheet Accounts Plan/Actual/Variance, as shown in Figure 8.104.

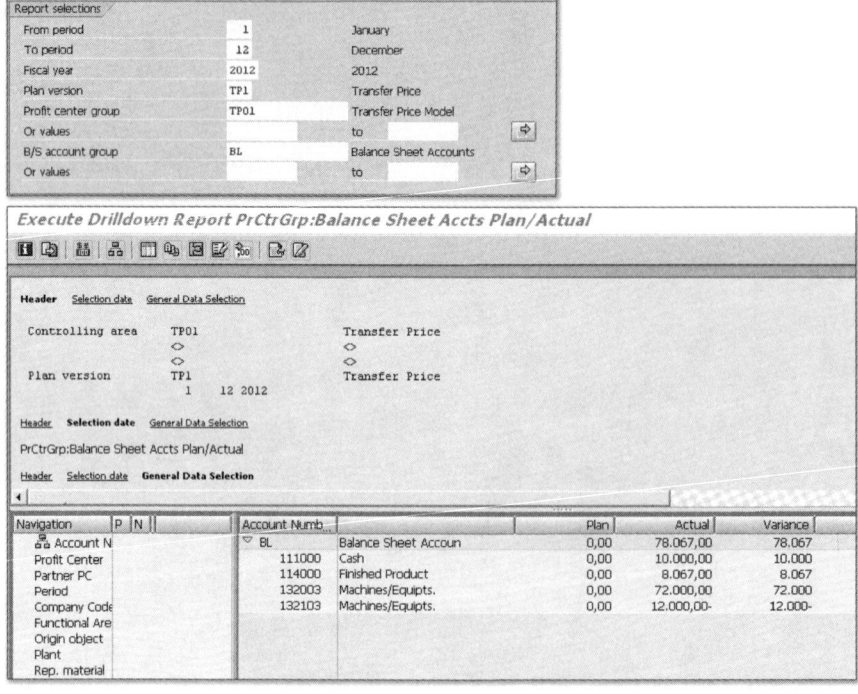

Figure 8.104 Balance Sheet Accounts Plan/Actual/Variance Report

The same report options are available as you saw previously for the P&L account report, but this report shows the balance sheet accounts.

You also have the option to run a report that shows both balance sheet and P&L accounts: Report S_ALR_87013340 – Profit Center Group: Plan/Actual /Variance as shown in Figure 8.105.

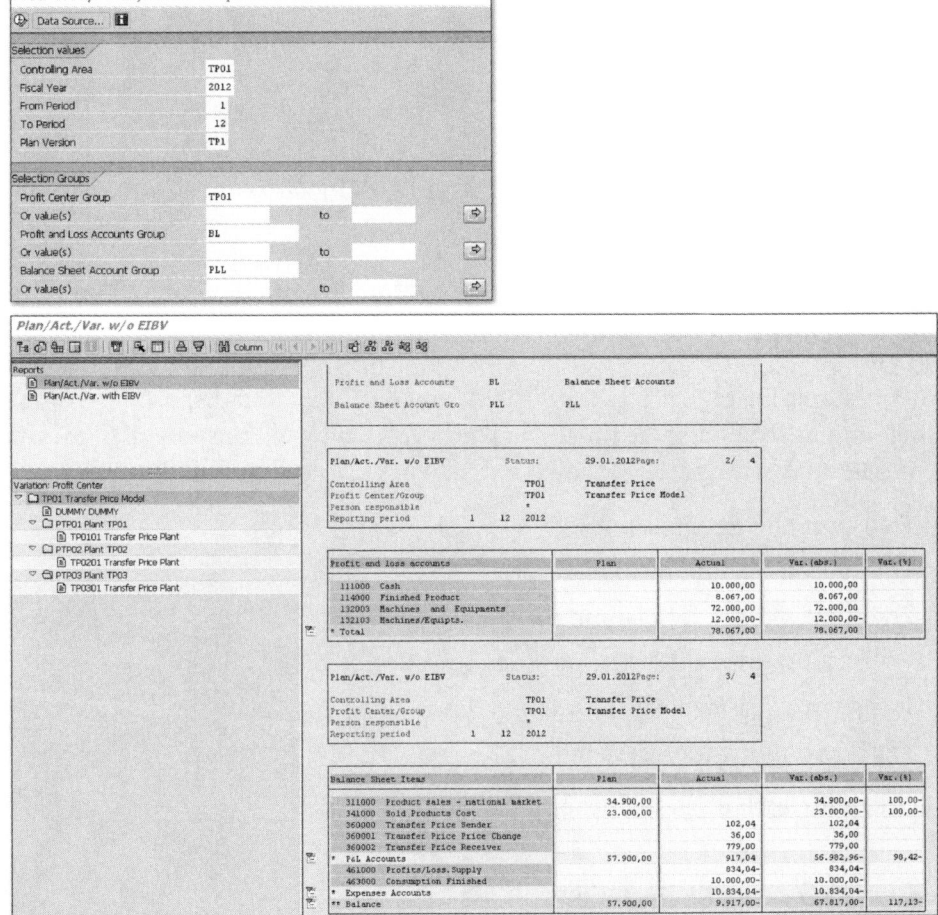

Figure 8.105 Profit Center Group Plan/Actual /Variance Report

In this report, you have the option to choose the balance sheet and P&L account group; the report result will show the group breakdown. We've been discussing the group functionality for controlling objects, and you can see in Figure 8.105 how it contributes value to your reporting analysis.

The following are some other good reports for EC-PCA:

▶ KE5Z: Profit Center: Actual Line Items

▶ KE5Y: Profit Center: Plan Line Items

▶ S_ALR_87013343: Profit Center: Receivables

▶ S_ALR_87013344: Profit Center: Payables

▶ 2KEE: Profit Center: Totals Records

▶ KE5X: Profit Center: Master Data Index

In the next section, which addresses tools for EC-PCA, you'll see how to transport the customizing settings for EC-PCA.

8.9 Tools

After customizing the settings for EC-PCA, you may want to transport the customizing settings all at the same time. You'll now learn how to transport all of the different EC-PCA settings. The following transport areas are explored further:

▶ Transport environment

▶ Transport master data

▶ Transport settings for planning

▶ Transport settings for actual postings

▶ Transport assessment/distribution cycles

▶ Transport information system

Let's explore each of these further.

8.9.1 Transport Environment

In the transport environment, you can choose to transport the following settings:

▶ Basic data and controlling area settings

▶ Business activities in PCA

▶ Statistical key figures from CO

To create the transport request for the environment, either use Transaction OKEP, or go to CONTROLLING • PROFIT CENTER ACCOUNTING • TOOLS • TRANSPORT CUSTOMIZING SETTINGS • TRANSPORT ENVIRONMENT. The selection screen is shown in Figure 8.106.

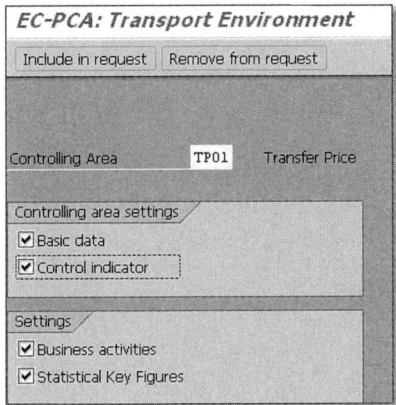

Figure 8.106 EC-PCA Transport Environment

Select the settings that you want to transport, and click on INCLUDE IN REQUEST. You can also remove settings from a transport request by choosing REMOVE FROM REQUEST.

> **Note**
>
> If you are transporting the EC-PCA settings at the same time as controlling area settings, make sure to first transport the controlling area settings and *then* transport the EC-PCA settings.

8.9.2 Transport Master Data

In this activity, you can select to transport the following EC-PCA definitions:

- Profit centers
- Standard hierarchy
- Time-based fields
- Profit center groups
- Substitutions for sales orders

To create the transport request for EC-PCA master data, either use Transaction 0KEQ, or go to CONTROLLING • PROFIT CENTER ACCOUNTING • TOOLS • TRANSPORT CUSTOMIZING SETTINGS • TRANSPORT MASTER DATA. You can see the selection screen in Figure 8.107.

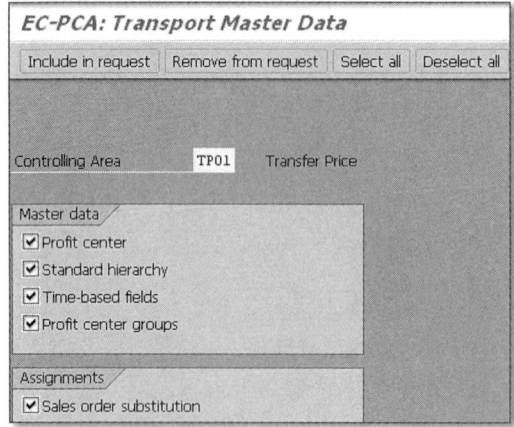

Figure 8.107 EC-PCA Transport Master Data

> **Note**
>
> We recommend that you always transport the settings for master data together. There are dependencies between the master data, and if you transport only part, and for some reason a dependent setting has not been assigned to the transport request, then it can lead to master data inconsistencies.

8.9.3 Transport Settings for Planning

In this customizing, you'll transport the settings for the following items:

▶ Plan version

▶ Distribution keys

▶ Planning layouts

To transport the plan version definition, either use Transaction 0KER, or go to CONTROLLING • PROFIT CENTER ACCOUNTING • TOOLS • TRANSPORT CUSTOMIZING SETTINGS • TRANSPORT SETTINGS FOR PLANNING • TRANSPORT PLAN VERSIONS. The selection screen is shown in Figure 8.108.

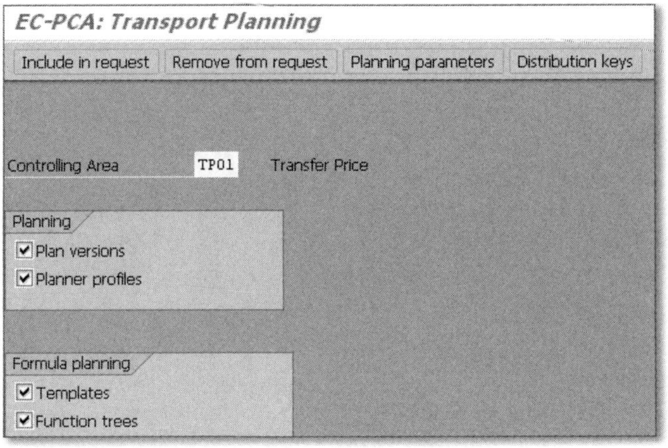

Figure 8.108 EC-PCA Transport Planning

Select the planning options, and click on INCLUDE IN REQUEST.

To transport the distribution key definitions, you can use Transaction GCT6, or go to CONTROLLING • PROFIT CENTER ACCOUNTING • TOOLS • TRANSPORT CUSTOMIZING SETTINGS • TRANSPORT SETTINGS FOR PLANNING • TRANSPORT DISTRIBUTION KEYS. Figure 8.109 shows the selection screen.

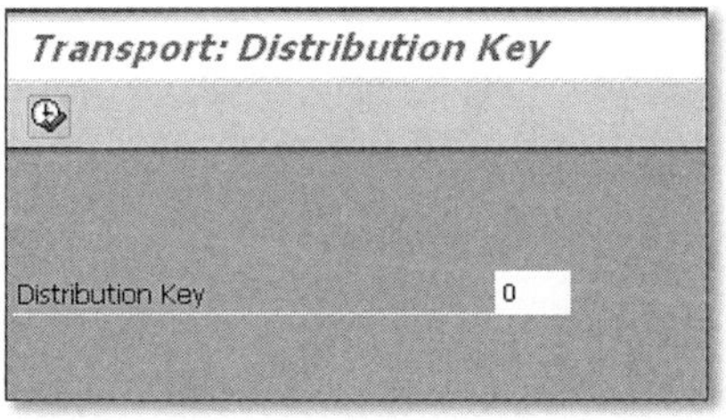

Figure 8.109 EC-PCA Transport Distribution Key

Select the distribution key, and execute.

To transport the planning layouts, either use Transaction 7KEI, or go to CONTROLLING • PROFIT CENTER ACCOUNTING • TOOLS • TRANSPORT CUSTOMIZING SETTINGS • TRANSPORT SETTINGS FOR PLANNING • TRANSPORT PLANNING LAYOUTS. You can see the selection screen in Figure 8.110.

Mark the planning layout you want to transport, and execute.

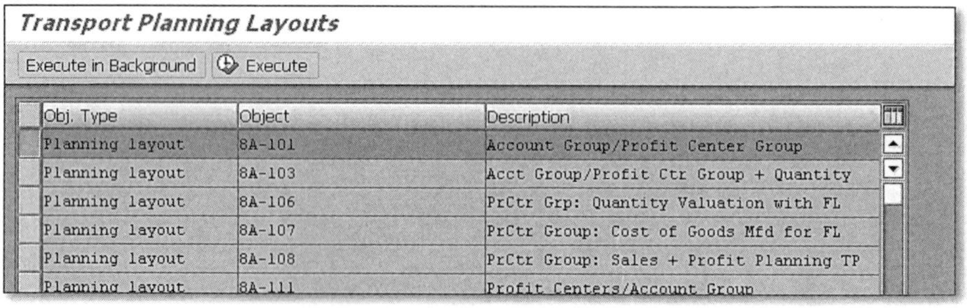

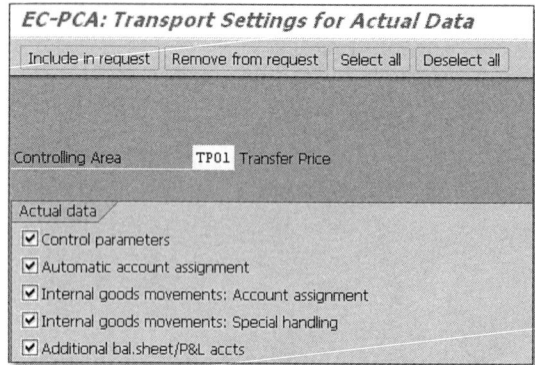

Figure 8.110 EC-PCA Transport Planning Layouts

8.9.4 Transport Settings for Actual Postings

In this step, you'll select the actual EC-PCA customizing to be transported. To transport actual settings for EC-PCA, use Transaction OKES, or go to CONTROLLING • PROFIT CENTER ACCOUNTING • TOOLS • TRANSPORT CUSTOMIZING SETTINGS • TRANSPORT SETTINGS FOR ACTUAL POSTINGS • TRANSPORT SETTINGS FOR ACTUAL POSTINGS. You can see the selection screen in Figure 8.111.

Figure 8.111 EC-PCA Transport Settings for Actual Data

In this screen, you select which EC-PCA actual customizing you want to transport.

> **Note**
>
> We recommend that you transport all settings together to avoid inconsistencies caused by dependencies between the customizing settings. When you transport the control parameters, it will directly change the target system. Make sure that all customizing required for EC-PCA (such as company code, controlling area, and CO-PA settings) is completed before sending the actual data.

8.9.5 Transport Assessment/Distribution Cycles

You already created definitions for distribution and assessment cycles. In this step, you'll transport these cycles. Use Transaction 0KEU, or go to Controlling • Profit Center Accounting • Tools • Transport Customizing Settings • Transport Assessment/Distribution Cycles. You can see the selection screen in Figure 8.112.

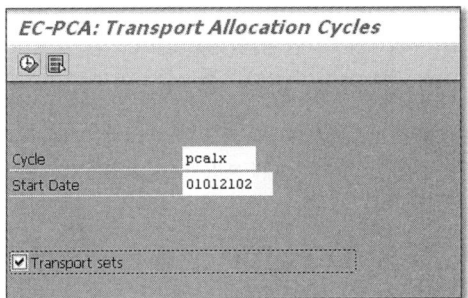

Figure 8.112 EC-PCA Transport Allocation Cycles

Enter the cycle and the start date. In the customizing of some cycles, you can use sets to define accounts, profit centers, and other fields. If you mark Transport sets, the system will include the sets used in the customizing in the transport request.

8.9.6 Transport Information System

In this transaction, you can transport the report definitions for EC-PCA. The system will transport the EC-PCA report tree and also the reports you've created using Report Painter. Use Transaction 0KET, or go to Controlling • Profit Center Accounting • Tools • Transport Customizing Settings • Transport Information System, as shown in Figure 8.113.

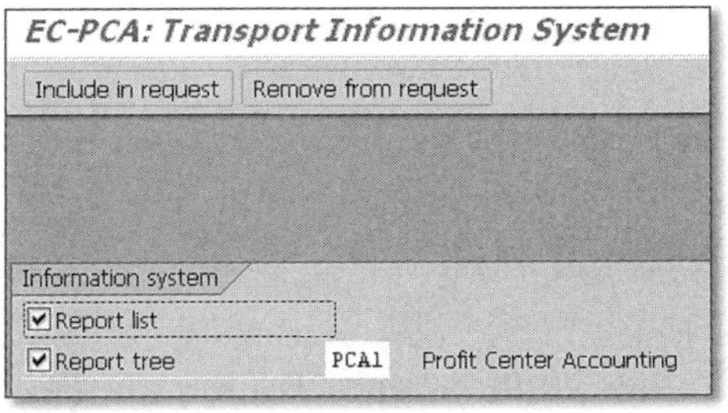

Figure 8.113 EC-PCA Transport Information System

If you mark REPORT LIST, all Report Painter reports related to EC-PCA will be included in the transport request. You can also transport the EC-PCA report tree.

8.10 Summary

EC-PCA brings a new dimension to the organization's business reporting and provides the option to create financial statements by business (or other organizational groupings) within the company and not only by legal entity.

In the basic settings, you learned how to complete all of the steps in the process to activate EC-PCA in SAP ERP, and how to use important tools to accelerate the master data creation process.

You've seen one of the most important advantages in using EC-PCA (the transfer price functionality, through which you can measure profit between businesses automatically) and have learned step by step how to customize it for your organization.

In the customizing for planning, you've learned that it's possible to import planning data from other subcomponents, such as CO-PA and CO-CCA, and how to use formula planning and allocations to better manage the planning data.

The section devoted to actual postings taught you which kinds of transactions automatically transfer to EC-PCA and how to expand the EC-PCA functionality to also include additional balance sheet and P&L accounts in your EC-PCA to best meet your needs. You've seen how to import actual data and which data must and must not be imported on a regular basis.

In preparation for consolidation, you learned how to derive the partner profit center for affiliated companies.

The section about tools showed you how to transport the EC-PCA settings to a target environment.

You should now have a good understanding of the available functionality in EC-PCA and be able to choose which options would add value to your company's business management reporting needs. With this knowledge, you now know which steps you need to complete to customize it in SAP ERP to meet those needs and also how to prepare for the production start-up of EC-PCA in your system.

If you understand the relationships and dependencies between the different Controlling subcomponents, you will be better equipped to use each one and to develop your CO implementation plan.

9 Conclusion

Now that you have learned about the SAP ERP CO component, the different functionalities it provides, and how to customize each of its subcomponents, let's briefly review each part and discuss how they interrelate and work together so that you can choose the best implementation combination to meet your needs.

The CO component of SAP ERP in a customized implementation can provide your organization with a full toolbox that enables you to better coordinate, monitor, and optimize all your business processes.

You are now familiar with the impacts of the controlling area definition on your CO implementation, and the key decisions you will make in establishing this main structural element of CO that reflect your organization's current and future needs.

For the Overhead Management subcomponent (CO-OM), using Cost Element Accounting (CO-CEL), Cost Center Accounting (CO-CCA), and Internal Orders (CO-OPA), you've learned how these subcomponents together can provide powerful analysis capabilities for monitoring and additional tools for controlling costs; you also learned how to establish them to maintain integrity in your management accounting and reporting system by easily reconciling back to your statutory accounting in FI.

Activity-Based Costing (CO-ABC) brings a new dimension of costing analysis to CO in which you can measure and control overhead costs by associating them with cost drivers, therefore adding transparency to your cost analysis and laying the foundation for a continuous improvement environment.

The Product Cost Controlling (CO-PC) subcomponent can help you understand, manage, and improve your production costs, including cost values from the other CO subcomponents and also from other SAP ERP components.

Profitability Analysis (CO-PA) can measure your profitability by segment, customer, product, and other business characteristics in a fully customized, multidimensional analysis tool. Profit Center Accounting (EC-PCA) lets you measure the profit and loss of internal areas in your company, including balance sheet measurements such as working capital and assets employed.

Since you learned about the functionality available from each of the subcomponents and the benefits that they can bring to your management accounting and reporting, you probably have determined that only some of them would add value to your organization. That is, you may not need all of the tools in the box.

The subcomponents within CO can be activated individually—and there is no requirement to implement all of them—but there are some interdependencies that we recommend you consider before you finalize your implementation plans. Figure 9.1 shows the relationship between the subcomponents and the objective of each one. Next we will discuss the relationships and highlight the interdependencies that will affect your implementation planning.

Starting at the bottom of Figure 9.1, you can see how information from other SAP ERP components feeds into CO. The components at the bottom are foundational; information from them is used in the subcomponents shown in the higher levels. Now you will learn which other subcomponents are required to activate each of the CO subcomponents.

You will require CO-CEL in order to transfer values received from other SAP ERP components (such as PP, MM, SD, QM, PM, AA, HCM, FI, or PS) to other CO subcomponents (such as CO-CCA, CO-OPA, CO-ABC, CO-PC, CO-PA, or EC-PCA), so it is therefore always required when activating any portion of CO.

CO-CCA, CO-OPA, and CO-ABC require only CO-CEL to be activated; you can choose to activate any or all of these subcomponents, depending on your needs.

CO-PC is optional. It requires CO-CEL and CO-CCA, CO-ABC, or both to serve as an activity type sender to transfer overhead costs to CO-PC.

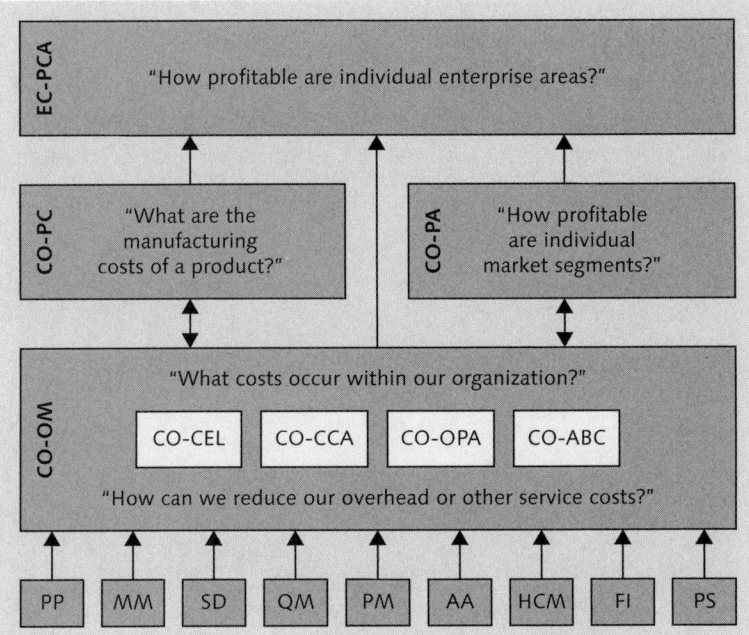

Figure 9.1 CO Subcomponent Purposes and Relationships

CO-PA is optional and can be used only with CO-CEL active. If you want to add more detailed analysis to your profitability reports, you may want to also add CO-PC to bring in product costing and CO-CCA, CO-OPA, or CO-ABC to bring overhead costs to your CO-PA.

EC-PCA is also optional, requiring only CO-CEL; however, if you use it in combination with other subcomponents, you will have more information available in your analysis and management reporting information system.

The relationships and interdependencies of the CO subcomponents are critical for you to consider before determining which subcomponents you will activate during your implementation. Throughout this book, as you've learned about each subcomponent, you have seen how they each can be useful (or not) for your organization. It's important not to make final decisions about your customization of any of the areas of CO until you have considered how they may impact your customizing of other subcomponents.

Now you are ready to plan your implementation of this powerful component of SAP ERP and draft your project blueprint, including the determination of which subcomponents you will activate, the options you will need, and the definitions of your key structures for each area. Remember to prioritize your organization's information needs when activating the SAP ERP CO component and customizing your chosen subcomponents.

The Authors

Rogerio Faleiros is an electronic engineer with an MBA in business management with an emphasis on information technology. He has been working with SAP ERP Controlling since 2005 and acquired significant experience in customizing this environment in businesses of several sizes and types, including multinational integration of systems and plants. He actively contributes to official SAP discussion forums, having used the tool in Brazil and worldwide. He has done customization to implement International Financial Reporting Standards (IFRS) and actual costing on international projects.

Alison Kreis Ryan has 25 years of experience in accounting, financial and management reporting, customization, and implementation of SAP ERP systems, process improvements, and information technology. She has a master's degree in accountancy, has worked as a CPA in public accounting, and for the past 20 years has worked in private industry in financial, operational and information technology management capacities. She has worked with SAP as a key user for 10 years, participating in a version upgrade and implementations to project management for design, customization, and initial implementations of Material Ledger, and SAP NetWeaver Business Warehouse and SAP BusinessObjects reporting systems.

Index

Learn how product costing works and integrates with other modules

Master integrated planning, product cost planning, manufacturing methods, reporting, and more

Reduce long run times during month-end processing and streamline controlling processes

John Jordan

Product Cost Controlling with SAP

This comprehensive resource is for anyone with an interest in the integrated areas of product costing. You'll learn how overhead costs flow from financial postings to cost centers and then on to manufacturing orders. In addition, you'll master the material ledger, transfer pricing, reporting, and discover how to address common problem areas, including month-end processing, long run times, and message and variance analysis. This new edition includes updated content on cost object hierarchies and engineer-to-order, as well as new case studies and real-world examples.

652 pp., 2. edition, 79,95 Euro / US$ 79.95
ISBN 978-1-59229-399-5

Understand the complete planning and consolidation solution from SAP

Master features, functions, and integration with other SAP components and applications

Completely updated for release 7.5, and includes coverage on consolidation and enhanced reporting features

Sridhar Srinivasan, Kumar Srinivasan

SAP BusinessObjects Planning and Consolidation

This new edition covers the major features, functions, implementation, and integration of SAP BusinessObjects Planning and Consolidation 7.5 for NetWeaver. Beyond the product functionality, you'll find best practices for budgeting, planning, forecasting, and consolidations, and master consolidation and business planning topics. With numerous screenshots and walkthroughs, this is the one-stop overview to understand what BPC is and what it can do for you.

446 pp., 2. edition 2011, 79,95 Euro / US$ 79.95
ISBN 978-1-59229-397-1

>> www.sap-press.com

Discover best practices for the design and configuration of SAP ERP Financials

Understand the configuration process by using a real-world, process-oriented approach

Completely revised to include extended coverage on account assignments, the new SAP General Ledger, and much more

Naeem Arif, Sheikh Tauseef

SAP ERP Financials: Configuration and Design

Master the issues involved in designing and configuring an SAP ERP Financials implementation using this overview guide. This is an invaluable reference that covers what you need for the configuration and design process, the enterprise structure, reporting, data migration, Accounts Payable and Receivables, Financials integration with other modules, and all other critical areas of SAP ERP Financials. This new edition is updated for SAP ERP 6.0, Enhancement Package 4.

664 pp., 2. edition 2011, 79,95 Euro / US$ 79.95
ISBN 978-1-59229-393-3

>> www.sap-press.com

Learn to easily navigate the SAP system

Work with SAP modules step-by-step

Includes many examples and detailed SAP illustrations

Olaf Schulz

Using SAP: A Guide for Beginners and End Users

This book helps end users and beginners get started in SAP ERP and provides readers with the basic knowledge they need for their daily work. Readers will get to know the essentials of working with the SAP system, learn about the SAP systems' structures and functions, and discover how SAP connects to critical business processes. Whether this book is used as an exercise book or as a reference book, readers will find what they need to help them become more comfortable with SAP ERP.

388 pp., 39,95 Euro / US$ 39.95
ISBN 978-1-59229-408-4

>> www.sap-press.com